THE DRAMATIC LIST

THE DRAMATIC LIST

A

RECORD OF THE PERFORMANCES

OF

LIVING ACTORS AND ACTRESSES

OF THE

BRITISH STAGE.

EDITED BY

CHARLES E. PASCOE.

SECOND EDITION, REVISED AND ENLARGED.

BENJAMIN BLOM, INC.

First Published 1880
Reissued 1969 by
Benjamin Blom, Inc., Bronx, New York 10452
and 56 Doughty Street, London, W.C. 1

Library of Congress Catalog Card Number 70-91911

Printed in United States of America
at Westbrook Lithographers, Inc.
Westbury, New York

PREFACE.

THE success of the first edition of 'The Dramatic List' has induced the publisher to issue a second and cheaper edition, revised and enlarged. In the preparation of this, I have received more assistance from actors and actresses themselves than fell to my lot while engaged on the original work. For this additional interest shown by members of the Profession, in the purpose and prosperity of 'The Dramatic List,' I am grateful. To collect from one series of contemporary journals, and substantiate by reference to others, the dates of the several stage performances of individual players is in itself a toilsome labour; but where no clue is at hand to mark the "first appearance" of actor or actress the work becomes doubly burdensome and intricate. I have been unable (without beginning my work anew, which for various reasons was impossible) to give a satisfactory account of some players owing to their omitting to provide me with this guide. I understand, however, that I have no reason to feel aggrieved at this remissness, it being almost as difficult to fix the exact date of an actor's first appearance as to obtain information respecting an actress's age.

By submitting each printed record of the first issue to the revision of the person whose professional services it enumerates, and who may be said to be equally interested with myself in its correctness, I have been enabled to make the present edition more complete than the last. It is gratifying to be able to say that the corrections were few and unimportant. In some instances complaints were made of my having inserted criticisms which were unduly severe; but as the excerpts from the journals were selected after very careful and impartial consideration, I have not thought it desirable to substitute others for those already printed. I have, however, largely curtailed this portion of the book, and the more material of the appended criticisms of the first edition stand as part of the narrative in the second.

More than a hundred additional names will be found recorded in the present issue of 'The Dramatic List.' Notwithstanding, however, this considerable increase, I am still compelled to repeat the statement of my former preface as to the book's incompleteness. It is almost impossible to render such a work as full and satisfactory as could be wished in two, or even three, editions. New players are constantly coming forward, old players are as constantly dropping out of sight. The old favourite in "the legitimate" of a few years back goes into retirement, and a younger professional brother in polite comedy takes his place. At my elbow as I write lie two lists of names of actors and actresses at present before the English public. The reader may be surprised to learn that five hundred and sixty represents the sum total of those names. Only a very small percentage of them have ever appeared, or probably ever will appear conspicuously writ on London play-bills; and it is without the power of any individual to reach every player who may make his or her appearance on the stage of a London theatre.

Through the kindness of a gentleman who has given much attention to dramatic matters, I have been permitted to look through a collection of London play-bills published within the period 1845–1877. On reading those bills I have been particularly struck with the number of names which are now utterly forgotten by the theatre-going public. Their owners came and went, and no one now cares to inquire whither they are gone. Yet, in their time, not a few of these now-forgotten actors and actresses drew forth as merry laughter and excited as much interest in their several performances as many a well-established comedian or prominent leading lady of the present. It seems to me that the purpose of 'The Dramatic List' is fairly fulfilled if it record the performances of our *principal* living actors and actresses. I believe that that result has been achieved in the present edition. It will be remarked that an *asterisk* stands here and there before a name in the book; I have used this mark to indicate where an actor or actress has withheld all information respecting his or her career. I have felt compelled to resort to this expedient to remove all misapprehension hereafter as to my having duly applied to all who would seem to have a fair claim to appear in the pages of 'The Dramatic List.' It is proper to add that my acknowledgments are due to several correspondents for information and advice, and especially to Mr. Fredk. E. Mawe, whose collection of newspaper notices of first performances has proved of much assistance.

CHARLES EYRE PASCOE.

London, *November*, 1879.

THE DRAMATIC LIST.

ADDISON, CARLOTTA (Mrs. CHARLES A. LA TROBE), younger daughter of the late Edward Phillips Addison, comedian, was born in Liverpool, July 1849. She was educated by her father for the dramatic profession, and as a child played in very juvenile parts at the Liverpool Amphitheatre. Miss Carlotta Addison made her *début* on the London stage Saturday, October 5, 1866, at the St. James's Theatre, under Miss Herbert's management, as *Lady F. Touchwood*, in a revival of 'The Belle's Stratagem.' Subsequently having joined the company of the New Royalty Theatre, in February 1868, Miss Addison played there the part of *Jessie Bell* in a three-act drama by Halliday, entitled 'Daddy Grey.' This was the first part of decided importance that this actress had sustained in London, and indeed more responsible than any of the others, inasmuch as *Jessie* happens to be the central figure of every situation, and the object of universal sympathy throughout the play. Miss Addison showed herself fully equal to the occasion : good speaking, graceful action, pathos, almost tragic but unexaggerated, were noticeable in her impersonation, while she never passed the limits proper to a simple country girl of Jessie's rank in life.

In 1868 Miss Carlotta Addison joined Mr. and Mrs. Bancroft's company at the Prince of Wales's Theatre, and in that year, a revival of T. W. Robertson's play 'Society,' sustained the part of *Maud Hetherington*. At the same theatre, Saturday, January 16, 1869, first performance of T. W. Robertson's comedy entitled 'School,' the part of *Bella* was sustained by Miss Carlotta Addison, "who in showing the good qualities of the pupil-teacher revealed some rare excellencies of the actress. There was not the slightest exaggeration in the display of her emotion, and the exquisite love scene in the third act, so full of purity and tenderness, owed much of its effect to the discreetly subdued style in which it was acted by Miss Addison and Mr. H. J. Montague." (*Daily Telegraph*, January 25, 1869.) On Saturday, April 23 of the following year, she sustained the part of *Ruth Daybrooke* in the same author's comedy entitled 'M.P.,' then first performed at the Prince of Wales's Theatre. After fulfilling an engagement at the Gaiety

Theatre, on Saturday, October 7, 1871, Miss Carlotta Addison appeared at the Globe Theatre in a leading *rôle* (*Fanny Smith*), first performance of H. J. Byron's comedy 'Partners for Life.' On the 9th of March, 1872, first performance at the same theatre of Albery's play 'Forgiven,' she sustained the part of *Mrs. Redruth;* and in the same year, at the same theatre, *Mrs. Cuthbert*, in a revival of H. J. Byron's comedy 'Cyril's Success.' In February 1873, first performance at the same theatre of Mr. Albery's comedy 'Oriana,' Miss C. Addison acted the part of *Peep* with great success. The play itself proved unattractive, but Miss Addison's acting in it received unqualified praise. In April 1875, in a revival of 'The Merchant of Venice' at the Prince of Wales's Theatre, which proved unsuccessful, though for the most part carefully acted and well put on the stage, she sustained the part of *Nerissa;* and in October of the same year played the heroine, *Ethel Grainger*, in Byron's comedy 'Married in Haste,' produced on Saturday, the 2nd of that month, at the Haymarket Theatre. A contemporary journal (*Athenæum*, October 9, 1875) remarked of this performance that Miss Carlotta Addison, as the heroine, had made a distinct stride in her profession. So concentrated and intense was the manner in which she displayed feeling, without going outside the bounds of social custom, that a high position might reasonably be predicted for her as an exponent of realistic drama.

Since her marriage, in September 1876, Miss Carlotta Addison has rarely appeared on the stage. At the Prince of Wales's Theatre, in 1877, she played *Grace Harkaway*, in a revival of 'London Assurance'; and at the Haymarket Theatre on Thursday, October 3, 1878, appeared as *Julia* in a revival of 'The Rivals.'

ADDISON, FANNY (Mrs. H. M. PITT), elder daughter of the late Edward Phillips Addison, comedian, and sister of the above-named Carlotta Addison, was born in Birmingham, December 1847. She was educated by her father for the stage in childhood, and acted frequently at the Doncaster Theatre in children's parts in the intervals between school vacations. At the age of fifteen Miss Addison commenced work in earnest at the Theatre Royal and Amphitheatre in Liverpool. She subsequently accepted an engagement as "leading lady," first at the Newcastle-on-Tyne Theatre Royal, and subsequently at the Bath and Bristol Theatres. She made her first appearance in London, Monday, November 19, 1866, at Her Majesty's Theatre in Falconer's drama, entitled 'Oonagh.' The part which Miss Fanny Addison sustained in the play was carefully acted, and received very favourable notice from the press. (See, especially, the *Morning Star*, November 22, 1866.) The play itself was withdrawn after but few representations. On Thursday, October 24, 1867, on the occasion of the opening of the New Queen's Theatre, Long Acre, London (now relegated to other uses), Miss Addison played the part of *Josephine de Beaurepaire*, in the first performance of 'The Double Marriage' (Charles Reade), founded on that author's story of 'White Lies.' In this play Miss Fanny Addison gave a fine and passionate representation of the heroine. Some portions of her acting were intensely tragic, and all of it was excellent.

In October 1868 Miss Addison appeared at Drury Lane Theatre in Halliday's drama 'King o' Scots,' performing the part of *Martha Trapbois* with considerable effect. This actress's most important and successful London engagements have been as follows, viz. : (1) *Rosa Dartle* in Halliday's 'Little Em'ly,' produced at the Olympic Theatre October 9, 1869, a part which she sustained with great force and earnestness. Her acting was thus commented upon in a London journal : "The highest compliment that could be paid to an artist was certainly paid to Miss Addison. So completely did she identify herself with the terrible *Rosa Dartle*, and so vile and powerful was her invective, that the audience, forgetting the courtesy due to a lady, and oblivious of the canons of criticism, actually hissed her *because* she acted so extremely well. Never was such a paradox heard of. But it was not only in the fierce and unbridled passion that Miss Addison showed herself such a consummate artist. The heartbroken accents in which she tells the frightened girl of her own love for Steerforth were exquisitely touching." (*Weekly Dispatch*, October 17, 1869.) (2) *Queen Elizabeth* in the same author's play of 'Amy Robsart,' produced at Drury Lane September 24, 1870 ; and (3) the *Countess Danischeff* in 'The Danischeffs,' produced at St. James's Theatre, January 6, 1877. At intervals between her London engagements Miss Addison has played in the provinces as " star leading lady " of the so-called 'Two Roses,' the 'Caste,' and the Pitt-and-Hamilton Comedy Companies, of the latter of which her husband is joint manager.

AMALIA, MISS, burlesque actress, made her *début* on the London stage at the Surrey Theatre, December 26, 1869, in the pantomime of 'St. George and the Dragon.' She subsequently played in other pantomimes, securing, conjointly with Miss Violet Cameron, the full honours of the evening on December 27, 1873, at Drury Lane Theatre, "for her acting and singing in a ballad called 'Buttercup Green,'" introduced into the burlesque opening. More recently Miss Amalia has been engaged at the Gaiety, and has played in many of the extravaganzas of Mr. Byron on which that theatre mainly, and for the most part profitably relies as its principal attraction.

ANDERSON, JAMES R, was born in Glasgow, May 8, 1811. In the early part of his professional career he "strolled" as a member of the company of the Theatre Royal, Edinburgh, under Mr. William Murray ; on the Nottingham Circuit with Mr. Tom Manly ; and as a member of the Theatre Royal, Newcastle-on-Tyne, Company with Mr. Sam Penley. Mr. Anderson was manager of the Leicester, Glo'ster, and Cheltenham Theatres in 1834-5-6, and at the latter theatre first met Mr. William

Macready, who offered him an engagement. Mr. Anderson made his *début* in London 30th September, 1837, at the Theatre Royal, Covent Garden, under Mr. Macready's management, in the part of *Florizel* ('A Winter's Tale'), winning golden opinions for the ease and propriety of his demeanour and delivery.

His next appearance was in 'The Novice,' a dramatic piece, which did not prove successful. The following year, May 23, 1838, Mr. Anderson played the part of *Sir Valentine de Grey* in an original drama by Sheridan Knowles, then for the first time performed at Covent Garden Theatre, entitled 'Woman's Wit; or, Love's Disguises.' Thursday, March 7, 1839, at the same theatre, he personated *Chevalier de Mauprat*, on the occasion of the first performance of Lord Lytton's play of 'Richelieu' with Macready, Warde, Phelps, Howe, and Helen Faucit in the principal characters. The performers exerted themselves so as to render selection for praise impossible. "Each seemed in possession of, and able to realize, the character that was professedly personated. . . . The irritability, the extremes of feeling, the vivacity and the earnestness of *De Mauprat*, were effectively presented by Mr. Anderson." (*Morning Chronicle*, March 8, 1839.) At the opening of Covent Garden Theatre under the Vestris-Mathews management, September 30, 1839, he played the part of *Biron* ('Love's Labour Lost'); and on March 16, 1840, for the first time, the character of *Romeo* at the same theatre. In September of the same year Mr. Anderson acted *Fernando*, in the first performance of Sheridan Knowles's play 'John of Procida.' He was also the "original" *Charles Courtly* of 'London Assurance,' by Dion Boucicault, first performed at Covent Garden Theatre May 4, 1841. Notwithstanding the not too favourable criticisms of the London press, this play was one of the most signal successes of the Vestris-Mathews management of that theatre. The *Examiner*, March 7, 1841, thus remarked upon the individual merits of the players in the original cast: "The degree of merit that appeared in the acting of the piece was a test of the incapacity of the actors for anything higher or better; a melancholy exhibition of the state of the stage. We would except from this remark Mr. Anderson, whose part was unsuited to him; Mr. Keeley, who is always an admirable comedian; and we are surprised to find ourselves add Mr. Mathews."

In January 1842 Mr. Anderson took part at Drury Lane Theatre in the opening performance which inaugurated Mr. Macready's management, sustaining the part of *Bassanio* ('Merchant of Venice'). During the month of February 1842 his name appeared in the original cast of Douglas Jerrold's comedy 'The Prisoners of War'; and on the 23rd of the same month he played *Titus Quintus Fulvius*, in the drama of 'Gisippus' (Gerald Griffin), at its first performance at the same theatre, Mr. Macready being in the title *rôle*. Mr. Anderson earned special praise for his performance in the last act. It was stated that his choking voice when he recognized the sword of Gisippus, and the horror that spread over his features and shuddered through his frame, as he staggered wildly off to rescue his friend, suggested much greater powers in Mr. Anderson than he had ever given any indication of before. He obtained repeated plaudits.

Monday, May 23, 1842, was the closing night of Macready's first season at Drury Lane, and Mr. Anderson played *Othello* then for the first time. He had been a rising star ever since he made his first appearance at Covent Garden under Mr. Macready's management. Said the *Times*, May 24, 1842 : " Mr. Anderson's *Othello* last night was what might have been expected from him ; it was manly, it was careful, it was eloquent. Probably no one could have delivered better the speech to the senate. Mr. Anderson has a good ear for rhythm and metre, he makes fewer slips than most of his colleagues, and this speech was beautifully spoken, with the calm dignity of the veteran soldier, and with a voice deepening into emotion as he came to the tale of love. The speech at the close of the tragedy, which terminates with *Othello's* death, the speech concluding with ' Othello's occupation's gone,' may likewise be cited as specimens of elocution, mournful and deeply impressive. . . . . The expression of countenance during the quieter stage of jealousy was well sustained ; it was a growing sorrow. . . . The first loud burst of anguish was effective—it was a startling contrast ; and as the Moor sank exhausted into a chair, the audience rose into loud and repeated applause."

During the season 1842-3, at Drury Lane (the second of Mr. Macready's management), Mr. Anderson played the following leading parts, viz. *Orlando* in ' As You Like It '; *Captain Absolute* in ' The Rivals '; *Harry Dornton* in ' The Road to Ruin '; *Faulconbridge* in ' King John '; *Posthumus* in ' Cymbeline.' On February 11, 1843, Mr. Browning's poetic melodrama ' A Blot on the Scutcheon ' was first performed at Drury Lane, and Mr. Anderson sustained the character of *Earl Mertoun ;* and on the 24th of April following, being the night of the first performance of Sheridan Knowles's ' The Secretary,' the title *rôle.* The following season, 1843-4, Mr. Anderson was engaged at Covent Garden Theatre, playing Shakespearian characters alternately with Vandenhoff and Phelps, viz., *Othello, Iago, Cassio,* &c. On October 20, 1845, at a performance of Lord Lytton's play of ' The Lady of Lyons ' at the Haymarket Theatre, Mr. Anderson sustained the part of *Claude Melnotte* with care and tact ; " but his voice," said the *Athenæum* (November 1, 1845), "that once fine organ, seems irreparably ruined ; it is husky and guttural, and requires excessive watchfulness to prevent its becoming inarticulate."

During the years 1846-7, and part of the year 1848, Mr. Anderson fulfilled various engagements in the United States, opening in the part of *Othello* at the Park Theatre, New York. Returning to England in 1848 he made a professional tour of the provinces in the early part of 1849, in company with Miss Huddart (Mrs. Warner), acting with great success in Birmingham, Manchester, Liverpool, Dublin, Edinburgh, and Glasgow. Following this he became manager of the Theatre Royal, Drury Lane, and "opened" December 26, 1849, with Shakespeare's 'Merchant of Venice,' and the pantomime of 'Good Queen Bess,' in Mr. Anderson's opinion one of the best and most successful examples of this species of entertainment ever produced. Among his company were included Mr. Vandenhoff and Mrs. Nisbett.

In the year 1850 Mr. Anderson produced various plays at Drury Lane Theatre, principally of the Shakespearian and poetic drama, —'As You Like It'; 'Othello'; 'The Hunchback'; Beaumont and Fletcher's 'The Elder Brother ; or, Love at First Sight'; Planché's adaptation of Schiller's 'Fiesco,' &c. In the following year, on January 16, he produced an original comedy, 'The Old Love and the New' (Sullivan), in which he played the part of *Captain Sidney Courtoun*. The piece was but a partial success. His next production, however, was a more profitable venture. It was a drama entitled 'Azaël, the Prodigal,' founded on MM. Scribe and Auber's 'L'Enfant Prodigue.' The English adaptation of this play, first performed at Drury Lane on Wednesday, February 19, 1851, is described in contemporary journals as "one of the most elaborately gorgeous exhibitions ever placed on the boards." It had a very successful run. Discussing its merits the *Athenæum* of February 22, 1851, remarked :—"We are next taken to Memphis, with its Egyptian architecture and processions, and especially its temple of Isis, the interior of which is shown with all its grandeur and mystical rites, voluptuous and picturesque to the extreme point of tolerance. As a splendid show the scene surpasses all examples of which we have any remembrance." Mr. Anderson played *Azaël*, the son; Mr. Vandenhoff the part of Reuben, the father. In April, 1851, the bill was changed, and the management produced 'The Queen of Spades' (Boucicault), founded on a French piece, 'La Dame de Pique.' In June 1851 Mr. Anderson produced another successful play, which brought money to the treasury, viz., Lovell's 'Ingomar,' in which he sustained the title *rôle*. Although a considerable success, it was not, however, sufficient to retrieve the falling fortunes of the theatre ; and on the 24th of the same month Mr. Anderson retired from the management of Drury Lane Theatre. During the two seasons he had held the lesseeship the speculation had resulted in a loss of 9161*l.* The number of nights the theatre was open was 232 (*Athenæum*, July 26, 1851).

Mr. Anderson now turned his attention to "starring," and down to the date of his retirement from the stage occupied himself with this more profitable and less speculative way of securing theatrical honours and pecuniary independence. He began his career as a "star" actor at the Britannia Theatre, under the management of Mr. Sam Lane, November 3, 1851. His first engagement here was made for six nights at 25*l.* a night. Afterwards he went to the City of London Theatre, and played a six-weeks' engagement at 80*l.* a week. In May 1852 Mr. Anderson returned to the Britannia Theatre for a four-weeks' engagement, concluded at the rate of 100*l.* a week. These figures will enable the reader to judge of the remuneration at one time afforded prominent actors by the London

East-end Theatres.* In 1853 he fulfilled an engagement at the Strand Theatre, appearing there Monday, January 17, in a piece originally produced at the City of London Theatre, and written by one of its "stock" actors, by name John Wilkins, under the title 'Civilization.' The play was founded on Voltaire's 'L'Ingénu,' and was a remarkable success. Mr. Anderson played in it the part of *Hercule*, an Indian of the Huron tribe.

In the year 1853 Mr. Anderson again went to America, and opened at the old Broadway Theatre in New York. It was stated as an item of gossip (*Athenæum*, October 8, 1853, p. 1197), that this engagement was effected at 16,000*l.* for four years, to perform 800 nights; this sum not including travelling expenses. Although Mr. Anderson was undoubtedly a great favourite in American cities, he was scarcely fortunate enough to realize these extraordinary terms, for in the year 1854 he had returned to England and was acting with "great success, for the most part in five-act tragedies," at the Standard Theatre, London. And he continued to perform at the same theatre, renamed the New National Standard Theatre, as a "star," with but few intervals of rest, down to November 1855. In November 1856 he revisited the United States, playing for some part of the time at Wallack's Theatre, New York; and again in 1858, and the year following, he went to America. He visited California, opening in San Francisco, March 9, 1859, in *Hamlet*, and playing 30 nights in that city; in Sacramento City he played 14 nights, and in Nevada City 6 nights. Making a second short trip to San Francisco he returned to New York after six months' absence, having netted over $10,000. In 1863 Mr. Anderson joined Mr. Richard Shepherd as part manager at the Surrey Theatre, which was unfortunately destroyed by fire in February 1865. During this joint management Mr. Anderson produced his own stirring drama of 'The Scottish Chief,' which had a run of 80 nights, and Shakespeare's 'Second Part of King Henry VI.' (the Wars of the Roses), which achieved a success of nearly 100 nights. This play had probably not been performed in England, until Mr. Anderson produced it, for a period of 200 years. The cast of the play is, as most persons are aware, very full, and all the actors at "the Surrey" had to double, treble, and quadruple their parts. Mr. Anderson himself played the *Duke of York* and *Jack Cade*. In May 1867 he made a voyage to Australia, *viâ* the West Indies, Panama, and New Zealand, playing at Melbourne, Ballarat, Sydney, Adelaide, &c., returning home by way of Ceylon, Aden, and Malta. Mr. Anderson was absent for 32 weeks, and had the good fortune to earn 3000*l.* by his trip round the world. In 1873-4 he once again appeared on the boards of his old house, Drury Lane, with much success, as *Antony* ('Antony and Cleopatra'), and as *Richard Cœur de Lion* in an adaptation of Sir Walter Scott's 'Talisman.' Mr. Anderson has written several dramatic pieces, none of which, however, have secured any permanent success, with the exception of 'Cloud and Sunshine,' and 'The Scottish Chief,' already mentioned.

* Letter from Mr. Anderson to the Editor.

ANDREWS, ALBERT GARCIA, was born at Buffalo, New York, U.S.A., and was educated in France and at the College of the City of New York. He has been more or less engaged in dramatic affairs since boyhood, under the guidance and instruction of his father, the late M. A. Andrews, who was for some years professionally connected with the Haymarket Theatre. Mr. Andrews's first important appearance on the stage was at the Gaiety Theatre, Dublin, with the so-called ' Chippendale Comedy Company,' on April 17, 1876. He remained with that company for two seasons, and then became a member of the "stock" company at the Theatre Royal, Newcastle-on-Tyne. Subsequently, June 1877, he joined the Haymarket company on tour, and "opened" as *Crabtree* in ' The School for Scandal,' to Mr. J. B. Buckstone's Sir Benjamin Backbite. Whilst with the same company Mr. Andrews played such characters as *Careless, Fag,* and *David* in ' The Rivals'; *Cool* in ' London Assurance'; *Captain Smart* in ' Overland Route,' &c. His first appearance on the London stage was made December 1877 at the National Standard Theatre in the aforesaid part of *Captain Smart.* Subsequently he was engaged by the management of the Lyceum Theatre to play in the revival by Mr. Irving of ' Louis XI.,' and sustained therein the character of *The Dauphin,* March 9, 1878. Mr. Andrews is still (1879) a member of the company of the same theatre, having recently personated the part of *Second Gravedigger* in the revival of ' Hamlet.'

*ANSON, GEORGE WILLIAM, son of the undermentioned John William Anson, was born in Montrose, N.B., November 25, 1847. He first appeared on the stage in December 1865 at the Theatre Royal, Edinburgh, and had achieved some success in the provinces (notably at Liverpool) as a "character actor" previous to his *début* in London, which took place at the Olympic Theatre, October 4, 1873, in the part of *Minadab* in H. J. Byron's four-act comedy ' Sour Grapes.' Mr. Anson's acting on this occasion made a favourable impression. In the following year, in February, he performed the *rôle* of *Verges* in a revival at the Olympic Theatre of Shakespeare's ' Much Ado About Nothing,' Mr. Righton playing *Dogberry,* Mr. G. Neville *Benedick,* and Miss Fowler *Beatrice.* At the same theatre, in March of the same year (1874), on the occasion of the first performance of Tom Taylor's four-act historical drama, entitled ' Lady Clancarty ; or, Wedded and Wooed,' Mr. Anson sustained, in a way which elicited high admiration of his dramatic powers, the part of *Scum Goodman.* In this drama Miss Cavendish "created" the leading *rôle,* and Miss Fowler the character of *Lady Betty Noel.* Mr. Anson was likewise in the original cast (1) of ' The Two Orphans,' "drama in six acts and eight tableaux," adapted from the French ' Les Deux Orphelines,' produced at the Olympic Theatre, Monday, September 14, 1874; and (2) of Mr. Albery's five-act comedy ' The Spendthrift; or, the Scrivener's Daughter,' first performed at the same theatre in May 1875. His acting in the latter play was remarked upon as " strikingly realistic."

Mr. Anson performed also in revivals of 'The Ticket-of-Leave Man' and 'Henry Dunbar' at the Olympic; his picture of light-hearted and ebullient villainy, as typified in the amusing *Major* of the last-named drama, was singularly life-like and unconventional, and formed not the least interesting and attractive element of the revival. It may be interesting to note that 'Henry Dunbar; or, a Daughter's Trial,' a four-act drama by Tom Taylor, founded on Miss Braddon's novel, was first produced at the same theatre in December 1865. At that time Miss Kate Terry (Mrs. Arthur Lewis) had not quitted the stage, and the play obtained a measure of success to which her acting as Margaret Wentworth the heroine, and that of Mr. Henry Neville as the so-called Henry Dunbar, largely contributed. This piece has always been a favourite with Olympic playgoers, who in general exhibit a nice appreciation of the trifling infirmities and cool impudence of the *Major*.

In 1875-6 Mr. Anson was engaged at the Court Theatre, and appeared there in burlesque with considerable *éclat*, and in a revival of the comedy of 'New Men and Old Acres,' in which he sustained the character of *Bunter*. In 1877-8 he had returned to the Olympic Theatre; and on Monday, June 10 of the latter year was in the original cast of Messrs. Tom Taylor and Paul Meritt's three-act domestic drama 'Love or Life.' The piece, however, proved unattractive. In the summer season of 1879 Mr. Anson was engaged at the Haymarket Theatre, and appeared there in April in Mr. W. G. Wills's unsuccessful five-act comedy 'Ellen; or, Love's Cunning,' subsequently revised by the author and reproduced at the same theatre as a three-act comedy under the title of 'Brag.' There were some admirable points in both these plays, but each lacked intelligibility and cohesion. The characters which secured most notice were those of *Tom Pye*, most amusingly played by Mr. Charles Kelly; a *Jesuit Priest*, superbly acted by Mr. Anson himself; and *Lady Breezy*, performed by Miss B. Henri. Miss Florence Terry "created" the title *rôle*. Following the withdrawal of 'Brag,' Mr. Boucicault's all-but-forgotten Adelphi drama 'The Life of an Actress' was placed on the Haymarket stage, Mr. Anson undertaking the *rôle* of *Grimaldi*, originally played by the author of the play. As an actor Mr. Anson is possessed of force and pathos, and is an excellent low comedian. He has acquired the facility of a foreign accent which in some pieces he has employed to advantage. On the whole, his broken English is the best that has been heard on our stage since the days of Mr. Alfred Wigan, with whom, in that actor's well-known impersonation of *Achille Talma Dufard*, Mr. Anson favourably compares. He has been recently (July 1879) appearing in this character at the Folly Theatre, London.

ANSON, JOHN WILLIAM, father of the above-named, was born in London, July 31, 1817. At the age of twenty he joined the Cambridge "Garrick Amateur Club," in whose theatrical performances he bore a leading part, and in 1843 entered the dramatic profession, first appearing at the Theatre Royal, Bath, as *Lissardo* in the comedy of 'The Wonder.' His *début* being a success, Mr. Anson joined the Ryde and Southampton, and afterwards the York, and later, the Belfast " circuits," of the latter of which organizations he was a member for four years. For some considerable period of his earlier career Mr. Anson was manager of the Dundee, Perth, Montrose, and Inverness theatrical companies. He made his first appearance in London in 1853, as a member of Mr. W. Cooke's dramatic company, then playing at Astley's. At that theatre Mr. Anson appeared in a dramatic piece entitled 'The Battle of the Alma'; and subsequently sustained there the character of *Falstaff;* and during a revival of 'Rob Roy' the part of *Baillie Nicol Jarvie.* For many years Mr. Anson was connected with the Adelphi Theatre under the lesseeship of Mr. Benjamin Webster. He has taken a prominent part in various enterprises designed to benefit members of his profession incapacitated through age or ill-health from following the active duties of their calling. In 1855 he founded the Dramatic, Equestrian, and Musical Sick Fund ; and he was also largely instrumental in promoting the foundation of The Dramatic College, an institution which, continuing for some years, resulted in failure, owing to the lack of adequate pecuniary support.

APPLEBY, THOMAS BILTON, was born at Howdon (New-castle-on-Tyne). He began his professional career August 3, 1866, at the Theatre Royal, Dundee, under the management of Mr. E. D. Lyons, as " first low comedian and principal burlesque actor," " opening " there as *Wormwood* in 'The Lottery Ticket.' Afterwards he fulfilled engagements at the Theatres Royal, Glasgow and Edinburgh, and at the Tyne Theatre (Newcastle-on-Tyne), where, at its first performance in England, Mr. Appleby played the part of *Sadlove* in Boucicault's drama 'Elfie ; or, the Cherry Tree Inn.' On March 4, 1872, he joined the late Mr. L. J. Sefton's company at the Theatre Royal, Leeds, selected to play 'Pygmalion and Galatea' throughout the provinces, and sustained the part of *Chrysos* during the very successful provincial "run" of the piece. Mr. Appleby played at the same theatre on the date above given the title *rôle* in Burnand's burlesque 'King Kokatoo ; or, Who is Who, and Which is Which?' afterwards altered and produced at the Opéra Comique, London, under the title of 'Kissi-Kissi.' Mr. T. B. Appleby made his *début* on the London stage August 15, 1874, at the last-named theatre as the *Governor* in the opera bouffe 'The Broken Branch.' At the conclusion of his engagement at the Opéra Comique, Mr. Appleby joined, successively, the companies of the Theatres Royal, Manchester and Hull, and of the Gaiety Theatre, Dublin, remaining at the latter theatre for two years, where his careful acting of the *First Grave-digger* in a revival of 'Hamlet' during an engagement of Mr. Irving secured well-merited approbation. Afterwards he joined the company of the late Mdlle. Beatrice to undertake "the character business." With that company he appeared at the Olympic Theatre August 5, 1878, as *Remy* in 'The Woman of the People'; and at the same theatre April 27, 1879, on the occasion of the first performance in London of an original "comedy-drama" by Frank Harvey, entitled 'Married, not Mated,' he played the part of *Matthew Lambert.*

ARCHER, FRANK (a *nom de théâtre ;* FRANK BISHOP ARNOLD), was born at Wellington, Salop. He began his dramatic career at the Theatre Royal, Nottingham. In September 1869 Mr. Archer appeared at the Prince's Theatre, Manchester, under Mr. Calvert's management, as *Polixenes* in a revival of 'A Winter's Tale'; and continued at the same theatre for several seasons, playing principally in the Shakespearian revivals introduced by Mr. Calvert, 1869–72. In March 1871 Mr. Archer appeared there as *Apemantus* in 'Timon of Athens,' the first time of its production in Manchester, concerning which performance the *Manchester Guardian* (March 8, 1871) wrote : " The rare perceptive power of the great poet, of the subtle differences between qualities which a common generalization would consider identical, is finely displayed in this drama. Timon the misanthrope is an altogether different being from *Apemantus* the cynic. In make-up, attitude, gait, and voice Mr. Archer realizes this latter character admirably. He is, however, a trifle too ready with his bitter badinage, and thus sometimes suggests rather a chiselled criticism than a flashing retort. He is too *au fait ;* but in all other respects he speaks and acts the part well."

The same year Mr. Archer accepted an engagement at Liverpool ; but returning to Manchester, played *Antonio* in a grand revival of 'The Merchant of Venice.' He made his first appearance in London at the Prince of Wales's Theatre, May 1872, as *Captain Dudley Smooth* in 'Money.' During May 1873 Mr. Archer appeared as the *King* in 'Hamlet' in a series of performances of that tragedy organized at the Crystal Palace, Sydenham, by Mr. Tom Taylor ; and on the 19th of the same month and year he represented the character of *Julian Gray* in Mr. Wilkie Collins's play of the ' New Magdalen,' then performed for the first time at the Olympic Theatre. This part was very ably sustained by him.

In November 1874 he returned to the Prince of Wales's Theatre, appearing as *Lord Ptarmigant* in the revival of ' Society.' At the same theatre, in April 1875, he enacted the part of *Antonio* in the unsuccessful revival of ' The Merchant of Venice ' ; and subsequently *Vane* in ' Masks and Faces.' In April 1876 Mr. Archer undertook the representation of *Wilfred Gordon* in Byron's play of ' Wrinkles,' also at the Prince of Wales's Theatre ; and in May of the same year played *Prince Perovsky* in a revival of T. W. Robertson's ' Ours.' In September 1876 he reappeared at the Olympic, under Mr. H. Neville's management, as *The Duke de Gonzagues* in ' The Duke's Device.' In the following year, on July 6, at the Princess's Theatre, Edinburgh, he played *Hamlet.* " Mr. Archer's impersonation of the greatest of all Shakespearian characters is original, not in the sense that he has placed a strikingly new interpretation on any scene or passage, but because he has manifestly devoted himself with earnestness to the study of the part, has thought out the meaning of every line, and strives, with a very considerable measure of success, to give a natural, spontaneous delineation of each phase of the character. . . . The chief fault of his impersonation arose from his anxiety to avoid rant, which made his reading of some of the louder and more stormy scenes too quiet, and wanting in fire, though rarely in depth of passion. Mr. Archer's delivery of the great soliloquies was excellent from the total avoidance of the 'set speech' style, and from the meaning and expression given, without artifice or effort, to every word." (*Scotsman*, July 7, 1877.)

On March 30, 1878, and during the subsequent " run " of the piece at the Royal Court Theatre, he undertook the part of *Burchell* in Wills's play of ' Olivia,' founded on a leading incident in Oliver Goldsmith's ' Vicar of Wakefield.' On September 23 of the same year, in a revival at the Olympic Theatre of ' The Two Orphans,' Mr. Archer played the *Count de Linière;* and on Monday, March 24, 1879, first performance at the same theatre of Mr. W. S. Gilbert's ' Gretchen,' he acted *Mephistopheles*. The play proved unattractive; its withdrawal, however, giving rise to some difference of opinion as to the expediency of that course between the author and the management of the theatre.

ARCHER, JOHN, was born in London 1835, and entered the dramatic profession in 1849. He was for some years member of a travelling company, first of the Kent, and afterwards of the York circuits, and has appeared at the various leading theatres in the provinces. In 1868 he entered upon an engagement as a leading member of the " stock " company of the Edinburgh Theatre. He subsequently appeared at the Lyceum Theatre, in London, under Mrs. Bateman's management, in various parts in the revivals originated by Mr. Henry Irving.

ASHFORD, CHARLES, born in Birmingham, was in early life apprenticed to an engraver. He entered the dramatic profession in 1871, making his first appearance, September 11 of that year, at the Theatre Royal, Nottingham, as *Genshette* in the drama of 'Notre Dame.' Afterwards, from 1871 to 1877, he fulfilled engagements as " low comedian, character and burlesque actor " at various provincial theatres. At the Theatre Royal, Hull, 1876–7, under Mr. Sefton Parry's management, Mr. Ashford established himself as a great favourite in such parts as *Barney O'Toole* (' Peep o' Day '), *Wackford Squeers* (' Nicholas Nickleby '), *Picard* ('The Two Orphans'), &c. He made his *début* on the London stage at the Olympic Theatre, Monday, April 2, 1877, as *Welsh* (the ship's carpenter) in Mr. Charles Reade's drama ' The Scuttled Ship,' " by his dancing and thoughtful acting contributing not a little to the general success of the piece." Subsequently, in August of the same year, he acted at the Criterion Theatre the character of *Sampson Burr* in a revival of ' The Porter's Knot'; and in September joined Mr. Alexander Henderson's company at the Folly Theatre, appearing as *Neptune* in Lecocq's ' Musical Romance,' ' The Sea Nymphs,' and as *Babillard* in Offenbach's comic opera

'The Creole.' In February 1878, at the same theatre, on the occasion of the first performance in London of Planquette's comic opera 'Les Cloches de Corneville,' Mr. Ashford performed the part of *Gobo*. He has continued to act the same *rôle* during the successful "run" of the piece, at the Globe Theatre, extending to the present time (July 1879).

ASHLEY, HENRY JEFFRIES, nephew of the late well-known author and contributor to English literature, Dr. Doran, was born in London, and was originally educated for the profession of a civil engineer, having passed nine years of studentship in the office of the firm of Maudslay, Sons, and Field. A predilection for the stage induced Mr. Ashley to enter the dramatic profession, and he studied the rudiments of the actor's art under the late Edmund Glover in Glasgow. With the exception of a brief season at Birmingham, Mr. Ashley remained at Glasgow acting minor parts until the opening of the St. James's Theatre, London, under the management of Mr. and Mrs. Alfred Wigan in 1860. His *début* on the London stage was made at that theatre the same year, in Tom Taylor's comedy entitled 'Up at the Hills.' It was during this engagement, extending over two years, that this actor first discovered a qualification for eccentric comedy in a farce called 'Under the Rose.' After a season at Liverpool, under Mr. Alexander Henderson's management, Mr. Ashley returned to the St. James's Theatre (under Benjamin Webster), and was subsequently transferred to the Adelphi, where Mr. Ashley remained for seven years. Among the successes obtained by him at that theatre, the part of *William* in Charles Reade's adaptation of Tennyson's 'Dora' is deserving of mention. After leaving the Adelphi he accompanied Mr. Toole on an extended tour, and subsequently fulfilled several successful engagements at Liverpool and Hull. During the performance of the play entitled 'The Great Divorce Case,' at the Criterion Theatre, Mr. Ashley performed for a time the part of *Geoffrey Gordon*. He has continued at the same theatre, appearing in prominent characters in the following pieces, viz. : 'Hot Water,' 'On Bail,' the 'Pink Dominos' (in the character of *Joskyn Tubbs*), and the 'Porter's Knot' (in the character of *Sampson Burr*).

AUBREY, KATE, was born at Stafford, and commenced her theatrical career in the provinces under the management of Mr. John Hudspeth, making her first appearance on any stage at Derby, December 24, 1874. She remained with Mr. Hudspeth's company for some months, and afterwards (September 4, 1875) accepted an engagement at the Theatre Royal, Hull, which continued until May in the year following. Here Miss Aubrey played a variety of parts of more or less importance, notably the character of *Mrs. Leslie* in a new piece written by W. F. Broughton, entitled 'A Labour of Love,' and that of *Rosa Dartle* in 'Little Em'ly.' In May 1876 she was engaged at the Prince's Theatre, Manchester, under Mr. Browne's management, and played there in a new opera entitled 'Nell Gwynne,' and the part of *Pedro* in 'Giroflé-Girofla ';

and subsequently acted with Mr. Irving, Mr. Toole, and Miss
Neilson during their several engagements at that theatre in 1876.
Miss Aubrey made her *début* on the London stage, December 2,
1876, at the Royal Court Theatre, in the character of *Fanny
Bunter* in a revival of 'New Men and Old Acres'; and subse-
quently appeared there in various plays produced between 1876 and
1878.   In the latter year, on 30th March, she performed the part of
Sophia on the occasion of the first representation of Wills's play
'Olivia,' and continued to appear in the same character during
the run of the piece.

BALFOUR, THOMAS, was born in London, October 1849, and adopted the stage as a profession in 1876, having previously passed through the usual routine of study with "stock" companies in the provinces. He made his first appearance on the London stage as the *Coroner* in 'Jo' at the Globe Theatre, and afterwards played there a round of various characters (including *Rawdon Scudamore* in Boucicault's 'Hunted Down'), terminating his engagement at the end of April 1878. Mr. Balfour has supported Mrs. Herman Vezin on tour, playing *George du Hamel* ('Cora'), *Mr. Oakley* ('The Jealous Wife'), *Fortescue* ('Miss Chester'), &c.; and with the so-called 'Dan'l Druce' Company has played "juvenile leading parts," *Archibald Herries* ('Heroes'), &c.

BANCROFT, MARIE EFFIE (*née* WILTON, MARIE), was born in Doncaster, and entered the dramatic profession in childhood, playing various children's parts in the provinces, principally at the Norwich, Bristol, and Bath theatres. She made her first appearance on the London stage September 15, 1856, at the Lyceum Theatre, as the boy *Henri* in 'Belphegor,' Mr. Dillon sustaining the title *rôle;* and on the same evening acted *Perdita*, in a burlesque by William Brough, then performed for the first time, entitled 'Perdita; or, the Royal Milkmaid.' On Monday, April 13, 1857, at the Haymarket Theatre, Miss Wilton played the part of *Cupid* in Talfourd's burlesque of 'Atalanta,' "with her usual vivacity, and aptitude for point making"; and in the following year, on Monday, August 9, the comedy of 'Court Favour' was revived at the Strand Theatre, in order to introduce her in the part of *Lucy Morton*, originally played by Madame Vestris. The ability of Miss Marie Wilton being admitted, she at once received offers of engagement from London managers, and in December of 1858 acted the leading character in Morton's play, 'The Little Savage,' at the Strand Theatre with considerable success. Without particularizing the many characters played by this actress in the first years of her connection with the London stage, it may be remarked, in general, that for some seasons she was one of the leading attractions at the Haymarket, Strand, Adelphi, and St. James's Theatres, chiefly as an impersonator of sparkling characters in farce and extravaganza. Some of the more sterling successes at the Strand Theatre—at one period of its history the home of English burlesque—were in a considerable degree attributed to Miss Wilton's admirable acting. Her metropolitan reputation being established, in 1865, in conjunction with Mr. H. J. Byron, she entered upon the management of the little theatre in Tottenham Street, Tottenham Court Road, now known as the 'Prince of Wales's.' Many first-rate associations had been connected with the building, which was originally opened as a melodramatic theatre on Easter Monday, April 23, 1810, with the result, however, of bringing about the ruin of Mr. Paul, a retired pawnbroker, who became its manager. Succeeding conductors fared little better, until in 1821 it came under the bâton of Mr. Brunton, the father of the celebrated Mrs. Yates. In the interval it had changed its name more than once, and was known successively as 'The Regency,' and 'The West London Theatre.' A French company occupied it for some time ; and here M. Frédéric Lemaitre made his *début* in England. Afterwards Mr. Thomas Dibdin assumed the reins with moderate success. On the accession of William the Fourth, the theatre was again re-named, and called 'The Queen's,' in compliment to Queen Adelaide ; but in 1833 it changed its title to 'The Fitzroy,' under the management of the Mayhews, when 'The Wandering Minstrel,' afterwards made so famous by the inimitable Robson, was produced. Mr. Henry Mayhew and Mr. Gilbert Abbott a'Beckett were the chief authors of the establishment. In 1835 it came under the management of the celebrated Mrs. Nisbett, who again called it 'The Queen's'; but after passing through the hands of Colonel Addison and Mr. George Wild, it finally came into those of Mr. Charles James, a scenic artist, who retained possession of it from 1839, and who retained the lesseeship while transferring its direction to Mr. Byron and Miss Wilton. On Saturday, April 15, 1865, it was opened as the Prince of Wales's Theatre. Burlesque—hitherto Miss Wilson's forte—was at the outset the *raison d'être* of the new establishment. The performances on the opening night comprised, 'The Winning Hazard' (J. P. Wooler) ; 'La Sonnambula! or, the Supper, the Sleeper, and the Merry Swiss Boy' (H. J. Byron) ; and Troughton's farce of 'Vandyke Brown.' Miss Wilton acted the *Merry Swiss Boy*, and in the course of the evening spoke a prologue to the audience, which was very neatly written and well received. It was not, however, by means of Mr. Byron's metrical hits, or the production of such skilful work as Mr. Palgrave Simpson's 'Fair Pretender,' that the new management achieved its most noteworthy triumphs. The elevation of the Prince of Wales's Theatre to the rank of what might be called, with every propriety, the most fashionable and best frequented theatre in London, dates from the introduction there of modern English comedy—of comedy of a kind hitherto unattempted by any graduate in the younger school of English dramatists. The genius of the late T. W. Robertson supplied the necessary plays for presentation. In their order those plays, as produced at the Prince of Wales's Theatre, stand as follows :—'Society' on Saturday, November 11, 1865 ; 'Ours' on Saturday, September 15, 1866 ; 'Caste,' Saturday, April 6, 1867 ; 'Play,' Saturday, February 15, 1868 ; 'School,' Saturday, January 16, 1869 ; and 'M.P.,' Saturday, April 23, 1870. In 'Society' Miss Wilton undertook the part of *Maud Hetherington ;* in 'Ours' she played the original *Mary Netley ;* and in 'Caste' created the part of *Polly Eccles*. And here it should be mentioned that at the close of the season of 1867, in December, Marie Wilton married Mr. S. B. Bancroft, one of the members of her company, who had from the first borne a principal part with her in representing the characters drawn by the skilful pen of Mr. Robertson.

Continuing the enumeration of the parts played by Miss Wilton (now Mrs. Bancroft), in the comedies of Mr. T. W. Robertson above-mentioned:—In 'Play,' she enacted the part of *Rosie Fanquehere;* in 'School,' she represented the girlish heroine *Naomi Tighe;* and in 'M.P.' she was *Cecilia Dunscombe*, the lighter-hearted of the two girls by whose bright eyes and pretty ways the whole of that pleasant piece was irradiated. With truth it may be said that, during the six years of their first performance at the Prince of Wales's, Mrs. Bancroft was the leading spirit of the Robertsonian comedies. Success followed success in her accurate and charming reproductions of the characters sketched by the author. The name of Bancroft will always be intimately associated with Mr. T. W. Robertson's dramatic triumphs; and assuredly these were sufficiently brilliant to mark an epoch in the history of the modern English stage.

Previous to the production of 'SOCIETY'—which, it may be noted, was first performed at the Prince's Theatre, Manchester—Mr. Robertson, one of the most indefatigable of dramatic writers,* had only produced one piece which achieved anything of a success. This was the play of 'David Garrick,' an adaptation of the French, 'Sullivan,' first performed at the Haymarket Theatre Saturday, April 30, 1864 with Mr. Sothern in the title *rôle*. His later work 'Society' was not only original, but in tone and construction so thoroughly English that even the suspicion of a foreign source was at once dismissed as absurd. Said the *Times* (November 14, 1865), in discussing its merits, and those of the players who performed in it at 'the Prince of Wales's': "What is most to be admired in this piece is the fresh, genial spirit in which it is written. We can fancy, as it progresses, that we can see the author pleased with the contrivance of his own plot, and chuckling over the jokes as they come spontaneously from his brain. Even his looseness of construction, his frequent change of scene, his deficiency in everything like Gallic finish, and the inartificiality of some of his motives, far from offending, suggests the pleasant notion of a perfect freedom from conventional trammels. Then the personages are well and distinctly drawn, and adequately acted. Sydney Daryl [played by Mr. Bancroft], by nature a spirited gentleman, by habit a semi-Bohemian, is a much less commonplace personage than the generality of stage lovers. . . . Next in importance [in the comedy] is Lord Ptarmigant, a remarkably thin nobleman of unmistakably aristocratic appearance [played by Mr. Hare], who less from weakness than from indolence, allows his wife to tyrannize over him, till he finds that he has to defend a righteous cause, and then surprises the audience by a sudden display of authority.

* Thomas William Robertson, born 9th January, 1829, died 4th February, 1871; was educated at Spalding in Lincolnshire, and in Holland. He wrote a number of dramas for the minor theatres, but none of them brought him much reputation. His first great success was 'Society.' Other noticeable plays of his, in addition to those enumerated in the present article, are 'For Love,' 'Shadow Tree Shaft,' 'Progress,' 'Dreams,' 'Home,' and 'War.'

. . . . *Maud Hetherington* is a young lady of delicate sensibilities, delicately represented by Miss Marie Wilton, and as John Chodd, Mr. J. Clarke cleverly spices insufferable vulgarity and insolence with an indication of deep malignity.   As for the 'Owls,' big and little, they are all capital fellows, capitally represented, from rough Tom Stylus who can't go to a patrician ball without a dirty meer-schaum in his pocket, and the eloquent president, Dr. Olinthus O'Sullivan, to a silent gentleman with snow-white hair and beard, who is said to be a professor of philanthropy."

To the last-named play succeeded 'OURS,' a three-act comedy, played with great success at Liverpool in the summer of 1866, and in the ensuing September placed on the Prince of Wales's stage. On the first night of the piece the little theatre in Tottenham Street was crammed, and the verdict of Liverpool was endorsed with enthu-siasm.   "From the author of 'Society,'" remarked the *Daily News* (September 18, 1866), "it was only reasonable to expect dramatic writing of a high order, and no reasonable expectations will be disappointed in 'Ours.' Mr. Robertson evidently relies more upon the brilliancy of his dialogue, and the originality of his situa-tions, than upon any subtleties of plot. The construction of the piece is exceedingly simple, and the story of it may be told in two or three lines. A poor ensign falls in love with a rich ward, and a rich brewer falls in love with a poor companion. The Russian war summons the former to the Crimea, and the latter follows as a volunteer. They are joined by the ladies—whose presence at the seat of war, by the way, is not satisfactorily accounted for—and the two couples ultimately become two units. A minor character is introduced in the person of a Russian prince, who proposes to the heiress, is rejected, and bears his mortification like a gentleman. There is also a highly amusing sergeant, the possessor of twins, whose domestic calamity forms the subject of some happy allusions . . . . The acting of the comedy was very near perfection ; every-body was fitted to a nicety.   Mr. Clarke, as the wealthy brewer [Hugh Chalcot], misanthropic in appearance, but in reality the kindest of creatures, was excellent ; Mr. Hare, in the small part of the Russian prince [Prince Perovsky], made up and played as admirably as usual. Mr. F. Younge made his first appearance here as the doubly paternal sergeant [Sergeant Jones], and acted the part with much humour.   The fair manageress (Miss Wilton), whose reception was overwhelming, played as well as she looked [*Mary Netley*] ; and Miss Louisa Moore looked as well as she played [Blanche Haye].   The comedy is remarkably well mounted, and the last scene—a Crimean hut—was very effective."

'CASTE' was the next of Mr. Robertson's comedies.   The materials of which its story was composed had often been used before, but never more effectively.   "The author," wrote a contem-porary journal, "has combined the geniality of Mr. Dickens, with the cynicism of Mr. Thackeray.   He has taken the ordinary ballet girl of the stage and made her his heroine, and an angel, and he has shown, as clearly as a dramatist can show, that marriages between persons of very different classes are often very uncomfort-

able, if not positively unhappy." The plot was excellently constructed for the purpose of exhibiting and grouping the various
characters. " The Hon. George d'Alroy, son of the Marquise de
Saint-Maur, an English lady of high birth, married to a French
nobleman, has fallen in love with Esther, daughter of Eccles (a
dissipated specimen of the working man, who does no work), and,
during the absence of his mother on the Continent, visits the
humble residence of the plebeian in the character of an honourable
suitor.   He is accompanied by his friend, Captain Hawtree
[Mr. Bancroft], who lectures him from a worldly point of view on
the danger he is encountering by entering into a family so much
below him in rank.   Old Eccles [Mr. Honey] is simply detestable ;
his two daughters support themselves and him by dancing at the
' Theatre Royal, Lambeth' (wherever that may be), and though
Esther [Miss Lydia Foote] the object of his choice, is a girl of
superior manners, the same cannot be said of her sister *Polly*
(Miss Marie Wilton), who is a damsel of very blunt manners,
engaged to Sam Gerridge [Mr. Hare], a worthy gas-fitter, who
neither tries nor even desires to elevate himself above his order.
. . . . Eccles is a degraded mortal, who is always howling about
the rights of labour, but who has scarcely been known to do a
' stroke of work' within the memory of his oldest friends.   He hates
the aristocracy in theory, but is ready to lick the shoe of a person
of quality if anything is to be made by the degradation.   That
democratic clap-trap which is amongst the leading nuisances of the
day is satirized in this character with the most unsparing severity,
and the moral effect of the part is heightened by the contrast of
Eccles with Sam Gerridge, intended as a good specimen of the
operative class.   A less conservative writer would have found an
opportunity for putting a little clap-trap into the mouth of honest
Sam, but such operations are not to the taste of Mr. Robertson.
Sam is not at all idolized, nor are his uncouth appearance or the
vulgar terpsichorean feats which he performs under the influence of
excessive joy accompanied by the possession of lofty sentiments.
He is honest, industrious, and good-natured, has an eye ever
directed to the main chance, and respects his own ' caste' without
less respecting that of others.   He has a fitting partner in *Polly
Eccles*, whose character is in the main similar to his own, though a
tinge of feminine coquetry gives her somewhat the tone of a fine
lady.   These three parts are as well played as they can possibly
be by Mr. George Honey, Mr. Hare, and Miss Marie Wilton."
(*Times*, April 11, 1867.)
    "The hero of ' PLAY' is very much like a blackleg; his com-
panion is one of those ' Honourables' of ancient family who are
not above earning a little money by billiard-sharping ; and round
these two characters revolve, at different distances, an old tradesman and toady ; an old woman who borrows from nearly everyone
she meets ; a young lover who has more money than brains ; a
silly impulsive girl, one of those ideal actresses who are all beauty,
goodness, virtue, charity, and affection ; a Prussian soldier, who
speaks seven or eight words, not languages ; and another Prussian

soldier, who is qualified for a deaf and dumb asylum. These are the characters who have to work out the story ; and the story may be told in a very few words—attempted bigamy. The blackleg hears the silly girl has come into a large fortune ; cuts the announcement of this fact out of a sporting paper to conceal it from her uncle and guardian ; then makes love to the girl, and is defeated by the unexpected appearance of his wife, who is only a trifle less silly than the other woman. . . . The acting leaves nothing to be desired." (*Daily News*, February 17, 1868.)

In noticing the first performance of ' SCHOOL,' the *Times* (January 18, 1869) wrote as follows : " The fact is not to be denied that the production of a new comedy by Mr. T. W. Robertson at the theatre which, once obscure, has become, under the direction of Miss Marie Wilton, one of the most fashionable in London, is now to be regarded as one of the most important events of the dramatic year. . . . The name of the piece might possibly recall to the memory of some elderly playgoers a delightful comedy by Mr. Douglas Jerrold, entitled ' The Schoolfellow,' which was produced on the same boards more than thirty years ago, when the theatre flushed into temporary celebrity under the nominal management of Mrs. Nisbett. . . . Although in four acts the piece may be said to lack plot altogether, if by plot is meant a complication of incidents. Nor is this peculiarity felt to be a defect. Four pictures, all striking and full of significance, though of unequal merit, are connected with an artistic hand, and when all is over an unwearied audience is aware that a perfectly organized whole has been contemplated with uninterrupted pleasure. . . . The dialogue between the young lord [Lord Beaufoy, played by the late Mr. H. J. Montague] and Bella [played by Miss Carlotta Addison], while they converse in the moonlight, contemplating their own strongly-cast shadows, and fancifully commenting upon them, is replete with the prettiest conceits, in which it is hard to say whether wit or sentiment has the mastery, and the effect of the situation is heightened by the perfect arrangement of the decoration and the contrivance of dramatic effect. The school-girl archness of *Naomi*, and the transformation of the stubborn cynic Poyntz [Mr. Bancroft] into an uncouth adorer are expressed, too, in the smartest talk, sparkling with natural yet unexpected touches of humour. The actors, too, should receive their full share of credit for the perfect manner in which they realize the refined conception of the author."

Mr. Robertson added another leaf to the garland he had so honestly and honourably won at this theatre, by the production of ' M.P.' " None of his ' first nights,' we should say, can have been more genuinely and pleasantly successful than that of his new comedy ' M.P.' . . . In the way of light comedy there is nothing in London approaching the pieces, and the *troupe* of the Prince of Wales's taken together. In a more spacious theatre, and by an audience more largely leavened with the usual pit and gallery public, these light and sparkling plays would probably be voted slow in movement, slight in texture, and weak in interest. But in this pretty little bandbox of a house, with such artists as Marie

Wilton, Hare, Bancroft, and their associates to interpret them, almost at arm's length of an audience who sit as in a drawing-room, to hear drawing-room pleasantries, interchanged by drawing-room personages, nothing can be better fitted to amuse. Author, actors, and theatre seem perfectly fitted for each other. . . . Paris itself furnishes no exact *pendant* to this theatre and these comedies. The Gymnase would be, on the whole, the nearest parallel; but the staple of pieces at that house is heavier and more solid than Mr. Robertson has created for the Prince of Wales's. These plays are, indeed, so unlike other men's work that they amount to a creation. Light as they are, there is in them an undercurrent of close observation and half-mocking seriousness which lift them above triviality. The worldliness, which is their predominant atmosphere, is corrected by fresh airs of unselfishness and better feeling, skilfully let in from time to time. They play about life, but not with it. There is no vulgarity in them, and no horseplay; and their *morale* is, on the whole, healthy, even when they most affect to disclaim 'purpose,' and laugh 'goodiness' to scorn. Mr. Robertson is perfectly seconded by his actors. Miss Marie Wilton is the actress who, of all now on the stage, has preserved most of the arch humour and shrewd significance of Mrs. Keeley, while her line of parts combines with these a refinement which in Mrs. Keeley's usual business would have been misplaced. . . . Miss Marie Wilton was charming in the mingled archness, sweetness, petulance, grace, and sauciness, which she threw into her part." (*Times*, April 25, 1870.)

"In Miss Marie Wilton's performance of *Cecilia* it would be difficult to hint any fault," remarked another contemporary journal (*Daily News*, April 25, 1870). "Its spontaneous, genuine, and unflagging vivacity, though, perhaps, the quality which recommended it most to the audience, is really the least of its charms, which lie still more in the rarer qualities of the artistic actress. The perfect command of appropriate gesture and movement; the subtler play of feature; the power to indicate, in spite of an exterior of frivolity and mirth, a deeper and more earnest nature, these are things which on our stage are unhappily given but to the few. As *Cecilia Dunscombe*, Miss Wilton has actually succeeded in dignifying the famous 'young lady of the period'; and by a happy revelation of a something beneath the surface of a character, has, in spite even of a double gold eye-glass, and a faint approximation to a 'Grecian bend,' raised that odious and half-fabulous personage to a point absolutely commanding our sympathy and admiration."

In May 1872, Mrs. Bancroft undertook the part of *Georgina Vesey*, in a revival of 'Money' at the Prince of Wales's Theatre, thus adhering to the principle which resulted in the strong casts of former days—the principle of making even the smallest parts as effective as possible. As pertinent to this admirable plan—so carefully followed at the Prince of Wales's Theatre, under Mr. and Mrs. Bancroft's direction, and, with justice it should be added, by the late management of the Royal Court Theatre—the following remarks may seem not inappropriate: "From the current blemishes of English acting the Prince of Wales's company is to a great extent free. No attempt is made by any one of its members to eclipse his fellows, or to monopolize either the space on the boards or the attention of the audience; no piece is presented in such a state of unpreparedness that the first dozen performances are no better than rehearsals; no slovenliness in the less important accessories of the play is permitted. A nearer approach, accordingly, than elsewhere in England can be found to that *ensemble* it is the boast of the Comédie Française to encourage, is witnessed. Actors are measured, so to speak, by their parts, and are only to take such as fit them. Miss Wilton herself, with an artistic feeling to be expected from her, accepts a subordinate character. The example she sets is followed, and, as a result, the performance takes the town with a sort of wonder." (*Athenæum*, May 18, 1872.)

Among later assumptions by Mrs. Bancroft, *Lady Teazle*, in 'The School for Scandal,' revived at the Prince of Wales's Theatre in April 1874, should be noticed. "At last we obtain—at least in modern days—a *Lady Teazle* who is the fresh, genuine, impulsive country maiden wedded to an old bachelor, and not the practised actress, with all her airs and graces. How often in *Lady Teazle* the character is forgotten, the actress and the whole business invariably remembered! In the scandal scenes we were presented with an archness and sly sense of humour, always evident but never superabundant, in which Mrs. Bancroft has a special patent; in the coaxing scene with Sir Peter Teazle, the child-like desire to kiss and make friends, the almost kitten-like content when the reconciliation is made, and the expressive change of the countenance from sunshine to storm when the wrangle commences again, were admirably conveyed. But it was reserved for Mrs. Bancroft to make her most lasting impression in the screen scene. With wonderful care and welcome art the impression conveyed to an innocent mind by the insinuating deceit of Joseph was accurately shown by expression to the audience, though the excellence of the general idea culminated in what is known as *Lady Teazle's* defence, when the screen has fallen and the *dénouement* has taken place. This was entirely new, and thoroughly effective. The tones, alternating between indignation and pathos, between hatred of Joseph and pity for her husband's condition, were expressed with excellent effect. It was the frank and candid avowal of a once foolish but now repentant woman. The womanly instinct which [bids *Lady Teazle* touch and try to kiss her husband's hand, the womanly weakness which makes *Lady Teazle* totter and trip as she makes for the door of the hated room, the womanly strength which steels *Lady Teazle* in her refusal of assistance from Joseph, and the woman's inevitable abandonment to hysterical grief, *just before* the heroic goal is reached, were one and all instances of the treasured possession of an artistic temperament." (*Daily Telegraph*, April 6, 1874.)

In November of the same year Mrs. Bancroft played the part of *Jenny Northcote*, in Mr. W. S. Gilbert's charming "dramatic contrast" 'Sweethearts,' then first performed. (See subsequent criticism.) And in November 1875 she sustained the part of *Peg Woffington*, in a revival of ' Masks and Faces.' In April 1877 she acted the part of *Mrs. Heygarth*, in ' The Vicarage ' ; and in September of the same year, the character of *Hester Grazebrook*, in a revival of ' The Unequal Match,' in which she gave further proof of her careful study of character and keen insight into peculiarities of temperament.

On Saturday, January 12, 1878, Mrs. Bancroft undertook the *rôle* of the *Countess Zicka*, in an English version of M. Sardou's play of ' Dora,' entitled ' Diplomacy,' then first performed at the Prince of Wales's. In a lengthy and well-considered criticism of this piece, the method of its adaptation, and of the acting of those set down in the original English cast, the *Saturday Review* (January 19, 1878) remarked, that in one particular of some importance the English had the advantage over the French performance : " Mdlle. Bartet, promising though her acting was, did not approach the complete mastery and finish which Mrs. Bancroft shows in her playing of the *Countess Zicka*. . . . Whatever sins may be chargeable to the adapters, however, they have not been able to spoil the play for acting purposes. Mrs. Bancroft, as we have hinted, reveals as *Countess Zicka* a power for which her previous performances have scarcely prepared one. Every emotion of the scheming woman who, in Mrs. Bancroft's interpretation, says with infinite pathos that she might have been as good as Dora had she been as fortunate, is given with rare skill and truth. In the last act, the shame of her detection commands pity, in spite of the baseness of her conduct ; and so great an interest is given by the actress to what has been left of *Countess Zicka's* account of her early life and its trials, that one cannot but regret its curtailment." The *Countess Zicka*, though always an important element in the piece, is not brought into any marked prominence till the last act, where the toils are gathered round her, and, struggling bravely to the last, she is brought to make confession and to sue for pardon. In this act Mrs. Bancroft, the representative of that character, exhibited in a degree which none of her later performances have permitted to her, all the admirable refinements and resources of the art in which she is acknowledged a mistress.

On Saturday, January 11, 1879, ' Caste,' on the whole, the best known of the comedies of Mr. Robertson, was revived at the Prince of Wales's Theatre and had a successful run of nineteen weeks, the last performance taking place on Friday, May 30. Mrs. Bancroft had not appeared at the Prince of Wales's as *Polly Eccles* since 1871 ; the brightness and dramatic force of " her last appearances in this character"* during the period indicated, were beyond all praise. Of the original representatives of the piece, three were in their old places—Mrs. Bancroft, Mr. Bancroft, who again performed the part of Captain Hawtree, and Mr. George Honey, who represented the drunken father

---

* The playbills advertised these as Mrs. Bancroft's last appearances in the part of *Polly Eccles*.

(*see* HONEY, GEORGE). Of this revival it was remarked that, while armies of supernumeraries fill the stage of the great theatres, eight people on the stage of the Prince of Wales's cause the benches to be full. On Saturday, May 31, the programme was altered by the substitution, for the last-named play, of W. S. Gilbert's dramatic idyll, 'Sweethearts' (in which Mrs. Bancroft sustained her original part of *Jenny Northcote*), and by the addition of Palgrave Simpson's comedietta 'Heads or Tails,' and Buckstone's comic drama 'Good for Nothing.' "The main burden of the rest of the evening falls upon Mrs. Bancroft," remarked the *Times* (June 2, 1879). "It is hardly necessary to say how she sustains it in 'Sweethearts,' a poetical contrast by Mr. Gilbert, sometimes charming and sometimes nearly revolting, as the feeling for beauty of form or the tendency to cynicism in meaning, which make up the two sides of the author's work, alternately prevail. In the first act two young people are in love, but the pride of the girl is roused on hearing that her lover has suddenly determined, without consultation with her, to go to India; she pretends that he is indifferent to her, and teases him by mere courtesy when he comes to her to say 'Good-bye,' full of vague hopes and tender sentiments. He asks for a flower, and she gives him a whole pot of pelargoniums, and congratulates him on his botanical tastes. When he is gone, disappointed, she runs to see him come back, sure that he will come, ready, now that she has punished him, to betray the secret of her heart. Her happy flutter of expectation when she thinks she sees him returning, her sudden tears when, like the knight in the ballad, he shakes his bridle-rein and rides away, had the old result upon the audience. The emotions of Mrs. Bancroft are magnetic, and draw laughter and tears from some to whom these are rare luxuries. In the next act she is an old lady with silver hair, and her lover has come back with the title and fortune of a retired Indian Chief Justice. He visits the old place without any precise consciousness or recollection of the particular circumstances which make it dear to him. To the charming old maid whom he converses with so unconcernedly, her petulant dismissal of her sweetheart has been the one event of her life, and she has treasured ever since his rosebud, in exchange for which she made him that ill-timed gift of pelargoniums. So there comes about the second contrast of the drama. The first is between the garden in the country in 1848 and the suburban grass-plot in 1878. The second is between the woman who throughout her quiet life has cherished and kept green her old passion and the man with the dust and ashes of a busy life accumulated over the once active volcano of his love."

In the little comic drama of 'Good for Nothing,' Mrs. Bancroft represented the heroine *Nan*, 'for the first time for thirteen years,' according to the playbill. 'Good for Nothing' was first produced at the Haymarket Theatre in 1851, and is understood to be founded upon the French vaudeville 'La Gamine.' *Nan*, first personated by the late Mrs. Fitzwilliam, has also found excellent interpreters in Mrs. German Reed and Mrs. Mellon. Mr. Buckstone in the part of

Tom Diddles has been followed by Mr. Toole and the late Mr. John Clarke ; the original Harry Collier was Mr. Howe. " Mrs. Bancroft's performance of *Nan* is delightful because of its drollery, its naturalness, its artistic touches of pathos. This female Cymon of the streets, whom love converts from gutter games, rags, and uncleanness, to decency and propriety of language, conduct, and aspect, has never been more expertly or whimsically presented. From her first entrance, when soiled with mud, and fresh from throwing stones at Master Simpson, the landlord's son, who had interfered with her ' hop-scotch,' she stands to be rebuked by her ' two fathers '—the gardener who begins like a lamb and ends like a lion, and the stoker who begins like a lion and ends like a lamb— *Nan* is assured of the hearty goodwill of the audience ; her rapid toilet, accomplished chiefly by the aid of a blacking brush, affords great amusement ; and genuine sympathy attends her ultimate union with her true love, Charley the carpenter." (*Daily News,* June 4, 1879.) During the season negotiations were opened between Mr. and Mrs. Bancroft and Mr. J. S. Clarke, which resulted in the former becoming lessees of the Haymarket Theatre. It is understood that Mr. and Mrs. Bancroft will enter upon their new and more responsible undertaking at the beginning of 1880, when, should ' Duty ' prove sufficiently attractive, that play will constitute the principal attraction.

BANCROFT, SQUIRE BANCROFT, was born in London, May 14, 1841, and entered the dramatic profession at the Theatre Royal, Birmingham, in January 1861. Subsequently, he accepted engagements in Dublin and Liverpool, playing almost every line of character at each place, notably, various Shakespearian parts at the Theatre Royal in the first-mentioned city during the " starring " engagements of the late G. V. Brooke and Charles Kean in 1862-3. At this period of his career Mr. Bancroft likewise personated with considerable success the widely-different characters of *Bob Brierly* (' Ticket of Leave Man '), *Monsieur Tourbillon, John Mildmay, Captain Hawkesley,* and *Murphy Maguire.* He made his first appearance on the London stage on the occasion of the opening of the Prince of Wales's Theatre, under the management of Mr. Byron and Miss Marie Wilton, April 15, 1865. His reception being favourable, he was selected to sustain the part of *Sydney Daryl* in Mr. T. W. Robertson's comedy ' Society,' first performed in the November following. This, as we have already noted, was the first of the series of plays written by that dramatist which so largely contributed to the success of the Prince of Wales's Theatre, and in no small measure to establish the Wilton-Bancroft company in the foremost rank of present English players. In each Mr. Bancroft may be said to have created one of the leading characters. In ' Society ' (1865) he appeared as *Sydney Daryl* and afterwards as *Tom Stylus ;* in ' Ours ' (1866) as *Angus McAlister ;* in ' Caste ' (1867) he was the original *Captain Hawtree ;* in ' Play ' (1868) the original *Chevalier Browne ;* in ' School ' (1869) the original *Jack Poyntz.* This latter play is generally acknowledged to be the masterpiece, as regards dialogue, of the six principal works (including 'M.P.,' in which Mr. Bancroft took the part of *Talbot Piers*), written by the late T. W. Robertson. 'School' had a consecutive run of nearly four hundred nights (381) by way of commencement, and has since been performed with unvarying success at every leading provincial theatre in the kingdom. Considering the care, skill, and originality brought to bear on the original presentment of the character of *Jack Poyntz*, it seems only proper to mention Mr. Bancroft as a principal contributor to the conspicuous success which attended the first presentation of that play.

In 1867 Mr. Bancroft married Miss Marie Wilton, and a large share of the management of the Prince of Wales's Theatre thenceforward devolved upon him. After the death of Mr. Robertson, in 1871, revivals of various plays were tried at this theatre with gratifying success, the more noteworthy of these being 'Money,' in May, 1872, followed by the revival of 'The School for Scandal,' in 1874. In the first Mr. Bancroft played the part of *Sir Frederick Blount*, in the second that of *Joseph Surface*. Both representations exemplified the ability and earnestness with which this actor pursues his art. Said the *Daily Telegraph* (April 6, 1874): "The *Joseph Surface* of Mr. Bancroft, in that it is one of the most original and reflective performances, will attract most criticism, will probably court the most objection. When Mr. Fechter played Iago, and discarded the hackneyed villain, there was a similar disturbance. According to stage tradition, Iago and *Joseph Surface* are such outrageous and obvious rascals that they would not be tolerated in any society. Mr. Bancroft reforms this altogether, and by a subtlety and an ease most commendable, valuably strengthens his position as an actor and his discrimination as an artist. *Joseph Surface* can be played as a low, cunning villain, or as a hungry, excited, and abandoned libertine. Mr. Bancroft adopts the golden mean. His deception is never on the surface, his libertinism is never for an instant repulsive. Not altogether striking or showy at first sight, it is, however, one of those instances of good acting which strikes the beholder when the curtain is down and the play put away."

Among important parts played by Mr. Bancroft at the Prince of Wales's Theatre since 1872, the following deserve notice, viz., *Triplet* in 'Masks and Faces'; *Sir George Ormond* in 'Peril'; *Dazzle* in 'London Assurance'; *Blenkinsop* in 'An Unequal Match'; and lastly, *Count Orloff* in the English version of M. Victorien Sardou's play of 'Dora,' entitled 'Diplomacy,' performed in London for the first time January 12, 1878. "Some time ago, when writing of the performance of 'Dora' in Paris, we [*Saturday Review*, January 19, 1878] expressed a doubt whether adequate interpreters could be found for the great scene between the three men. We may as well say at once that we are delighted to find this doubt need not have been entertained. This scene, which is no doubt the one upon which the play depends, is played as admirably here as it was at the Vaudeville in Paris. . . . Mr. Bancroft's performance in this scene as *Count Orloff* (the Teckly of the original play) could hardly be improved, and his playing of the part throughout gives a fresh proof of Mr. Bancroft's fine power of impersonation— a thing somewhat different from acting in the loose sense which is too commonly attached to the word. The character demands an unusual capacity for indicating rather than expressing a passionate emotion, and in Mr. Bancroft's rendering of it we can find no fault." In the first of the great scenes of the play the acting of Mr. Bancroft, Mr. Kendal, and Mr. Clayton, respectively impersonating the friend, the husband, and the brother, could not well have been bettered. The situation is in itself very striking, and presented as it was by these three gentlemen, it brought down applause from all quarters of the house. The play was a great success.

In a revival of 'Caste,' January 1879, Mr. Bancroft resumed his original part of *Captain Hawtree;* and in June of the same year, in a revival of W. S. Gilbert's 'Sweethearts,' he sustained the character of *Harry Spreadbrow*, originally played by Mr. Coghlan.

Mr. Bancroft, it may be remarked, has devoted much time and energy at the Prince of Wales's Theatre to, what may be not unfitly termed, the art of stage management. Towards the end of the present year he becomes joint-lessee with his wife of the Haymarket Theatre.

BANDMANN, DANIEL EDWARD, was born at Cassel, Germany, and entered the dramatic profession at the age of 18, making his professional *début* at the Court Theatre of New Strelitz. He afterwards performed in various towns of Germany and Prussia, and in Vienna, and acquired considerable reputation as an actor in Shakespearian drama. Subsequently, going to the United States, Mr. Bandmann acted for the first time in English January 15, 1863, at Niblo's Garden in New York, where he created a very favourable impression as *Shylock*. He remained for five years in the United States acting in the principal cities. At Philadelphia (where his tragic power attracted the notice of the distinguished tragedian Edwin Forrest) he was selected to play *Hamlet* at a commemorative celebration of the tercentenary birthday of Shakespeare. Mr. Bandmann performed the same part at San Francisco during a "run" of the play, which extended to a month. He made his first appearance on the British stage at the Lyceum Theatre, on Monday, February 17, 1868, in a play called 'Narcisse,' which had already acquired much reputation in Germany and America. Its author, Herr Brach Vogel, a Berlin dramatic writer of some note, founded its chief incidents on M. Diderot's well-known story 'Neveu de Rameau.' Mr. Bandmann played the title *rôle*. The following notice of the performance was published in the *Times* (February 21, 1868) :—"On Monday night this theatre (the Lyceum) was crowded to an extraordinary degree by an audience anxious to witness the performance of Herr Bandmann, a German actor, who, though he had never been seen in London, had acquired in his own country and the United States a fame which had travelled to England. Herr Bandmann, by birth a Prussian, commenced his professional career by a tour through Bohemia, Austria, and Hungary, and then crossing to America came out at the *Stadt-theater*, New York, a house in the Bowery exclusively appropriated to German performances. So great was his success, that he was advised to study the English language. The counsel was followed, and its soundness was proved by a successful performance in English at Niblo's Garden, then the chief house for the higher class of drama, though now apparently doomed to the perpetual representation of spectacle. Herr Bandmann brings with him to England the translation of a German play, entitled ' Narcisse,' being the work in which his great successes, European and American, have been achieved. The hint for this piece was taken by the author, Dr. Brach Vogel, from the remarkable dialogue entitled 'Rameau's Neffe,' which was published by Goethe in 1805, and always has a place in his collected works. The history of this dialogue is curious. ' Le Neveu de Rameau ' was written by Diderot—of course in French—about the year 1760, and the original MS., we read, is still to be found in the Imperial library at St. Petersburg, where it is numbered 381. A copy of this MS. fell into the possession of Schiller, and was by him handed over to Goethe, who translated it, and published it with a highly instructive appendix. A re-translation from Goethe's German into French, by M. de Saur, published in 1821, first rendered the dialogue accessible to the French public, and was for a time regarded as the genuine production of Diderot. However, shortly afterwards the real original, taken from a copy in the possession of the only surviving daughter of Diderot, was published in the collected works of the atheistical *philosophe*, edited by Brière. . . .

" In the elaborate book on the life and works of Diderot, written by Dr. Carl Rosencranz, and published rather more than a twelvemonth since, Brach Vogel's ' Narcisse ' is mentioned as one of the most popular plays of the modern German repertory. That it could ever become very popular in England, save as a vehicle for the actor who plays *Narcisse*, is extremely doubtful. The numerous *dramatis personæ* are neither strongly marked, nor are they of a kind that greatly appeals to British sympathies, inasmuch as these generally lie dormant in the atmosphere of a theatrical French Court. The dialogue, too, the repartees of *Narcisse* included, is marked by that absence of sparkle which is not unfrequent in Teutonic wit. This latter defect is rendered most apparent by a scene representing Madame de Pompadour at her toilette, which has been written in by the last French adapter, and which in point, purpose, and historical significance is so far superior to the rest of the work, as far as dialogue is concerned, that we should hazard a wish that the same gentleman had rewritten the whole, from beginning to end, did we not take into consideration the immense trouble that would have been encountered by Herr Bandmann had he been subjected, after performing the piece for hundreds of times, to a study of new words. It is on Herr Bandmann himself that the success of ' Narcisse ' depends. Not that the nephew of Rameau is a personage whom any actor desirous to

make a display would choose to represent; for, strange to say, he
is not involved in a single dramatic situation till within a few
minutes before the fall of the curtain, nearly the whole of his effect
being produced by speeches of a narrative and reflective kind.
Herr Bandmann, however, has manifestly taken a strong fancy to
the part, and so completely has he identified himself with its
peculiarities, that the result is one of the most highly finished and
original performances to be seen on any stage.   There is a light
easy grace in his early scenes, which at once prepossesses the
public in his favour, and the sarcasms which he utters, and which
are not of the most pungent, gain a strange significance from the
glib manner in which he rolls them off his tongue.   With all his
merriment there is something weird in his aspect, as though he
was talking under the influence of a dream, and it was altogether
uncertain what odd phrase would follow the last one uttered.   His
pathos in the delivery of an affecting narrative is deep and quiet—
so quiet indeed, that it at first leads to a belief that he is deficient
in physical power.   But the fallacy of the inference is amply proved
before the end of the play.   The rush into the arms of the Marquise, when *Narcisse* first recognizes her amongst the audience of
the play; the change of the love, so passionately and so spontaneously expressed, into absolute abhorrence, and the further
change to despair, tell with a force that could scarcely be surpassed.   In this situation occurs the only opportunity for a display
of gesticulatory talent, and Herr Bandmann avails himself of it to
the utmost.   There is not one of his attributes that is otherwise
than picturesque, and, strange to add, that is otherwise than
natural.   In some of his impassioned utterances, where love is the
theme, he will remind many of Mr. Fechter, but in his command
of the English language he is far superior to that celebrated actor.
Indeed there is little in his accent to indicate that he is a German
at all, the slight peculiarity in his pronunciation apparently indicating the influence of his visit to America rather than that of
his birth in Fatherland."

On Saturday, October 3, 1868, on the occasion of the first
performance at the Lyceum Theatre of 'The Rightful Heir' (Lord
Lytton), Mr. Bandmann sustained the character of *Vyvyan*, and
on the 30th of November of the same year at the Lyceum he
played *Othello*.   In the year 1869 he visited the Australian colonies,
remaining there for twelve months, and appearing in various *rôles*
in the legitimate drama during that period.   Subsequently (1870–1)
he made a second tour through the United States, which was
equally successful as his first.   Returning to England in June 1871,
he reappeared in 'Narcisse' at the Queen's Theatre, and also in a
new play by Mr. Tom Taylor entitled 'Dead or Alive.'   On
Monday, February 10, 1873, he made his third appearance as
Hamlet, in London, at the Princess's Theatre, having already
performed the character at the Standard Theatre, Bishopgate, and
in Manchester and several provincial towns in England, Scotland,
and Ireland.   Judging from the criticism of Mr. Bandmann's acting
of the part, published in several provincial journals of repute, his

Hamlet has been keenly appreciated by large audiences, and ha
been rewarded with a larger measure of praise than falls to the lo
of most actors. His success in London in this and other Shake
spearian parts has perhaps not been so decided, at least in th
view of some whose judgment is entitled to respect. The *Athenæum*
(February 15, 1873) remarked as follows : "So far as Mr. Band
mann's presentation of *Hamlet* has any interest, it is an embodi
ment of the views of the character prevalent among German actors
The value of the exposition is greatly diminished by want of grace
and refinement. Mr. Bandmann not merely lacks the chivalrou
bearing, which in Mr. Fechter does duty for passion, but is ir
scenes almost slouching. The princeliness of *Hamlet* disappears
and is replaced by a weak sentimentality. No touch of the irony
pathetic and savage in turns, of *Hamlet* is found in the actor'
performance. No sign is there, moreover, of the working of fate
upon the mind. At the outset of each separate scene the life o
Hamlet seems to start afresh,—

> " ' This year knows nothing of last year ;
> To-morrow has no more to say
> To yesterday.'

" Especially noticeable is this in the bearing of Mr. Bandmanr
when he sees the funeral of Ophelia. The first shock over, he
moralises as calmly as though the interest he felt in the dead body
before him was as remote as that in the skull of Yorick he had
previously exhibited. Though the inadequacy of the acting de
tracted thus from the value of the experiment, the experiment
itself is not without interest. Since the days of Emil Devrient the
German rendering of Hamlet has been much tamer than that
customary in England. The points on which the English actor
most insists are omitted, and the stage business judged of most
consequence is allowed to lapse. This is not wholly loss, if indeed
it is loss at all. There is something almost ludicrous in the notion
of an audience waiting for a certain elevation or inflexion of voice
at a fixed word, and bursting into applause as soon as it hears it
Some tameness, however, seems inseparable from the best ren
dering of the part after the German fashion. The tendency to
monotony Mr. Bandmann tries to counteract by inventing 'busi
ness' of his own. This is wholly bad. His addressing to the
picture of Claudius the strong words employed by *Hamlet* in his
interview with the Queen has some ground of reason, but his
sudden recoil and fall when the Ghost appears, and his delivery in
a recumbent attitude of the advice to his mother, are equally
meaningless and ineffective. The omissions from the text, whether
due to carelessness or inattention, are alike unjustifiable. The
most noteworthy occurs in the scene to which reference has just
been made. In this the words following *Hamlet's* ' Good-night,'—

> " ' But go not to my uncle's bed,
> Assume a virtue if you have it not,' &c.

are omitted.   A little previously the actor left out the lines —

> " 'A station like the herald Mercury,
> New-lighted on a heaven-kissing hill.'

Some scenes usually excised are, however, introduced. . . . That the experiment is wholly a failure is due to want of judgment in certain scenes, and of expository power in all. To partial failure such an essay is doomed from the first."

The *Examiner* (February 23, 1873), while concluding that Mr. Bandmann is an accomplished and capable actor, practised in all the resources of his art in a thorough manner, which is characteristic of his nation, considered that he did not evince that critical ability by which some of his countrymen have been able to throw considerable light on the works of the great poet. " His representation is careful, and shows conclusively that much thought has been expended upon it ; but the thought seems to have been turned rather towards matters of detail than towards the central idea, the result being a number of small innovations which, on consideration, appear unmeaning and useless, when not absolutely detrimental to the true effect. This constant striving after novel readings and ' business ' is becoming a characteristic of our revivals of Shakespeare's plays. To speak a passage with an unexpected accent, and to accompany it with some gesture not before used, seems to be the great object of most modern actors. It should be needless to point out that this method is at variance with the true order of procedure. Let the actor first grasp the main idea of the character he has to portray, and the smaller points in behaviour and speech will become clear to him, so that it is impossible to conceive them in two ways. Mr. Bandmann's *Hamlet* gives us no evidence of this process ; on the contrary, he would appear to have taken up each passage separately, and devised some mode of interpretation which should be peculiar, without any special reference to the nature and inner feelings of the speaker. In restoring some scenes usually omitted Mr. Bandmann shows, however, excellent judgment. One of these, in which *Hamlet* refuses to take the opportunity of killing the King while he is praying, because his soul might go to heaven, gives a necessary touch to the portrait, and is of the utmost importance as being the only instance in the play of the trait it illustrates. It has been said that such cruelty was inconsistent with the soft and affectionate disposition of the Prince—a criticism showing, we think, a want of acquaintance with peculiar developments of such a character. The entrance of Fortinbras with the soldiers, after the death of *Hamlet*, now closes the play, and here also the return to the original form is to be commended. From a certain point of view the usual conclusion with the words, ' The rest is silence,' is doubtless impressive, but a larger effect is made upon the imagination by this glimpse of the fighting, practical world. Like a breath of fresh air in a heated room, it braces the nerves, and enables us to see the occurrences of the drama in their true light ; it adds a salient colour to the picture, giving to the whole a broad and comprehensive harmony."

In January 1877 Mr. Bandmann appeared as *Hamlet* and *Othello* in Berlin with considerable success. He has since been acting in the provinces, mainly, and is now (1879) in the United States.

BANDMANN, MRS. (*née* PALMER, MILLICENT), born in Lancaster, England, was an actress of considerable repute at the Liverpool Theatre Royal, previous to her first appearance on the London stage, which took place November 7, 1864, at the Strand Theatre. She played on that occasion the part of *Pauline* in a piece entitled ' Delicate Ground.' " The romance and simplicity of *Pauline* were exquisitely represented by Miss Palmer (*Standard*, November 9, 1864), who, without an effort, and in a style very different to what the visitors to the Strand Theatre have been accustomed to see, made a deep impression, and appealed to all hearts. The tenderness of the character, too, was exquisitely realised, nor were energy and spirit wanting when required. There is, moreover, infinite grace and elegance in Miss Palmer's motions and attitudes which stamp her in a moment as a veritable queen of comedy ; added to which, her appearance is prepossessing in the highest degree. Need we say that Miss Milly Palmer is an invaluable acquisition to the Strand Theatre ? We may go even beyond this, and assert that Miss Palmer is one of the most accomplished actresses whom the London stage has witnessed for many years." She remained a member of the ' Strand ' company until the end of the season 1864-5. During her connection with that theatre she appeared in two pieces by J. P. Wooler, viz. ' The Wilful Ward ' and ' Laurence's Love Suit,' in both of which her acting secured special attention. In the latter play she sustained the part of *Eva*, the main purpose of this piece, according to the *Athenæum* (January 14, 1865), being the provision of an opportunity for Miss Palmer for the display of her pathetic powers. " The same lively sensible girl to whom humour seemed as natural as the most spontaneous act of her daily life, possesses also a fund of pathos so genuine in character, so unstudied, yet so effective, that it commands voluntary sympathy from all classes of spectators. The situation devised for her is of the simplest sort, scarcely sufficient for the supply of the most elementary conditions of dramatic structure ; but meagre as it is Miss Palmer charges it with a subtle vitality that acts on all within its reach. . . . Enough has been done to prove that Miss Palmer, with a more carefully drawn character, and in a more elaborately constructed drama, will rise into an estimation with which few will be able to compete."

In October 1866 Miss Palmer played the leading female *rôle* in Tom Taylor's drama, ' The White Boy,' then first performed at the Olympic Theatre, and on November 18, 1867, she appeared as *Juliet* at the Lyceum Theatre and played the part for five weeks with great success. Subsequently, February 17, 1868, Miss Palmer appeared at the same theatre as *Doris Guinault* in ' Narcisse '; and on October 3 of the same year as *Eveline*, first performance of ' The Rightful Heir.' Since her marriage with Mr. Bandmann (February 9, 1869) Mrs. Bandmann has appeared in the several plays in which her husband has acted a principal part. She accompanied him to the Australian colonies and the United States, and during his lengthened tour performed, among others, the following characters of the Shakespearian drama, viz. *Juliet, Beatrice,* and *Portia;* and in addition, *Pauline* in ' The Lady of Lyons.' Returning to England she appeared at the Queen's Theatre (Long Acre) July 6, 1872. In 1873 (February 10) she commenced an engagement at the Princess's Theatre, and then acted for the first time *Lady Macbeth* (see an appreciative notice in the *Era,* March 9, 1873). Since that year Mrs. Bandmann has played several successful " starring "engagements in the provinces, having appeared at various times in the characters already named, and as *Ophelia, Rosalind, Desdemona, Mrs. Haller* (' The Stranger '), and *Lady Teazle.* Her last London engagement was in the play of ' Proof; or, a Celebrated Case,' first performed at the Adelphi Theatre, Saturday, April 20, 1878.

BARNES, JOHN H., made his first appearance on any stage November 1871, at the Lyceum Theatre, in a subordinate part in ' The Bells.' After filling minor engagements at the Globe Theatre (December 1871), and at Scarborough, he appeared, September 1872, as *Captain Lewis* in ' The Lady of the Lake ' at Drury Lane. Subsequently at the Strand Theatre, during the winter of 1873, he performed with some success the character of *Gordon Lockhart* in ' Old Soldiers.' The following summer, while playing at the Globe Theatre, then under the management of Mr. E. Saker, he was engaged by Mr. R. H. Wyndham to take leading parts at Edinburgh. His successful impersonations of *Romeo, Claude Melnotte, Iago,* and other characters established his position as an actor of ability. At Mr. Byron's solicitation he appeared at the opening of the Criterion Theatre in 1874 as *Geoffrey Greville* in ' An American Lady.' In September 1874 he was engaged for a tour with Miss Neilson in America, and supported that lady in the well-known plays with which her histrionic fame is identified. During the summer of 1875 Mr. Barnes played leading comedy parts with his own selected company in the principal towns and cities of Canada. Returning to England, he sustained leading characters at the Theatre Royal, Manchester, and in a revival there of ' The School for Scandal ' appeared as *Charles Surface.* After playing *Captain Molyneux* in ' The Shaughraun,' he returned to London, appearing in May 1876 at the Princess's Theatre, where he achieved success as *Chateau Renaud* in a revival of ' The Corsican Brothers.' Since then he has appeared as *Sir Leicester Dedlock* in ' Jo ' at the Globe Theatre, and in various pieces at the Park, the Gaiety, the Opéra Comique, and the Aquarium (now Imperial) Theatres. During the autumn of 1878 Mr. Barnes acted in the provinces as *Captain Julian Beauclerc* in ' Diplomacy.' He appeared at the Olympic Theatre in Mr. Frank Harvey's play ' The Mother,' April 14, 1879, and as *Henry IV.*, at a morning performance, May 3, 1879. When Miss Genevieve Ward took the Lyceum at the close of Mr. Irving's season August 1879, Mr. Barnes supported her in ' Lucrezia

Borgia' and other plays; and September 20, in 'The Boarding School,' appeared at the reopening of that theatre under Mr. Irving's management. In 'The Iron Chest,' at the same theatre, Mr. Barnes appeared as *Captain Fitzhardinge.*

BARRETT, MRS. WILSON. *See* HEATH, CAROLINE.

BARRETT, WILSON, previous to assuming the management of the Court Theatre, had acquired considerable reputation in the provinces as an actor and manager, and is well known as the lessee of the Grand Theatre, Leeds, and Theatre Royal, Hull. He appeared as the advocate *Pomerol* in 'Fernande' at the reopening of the Court Theatre under his management, Saturday, September 20, 1879.

BARRINGTON, RUTLAND (a *nom de théâtre;* GEORGE RUTLAND FLEET). Born at Pénge, Surrey, January 15, 1853. Made his professional *début* at the Olympic Theatre, London, September 1, 1874, as *Sir George Barclay* in 'Clancarty.' At the same theatre during the same month and year he played *Lafleur* in 'The Two Orphans' ('Les Deux Orphelines' of M. d'Ennery), by John Oxenford. In connection with "readings" given in 1875 at the Egyptian Hall by Miss Emily Faithfull, Mr. Barrington played in a comedietta (adapted from the French by Miss Ella Dietz) entitled 'Lessons in Harmony.' Afterwards he joined the late Mrs. Howard Paul in her "Entertainment," travelling through the provinces 1875-7. At the Opéra Comique, November 17, 1877, first performance of Gilbert and Sullivan's comic opera 'The Sorcerer,' Mr. Barrington played *Dr. Daly,* the Vicar; and on Saturday, May 25, 1878, first performance at the same theatre of 'H.M.S. Pinafore,' comic opera (Gilbert and Sullivan), he played *Captain Corcoran,* a part which he has sustained during the very successful "run" of the piece.

BARRY, HELEN (Mrs. ALEXANDER ROLLS), was born in Kent, and entered the dramatic profession in August 1872, appearing at Covent Garden Theatre as the *Princess Fortinbrasse* in "a new fantastic musical drama" by Boucicault and Planché, entitled 'Babil and Bijou.' In 1872-3 at the Court Theatre she personated a leading character in Gilbert's play entitled 'The Happy Land'; and in the latter year was engaged by Mr. Tom Taylor to play *Margaret Hayes* in his drama of 'Arkwright's Wife' on its first production at the Leeds Theatre Royal. Subsequently, October 1873, Miss Barry sustained the same character at the Globe Theatre in London, "expressing the tenderer emotions with good effect, and her even passages being delivered with judgment" (*Times,* October 8, 1873). In December of the year following Miss Barry was engaged by the late Andrew Halliday to personate *Edith Dombey* in his play of 'Heart's Delight,' adapted from Charles Dickens's 'Dombey and Son,' and proved herself an efficient representative of the character. She was specially engaged by Mr. Boucicault to play *Armande* in his play of 'Led Astray' on its production at the Gaiety Theatre

July 1, 1874, following which she went on a "starring" tour in the provinces.   Returning to London, Miss Helen Barry was engaged to play the leading part in 'Round the World in 80 days' ('Le Tour du Monde en 80 jours'; MM. d'Ennery and Verne) at the Princess's Theatre.   Subsequently, in June 1875, at the same theatre she sustained the leading *rôle* in Mortimer's unsuccessful play entitled 'Heartsease,' afterwards performing the part of *Lady Clancarty* at the Queen's Theatre with considerable success.   In 1876 she appeared in London at the Haymarket in the title *rôle* in the English version of 'L'Étrangère,' and afterwards at the Standard Theatre as *Donna Carmen* in Hugh Marston's 'True Till Death,' an adaptation from the French.   Among important principal parts sustained with success by Miss Helen Barry the following may be selected for mention, viz. *Lady Macbeth* (at the Theatre Royal, Edinburgh), *Lady Teazle* (at the same theatre), *Lady Gay Spanker* (at Plymouth and Brighton Theatres, &c.), and *Mrs. Sutherland* in Cheltnam's comedy 'A Lesson in Love' (at Aberdeen).   September 23, 1878, she began an engagement at the Olympic, playing *Countess de Linière* in a revival of 'The Two Orphans.'   Miss Helen Barry is married to Major Alexander Rolls, formerly of the 4th Dragoon Guards, J.P. and D.L. for Monmouthshire.

BARRY, SHIEL, was born in Kildare County, Ireland, and first appeared on the stage in 1859, in the Australian colonies, as *Dr. O'Toole* in 'The Irish Tutor.'   Mr. Barry remained in Australia for some years.   Returning to England he played several engagements, principally in Irish comedy, in the provinces, and made his first appearance on the metropolitan stage September 7, 1870, at the Princess's Theatre, as the *Doctor* in Boucicault's drama entitled 'The Rapparee.'   Mr. Shiel Barry first attracted notice in London as an exponent of Irish character, his principal successes being in Boucicault's plays.   He has appeared at the Gaiety Theatre, London, in support of that actor in 'Arrah-na-Pogue' and 'The Colleen Bawn'; and with him has performed at the principal theatres in the United States (including Booth's at New York) and in Canada.   After various fortune Mr. Barry went to Demerara in British Guiana and visited the principal West Indian Islands.   Returning by way of New York, he was engaged by Mr. Boucicault to act in England in 'The Shaughraun.'   In the latter drama Mr. Shiel Barry appeared on the occasion of its first performance in London at Drury Lane Theatre, Saturday, September 4, 1875, as *Harvey Duff*, a police spy.   He met with his greatest success on the metropolitan stage in February 1878, at the Folly Theatre, when he acted the part of *Gaspard*, first performance of Messrs. H. B. Farnie's and R. Reece's English adaptation of M. Planquette's opéra comique, 'Les Cloches de Corneville.'   The piece proved most attractive.   On Saturday, August 31 of the same year, it was transferred to the stage of the Globe Theatre, the services of Mr. Shiel Barry being still retained for the principal character.   "So exceptionally encouraging was the reception which awaited it in its new abode, that it would seem in a fair way to rival in popularity the original version, which has already achieved in Paris a success as remarkable in its way as that of ' Our Boys ' itself, when it is borne in mind that long ' runs ' are comparatively rare upon the French stage.   More than one cause may be said to have contributed to this satisfactory result.   The distinctness of its incidental melodies, the real dramatic interest centred in the character of the old miser *Gaspard*, and the scope afforded to the scenic artist and his ally the costumier, all served to attract attention to M. Planquette's work. . . . Few who have once heard it will forget the guttural laugh of Mr. Shiel Barry in his powerful delineation of the miser—a performance which belongs to the very highest order of eccentric comedy." (*Daily News*, September 3, 1878.)   In the summer season of 1879 this piece was still being performed at the Globe Theatre, Mr. Shiel Barry in his " original " character.

BATEMAN, ISABELLA, third daughter of the late H. L. Bateman, formerly of New York, and subsequently lessee of the Lyceum Theatre, London.   As a child, on the 22nd December, 1865, she appeared at Her Majesty's Theatre, in a piece entitled ' Little Daisy,' in the character of *Diggory Dawdlegrace*, her sister, Miss Virginia Bateman [Francis], playing the part of *Little Daisy*. Miss Isabella Bateman made her professional *début* at the Lyceum Theatre on Monday, September 11, 1871, as the heroine in ' Fan-chette ; or, the Will o' the Wisp,' an adaptation of the German ' Die Grille.'   In the opinion of the *Athenæum* (September 16, 1871), a character less suited to a young actress whose talents are not of the highest order could not readily have been found.   " Miss Isabella Bateman has stage aptitudes.   Her first appearance should have been made, however, in a part far less exacting.   A face which can be charged with fine sorrow, movements cultivated almost too carefully, youth, brightness, and intelligence constitute her gifts. Against these must be opposed a certain hardness, such as her sister never conquered, and an unsympathetic voice.   In the per-formance of *Fanchette*, the later scenes, wherein the mischievous nature of the child was overcome, were decidedly the best.   The early scenes were decidedly wanting in girlishness, ease, and spontaneity."

On Saturday, September 28, 1872, Miss Isabella Bateman played the part of *Queen Henrietta Maria*, first performance at the Lyceum Theatre of Mr. W. G. Wills's historical drama ' Charles I.,' with real ability, and carried all the sympathy of the audience with her.   Her entry with the cavaliers at the close of the second act was accompanied with admirable fire of voice and gesture, and in the pathetic scenes her emotion was never out of place. The prettiness of her French-English constituted one of the charms of this impersonation (*Daily News*, October 1, 1872).   In October 1874, in a revival of ' Hamlet ' at the same theatre, she performed, during the unprecedented run of that tragedy, with Mr. H. Irving in the principal character, the part of *Ophelia ;* and in February 1876, in a revival of ' Othello,' the character of *Desde-mona*.   In June of the same year, on the occasion of a revival of

'The Belle's Stratagem,' she performed the part of *Letitia Hardy;* and in June 1878 that of *Thekla*, first performance of 'Vanderdecken' (Messrs. Fitzgerald and W. G. Wills), founded upon 'Der Fliegende Holländer.'

BATEMAN, KATE JOSEPHINE (Mrs. CROWE), eldest daughter of the late H. L. Bateman, formerly of New York, and subsequently lessee of the Lyceum Theatre, London, was born in Baltimore, October 7, 1842. She first appeared on the London boards as one of the so-called "Bateman Children," at the St. James's Theatre in 1851, under the auspices of Mr. P. T. Barnum. During that engagement Miss Bateman played in 'The Young Couple' (a comic French piece written for the child Léontine Fay, by M. Scribe); and also in selected scenes from Shakespeare's 'Richard III.' in conjunction with her sister, Miss Ellen Bateman, the characters enacted being *Richard III.* and *Richmond.* Miss Bateman's first appearance on the stage proper in London was made Thursday, October 1, 1863, at the Adelphi Theatre, as *Leah*, in the tragedy of that name, an adaptation of Mosenthal's 'Deborah,' of which Madame Ristori was the original heroine. In this character Miss Bateman supported by her own exertions a drama which, left entirely to its unassisted merits, might weary many and offend a chosen few. "Her speech," said the *Saturday Review* (October 10, 1863) in a criticism of the performance, "is not altogether free from the Transatlantic accent, and the delivery of her more quiet speeches, clearly as they are articulated, is not without an appearance of studied formality. But her power of abandonment to the influence of a strong passion is very great, and having first made an impression on her audience by her picturesque aspect, she rivets their attention when they least expect it by the intensity with which she expresses her emotions. Her poses, evidently the result of a somewhat severe study, are extremely striking; and the peculiar costume which heightens their effect shows that the idea of forming part of an effective tableau has been uppermost in the young artist's mind. 'Leah' is not the 'tendency-drama' that 'Deborah' was when it issued fresh from the hands of Mosenthal, whose dialogue almost looks like a *consommé* of the Old Testament. On the contrary, the Judaical tone is softened, and a few practical expedients bring the work to a more melodramatic level than originally belonged to it. But still, for acting purposes, the impassioned, wronged, vindictive, and penitent Jewess remains showy and effective as ever. Miss Bateman hurls down the great solemn curse with *aplomb*, and everybody shrinks. She reappears in enfeebled condition and murmurs forth forgiveness, whereupon everybody weeps. The means to the end are broad rather than subtle, but they are forcibly and skilfully employed, and when the curtain falls the actress has fairly subjected her audience."

The play was a great success. Miss Bateman's first engagement at the Adelphi terminated Saturday, June 11, 1864. On Monday, January 30, 1865, at the same theatre, she played the part of *Julia* in 'The Hunchback.' "We (*Daily Telegraph*, February 1, 1865) regard Miss Bateman's performance of *Julia* as falling short of that high standard by which it is apparently the lady's laudable ambition to be judged. A fine figure and a command of statuesque attitudes will do much to enchain the attention of the eye; but the heart requires to be warmed by that glow of sympathy which is only felt when a strong belief is impressed in the reality of the emotions so completely simulated. Miss Bateman is certainly not to be charged with a slavish adherence to what is called theatrical tradition, and rather too frequently gives a bold rendering of passages in a manner which is entirely her own; but taken in its entirety the performance lacked that individuality which endows with a fresh interest a familiar part. In the mechanism of acting Miss Bateman is thoroughly proficient, and the tone with which a word is spoken, or the gesture by which it is accompanied, appear to have been adopted only after much consideration. The study by which certain results are sought to be obtained is, indeed, too evident. The natural impulse of the moment is not suggested by measured cadences and obviously premeditated movements of the hands and arms. The perfection of art lies in the fidelity with which nature is presented; and it is precisely this point of her profession which the actress has yet to pass. For this reason the first act of the play, where *Julia* is shown as a guileless girl, happy in her rustic retirement, and content with the simple pleasures of a country life, was that which was least effective. When town is reached, and the giddy maiden, yielding to the frivolities of fashion, estranges her affianced lover, Miss Bateman portrayed the influences of an artificial life much more accurately. The interview with Clifford, where he first appears as the secretary, and which forms the crucial test of the actress who plays *Julia*, was characterized by a force of expression which secured the first really deserved recognition of an imparted sensation. In depicting the struggle between love and pride Miss Bateman somewhat elaborately marked the transitions; but her energy in the delivery of the fine speeches which are allotted to *Julia* in this scene carried the audience with her, and caused the fall of the act-drop to be followed by a vigorous recall. The last scene, in which the impassioned appeal is made to Master Walter to release her from the engagement to the Earl of Rochdale, was marked by more power than delicacy of treatment; but the crowded audience, strongly predisposed in her favour, accepted every outburst of feeling as an indication of fresh evidence of ability, and as the curtain descended, strewed the stage with bouquets amidst vehement applause. That Miss Bateman's *Julia* will prove as attractive as *Leah*, her most sanguine admirers would hardly dare to anticipate. It is a performance that illustrates the talents of a lady who has assiduously cultivated the means at her disposal, but it cannot be described as an embodiment which will give the town a new topic for conversation. The other parts in the play were not sustained in a manner likely to overshadow the heroine by their superior excellence."

The following appears in *Journal of a London Playgoer*, by Henry Morley, Professor of English Literature in University College, London, pp. 362-5:—

"March 18, 1865.—Having now seen Miss Bateman in two characters, one may estimate the measure of her ability. Her acting as *Julia* in 'The Hunchback' too exactly repeats the impression made by her *Leah*. In *Leah* it was only for a strain of pathos in the last act, and for a few touching notes of the voice there, that she was to be credited with a power of pathetic expression that came of her own genius, and not of mere stage drilling. But in other respects I find Miss Bateman as monotonous in the part of *Julia* as she was in the part of *Leah*, showing no original ability of any sort save when she has to give pathetic expression to her voice, and there, and there only, again succeeding. She says marvellously well the words of distress, 'Clifford, why don't you speak to me?' but acts lifelessly in the first scenes of country simplicity, and almost lumpishly, certainly without a trace of real vivacity, in the succeeding scenes of town gaiety, standing almost unexpressive while Clifford is cruelly wounding her pride, and putting only the monotone of her pathos into the few words she utters. . . . Now that I have seen her in two plays, I do not hesitate to rank Miss Bateman among the clever actresses whose special excellence is bounded within limits so narrow that although, once carefully and exclusively presented, it may win for a short time a deserved success, it does not enable them permanently to hold their own among performers of the highest class."

In the same year, 1865, on Monday, May 8, Miss Bateman appeared as *Bianca* in a revival of Milman's tragedy of 'Fazio,' at the Adelphi Theatre. At Her Majesty's Theatre, on December 22, 1865, advertised as "her last appearance prior to her departure for America and retirement from the stage," she sustained the character of *Juliet* for the first time in London. "Farewell benefits, when the actor or actress is an old and well-tried favourite of the public, retiring into private life after a prolonged theatrical career, are generally very melancholy things. . . Farewell benefits, however, when the actress is young, and the retirement is only a prelude to a happy marriage, is a very different ceremony ; and such a benefit was taken last night by Miss Bateman at Her Majesty's Theatre. Miss Bateman came to us a few seasons ago with an Anglo-German play, called 'Leah,' and made her first bow to an English public (if we except her juvenile performances in England) at the Adelphi Theatre. The pastoral simplicity and emotional power of the play secured its popularity with mixed audiences, not only at the Adelphi, but throughout the country, and the fortunate actress gained a firm footing on the English stage, partly by her own merits, and partly by the merits of the drama. The unfortunate Jewish heroine became the talk of the town and the idol of the picture-shops. Miss Bateman performed other characters with more or less success ; but the statuesque grace which probably helped to make 'Leah' popular was hardly so effective in 'Fazio' or 'The Hunchback.' The character chosen last night by Miss Bateman for her final appearance in England was *Juliet*. . . . A performance of this nature is beyond the pale of criticism ; it would be useless to praise it and ungracious to condemn it. The house was crowded and friendly ; every entry and every point was loudly applauded ; and the balcony and potion scenes were received with the loudest applause. Her powerful passages were the most effective. . . . It is a singular fact connected with Miss Bateman's former representation of this character in America that her Romeo was Wilkes Booth, the assassin of President Lincoln." (*Daily News,* December 23, 1865.)

"Those acquainted with the previous performances of Miss Bateman would readily surmise in which portion of the tragedy her talent was most effectively exhibited. It was not as the impulsive Italian maiden in the early awakening of her heart to the feelings of an ardent passion that the actress best deserved the applause of her admirers. The girlish *Juliet* which Shakespeare has presented to the imagination is rarely realized on the stage. The balcony scene showed rather the statuesque effect of certain attitudes than the delicate tenderness of the love-inspired maiden who there confesses the warmth of her affection. In the soliloquy of the fourth act, when the contents of the phial are drained amidst the shuddering anticipation of the horrors of the charnel-house, the actress was much more successful ; and in portraying the excitement of frenzy and the desolation of despair Miss Bateman fairly justified the warmth of the applause received. The last scene was very carefully acted, and when the curtain fell on the form of *Juliet* prostrate over the body of her lover, the audience would not be appeased until both were resuscitated, and the *Juliet* was brought smiling by Romeo before the curtain to receive the usual compliment in a more than ordinary emphatic form." (*Daily Telegraph,* December 23, 1865.)

On Monday, October 19, 1868, Miss Bateman reappeared as *Leah*, in a revival of that play at the Haymarket Theatre, and on December 7 of the same year, at the same theatre, she sustained the character of *Pietra*, in an adaptation of Dr. Mosenthal's tragedy of that name. At the Haymarket Theatre, June 21, 1869, on the occasion of the first performance of Tom Taylor's play ' Mary Warner,' Miss Bateman played the heroine, *Mary Warner*, on the whole the most finished performance with which she had as yet favoured the public. "She does not capture her audience with a start, as when she rushes across the Styrian bridge to then fall into an attitude singularly picturesque ; but in the dress of very humble life she has to begin with the quiet delineation of a very pattern wife and mother, and then gradually to render a person whose highest virtue appears to be frugality, an object of the most intense interest. The scene in the prison, when in a subdued tone she almost implores her husband to cheer her with a kind word, is singularly beautiful, through the depth of sorrow expressed, and the perfect nature of the expression ; and throughout the piece the manner is homogeneous. The indignation felt by *Mary* at George's supposed contumely is mild in its intensity, and a resignation qualifies the almost despair with which she sits down to die at the door of her residence. The scene with the child is given with all the tenderness which distinguished Leah's interview with the child of her rival, and with those additional touches that the change in the situation requires." (*Times*, June 24, 1869.) In the autumn of 1869 Miss Bateman appeared at Booth's Theatre, New York, as *Leah*, and in the following May (1870) reappeared on the London boards at the Olympic Theatre as *Mary Warner*. In May 1872 she again appeared in London in her favourite character of *Leah* at the Lyceum Theatre, and in July 1872 she played there the part of *Medea*, in an adaptation of the ' Medea in Corinth,' by Mr. W. G. Wills.

The *Examiner* (July 13, 1872) considered that in this impersonation Miss Bateman greatly surpassed all her previous successes. In one or two scenes she was perhaps rather too violent ; but the part was admirably suited to her powers, and her acting of nearly all of it was admirable. " ' Medea in Corinth' ought to last her as long as ' Leah ' has done ; and when she ceases to play in it, it deserves to maintain a lasting place among the best productions of modern English dramatists." The *Saturday Review* of the same date, however, entertained a different opinion of the actress's performance of *Medea*.

In October 1873, in a new drama by Mr. Dubourg, entitled ' Bitter Fruit,' first performed at the Alexandra Theatre, Liverpool, Miss Bateman played the leading female *rôle ;* and in September 1875, in a revival of Shakespeare's tragedy of ' Macbeth ' at the Lyceum Theatre (Mr. H. Irving as Macbeth), she played the part of *Lady Macbeth*.

In February 1876, at the same theatre, she acted the part of *Emilia* (' Othello ') ; and in April of the same year, first performance at the Lyceum Theatre of ' Queen Mary ' (Tennyson), Miss Bateman sustained the title *rôle*. " The nature of *Mary* is a hard and unlovely one, albeit weak as water before the slightest breath of Philip, and she is unable, as we see her on the stage, to create sufficient interest for her own sake to compensate for the want of other interest. This character is represented by Mrs. Crowe, who struggles hard with a hard task, and with far more success than we confess we should have thought possible. Despite a certain conventionality of voice and action, which would seem to be rather the property of the Lyceum company, her acting must on the whole be commended. In the fifth act especially is she to be praised, not because she is seen there at her best—in the first act we were most pleased with her—but because she does not altogether fail in one of the most difficult tasks which, perhaps, were ever set to any actress. Nearly the whole of this act is occupied with *Mary's* death, and that Mrs. Crowe was enabled to command the patience of her audience in such circumstances speaks, as we conceive, very highly for her powers. . . ." (*Times*, April 20, 1876.) In January 1877, in a revival of ' Fazio ' (Milman), at the same theatre, she played *Bianca*. On Thursday, October 9, 1879, Miss Bateman played *Helen Macgregor* (' Rob Roy ') on the occasion of the opening of New Sadler's Wells.

BATEMAN, VIRGINIA FRANCES. *See* FRANCIS, VIRGINIA.

BEAUMONT, ALLEN, has for the last six years been a member of the Lyceum company, where he has, under Mrs. Bateman and Mr. Irving's management, appeared in various parts, among which may be mentioned the *King* in 'Richelieu'; *First Player* in 'Hamlet'; *Comines* in 'Louis XI.'; and *Didier* in 'The Lyons Mail.'

BELFORD, WILLIAM ROWLES, was born at Easton, near Bristol. He made his first professional appearance on the stage at the Adelphi Theatre, Glasgow, in 1847, as *Sir Thomas Clifford* in 'The Hunchback,' having, in the previous year, already acted (as an amateur), at Pym's private theatre in Gray's Inn Road, the character of *Gratiano* ('Merchant of Venice'). Mr. Belford was a member of the late Mr. Samuel Phelps's company at Sadler's Wells for twelve years, and performed during that period in no less than thirty-two of Shakespeare's plays, besides several of the older comedies presented on its stage. In the year 1855, at the Marylebone Theatre, Mr. Belford acted *Romeo* to the Juliet of Miss Cushman, and in 1856 went on a provincial tour with the late Charles Mathews. At the Strand Theatre in 1856 and 1858 Mr. Belford appeared in the following plays, namely, 'Hard Times' (as *Harthouse*), 'Nothing Venture, Nothing Win' (*Duke de Vendome*), 'The Country Squire' (*Horace Selwood*), 'Court Favour' (*David Brown*). In the following year he went on tour with Mr. Phelps, and acted with him in Berlin, Leipsic, and Hamburg. In 1860, at the St. James's Theatre, he performed with much success the part of *Harry Sparkly* in 'A Friend in Need,' and, during the same year, various parts in Shakespearian and other revivals, for which the public were indebted to Mr. Charles Kean. In the course of thirty years' connection with the metropolitan stage Mr. Belford has played many "original" parts in plays of more or less importance, and has fulfilled engagements at nearly every leading theatre. He was well known at the Strand Theatre some sixteen years ago as a painstaking and efficient actor in such pieces as 'My Preserver,' 'Kind to a Fault' (*Frank Goldsworthy*), 'Miriam's Crime' (*Scumley*), 'One Tree Hill' (*Tom Bubble*), &c., &c. On the occasion of the opening of the Court Theatre under Miss Litton's management, January 25, 1871, Mr. Belford "created" the leading *rôle* in W. S. Gilbert's comedy 'Randall's Thumb,' and at the same theatre sustained the character of *Orlick* in the dramatic version of 'Great Expectations.' More recently Mr. Belford was engaged by the late Mr. Charles Calvert, and acted the character of *Henry the Eighth* at several provincial theatres.

BELL, PERCY, born at Peterborough, January 4, 1848, and entered the dramatic profession in 1869, first appearing on the stage at the Theatre Royal, Exeter. After fulfilling various engagements in the provinces (Leeds, Belfast, Scarborough, &c.), in 1875 Mr. Bell was engaged at the Royal Edinburgh Theatre, and appeared there as *Captain Thornton* in a revival of 'Rob Roy,' and as *Dick Evergreen* in Charles Mathews's comedy 'My

Awful Dad.' For his judicious performance of this part Mr. Bell was recommended by Mr. Mathews to the management of the Gaiety Theatre, London. He made his first appearance on the London stage at that theatre, April 17, 1876, in the above-named piece, with the late Mr. Charles Mathews in the principal character, and was very favourably received.

After playing the part for a "run" of nearly 100 nights he was engaged by Mr. F. B. Chatterton for the season 1876-7, at Drury Lane Theatre, performing important parts in 'Richard III.,' 'Macbeth,' &c., with Barry Sullivan. In September 1877 Mr. Bell again played the part of *Dick Evergreen* on tour with the late Mr. Charles Mathews, during which tour Mr. Bell acted as stage-manager. In April 1878 he was engaged at the Queen's Theatre, London, appearing as *Chevalier de Favre* in 'Madeleine Morel'; and on February 10, 1879, joined the company of the Duke's Theatre, Holborn, to play in 'The New Babylon.'

BELLEW, HAROLD KYRLE, younger son of the late J. C. M. Bellew, the well-known public reader of dramatic and lyrical pieces. Mr. H. K. Bellew passed part of his early life in the Mercantile Marine; and, subsequently, in 1871, at Melbourne, he appeared before the public as reader of a lecture written by Dr. Russell (*Times* correspondent) on the events of the Franco-Prussian War. In the following year he joined a company of strollers and played at the Northern Diggings in New South Wales and Queensland. Mr. Bellew first appeared on the stage in England in August 1875, at Brighton Theatre, performing the part of *Woodstock* in 'Clancarty,' and made his *début* in London at the Haymarket Theatre, where he was subsequently engaged for a period of three years. In 1876, on February 5, he acted there the part of *Lord Percy*, first performance of Tom Taylor's drama 'Anne Boleyn,' and was afterwards in the original cast of Mr. Gilbert's comedy 'Engaged,' produced at the same theatre. During the engagement there of Miss Neilson in 1878 Mr. Bellew appeared as *Claudio* ('Measure for Measure'), and as *Beauseant* ('Lady of Lyons'). In January 1879 he joined Mr. Irving's company at the Lyceum Theatre, "opening" as *Osric* in the very successful revival of 'Hamlet.' Mr. Bellew is now (October 1879) a member of Miss Litton's company at the Imperial Theatre.

BENTLEY, WALTER (a *nom de théâtre*), fourth son of the Reverend Dr. Begg, of Edinburgh, was born in that city, and entered the dramatic profession at Dunedin, New Zealand, in 1870, making his first appearance as *Potter* in Tom Taylor's comedy 'Still Waters Run Deep.' Subsequently he played at several colonial theatres all classes of parts, and for a season was lessee of the Prince of Wales's Theatre, Auckland, New Zealand. Arriving in England in October 1874, in that month Mr. Bentley first appeared before a London audience, at the Royal Court Theatre, in the character of *Stephen Tickle* in Herman Merivale's 'Peacock's Holiday.' On February 22nd, 1875, he appeared at the

Princess's Theatre, Edinburgh, as *Alfred Evelyn* in ' Money,' sustaining also, during this and ensuing engagements in other Scotch towns, the following characters, viz., *Hamlet, Macbeth, Richard III., Othello, Iago, Shylock, Claude Melnotte, Richelieu, John Mildmay,* &c. Mr. Bentley's first important London engagement was at the Lyceum Theatre, under Mrs. Bateman's management, where he made his *début* as *Noailles,* the French Ambassador, in Tennyson's ' Queen Mary.' At the same theatre, subsequently, he sustained various leading parts in the several plays revived and produced during Mr. Irving's engagement, notably, *Laertes* in 'Hamlet,' *Lord Moray* in 'Charles I.,' *Christian* in ' The Bells,' *Clarence* in ' Richard III.,' and *Tristan L'Ermite* in ' Louis XI.'

BERNARD-BEERE, MRS., daughter of Mr. Wilby Whitehead, of Norfolk, and widow of Captain E. C. Dering, a son of Sir Edward Dering, Bart., was a pupil of Mr. Herman Vezin. She first appeared on the stage at the Opéra Comique when Mr. Kingston was manager of that theatre. After her marriage she left the stage for a time, but returning to it gave a very successful impersonation of *Julia* in ' The Rivals ' at the St. James's Theatre, then under the management of Mr. Hayes. At this theatre Mrs. Bernard-Beere played *Lady Sneerwell, Grace Harkaway,* and *Emilia* with much success. Afterwards she appeared at the Royalty Theatre, when Miss Fowler was manager, as *Lady Mantonville* in ' Scandal,' and at the Crystal Palace as *Constance* in ' The Love Chase.' In the autumn of 1878 she made a tour of the provinces with Mrs. Chippendale's company, and played leading parts. Her principal appearances in London since have been, as *Constance* in ' The Love Chase ' at a morning performance, January 25, 1879, at the Olympic ; as *Lisa* in W. S. Gilbert's ' Gretchen,' March 24, at the same theatre ; as *Lady Teazle* and *Lydia Languish* at the Haymarket ; and at a matinée at the Criterion Theatre, May 24, when she took the leading part in a comedy called ' Campaigning.'

BEVERIDGE, JAMES, was born in Dublin, October 28, 1844, and first appeared on any stage August 31, 1861, at the Theatre Royal, Oldham. Having studied the various lines of an actor's profession at the Theatres Royal, Newcastle-on-Tyne, Glasgow, Plymouth, Belfast, &c., he made his *début* in London, October 3, 1869, at the Adelphi Theatre, as *Lord Alfred Colebrooke,* in a drama written in collaboration by Messrs. Boucicault and Byron, entitled ' Lost at Sea.' At the same theatre Mr. Beveridge played various parts, original and otherwise, during the season 1869–70, and in the summer of the latter year went on tour with Mr. H. J. Byron ; and afterwards, owing to the death, in a railway accident, of Mr. Frederick Younge, filled the place of that gentleman in Mr. Richard Younge's company of comedians. This engagement continued for three years, during which time Mr. Beveridge sustained various leading characters in the comedies of Mr. T. W.

Robertson in all the principal towns in the kingdom. In May 1873, at the Charing Cross Theatre, he was the original *Claude Ripley*, in a comedy of H. J. Byron's, entitled ' Time's Triumph.' Afterwards he accepted an engagement at the Lyceum Theatre for two years, under the late H. L. Bateman's management. At the end of his engagement at the Lyceum Mr. Beveridge fulfilled various metropolitan and provincial engagements ; at the Queen's Theatre, Manchester, he appeared as *Marc Antony* in a revival of ' Julius Cæsar.' In the autumn of 1878 he was engaged as stage-manager for Mr. Vance's company of comedians, and to sustain the character of *Beauclerc* in ' Diplomacy,' a part which he is still (July 1879) playing in the provinces.

*BILLINGTON, JOHN, was born in 1830. Having earned in the provinces the reputation of being a painstaking and efficient actor, he made his first appearance on the London stage April 14, 1857, at the Adelphi Theatre, in the character of *Harry Mowbray*, in a play entitled ' Like and Unlike.' From that date down to the year 1868, a period of eleven years, Mr. Billington remained a member of the company of the Adelphi Theatre, under Mr. Benjamin Webster's management. He appeared in nearly every play of importance originally performed at that theatre during the term of this long engagement. The following, among the various " original " parts sustained by him, are deserving of record, viz. : *Walter*, nephew of *Michael Cassidy*, first performance of ' The Poor Strollers ' (Watts Phillips), on Monday, January 18, 1858 ; *M. Dubois*, first performance of ' Ici on Parle Français,' on Monday, May 9, 1859 ; *Frederick Wardour*, first performance of ' The House or the Home ' (Tom Taylor), on Monday, May 16, 1859; *Beaumont Fletcher*, first performance of ' One Touch of Nature,' &c., on Saturday, August 6, 1859. On Monday, September 10, 1860, on the occasion of the first performance in London of ' The Colleen Bawn ' (Boucicault), he sustained the part of *Hardress Cregan*. In the first performance of ' Magloire, the Prestigiator,' on Monday, April 1, 1861, he performed the character *Count D'Arcy ;* and on Monday, November 18, 1861, in the first performance in London of ' The Octoroon ' (Boucicault), the part of *George Peyton*. In 1862, on Monday, April 14, first performance of Mr. Boucicault's dramatized version of ' The Cricket on the Hearth,' entitled ' Dot,' Mr. Billington performed the character of *Ned Plummer*. In March 1863, in a version of ' Aurora Floyd,' dramatized by Mr. Benjamin Webster, junr., he played *John Mellish*, and realized the character in a style so effective that this eccentric individual became the legitimate hero of the drama. " We use the word ' individual ' purposely ; for the part is by the actor, and, in the intention of the adapter, *individualized* in the strictest sense of the term ; and the uxorious Yorkshire squire, not only fond but proud of being hen-pecked by a wife who possesses the business habits in which he is deficient, is drawn with a fidelity to nature that does credit to the author and actor." (*Athenæum*, March 28, 1863.) On Monday, Jan. 30, 1865, in a revival of ' The Hunchback,' at the Adelphi (Miss Bateman as Julia), Mr. Billington played *Modus*, and in July of the same year, first performance of Walter Gordon's play 'Through Fire and Water,' sustained the part of *Kit Coventry*. On Thursday, December 26, 1867, first performance at the Adelphi of 'No Thoroughfare' (Charles Dickens and Wilkie Collins), he played *Walter Wilding*. In 1868 Mr. Billington's long connection with the Adelphi Theatre terminated. Since that date he has principally devoted his time to playing "star" parts in the provinces, and leading *rôles* in London. On Monday, October 9, 1871, first performance at the Olympic Theatre of 'The Woman in White' (Wilkie Collins), Mr. Billington sustained the character of *Sir Percival Glyde*. On January 31, 1874, at the Adelphi Theatre, London, in a drama by Mr. Paul Meritt, entitled 'Rough and Ready,' he played the part of the hero, *Mark Musgrave*, with marked excellence. On Monday, July 19, 1875, he entered upon the management of the Globe Theatre for a brief season, and produced there the last-mentioned play, sustaining the same character, and also appearing in his original character of *Alfred Casby*, in an old comic drama by Mr. Benjamin Webster, entitled 'The Hen and Chickens.'

*BILLINGTON, ADELINE, wife of the above-named, was for many years connected with the Adelphi Theatre under Mr. Benjamin Webster's management, appearing there in the various plays and revivals of plays produced in the decade 1858–1868. In August 1859 she sustained the part of *Cynthia*, in a revival of the popular Adelphi drama 'The Flowers of the Forest.' On Monday, September 10, 1860, first performance in London of 'The Colleen Bawn,' Mrs. Billington played the character of *Mrs. Cregan*. On Saturday, March 1, 1862, first performance at the Adelphi of 'The Life of an Actress,' by Mr. Boucicault, she played the part of *Julia;* and in the same year appeared in the same author's dramatized version of 'The Cricket on the Hearth,' entitled 'Dot.' In March 1863, in a version of 'Aurora Floyd,' by Mr. Benjamin Webster, junr., she played the part of *Mrs. Powell*. On Monday, March 8, 1865, revival of Milman's tragedy of 'Fazio,' at the same theatre (Miss Bateman in the character of Bianca), Mrs. Billington sustained the part of *Aldabella* "with great force of style, that frequently extorted loud plaudits from the pit." On Monday, September 4, 1865, first appearance of Mr. Joseph Jefferson at the Adelphi Theatre in his famous impersonation of Rip Van Winkle, Mrs. Billington played *Gretchen*. In 1867, Thursday, December 26, first performance of 'No Thoroughfare' (Messrs. Charles Dickens and Wilkie Collins), she performed the character of the *Veiled Lady*. In 1868 Mrs. Billington and her husband ceased their long connection with the Theatre Royal, Adelphi.

On Saturday, September 9, 1871, first performance at the Queen's Theatre, Long Acre, of Mr. W. G. Wills's drama of 'Hinko,' Mrs. Billington played the part of *Margaret*. In July 1872, production at the Gaiety Theatre of Mr. Boucicault's version of Colman's comedy 'John Bull,' she sustained the character of *Mrs. Brul-*

gruddery. On January 31, 1874, at the Adelphi Theatre, in a drama by Mr. Paul Meritt, entitled 'Rough and Ready,' she played *Mrs. Valentine,* and the same character, in a revival of that play at the Globe Theatre, Monday, July 19, 1875, during the temporary management of Mr. Billington. Since her retirement from the company of the Adelphi Theatre Mrs. Billington has, with her husband, fulfilled several important provincial engagements.

* **BISHOP, KATE,** has been connected with the London stage for some twelve years. Her acting of the part of *Alice Barlow* in a revival of Mr. Byron's comedy of '£100,000' at the Charing Cross Theatre in 1868 received favourable notice. In 1869-70 she was a member of the company of Miss M. Oliver at the New Royalty Theatre, and later was engaged at the Holborn Theatre. On the occasion of the opening of the Court Theatre under Miss Litton's management, 25th January, 1871, Miss Bishop sustained the part of *Edith Temple,* first performance of W. S. Gilbert's comedy 'Randall's Thumb.' She also performed with considerable success in the other plays produced at that theatre during Miss Litton's management—'Great Expectations,' 'Creatures of Impulse,' &c., &c. Miss Kate Bishop was in the original cast of 'Our Boys,' produced at the Vaudeville Theatre on January 16, 1875, in the character of *Violet Melrose.* On the withdrawal of the last-named comedy, after an extraordinary "run" extending over a period of three years, Miss Bishop "created" the part of *Mabel Clench* in the same author's play 'Our Girls,' first performed at the Vaudeville, April 19, 1879, and subsequently appeared as *Ida* in the revival of 'The Two Roses.'

BISHOP, ROSE. *See* EGAN, ROSE.

BLANDFORD, PERCY (a *nom de théâtre*), was favourably known as a concert singer at Brighton and other provincial towns previous to his entering the dramatic profession. His earliest reputation on the stage was gained as *Ralph Rackstraw* in 'H.M.S. Pinafore' at the Imperial Theatre. He has since appeared in the same character at the Olympic with the Comedy-Opera Company's artists.

BLUNT, ARTHUR CECIL. *See* CECIL, ARTHUR.

BOLEYN, RICHARD SMITH (a *nom de théâtre*). Born at Edgbaston, near Birmingham. He served for a time in the Mercantile Marine ; but entered the dramatic profession in 1870. Mr. Boleyn has been frequently engaged to play leading parts in the provinces, viz., at the Theatres Royal, Nottingham, Scarborough, and Bradford, and made his first appearance on the London stage October 8, 1872, at the Globe Theatre as *Major Treherne* in Byron's comedy 'Cyril's Success.' He subsequently fulfilled a short engagement at the same theatre, and afterwards at the St. James's Theatre, with success. Mr. Boleyn has been a member of the following travelling companies, viz. : the late Mr. H. J. Montague's, playing Albery's comedies ; Mr. R. Younge's, playing Byron's comedies ; in Mr. Duck's so-called ' Our Boys ' company ; and Mr. C. Wyndham's " Crisis " company, of which he was also stage-manager.

BOLEYN, MRS. R. S. *See* BROUGH, FANNY WHITESIDE.

BOND, JESSIE CHARLOTTE. Born in London. Previous to her appearance on the stage had attracted favourable notice as a pianiste and contralto singer at various public concerts ; Hope Hall, Liverpool; St. James's Hall, London ; the Crystal Palace, Sydenham ; Free Trade Hall, Manchester, being among places where Miss Bond has sang with success. She made her theatrical *début* May 25, 1878, at the Opéra Comique, London, in the character of *Hebe*, first performance of W. S. Gilbert and A. Sullivan's comic opera ' H.M.S. Pinafore.' At the same theatre in the season 1878-9 she played *Maria* (original) in a vaudeville in one act, by Desprez and A. Cellier, entitled ' After All.'

BOUCICAULT, AGNES (*née* ROBERTSON), was an actress of juvenile comedy at the Princess's Theatre, London, during the first period of the management of Mr. Charles Kean. She appeared there during the seasons 1851-2-3 in ' Our Clerks,' by Mr. Tom Taylor ; in a burlesque by the same author entitled ' Wittikind and his Brothers,' and as *Margaret* in a two-act drama by Mr. Boucicault, entitled ' The Prima Donna.' " *Margaret,* a character of quite an opposite temperament, a being of girlish impulse, absorbed in the object of her passion, and innocently blind to every other consideration, was charmingly acted by Miss Robertson, whom we almost look upon as a *débutante*, so slight have been the characters in which she has hitherto appeared. The scene in which she was the invalid, apparently on the limit of the grave, yet trying to sustain her spirits in the presence of her father, was given with a truth and delicacy which left nothing to desire." (*Times*, September 20, 1852.) Having previously resided for some years with her husband in the United States, performing in the various plays written by him, and originally produced there, in the year 1860 Mrs. Boucicault made her reappearance on the London boards. On Monday, September 10, 1860, first performance in London of ' The Colleen Bawn' (Boucicault), at the Adelphi Theatre, she played the part of *Eily O'Connor*, concerning which performance the *Daily Telegraph* (September 11, 1860) remarked as follows : " Mrs. Boucicault is the same graceful, intelligent actress she ever was, and in her embodiment of the charming Irish beauty showed that a Transatlantic experience had not lessened the force of her talents. Nothing could be more simple and artless than her manner as the charming peasant girl, nothing more touching than her unrepining sorrow when she feels that her husband no longer loves her." On Monday, November 18, 1861, Mrs. Boucicault appeared at the same theatre as *Zoe*, in ' The Octoroon' (Boucicault), first performance of that play in London, surprising the public by the force of her delineation. " Indeed, such a popular person was the Octoroon in her hands that several of the audience were dissatisfied with her unfortunate end, and refused to understand why George could not marry his devoted ' Yellow Girl ' in one of the many happy States where Louisiana law does not prevail, especially as the remittances from Liverpool had set him on his legs. To this feeling alone can we ascribe the few sounds of disapprobation which followed the descent of the curtain last night, and contrasted so strangely with the enthusiastic applause that had accompanied the first four acts." (*Times*, November 19, 1861.) It is interesting to note that the author, in obedience to a very general request that *Zoe* should be saved, altered the drama and brought the story to a happy conclusion. The following advertisement appeared in the daily papers in the first week of December 1861: " Mr. Boucicault begs to acknowledge the hourly receipt of many letters entreating that the termination of ' The Octoroon ' should be modified and the slave heroine saved from an unhappy end. He cannot resist the kind feeling expressed throughout this correspondence nor refuse compliance with a request so easily granted. A new last act of the drama, composed by the public and edited by the author, will be represented this evening. He trusts the audience will accept it as a very grateful tribute to their judgment and taste, which he should be the last to dispute."

On Monday, February 10, 1862, at the same theatre, Mrs. Boucicault played the leading *rôle* in ' The Dublin Boy,' a version by Mr. Boucicault of Vanderburch's ' Le Gamin de Paris.' " The character of the reckless hero—the mischievous but good-hearted boy—exactly suits the mingled dash and delicacy of Mrs. Boucicault's style." (*Athenæum*, February 15, 1862.) Her assumption of the Irish *patois* and the juvenile indifference to consequences were admirably realized. But when the occasion calls on the lad's intrinsic qualities and his undoubted courage, mere vivacity is exchanged for earnestness and determinate purpose, and the excited youth nobly vindicates his sister's honour. On Saturday, March 1, 1862, first performance at the Adelphi of the ' Life of an Actress ' (Boucicault), she played the part of *Violet*, Mrs. Boucicault's impersonation of the heroine being nothing less than perfect. " Her ingenuous *naïveté* and the sweetness of her voice, when she appears as the poor street singer, enlist at once all sympathies. The increased refinement in her manner after she has become more educated is most delicately delineated ; and although the slight elegance of her figure does not seem altogether adapted to the character of Corneille, she wears the classic costume with truly classic grace. Again, when *Violet* is falling under the influence of the opiate, Mrs. Boucicault's gentle demeanour robs an unpleasing situation of more than half its repulsiveness." (*Daily Telegraph*, March 3, 1862.)

In the same year, at Drury Lane, on September 15, she acted the heroine, *Jessie*, in a spectacular drama by her husband entitled ' The Relief of Lucknow.' and appeared in the same piece on its production by Mr. Boucicault at the Theatre Royal, Westminster (Astley's), on Monday, December 22, 1862, and on the same occasion as *Bob Nettles* in 'To Parents and Guardians.' On Monday, January 26, 1863, at the same theatre she sustained the part of *Jeannie Deans*, first performance of Mr. Boucicault's dramatic version of 'The Heart of Midlothian.' "Mrs. Boucicault is charmingly graceful and natural as *Jeannie Deans*," remarked the *Times*, (January 29, 1863); "so perfectly free indeed from all exaggeration and appearance of effort that the arduousness of the character is likely to be overlooked. She is content to let the part speak for itself when she has embodied its full meaning, and simplicity and firmness of purpose are admirably blended. Worthy of especial commendation is her conduct in the witness box, where the expression of intense anguish is checked by native timidity; but the impersonation is excellent throughout." On Wednesday, March 22, 1865, at the Princess's, first performance in London of Mr. Boucicault's drama 'Arrah-na-Pogue,' she played the part of the heroine, and secured hearty commendation for her acting. At the Lyceum, in September 1866, in a play by her husband entitled 'The Long Strike,' Mrs. Boucicault sustained the character of *Jane Learoyd*. On Saturday, May 4, 1872 (having returned in the interval to the United States), she reappeared in London at the Gaiety Theatre, in her original part in a play by her husband founded on 'La Joie fait Peur,' entitled 'Night and Morning'; she acted at the same theatre during 1872 in various revivals of Mr. Boucicault's plays. On Saturday, September 4, 1875, first performance in London (at Drury Lane) of 'The Shaughraun,' she played the part of *Moya*. In 1878, on Monday, June 10, Mrs. Boucicault appeared at the Olympic Theatre in the leading female *rôle*, in a piece dramatized from one of Crabbe's 'Tales of the Hall,' entitled 'Love or Life.'

BOUCICAULT, DION, youngest son of the late S. S. Boucicault of Dublin, was born in that city, December 20, 1822. He was educated partly in Dublin and partly at the London University, and became connected with the dramatic profession in the year 1841, as author of 'London Assurance,' a play in five acts, first performed at Covent Garden Theatre on Thursday, March 4, of that year. The piece was presented to the public as the work of "Mr. Lee Morton," and the following were the principal actors in the original cast, namely, *Dazzle*, Mr. Charles Mathews; *Sir Harcourt Courtly*, Mr. Farren; *Charles Courtly*, Mr. Anderson; *Lady Gay Spanker*, Mrs. Nesbitt; *Grace Harkaway*, Madame Vestris. The *Times* (March 5, 1841) thus remarked upon the performance:— "A five-act piece called 'London Assurance' was produced last night, sustained by nearly every actor in the company, and each part one which the sustainer would, of his own free will, have chosen. An easy, flippant man about town, pretending to be a relation to everybody on account of a marriage between a remote ancestor and ancestress, whom he admits in an 'aside' to have been Adam and Eve, with much cool impudence, and flexibility of limb, is Charles Mathews, under the name of Dazzle; while his friend, a son of Sir Harcourt, Mr. Charles Courtly, a gentleman of more stamina and less nimbleness—a puller-off of knockers in the first part, and an ardent lover in the latter part of the drama— gives room for the energies of Mr. Anderson. . . . Such a plot might seem but meagre to sustain a piece in five acts, but the author has contrived to make it a vehicle for oddities both of situation and dialogue, and he contrives to keep his audience in a roar from the beginning to the end with very few interruptions. This is his first attempt in the dramatic line, and he shows us great qualification for the art he has chosen—strength, animation, and a full flow of spirits. It is true his work is a five-act farce, whereas it is called a comedy. . . . yet with all this, in the use of his strange materials the author has displayed a vivacity, a fearless humour to strike out a path for himself, an enjoyment of fun, a rapidity in loading his speeches with jokes, a power of keeping up his spirits to the last, which distinguish this piece from every work of the day. . . . . Mr. Charles Mathews announced the piece for repetition amid tumultuous applause, which was only interrupted by calls for Mr. Lee Morton, the author, who was led forward eyeing the enthusiastic multitude with considerable nervousness." In February of the following year Mr. Boucicault produced, under his own name at the same theatre, ' The Irish Heiress,' a play which was not a success. On Monday, September 19, 1842, was performed at the Haymarket Theatre, for the first time, ' Alma Mater ; or, a Cure for Coquettes,' by Mr. Boucicault.

"Writing for the stage," said the *Athenæum* (September 24, 1842), " is either easy or difficult according to the way in which the dramatist sets about it. To the few who desire to represent human life and character in action without violating the consistency of nature it is so difficult that the instances of success may be soon numbered ; to the mass of playwrights who take the shorter method of disregarding truth and originality, and seek their materials, not in the world, but in plays, the task ' is as easy as lying ' ; one turn of the theatrical kaleidoscope, with the addition of a few bits and scraps of modern phantasmagoria, accomplishes the feat. The public are taken with the trick and seem never tired of seeing it performed ; they like the artificial subjects which they have been used to ; nature ' puts them out,' and no wonder since they so seldom get a glimpse of it on the stage which ' holds as 'twere the mirror up to itself.' This short way to success, Mr. Bourcicault * treads with the ease and confidence of experience. ' London Assurance ' was a triumph of the instinct of appropriation, and though his second attempt proved a failure, it was not without merit of the same kind. ' Alma Mater ; or, a Cure for Coquettes,' a less ambitious exploit, has been completely successful, if to elicit applause and laughter from the portion of the audience whose taste was hit, and to be called forward to receive the greetings of

---

* Mr. Boucicault used, about this time, to spell his name as it is here printed.

delighted admirers, be success : why should it not, since the piece pleases the public? and those who live to please must please to live."

The *Times*, September 20, 1842, considered that had this piece been one of the highest productions of dramatic genius the success could not have been more distinguished. Yet the play was not first rate, nor even third rate, indeed, the journal quoted could not conceive a more humble effort of a mind accustomed to the business of the stage than 'Alma Mater.' "The whole artifice has been to keep the stage in a kind of 'row,' to rattle away all sorts of phrases at random, without any regard to the person who has to utter them ; and such is the state of a London audience at present that there can be found persons not only willing to allow themselves to be carried away for a moment, but even to pay honour to this kind of thing. . . . There is one merit which is not to be denied to the author, namely, an occasional smartness of dialogue. He sometimes utters a rapid series of 'good things' which produce a legitimate laugh. But the worst of it is these good things seem to be uttered in the course of saying everything that comes uppermost, and there is no doubt that the man who makes up his mind to talk away all day, right or wrong, will be sure to pop out a brilliant speech . . . . It professes to be a representation of college life . . . . but it is a representation of no life at all, there is not a breath of vitality from beginning to end. . . . . Wherever we turn we meet an old acquaintance, and we are not gratified at the meeting, because we distinctly recollect that we have seen him look much better somewhere else. . . . . Mr. F. Vining was a sketchy reproduction of Gradus in 'Who's the Dupe?' and strange to say he was called Gradus here. . . . . The college supper was but a scene out of 'Charles O'Malley,' played at the Olympic, and singularly like one in a piece called 'King O'Neill,' played at this house. . . . . Nothing could be such mere patchwork. . . . There is, however, one feature in the piece which we would remark before we dismiss it altogether, and that is a want of proper feeling, which seemed to pervade it. . . . . It is true that in the most brilliant plays of Congreve we are repulsed by an equal want of heart, but an author must have all the wit of Congreve, and be able to raise a gorgeous structure of epigrams, before he can plead his example as an apology. We repeat the audience were delighted ; the author had measured them well, and the manager had done his part admirably. . . . . But let us hope that the author, who (if we mistake him not) once gave promise of better things, and who last night displayed much real wit, may turn his talents to some higher purpose than the mere vamping of disjointed, unartistical, and rakish extravaganzas, which though they may be uproariously hallooed at for a week or two, cannot elicit the approbation of a single judicious friend."

On Monday, October 2, 1843, Mr. Boucicault produced "a romantic and sentimental drama," entitled 'Woman,' at Covent Garden Theatre. This piece was not successful. On Monday, November 18, 1844, he produced at the Haymarket Theatre 'Old

Heads and Young Hearts.' In a long criticism of this play, the *Athenæum*, November 23, 1844, published the following :—" The talent and wit undoubtedly possessed by the author, and his quali- fications in many obvious respects for a successful dramatist, induce us to press upon him the necessity of re-examining the laws of the species of composition in which up to a certain point he has shown himself a skilful student, and by a thorough and de- liberate appreciation of its nobler ends he may in his future efforts secure a degree of merit to which now he makes but distant approximation."

The *Times*, November 19, 1844, expressed the opinion that the comedy of ' Old Heads and Young Hearts ' was the most amusing five-act production that had been seen for years, and that it had pleased—honestly pleased—the public to a degree that might defy the exertions of any opposing theorist to dispute its claim to popu- larity. The improvement which Mr. Boucicault had manifested in this piece, as distinguished from those of former times, was immense. He used to be addicted to a sort of random writing that sometimes turned out well, sometimes the reverse. " Of this fault he has entirely cured himself. His piece is carefully written throughout, and he has introduced points in his dialogue which are worthy of any author. . . . . The creation of character, strong individual character, totally different from any conventional class, is not Mr. Boucicault's greatest *forte*. . . . . But he can give appropriate and characteristic dialogue to personages of a more familiar description, and make them vigorously assert their posi- tion in his comedy. He loves the stout bustle and equivoque that distinguished the intrigue school of comedies, and that he may work his characters for these purposes he is inclined to colour them, particularly his women, a little coarsely. But how wrong it is to be over severe on this point. How difficult it would be to get reasonable quantity of action within three hours, without some of the characters proceeding with a suddenness which oversteps the modesty of nature. . . . . No drama could have been more suc- cessful. And we must say the success was fully deserved. The author has produced a work that has more elements of popularity than any of equal length that we have seen for a long, long time."

On Thursday, February 4, 1847, Mr. Dion Boucicault produced at the Haymarket ' A School for Scheming,' regarded, at the time, as one of the author's happiest efforts in dramatic composition. The play, however, was but a partial success. On Tuesday, May 2, 1848, he produced, at the same theatre, a comedietta adapted from the French, under the title of ' Confidence '; and on Wednesday, November 22, 1848, at the same theatre, ' The Knight of Arva.' In the year 1851, ' The Broken Vow,' adapted from the French. ' L'Abbaye de Castro,' by Mr. Dion Boucicault, was, in February, performed for the first time at the Olympic ; and in April of the same year he produced at Drury Lane, ' The Queen of Spades,' an adaptation of the libretto of ' La Dame de Pique.'

On Monday, June 14, 1852, Mr. Boucicault made his *début* on the London boards at the Princess's Theatre, under Mr. Charles

Kean's management, in an after-piece in three acts (or "dramas," as announced in the play-bills), written by himself, entitled 'The Vampire.' The piece proved fairly attractive, but there were differences of opinion as to its merits. "If there is truth in the old adage, that 'When things are at the worst they must mend,'" remarked the *Examiner* (June 19, 1852),* "the amelioration of spectral melodrama is not distant, for it has reached the extreme point of inanity in the new piece which was produced on Monday at the Princess's Theatre, under the attractive title of 'The Vampire.' Its plot is chiefly copied from a piece which, some years ago, turned the Lyceum into a Chamber of Horrors; but it has been spun out into three parts, facetiously designated as 'three dramas'; the little period of a century has been interposed between each part; and, in order that the outrage on the *possible* shall be complete, the third part is projected forward into the year that will be in 1860! By this ingenious arrangement, the resuscitation of the original Vampire has been enabled to supply the lovers of the revolting at the Princess's with three acts of murder—that is two consummated, and one attempted; but, as the delicate process of vampirical killing is exactly after the same pattern in each case, the horror is quite worn out before the career of the creature terminates. Nothing but tedious trash remains. . . . The monster of absurdity was personated by its reviver, Mr. Boucicault, with due paleness of visage, stealthiness of pace, and solemnity of tone; the scenery, especially a moonlit ridge amidst the heights of Snowdon, was beautiful, and the costumes were prettily diversified: but the dreary repetition of fantastical horror almost exhausted even the patience which a benefit enjoins. Unfortunately the mischief of such a piece, produced at a respectable theatre, does not end with the weariness of the spectators, who come to shudder and remain to yawn; for it is not only 'beside the purpose of playing,' but directly contravenes it; and though it may be too dull to pervert the tastes of those who witness its vapid extravagances, it has power to bring discredit on the most genial of arts."

The same year, on Saturday, September 18, Mr. Boucicault produced at the Princess's a new two-act drama, entitled 'The Prima Donna'; and in 1853, in June, at the Adelphi, 'Géneviève; or, the Reign of Terror,' adapted from MM. Dumas and Maquet's 'Le Chevalier de la Maison Rouge.' The same year Mr. Boucicault went to the United States of America, and superintended various revivals of his plays at Wallack's Theatre, New York; and, in November 23, 1853, produced at Burton's Theatre, in the same city, a piece entitled 'The Fox Hunt; or, Don Quixote the Second.' The success of this play was very considerable, and in a speech from the stage, Mr. Boucicault informed his audience that "it was his intention to stay in America for a long time, if they would let him." In 1854 he produced, in New York, a version of the 'Louis Onze' of M. Casimir Delavigne, which was first read by Mr.

* Compare with *Journal of a London Playgoer*, by Henry Morley, Prof. Eng. Lit. in Univ. Col. Lond., pp. 54-5.

Boucicault in Hope Chapel, in that city.   Returning temporarily to
England, on the 1st January, 1855, he produced at the Theatre
Royal, Drury Lane, then under Mr. E. T. Smith's management,
'Eugenie,' a drama ; and on Monday, February 5, 1855, at the
Adelphi, 'Janet Pride,' a play which had been already performed
with much success in the United States.   (*See* CELESTE, MADAME.)
On Wednesday, June 3, 1857, he produced at the same theatre a
drama under the title of 'George Darville,' which was recognized
as being full of stage interest, and a very effective drama, "based
on an extreme moral which affords no hope to crime, but carries
strictly out the punishment incurred, however the one may be
delayed or the other repented of."

    'In September 1860 Mr. Boucicault and his wife, Mrs. Boucicault
(*née* ROBERTSON, AGNES), commenced an engagement at the
Adelphi Theatre, London.   The drama produced on the opening
night, Monday, September 16, was written by Mr. Boucicault,
and entitled 'The Colleen Bawn.'   For its plot he was in the main
indebted to Mr. Gerald Griffin's Irish story 'The Collegians.'   In
the cast Miss Agnes Robertson (Mrs. Boucicault) was the heroine,
Eily O'Connor; and Mr. Boucicault, *Myles-na-Coppaleen;* Mr. E
Falconer played *Danny Mann;* Mrs. Billington was *Mrs. Cregan;*
Mrs. A. Mellon, *Anne Chute;* Mr. Billington, *Hardress Cregan;*
and Mr. David Fisher, *Kyrle Daly*.   The play was eminently successful.   When the novel ('The Collegians') was yet new, a version
of it, entitled 'Eily O'Connor,' had been played at one or more of
the minor theatres.   The early version, however, had been long
forgotten by the public, who found in Mr. Boucicault's work one of the
best constructed and most striking dramas of domestic life that had
ever been put upon the stage.   "The interest rises as the story progresses, and the acts, in accordance with a valuable rule, invariably
terminate with strong situations.   The attempted drowning of Eily
O'Connor, in a very picturesque lake, is, perhaps, too really horrible ;
but this is a fault on the right side ; and the concluding scene, in
which Hardress Cregan is first charged with murder, amid the preparations for his wedding, and is then released on the appearance
of his supposed victim, is wrought with a skill which none but an
experienced dramatist could attain.   For himself, Mr. Boucicault
selects the character of *Myles-na-Coppaleen*, the plebeian Irishman
of scampish propensities, who alternates native shrewdness and
pathos after a fashion familiar to those who are accustomed to the
theatrical Hibernian.   His consummate slyness, his dexterity at
prevarication, and his evident enjoyment when he feels that he has
baffled too curious an investigator, are admirably delineated, though
he is less 'rollicking' than most of the artists who have shown in
Milesian character."   (*Times*, September 11, 1860.)   'The Colleen
Bawn' is a genuine Adelphi drama.   It presents a succession of
highly-wrought domestic scenes, introduces many very effective
situations, and affords good scope to the artist for the display of
effective pictorial accessories.   From first to last it was admirably
acted.   At the close of the Adelphi season 1860-1, Mr. Benjamin
Webster announced from the stage that Mr. and Mrs. Boucicault

had performed in 'The Colleen Bawn' (in London and the provinces) for more than 360 consecutive nights—at that time one of the longest "runs," if not altogether the longest, on record. It may be added that 'The Colleen Bawn' was first performed in New York, with Mr. and Mrs. Boucicault in the characters already mentioned. On Monday, November 18, 1861, Mr. Boucicault produced at the same theatre another play originally performed in America, entitled 'The Octoroon,' in which he sustained the part of *Salem Scudder*, and his wife that of Zoe, the Octoroon. The house was crammed in every nook. "Though the title of the piece did not in the least refer to the Green Erin, and the public had been made duly acquainted with the fact that the word 'Octoroon' denotes the child of a Quadroon by a white, there was a sort of vague notion that another 'Colleen Bawn' would be presented, so completely had the name of the author been identified with that most famous of modern dramas. It may be as well, therefore, to state that the new piece is not a 'Colleen Bawn,' nor anything like a 'Colleen Bawn,' but that it exhibits a picture of life in the Southern States, not shown even during the mania for 'Uncle Tom.' . . . . The 'sensation scenes' which most appeal to the public in the representation of 'The Octoroon,' are the slave sale that takes place in Peyton's house, and the destruction of the steamer by fire. Of these the former is completely novel. Pete, an old negro, gives a vein of drollery to the situation by boasting his own qualities in order to fetch a handsome price, while the competition that arises with respect to Zoe is most exciting. The whole body of planters wish to preserve the daughter of their old friend, the judge, from falling into the hands of McClosky, even Dora, the young lady who has set her heart upon George, coming generously forward to the rescue of her rival, till at last the whole affair is nearly settled by a skirmish with bowie-knives. The acting throughout is very good. Mr. Boucicault, as the shrewd, cool Yankee, *Salem Scudder*, appears in a line, to him, entirely new, and succeeds to perfection." (*Times*, November 19, 1861.) During one week in December of this year, the author and his wife appeared at the Adelphi in both 'The Colleen Bawn' and 'The Octoroon' on the same night. The last-named play commenced at seven and ended at ten minutes past nine; 'The Colleen Bawn' followed, and ended at half-past eleven. It has been already mentioned (BOUCICAULT, AGNES) that the author in answer to a general request modified the original termination of 'The Octoroon,' by saving Zoe's life.

On Monday, February 10, 1862, Mr. Boucicault produced at the same theatre 'The Dublin Boy'—a version of Vanderburch's 'Le Gamin de Paris'; and on Saturday, March 1, 1862, at the same theatre, a drama in five acts, under the title of 'The Life of an Actress,' which had been already performed in America. Mr. Boucicault in this play sustained the character of *Grimaldi*. "The new play was exceedingly successful up to the end of the third act. Mr. Boucicault's portraiture of the, by turns, obsequious, courteous, and indignant *Grimaldi* was in all respects a masterpiece of histrionic ability. What is technically called the 'make-up' was complete; and his manner throughout was true to the natural bearing of a man fallen into misfortune, but conscious of noble birth and noble feelings. He showed, too, some extraordinary powers. While teaching his pupil he has to point out to her how Rachel delivered a particular speech, and finds it necessary to resort to the original French. This feat he brilliantly accomplished. His nervous anxiety for his *débutante's* success on the provincial stage, and his passionate disappointment when he misses her from the next scene and learns the story of her abduction, were both admirably delineated. These things place Mr. Boucicault in the front rank as an artist of versatile abilities and a comprehensive mind. . . . . We are not quite sure that the drama itself (which is partly compilation and partly adaptation) will add much to his reputation as a dramatist; but his reputation as an actor must be augmented by the skill and tact with which he has embodied and supported the part of its hero." (*Athenæum*, March 8, 1862.) In the original cast of this play Mrs. Boucicault acted the part of Violet, Mr. Toole that of Wopshot ("a low comedian"), and Mrs. Billington the *rôle* of Julia (a "star," leading lady).

On Monday, April 14, 1862, at the Adelphi, Mr. Boucicault produced a dramatic version of Charles Dickens's 'The Cricket on the Hearth,' under the title of 'Dot.' Becoming sub-tenant of Drury Lane Theatre for a few months in the autumn of 1862, he produced there a spectacular drama entitled 'The Relief of Lucknow,' in which he sustained the part of *Corporal Cassidy*. Vacating that theatre in December of the same year, on Monday, the 22nd of that month, he opened Astley's Theatre as "The Theatre Royal, Westminster," and produced on the opening night, 'To Parents and Guardians' (in which he played the part of *M. Tourbillon*), and a revival of 'The Relief of Lucknow,' sustaining in this piece his original character before mentioned. On October 2nd, 1862, a letter was published in the *Times* over the signature "Dion Boucicault," advocating improvements in theatre building, and contrasting the working expenses, the dinginess, ill-ventilation and general discomfort of the London theatres of that time with the Winter Garden Theatre in New York, which Mr. Boucicault held in 1859. In that letter he offered to head a subscription with 5000*l.* for the purpose of erecting a suitable and comfortable London Theatre. It may be reasonably assumed that the alterations which Mr. Boucicault effected in the general arrangements of old Astley's were in some sort to be accepted as a practical exemplification of his views of what a house devoted to theatrical entertainment should be. He converted the old "ring" into an elaborate arrangement of stalls and pit; the bygone Adelphi system of intermediate "pit stalls" he also introduced. The immense size of the *salle* admitting of greater alterations, Mr. Boucicault placed between the stalls proper and the orchestra a sort of miniature garden of shrubs, flowers, and fountains, the effect of which in hot weather was extremely pleasant. Adjoining the theatre, and on the site of what was known as "Astley's cottage," Mr. Boucicault had projected a vast *café*, which was to be constructed of iron and glass with *foyers* for promenaders between the acts, and an open-air restaurant on the flat Moorish roof commanding a view of the river. The affairs of the theatre becoming involved in litigation, this part of Mr. Boucicault's scheme was left unfulfilled ; but during his short term of management he effected immense improvements in the interior of old Astley's. On Monday, January 26, 1863, he produced at the Westminster Theatre a dramatic version of 'The Heart of Midlothian,' under the title 'The Trial of Effie Deans,' in which play he performed the part of *Counsel for the Prisoner.* On Wednesday, May 11, 1864, at the St. James's Theatre, he produced a drama in five acts entitled ' The Fox Chase,' already performed in New York. This play was not very successful in London. In the same year, on the 5th of August, at the Princess's Theatre, he produced 'The Streets of London,' a sensational drama, not exactly new to the English boards, the substance of it having been supplied by Mr. Stirling Coyne to the Surrey stage in 1857, and shortly afterwards to the Strand, by Mr. R. Barnett, under the respective titles of 'Fraud and its Victims,' and ' Pride and Poverty.' The original, it may be remarked, of these adaptations, is a seven-act French drama, entitled ' Les Pauvres de Paris,' by MM. E. Brisebarre and Eugène Nus, acted in 1856 at the Ambigu Comique. Before being performed in London Mr. Boucicault had produced a version of ' The Streets of London ' in New York, and in Leeds and Liverpool.

On Wednesday, March 22, 1865, at the Princess's Theatre, Mr. Boucicault produced, for the first time in London (having originally presented it on the stage, in November 1864, in Dublin), a drama entitled ' Arrah-na-Pogue ; or, the Wicklow Wedding,' in which he sustained the part of *Shaun, the Post.* "The story in this instance, not derived from a novel, but alleged to be the dramatist's own invention, is simple in form, but very ingeniously treated, so as to afford a diversity of situations, all possessing more or less a hold over the sympathies of the audience. Thoroughly versed in the important art of construction, and expert at framing those effective speeches which convey their purpose in the fewest words, the author keeps his characters constantly in action, and suffers neither the ear nor the eye to grow weary. The lines sparkle sometimes with wit, at others glow with good humour, but are always terse, naturally in keeping with the exigencies of the situation, and fitted to the characters from whose lips they proceed. The principles which command success in dramatic composition, and without which the most brilliant dialogue and the most fertile fancy would be of little avail, have seldom received a clearer elucidation than in the management of the plot of ' Arrah-na-Pogue.' . . . "The character of *Shaun, the Post,* a Wicklow carman, which Mr. Boucicault has allotted to himself, is rendered with considerable artistic power, guided by a thorough knowledge of the peculiarities of the Irish temperament, which finds full expression in a mixture of humour and pathos, very felicitously depicted. The readiness of repartee, coloured with a tinge of poetry, and associated with a warm heart full of trusting con-

fidence in the girl he loves, gives the actor the fullest possession
of the sympathies of his audience." (*Daily Telegraph*, March 23,
1865.) ' Arrah-na-Pogue' was a great success, and was represented in Paris,'and throughout the French provinces, the United
States, and Australia.   The French version, ' Jean la Poste ;
ou, les Noces Irlandaises,' was performed at the Gaieté for 140
nights.

In May 1866, Mr. Boucicault produced at Manchester an " original " three-act play entitled ' The Parish Clerk,' the piece having
been written expressly for Mr. Joseph Jefferson.   At the Lyceum
Theatre in London, in September 1866, during the management of
Mr. Charles Fechter, Mr. Boucicault produced ' The Long Strike'
(partly founded on the story of ' Mary Barton,' and partly on that
of ' Lizzie Leigh '), in which he played *Johnny Reilly*.   In the
same year on Saturday, October 6, on the occasion of the opening
of the Holborn Theatre, he produced ' The Flying Scud ; or, a
Four-legged Fortune' ; and in November of the same year, at the
St. James's Theatre, ' Hunted Down,' a drama.   (*See* HERBERT,
LOUISA.)   In 1868, on Wednesday, August 12, at the Princess's,
he produced ' After Dark ; a Tale of London Life ' ; and in the
year following, in May, at the same theatre, ' Presumptive Evidence,' a drama ; and in August, at Drury Lane, ' Formosa,' a
drama.   In 1870, likewise at the Princess's Theatre, the three
following pieces from his pen were placed on the stage, viz. ' Paul
Lafarge ' ; ' A Dark Night's Work ' ; and ' The Rapparee ' ; and in
December of the same year, at the Holborn Theatre, ' Jezebel ; or,
the Dead Reckoning,' founded on ' Le Pendu,' a play by MM.
Michel Masson and Anicet Bourgeois.   Neither of these plays was
altogether successful.   After sojourning in the United States for
a brief period, in 1872 Mr. Boucicault returned to England, and on
Saturday, May 4, of that year, reappeared with Mrs. Boucicault on
the London boards at the Gaiety Theatre, in a rendering of ' La
Joie fait Peur,' entitled ' Night and Morning,' and in their original
characters in a revival of ' The Colleen Bawn.'   During the same
year at the same theatre, Mr. Boucicault and his wife appeared in
various revivals of his plays ; and in July in a version by himself
of Colman's comedy of ' John Bull,' produced also at the Gaiety
Theatre, Mr. Boucicault sustained the part of *Dennis Brul-
gruddery*.   In 1874 (June) at the same theatre, he produced ' Led
Astray,' a play adapted from ' La Tentation,' of M. Octave Feuillet.
In the following year (Saturday, September 4, 1875) at Drury Lane
he produced, for the first time in London, ' The Shaughraun,' in
which he performed the part of *Conn O'Kelly*.   " The acting in
two or three characters was admirable.   Mr. Boucicault is probably the best stage Irishman that has been seen.   It is impossible
to make drollery more unctuous and blarney more attractive than
they appear in his rendering.   To the vitality he imparts to the
character of *Conn* the success of the piece is largely attributable."
(*Athenæum*, Sept. 11, 1875.)

In 1876 Mr. Boucicault returned once more to the United States,
where he resides.   It may be said that he reached the climax of

his fame as an actor and dramatic author in 1860 with the production of ' The Colleen Bawn.' His merits as an actor were probably best exhibited in that play, in ' The Life of an Actress,' and in his later production, ' The Shaughraun.' It cannot be said that Mr. Boucicault is entitled to the distinction of being designated an original writer. His most popular plays are adaptations ; but no modern dramatic author has said better things on the stage than has Mr. Boucicault in those plays.

BRENNAN, MAGGIE, made her *début* on the London stage Saturday, November 28, 1868, at the Globe Theatre, as the *Hon. Fred Titeboy* in Byron's play, ' Cyril's Success,' performing one of those parts in trousers and frock coats, which are so often a snare to ambitious actresses, with a self-command and an absence of anything like vulgarity which certainly did not suggest immaturity. Her acting in the part of the *Hon. Fred Titeboy*, a musical amateur, who is a good-natured but somewhat weak-minded "star" of fashionable circles, was indeed clever throughout, and at once established her in the favour of the audience. In April of the following year she played the part of *Miss Honor Molloy*, first performance of Mr. T. W. Robertson's comedy, ' A Breach of Promise.' " Feminine acting is seldom intrinsically comic. Miss Brennan's power of changing her expression, however, is very humorous and her mimetic skill is remarkable." (*Athenæum*, April 17, 1869.) Miss Maggie Brennan has since played original parts in various plays, of which the following will suffice as examples, viz. ' Formosa' (*Earl of Eden*), ' On Guard' (*Guy Warrington*), ' Randall's Thumb' (*Miss Spinn*), &c.

BRENNAN, MAUDE, sister of the above-named, was born at Hurst Castle, Hampshire, in 1855. She became a pupil of Edward Stirling, of the Theatre Royal, Drury Lane, in 1869, and entered the dramatic profession at the Brighton Theatre in 1871. After a tour through the provinces, Miss Brennan was engaged by Mr. W. Sidney for the Prince of Wales's Theatre, Glasgow, 1872, to support Mr. Barry Sullivan, and during that engagement played various leading parts, including *Lady Macbeth*. She afterwards fulfilled various engagements at the principal provincial theatres. Her first appearance in London was made in 1876, at Covent Garden Theatre, as *Portia* in the ' Merchant of Venice.' Subsequently she played at the Gaiety Theatre, Glasgow, under Mr. C. Bernard's management, and was by him sent on tour with Mr. H. J. Byron. Miss Brennan has lately concluded a " starring " engagement at Belfast, where she presented the character of *Leah* in the tragedy of that name, with some success. During the latter part of 1878 Miss Brennan supported Mr. Henry Irving on his provincial tour as " leading lady," appearing as *Ophelia* (' Hamlet'), *Julie* (' Richelieu '), &c.

BROMLEY, NELLIE, first attracted notice as an actress in burlesque at the Royalty Theatre under the management of Miss M. Oliver in 1868. Here she played with some success in

Burnand's 'Latest edition of Black-eyed Susan,' as *Dolly May-flower*, and the same author's ' Claude Du Val,' as *Nimble Ned.* In 1871 she was acting at the Court Theatre. In 1873 she was engaged at the Gaiety Theatre, and appeared there as *Praline de Patoche* in H. B. Farnie's burlesque ' Nemesis,' and in the following year as *The Plaintiff*, in Gilbert and Sullivan's comic opera, ' Trial by Jury.' Miss Bromley was likewise in the original cast of ' Pink Dominos,' and first performed at the Criterion Theatre, Saturday, March 31, 1877. She acted the part of *Rebecca*. Subsequently she has been engaged at the Royalty Theatre, playing in an extravaganza by E. Rose and A. Harris, entitled ' Venus.'

BROUGH, FANNY WHITESIDE (Mrs. R. S. BOLEYN, a *nom de théâtre*), only daughter of the late Robert Brough (better known as one of " the Brothers Brough "), the author, was born in Paris and entered the dramatic profession in 1869, as a member of Mr. Charles Calvert's company at the Prince's Theatre, Manchester. She remained at that theatre for two years, and during the engagement played *Ophelia* (' Hamlet') with considerable success, Mr. Barry Sullivan acting the title *rôle*. Miss Fanny Brough made her first appearance on the London stage at the St. James's Theatre, Saturday, October 15, 1870, as *Fernande*, in Sutherland Edwards's adaptation of V. Sardou's play of that name, "playing with great intelligence and giving the character much sweetness and gentleness " (*Examiner*, November 12, 1870). During her engagement at St. James's Theatre Miss Brough appeared as *Fanny Parkhouse*, the first performance of Albery's ' Two Thorns,' and as the heroine in Mr. T. W. Robertson's comedy entitled ' War,' first performed at the same theatre. She also played in the several comedies revived by Mrs. John Wood during the first period of that lady's management of St. James's Theatre. She was engaged to play leading parts with Mr. R. Younge's so-called ' Caste' company of comedians ; and subsequently appeared at the Prince of Wales's Theatre, London, under Mr. and Mrs. Bancroft's management, as *Clara Douglas* in ' Money' on its first revival there. At the Gaiety Theatre, under Mr. J. Hollingshead's management, Miss Brough has personated important characters with Mr. Toole and the late Mr. C. Mathews, those gentlemen acting the principal *rôles*. She has been a member of Mr. L. J. Sefton's so-called ' Pygmalion and Galatea' company, and more recently (April 1878) of Mr. Duck's ' Our Boys' company. Miss Brough's most pleasing successes on the provincial stage have been in the characters of *Mary Melrose* (' Our Boys') and *Ethel Grainger* (' Married in Haste'). She has recently (June 1879) been playing the part of *Haidee Burnside* in ' The Crisis' in the provinces, and has met with considerable favour.

BROUGH, LIONEL, was born at Pontypool, Monmouth, 10th of March, 1836. Son of Barnabas Brough, once well known as a dramatic author of some note, writing under the *nom de plume* of " Barnard de Burgh"; and brother of the late William and

Robert Brough (known as "the Brothers Brough"), authors, and of the late John C. Brough, some time Secretary of the London Institution, and a frequent contributor to scientific literature. Lionel Brough began life in the office of John Timbs, when that gentleman was editor of the *Illustrated London News*, and when, among its chief literary contributors, were included Douglas Jerrold, Albert Smith, Angus Reach, Charles Dickens, W. M. Thackeray; and among its artists John Leech and Sir J. Gilbert. He was, in the earlier years of its existence, assistant publisher of the *Daily Telegraph*. In that capacity Mr. Brough lays claim to having originated the present system of selling newspapers in the streets, having organized in London for the *Daily Telegraph* a staff of 240 boys for that purpose. He made his first appearance on any stage, in December 1854, at the Lyceum Theatre, London, under the management of Madame Vestris and Mr. Charles Mathews, in an extravaganza by his brother, William Brough, entitled ' Prince Pretty Pet,' and a farce, ' My Fellow Clerk.' Leaving the stage for a time after the death of Madame Vestris, he returned to the Lyceum in 1858, under the management of Mr. Edmund Falconer, and in that year played in the ' Siege of Troy ' (burlesque by R. B. Brough) under the pseudonym of " Lionel Porter," and in Falconer's drama ' Francesca.' He retired from the stage for five years, during which time Mr. Brough was on the staff of the *Morning Star*, London daily newspaper, from the date of its first publication until its fifth anniversary. Afterwards he gave an entertainment in London, of which the *pièce de résistance* was ' Cinderella,' written by Byron, Leicester Buckingham, the Brothers Brough, Frank Talfourd, Andrew Halliday, and others, and presented by the authors to Lionel Brough. Subsequently he was at the Polytechnic Institution for a year, giving various entertainments, and was the first who travelled the provinces with the " Ghost" exhibition. Lionel Brough played with the members of the Savage Club before the Queen, Prince Consort, and Royal Family in aid of the "Lancashire Famine Relief Fund," and afterwards in Manchester and Liverpool for the same object. In February 1864 he joined Mr. Alex. Henderson's company at the Prince of Wales's Theatre, Liverpool, and remained a leading member of that company for more than three years. Subsequently he was at the Amphitheatre under the respective managements of Copeland, and Henderson, and Byron, and then became associated with Mr. Saker of the Alexandra Theatre in that town. In October 1867 Mr. Brough played *Dard* in ' The Double Marriage ' on the occasion of the opening of the new Queen's Theatre in London, being recognized as an actor of genuine ability, well deserving the favourable reception he obtained. Lionel Brough's first important London success was in the character of *Ben Garner* in Byron's comedy, ' Dearer than Life,' first performed at the Queen's Theatre, Long Acre, on 8th January, 1868, in which he made one of those "hits" which mark a decided stride in the career of a rising actor. " Next to the principal part, one of the most striking was that assigned to Mr. Lionel Brough, who only wants fair opportunity to become one of the most successful comic or character actors of the day. His impersonation of the drunken old sot, *Ben Garner*, was marvellously worked out, and at the end of the first act, he more than divided the applause with Mr. Toole. All throughout he helped the piece by the individuality and the humorous force of his impersonation." (*Standard*, January 9, 1868.)

Among noteworthy successes achieved by Lionel Brough about this time the parts sustained by him in the following plays may be selected for mention, viz. : In ' The Lancashire Lass,' ' Not Guilty,' the burlesques ' La Vivandière ' (Gilbert), ' Stranger ' (Reece), and ' Foul Play ' (Burnand). Under the auspices of Mr. J. L. Toole, Lionel Brough travelled some time with the company of which Henry Irving was a member. On March 29, 1869, he commenced a series of engagements under Mrs. John Wood's management, at the St. James's Theatre, performing the character of *Tony Lumpkin* for a " run " of nearly 200 nights, and *Paul Pry* for a run almost equally as long. Mr. Brough played in ' La Belle Sauvage ' (burlesque) the part of *Captain John Smith*, and in ' My Poll and My Partner Joe ' (burlesque) the part of *Black Brandon*, each performed with much success at the St. James's Theatre. Afterwards he joined Mr. Fell at the Holborn Theatre (now " the Duke's "), where he played in ' La Vie Parisienne,' ' Petit Faust,' and other pieces. In August 1872 Mr. Brough was selected by Mr. Boucicault to be " first low comedian " and stage-manager of Covent Garden Theatre on the production there of the stage spectacle of ' Babil and Bijou.' He was subsequently engaged at the Gaiety Theatre for a period of twelve months, playing in such pieces as ' Bib and Tucker,' ' London Assurance,' &c., and in various opera bouffes and burlesques produced there. Mr. Brough then became attached to the companies of the Globe and Folly Theatres, playing *Blue Beard* (over 300 nights), *Robinson Crusoe*, &c. ; and on April 28, 1878, he concluded an engagement at the New Royalty Theatre, afterwards, in September 1878, entering upon an engagement at the Folly Theatre. During this period Mr. Brough played also in various morning performances at the Crystal and Alexandra Palaces and at the Aquarium Theatre. At the latter place of amusement he repeated his performance of *Tony Lumpkin* with Mrs. Stirling, Miss Litton, Mr. W. Farren, and Mr. John Ryder in the cast. At the latter theatre, renamed, in April 1879, " The Imperial Theatre," he entered into an engagement, as " first low comedian." On April 23, 1879, a new burlesque of ' The Lady of Lyons ' (W. Younge) was produced, Miss Lydia Thompson playing Pauline, Mr. Brough *Claude Melnotte*. The most successful scene in the piece was a *pas de deux*, in which these two struck successive attitudes, interpreted alternately by the two performers to the audience, partly in caricature of mythological heroes, partly of political leaders of the day.

BROUGHAM, JOHN, was born May 9, 1814, in Dublin, where he was educated with the view of following medicine as a profession. This intention, however, was not carried out. Mr. Brougham's tastes were more in the direction of the stage, on which he first appeared in the year 1830. The place of his *début* was the Queen's Theatre, now the Prince of Wales's, in Tottenham Street, Tottenham Court Road, London, and the piece in which he first made his appearance, Moncrieff's operatic extravaganza, 'Tom and Jerry.' During Madame Vestris's management of the old Olympic Theatre Mr. Brougham was a member of her "stock" company, and in that position earned for himself considerable reputation. He was afterwards a member of her company at the Theatre Royal, Covent Garden. In 1840 he entered upon the management of the Lyceum Theatre, and commenced in the same year his career as a dramatic author by the production of an extravaganza entitled 'Life in the Clouds,' first performed there. Two years later Mr. Brougham went to the United States, where he subsequently took up his residence, and followed his profession of dramatist and actor with great success.* Returning to London in 1859, he subsequently joined the company of the Lyceum Theatre, under Mr. Charles Fechter's management, and furnished that admirable actor with two of his most popular plays, taken from the French, viz. 'The Duke's Motto,' an adaptation of 'Le Bossu,' a romantic drama, by Paul Feval, originally performed at the Porte St. Martin, and 'Bel Demonio,' founded on a five-act drama called 'The Broken Vow ; a Romance of the Times of Sixtus the Fifth,' which, in its turn, was taken from 'L'Abbé de Castro.' The first was produced at the Lyceum Theatre on Saturday, January 10, 1863 ; the second on Saturday, October 31, of the same year. Mr. Brougham was in the original cast of both these plays. In 'The Duke's Motto' Mr. Brougham played *Carrickfergus*, an Irish soldier of fortune ; in 'Bel Demonio' he acted the character of *Cardinal Montalto*. "As a drama it ('Bel Demonio') has this quality in common with 'The Duke's Motto,' that it interests the audience more by the exhibition of a series of extraordinary adventures than by the development of an idea or the delineation of character. . . . While 'The Duke's Motto' and 'Bel Demonio' are dramas constructed on precisely the same principles, the differences between them are not in favour of the latter. The adventures of the first six tableaux are exciting enough, but in his endeavours constantly to renew an interest, the author has made the latter scenes of his play too long. . . . Angelo is not nearly so good a part as Captain Lagardère for the display of Mr. Fechter. With the exception of a love scene in the third tableau, played with all that ardour which is peculiar to

* "A class of important characters, the *Sir Oliver Surfaces* and other uncles from India, the *Sir Lucius O'Triggers* and other gentlemen from Ireland, are held at Wallack's Theatre [New York] by the gentle and genial John Brougham. For more than thirty years the name of John Brougham has held a high place in the play-bills of America, as author, or actor, or manager, or as all three at once. When he made his first appearance in New York in 1842 as the 'Irish Lion,' he was at once accepted as the successor of the lamented Tyrone Power, who had been lost in the steamer 'President' the year before."—*Scribner's Monthly*, April 1879, p. 781. ('Actors and Actresses of New York,' by J. B. Matthews.)

this fascinating actor, and a few passages of pathos on the discovery of Lena in the crypt, Angelo is rather a thread by which a
number of incidents are connected together than a character of
importance on his own account. Indeed, the *Cardinal*, excellently
made up and acted by Mr. John Brougham ; and Ranuccio, played
with bluff humour by Mr. Emery, are the only two marked characters in the play." (*Times*, November 2, 1863.)

Subsequently Mr. Brougham appeared at the Princess's Theatre,
and on the occasion of the first performance there, Wednesday,
March 22, 1865, of Boucicault's drama ' Arrah-na-Pogue,' he
played the part of *Colonel Bagenal O'Grady*. Perhaps the most
favourable example of Mr. John Brougham's powers as a dramatist is found in his comedy ' Playing with Fire,' produced at the
Princess's Theatre on Saturday, September 28, 1861. Mr. Brougham
himself sustained the principal character, *Dr. Savage*. Enough
was known of the previous fortunes of the piece to awaken considerable curiosity as to its merits. It had been produced with
great success in America, and though a New York theatre is
scarcely regarded as a passport office that will secure the hos-
pitable reception of a drama in the old country, this particular play
had been mentioned in such remarkably high terms that much was
expected of it. A subsequent performance in Manchester had
procured from a public claiming some authority in theatrical
matters a confirmation of the verdict pronounced in the United
States. ' Playing with Fire' was in all respects a legitimate success. Mr. Brougham was heartily welcomed, and made a most
favourable impression.

BRUCE, EDGAR, entered the dramatic profession in 1868,
making his first appearance at the Prince of Wales's Theatre, Liverpool, where he subsequently acted for a season. He made his *début*
on the London stage August 30, 1869, at the Strand Theatre, as
Chateau Renaud, in a burlesque entitled ' The Pilgrim of Love.'
" After two years' hard work in the principal country theatres and
in London," Mr. Bruce became, in 1871 (August), a member of the
" Wyndham Comedy Company," performing in America, and played
leading parts in various theatres in the United States and Canada,
his most successful impersonations during this engagement being
D'Alroy and *Hawtree*, in ' Caste'; *McAlister* and *Chalcot*, in
' Ours '; and *Lord Beaufoy*, in ' School.' In March 1873 Mr.
Bruce joined the company of the Court Theatre, where he appeared
in the following among other plays : ' About Town,' 'Marriage
Lines,' 'Alone,' 'Wedding March,' &c., &c. In March 1875 he
was engaged at St. James's Theatre. The same year, in June, he
opened the Haymarket Theatre under his management for a season
of six weeks ; and on 21st February of the following year (1876)
the Globe Theatre, producing there a drama, founded on Charles
Dickens's novel ' Bleak House,' entitled ' Jo,' with Miss Jennie Lee
in the title *rôle*. At the same theatre during the following season
Mr. Bruce produced ' Cora,' with Mrs. Herman Vezin in the
leading character. During the early part of 1878 he acted the

character of *Greythorne* (in succession to Mr. Wyndham) in 'Pink Dominos' at the Criterion Theatre, and afterwards went on tour with Mr. George Honey to play in Gilbert's comedy 'Engaged.' In April 1879 Mr. Bruce entered on the management of the Royalty Theatre, and "opened" on the 14th of that month with "A Comedy of the Day, in three acts," entitled 'Crutch and Tooth-pick,' adapted by Mr. Geo. R. Sims. The piece proved successful.

*BRUCE, EDITH, began her theatrical career in the provinces, and made her first London appearance at Covent Garden Theatre, August 29, 1872, as *Wanda* in 'Babil and Bijou.' She performed at the Strand Theatre, for two seasons at Brighton, and afterwards at the Criterion Theatre, at the latter of which she exhibited some amusing qualities as *Parker* in 'The Great Divorce Case.' The principal plays in which she has since appeared at the Criterion Theatre are, 'Hot Water,' 'On Bail,' and 'The Pink Dominos.' At the Crystal Palace she played the leading parts in some of the pantomimes produced there, and also performed in several of the plays presented there under the management of Mr. Charles Wyndham. She was engaged by Miss Fanny Josephs for the Olympic, and is now (October 1879) a member of the Gaiety Company.

BUCKSTONE, JOHN BALDWIN, was born at Hoxton, near London, September 1802, and entered the dramatic profession in the year 1821 as member of a travelling company of players, and first appeared upon the stage at Wokingham, Berks. He made his *début* in the part of *Gabriel* in 'The Children of the Wood.' Afterwards he joined the "Faversham, Folkestone, and Hastings Circuit," and remained a member of that association for three years. At the anniversary dinner of the Royal General Theatrical Fund in 1855, Mr. Buckstone, in proposing the toast of the evening, gave the following amusing account of his earlier struggles as an actor. "I am enabled," said he, "truly to depict what performers endure, because I was a country actor, and, amongst other vicissitudes, once walked from Northampton to London—72 miles—on 4½*d*. I had a companion in the same plight, and on comparing our pecuniary resources we discovered ourselves masters of the sum of 9*d*.— 4½*d*. each. As it may interest you, gentlemen, I will describe my costume on that occasion, and how we got to London. My costume consisted of a threadbare whity-blue coat, with tarnished metal buttons, secured to the throat, because I wore underneath what we term a flowered waistcoat, made of glazed chintz, and of a very showy pattern, generally adopted when playing country boys and singing comic songs, which at that time was my vocation. I will not attempt to describe my hat; while my trousers must only be delicately alluded to, as they were made of what was originally white duck, but as they had been worn about six weeks, and having myself been much in the fields, there was a refreshing tint of a green and clay colour about them, which imparted to that portion of my attire quite an agricultural appearance. I carried a small bundle. I will not describe its entire contents, except that it held a red wig and a pair of russet boots. Under my arm was a portfolio, containing sketches from nature and some attempts at love poetry; while on my feet, to perform this distance of 72 miles, I wore a pair of dancing-pumps, tied up at the heels with packthread. Thus equipped, I started with my companion from Northampton, and before breakfast we accomplished 15 miles, when we sat down to rest ourselves under a hedge by the roadside. We felt very much disposed to partake of the meal I have alluded to, but were rather puzzled how to provide it. Presently a cowboy appeared, driving some lazy, zigzag-going cows, and carrying two large tin cans containing skimmed milk. We purchased the contents of one of the cans for one halfpenny. A cottage was close at hand, where we applied for bread, and procured a very nice, though rather stale, half-quartern home-baked loaf for one penny. The cowboy sat by us on that roadside to wait for his can. The cows seemed to regard us with a sleepy look of mingled pity and indifference, while with the bottom crust of that loaf and three pints of skimmed milk I assure you I enjoyed the roadside breakfast of that summer morning more than I have enjoyed the sumptuous banquet of this evening. On the first day we walked 40 miles, in which my pumps and what they covered, as the Yankees say, 'suffered some.' Our bed for the night was in one of those wayside hostelries called 'a lodging-house for travellers,' for which accommodation we disbursed twopence. Late in the evening of the next day we completed the remaining 32 miles, and found ourselves at the 'Mother Red Cap,' at Camden Town, with enough in our pockets to procure half a pint of porter. Thus you see, gentlemen, I have experienced some of the vicissitudes of a country actor." Whilst strolling Mr. Buckstone made the acquaintance of the late Edmund Kean, to whose encouragement he owed, in some part, his early success as a comedian. His first appearance on the London stage took place at the Surrey Theatre in the year 1824, in the part of *Peter Smink* in a play entitled 'The Armistice.' Having shown considerable ability in the line of low comedy at that theatre Mr. Buckstone was offered various engagements in London. He became connected with the company of the old Adelphi Theatre in 1828, in the days of Frederick Yates and John Reeve, and first appeared there as *Bobby Trot* in his own drama of 'Luke the Labourer.' At this and a somewhat later period of his career Mr. Buckstone devoted much of his time to writing and adapting pieces for the stage, and especially for the Adelphi and Haymarket Theatres. For the first-named he wrote two plays in particular—'The Green Bushes,' first performed at the Adelphi, January 27, 1845, and 'The Flowers of the Forest,' produced March 11, 1847—which still remain important examples of popular English melodrama. To these may be added a lengthy list of comedies, dramas, and farces, some of which in their day attained considerable popularity. Among the number may be specially mentioned a drama entitled 'The Wreck Ashore,' first performed at the last-named theatre in October 1830. On the 5th of March, 1832, was produced at the Adelphi a domestic drama entitled 'Forgery; or, the Reading of the Will,' by J. B. Buckstone ; spoken of in contemporary journals as "a good story with some powerful situations, well relieved by the broad comicalities of Mr. Buckstone." In the year 1833 he produced at the same theatre a successful three-act piece founded on Cooper's novel, 'The Bravo.' The same year at the Haymarket he produced a drama entitled 'Ellen Wareham'; the heroine acted by Mrs. Yates. Wednesday, July 17, 1833, he acted at the Haymarket in a piece by Douglas Jerrold—then performed for the first time—entitled 'The Housekeeper ; or, the White Rose,' described as "a love story, the hero and heroine (Mr. F. Vining and Miss Taylor) being mixed up with a portion of the political intrigues of the early part of the reign of George the First." Both Mr. Buckstone and Mr. Benjamin Webster were in the original cast.

The following month Mr. Buckstone performed at the same theatre with the late Mr. Charles Mathews, the younger, in one of many plays written by that admirable comedian, entitled 'Pyramus and Thisbe'; and in the following October in a piece from his own mirth-provoking pen, entitled 'Uncle John.' Besides the author himself, the elder Farren, Benjamin Webster, and Mrs. Glover were in the cast. In the month of January 1834 was produced "with complete success," at the Adelphi Theatre, a drama entitled 'Thirty Years of a Woman's Life,' by J. B. Buckstone ; and the same year at the Haymarket he produced the two following plays, viz. 'Rural Felicity' and 'Married Life.' In the latter Mr. Buckstone himself acted, together with Mrs. Faucit, Mrs. Glover, and Mrs. Humby, and Messrs. Farren and F. Vining. In November 1834 Mr. Buckstone produced, at the Adelphi, a drama entitled 'Agnes de Vere ; or, the Broken Heart,' adapted from the French, in which he and Mrs. Keeley sustained the comic parts ; and the following month, at the same theatre, a dramatization of 'The Last Days of Pompeii.' Of this effort it is stated in a contemporary journal, that "it was enthusiastically received, and will draw, no doubt, plenty of money to the theatre." About this time Mr. Buckstone was permanently enrolled a member of the company of the Haymarket Theatre, as its principal low comedian, and continued to provide for that theatre farces "bearing the droll impress of the broad Buckstonian stamp." In June 1835 he produced there 'Good Husbands make Good Wives'; and in July 1835, 'The Scholar,' an adaptation from the French. In November 1835 was performed for the first time, at the Adelphi Theatre, 'The Dream at Sea,' an original three-act drama by J. B. Buckstone. In January 1838 he produced two new farces in the same week ; viz., at the Olympic, 'Shocking Events,' and at Drury Lane, 'Our Mary Anne.' In May 1838 was performed at the Haymarket, for the first time, a clever little farce called 'The Irish Lion,' by J. B. Buckstone—"a hit at the absurd fashion now prevalent of exhibiting at *soirées* and evening parties a literary lion on all occasions."

In the year 1840 Mr. Buckstone fulfilled a farewell engagement at the Haymarket Theatre, previous to visiting the United States of America, whither he went in June of that year, and whence he returned in the summer of the year 1842. His American tour was but a partial success.

At the Haymarket "Buckstone showed his comic phiz again on Wednesday, after his long absence in America, and literally 'tipped the wink' to the audience, who responded with a roar of laughter. After playing *Dove* in his own grotesque piece, 'Married Life,' he was called forward, and expressed, in a becoming and feeling manner, his acknowledgments of the welcome." (*Athenæum*, October 22, 1842.)

During the seasons 1842-3-4 Mr. Buckstone was playing at the Haymarket in various French vaudeville pieces and dramas written principally for Madame Celeste ; and in the latter year he played *Grumio* in a revival of 'The Taming of the Shrew.' On June 18, 1844, the long anticipated prize comedy of Mrs. Gore, entitled 'Quid pro Quo ; or, the Day of Dupes' (*see* WEBSTER, BENJAMIN), was produced at the Haymarket, Mr. Buckstone being in the original cast. November 18, 1844, he played the "original" *Bob*, first performance at the Haymarket of Dion Boucicault's play, 'Old Heads and Young Hearts.' In September 1845 he played the part of *Sir Peter Redwing*, first performance at the Haymarket "of an original comic drama by the author of 'Paul Pry.'" January 6, 1846, first performance of Benjamin Webster's dramatic version of 'The Cricket on the Hearth,' he played the part of *Tilly Slowboy* ; and, during the same year, *Golightly*, first performance of the now well-known farce, 'Lend Me Five Shillings'; *Dan*, in a revival of 'John Bull'; and *Sir Andrew Aguecheek* ("most effectively played "), in a revival of 'Twelfth Night,' with the two Misses Cushman as Viola and Olivia.

For many years the weight of the farces produced at the Haymarket rested on the shoulders of Mr. Buckstone, and he was constantly being received before the curtain and "greeted with roars of laughter and shouts of applause." Thursday, February 4, 1847, he played *The MacDunnum of Dunnum*, first performance at this theatre of Dion Boucicault's comedy, 'A School for Scheming.' After taking a farewell benefit at the Haymarket, Wednesday, July 21, 1847, on which occasion he sustained the part of *Scrub* in 'The Beaux' Stratagem' (at that time one of Mr. Buckstone's most famous impersonations), in the month of October following he joined the company of the Lyceum Theatre, then under the management of Madame Vestris and Mr. Charles Mathews. Monday, November 1, 1847, was produced there "an amusing interlude" entitled 'Box and Cox,' by Mr. Morton, "with the evident purpose of giving Mr. Buckstone and Mr. Harley some special fun to enact." Tuesday, December 7, 1847, Mr. Buckstone took a part, with all the eminent actors of the day, in the special Shakespearian performances arranged for providing a fund for the purchase of Shakespeare's house at Stratford-on-Avon. On that occasion he played *Speed* ('Two Gentlemen of Verona,' act iii., sc. 1). In the season 1848-9 he had returned to the Haymarket Theatre, and was there playing in the Shakespearian revivals introduced during the temporary engagement of Mr. and Mrs.

Charles Kean. Saturday, June 2, 1849, revival of 'Macbeth,' Mr. Buckstone sustained the part of one of the Weird Sisters—be it recorded, much to the amusement of the audience and to the no little dismay of the principal performers concerned. Thursday, July 11, 1849, he produced at the Haymarket "one of the raciest little dramas imaginable," under the title 'An Alarming Sacrifice,' in which he himself performed the part of *Bob Ticket*. Tuesday, October 30, 1849, was performed for the first time at the Haymarket 'The Serious Family,' adapted from the French 'Le Mari à la Campagne,' in which Mr. Buckstone personated the character of *Aminadab Sleek* with great success.

In January 1850 (Tuesday, the 15th), Mr. Buckstone produced at the Haymarket a domestic drama, which was eminently successful, entitled 'Leap Year.' In this play he himself acted, together with Mr. and Mrs. Charles Kean. The same year he played (in April) *Moses*, in Stirling Coyne's dramatic version of 'The Vicar of Wakefield'; and (in May) *Appleface*, first performance of Douglas Jerrold's comedy 'The Catspaw.' Saturday, February 12, 1853, first performance at the Haymarket of Lord Lytton's play, 'Not So Bad As We Seem,' Mr. Buckstone sustained the part of *Shadowly Softhead*. (*See* WEBSTER, BENJAMIN.) "Mr. Buckstone abounded in that rich and eccentric humour with which he usually vitalizes absurdity, and which, in this instance, gave the effect of a full-length portrait to a simple and meagre sketch." (*Athenæum*, February 19, 1853.) In the year 1853 Mr. Buckstone entered upon the lesseeship and management of the Theatre Royal, Haymarket, on the retirement of Mr. Benjamin Webster, and from that time to the year 1876 devoted himself largely to managerial duties. On Easter Monday, 1853, he opened the theatre with the following company, viz.: Mr. Barry Sullivan, Mr. Compton, Mr. Chippendale, Mr. Corri, Mr. Howe, Mr. Wm. Farren, junr., Mr. Tilbury, Mr. Rogers, and Mr. Arthur Payne; and Miss Reynolds, Miss Louisa Howard, Mrs. Buckingham, Mrs. Poynter, Mrs. Stanley, Miss A. Vernon, Miss E. Romer, Miss A. Vining, Mrs. Caulfield, Miss E. Bromley, Miss Grace Leslie, and Miss Laidlaw. The opening performances were 'The Rivals,' and a new and original extravaganza by Planché, entitled 'Buckstone's Ascent of Mount Parnassus.' Mr. Buckstone expressed his intention of confining the performances of the theatre as far as possible to comedy and farce, which constituted its principal characteristics in former periods. Saturday, May 20, 1854, in pursuance of this resolve, he produced 'The Knights of the Round Table,' by J. R. Planché. The piece had the advantage of admirable acting; Mr. G. Vandenhoff and Mr. Buckstone being selected for special praise. "*Tom Tittler*, who combines the usually separate functions of 'funny man' and *Deus ex machinâ*, and who is in his latter capacity the natural foe to the clever captain, is a most gallant little fellow in the hands of Mr. Buckstone, and it should be observed that that grotesque style which is so irresistibly droll in so many of the actor's comic parts is here in a great measure suppressed. Mr. Buckstone gives us a specimen of sound legitimate acting, in which the oddity of the

poor but valiant *Tittler* by no means obscures the chivalric foundation of his character." (*Times*, May 22, 1855.)

Among noteworthy plays first performed at the Haymarket during
the period of nearly a quarter of a century Mr. Buckstone held the
reins of management, the following are entitled to mention, viz.
on Wednesday, July 8, 1857, a comedy entitled 'The Victims,' by
Mr. Tom Taylor ; on Saturday, November 7, 1857, 'An Unequal
Match,' by Mr. Tom Taylor, in which Mr. Buckstone played the
part of *Dr. Botcherby;* on Saturday, April 2, 1859, a comedy by
Mr. Stirling Coyne, entitled 'Everybody's Friend,' in which Mr.
Buckstone was the original *Major Wellington de Boots;* June 29,
1859, a comedy by Mr. Tom Taylor, entitled 'The Contested
Election,' in which Mr. Buckstone played *Mr. Peckover;* on
Thursday, February 23, 1860, 'The Overland Route,' by Mr. Tom
Taylor, in which Mr. Buckstone was the original *Lovibond;* on
Wednesday, May 9, 1860, 'The Family Secret,' by Mr. Edmund
Falconer, Mr. Buckstone as *Bubble;* on Saturday, May 10, 1860,
'The Babes in the Wood,' by Mr. Tom Taylor, Mr. Buckstone
performing the part of *Beetle;* Monday, April 22, 1861, a comedy
entitled 'Black Sheep,' by Mr. Stirling Coyne, in which Mr. Buck-
stone played the character of *Mr. Bunny;* on Monday, November
11, 1861, 'Our American Cousin,' a comedy by Mr. Tom Taylor,
Mr. Buckstone as *Asa Trenchard;* on Monday, March 10, 1862,
'The Wife's Portrait,' by Dr. Westland Marston ; on Saturday,
November 14, 1863, a play entitled 'Silken Fetters,' by Mr.
Leicester Buckingham; on Saturday, April 30, 1864, 'David Garrick,' by T. W. Robertson, in which Mr. Buckstone was the
original *Squire Chevy;* on Monday, June 13, 1864, 'Lord Dun-
dreary Married and Done For'; in May 1865, 'Brother Sam,'
in which Mr. Buckstone played *Mr. Jonathan Rumbelow;* on
Monday, April 2, 1866, Dr. Westland Marston's comedy 'The
Favourite of Fortune,' in which Mr. Buckstone sustained the part
of *Tom Sutherland;* on Saturday, March 14, 1868, 'A Hero of
Romance,' by Dr. Westland Marston, Mr. Buckstone playing *Dr.
Lafitte;* on Monday, October 25, 1869, 'New Men and Old Acres,'
by Mr. Tom Taylor, in which Mr. Buckstone was the original
Bunter; on Saturday, November 19, 1870, 'The Palace of Truth,'
by Mr. W. S. Gilbert ; on Saturday, December 9, 1871, a comedy
entitled 'Pygmalion and Galatea,' by the same author ; on Saturday, January 4, 1873, 'The Wicked World,' by the same ; and on
Saturday, January 3, 1874, a play called 'Charity,' also by the
same author.

It may be said that Mr. Buckstone has played almost all the
principal low comedy parts of the English Drama presented on the
London stage within living memory. His name will be inseparably
associated with some of the more amusing characters in the higher
range of old English comedy, such, for example, as *Grumio, Speed,
Touchstone, Sir Andrew Aguecheek, Zekiel Homespun, Scrub,
Tony Lumpkin*, and *Bob Acres;* and it may be added that the
varied attributes of those characters have invariably received at his
hand the happiest illustration. Since the year 1877 Mr. Buckstone

has ceased to take any active part in the duties of his profession. In August 1879, through the generosity of Mr. J. S.
Clarke, lessee of the Haymarket Theatre, a series of five benefit
performances were arranged at that house as a testimonial to Mr.
Buckstone. [Mr. Buckstone died on October 31, 1879, while this
edition was passing through the Press.]

BUCKSTONE, JOHN COPELAND, son of the above-named
J. B. Buckstone, was born December 9, 1858. He made his first
appearance on the stage at the Gaiety Theatre, Dublin, April 17,
1876, when a member of Mr. and Mrs. Chippendale's company, as
Bertie Fitzurse in 'New Men and Old Acres.' During two provincial tours with the same company he played walking gentleman
parts in old and modern comedy. His next engagement was with
Edward Terry, when he played *Arthur Medwyn* in Byron's 'Weak
Woman,' *Frank Hardy*, &c., at the Aquarium Theatre, Westminster, and in the country. On June 11, 1877, he accompanied
his father on his farewell tour ; and on September 20 of the same
year sailed for India with Mr. George Anderson's company, where
he played a five months' season at the Corinthian Theatre, Calcutta, appearing during that time in several well-known characters.
On his return to England he accompanied Mr. Chippendale on
his farewell tour, commencing at Birmingham, September 2, 1878,
and playing *Master Trueworth, Charles Courtly, Sir Benjamin
Backbite, Sir Charles Cropland*, &c. On his return to town he
was engaged by Mrs. Bernard-Beere for her series of matinées
at the Olympic Theatre, commencing January 25, 1879. After
playing for a short time at the Folly Theatre, he was engaged by
Mr. J. S. Clarke to sustain the part of *Henry Moreland* in 'The
Heir-at-Law' during its run at the Haymarket Theatre, commencing August 25, 1879. Mr. J. C. Buckstone has also played at various
times at the Alexandra and Crystal Palaces *Young Marlow* in 'She
Stoops to Conquer,' the *Hon. Augustus Adolphus* in 'Extremes,'
and in other parts.

BUCKSTONE, LUCY ISABELLA, daughter of the above-
named J. B. Buckstone, was born in 1859. She made her first
appearance on any stage at the Croydon Theatre as *Gertrude* in
'The Little Treasure,' and afterwards accompanied her father and
Mr. Sothern on a provincial tour, appearing at the Theatre Royal,
Dublin, in the following characters, viz. *Florence Trenchard* in
'Our American Cousin'; *Lucy Dorrison* in 'Home'; and *Ada
Ingot* in 'David Garrick,' in which part she made her *début* at
the Haymarket Theatre, on December 26, 1875. Miss Buckstone
subsequently accepted an engagement at the Lyceum Theatre,
where she played *Annette* in 'The Bells,' and, in a revival of
'The Belle's Stratagem' in June 1876, the part of *Lady F. Touch-
wood*. During the same year she appeared at the Prince of Wales's
Theatre as *Lucy Ormond* in 'Peril.' On January 6, 1879, at St.
James's, Piccadilly, Miss Buckstone was married to Mr. H. E.
Smithes.

BUFTON, ELEANOR (Mrs. ARTHUR SWANBOROUGH), was born in Wales in 1840. She became connected with the stage at a very early age, and made her professional *début* at Edinburgh as the *Servant* in 'The Clandestine Marriage.' Shortly afterwards Miss Bufton came to London, and made her first appearance on the metropolitan boards at the St. James's Theatre. Subsequently she became a member of the company of the Princess's Theatre, under Mr. Charles Kean's management, and appeared in various Shakespearian plays produced there by that distinguished actor. In *A Journal of a London Playgoer*, Henry Morley, p. 156, appears the following entry :—" October 25, 1856.—The beautiful mounting of the 'Midsummer Night's Dream' at the Princess's Theatre attracts, and will attract for a long time, crowded houses. The words of the play are spoken agreeably, some of the sweetest passages charmingly, and much of Shakespeare's delicate pleasantry is made to tell with good effect upon its hearers. The 'Midsummer Night's Dream' is full of passages that have only to be reasonably well uttered to be enjoyed even by the dull; and with so fair a *Hermia* as Miss Bufton, so whimsical a Bottom as Mr. Harley, who seems to have no particular conception of the part, but, nevertheless, makes it highly amusing—with a generally good delivery of words and songs—the play speaks for itself in a great measure."

On Wednesday, July 1, 1857, Miss Bufton played, at the Princess's Theatre, the part of *Ferdinand*—the first time this character had ever been played on the London stage by a woman—in a grand revival of 'The Tempest.' From the Princess's Miss Bufton went to the Strand Theatre, where she was for a long period one of its leading and most popular actresses, appearing there in many original parts in the numerous comedies and burlesques produced under Mr. W. H. Swanborough's management. Among plays in which Miss Bufton especially distinguished herself, the following may be mentioned, viz. 'Christmas Boxes' (Sutherland Edwards and Augustus Mayhew), produced at the Strand in January 1860 ; 'Observation and Flirtation' (Horace Wigan), produced in July of the same year ; 'The Post Boy' (Craven), first performed October 31 of the same year ; 'The Old Story' (H. J. Byron) ; and 'The Idle 'Prentice' (Farnie). On Wednesday, April 4, 1866, at the St. James's Theatre, Miss Bufton appeared as *Hero*, in a revival of 'Much Ado About Nothing'; and at the same theatre, in the following month (May 1866), she appeared as *Julia*, in a revival of 'The Rivals.' In the year following, on Saturday, February 9, at the same theatre, she sustained the part of *Sophia* in a revival of 'The Road to Ruin.' On Saturday, February 5, 1870, at the Strand Theatre, in a revival of the younger Colman's comedy of 'The Heir-at-Law,' she played *Cicely Homespun.* On Wednesday, January 25, 1871, on the occasion of the opening of the Royal Court Theatre, Sloane Square, London, Miss Bufton played the part of *Miss Flamboys* in the first performance of W. S. Gilbert's comedy entitled 'Randall's Thumb '; and at the same theatre, in May 1871, first performance of a dramatic version of Mr. Charles Dickens's ' Great Expectations,' she sustained the character of

Estella. Shortly after the termination of her engagement at the Court Theatre, Miss Bufton had the misfortune to meet with a severe railway accident, which incapacitated her from following her profession for two years. Since 1876 she has appeared only at intervals on the London stage ; in 1879, however, she was engaged at the Lyceum Theatre, under Mr. Henry Irving's management, appearing in a comedietta entitled ' Book the Third, Chapter the First.'

BURNETT, MRS. *See* LEE, JENNIE.

BURNETTE, AMY, was born in London. Her first engagement of importance was fulfilled in 1871 with Miss Thorne's so-called ' Palace of Truth ' company. Previous to this she had played minor characters at some of the London theatres, viz. the Adelphi, Olympic, and Holborn. In the autumn of 1871 Miss Burnette joined Mr. Rice's company at the Theatre Royal, Bradford, and played the parts of *Amy Robsart, Esmeralda,* &c. On March 4, 1872, she was specially engaged by Mr. L. J. Sefton to perform the character of *Cynisca* (' Pygmalion and Galatea '), and remained a member of his company until 1874. After fulfilling engagements at Cheltenham and Liverpool, and again with Mr. Sefton's company, in October 1875 Miss Burnette joined the company of the New Theatre Royal, Bristol, under Mr. Chute's management. She remained at that theatre until 1876, and subsequently entered upon an engagement at the Theatre Royal, Birmingham, where during the season she appeared with success in the following leading characters, viz. *Lady Macbeth, Ophelia, Desdemona, Mrs. Haller, Pauline, Clara Douglas,* &c. Miss Burnette travelled on tour in the spring of 1877, playing *Claire Ffolliott* in ' Shaughraun '; and in June of the same year joined Miss Lee's so-called ' Jo ' company, being specially engaged for the part of *Lady Dedlock.* Since 1877 Miss Burnette has fulfilled engagements in London and Liverpool.

BURVILLE, ALICE, first attracted notice as a singer in an operetta by Suppé, at the Theatre Royal, Drury Lane, December 3, 1874. In 1875 she performed at the Charing Cross Theatre in ' Dagobert,' and afterwards at the Criterion Theatre in ' Fleur de Thé,' taking the title *rôle.* Previous to going on a tour in the provinces she sang in operetta at the Gaiety Theatre. Returning to London, she appeared in ' Der Fledermaus,' and in ' Orphée aux Enfers ' at the Alhambra Theatre; and after a short tour in America with Miss Lydia Thompson, took the character of *Généviève de Brabant* in Offenbach's opera at the Philharmonic Theatre in January 1878. Miss Burville succeeded Miss Howson, the original *Josephine* in ' H.M.S. Pinafore,' at the Opéra Comique.

BUTLER, MRS. FANNY. *See* KEMBLE, FRANCES ANN.

BYRON, HENRY JAMES, son of Henry Byron, Esq., of her Majesty's Consular Service, was born in 1834. He had gained reputation as a dramatist long previous to his appearance on the stage as an actor. His merits in the first direction are, perhaps, fairly summed up in the following criticism :—" Of our younger dramatists Mr. Byron is the one to whom we should most readily turn in expectation of receiving a contribution to genuine comedy. He is destitute of invention, a deficiency he shares in common with every English dramatist of the last fifty years. He has wit, however, dramatic perception, a certain power of character painting, and a talent, quite unrivalled in England, of turning to fresh account well-used materials. His defects are want of patience, and an irresistible tendency to wander from the course he has chalked out. Let him bestow upon one work the labour he now spends over three, and let him restrain a vagrant fancy, and he might yet give us good work. Better still, perhaps, would it be for him to associate himself with a *collaborateur*, whose steady pace would check his erratic movements, and whose invention might strengthen the singularly weak fabric of his plays." (*Athenæum*, No. 2362, p. 156, Feb. 1, 1873.) Mr. H. J. Byron's reputation as an actor rests on his impersonation of the part of *Sir Simon Simple* in his own drama ' Not Such a Fool as He Looks,' in which he first appeared on the London stage, at the Globe Theatre, Saturday, October 23, 1869. Although not an event without precedent, the announcement that a well-known dramatic author would perform at a London theatre the principal part in a play of his own writing was remark-able enough to draw a crowded audience to the theatre. The drama, which had been performed for some months in provincial cities, was entirely new to London. With regard to Mr. Byron himself, although he had once or twice taken a part in amateur performances in London, and had sustained in Manchester and Liverpool the same character of *Sir Simon Simple*, he, too, was entirely unknown on London boards. Such a combination of novel circumstances constituted a dramatic event, and suffi-ciently explained the enthusiasm with which the audience of the Globe greeted the rising of the curtain. Said the *Daily News* (October 25, 1869) : " Mr. Byron's performance certainly needs no apology on the ground of inexperience in the actor. Though a little weak in its effect in the first act, it rose in the second to a high degree of dramatic art. Nothing could be better than his struggle between the desire to maintain a dutiful regard for his new-found mother and his horror of her vulgarity and hypocrisy ; nor would it be easy to name an actor who could render with more dramatic power the situations in which he makes the audience feel that *Sir Simon* is, after all, ' not such a fool as he looks.' The scene in which he defies Murgatroyd, and breaks across his knee the stick with which the bill-discounter has threatened him, is an example." ' Not Such a Fool as He Looks,' although in three acts, is a drama essentially farcical in structure (according to the *Daily Telegraph* of the date last quoted), making no pretension whatever to engage the attention by working out an intelligible story. The sole object of the author seems to have been the contrivance of situations which shall excite mirth by a whimsical defiance of the laws of probability. An improbable plot is so treated that the impossibility of anything taking place in the manner indicated merely increases the enjoyment of the spectator as the play proceeds ; and it is only because the absurdities of position are not heightened at the end that a slight feeling of disappointment is felt when the curtain falls. "The hero of 'Not Such a Fool as He Looks' has his attributes foreshadowed in the title of the drama. His peculiarities, defined very clearly by Mr. Byron as the author, are depicted very cleverly by Mr. Byron as the actor. *Sir Simon* is a fair-haired young gentleman, quick in perceiving the right thing to do, but so slow in finding the right thing to say that he has come to be regarded as a simpleton. He wears an eyeglass through weakness of vision, not for foppery, and his languid manner and drawling tone are both plainly referable to his tardiness of apprehension and not to his love of affectation. He is a slow talker because he is a slow thinker, and the sound and the sense of words get so confused in his speech that he makes, unconsciously, the most desperate puns in the most deliberate manner. This apparent stolidity is, however, but the veil thrown over a truly generous nature. . . . . The ability of Mr. Byron to give this character the fullest expression was quickly recognized by the audience, and in the repeated recalls and the protracted plaudits at the end of the piece, the best assurance was afforded of the double triumph gained." Mr. Byron represented the character of *Sir Simon Simple* again in the following year (February 1870) at the Adelphi Theatre in a revival of the play.

On March 23, 1870, at the Adelphi, first performance of his four-act drama entitled 'The Prompter's Box,' Mr. Byron sustained the leading *rôle*, *Fitzaltamont*, an unfortunate provincial comedian, who is always bewailing his own miseries with the most ludicrous sorrow, and who, having long been an object of universal pity, astonishes the world by becoming, when heroism is required, a hero. The character was original in conception, and Mr. Byron's acting in it was considered the best histrionic representation he had yet given.

Two years later, in October 1872, at the Strand Theatre, Mr. Byron played the same part in the same piece, slightly altered, and with the changed title 'Two Stars ; or, the Footlights and the Fireside.' In January 1873 he produced a new three-act comic drama, entitled 'Old Soldiers,' at the Strand Theatre, in which he sustained the part of *Lionel Leveret* with decided success, the ingenious author having once more fitted himself with one of those peculiar characters whom it had lately been his study to create and elaborate. *Lionel Leveret* is a young country gentleman, resident in Devonshire, who having a reputation for dullness and indecision, is therefore the object of the attack of the "old soldiers," but who, like his predecessor, Sir Simon Simple, is not such a fool as he looks. Mr. Byron acted with admirable repose, delivering smart repartees with a quiet, unconscious air which, contributing to their effectiveness, softened sometimes their rudeness and occasionally helped to atone for their extravagance.

On Saturday, March 21, 1874, Mr. Byron produced his comedy, 'An American Lady,' at the Criterion Theatre, Piccadilly, on the occasion of its first opening, and played the part of *Harold Trivass.* On Saturday, October 2, 1875, his comedy, 'Married in Haste,' was performed for the first time at the Theatre Royal, Haymarket, Mr. Byron himself sustaining the part of *Gibson Greene.* Concerning this play the *Daily News* (October 4, 1875) indulged in the following reflections :—

"The story of Mr. Byron's comedy, it must be confessed, is not remarkable for originality or for dramatic qualities of a robust kind. It is, in fact, only the old theme of a young couple who part on a misunderstanding, or at least upon very slender grounds, and who are subsequently brought together again by rather obvious devices. How often this notion has served the dramatist's turn, or even how many times Mr. Byron himself has in this way involved hero and heroine in troubles too manifestly predestined to be only of a temporary nature to excite serious apprehensions in the breast of the spectator, it would be hard to tell. But it is now rather late in the day to expect from Mr. Byron either boldness of design or vigorous handling of old elements of dramatic story-telling. Strictly speaking, there is in his pieces scarcely any construction at all. His scenes are clever ; his characters, though not profoundly conceived, are sketched with true humour, and some observation of life, and no one who is in the habit of going to theatres need be told that his dialogue is a perpetual feast of entertainment. But of the art of laying out a story and of giving to its parts that coherence and inter-dependence which are the secret of the success of so many plays, not remarkable for other qualities, he has hitherto exhibited scarcely a token. From the title of 'Married in Haste,' it may be inferred that the author's original notion was to show in action the truth of the proverb that those who join hands for life without due reflection are destined to long repentance; but his first act provides no basis for a moral of this kind. His hero is not only a very well-favoured, but a very honourable, indeed a chivalrous, young gentleman. . . . In brief, Mr. Byron's incidents, instead of standing to the foundation of his story in the relation of effect to cause, are more like a series of 'happy thoughts' by which, while invention holds, his piece might be continued through as many acts as the patience of audiences would allow. Meanwhile, what is presumably the fundamental notion of the piece is allowed to evaporate ; and finally, instead of showing how those who 'marry in haste' are doomed to 'repent at leisure,' Mr. Byron enforces no moral at all, unless it be that a hasty marriage ought not to be repented of in a hurry.

"We have thought it worth while, in the interest of dramatic art, to offer these observations upon Mr. Byron's plots generally ; but it is really ungracious to make complaint of a gentleman who is able to amuse us by so many legitimate ways. Following his established fashion, he has imagined for himself a character which, though only loosely connected with the story, is never without reasonable excuse for presenting himself and saying those clever things which, in or out of season, rarely in Mr. Byron's mouth miss their effect. *Mr. Gibson Greene* is the latest name of this not unwelcome intruder. His hair, since we met him first, has become slightly dashed with grey; he is described as 'a mature man about town,' and he is, on this occasion, not a mere visitor or hanger-on, but a gentleman, who, by his kind-hearted devices and his ready wit, renders substantial aid to the hero and heroine, and thus may be said to keep the story always in his own hands. But it is as impossible to fail in recognizing him as to be blind to the fact that the real cause of his frequent appearance is his irresistible passion for saying good things. In point of acting there is little to say for these personages; Mr. Byron has never acquired either perfect ease on the stage, nor that variety of tone, movement, and expression which are the triumph of the finished actor. But then he rarely takes to himself a part connected with the serious action of his pieces, and he is apparently ambitious of success chiefly in the art of quietly dropping those witty and whimsical observations in the invention of which his powers have certainly undergone no deterioration."

On Monday, September 16, 1878, in a comedy-drama from his own pen, entitled 'Conscience Money,' then first performed at the Haymarket Theatre, he acted the part of *Dick Simpson*, "a character such as he has frequently presented." This play proved unattractive.

In a record of Mr. Byron's dramatic services extending to the present time (1879), although that record does not profess to take account either of his innumerable contributions to periodical and dramatic literature or of his services as a dramatic author, it seems only proper that note should be made of the extraordinary success attained by his comedy, 'Our Boys.' That play was originally produced at the Vaudeville Theatre, London, on Saturday, January 16, 1875, and its last performance took place at the same theatre on Friday, April 18, 1879—an unbroken "run" in the metropolis of over four years and a quarter. It has been played by a travelling company of comedians for over 1200 nights, and is still (June 1879) being played by the same company in the provinces. It has been successfully produced in the principal American and colonial cities and towns, and has been adapted or translated and played in Norway, Denmark, Switzerland, Holland, Bavaria, and France. Such a career is unparalleled in the history of the drama.

CALHAEM, STANISLAUS, became early connected with the stage, having in his fifth year played the part of *Young Norval* at the Queen's Theatre, Liverpool. During the ensuing seven years young Calhaem, under the *sobriquet* of the "Infant Roscius," performed the parts of *Hamlet, Shylock, Richard III., Rolla, Sir Giles Overreach*, in various parts of the country. He then left the dramatic profession for a time, but in August 1846 rejoined it, appearing at the Liver Theatre, Liverpool, under Mr. C. F. Marshall's management, as *Hamlet*, in a drama by C. H. Somerset entitled ' Garrick, the King's Jester ; or, the Early Days of Hamlet.' Thence Mr. Calhaem went to Belfast, Carlisle, &c., and was for some time a member of the York Circuit and of Samuel Roxby's company. From 1853 to 1855 he was stage-manager and principal comedian of the T. R. Sheffield, during which period was produced there ' Slavery,' a successful stage version of ' Uncle Tom's Cabin,' in which Mr. Calhaem personated the triple parts *Sam* (a nigger), *Phineas Fletcher*, and *St. Clair*. At the opening of the " Queen's Theatre and Opera House," Edinburgh, under Mr. Black's management, in December 1855, he performed the *rôle* of *St. Lo* in ' Love's Sacrifice.' Mr. Calhaem made his *début* on the London stage at the Lyceum Theatre, under Charles Dillon's management, September 15, 1856, as *Leontes* in the burlesque of ' Perdita,' and continued a member of the Lyceum company for two seasons, appearing chiefly in burlesque and farce. During a subsequent engagement at the same theatre, commencing Easter Monday, 1860, Mr. Calhaem acted the character of *Morgiana* in the " Savage Club " burlesque of ' The Forty Thieves.' In the two following years he was stage-manager to Mrs. E. Glover at the Prince's Theatre, Glasgow, and T. R. Greenock, and subsequently, in 1862-3-4, was acting on the metropolitan stage, at Drury Lane and Astley's.

In 1864 Mr. Charles Reade's drama ' It's Never Too Late to Mend ' was first performed at Leeds Theatre Royal, Mr. Calhaem appearing in the original cast as *Jacky*. On October 4, 1865, the play was produced in London at the Princess's Theatre, under Mr. Vining's management, Mr. Calhaem being selected to sustain the same character. It was generally admitted that his was the most remarkable performance in the play. "We have seldom seen," remarked the *Times*, October 5, 1865, "a more sterling piece of acting, or a piece in which the talent of the actor so completely fleshed and clothed the author's skeleton idea. *Jacky* is one of those embodiments which are sufficient to make the reputation of any actor, and Mr. Calhaem's performance will be talked about for some time to come." It was the marked success of the evening; and it would hardly be an injustice to the distinguished author of the drama to say that the ability displayed by Mr. Calhaem con-duced in no slight degree to the success of ' Never Too Late to Mend ' on the occasion of its first representation in London. Probably no play met with a more equivocal reception than did Mr. Reade's on the first night of its performance at the Princess's Theatre. A considerable section of the audience denounced the second part of the drama ("Prison Life ") in the strongest possible manner. Not only were loud cries of " Shame, shame," " Off, off," " Disgusting," " Degrading," and " Disgraceful " made use of; but several gentlemen got up in the stalls and called upon Mr. Vining to come forward and apologize for introducing such scenes upon the stage.* The expression and contest of opinion ultimately became so strong that the performance was for a time suspended; and Mr. Vining came forward, and, having with difficulty obtained a hearing, declared that he had produced the play " on a high principle, coinciding, we (*Morning Advertiser*) presume, with Mr. Reade's notions as to the treatment of criminals. An altercation thereupon took place, and we are free to confess that we ourselves denounced the introduction of so complex a question as prison discipline into a melodrama, especially backed up as it is by such dismal and revolting representations of horrors. The unnecessary introduction of a clergyman into the piece, and of the most serious discussions as to religion and morality, also added to the disgust which many of the audience felt." † This interruption served as a test, after all, of the powerful attraction of the piece, inasmuch as the succeeding act entirely restored the equanimity of the audience, and the curtain fell, at length, "to the most warm and decided testimonies of success." In this, the third act, *Jacky* (Mr. Calhaem) " gave one of the most perfect examples ever seen of a peculiar class of acting."

During Mr. Calhaem's engagement at the Princess's Theatre he played, November 12, 1866, *Simon Tappertit* in a version of ' Barnaby Rudge ' (Watts Phillips and Vining), which was unsuccessful. In the last season of Mr. Fechter's management of the Lyceum Theatre, Mr. Calhaem became a member of his company, and played *Glavis* in ' The Lady of Lyons,' in succession to Mr. H. Widdicombe, who was a very excellent "low comedian " in his day. Subsequently Mr. Calhaem joined Mr. John Coleman on the York " Circuit," and played *Jacky* in the provinces. In 1871 he joined the company of the T. R. Adelphi, and appeared as *Solomon* in ' The Hidden Treasure '; in 1872-3-4 he was at the Princess's, and played in ' Haunted Houses,' H. J. Byron ; ' Griselda,' Miss Braddon ; ' Puss in Boots,' R. Reece ; ' Mary Stuart,' W. G. Wills. On September 28, 1874, he " reopened " at the Adelphi Theatre as *Ezekiel Homespun*, after which date he was connected with the

* *Standard*, October 5, 1865. See also *Daily Telegraph* of same date ; *Times* (*ibid*) ; *Weekly Dispatch*, October 7, 1865.

† *Morning Advertiser*, October 5, 1865. See also *Sunday Times*, October 8, 1865. " The nauseous second act of Mr. Charles Reade's new drama ' It's Never Too Late to Mend ' was freed from a few of its most intensely revolting features last evening, when the piece was played for a second time."—*Morning Star*, October 6, 1865.

Adelphi, Princess's, and Drury Lane Theatres under Mr. Chatterton's management. On December 26, 1878, in a revival at the Princess's Theatre of 'Never Too Late to Mend,' Mr. Calhaem played his "original" part of *Jacky*, "with the familiar effect, and acted with a quiet humour and a degree of unaffected pathos that could not easily be surpassed."

CALTHROP, JOHN ALFRED CLAYTON. *See* CLAYTON, JOHN.

CAMERON, VIOLET, an actress who has fair claim to the distinction of "prima donna" in comic opera and burlesque, first appeared on the stage Easter, 1870, at the Princess's Theatre, London, in the character of *Karl* in 'Faust and Marguerite.' She played as a child in pantomime at Drury Lane and the Adelphi Theatres 1871–1874; and in 1875 was acting at the Globe Theatre. At the Criterion Theatre in February of the following year "created" the *rôle* of *Joconde* in Farnie's burlesque of 'Piff-Paff.' In September of the same year, at Alexandra Theatre, Liverpool, Miss Cameron acted the part of *Perdita* in 'A Winter's Tale' with gracefulness, intelligence, and feeling. From 1876 to 1878 she was engaged at the Folly Theatre, playing in burlesque and comic opera, as to which the following will suffice as examples: 'Robinson Crusoe' (Farnie), as *Polly Hopkins;* 'Sea Nymphs' (Lecocq), *Pearlina;* 'La Créole' (Offenbach), *Antoinette;* 'Les Cloches de Corneville' (Planquette), *Germaine:* this latter character Miss Cameron performed with more than ordinary excellence. "The young actress sang charmingly, and acted with a delicacy and grace very rarely found in the heroine of a comic opera" (*Standard,* February 1878). In the same year (October) she acted in 'Nemesis' (Farnie) at the Strand Theatre; and in April 1879 at the same theatre sustained the *rôle* of *Suzanne,* first performance there of 'Madame Favart' (Offenbach).

CARTER-EDWARDS, JAMES (EDWARDS, JAMES), was born at Birmingham, and claims descent on his father's side "from 'Old Edwards,' Keeper of the Crown Jewels at the time of Colonel Blood's attempt to steal them." He first appeared on the stage September 17, 1859, at the Garrick Theatre, under the management of his brother George Henry Edwards, as *Leonardo Gonzago* in 'The Wife.' In July 1861 he adopted the stage as a profession, accepting an engagement at the Queen's Theatre, Hull. During his first season Mr. Carter-Edwards acted with Mr. and Mrs. Charles Kean, who were passing through the town on a starring tour. Subsequently he went to Aberdeen, and remained there for four years under McNeill's management, and "acquired a very high reputation there, chiefly in heavy parts, and was a great favourite." Was for two years under George Hodson, the Irish comedian, and during this engagement played *Shylock* to Miss A. Sedgwick's

Portia.* Mr. Edwards was for a short season at the Theatre Royal, Birmingham (where he acted with Miss Helen Faucit), and afterwards joined Mr. Coleman's company at Theatre Royal, Hull, and New Theatre, Leeds, 'Hamlet' being the "opening" play, in which Mr. Edwards acted the *Ghost.* At the latter theatre Charles Reade's dramas 'Foul Play' and 'Put Yourself in His Place' were first produced (1868–70). In the first-named Mr. Edwards was the "original" *Arthur Wardlaw,* in the last-mentioned the original *Mr. Coventry.* He then "went to Edinburgh Theatre Royal for 'leading business,' and played there original parts in the Scott Centenary plays—*Fergus McIver, Balfour of Burley,* and *Varney*—also as *Rashleigh* in 'Rob Roy.' Remained at this theatre over two years, and made a capital reputation as a Scotch and English reader at St. George's Hall." In 1873 he was engaged by the late Mdlle. Beatrice for her company of comedians, of which Mr. Carter-Edwards still (July 1879) remains a member. During his long connection with Mdlle. Beatrice's company he has played the following among other "original" parts with success, viz. *Arthur Lejardie* in the English version of 'The Sphinx'; *John Jasper* in 'John Jasper's Wife'; *Appiani* in 'A Woman of the People'; *Sir Harold Pentreath* in 'Married, not Mated.'

CARTON, R. C. (a *nom de théâtre;* RICHARD CLAUDE CRITCHETT). Born in London, and made his first appearance on any stage at the New Theatre Royal, Bristol, Monday, March 29, 1875, as *George de Laval* in 'The Sea of Ice.' On June 19, 1875, he made his *début* on the London stage at the Lyceum Theatre in the character of *Osric,* in a revival of 'Hamlet' by Mr. Irving, and afterwards, during the same year, accepted an engagement under Mr. Sefton Parry's management at the Theatre Royal, Hull. Returning to London he reappeared at the Lyceum as *Osric,* and subsequently as *Courtenay,* first performance of Tennyson's 'Queen Mary.' In the summer of 1876 Mr. Carton appeared at the Alexandra Theatre, Liverpool, to support Mr. G. H. Brooke, and played a round of characters in the Shakespearian drama, and in the autumn of the same year accompanied Mr. Irving on his first provincial 'Hamlet' tour. In July 1877, at the Amphitheatre, Liverpool, he created the part of the *Rev. Alfred Lonsdale* in the drama of 'Liz,' and "opened" in this character on the production of the play in London. In November 1877 Mr. Carton accepted an engagement at the Royal Aquarium Theatre, and played *Sir Benjamin Backbite* in 'The School for Scandal' for a run of six

* "My first really great success was here. I played *Shylock* to Miss Sedgwick's Portia, and the night is well remembered by me for the startling success I made ; indeed, I seemed to have been like one of those who had suddenly woke up to find myself famous. I played the whole leading business during this engagement, and was stage-manager during the second year, acting with James Anderson, Neil Warner, Miss A. Sedgwick, Belle Boyd ('The Confederate Heroine'), Mrs. G. V. Brooke (Avonia Jones), Menken, H. Talbot, Charles Harrison, the Keans, and Toole."—*Letter from Mr. Carter-Edwards to the Editor.*

weeks. In February 1878 he appeared at the Court Theatre in
'New Men and Old Acres'; and in April following played the
part of *Johnny Fosbrooke*, first performance of 'Such is the Law'
(Taylor and Meritt) at St. James's Theatre. He remained a
member of the company of the same theatre until the end of the
season, and for the following (the winter) season, 1878, was engaged
by Mr. Henderson.

CATHCART, MAUD, daughter of the under-mentioned Rowley
Cathcart, entered the dramatic profession at the Royal Court
Theatre March 30, 1878, on which date she appeared as *Polly
Flamborough* in Wills's play of 'Olivia.' Miss Cathcart continued
to play the part during the successful " run " of the piece. She was
re-engaged by Mr. Hare for the season 1878-9, and reappeared at
the Court Theatre as *Mary Sullivan* in 'A Quiet Rubber.'

CATHCART, ROWLEY, born at Chichester, January 15, 1832,
and entered the dramatic profession when a child, playing boys'
parts under his father's instruction at various theatres in the provinces. In the year 1845 he first appeared in a part of importance,
playing at Glasgow, *Franco* in 'Guy Mannering,' with Mackay
and John Alexander in the cast. In 1847 he was engaged at
Liverpool, and thence went on tour with his father to perform at
Bristol, Bath, Manchester, Brighton, &c. In 1850 the late Charles
Kean enrolled Mr. Cathcart as a member of the company of the
Princess's Theatre. He continued to act at that theatre during the
whole of Charles Kean's management and that of his immediate
successors, Augustus Harris and George Vining. In 1868 Mr.
Cathcart joined the so-called 'Caste' company in the provinces,
and, returning to London, in the following years fulfilled engagements at the Globe, Olympic, Queen's, Royalty, Prince of Wales's,
and Royal Court Theatres. Among important characters sustained
by him during his long career on the stage, the following may be
selected as deserving honourable mention:—*The Prince of Morocco,*
'Merchant of Venice,' at the Princess's Theatre in 1858; *Tremoroso*
in 'Jack the Giant Killer' at the same theatre, 1859-60; *Launcelot
Gobbo* in 'Merchant of Venice' at the same theatre, 1863; *Grumio*
in 'Taming of the Shrew' at the Globe Theatre, 1870; *The Old
Fiddler* in 'Amos Clark' at the Queen's Theatre, 1872; *Rowley* in
'The School for Scandal' at the Prince of Wales's Theatre, 1874;
and *Farmer Flamborough* in Wills's play of 'Olivia' at the Royal
Court Theatre, 1878.

CAVENDISH, ADA, first attracted attention in London as an
actress in burlesque, at the Royalty Theatre, under the management of the Misses Pelham, where, in May 1865, she first appeared
in a leading part, that of *Hippodamia*, in a burlesque by F. C.
Burnand, entitled 'Pirithous, the son of Ixion.' On Thursday,
February 15, 1866, she acted for the first time at the Haymarket
Theatre, in a comedietta entitled 'A Romantic Attachment,' and
met with an extremely favourable reception. At the same theatre,

on Thursday, January 14, 1869, first performance of Mr. T. W. Robertson's comedy of 'Home,' she sustained the character of *Mrs. Pinchbeck*, in which she may be said to have first earned reputation. In 1870, Saturday, April 16, on the occasion of the opening night of the Vaudeville Theatre, Strand, under Messrs. Montague, James, and Thorne's management, Miss Cavendish appeared in a comedy by Andrew Halliday, entitled 'For Love or Money.' At the Globe Theatre the same year, on Saturday, October 8, she played the part of the *Marchesa San Pietro*, in a revival of Palgrave Simpson's 'Marco Spada'; and on Monday, September 11, 1871, in a revival at the Gaiety Theatre of Westland Marston's drama of 'Donna Diana,' Miss Cavendish sustained the title *rôle*, the piece going admirably—a fact for which the acting of Miss Ada Cavendish was largely responsible. "In dignity and grace of bearing Miss Cavendish has no superior. Her presentation of the haughty princess whom no prayers can move had singular beauty and refinement. In the early scenes pride of conscious superiority was well worn, and in the later the strife with nascent tenderness was cleverly revealed." (*Athenæum*, April 16, 1871.) On Monday, March 25, 1872, at the same theatre, she performed the part of *Julia* in 'The Hunchback,' deservedly gaining the approval of a very numerous audience; and shortly afterwards, at the Court Theatre, first performance of Dr. Westland Marston's and Mr. W. G. Wills's play 'Broken Spells,' she undertook the character of *Estelle*. At the Olympic Theatre, in May 1873, first performance of Mr. Wilkie Collins's play 'The New Magdalen,' Miss Cavendish sustained the leading part of *Mercy Merrick*. "There is considerable merit in Mr. Wilkie Collins's 'New Magdalen,'" remarked the *Examiner* (May 21, 1873), "though it may be doubted whether, apart from its dramatic power, it can bear the test of criticism. The story is a simple one. . . . Mr. Wilkie Collins has ingeniously managed to enlist the sympathies of the audience not with the victim of fraud but with the impostor; and the moral of the 'New Magdalen' appears to be that a young-woman may stray from virtue's path, and lie and steal and cheat, but if she repents in the end, she is sure not only to be forgiven but to be glorified as a saint, and married to a clergyman of the Church of England. . . . The reception of the piece by a very crowded house could not fail to be flattering to the author, who was twice called before the curtain on the occasion of the first performance; but we are bound to say that this success was mainly attributable to the admirable acting of Miss Cavendish and Mr. Archer. High as we rate the talents of Miss Cavendish, we were startled by the power no less than the versatility of her acting in the part of *Mercy Merrick*. The transition from security to doubt and fear; the struggle between pride and her newly-awakened conscience; the grandeur of her scorn and rage when goaded by the insults of her victim into renouncing her intentions of making confession and restitution; and, finally, the deep pathos of her honest repentance and self-sacrifice, make up a finished piece of acting such as in these days is rarely seen upon the English stage."

On Friday, September 26, 1873, at the Olympic Theatre, on the occasion of her benefit, Miss Cavendish appeared for the first time in London as *Juliet,* in Shakespeare's tragedy. "Her performance of the part was creditable in the extreme ; she showed the greatest intelligence in the delivery of the language, there was manifestly intention in every word she spoke, and the scenes which most require strength of expression were given with a force scarcely to be expected from an actress to whom tragedy presents a world entirely new." (*Times,* September 29, 1873.) In March 1874, first performance at the Olympic of Mr. Tom Taylor's play ' Lady Clancarty ; or, Wedded and Wooed,' Miss Ada Cavendish performed the part of the heroine. At the Gaiety Theatre, in April 1875, for the first time she sustained the character of *Beatrice* in a revival of ' Much Ado About Nothing '; and in 1876, at Easter, at the Globe Theatre, first performance in London of Wilkie Collins's ' Miss Gwilt ' (the play was originally produced in Liverpool), Miss Ada Cavendish performed the character *rôle,* playing it throughout " with deliberation in the calmer scenes, and in the more passionate passages with an impetuosity and dramatic fire which met with sincere appreciation. There are scenes in the play taken with such a firm grasp that hope may well be held out that the career of this young actress is likely to be as ambitious as it cannot fail to be successful." (*Daily Telegraph,* April 18, 1876.)

On Saturday, January 13, 1877, at the Olympic, first performance of a comedy-drama, in four acts, entitled ' The Queen of Connaught,' she played the heroine. At various times Miss Cavendish has undertaken for brief periods in London the lesseeship of the Olympic, St. James's, and other theatres. She has performed with much success in the provinces, and in August 1878 went to the United States. She made her *début* at the Broadway Theatre, New York, in the following month in the character of *Mercy Merrick* (' The New Magdalen '), and was received with much favour. Afterwards she made a " starring" tour through the country, visiting, among other cities, San Francisco, Chicago, St. Louis, appearing as *Rosalind, Juliet, Lady Teazle, Miss Gwilt,* &c.

CECIL, ARTHUR (a *nom de théâtre ;* ARTHUR CECIL BLUNT). Born near London in 1843, and first appeared on the stage, as an amateur, at the Richmond (Surrey) Theatre Royal, in the parts of the young *King Charles* in ' Faint Heart Never Won Fair Lady,' and *Bundle* in the musical farce of ' The Waterman.' He made his professional *début* in London, Easter Monday, 1869, at the " Gallery of Illustration," with Mrs. German Reed's company, as *Mr. Churchmouse* in ' No Cards,' by W. S. Gilbert, and *Box* in the musical version of ' Box and Cox,' by Messrs. Burnand and A. Sullivan. In 1874 he joined the company of the Globe Theatre, and appeared there during that year as *Jonathan Wagstaff,* in W. S. Gilbert's comedy ' Committed for Trial,' and as *Mr. Justice Jones* in Albery's comedy ' Wig and Gown.' In the same year, on December 19, at the Gaiety Theatre, in a revival of ' The Merry

Wives of Windsor,' Mr. Cecil played the part of *Dr. Caius;* and
the following year (1875), February, at the Opéra Comique, in a
revival of Shakespeare's 'As You Like It,' he played *Touchstone.*
At the Gaiety Theatre, during the same year, he appeared as *Duke
Anatole* in 'The Island of Bachelors,' by Messrs. Reece and
Lecocq, and as *Charles* in 'Oil and Vinegar,' by H. J. Byron.
January 1876, at the same theatre, on the occasion of his benefit,
Mr. Arthur Cecil played *Monsieur Jaques* in the musical piece of
that title, and *Sir Harcourt Courtly* in a revival of 'London
Assurance.' "Mr. Cecil's performances for his benefit of *Monsieur
Jaques* in the musical comedy of that name, and *Sir Harcourt
Courtly* in 'London Assurance' (*Athenæum,* January 22, 1876),
show how admirably careful and artistic he is in his style, and
maintain his reputation at the high point it has reached. He is
still wanting in breadth, and his voice is at times scarcely audible.
When he acquires more force, his position in light comedy will be
little short of the highest." The part of *Tourbillon* in 'To Parents
and Guardians,' a character of which Mr. Alfred Wigan was the
original exponent, is one which deserves to be included in any
notice of the principal services on the London stage of Mr. Arthur
Cecil. The *Saturday Review* speaks of his acting in this part as
being little short of "marvellous," which, doubtless, means that in
this particular character Mr. Cecil has shown himself superior to
the majority of actors who have undertaken it.

At the Globe Theatre, Easter Monday, 1876, first performance
of Wilkie Collins's play of 'Miss Gwilt,' adapted from his novel
of 'Armadale,' Mr. Cecil sustained the part of *Dr. Downward.*
On Saturday, February 5, 1876, first performance at the Haymarket Theatre of 'Anne Boleyn,' by Tom Taylor, he played
Chapuis with great force and originality; and the same year
at the Prince of Wales's Theatre, in 'Peril,' adapted by Messrs.
Savile Rowe and Bolton Rowe from M. Sardou's 'Nos Intimes,'
the part of *Sir Woodbine Grafton,* which in the hands of Mr.
Arthur Cecil was presented as a very highly-finished piece of
miniature painting—one of those delicate little bits of character
which Mr. Cecil knows so well how to treat. "He is as good
as he can be in the first act; but as the play proceeds there
peeps out here and there a glimpse of something we have seen
before, and *Sir Woodbine Grafton* is once or twice very nearly
giving place to *Dr. Downward.* In this particular school of acting,
'character acting,' as it is called, to avoid any repetition and
carefully define each successive character must be a task of more
than ordinary difficulty—it would seem, indeed, to be a task of
great difficulty in many other schools of acting where this excuse
cannot be offered—and the difficulty is of course much enhanced
by a protracted representation of one particular character. It is a
mistake, however, to be avoided by all means, and more, perhaps,
in this style of acting than in any other. Mr. Cecil indeed was,
considering what we so often see, a very slight offender, and in
saying what we have said we do not wish for a moment to detract
from his performance, which was very amusing and very clever."

(*Times*, October 3, 1876.) In April 1877, at the same theatre, first performance of 'The Vicarage,' by Savile Rowe, Mr. Cecil undertook the part of the *Rev. Noel Haygarth;* and in the following year (1878), January 12, first performance of 'Diplomacy' (Messrs. Savile Rowe and Bolton Rowe), the part of *Baron Stein*, "Mr. Cecil's rare talents for disguise of speech, manner, and appearance being shown in their fullest significance in the small but highly finished part of the Russian agent" (*Times*, January 21, 1878). In a revival of 'Caste' at the Prince of Wales's Theatre in January 1879 (continuing to May of the same year), Mr. Cecil played the part of *Sam Gerridge*, originally sustained by Mr. Hare ; and in a subsequent revival, in June 1879, of Buckstone's comic drama 'Good for Nothing,' the part of *Tim Dibbles* was acted by him.

CELESTE, MADAME (CELESTE ELLIOTT), was born in Paris, August 16, 1814. Entered the classes of the Academy of Music in that city as a child, and at the age of fifteen commenced an engagement in the United States, where she subsequently married Mr. Elliott. She first appeared on the English stage, in 1830, at Liverpool, as *Fenella* in 'Masaniello,' and the same year appeared at Drury Lane Theatre in the ballet of 'La Bayadere.' Madame Celeste made her professional *début* in London, at Drury Lane Theatre, in the year 1837 (October), as *Maurice*, the dumb boy, in Planché's 'Child of the Wreck.' "The whole weight of the drama rested on Madame Celeste, whose 'dumb show,' unlike that of Shakespeare, is anything but inexplicable. She expressed by her varied and appropriate action, and by her swiftly changing features, the various passions of love, despair, indignation, and joy, with touching fidelity. She was much applauded." (*Times*, October 9, 1837.) The same month of the same year she appeared at Drury Lane Theatre as the heroine in a piece entitled 'The Indian Girl.' From time to time during the years 1838-9 and 1840-1, Madame Celeste performed at the Haymarket Theatre, and for the most part in characters involving only mute action. On May 30, 1841, at that theatre, she appeared in a melodrama entitled 'Marie Ducange,' written expressly for her by Mr. Bernard. In November of the same year she performed at the same theatre in a piece entitled 'The Quadroon Slave.' In the following year she returned to the United States for a brief period, reappearing at the Haymarket Theatre on December 7, 1842, in a one-act piece from the French, entitled 'The Bastille.' On June 3, 1843, at the Haymarket, Madame Celeste played a principal part with Mr. Benjamin Webster in 'Louison,' a version of 'The Angel of the Attic' (then being performed at the Princess's Theatre) ; and subsequently, at the same theatre, with the same actor, the heroine in 'Victor and Hortense,' another French vaudeville. In 1844, in conjunction with Mr. Benjamin Webster, she entered upon the management of the old Adelphi Theatre, and may be said to have been the originator of the success which for so many years attended the production of so-called domestic drama at that theatre. Madame Celeste was the creator of leading parts in many well-known

Adelphi dramas, in not the least noteworthy of which, 'The Green
Bushes,' by J. B. Buckstone, first performed January 27, 1845, she
was the original *Miami*—a character which she invariably acted
with uncommon vigour and pathos. This play is so intimately
associated with the history of the " Old Adelphi " that we may be
pardoned for giving the subjoined outline of its plot, together with
the names of those who were in the original cast :—

" The scene of the first act of ' The Green Bushes ' is Ireland—
the coast of Galway; the time 1745. Connor O'Kennedy (Selby),
an Irish gentleman, is obliged to fly his country for political
reasons. He continues to linger as long as he can near his wife,
Geraldine (Mrs. Yates), and his home. His younger brother,
George (Mr. Hudson), anxious to gain possession of the family
estates, eagerly counsels flight, trusting that Connor once away will
never return. Wild Murtoch (Mr. O. Smith), a rascally horse-
stealer, is the accomplice of the younger brother in his nefarious
schemes. Traitor, however, to all, he tries to surprise and take
Connor with the view of obtaining the reward offered by Government for his apprehension ; but the plot fails ; the soldiers, when
they make their appearance at the moment of the fugitive's em-
barkation, are overpowered by the peasantry, and Connor escapes
to America, leaving his wife and infant child under the protection
of the former's foster-sister, Nelly O'Neil (Mrs. Fitzwilliam). These
matters, interspersed with an Irish row, and some pretty Irish
singing by Mrs. Fitzwilliam and Mr. Hudson, form the somewhat
barren materials of the first act. With the second the real interest
of the piece commences. Two years have elapsed, and we find
ourselves in America, near a log cabin by the Mississippi. Here
Connor dwells ; but, alas! not alone. He has been unfaithful, and
lives with *Miami* (Madame Celeste), the ' Huntress of the Mississippi,' a sort of wild woman of the woods, half Indian, half French,
but, withal, a very pretty specimen of a coquette of the wilderness,
as skilled, too, in the rifle as she is witching in her sweet looks and
untutored words. But Connor is not happy; he yearns for his
forsaken wife and his own land. He treasures as a holy prize the
only letter which has reached him from her, cons it over every
moment he is alone, and has enough to do to allay the suspicions
and rising jealousy of his half savage partner. At length comes a
catastrophe, in the shape of the deserted wife. She has arrived
in America to trace her husband. The meeting scene is well
managed ; but while she is still half fainting in his arms, *Miami*
appears behind. In a moment all her savage blood is roused.
Half-a-dozen times is the rifle carried to her shoulder, and as often
is the point let fall. Geraldine, weary and footsore, faints; her
husband carries her to a neighbouring spring ; *Miami* follows the
pair. At length, unable to control her fierce jealousy and passion,
she fires, and Connor is shot through the heart. His wife frantic-
ally flies for assistance, and unknowing whence the fatal blow has
been struck, supplicates on her knees the aid of her husband's
assassin. The last scene in the act represents Connor's death.
His wife flings herself distractedly over the body. *Miami* stands

by unmoved, the 'stoic of the woods.' With his last breath Connor
entreats the murderer of the husband to protect the wife. He dies.
Miami leaps madly into the river, and the drop falls upon the
scene of her rescue by a party of French soldiers proceeding down
the stream on a raft. We ought to mention that the tragic part
of the act is relieved by the vagaries of Master Grinnidge (Wright),
and Jack Gong (Paul Bedford), a showman and his *factotum*, who
have arrived in America in search of a wild Indian, to clap into
their caravan of curiosities at home; unfortunately, however,
getting caught by the Indians instead of catching any themselves.

"The third act, and we are in Ireland again; two years more
have elapsed; George, the younger brother, is in possession of the
family estates. The daughter of Connor, confided, when his wife
went to America, to the care of Nelly O'Neil, has been stolen from
her by the agency of George and Wild Murtoch, still his worthy
accomplice; the child is placed under the care of a village blacksmith. An accident happening to a passing carriage introduces
a stately lady beneath the smith's roof, but who, wonderful to tell,
is no other than *Miami*, the mocassined, rifle-bearing huntress,
however, sunk in the brocaded and polished French lady of quality.
Saved by French soldiers, and brought home to her fatherland, she
has claimed and obtained her heritage, and then proceeded to
Ireland to make what atonement she could to the surviving child
of her murdered lover. In the little girl in the blacksmith's shop
she believes she recognizes the object of her search, and brings the
child with her. Meantime, poor Nelly O'Neil is wandering dis-
consolately about searching for the stolen girl, and continually
singing an old Irish song which she had taught the child, the
burden of which touches certain 'Green Bushes,' the only link, by
the way, between the piece and its name.

"George, meanwhile, hopes, by means of *Miami*, whose arrival
he has heard of, to obtain more authentic accounts than he has
yet had of his brother's death. Pending an interview, which is
arranged, Geraldine, the widow of Connor, arrives, and falls in with
Nelly O'Neil. George and *Miami* meet. The child is present. In
the course of the interview Nelly sings 'Green Bushes' outside; the
little girl recognizes the voice, flies to the window, and is as suddenly
recognized by the wandering minstrel. Much of what remains can
easily be conceived. The mother rejoins her daughter, and *Miami*,
the murderer of her father, having accomplished her work of atonement in endowing the child with all her possessions, suddenly dies
—we could not exactly make out how or why; and so the curtain
falls upon 'Green Bushes.' In all this there is, of course, plenty of
extravagance and improbability; but the energy of some of the
scenes, and the effect of some of the situations tell well, and carried
off the piece triumphantly. It was generally extremely well acted.
Celeste played with great energy and spirit, interpreting the wild
love of the Indian girl with feeling and effect." (*Morning Chronicle*,
January 29, 1845.)

On March 11, 1847, Madame Celeste played the part of *Cynthia*,
first performance at the Adelphi of Buckstone's 'Flowers of the

Forest.' "'The Flowers of the Forest' is a perfect Adelphi melodrama," remarked the *Examiner* (March 20, 1847), "in which the exact strength and resources of the company are exquisitely measured. There is picturesque power for Madame Celeste and Mr. O. Smith; laughter and pathos for Mrs. Fitzwilliam; the broadest drollery for Messrs. Wright and Bedford; and a part for Miss Woolgar which gives admirable scope to her cleverness and versatility. She plays a gipsy lad, on whose murder of one of the characters (under provocation of a horse-whip) the interest turns. The murder is seen by an Italian gipsy, who, with his daughter, has joined the English tribe, and in his hatred to the white race, not only screens the culprit, but diverts suspicion to an innocent man. But this purpose is foiled by his daughter, who sacrifices herself to bring justice home. The English gipsy girl, who protects the poor Italian whose sense of right had deprived her of her own lover, is a very pretty notion; and though Miss Woolgar is a somewhat young lover for the now (alas! that we should say it) elderly Mrs. Fitzwilliam, the acting of both is delightfully natural."

In 1853 Madame Celeste was at the height of her popularity at the Adelphi Theatre, acting "with that high finish that elevates even melodramatic acting to the dignity of histrionic art." In June of that year, at the Adelphi, she personated the heroine in the first performance of Dion Boucicault's drama 'Géneviève; or, the Reign of Terror.' The drama, which embraced all the strength of the company, was acted to perfection. Mr. Webster, as the noble-hearted, generous Sorin; Mr. Wigan, as the subtle, vindictive Dismer; and Mr. Leigh Murray, as the impetuous, ardent Maurice, were all that might be expected from such artists—while Madame Celeste, as the sorrowing, heart-broken *Géneviève*, gave all possible pathos to the part. Mr. and Mrs. Keeley were also in the original cast.

On Monday, March 20, 1854, at the Adelphi, Madame Celeste played the original *Ruth Ravensear*, first performance of Messrs. Tom Taylor's and Charles Reade's drama 'Two Loves and a Life.' The *Examiner* (March 25, 1854),* alluding to the play, said: Madame Celeste never displayed more energy and spirit, more power of depicting half-untutored passion than in the part which she here sustains.

On Monday, May 20, 1854, she performed the character of *Mdlle. Marco*, first performance at the Adelphi of 'The Marble Heart,' adapted from 'Les Filles de Marbre' (Barrière and Theboust), by Mr. Selby. "Madame Celeste was admirable as the callous woman of the world, spurning all human feeling in the insatiate pursuit of wealth." (*Daily News*, May 24, 1854.) On Monday, February 5, 1855, first performance at the Adelphi of 'Janet Pride' (Boucicault), Madame Celeste played the title *rôle;* and on Wednesday, June 20, 1855, first performance at the Adelphi Theatre of 'Helping Hands,' by Tom Taylor, she sustained the character of *Margaret Hartmann.* In the Christmas pantomime of the

---

* Compare with *Journal of a London Playgoer*, Henry Morley, p. 82.

same year ('Jack and the Beanstalk'), at the same theatre, she played Harlequin. In 1858, Monday, January 18, she was the original *Marie Leroux*, first performance of Watts Phillips's 'Poor Strollers,' likewise at the Adelphi Theatre.

In the following year, 1859, Madame Celeste entered upon an engagement at the Lyceum Theatre, and "opened " there, Monday, January 3, as the heroine, *Marion de L'Orme*, in the drama of that title, translated from M. Emile de la Roche's play. In the following November she became the lessee of the Lyceum Theatre, and. inaugurated her management, on the 28th of that month, with a piece entitled 'Paris and Pleasure ; or, Home and Happiness.' At the same theatre she produced, on Monday, January 30, 1860, a play founded on Charles Dickens's 'Tale of Two Cities,' and sustained in it the character of *Madame Defarge*. On Monday, March 19 of the same year, at the Lyceum, she performed the part of the *Abbé Vaudreuil* (afterwards a favourite character with Madame Celeste) in a play of that title by the late Colonel Addison ; and on Monday, November 12 of the same year, *Adrienne de Beaupré*, in a drama entitled 'Adrienne ; or, the Secret of a Life,' which proved the most successful piece which Madame Celeste had brought out since her accession to managerial power. "The incidents are not, perhaps, always original, but they are so cleverly arranged with a view to effect, and the story is developed with so much artistic management, that the interest awakened almost immediately after the curtain rises is pretty evenly sustained until it falls. . . . . The piece was admirably played throughout. Madame Celeste, in *Adrienne*, has one of those parts in which she appears to the utmost advantage ; and Mrs. Keeley, as the Italian serving-maid, cast in an English mould, was fitted to a nicety, and played with infinite animation and humour." (*Daily Telegraph*, November 13, 1860.)

On Monday, February 11, 1861, was produced at the Lyceum 'The House on the Bridge of Notre Dame' (translated from the French of MM. T. Barrière and H. de Kock), in which Madame Celeste sustained the part of *Ernest de la Garde*, which subsequently became one of her most famous impersonations.

In 1863 Madame Celeste embarked on a lengthened foreign tour, and did not appear again on the London stage until 1868, in which year, on Easter Monday (April 13), she inaugurated a series of twelve farewell performances at the St. James's Theatre with a representation of the character of *Rudiga* in Stirling Coyne's drama of 'The Woman in Red.' The year 1868 did not, however, bring Madame Celeste's long professional career to an end. In May 1869, at the Princess's Theatre, she played *Josephine Dubosc*, first performance of Dion Boucicault's drama ' Presumptive Evidence ' ; and in the following year, on Saturday, October 22, 1870, at the Adelphi Theatre, in a revival of 'The Green Bushes,' her original character of *Miami*, a part which, perhaps, more than any other contributed to establish her popularity as an actress. "Of Madame Celeste's last representation," said the *Athenæum* (October 29, 1870), "it may safely be said that it can scarcely be told from the earliest. When the actress crossed the familiar bridge behind the log cabin, her appearance was precisely that of former years, and neither voice, accent, nor bearing dispelled the illusion created." On Saturday, December 17, 1870, Madame Celeste again made her appearance on the Adelphi boards for her " farewell benefit." The characters she selected to represent on the occasion were the *Abbé Vaudreuil* and *Miami.* "Amidst the warmest wishes for her welfare that a very crowded, exceedingly enthusiastic, and a most sympathetic audience could express, Madame Celeste closed on Saturday night, with a farewell benefit, a long professional career, associated with a host of pleasurable recollections. Some forty years have passed away since the actress who came on Saturday evening before the public for the last time made her *début* on the Drury Lane boards as a dancer who had then scarcely numbered fifteen summers. During this interval the reputation of the artist has steadily advanced, and, despite the difficulty, which was apparently insuperable, of the Parisian girl effectually mastering the English accent, few performers have ever become more closely identified with a long series of dramatic successes on the London stage. The remarkable power of pantomimic expression which was evinced at a very early stage of her histrionic progress suggested the construction of a number of dramas expressly designed to give employment to this special talent. What Mdlle. Celeste could accomplish as an intelligent interpreter of the mysteries of the ballet was sufficiently manifested in her performance of the dumb girl *Fenella* in the opera of ' Masaniello,' her graceful evolutions as *Zelica* in the opera of ' Maid of Cashmere,' her earnestness of manner in the famous Covent Garden spectacle of ' The Revolt of the Harem,' and her lively action as the leader of the ' Danse des Folies ' in the opera of ' Gustavus the Third.' Dramatists, however, soon recognized the advantage of turning these capabilities to greater account ; and in such pieces as ' The Arab Boy,' ' The French Spy,' ' Prince Le Boo,' and ' The Child of the Wreck,' Mdlle. Celeste not only became a great favourite in this country, but obtained a repute which enabled her to acquire a large fortune and a widely extended fame in the United States.

" At the old Adelphi, with which her later triumphs have been more intimately connected, her histrionic powers have been much further developed ; and in ' St. Mary's Eve,' ' Marie Ducange,' ' Two Loves and a Life,' ' Janet Pride,' and ' Tartuffe,' her abilities as an actress have been conspicuously displayed ; whilst as *Miami* in ' The Green Bushes,' and *Cynthia* in ' The Flowers of the Forest,' her valuable assistance has been so distinctly felt that these dramas could never be revived without a reference to the accomplished actress who had originally given them their early popularity. Recalling these and many other such memories of a brightly-illuminated theatrical past, elder playgoers mingled on Saturday night with those of the present generation, and shared together sympathies, regrets, and congratulations.

" That Madame Celeste now retires from us in full possession of all her powers was sufficiently evinced by her admirable performance of the *Abbé Vaudreuil* in the fantastic drama of that name, which, adapted from the French by Colonel Addison,* was brought out at the Lyceum about ten years since, when the theatre was under her management. The encored minuet, danced with Miss Furtado, afforded a substantial proof at least that no experience of physical deficiencies had enforced retirement from the stage. As *Miami* in ' The Green Bushes ' Madame Celeste, moreover, again showed that the Indian huntress still retained all the brilliancy of eye and force of expression which had long rendered this assumption one of the most noted in the repertory of the *bénéficiaire*. The second act was alone performed, but it need hardly be stated that in this portion of the drama the very fullest demand is made on the powers of the actress. At the termination of each piece Madame Celeste was enthusiastically recalled, and greeted with prolonged plaudits." (*Daily Telegraph*, December 19, 1870.) Madame Celeste appeared subsequently at the Adelphi Theatre, in September 1872, for twelve nights ; in November 1873 for eleven nights ; and in October 1874 for twelve nights. On each occasion *Miami* in ' The Green Bushes ' was the character in which she was advertised to appear. Madame Celeste has now finally retired from the stage, and resides in Paris.

CHALLIS, EDITH, first appeared at Niblo's Garden, New York, in ' After Dark '; subsequently coming to London she took the part of *Mrs. Seabright* in ' The Overland Route ' at the Haymarket. Having revisited America, and appeared in ' The Two Roses,' ' Lalla Rookh,' ' Money,' and other plays in New York, Philadelphia, &c., Miss Challis returned to London, where she appeared at the Court Theatre in ' Brighton.' She also played in the ' Danischeffs ' at the St. James's Theatre, in ' The Widow Hunt ' with Mr. J. S. Clarke at the Haymarket, in ' The Vicar of Wakefield ' at the Aquarium Theatre, in ' The American Cousin ' at the Haymarket, with Mr. Sothern, and in ' Family Honour ' at the Aquarium Theatre.

CHAMBERS, EMMA, first attracted notice in the dramatic profession by her spirited performance of the part of *Harry Halyard* in ' Poll and My Partner Joe ' at St. James's Theatre in May 1871. The following Christmas at the Alexandra Theatre she played the title *rôle* in the pantomime of ' Jack the Giant Killer,' and afterwards was engaged at the Strand and Olympic Theatres ; at the latter she was in the original cast of ' Sour Grapes ' (H. J. Byron), and created a favourable impression by her realistic impersonation of a young country girl. In 1875 Miss Chambers accepted a three years' engagement from the directors of the Royal Alhambra Theatre. She played there in various operas, and at the expiration of her Alhambra engagement appeared at the

---

* See *ante*. Madame Celeste informs me that this play was the " original " work of Colonel Addison, and not an adaptation from the French. —ED.

Philharmonic Theatre as the *Directrice of the Convent*, her original part, in ' Le Petit Duc.' Upon the withdrawal of ' Le Petit Duc,' she was engaged by Mr. Alexander Henderson to play *Serpolette* in ' Les Cloches de Corneville ' at the Globe Theatre. Christmas 1878 she appeared at the Prince's Theatre, Manchester, and is at present (July 1879) engaged at the Alhambra Theatre, acting in the operatic spectacle entitled ' Venice.'

CHIPPENDALE, WILLIAM HENRY, born in London in 1801. He was partly educated at the High School of Edinburgh, and was designed by his father (an actor of the Haymarket Theatre) for a printer. Young Chippendale was placed in James Ballantyne's office, and here he read ' Waverley ' for the press, and thus attracted the notice of Sir Walter Scott, who treated the lad on all occasions with much kindly notice as a " *chip* of the old block," the elder Chippendale being well known to Sir Walter. In the printing office young Chippendale became ill, and was removed and apprenticed to John Ballantyne, the celebrated publisher and literary auctioneer, in whose sale rooms he became familiar with many distinguished authors and literary men of the day, notably Wilson, Lockhart, Patrick Robertson, James Hogg, and other characters in the ' Noctes Ambrosianæ,' and contributors to ' Blackwood.' He afterwards entered the service of a commercial firm, which failed, and thereupon became an actor. Prior to this the younger Chippendale had played under the auspices of his father at the Haymarket Theatre, in various children's parts to several members of the Kemble family. He entered the dramatic profession proper in 1819, appearing at Montrose as *David* in ' The Rivals.' In the year following, Mr. Chippendale became a member of Mr. Alexander's company in Scotland, playing in Glasgow, Carlisle, Whitehaven, and other towns of his " circuit " up to the year 1836. He was principal comedian in the Lincoln, York, and Worcester Circuits, and in Edinburgh, Bristol, and Bath, where he met Edmund Kean, the elder Mathews, Mr. Macready, Miss Duncan, Kitty Stephens, and a host of celebrities. He worked in his early days with many actors with whom he was associated in later life, Mr. Compton, Messrs. Clark, Cullenford, &c., of the Theatre Royal, Haymarket. In the year last mentioned, having accepted an offer from Mr. Stephen Price, of the Old Park Theatre, New York, Mr. Chippendale went to the United States, where he remained for seventeen years, occupying at the Park Theatre very much the same position which the elder Farren at that time did in London. Returning to England in 1853 on Easter Monday, March 28 of that year, Mr. Chippendale made his *début* on the London stage at the Haymarket Theatre as *Sir Anthony Absolute* in ' The Rivals.' " It was a careful, measured, predetermined piece of acting. The passion was in no degree exaggerated, nor did it seem to fall short of the natural expression. But the character did not secure that marked prominence among the *dramatis personæ* which we have seen it assume with our greater English actors." (*Athenæum*, April 2, 1853.)

For a period of twenty years Mr. Chippendale worked con-
tinuously at the Haymarket Theatre, playing all the characters in
his own line of business, and fulfilling, for a part of the time, the
duties of stage-manager. The following, among other leading
parts played by him during his long engagement at the Haymarket, are deserving of being mentioned, viz. *Lord Betterton*,
in ' Elopements in High Life,' first performed at the Haymarket
Theatre, Thursday, April 7, 1853; *Sir Francis Gripe*, in Mrs.
Centlivre's comedy 'The Busybody,' "revived" at that theatre
in July 1855; *Sullen*, in 'The Beaux' Stratagem,' "revived"
January 5, 1856; *Hill Cooley, Esq.*, in Mr. B. Bernard's comedy
' The Evil Genius,' first performed at the Haymarket, Saturday,
March 8, 1856; *Malvolio*, in a revival of Shakespeare's ' Twelfth
Night,' July of the same year; *Old Adam*, in a revival of ' As You
Like It,' at the same theatre, September 4, 1856; *Old Mirabel*, in
a revival of ' The Inconstant,' September 20, 1856; and *Honeybun*,
in ' The Contested Election,' by Tom Taylor, first performed at
the Haymarket Theatre, June 29, 1859. In 1860, on Thursday,
February 23, first performance of Tom Taylor's comedy 'The
Overland Route,' Mr. Chippendale sustained the character of *Com-
missioner Colepepper*. He played the part of *Ingot*, first performance at the Haymarket of ' David Garrick,' Saturday, April 30,
1864; and *Mr. Fox Bromley*, first performance at the same
theatre, Monday, April 2, 1866, of Westland Marston's play ' The
Favourite of Fortune.' In October of the same year, in a revival
of the younger Colman's ' The Heir-at-Law ' at the Haymarket,
Mr. Chippendale played *Lord Duberly*. January 1867, first
formance of Tom Taylor's comedy 'A Lesson for Life,' he sustained the part of *Dr. Vivian*. March 1868, first performance of
' A Hero of Romance ' (Westland Marston), he performed the
character of *M. Dumont*. Monday, October 25, 1869, first performance at the Haymarket Theatre of Mr. Tom Taylor's comedy
' New Men and Old Acres,' Mr. Chippendale sustained the part of
Mr. Vavasour.

In 1871, Monday, October 16, he appeared at the Haymarket in
his old impersonation of *Sir Anthony Absolute*, upon the merits of
which the *Athenæum* of the ensuing week made the following
remarks : " The best impersonation in the entire performance is,
however, the *Sir Anthony* of Mr. Chippendale. A little stiffness
and formality which distinguished Mr. Chippendale's early representations has worn off. His general style has mellowed, and he
is now one of the best of the very few actors we possess who can
play the characters of old comedy. His laugh at his own jokes
is quiet, undemonstrative, and unforced, and the whole representation has the courtliness without which a character such as
this is apt to grow unpleasant." Perhaps the most important and
best appreciated impersonations of Mr. Chippendale in "classic"
comedy have been, in addition to the character already mentioned,
Sir Peter Teazle, Sir Harcourt Courtly, and *Mr. Hardcastle*.
During the long run of ' Hamlet' at the Lyceum Theatre (September 1874–June 1875), Mr. Chippendale played the part of

Polonius. Since that time he has appeared on various occasions at London and provincial theatres. In August 1878 he organized the " Chippendale Comedy Company " for a series of performances, in the provinces, of those plays in which his reputation was first made, " previous to his retirement from the stage." At the commencement of Mr. Irving's season 1878–9 at the Lyceum Mr. Chippendale played *Polonius* in the revival of ' Hamlet.' On Monday, February 24, 1879, he made his farewell of the stage at the same theatre in the same character (Mr. Irving acting Hamlet), the total receipts of the evening's performance, through Mr. Irving's generosity, being reserved to the veteran actor, who spoke a few words of farewell at the end of the play. It may be interesting to note, that in the course of his long career Mr. Chippendale has, in the character of *Polonius,* supported Edmund Kean, Charles Kemble, Charles Young, Harry Johnson, Macready, John Vandenhoff, Charles Kean, Barry Sullivan, Edwin Forrest, Booth, Creswick, and, finally, Henry Irving.

CHIPPENDALE, MARY J. (*née* SNOWDON), wife of the above-named, was born at Salisbury. She entered the dramatic profession in 1855 as member of a company of comedians performing in a small circuit of towns in the north of England, afterwards joining the Theatre Royal, Dublin, and continuing a member of the company there for two years. She made her professional *début* on the Manchester stage, in the name of " Seaman," in the autumn of 1859, appearing as *Mrs. Major de Boots,* in Stirling Coyne's comedietta ' Everybody's Friend.' In 1863, in the name of Snowdon, her first appearance on the London stage was made at the Haymarket Theatre in the part of *Mrs. Malaprop* in ' The Rivals.' In 1866 Miss Snowdon was married to Mr. Chippendale of the same theatre. Mrs. Chippendale continued to play at the Haymarket Theatre from 1865 to 1874 in the various original pieces and revivals of the older comedies produced during that period under the superintendence of Mr. J. B. Buckstone. In 1875 she fulfilled an engagement at the Court Theatre; and subsequently, in 1878, joined the company of the Lyceum Theatre, where she performed the character of *Martha* (wife of *Marcel*) in a revival of ' Louis XI.' Two of the most important of Mrs. Chippendale's impersonations are *Mrs. Candour* (' The School for Scandal ') and *Mrs. Malaprop* (' The Rivals ').

CLARKE, JOHN S., was born in Baltimore, Maryland, United States of America, in 1834, of English extraction; his mother was a grand-daughter of John King, who held an official position under the East India Company, and his grandfather, Stephen Clarke, was a London merchant. Mr. Clarke was educated with a view of practising law in the United States; but in 1852 adopted the stage as a profession. In that year, August 28, he made his professional *début* at the Old Chestnut Street Theatre, Philadelphia, in the part of *Soto,* in a revival of Cibber's play ' She Would and She Would Not.' Subsequently he became leading comedian of the Front Street Theatre in that city ; and afterwards, until 1861, joint lessee with Mr. Wheatley of the Arch Street Theatre. In that year Mr. J. S. Clarke appeared with considerable success in New York at the Winter Garden Theatre, of which he subsequently became joint lessee, and so continued until 1867, when the theatre was destroyed by fire. In 1865, in conjunction with his brother-in-law, Edwin Booth, he purchased the Walnut Street Theatre, Philadelphia, and in 1866 became joint lessee of the Boston Theatre for a brief period. In October 1867 Mr. J. S. Clarke made his first appearance on the London stage at the St. James's Theatre as *Major Wellington de Boots* (a very eccentric part, originally sustained by Mr. Buckstone) in Stirling Coyne's comedietta 'Everybody's Friend,' altered to the title of 'A Widow Hunt.' Mr. Coyne had remodelled the play and strengthened the part especially for Mr. Clarke. Although originally sustained by Mr. Buckstone, the character was not certainly considered, at the period of its first introduction to the Haymarket, in April 1859, remarkable as being the central figure of the drama. In America it had, however, grown up apparently into a figure of overshadowing magnitude, which, as in the case of Lord Dundreary in 'Our American Cousin,' completely overwhelmed the other personages of the play. Mr. J. S. Clarke had manifestly made the attributes of the really timorous, but professedly valiant, militia major the subject of earnest study. By a free use of flexible and humorously-expressive features, abundantly employing illustrative gesture, and filling up the action with a multitude of small details, which, if occasionally extravagant, were invariably funny, he established the character in a higher position than it had hitherto held in London. " The affected swagger, with the consciousness of cowardice, and the domineering manner controlled by the sense of marital subjection, could hardly have found more emphatic expression. To the constant laughter created among the audience the actor may confidently refer in evidence of his complete success." (*Daily Telegraph*, October 17, 1867.)

In February 1868, at the Princess's Theatre, Mr. Clarke played the part of *Salem Scudder* in a revival of ' The Octoroon '; subsequently, in the same year, he appeared at various towns in the provinces, and afterwards returned to the Strand Theatre, where he acted *Young Gosling* in a piece entitled 'Fox *versus* Goose.' "*Jack Gosling*, as executed by Mr. J. S. Clarke, is a most remarkable specimen of grotesque humour. Silly good humour and unreasonable irascibility alternate with each other, and when the unfortunate youth is left alone, thoroughly 'done over,' his drollery becomes irresistible. There is genius in every patch of colour. . . . It is wonderful how the comic genius of Mr. J. S. Clarke breaks through difficulties when its manifestation is least expected. Sometimes the influence of cumbrous matter threatens to make all dramatic peculiarity fade out, and its sudden reappearance is almost startling. In the scene of the duel, *Gosling*, whose sole object it is to make mortal combat impossible, objects to the rifles, which he himself has previously selected. He is asked what weapons he would prefer. ' Cannons,' he thunders forth, astounded at the brilliancy

of his own notion.   His adversary sneeringly suggests that he
would not even fight with 'pop-guns,' whereupon he vehemently
declares that he *would*.   The pop-gun is even better than the
cannon, and the avidity with which he jumps at the new means of
escape is surprisingly droll."   On Monday, July 26, 1869, at the same
theatre, he appeared in a leading *rôle* (*Babington Jones*), in a
comedy by John Brougham, entitled 'Among the Breakers.'   Wrote
the *Athenæum* (July 31, 1869) :—" Mr. J. S. Clarke played his part
in a very laughable fashion.   His facial play is always droll, and
his manner of bearing his unmerited misfortunes was as funny as it
could be.   Mr. Clarke has a curious power of changing rapidly his
expression, which he often employs.   His mouth widens, his eyes
distend, and his whole face is expressive of unrestrained merriment.
Suddenly, with a sort of self-rebuke, as though he had committed
himself, he assumes the preternaturally grave countenance of a wag
who had forgotten himself and made a joke at a funeral.   The
effect of this is very comic."

Afterwards, at the same theatre during the same year, he played
Toodles (one of his favourite and best known characters) in the
farcical comedy entitled 'The Toodles.'   On Saturday, February 5,
1870, he sustained the part of *Dr. Pangloss*, in a revival, at the
Strand, of the younger Colman's comedy of 'The Heir-at-Law.'   As
to this performance the *Daily News* (February 7, 1870) remarked :—
" The success of the comedy, which was produced for the first time
in 1797, at the Haymarket, is sufficiently explained by the original
cast, which included such stars as Snett, Palmer (whether John or
Robert we know not), Fawcett, Charles Kemble, and Munden ; but
it is remarkable that the original *Pangloss*, whose character is the
very pivot of the play, was not regarded as satisfactory, the best
critics considering John Bannister, Fawcett's successor in the part,
as superior in that 'stiff solemnity and slowness of utterance'
appropriate to the obsequious tutor.   Mr. J. S. Clarke's *Pangloss*
is probably different in numerous points from either of those
originals.   It is full of those abrupt transitions from slow utterance
to quick, from a low tone to a high, from repose to activity, which
are only saved from degenerating into mere mannerisms by the
real comic genius of the actor.   In his peculiar roll of the eyes, his
smiles suddenly checked at full height, his eccentric inflections of
voice, and grotesque exits, it is, indeed, easy enough to recognize,
even under the quaint wig and Georgian clerical costume, our old
friends *Wellington de Boots* and *Timothy Toodles ;* but there are
still abundance of touches in his performance—like his sudden and
serious contemplation of the old chandler's countenance to watch
the effect of his magnificent Latin and Greek quotations—which
are really artistic and new."   Said the *Times* of the same date :—
" Those who associate this mirthful little theatre with entertainments of the lightest class will be surprised to learn that the old
standard comedy, 'The Heir-at-Law,' of the younger Colman,
decidedly the best work of an indifferent school, attained a most
decided success when revived in three acts on Saturday night.
Folks are in the habit of laughing loudly at the Strand, but never

did they laugh more loudly than at this 'legitimate' farce. Let us remark, by the way, that certain obstacles to mirth which occur in the five-act play, and which were apparently relished by our fathers, are removed in the compressed version. The purpose of the revival is obviously to furnish Mr. John S. Clarke, the American comedian, with a new part of strongly marked character. He plays *Dr. Pangloss*, and takes a view of that model tutor which is perfectly consistent with the text, and which affords occasion for the display of the broadest humour. According to Mr. Clarke, *Pangloss* is not a dry pedant, but a genial swindler with pedantic embellishments, who has the greatest difficulty in concealing the delight afforded by the triumphant success of his own dishonesty. An urbane man, too! He chuckles inwardly at the cacology of his noble patron, but he corrects his mistakes with the utmost delicacy, rather suggesting than demanding an amendment, the embodied spirit of insinuation. On one occasion only is he thoroughly grave, and that is when he is compelled by Dick Dowlas to dance in the streets, and he sees in that dance the ruin of his prospects. The legs partially move, but the face is sad."

Mr. Clarke reappeared with considerable *éclat* in New York on April 17, 1870, and subsequently performed with much success during the same year at the various principal cities in the United States. In July 1871 he returned to England, and on the 29th of that month "opened" at the Strand Theatre as *Dr. Pangloss*, which character he sustained for a "run" of one hundred and fifty nights. His next appearance in London was at the same theatre on Saturday, March 9, 1872, as *Dr. Ollapod*, in the younger Colman's comedy of 'The Poor Gentleman.'

The great success of 'The Heir-at-Law,' in which Mr. Clarke's *Pangloss* will be long remembered, had probably suggested to the management to revive another comedy of George Colman's. "From *Pangloss* to *Ollapod* is an easy transition. Until lately these two stage figures, once so familiar in the eyes of English playgoers, had become somewhat indistinct, for the Haymarket, which may be said to have been the last home of the old comedies, has, of late years, consigned the plays of George Colman to a sort of honourable superannuation. No one, however, who witnessed the performance of 'The Heir-at-Law' at the Strand will be disposed to deny that there are qualities in these pieces which not only explain their old popularity, but are quite sufficient to give them new life when they are put upon the stage with tolerable care. *Ollapod*, it must be confessed, is a character neither so amusing in itself nor so completely worked out as the part of the obsequious tutor. Neither character has the slightest pretence to depth. The country apothecary and cornet of volunteers and the time-serving pedantic private tutor are both rather compounds of oddity than studies from life. Their eccentricities, however, are at least conceivable ; and it would be a great mistake to condemn them simply because they are artificial creations. The fact is, that our capacity for enjoying the inventions of the novelist's or the dramatist's brain is by no means strictly limited to the probable, much less to average

types of men. Some of the most successful of stage characters—
Paul Pry and Lord Dundreary for example—are personages
certainly not to be found off the stage. Yet they could hardly be
called characters of farce, for their attributes are rather humorous
than broadly comic, and their elements, if strangely mixed, are not
entirely remote from human traits. Thus the toadying and pliant
'bear-leader' of old times is, after all, the foundation of *Pangloss,*
as is the country apothecary of Colman's days, with his narrow
views of life, his bland servility and fussy patriotism, the foundation
of *Ollapod.* The queer habits and sayings with which they are invested are the mannerisms of the author, whose thorough knowledge of the essentials of stage success saved him from going too
far in this way, while his hearty relish for odd people and quaint
dialogue is manifested in the overflowing drollery of the scenes.

"Mr. J. S. Clarke is a mannerist, as nine comic actors out of ten
have ever been, and this is, to a certain degree, a disadvantage
when performing in succession two characters having so many
superficial points of resemblance as *Pangloss* and *Ollapod.* When
he stops abruptly with the frequent exclamation, 'Thank you, good
sir, I owe you one,' the spectator cannot fail to be reminded of
Pangloss's abrupt mention of the names of the authors whom he
delights to quote ; and, as all Mr. Clarke's admirers will understand,
the same constrained walk, and frequent chuckle, and self-admiring
smile, and frequent roll of the eye which were conspicuous in
Pangloss and *Wellington de Boots* flourish again in the case of the
eccentric apothecary. But all these things are very droll in themselves, and the ungainly attitudes of the proprietor of the Galen's
head when in his full regimentals—including the traditional large
brass helmet—are irresistibly comic. Mr. Clarke received from
a crowded audience an enthusiastic welcome." (*Daily News,*
March 11, 1872.)

On Thursday, June 27, 1872, at the Strand, he performed the
part of *Paul Pry* in Poole's well-known comedy ; and, subsequently, *Robert Tyke* in 'The School of Reform,' exhibiting in
the part "a remarkable mastery of the Yorkshire dialect and a
power of expressing strong emotional feelings, which prove his
range to be by no means limited to eccentric comedy." During
the several seasons Mr. Clarke has played in London he has taken
up, one after the other, most of the leading characters of broad
comedy. His representations, depending largely upon facial play,
have a generic likeness, and it is rather by aid of such accessories
as costume than by means of any special portrayal of character
that the spectator distinguishes one from the other. The impersonation of *Paul Pry*, the hero of Poole's well-known comedy, has
much in common with his *Dr. Ollapod* and *Dr. Pangloss.* In
absolute extravagance of drollery Mr. Clarke approaches nearer
Liston perhaps than any subsequent interpreter of the character
first named.

In November 1872 he opened the Charing Cross Theatre under
his management, and produced 'The Rivals,' in which he sustained
the part of *Bob Acres.* Since the above date Mr. Clarke has

appeared from time to time in London in the round of characters already specified. In April 1874 he appeared at the Holborn Theatre as *Phineas Pettiephogge* in a five-act melodrama by H. J. Byron, entitled ' The Thumbscrew.' In the autumn of 1878 he assumed the lesseeship and direction of the Haymarket Theatre. On Monday, December 2, 1878, he produced there ' The Crisis ' (a version of M. Emile Augier's ' Les Fourchambault '), by Mr. James Albery. The principal players in the piece were Messrs. Charles Kelly, Terriss, and Howe, and Mesdames John Wood, Eastlake, and Louise Moodie. The acting was in some instances exceptionally good, and the play was a success. On Easter Monday, April 14, 1879, Mr. Clarke produced an original "comedy-drama," in five acts, by W. G. Wills, entitled ' Ellen ; or, Love's Cunning.' Though one or two of the scenes of this play were excellent (notably those in which Thomas Pye (Charles Kelly) and Lady Breezy (Miss B. Henri) bore a principal part), considered as a whole it was a conspicuous failure, and was removed from the bills after a week's performance, giving place to ' The Rivals,' in which Mr. J. S. Clarke resumed his old part of *Bob Acres*. Subsequently, in May, ' The Crisis ' was revived ; and on Thursday, June 12, 1879, ' Brag ' (W. G. Wills), an amended version of the same author's ' Ellen.' This piece, like its predecessor, was unsuccessful. The summer season 1879 ended Tuesday, June 24, and with it Mr. Clarke's lesseeship of the Haymarket Theatre, which was transferred to Mr. and Mrs. Bancroft.

CLAYTON, JOHN (a *nom de théâtre;* JOHN ALFRED CLAYTON CALTHROP), was born at Gosberton, Lincolnshire, February 14, 1845, and made his first appearance upon any stage, February 27, 1866, at St. James's Theatre, London, in the character of *Hastings* in ' She Stoops to Conquer.' In the following year (in August), at the Olympic Theatre, Mr. Clayton appeared in a comedietta entitled ' Six Months Ago,' in which his acting was favourably commented on. The same month of 1867, at the same theatre, he played the part of *Laudry Barbeau* in ' The Grasshopper,' a dramatization of Madame Dudevant's story ' La Petite Fadette.' The piece had already been presented in America. On March 27, 1869, first performance of T. W. Robertson's comedy ' Dreams,' he played the part of *Earl Mount Forrestcourt;* and at the Gaiety Theatre in the July following, first performance of W. S. Gilbert's comedy ' An Old Score,' the part of young *Calthorpe.* The same year, Monday, October 11, at the same theatre, first performance of ' A Life Chase ' (by Messrs. Oxenford and H. Wigan), Mr. Clayton played *Vaubert.* In December of the same year, at the Gaiety, he was the original *Joe Lennard*, first performance of ' Uncle Dick's Darling.' In February 1876, at the Princess's, he played *Nigel* in a revival of ' The King o' Scots ' ; in May of the same year, at the Court Theatre, in a dramatic version of ' Great Expectations,' the part of *Jaggers;* and in the ensuing November the part of *Mr. Jormell*, first performance at the same theatre of H. T. Craven's comedy ' Coals of Fire.' In July 1872, at the

Vaudeville Theatre, in a revival of 'The School for Scandal,' Mr. Clayton played the part of *Joseph Surface.* The piece was performed for four hundred and twelve consecutive nights, being the longest " run " Sheridan's comedy has yet obtained. In a second adaptation of ' Marcel ' (MM. Sandeau and Decourcelle), entitled ' Awaking,' first performed at the Gaiety Theatre, December 14, 1872, Mr. Clayton sustained the leading *rôle* with great power. " Though his [Mr. Clayton's] voice was wanting in that quality at once grave and tender, which, as we have already said, would be necessary to give due effect to the part, and he seemed, unfortunately, unable to shake off some mannerisms—a peculiar rolling gait, for example—in many passages he fairly surmounted all disadvantages. The fine gradations of the father's return to reason, and his horror at the imaginary picture of the child lying dead at his feet, were depicted by him with much subtlety and power ; but the most touching part of his performance was in the closing scene, when a simple exclamation indicates both his return to reason and his perception of the fact that the little child before him is another son born to him in the early days of his insanity, and now destined to fill the place of his lost brother in his affections." (*Daily News,* December 17, 1872.) In 1873, on Saturday, September 27, in a revival at the Lyceum Theatre of ' Richelieu,' Mr. Irving in the title *rôle,* Mr. Clayton sustained the part of *Louis XIII.* The following year (1874), on Saturday, February 7, in a new drama produced on that date at the Lyceum Theatre, entitled ' Philip (Hamilton Aïdé), he played *Juan de Miraflore.* On Saturday, March 13, 1875, the opening night of the Court Theatre under Mr. Hare's management, in a new comedy by Mr. Charles Coghlan, entitled ' Lady Flora,' Mr. Clayton sustained the part of *George de Chavannes.* The same year, on Monday, October 18, at the Mirror Theatre, London, first performance of ' All for Her' (Messrs. Palgrave Simpson and Herman Merivale), he sustained the part of *Hugh Trevor.* Mr. Clayton's presentation of the character was so successful that he afterwards performed it in London and the provinces for a period of nearly two years. The *Daily Telegraph* (October 20, 1875) thus remarked on the performance :—" Mr. Herman Merivale, cordially assisted by his friend, Mr. J. Palgrave Simpson, has once more enriched the literature of our modern stage with a play glowing with the rich warmth of poetical feeling and of serious dramatic value. Once more has a young actor come boldly to the front, and shown himself not only capable of appreciating the high intention of his authors, but of interpreting it to the complete satisfaction of his audience. The actor is Mr. John Clayton, who has won his position by intense application and rare industry, and has secured his success by one of those impulsive bounds which are as surprising to the public as they are delightful to all who make the drama their special study. It will be needless, we trust, to waste many words upon steady playgoers in urging particular attention to this new play, ' All for Her.' It will be superfluous, we believe, to demand healthy and hearty criticism upon an art-study so meritorious as the *Hugh Trevor* of

Mr. Clayton. But there are times when it appears to be the duty of the critic to abandon the dull office of chronicler, and to lead a cheerful chorus of congratulation. All who know Mr. Merivale's work, and appreciate the value of such an author, will lose no opportunity of seeing the new play." And the *Times* (January 13, 1876), noticing the same play after it had been before the public for some weeks, expressed the following opinion upon its merits and Mr. Clayton's acting :—"' All for Her ' is certainly the most powerfully written play which has been on the English stage for some years. . . . . 'All for Her' was well played in Holborn, but it is still better played in St. James's. It does not often fall to the lot of an actor to have such a part as that of *Hugh Trevor* assigned to him ; but, on the other hand, it is not everyone who can grasp his opportunity when it is before him. This Mr. Clayton has done. It would have been easy to make *Trevor*, the poor, reckless, good-for-nothing drunkard, a very repulsive person ; but this Mr. Clayton has not done. Philip, drunk or sober, is still a gentleman, and from first to last this fact is kept before us with exceptional art. So skilfully managed, too, both by author and actor, is the birth and growth of *Trevor's* hopeless love for the woman who is to be his brother's wife, that the burning of the only proof of his legitimacy, and the last great sacrifice at the close of the play, seem to us, while we fully recognize their nobility, hardly more than a man placed in *Trevor's* position would have done. We are pleased, too, to note another point, and no common one, in Mr. Clayton's acting. Such a part, demanding the exercise of physical as well as other powers, when played night after night, is terribly susceptible, as we have many proofs, of exaggeration ; but we can discover no sign of this at the St. James's any more than was to be seen at the Mirror. On the contrary, it seems to us that Mr. Clayton has modified one or two little trifling excesses of voice and gesture which were apparent in the earlier representations."

On Saturday, January 6, 1877, first performance at St. James's Theatre of the English version of ' The Danischeffs,' Mr. Clayton sustained the character of *Osip.* In 1878, January 12, first performance at the Prince of Wales's of ' Diplomacy,' he played the part of *Henry Beauclerc.* "The two great scenes in this play are the second and third acts. On these rested the fame of the French piece, which, in other respects, was considered to be occasionally too diffuse and slightly deficient in vitality. The first of these scenes, however, has acquired a distinction unusual even among the great traditions of the French stage, and the corresponding scene in the English piece may well attain an equal honour in the annals of our own stage. In this, the husband learns on his wedding day, from the lips of a friend ignorant of the marriage, that he has taken to wife a traitress and a spy. The friend, learning too late the indiscretion of which he has been guilty, would retract his words, but he is forced to speak, and establishes what cannot but seem conclusive proof of the truth of what he has said. The husband refusing to believe, and yet scarcely daring to disbelieve, what he has heard, spares no effort to establish his wife's innocence ; but the secret enemy at work is too strong for him, and all his efforts unfortunately tend to establish but too clearly her guilt.   Then ensues the second of the famous scenes where the husband and wife, after mutual apologies, offers of forgiveness, and recrimination, alternately advanced and withheld, part to meet, they vow, no more.   The closing act is occupied with the restoration of the wife's innocence and the conviction of the real criminal—a Russian Countess in the pay of the Russian police, whose rejected love for the husband has led her to take this terrible vengeance on the wife and through her on him.   The means by which a happy conclusion is attained, though somewhat weak in art, and apt, perhaps, to strike the spectator as more ingenious than ingenuous, are skilfully contrived to further those ends of justice which the stage of comedy requires.   In the first of the great scenes, the acting of Mr. Bancroft, Mr. Kendal, and Mr. Clayton, respectively impersonating the friend, the husband, and the brother, could not well be bettered.   The situation is, in itself, very striking, and presented as it is by these three gentlemen, it brought down from all quarters of the house such applause as is seldom heard in this theatre, where satisfaction is wont to be expressed after a somewhat languidly decorous fashion.   [*See also* BANCROFT, S. B.] . . . On Mr. Clayton's shoulders devolved, perhaps, the hardest share of the scene, for he has much to do but scarcely a word to say.   It is his business to watch and control his brother, to soften the severity of the blow, and to temper indignation with reason.   In this he is assisted but little by the authors, his words are of the fewest and the simplest, his manner and his action are his own, and both are marked with true and natural propriety of expression.   Mr. Clayton's performance, indeed, is throughout one of the soundest and most consistent among so many good ones, and the only exception we could probably take to him would be in the closing scene, where we doubt whether he might not soften his manner towards the wretched woman from whom his craft has drawn a full confession of her crime.   Here, however, his conduct is, we suppose, more directly indicated by the text." (*Times*, January 21, 1878.)

On Saturday, January 11, 1879, in a revival of ' Caste ' at the Prince of Wales's Theatre, Mr. Clayton played *George D'Alroy* (his predecessors in the part being Frederick Younge, H. J. Montague, and Charles Coghlan) ; and on Saturday, May 31 of the same year, at the same theatre, he played in a revival of W. S. Gilbert's ' Sweethearts.'   It is understood that at the end of the summer season 1879 Mr. Clayton joins Mr. Boucicault's company at Booth's Theatre, New York.

CLEMENTS, FRANK, was born in Aberdeen, July 8, 1844. He studied for the Church of Scotland at King's College, Aberdeen, for some time ; but, finally, in 1861 left that University and entered the dramatic profession.   In the same year he appeared on the stage for the first time at the New Theatre, Birmingham, and afterwards entered upon engagements at various theatres in the provinces. His first appearance as "leading actor" was at the Theatre Royal, Birmingham, where Mr. Clements remained during two years, performing from time to time in the following parts, viz. *Macbeth, Iago, Claude Melnotte, Master Walter, Romeo, Richard III.,* &c. He undertook in 1869 the management and leading business at the Theatre Royal, Nottingham, for one year. In 1870 he returned to the Theatre Royal, Birmingham, as "leading actor," and remained a member of the company of that theatre until December 1873, afterwards joining Mr. Sefton's travelling company to play leading parts in 'Pygmalion and Galatea' and 'The Palace of Truth.' In July 1874 Mr. Clements made his first appearance in London at the Lyceum Theatre as *Lord Moray* in 'Charles I.' In March 1875 he commenced a "starring" tour in the provinces, which continued until July 1877, during which time Mr. Clements visited the principal towns and cities of the United Kingdom, playing nearly every leading legitimate and Shakespearian character. The *Liverpool Daily Post* noticed his performance of *Macbeth* as follows :—" Mr. Clements played *Macbeth* with an intellectual power and dignity far above the average, and with an absence of staginess which cannot be too highly commended." Mr. Clements rejoined the Lyceum company on its provincial tour in 1877 ; and in 1878 in London sustained the part of *Philip de Commines* in the revival of ' Louis XI.' at the Lyceum Theatre.

CLIFFORD, EDWIN, was born at King's Cliffe, Northamptonshire, and entered the dramatic profession in 1867. He accepted an engagement for three successive seasons at the Theatre Royal, Dundee, and subsequently passed into the company of Mr. Wilson Barrett. He made his first appearance in London at the Victoria Theatre, September 24, 1876, in the character of *Ishmael the Zingaro*, in a romantic drama entitled ' The Shadow of Death.' Mr. Clifford has devoted himself chiefly to the impersonation of the characters of Shakespearian tragedy, and his performances of *Hamlet, Macbeth, Othello,* and other leading *rôles* have been appreciated in a large circle of provincial towns.

CLIFTON, FREDERIC, was born May 29, 1844, and entered the dramatic profession in 1861, making his first appearance at the Theatre Royal, Reading. After a varied experience in almost every line of theatrical business, he accepted an engagement in 1865 as musical lecturer and entertainer at the Royal Polytechnic Institution. Subsequently he fulfilled an engagement of a like character at the Crystal Palace. In 1868 Mr. Clifton appeared in London as the English original *Krakwitz* in Offenbach's ' Last of the Paladins.' Since then he has sustained original parts in various operas and opera bouffes, &c., at the Criterion Theatre, the Egyptian Hall, the Royalty, Alhambra, and Gaiety Theatres, and at the Crystal Palace. He has been from the commencement of Mr. D'Oyley Carte's management (November 1877), and is still (July 1879), engaged at the Opéra Comique, London, performing in Messrs. Gilbert and Sullivan's successful comic operas. Mr.

Clifton was in the original cast of 'H.M.S. Pinafore,' by the same author and composer, produced at that theatre Saturday, May 25, 1878, as *Bill Bobstay* (boatswain's mate). He is the author of 'A Theory of Harmony,' published by Boosey and Co., and has composed the incidental music for several works favourably noticed by the London press.

COBB, RICHARD. *See* TEMPLE, RICHARD.

*COGHLAN, CHARLES F. A leading actor of considerable merit in modern comedy, whose most noteworthy appearances on the London stage are associated with the period of his engagements at the Prince of Wales's Theatre, 1870–6. Previous to the year first named he had acted in London, with more or less success, at the Olympic, St. James's, Lyceum, and Holborn Theatres. In 1870, on Saturday, April 23, at the Prince of Wales's Theatre, first performance of 'M.P.' (T. W. Robertson), Mr. Coghlan acted the part of *Chudleigh Dunscombe.* The same year, November 26, at the same theatre, he played, in a revival of 'Ours,' *Angus McAlister,* the part originally taken by Mr. Bancroft; and in the following year, in a revival of ' Caste,' *George D'Alroy,* his predecessors in this character being Mr. F. Younge and Mr. Montague, both deceased. In May 1872, in a revival of ' Money,' and during the "run" of the play at the Prince of Wales's Theatre, he sustained the part of *Alfred Evelyn,* and "succeeded well in giving life to that very difficult character. To speak naturally some of the stilted speeches put into *Evelyn's* mouth is beyond the powers of mortal man, and it is most creditable to Mr. Coghlan's art that the discursive philosophy is rarely tedious, and sometimes even interesting." In April 1874, in a revival at the same theatre of ' The School for Scandal,' Mr. Coghlan performed the part of *Charles Surface,* as to which the *Daily News* (April 6, 1874) remarked :— " Mr. Coghlan's *Charles* comes perhaps nearest of all the male parts to the ideal of the character. His high spirits and frank *insouciance* had a genuine tone about them, heightened, however— as they ought to be—by that dramatic colouring in which some of the minor characters were sadly wanting. A few performances before real audiences will doubtless add a completeness to the representation, which even the careful rehearsals bestowed on all pieces brought out at this theatre are sometimes powerless to give." " Of Mr. Coghlan's *Charles Surface* there cannot be two opinions. He is easy, elegant, buoyant, gentleman-like, without any of the coarseness which frequently disfigures him ; and his smallest touches indicate a profound conception accompanied by facility of execution. Had ' The School for Scandal ' been performed in the old instead of the new fashion, there is no doubt that Mr. Coghlan would still have shown his pre-eminence." (*Times,* April 9, 1874.) In November of the same year, first performance at the Prince of Wales's of an "original dramatic contrast," written by W. S. Gilbert, entitled ' Sweethearts,' Mr. Coghlan performed the part of *Harry Spreadbrow,* Mrs. Bancroft as Jenny Northcote. In April

1875, at the same theatre, he acted the part of *Shylock* in a revival of 'The Merchant of Venice,' which was a failure, though placed on the stage in the most sumptuous manner. "With the success of the revival Mr. Coghlan's *Shylock* will have little or nothing to do. It is a failure, not through lack of intelligence, but in consequence of the application of an unsound theory. In a house where Mr. Robertson's name so long predominated, and where the grand object has been an imitation of the manners of modern life, Mr. Coghlan has evidently formed the opinion that the style of acting suitable to Robertsonian comedy would equally fit the stormiest creations of the Elizabethan era. He deliberately avoided not only traditional points, but all point whatever, and when emphasis was naturally suggested it seemed that he purposely shunned it. Sometimes one was inclined to hope that, like Signor Salvini, he was holding his forces in reserve, and would break out at an unexpected moment, but the moment never came. The suppressed rage at *Shylock's* final exit showed that the actor perfectly understood the meaning of the situation, but his theory forbade him to give it effect. And in the soft, but not less crushing embraces of the same theory were nearly all the performers held, exciting less mirth, less grief, less terror, than could be produced by persons of far inferior attainments acting under ordinary circumstances." (*Times*, April 19, 1875.) The same year, in August, at the Princess's Theatre, Mr. Coghlan sustained the part of *Claude Melnotte* to Miss Ellen Terry's Pauline in 'The Lady of Lyons.' This impersonation calls for no special comment. It was not very successful. Mr. Coghlan left for the United States in the year following, and after a career there of unusual success returned to London in July 1879. He has some reputation as a dramatist, having written 'Lady Flora' and 'Brothers,' and a clever little version of 'La Partie de Piquet,' entitled 'A Quiet Rubber,' all produced at the Court Theatre under Mr. Hare's management in 1875–6. Mr. Coghlan also completed and revised for the stage Lord Lytton's play 'The House of Darnley,' first performed at the same theatre.

*COGHLAN, ROSE, first attracted notice on the London stage by her excellent acting of the part of *Lady Marsden* in Messrs. Palgrave Simpson and Herman Merivale's three-act drama 'All for Her,' first performed at the Mirror (Holborn) Theatre, Monday, October 18, 1875. "'All for Her' was received on the first night with acclamations of more than ordinary warmth, and the authors were enthusiastically summoned to appear before the curtain. Mr. Merivale was not present, but Mr. Palgrave Simpson responded to the call, and in the course of a few remarks said that but for the excellence of the acting the success of the piece would not have been so great. In this he only rendered justice to Miss Coghlan and Mr. Clayton, the full measure of whose deserts, it may be confidently asserted, have never been known until now. Miss Coghlan's *Lady Marsden* is remarkable for vigour of conception, forcible expression of totally distinct feelings, earnestness of purpose, and natural dignity of demeanour. Her treatment of the scene with Hugh in the second act is characterized by much delicacy, and it was difficult to believe that the actress who had appeared to advantage in the light-comedy scene with Colonel Damer could display such power as is witnessed when, at the end of the second act, she hears that Hugh has been playing a part in order to capture her lover. Her pathos and tenderness in the last act, too, created a perceptible effect upon the audience." (*Times*, ˙October 22, 1875.) Since the last-mentioned year Miss Rose Coghlan has been engaged on the American stage.

COLLETTE, CHARLES, was born in London, July 29, 1842. He was educated for the Army, and held a commission for seven years in the 3rd (Prince of Wales's) Dragoon Guards. Having retired from the service in 1866, two years afterwards (November 1868) he entered the dramatic profession, and made his first appearance in London the same year at the Prince of Wales's Theatre in Edmund Yates's comedy 'Tame Cats.' Among important impersonations sustained by Mr. Collette, subsequently, at that theatre, the following, in the "revivals" and productions of the several plays to which each character relates, are deserving of being mentioned, viz. *Colonel Berners, Sir Oliver Surface, Old Sowerberry, Chillichutney, O'Sullivan* (in 'Society'), *Sir John Vesey,* and *Serjeant Jones* (in 'Ours'). As *Sir Patrick Lundie,* in a revival of Mr. Wilkie Collins's play of 'Man and Wife,' Mr. Collette has also attracted favourable notice. In addition to the Prince of Wales's, this actor has appeared at the following London theatres in leading parts, viz. at Drury Lane, Strand, Gaiety, Olympic, Vaudeville, Alhambra, Surrey, Royal Park, Princess's, Opéra Comique, and at the principal theatres in the provinces. He has attracted favourable notice for his acting as *Sir Fretful Plagiary* and *Puff* in 'The Critic'; *Old Tom* in 'After Dark'; *Micawber* in 'Little Em'ly'; *Felix Featherstone* in 'The Snowball'; and *Professor Lobelia* in 'Love Wins.' Mr. Collette is the author of a farce entitled ' Cryptoconchoidsyphonostomata,' the principal character in which (*Plantagenet Smith*) is a stage-creation of his, and, it may be added, one in which he has secured well-merited popularity.

COMPTON, EDWARD, son of the well-known comedian, the late Henry Compton, of the Theatre Royal, Haymarket, and brother of the under-mentioned Katherine Compton, was born in London. He first appeared on the stage at the New Theatre Royal, Bristol, September 22, 1873, in a subordinate part (*Long Ned*) in a play entitled 'Old London,' and remained six months at that theatre. In April 1874 he went on tour in Mr. Francis Fairlie's company, "ostensibly for 'walking gentlemen,' but playing such mixed 'business' as *Richard Hare* and *Earl Mountsevern* ('East Lynne'), *Dr. Brown* ('Progress'), *Crabtree* and *Careless* ('School for Scandal')." At the Bristol Theatre Royal, on the occasion of a benefit performance, he appeared in the part of *Malvolio* ('Twelfth Night'), Mr. Henry Compton, Mr. Chute, and Mrs. Kendal being in the cast. After playing many leading parts in the legitimate drama at Blackpool, Newcastle-on-Tyne, and elsewhere, going through what the subject of this record in a letter describes as "awful work," but which, doubtless, represents only the common experience of all actors at the outset of their career, Mr. Compton entered upon a long engagement with Mr. Glover at Glasgow and Kilmarnock. At these places he became extremely popular, and largely increased his knowledge of stage art by the opportunities which were presented him of supporting well-known players in their "starring" engagements. On March 6, 1876, Mr. Compton "opened" at the Prince of Wales's Theatre, Liverpool; and in the following September at Theatre Royal, Birmingham, as "leading gentleman." On the occasion of a Benefit to Mr. Henry Compton at Drury Lane Theatre, March 1, 1877—in all respects one of the most remarkable ever tendered to an actor*—Mr. Edward Compton played the character of *Evelyn* in the first act of Lord Lytton's 'Money.' Following the termination of the season at Birmingham he entered upon a long engagement with Mr. H. J. Byron to play in 'Cyril's Success' (*Cyril*) and other of his plays. On October 22, 1877, at Prince's Theatre, Manchester, he appeared for twelve nights in support of Miss Wallis in Shakespearian parts, *Romeo, Orlando,* &c., with considerable success, after which he went on tour with the same lady, and appeared in the following among other characters, viz. *Romeo, Benedick, Charles Surface, Claude Melnotte, St. Lo, Master Wildrake,* and *Ingomar.* In the presentation of these Mr. Compton was equally successful. September 28, 1878, in a revival of the 'Winter's Tale' at Drury Lane Theatre, he enacted the part of *Florizel.* In other Shakespearian revivals that followed at the same theatre in the same year Mr. Compton appeared as *Cassio* ('Othello'), *Malcolm* ('Macbeth'), *Leonatus* ('Cymbeline'), *Romeo* ('Romeo and Juliet'), &c. In the summer season 1879 Mr. Compton joined the company of the Theatre Royal, Adelphi, where he appeared as *Sir Benjamin Backbite* in a revival of 'The School for Scandal.' He is the author of a modern comedy in three acts, entitled 'A Strange Relation,' first performed at the Prince of Wales's Theatre, Liverpool, May 22, 1876, and of a comedietta in one act, entitled 'A Mutual Separation,' produced at the Princess's Theatre, Edinburgh, December 7, 1877, the leading parts being played by the author and Miss Wallis. In conjunction with his brother he published in May 1879 a biography of the late Mr. Henry Compton.

---

* The Treasurer of the Committee entrusted with the general arrangements of the performances stated from the stage on the day of the Benefit that no less a sum than 4250*l*. had been realized in London and Manchester. This amount was considerably increased afterwards by private subscriptions. Hardly a name of note on the English stage was absent from the programme of the occasion.

COMPTON, KATHERINE MACKENZIE (KATHERINE MAC-KENZIE CRITCHETT), sister of the afore-named, and daughter of the well-known comedian, the late Henry Compton, was born in London. She made her first appearance on any stage October 1874, at the New Theatre Royal, Bristol, as *Maria*, in 'The School for Scandal.' Miss Compton remained at Bristol playing a round of characters until April 1875, and in the following month accepted an engagement in Mr. Wybert Reeve's travelling company of comedians. October 18, 1875, under Mr. Sefton Parry's management, at the Theatre Royal, Hull, she played the *Dauphin* ('Louis XI.'), Mr. Charles Dillon in the title *rôle;* and in July of the same year, at the Theatre Royal, Manchester, sustained the character of *Emily Worthington* in a revival of the comedy of 'The Poor Gentleman,' for her father's benefit. Miss Compton made her first appearance on the London stage at the Gaiety Theatre, May 2, 1877, as *Julia* ('The Rivals'), on the occasion of a benefit performance for Mrs. Chippendale. During the same year she played at the Globe and Aquarium Theatres : at the last-named, the character of *Maria* ('The School for Scandal') for a run of six weeks ; and on April 20, 1878, at the St. James's Theatre, created the part of *Lucy Merivale*, in the drama of 'Such is the Law' (Taylor and Meritt), being thoroughly successful. The part was played by Miss Compton until the termination of the season.

CONQUEST, GEORGE (the Elder), was born in London, and first appeared on the stage at the Grecian Theatre in pantomime "about twenty-five years ago." Has attracted notice by his clever acrobatic performances, having at various times personated with equal success "an octopus, a crab, a bat, a porcupine," and last, not least, "a tree," and being possessed of the most marvellous facilities for changing "instantaneously from a dwarf to a full-grown man, &c." From the foregoing it will be at once admitted that Mr. Conquest's abilities as a pantomimist are of no mean order ; and to judge from contemporary journals his remarkable illustrations of animal and still life have been greatly relished by the playgoing public.

CONQUEST, GEORGE (the Younger), son of the above-named, first appeared on the stage at the age of eight years in the pantomime of 'Robinson Crusoe,' in which he sustained the part of "The Dog" with admirable ability. Mr. Conquest has acted in various pantomimes with his father, and generally "in acrobatic parts," and, like him, has attained a considerable reputation by his skilful performances in that direction.

*****CONWAY, H. B.** (a *nom de théâtre;* H. B. COULSON), was born in 1850, and educated at Rossall School and the University of Berlin. He made his first appearance on the stage at the Olympic Theatre in November 1872 in the part of *Bernard*, in Dubourg's play 'Without Love.' Subsequently he sustained the part of *David Copperfield* in a revival of 'Little Em'ly.' In 1873,

September 27, in a revival of 'Richelieu' at the Lyceum Theatre, Mr. Conway acted the part of *François*. At the same theatre, during subsequent seasons, he appeared in the following parts, viz. *Christian*, in 'The Bells' (Leopold Lewis); *Lord Moray*, in 'Charles the First' (Wills); *Comte de Flamarens*, in 'Philip' (Hamilton Aïdé); and as *Osric*, during the long "run" of 'Hamlet.' In August 1875 he joined the company of the Haymarket Theatre, and "opened" there as *Dick Dowlas*, in a version of the younger Colman's comedy 'The Heir-at-Law.' On Monday, January 17, 1876, he sustained the part of *Romeo*, in a revival of Shakespeare's tragedy at the same theatre, a performance which, in the opinion of the *Athenæum* (January 22, 1876), might "be considered the first effort in imaginative art of a young actor who has shown, hitherto, few qualifications beyond youth and good looks, with a moderation of style which, if not ascribable to timidity, is a sign of intelligence. As such it was a creditable impersonation. Mr. Conway's bearing is gallant, his speech is not wanting in passion, and his general rendering, except in the scene in the Friar's cell—one of the most difficult in the drama—was effective." At the Haymarket Theatre Mr. Conway has at various times acted the following parts:—*Orlando*, in 'As You Like It'; *Lucio*, in 'Measure for Measure'; *Lord Tinsel*, in 'The Hunchback'; *Sebastian*, in 'Twelfth Night,' in addition to various characters in less important pieces. In 1876 he joined the company of the Royal Court Theatre, and, on November 2, played there the part of *Fred Meredith* in a piece entitled 'The Brothers.' His careful acting of this character received favourable notice. In August 1878 Mr. Conway joined the company of the Prince of Wales's Theatre for "juvenile lead." He has since that date appeared there as *Julian Beauclerc* in 'Diplomacy'; and on Saturday, May 31, 1879, in a revival of Mr. Buckstone's comic drama 'Good for Nothing,' Mr. Conway played the part of *Charlie*, and in Palgrave Simpson's farce 'Heads or Tails,' *Harold Dyecaster*.

*COOPER, F., son of the under-mentioned Thomas Cooper, is a member of the Lyceum company, and has appeared in subordinate parts in the series of dramas and tragedies brought out under Mr. Henry Irving's management during 1879.

*COOPER, HARWOOD, son of Mr. Fox Cooper, made his first appearance on the London boards at the City of London Theatre, May 5, 1845. He was at the Olympic Theatre for a long period, when Mr. Robson was playing there with Mr. Alfred Wigan as manager. Mr. Cooper has generally appeared in small character parts, in the rendering of which he has shown himself a competent actor. He has been for some years connected with the Adelphi Theatre.

COOPER, THOMAS CLIFFORD, was born in London, and is the son of a pianoforte manufacturer, who, being killed by the overturning of a stage coach, left a large family unprovided for.

Mr. T. C. Cooper, having a predilection in that direction, thereupon turned his attention to the stage for a means of livelihood, and joined a dramatic club of which the late Leigh Murray, W. H. Eburne, J. Kinloch, and others were some time members. Afterwards he entered the dramatic profession proper, and passing through "the usual struggles and vicissitudes incidental to a country actor's life," was engaged by Mrs. Warner at the Marylebone Theatre, of which that lady had the management during 1847–8. Mrs. Warner, it may be remarked, was one of the most distinguished and respected of our actresses, who for years maintained her family by her exertions in the highest departments of dramatic art. Professor Henry Morley, in his *Journal of a London Playgoer*, relates a very touching incident, showing the esteem in which Mrs. Warner was held by those who knew her and had the privilege of witnessing her admirable acting some thirty years ago. When Mrs. Warner relinquished the management of the little theatre off the Edgware Road, Mr. Cooper became a member of the company of her successor, Mr. Watts, and subsequently was engaged by Madame Vestris and Charles Mathews when they leased the Lyceum Theatre in 1851. For some years Mr. Cooper undertook the responsibilities of a provincial manager, and in such capacity introduced Italian opera (and one of its most admirable exponents, Mdlle. Piccolomini) to the notice of the playgoers of Hull and other large towns in the north of England. He was for twelve years a member of the stock company of the Theatre Royal, Manchester, and " in the off season conducted the little theatre at Oxford." At Manchester Mr. Cooper became very popular. Among original parts sustained by him in recent years the following are entitled to notice, viz. *Colonel Challice*, in a play entitled ' Alone '; *Colonel O'Fipp*, in ' Tom Cobb,' a *rôle* played by him with much care and humour; *Mortiboy*, in ' Ready-Money Mortiboy '; *Cobham Brown*, in ' Tottles,' &c. Mr. Cooper has been recently engaged at the Lyceum Theatre under Mr. Irving's management, and has appeared during the season of 1879 as *Polonius*, in ' Hamlet '; *Parson Meadows*, in ' Eugene Aram '; *Joseph*, in ' Richelieu,' &c.

CORNOCK, J. R. *See* CRAUFORD, J. R.

COULSON, H. B. *See* CONWAY, H. B.

COVENEY, HARRIET (Mrs. JECKS), was born in London, and is the youngest of thirteen children, all of whom have appeared on the stage; Miss Coveney's parents having been for many years connected with the Theatre Royal, Haymarket. She made her first appearance on the stage, at the age of seven, at the Adelphi Theatre, Edinburgh, as *Zoe*, in 'The Pet of the Petticoats'; and continued to play children's parts there and at other theatres in Scotland for some time, making a decided success at the Theatre Royal, Glasgow, in the character of *Oliver Twist*. She became a very proficient dancer under the instruction of Leclercq. Miss Coveney made her *début* on the London stage at the Victoria

Theatre, where she gained considerable reputation as a spirited character dancer, vocalist, and performer of children's parts. After playing in the provinces, she " opened " at the Adelphi Theatre on " Boxing Night " (Christmas), 1849, as *Princess Agatha*, in the burlesque of ' Frankenstein,' by the Brothers Brough; and in 1850–51–52, and later, appeared at the Surrey and at Drury Lane Theatres in pantomime, in which Miss Harriet Coveney has always excelled. Among her impersonations of more recent years, the following are entitled to mention as having secured special recognition for their artistic excellence, viz. *Mother Shipton*, in E. L. Blanchard's pantomime ' The Dragon of Wantley,' performed at Drury Lane Theatre, 1870–1 ; *Polly Mittens*, in ' The Water Witches,' played at the Globe Theatre, May 1871 ; the page *Adolphe*, in ' Falsacappa,' an English version of Offenbach's ' Les Brigands'; the title *rôle* in R. H. Edgar's extravaganza of ' Crichton,' produced at the Charing Cross Theatre in August 1871 ; *Sunbeam*, in E. L. Blanchard's ' Legend of Spring ; or, the Victory of the Sunbeam,' performed at the Crystal Palace, Sydenham, Easter, 1872.

In the autumn of 1872, at the Opéra Comique, Miss Harriet Coveney played the part of the *Marquise* in ' L'Œil Crève.' " Miss Harriet Coveney's part of the mysterious *Marchioness* is altogether dramatic, or perhaps we ought to say melodramatic. The wonderful thing about it is the manner in which it is played, the performance being, in its way, as good as Rachel's Phèdre or Ristori's Medea—as good, that is to say, as can be imagined. Any sort of liberty is, by convention, allowed to a burlesque actress, but the mysterious *Marchioness* never steps beyond the strictest limits of her part, which she renders with a burlesque-tragic feeling almost poetical from its intensity." (*Pall Mall Gazette*, October 24, 1872.) Miss Coveney is an artist of considerable versatility. For a number of years she has been almost indispensable at Drury Lane in the Christmas pantomime. She has been recently acting the part of *Flibbertigibbet* in a revival of Andrew Halliday's drama ' Amy Robsart,' at the Adelphi Theatre, London.

CRABBE, MRS. *See* HERBERT, LOUISA.

CRAUFORD, J. R. (a *nom de théâtre;* CORNOCK), first appeared on the stage at the Princess's Theatre, Edinburgh, and played through the "stock" season of 1873–4. Various country engagements followed. He made his *début* in London at the Mirror Theatre, Holborn, when it was under the management of Mr. Horace Wigan, and subsequently appeared at St. James's, Princess's, Gaiety, Olympic, and Globe Theatres. For the " stock " season of 1866–7 he played at the Corinthian Theatre, Calcutta. He has been on several provincial tours with theatrical " stars " ; and in 1879 was engaged to support Mr. E. A. Sothern. Mr. Crauford is the author of some successful farces.

CRAUFORD, MRS. J. R. *See* INGRAM, ALICE.

CRAVEN, HENRY T., dramatist and actor, was born in London, February 26, 1821, and entered the dramatic profession in 1840, making his *début* on the London stage in 1850 at Drury Lane Theatre, on which occasion he played *Orlando* in a revival of 'As You Like It,' Mrs. Nesbitt sustaining the part of Rosalind. The year following he appeared at the Strand Theatre in an operetta which attained some success, and of which he was the author, entitled 'The Village Nightingale.' In 1854 Mr. Craven went to Australia, where he remained until 1859. In the year following he appeared at the St. James's Theatre in a little one-act comic drama, 'A Border Marriage,' first performed at the Adelphi Theatre. "The piece in itself is trifling, and it secures the suffrages of the public by the spirit with which it is acted ; and certainly on its revival the authors have no ground of complaint against the executants, for every one engaged in the piece enters *con amore* into his or her part, and the result is that 'A Border Marriage' amuses the audience. The plot of the piece simply turns upon a widow being entrapped into a marriage with one of six needy cavaliers, who, after the battle of Worcester, find themselves in the castle of one of their number without a maravedi in their pockets ; and the chief interest is gained by the after-marriage wooings of the hero and heroine, which pass through changes varying from stormy to fair, and terminate, finally, at 'set fair.' . . . Mr. Craven, as the hero, embodies the character with great vivacity; he is the genial cavalier with his jolly companions, and alternately a playful and an impassioned lover when in the presence of his wife. . . . Judging from the manner in which the piece was received last night, 'A Border Marriage' seems likely to keep its place on the bills of the St. James's Theatre for some time to come." (*Standard,* February 1, 1860.)

Mr. Craven had decided upon retiring from the stage in this year; but the death of Mr. Robson, for whom he had prepared the character of 'Milky White,' induced him later to reconsider his decision. Already he had won reputation as the author of three plays which had attained considerable popularity :—' The Post Boy,' produced at the Strand Theatre, October 31, 1860; 'The Chimney Corner,' first performed at the Olympic, February 21, 1861 ; and 'Miriam's Crime,' first performed at the Strand Theatre, October 9, 1863. In 1864, on Wednesday, September 28, a new two-act play from his pen, entitled 'Milky White,' was produced at the Strand, in which Mr. Craven himself undertook the *rôle* that he had intended for Mr. Robson. The piece obtained a decided and deserved success. "The author," remarked the *Daily Telegraph* (September 29, 1864), "has not only to be congratulated on the literary power and constructive skill with which he has worked out an exceedingly original idea, but he has also to be complimented on the cleverness with which he has embodied the effective character who is the hero of the story so happily imagined. Already well known as a dramatist who has furnished the stage, in 'The Chimney Corner' and 'The Post Boy,' with two excellent specimens of this class of composition, his histrionic achievements have, in this country at least, scarcely been considered as prominently associated with his name. As an actor as well as an author Mr. Craven will henceforth find himself well remembered by the public. It would be difficult to name any comedian who could have more thoroughly realized the part. . . . The ingenuity with which the piece is constructed can only be faintly suggested by an outline of the story; but equally touching the sympathies and rousing the mirth of the audience, it secures their interest and amusement to the very last. The writing abounds in quaint turns of expression, some of them so daringly tipped with verbal flippancies that the serious situations are occasionally endangered by their utterance. . . . Mr. Craven has rendered 'Milky White' one of the most original and effective stage portraitures of real life which has been ever included in the theatrical gallery."

This play had a "run," not only in London, but in the provinces, and was revived at the Strand Theatre, with Mr. Craven in his original character, in the following year. On April 17, 1865, he produced at the Strand a new drama entitled 'One Tree Hill,' in which he sustained the part of *Jack Salt*. On Monday, June 4, 1866, Mr. Henderson, of the Prince of Wales's Theatre, Liverpool, tested the merits of a five-act comedy called 'The Needful,' afterwards transferred to the St. James's, London; the author, Mr. H. T. Craven, in both instances playing the character of *Abraham Store*. On October 17, 1866, Mr. Craven produced at the Royalty Theatre a new play entitled 'Meg's Diversion,' in which he appeared as *Jasper*. 'Philomel,' a romantic drama by him, was first represented at the Globe Theatre, February 10, 1870, and 'Barwise's Book' (likewise written by Mr. Craven), at the Haymarket, April 20, 1870. On Monday, November 20, 1871, at the Court Theatre, he produced 'Coals of Fire,' in which he sustained the character of *Job Ricketts*. His latest dramatic production was an historical play called 'Too True!' at the Duke's Theatre, January 22, 1876. Mr. Craven is a genuine humorist, and contrives to blend the pathetic and comic sides of human nature in a manner that places him in the front rank of living actors. Since Mr. Robson, whose style Mr. Craven recalls, no English actor has equalled him in presenting beneath a droll exterior underlying touches of subtle pathos. He is the author of a novel entitled 'Old Time,' published in 1876.

CRESWICK, WILLIAM, was born in 1813, and made his first appearance on the London stage in 1835 at the Queen's Theatre (now the Prince of Wales's), at that date under Mrs. Nesbitt's management. He played the part of *Horace Meredith* in a piece of Douglas Jerrold's called 'The Schoolfellows.' In 1836 there was a so-called theatre in Magdalen Street, Oxford, open when there were none but townfolk to go to it. In this unpretending building Mr. Creswick and Mr. H. Marston were accustomed at times to perform *Macbeth* and *Banquo* together, and those who wished to see the performance from the boxes were directed to go through "the door adjoining Mr. R. Stevens's, Fruiterer's, No. 9, Magdalen

Street." Thus early did Mr. Creswick essay Shakespearian character, in the presentation of which he became, in a few years, one of the most proficient of English actors. After playing in Mr. Downe's company on the York, Leeds, and Hull "Circuit," he visited the United States and Canada, where he remained about three years. On his return to England he undertook the "leading business" successively at Newcastle-on-Tyne, Liverpool, and Birmingham. He first appeared on the London stage, in Shakespearian drama, July 25, 1846, at Sadler's Wells Theatre, during the third season of Mr. S. Phelps's management, in the part of *Hotspur*, Shakespeare's 'Henry IV.' "The appearance of this gentleman (Mr. Creswick) on the London stage had excited considerable interest in the theatrical profession; and the expectations formed of him have not been disappointed. He seized the chivalric and poetic in the character with an enthusiastic readiness full of promise. With his qualifications there can be little doubt that Mr. Creswick will become a highly popular actor; and to the theatre where he has now made his *début* he is unquestionably an important acquisition." (*Athenæum*, August 1, 1846.) On the second occasion of Mr. Creswick's appearance at the same theatre he sustained the character of *Master Walter* in 'The Hunchback.' In 1847, Monday, April 26, at the Princess's Theatre, he performed the same part with remarkable success, on the night of Mrs. Butler's (Fanny Kemble) reappearance on the London stage after her long absence in America. At the same theatre, during the following month, he performed the part of *St. Pierre*, in Sheridan Knowles's then popular play 'A Tale of Mantua.' In July of the same year Mr. Creswick accepted a three years' engagement at the Haymarket Theatre, under Mr. Benjamin Webster's management, and "opened" the season by playing *Claude Melnotte* (with Miss Helen Faucit) in 'The Lady of Lyons,' and subsequently *Trueworth* in 'The Love Chase.' October 4, 1847, first performance of Westland Marston's drama 'The Heart of the World,' at the Haymarket, Mr. Creswick sustained the character of *Vivian Temple*, Miss Helen Faucit acting the part of *Florence Delmar*. The following year, at the same theatre, Monday, October 23, in a revival of 'The Patrician's Daughter' (Westland Marston), he played the part of *Mordaunt*. Thursday, December 14, 1848, at the Princess's Theatre, Mr. Creswick played *Proteus*, in a revival of 'The Two Gentlemen of Verona'; and subsequently *The Ghost* in 'Hamlet,' and *Cassio*, and other important characters in the various Shakespearian revivals produced during the year 1848 by Mr. Charles Kean at that theatre. In 1849 Mr. Creswick entered upon the management of the Surrey Theatre in conjunction with Mr. R. Shepherd, and on the opening night of his first season, Monday, September 17, sustained the character of *Alasco*, in Sheridan Knowles's 'Rose of Arragon.' On Monday, September 24 of the same year, he played *Virginius* in the drama of that title, followed by *The Stranger*, and justified his "character of a meritorious and well-informed actor." In the same year, in October, at the Surrey Theatre, he placed 'Richelieu' upon the stage, restoring to that drama "those poetic passages that, from its first presentation to its last, had always been omitted . . . . the result to be recorded is that these restorations are among the passages most applauded—that the poet's sympathies had all along been right, and the actor's conventional prejudices wrong." Mr. Creswick's *Richelieu* is one of the best of his assumptions. It has many fine points, and is marked throughout by steady execution and clear characterization.

On Monday, October 12, 1849, Mr. Creswick played *Hamlet* with great success. In the following year, at the Surrey Theatre, in a new play entitled 'Old Love and New Fortune' (H. F. Chorley), performed for the first time February 18, he sustained the part of *La Roque*. Among noteworthy plays produced by Mr. Creswick during his management, and in which he played a leading part, the following are entitled to mention, viz. a dramatization of 'David Copperfield,' first performed Wednesday, November 13, 1850; 'The Woman of Colour; or, Slavery in Freedom,' first performed in November 1853; 'Dred' (F. Phillips), produced in October 1856; 'Cromwell,' a tragedy by the same author, based on Victor Hugo's play of that title, first performed in February 1859; 'The Changed Heart,' founded on a French drama, 'Le Comtesse de Noailles,' first performed in January 1860; a revival of the tragedy of 'Damon and Pythias,' produced February 7, 1860 (Mr. Creswick in the first-named character); a dramatic version of George Eliot's 'Adam Bede,' first performed February 28, 1862, Mr. Creswick playing the title *rôle;* and a drama in four acts, entitled 'The Four Stages of Life,' first performed in April of the same year. In September 1862 Mr. Creswick retired from the management of the Surrey Theatre in favour of Mr. Shepherd, and for a time devoted himself to "starring" in London and the provinces. In this way he became one of the established favourites of the Standard Theatre in London, always drawing a full house whenever his name was announced on the bills. On Thursday, November 6, 1862, on the occasion of a farewell performance of Mr. S. Phelps, "previous to his retirement from the management of Sadler's Wells Theatre," Mr. Creswick played *Cassius* to the *Brutus* of that accomplished player. During the Falconer-Chatterton management of Drury Lane, on September 24, 1864, Mr. Creswick appeared as *Hotspur* in a revival of 'Henry the Fourth' at that theatre; and subsequently, during the same engagement, as *Othello, Iago, Macbeth, Macduff,* and *Iachimo.* In 1865 he fulfilled a successful "star" engagement at the City of London Theatre; and in the following year, in conjunction with Mr. Shepherd, once more entered upon the management of the Surrey. On the opening night, September 8, 1866, was produced "the T. P. Cooke's Prize Drama," by Mr. Slous, entitled 'True to the Core,' in which Mr. Creswick "created" the part of *Martin Truegold.* This drama was a great success. The year following it was performed with the original cast at the Princess's Theatre. Since 1868 Mr. Creswick has fulfilled various engagements, and appeared in many "revivals" of Shakespeare's plays, and of the legitimate and poetic drama in London and the provinces. In 1871 he made his second visit to the United States, making his first appearance in the part of *Joe*, in 'Nobody's Child'; and afterwards, in conjunction with Charlotte Cushman and Edwin Booth, acted in 'Henry VIII.' and 'Julius Cæsar,' and several other standard plays. In May 1877 he left England for Australia, and opened at Melbourne as *Virginius* in the following August. Since then he has played at Sydney, Adelaide, Hobart Town, &c.

CRITCHETT, KATHERINE MACKENZIE. *See* COMPTON, KATHERINE MACKENZIE.

CRITCHETT, RICHARD CLAUDE. *See* CARTON, RICHARD CLAUDE.

CROWE, MRS. *See* BATEMAN, KATE JOSEPHINE.

DALLAS, MRS. E. S. *See* GLYN, ISABEL.

DE FIVAS, SIDNEY. *See* GLOVER, AUGUSTUS.

DIETZ, LINDA, was born in New York, and made her first appearance on the stage at the old Fifth Avenue Theatre in 1870, as *Georgette* in 'Fernande.' Her first appearance in England was at the Haymarket Theatre, August 30, 1873, in the parts of *Caroline Dormer* in 'The Heir-at-Law,' and *Mrs. Featherley* in 'The Widow Hunt,' with Mr. J. S. Clarke in the principal part. She appeared at the Haymarket the following season, and again at the Holborn Theatre, in 1874, with Mr. Clarke. Subsequently she played a short engagement at the Globe Theatre under the management of Mr. H. J. Montague. She then made a tour of the provinces as leading lady with Mr. E. A. Sothern, and travelled with him for a year in America. Miss Dietz gained her first theatrical success at the Union Square Theatre, New York, in the part of *Valentine* in 'A Celebrated Case,' and as *Marcelle* in 'Mother and Son,' an adaptation of 'Les Bourgeois de Pont-Arcy,' which part she played at the Prince of Wales's Theatre, September 27, 1879, in a version of the same play entitled 'Duty.' Previous to appearing at the Prince of Wales's Theatre Miss Dietz had been supporting Mr. Clarke at the Haymarket in his farewell performances of 'The Heir-at-Law' and 'The Widow Hunt.'

DILLON, CHARLES, was born at Diss, Suffolk, in 1819. Prior to his appearance on the metropolitan stage he had made a considerable reputation as an actor in the legitimate drama in Dublin, Manchester, Liverpool, and Edinburgh. His first appearance on the London stage took place Monday, April 21, 1856, at Sadler's Wells Theatre, in the part of *Belphegor*, in the drama of that title. The part had already been made familiar to one class of playgoers by the acting of Lemaître, and to another by a long run of the play at the Adelphi. The *Athenæum* (April 26, 1856), noticing the performance, remarked as follows :—"Mr. Dillon has a good stage figure, of the middle height, with an expressive countenance and a flexible voice, which enables him to deliver familiar dialogues without effort. He is no declaimer, but speaks naturally, and even in phrases of the highest passion is never noisy, substituting intention for stormy vehemence. In these particulars he presents new points, and differs from nearly all the English artists who have obtained reputation. His power over the feelings is extraordinary. In the first act of the present play he gradually melted his audience from scene to scene, and long ere the fall of the curtain every eye was moist with sympathetic tears."

Said the *Times* (April 22nd of the same year) : "Mr. Charles Dillon gives such evidence of the true material, and the impression he made was of such a genuine kind, that even if his temperament is not remarkably sanguine, he has a right to expect that his *début* —albeit taking place in remote Pentonville—will become a topic of conversation amongst all whose discourse turns upon the merits of plays and players."

In September of the same year Mr. Dillon entered upon the management of the Lyceum Theatre, and "opened" with a revival of 'Belphegor' (in which he played the title *rôle*), and a burlesque by William Brough, entitled 'Perdita; or, the Royal Milkmaid,' in which Mr. J. L. Toole played *Autolycus*, Miss Marie Wilton *Perdita*, Miss Woolgar *Florizel*, and Mr. William Brough *Polyxenes*. Concerning the first-named performance the following criticism appeared:—"Mr. Dillon's *Belphegor* is entitled to the praise of distinct originality; indeed, it is so strongly impressed by the actor's individuality that we cannot fancy him playing any other part in any other manner. It is obvious, however, that he has no very accurate conception of the character, from the fact that he presents it throughout in a uniform reading, instead of emphatically marking the different phases through which it passes. There are great moral and physical changes wrought in *Belphegor;* but they demand a versatility of powers beyond the reach of Mr. Dillon. His showman of the first act, and his chevalier of the last, are distinguishable from each other by little more than their costume. We lack in the one the *abandon*, freedom, and reckless animal spirits which the author bestowed upon him to make his subsequent wretchedness the more striking; and, in the other, the finesse and by-play which constitute the dramatic interest of the situation. It is in the middle distance of the picture, so to speak, that Mr. Dillon is most successful. The whole of that scene where *Belphegor* is deserted by his wife was finely acted. Profoundly touching, without the least violence or excess, it approached more closely to a reality than any passage of domestic pathos we remember on the stage since the days of Miss Kelly, with whom what may be called the literal school of acting went out. Excellent, too, and no less meritorious in parts, although not so true or effective as a whole, was the haggard exhibition of the conjurer and his son in the gardens, before the fine gentlemen of the *ancien régime*. Mr. Dillon, greatly to his credit, never gives way to the melodramatic temptations of a part abounding in sudden transitions of moods and passions. He preserves, in the depths of his wrongs and sorrows, a gentleness as rare as it is piteous. This is a conspicuous virtue; but virtues have their extremes, which are as much to be avoided as their opposites. The performance requires relief; it is too quiet, in spite of many isolated passages of considerable merit, and it leaves a final impression of want of power." (*Saturday Review*, September 27, 1856.)

On Thursday, October 16, 1856, at the same theatre, Mr. Charles Dillon sustained the character of *D'Artagnan*, first performance of 'The Three Musketeers,' by Messrs. C. Dillon, C. Rice, and the late Aug. Harris, adapted from M. Dumas' novel 'Les Trois Mousquetaires.' The production of the piece proved of the highest

importance to the histrionic reputation of Mr. Dillon. His great
success in *Belphegor*, which had remained in the Lyceum bills ever
since the opening of the theatre, had so completely identified him
in the public mind with the figure of the starving Paillasse, that
his impersonation of a new part was anticipated with more than
ordinary curiosity. "He had, indeed, played other characters
at Sadler's Wells; but then the Pentonville establishment, during
Mr. Phelps's season of repose, was not a focus of general attraction,
and the West-end *connoisseurs*, satisfied with the merits of the provincial *débutant* in his first part, did not care to pursue their inves-
tigations by repeated journeys in an unusual direction. To these
Mr. Dillon remained Paillasse, and nothing but Paillasse, till the
middle of the present week; and it was not surprising that, amid
the theatrical gossip of the day, the question should have been
asked whether the gentleman who is celebrated in Parliament as
'One-speech Hamilton' had not found a histrionic ectype in a one-
part actor. The character of Paillasse is, after all, of the most
exceptional kind, and it is quite possible that an artist, by dint of
hard study, might master its peculiarities without decided qualifications for what is called 'general business.' Now, by his impersonation of the young Gascon, *D'Artagnan*, in 'The King's Musketeers,' Mr. Charles Dillon has utterly dispelled all fears that his
talent would prove *singular*, in the least favourable sense of the
word. There could not be in the range of humanity two personages
more thoroughly the antipodes of each other than the mountebank
and the Gascon. The existence of the former is passed between
anxious care and unmitigated misery; the latter is one of those
happily constituted individuals whom no misery could reach, and
who, whether he had to ascend the steps of a throne or a scaffold,
would ever preserve his joyous aspect. This state of chronic
hilarity has been most felicitously apprehended by Mr. Dillon.
His *D'Artagnan* has about it the true spirit of a sanguine adventurer, to whom every windfall is a source of bliss, and no obstacle
is a cause of terror. The employment of his sword 'Bobadillo,'
which was left him by his father with the strict injunction that he
is never to refuse a challenge, seems the main end of his existence,
but yet there is nothing cruel or bloodthirsty in his temperament.
If he can fight three duels in a day he is delighted at the opportunity, not because he harbours ill-will against any three of his
fellow-creatures, but because he is gratifying a natural disposition
to pugnacity, and, moreover, showing a pious regard to his father's
memory. True, he may take life in the course of the several encounters, but with him life itself is but a trifle, to be staked on
every occasion when fortune commands a game of chance, and
death is a slight balk the prospect of which need not in the least
disturb the equanimity of a sensible man. To the modern Lon-
doner, who regards length of days as all-important, and to whom a
railway accident by which half-a-dozen lives are lost appears a most
appalling occurrence, such a totally careless personage as a French
soldier of the seventeenth century, who is quite as ready to shed
his blood for 'fun' as for duty, would almost seem a being beyond

the limits of moral possibility. . . . That jovial fellows, whose entire attributes might be summed up in the compound adjective 'devil-may-care,' were plentiful in Paris during the reigns of Richelieu and Mazarin, and that at that period duelling was regarded as a pleasant sport, are historical facts, proved beyond the reach of a doubt. It is the great merit of Mr. Dillon that he makes such a character appear probable *now*, and thoroughly amiable in the bargain. He becomes the child of a certain period with such thorough efficiency that the period itself is revived, and we can think and feel according to the moral code of the seventeenth century. Nay, he is even a somewhat *childish* child; there is an innocence in his very pugnacity, and one may compare him to a generous, good-humoured schoolboy, who is at the same time the 'best fighter' of his class, and who, totally destitute of anything like an 'itching palm,' makes up for the deficiency by the indubitable possession of an itching fist." (*Times*, October 18, 1856.)

On Monday, November 10 of the same year, at the Lyceum, he played *Claude Melnotte* in 'The Lady of Lyons,' and so entirely successful was he in developing all the sensibility of which the character of *Melnotte* is susceptible, that he was frequently called before the curtain during the progress of the play to receive the plaudits of the audience. On Monday, December 1, 1856, in a revival of 'Othello' at the Lyceum Theatre, Mr. Dillon played the title *rôle*. " From the actor to the *mise en scène* all the usual conventionalities of the stage were set at naught (*Athenæum*, December 6, 1856). The *Othello* was natural, not all declamatory, sometimes familiar, always domestic, and rather intensely passionate than vehemently demonstrative. The great scenes between the Moor and his tempter were for the most part gone through in a sitting position; and constant attention was paid to every indication in the text of a deeper sentiment than appears on the surface of a passionate dialogue. All was surprisingly fresh and original, and much that was like a new revelation of the Shakespeare mind. . . . The last scene of the tragedy was a triumphant display of originality, passion, feeling, and beauty of style on the part of the actor. Sometimes his pathos in its intensity became sublime."

The *Times* (December 2, 1856), in a carefully written criticism of Mr. Dillon's *Othello*, said : " The declamatory part of histrionic art seems to accord least of all with Mr. Dillon's idiosyncrasy, and therefore, though the address to the Senate was carefully delivered, it still seemed that the artist was outside the character he assumed. As the famous dialogues with Iago progressed it became evident that he warmed into the business of the scene. The blank misery with which he listened to the tempter's description of jealousy, and the manly effort of self-possession with which he gathered himself together were well conceived. The air of painful attendance with which he listened to unpleasant tidings was remarkable for its truthfulness. However, it was only by degrees that his particular interpretation of the entire part was made apparent. A tender affection for Desdemona was the one feeling which he intended to be predominant over all the rest, and the manifestation of this feeling was constantly to be found, even when it might be least expected. His grief was always greater than his rage; if he could find a pretext for returning tenderness he seized it with avidity, and we might fancy that *Othello* was ever anxious to look upon the revelations of Iago as part of a hideous dream, from which with a mental effort he could awaken. The great ranting passage, 'Whip me, you devils,' &c., was given with a power which could scarcely be surpassed; but its chief effect was produced by the transition to grief at the end, the sudden change from noisy despair to deep, unutterable anguish. The concluding portion of the last act was perfect in its minutest details, the general conception being that the Moor, on the revelation of the deceits practised upon him, had ceased to take interest in external events, and was absorbed in the mental preparation for his own death. In the concluding speech every line had its due value ; and to those of the audience who had the earlier part of the play in their remembrance, most striking was the contrast between the declamation of the actor, who had not identified himself with the character, and the elocution of the same actor when the feelings of *Othello* had become his own. From the beginning to the end of the tragedy Mr. Dillon made, as it were, a constant encroachment on the sympathies of his audience, and when the curtain had fallen his sway had become universally acknowledged. It was impossible to misinterpret the hearty cheers that saluted the actor as he crossed the stage in response to general acclamations."

At the Lyceum, on Monday, February 16, 1857, Mr. Dillon performed the part of *Lord Revesdale*, first performance of Westland Marston's drama 'A Life's Ransom'; and on Friday, the 13th of March following, *Virginius*, in the tragedy of that title. On Friday, the 27th of the same month, he performed *Hamlet* for the first time in London. "From what had been seen of Mr. Dillon's previous characters, it was not difficult to foresee which side of *Hamlet's* character he would make prominent—or foresee that the emotional rather than the intellectual element in the Danish prince would be uppermost in his thoughts (*Times*, March 23, 1857). To take up a speech as a thing external, and to display ingenuity by carrying it through infinite varieties of emphasis and expression, would obviously be foreign to his theory of histrionic art. You do not listen to him to study his 'readings,' but to discover how soon his emotions will be identified with those of the character —and we may truly say that the greater the warmth required, the more he 'warms up.' Thus in 'Hamlet,' although the first two acts are carefully and conscientiously performed, it is not till the third act that Mr. Dillon's peculiarity is revealed. The tenderness with which he surveys Ophelia in the midst of his ravings about the 'nunnery,' and to which he gives extreme expression by dropping on his knee and fondly kissing her hand, is natural from its spontaneous appearance; and his welcome to Horatio, on the entrance of the latter, has a frankness about it that is singularly touching. Nothing of great moment occurs at this meeting of the two friends, but the notion is conveyed that a kindly heart, long placed amid uncongenial spirits, has at length found a sympathetic being on which it can repose. The watching of the King during the play scene is carried out, through all its details, with immense earnestness, and the burst of triumph in which it results is most powerful. In the 'closet scene' a new arrangement is made, which leads to a new histrionic effect. The ghost does not cross the front of the stage; but the lower part of the side and back scene becomes transparent, and the spectre is seen passing from behind the picture of the deceased King to the point where it vanishes. Its steps are followed by *Hamlet*, who thus leads his mother round the apartment in a state of rapt attention; and the explosion with which he utters the words 'Out at the portal,' and sinks into a chair exhausted with the mental strain, is terrific. Throughout the whole of this act the actor has more and more entered into the spirit of the scene, and here is his climax. He has gained his audience, and now he may fearlessly pursue his victory through the two remaining acts."

Mr. Dillon's first season at the Lyceum Theatre, which closed April 2, 1857, proved a profitable one. On the last night of the season he played *Richelieu*. During the same month he appeared at Drury Lane in that character, and in the parts of *Othello* and *Hamlet*. The following year (1858) he again rented the Lyceum Theatre, and on January 20th produced there a pleasant drama of Leigh Hunt's entitled 'Love's Amazements,' in which Mr. Dillon played the part of *Captain de la Rousse*. On Monday, February 1 of the same year, in a play by Westland Marston, then first performed, entitled 'A Hard Struggle,' he sustained the character of *Reuben Holt*.[*] The same month Mr. Dillon played the parts of *Rover* ('Wild Oats') and *Iago* ('Othello'). On Thursday, February 25, 1858, he performed, for the first time in London, *Macbeth*, Miss Helen Faucit sustaining the part of Lady Macbeth. In the opinion of the *Athenæum* (February 27, 1858), Mr. Dillon's *Macbeth* was the best performance he had yet given in London. It was remarkably fresh and original; it was moreover impulsive, and leant in no degree on theatrical conventions. "In the first place, the actor presents the brave Scotchman of the poet, whose nobility of disposition is the theme of general admiration in the earlier scenes; and not the hesitating coward of the boards, who trembles at every step of his progress. Fate urges on the valiant Thane to

---

[*] Through the courtesy of a correspondent I have been shown a letter in which, writing to the author of the play, Dr. Westland Marston, the late Charles Dickens says:—"I have witnessed twice the representation of your charming little piece 'The Hard Struggle.' . . . You ask me what I think of Charles Dillon as an actor. His representation of *Reuben Holt* was exactly what acting should be—Nature itself. I can't call to mind any living actor who could have played it so well. So closely did I watch him on both occasions that I could only discover one slight defect: on receipt of the letter from his love announcing the arrival of Lilian, in his emotion he crumpled the paper in his hand. I think it would have been more consistent had he folded the letter carefully and placed it in his breast."—Ed.

commit for a political motive a crime at which his moral nature revolts. The necessity to which he is subject makes him writhe with remorse, and reluctant to act. The crime once committed, the first rebound is fearful; but that once surmounted, his sole care is for the security of himself and his power; and to this he sacrifices victim after victim, till the land groans with his tyranny. Throughout a superstitious frame of mind colours his conduct, and tinges his thoughts with the hues of imaginative sentiment. Thus regarded, the character abounds in variety, and phases of emotion."

On Monday, March 22, 1858, Mr. Dillon performed, for the first time before the London public, *Louis XI.*, on the occasion of a complimentary benefit given by the company to himself and Mrs. Charles Dillon. "All that the part required he gave with the care, the elaboration, and thorough appreciation of the spirit of the scene which distinguish a true artist; and his task was a really fine picture of sustained acting. Mr. Dillon, who is eminently a natural performer, has shown by this embodiment that he can ably render the purely artificial drama." (*Daily News*, March 23, 1858.) From 1858 to 1860 Mr. Dillon was fulfilling various engagements as a "star" actor, in the provinces and elsewhere. He reappeared in London, Monday, February 6, 1860, at Drury Lane Theatre, as *William Tell*, in the tragedy of that title.

After an absence of several years, during which Mr. Dillon had made the tour of the world, on Monday, February 17, 1868, at Sadler's-Wells Theatre, he presented the character of *King Lear*. The part was one in which he had not acted in London previous to his departure for Australia, and therefore the performance was quite new to playgoers. It was considered successful. At the same theatre during the same year he played a round of Shakespearian characters and appeared also as *Richelieu*. In the spring of 1869 Mr. Dillon fulfilled an engagement at Drury Lane, playing his usual parts in the higher drama. In March of the same year, in 'The Man of Two Lives,' the second play adapted for the English stage from Victor Hugo's 'Les Miserables,' he sustained the part of *Jean Valjean*. On Saturday, August 16, 1873, in a revival of 'Manfred' at the Princess's Theatre, he appeared in the character *rôle*. Since the above date Mr. Dillon has played but seldom in London. On Saturday, September 28, 1878, however, he reappeared at Drury Lane Theatre as *Leontes* in a revival of 'A Winter's Tale.' This performance was scarcely so successful as had been anticipated. Since the last-mentioned date Mr. Dillon has been acting in the provinces.

DOLARO, SELINA (a *nom de théâtre*). Born in London, and made her first appearance on any stage, January 20, 1870, at the Lyceum Theatre, London, as the *Spanish Princess* in 'Chilperic.' Subsequently at various theatres in London Madame Dolaro has appeared as *Généviève* ('Généviève de Brabant'), *Clairette* ('Madame Angot'), *Périchole* ('La Périchole'), *Carmen* (in the opera of that name), in the English versions of each. On Wednesday, May 14, 1879, she entered, for a brief period, on the management of the Folly Theatre, and produced there that evening an English version by Mr. Henry Hersee of Maillart's 'Les Dragons de Villars.' In July 1879 at the same theatre she appeared as the heroine in ' The First Night,' Mr. G. W. Anson sustaining the part of Achille Talma Dufard, both actors being seen to great advantage in this play, a burlesque scene between the two being considered quite excellent.

DRUMMOND, DOLORES (DOLORES DRUMMOND GREEN). Born in London 1840. Daughter of the late Mr. and Mrs. Charles Green, and grand-daughter of the late Samuel Drummond, A.R.A. Was originally educated as an artist, and went with her mother to Australia with the intention of practising art as a profession. Having taken a special interest in stage matters while in that country, she was offered an opportunity of appearing at the Theatre Royal, Melbourne, and first acted there an important character,— *Desdemona*, under the auspices of G. V. Brooke. Miss Drummond returned to England in 1874, and made her appearance in London, November of the same year, at the Standard Theatre in the part of *Hermione* ('A Winter's Tale') with gratifying success. In 1876 (having fulfilled engagements in the interval) she appeared at the Globe Theatre as *Hortense* in the play of ' Jo,' and " obtained deserved recognition for a fine piece of acting." During 1878 she appeared at the Standard Theatre as *Lady Isabel* in ' East Lynne '; and played also at the Royal Park, Princess's, and Adelphi Theatres.

DUPLANY, CLAUDE MARIUS. *See* MARIUS, CLAUDE.

DYAS, ADA, daughter of the late Mrs. Edward Dyas, who was an actress of some ability attached to the London theatres. Miss Ada Dyas made her *début* on the metropolitan stage in 1861, as *Prince John of Lancaster*, in Shakespeare's ' Henry the Fourth.' Subsequently she earned popularity as a member of " Miss Marie Wilton's London Comedy Company," with which company she acted in the provinces in Mr. T. W. Robertson's play of ' Caste,' as *Esther Eccles*. In 1871 she was in the original cast of Wilkie Collins's 'Woman in White,' first performed àt the Olympic Theatre on October 9 of that year. She sustained in this play the dual parts of *Laura Fairlie* and *Anne Catherick*, and " accomplished a very difficult task with much propriety and truthful feeling." In 1873 she was performing at the Vaudeville Theatre ; but subsequently went to the United States of America, where she has since attained considerable popularity as an actress.

EDGAR, EDWARD FISHER, made his first appearance on the stage at the Victoria Theatre as a child, in 'The Stranger'; and he continued to play children's parts till old enough to take other characters. Then for a time he was with Mr. E. D. Davis, of Barnstaple, and played in different theatres in that vicinity. After a very extensive experience of some years in the provinces he returned to London in 1852, and appeared at the Olympic Theatre as *André* in 'Lucille; or, the Story of a Heart,' under the elder Mr. Farren. He has been the lessee of the Marylebone Theatre, and also of the Surrey Theatre in conjunction with Mr. Shepherd. He played an original part in numerous pieces at the Surrey, Princess's, Lyceum, Globe, Adelphi, Royalty, Olympic, and other theatres; among others may be mentioned 'Nobody's Child,' by Watts Phillips; 'True to the Core,' by Slous; 'The Rapparee,' by Boucicault; 'Eugene Aram,' by Wells; 'Philomel,' by Craven; 'Family Honour,' by Frank Marshall, &c., &c. He has more recently been connected with the Imperial Theatre; and in 1879, during the long run there of 'She Stoops to Conquer,' played the part of *Hastings*. In September 1879 he appeared at the Imperial Theatre as *Aimwell* in a revival of 'The Beaux' Stratagem.'

EDGAR, MRS. R. *See* MARRIOTT, ALICE.

EDWARDS, JAMES. *See* CARTER-EDWARDS, JAMES.

EGAN, ROSE (Mrs. BISHOP), born in Birmingham; daughter of Mr. F. B. Egan, for sixteen years manager of the old Queen's Theatre, Manchester. Having already had some experience on the provincial stage, Miss Egan made her *début* in London at the Court Theatre, in June 1873, in the part of *Florence* in the play of 'About Town.' The following "original" parts were performed by her during her engagement (1873–5) at the same theatre, viz. *Mrs. Carter* in Bronson Howard's comedy 'Brighton'; *Mrs. Bun-thunder* in W. S. Gilbert's comedy 'The Wedding March'; *Lady Isabelle* in Herman Merivale's play 'The White Pilgrim.' Miss Egan afterwards played her "original" part in 'Brighton' at the Standard, Haymarket, Criterion, and St. James's Theatres. In 1877, during the summer season at the Aquarium (now the Imperial) Theatre, Westminster, she appeared as *Mrs. Singleton Bliss* in 'Cyril's Success' and *Lamorce* in 'The Inconstant'; and on April 8, 1879, commenced an engagement at the Criterion Theatre to play *Lady Compton* in Bronson Howard's comedy of 'Truth.'

ELDRED, JOSEPH, was born in London. In 1860 he acted as agent for the Rev. J. M. Bellew, the elocutionist, on a reading tour through the provinces. About five years later he was performing as a low comedian in Dublin. Afterwards he went to Liverpool, and soon made an impression there as actor and manager. He made his first appearance on the London stage as *Major Regulus Rattan* in 'Ici on parle Français,' June 15, 1868 at the Olympic Theatre. When Mr. W. H. Liston opened the Olympic Theatre in October 1869 with 'Little Em'ly,' Mr. Eldred appeared as *Micawber.* Among the many parts he has acted this is one of his best. He has played starring tours throughout the provinces, notably with the late George Belmore in 'The Flying Scud,' and has everywhere made a reputation as an enterprising manager.

EMERY, SAMUEL ANDERSON, son of the late John Emery, a well-known comedian on the London stage in the second decade of the present century, was born in 1814. Mr. Samuel Emery made his first appearance at a London theatre on the 17th of April, 1843, in the part of *Giles,* in a piece entitled 'Miller's Maid,' and first attained popularity as an actor during the Keeley *régime* of the Lyceum Theatre, 1844–7. He was the "original" of the following characters, viz. *Jonas Chuzzlewit,* in Stirling's adaptation of Charles Dickens's novel 'Martin Chuzzlewit'; *Will Fern,* in an adaptation of the same author's Christmas story of 'The Chimes'; and *John Peerybingle,* in a dramatic version of the same author's story 'The Cricket on the Hearth.' These plays were first produced at the Lyceum Theatre, under the superintendence of Mr. and Mrs. Keeley, within the period above mentioned. Mr. Emery "created" the part of *Antony Latour,* in Shirley Brooks's drama of 'The Creole,' first performed at the same theatre in April 1847. This was one of the most striking impersonations of Mr. Emery's earlier professional career.

Having joined the company of the Olympic Theatre in the first year of Mr. A. Wigan's management, Mr. Emery was in the original cast of two of the most popular dramas produced there under Mr. A. Wigan's supervision, viz. 'Plot and Passion,' written by Mr. Tom Taylor, in conjunction with Mr. John Lang, first performed Monday, October 17, 1853; and 'Still Waters Run Deep,' by the first-named author, first performed Monday, May 14, 1855. Mr. Emery was also in the original cast of certain of Mr. Boucicault's plays on the occasion of their first performance in this country, of which, perhaps, 'The Octoroon,' 'Arrah-na-Pogue,' and 'The Long Strike,' have furnished the best examples of Mr. Emery's abilities and skill as an actor of what are known as "character" parts. His latest most important impersonations have been *Dan'l Peggotty,* in Andrew Halliday's version of Charles Dickens's story 'David Copperfield,' dramatized under the title of 'Little Em'ly'; and *Cap'n Cuttle,* in Andrew Halliday's play 'Heart's Delight,' founded on Mr. Dickens's novel of 'Dombey and Son.' The first-named play was first performed in London at the Olympic Theatre, Saturday, October 9, 1869; the second, at the Globe Theatre in December 1873. "The *Captain Cuttle* of Mr. S. Emery," said the *Daily Telegraph* (December 19, 1873), "is one of those admirable performances which so delight the playgoer and do such credit to the English stage. There is no need for the

orchestra to strike up a merry nautical tune in order to add zest to
the welcome of *Captain Cuttle.* When Mr. Emery comes rolling
on to the stage, made up to the very life, after the pictures by
' Phiz,' with the rubicund face and the bald pate, the coarse canvas
open shirt, and the hook instead of a right hand, the roar that
greets the old favourite shows that half the actor's work is over.
He looks the part, and there is no prejudice on that account. Few,
however, could have hoped for so thorough and masterly a specimen
of acting. It is not an actor walking upon the stage cleverly made
up and assuming a nautical or seafaring air; it is the very man
before us. He fills the stage with his bluff boisterous bearing, and
his hearty cheeriness is refreshing to all about him. His spirits are
so invigorating that our eyes, a little moist after some affecting
scene, are instantly dried, and his rough honesty is so apparent
that it serves as a pleasant reaction after scenes of misery and
villany. And then, when the actor has made our sides ache with
laughing, with consummate skill he rushes off to the opposite extreme, and makes the success of the evening with that pathetic
lament over drowned 'Wal'r,' which is a prose poem in the text of
Dickens, and in the hands of Mr. Emery a masterpiece of natural
and pathetic expression. ' Gone down with Wal'r,' sobs poor old
Cuttle, as the refrain to his wail over the lost boy, and the dirge
was a struggle between joviality and grief which few who heard it
are likely to forget. Mark how natural and gradual is this breakdown of *Captain Cuttle.* Another actor, with a trick of voice or a
gurgle in the throat, would assume the requisite pathos. But true
pathos is far more than trick of voice. You see the grief coming
upon the old fellow in spite of himself. He is laughing to the last
even in his tears ; but all at once the grief gets the mastery, and
the half-gulp, half-hysterical sob of the artist commands the attention even of the dullest audience. Equally admirable was Mr.
Emery's acting in the scene of the return of Walter Gay. The art
here is so complete and subtle that not a look, movement, or gesture, is lost upon the audience. They tell us of the *Captain Cuttle*
of Burton, an American actor, and speak of it in terms of unqualified praise. It must have been a masterly performance indeed
to rival that of Mr. Emery, a genuine study and a rare contribution
to dramatic art." It has been remarked of Mr. Emery that " he is
full of genuine humour, and knows full well how and when to give
it due expression. His delineations are most powerful whenever
deep feeling and pathos are to be exhibited. He can display
artistically, because naturally, the strongest of human passions,
and he is equally at home in whatever is genial, and quiet, and
humorous." He last appeared on the London stage at the Globe
Theatre, on July 20, 1878, in the part of *Cap'n Cuttle,* in the play
already alluded to.

ERNSTONE, HELENA CECILE (a *nom de théâtre*), daughter
of Adam Joseph Schott, of Mayence-on-the-Rhine, of the well-
known publishing firm of that name. Miss Ernstone received her
early education, which was mainly musical, at Bayreuth, and in 1863,

when but a mere girl, she was chosen to sing a contralto solo by Cherubini during the Mass celebrated in the cathedral of Frankfort-on-the-Maine before the European Princes then assembled in Congress in that city. "Under the German system of forcing the upper register her voice gave way, and she was advised to turn her attention to dramatic art." In 1867 she made her first appearance on the English stage at Canterbury Theatre as *Geraldine* in 'The Green Bushes.' Afterwards Miss Ernstone played a round of leading characters at various provincial theatres; and in 1869 made her *début* in London at the Charing Cross Theatre as *Ada Vavasour* in Cheltnam's drama of 'Edendale.' Miss Ernstone's next engagement was at the Olympic Theatre, where, Saturday, October 9, 1869, she "created" the part of *Martha*, first performance of Andrew Halliday's version of Charles Dickens's story of 'David Copperfield,' dramatized under the title of 'Little Em'ly.' Her accurate conception of the character attracted the notice of the famous novelist, who personally expressed his appreciation of Miss Ernstone's excellent acting in the drama. After fulfilling engagements at the Globe and Lyceum Theatres and Opéra Comique, Miss Ernstone's health gave way, and she was advised to take a long sea-voyage. Acting on this suggestion, she sailed for Australia, and performed in Melbourne for a short time. Returning to England, she reappeared on the London stage in March 1873, at Astley's Theatre, in the title *rôle* in W. M. Akhurst's historical drama of 'Fair Rosamond; or, the Days of the Plantagenets.' The same year, in May, at the Olympic Theatre, Miss Ernstone "created" the *rôle* of *Grace Roseberry* in Wilkie Collins's drama of 'The New Magdalen,' playing the part in a telling and straightforward manner, and aiding in no slight degree to make the piece a success. Her next "original" *rôle* was that of *Henriette* in 'The Two Orphans,' in which she was also successful. In May 1879, at the Olympic Theatre, Miss Ernstone played the part of the heroine (*Marguerite Duval*) in the drama of 'The Mother' with considerable force, earnestness, and pathos.

*EVERARD, H., made her first appearance on the stage at the Theatre Royal, Exeter, and for years has performed in burlesque, pantomime, comedy, and light opera characters in London and the provinces. In 1869 she was playing at the Royal Alfred Theatre. She subsequently appeared at the Queen's and the Royalty Theatres in many pieces, and later at the St. James's, Princess's, and other theatres. She was the original *Little Buttercup* in 'H.M.S. Pinafore' at the Opéra Comique, where that popular light opera was first represented.

EVERILL, FREDERICK AUGUSTUS. Born in London, February 6, 1829. He made his first appearance on any stage at the Ryde (Isle of Wight) Theatre, July 12, 1852, in the part of *Baron Steinfort* in 'The Stranger.' Subsequently he joined the company of the Southampton Theatre, where he acted for six seasons; and on October 1st, 1859, accepted an engagement at

the Theatre Royal, Manchester, with which Mr. Everill was connected for a period of eleven years.   During this protracted term
he appeared in many important characters, among which the
following deserve mention for the general excellence of their
presentation, viz. *Falstaff* ('Merry Wives of Windsor'); *Launce*
('Two Gentlemen of Verona'); *Dogberry* ('Much Ado About
Nothing'); *Gratiano* ('Merchant of Venice'); *Polonius* ('Hamlet'); *Mercutio* ('Romeo and Juliet'); *Desmaret* ('Plot and
Passion'); *Andrew Wylie* ('A Bachelor of Arts'); *Old Goldthumb* ('Time Works Wonders').   Mr. Everill made his *début*
on the London stage, June 30, 1870, as *Felix Trimmer* in Tom
Parry's farce 'A Cure for Love.'   Of important original parts
played by Mr. Everill during his connection with the Haymarket
Theatre, continuing to 1879, *Chrysal*, in W. S. Gilbert's "fairy
comedy" 'The Palace of Truth,' affords a satisfactory example.
The play was first performed at the Haymarket, Saturday, November 19, 1870.   "He acted excellently, indeed he was the only one
who, consistently, when in the 'Palace of Truth,' spoke the truth
as if he did not understand what he was saying.   Many of the
others made their action identical with their words." (*Observer*,
November 20, 1870.)

FAIRS, JOHN. *See* HARE, JOHN.

FARREN, ELLEN (Mrs. R. SOUTAR). Born in Lancashire. Daughter of Henry Farren, and grand-daughter of William Farren the elder. She made her first appearance on the London stage at the Victoria Theatre, under Mr. Cave's management, March 28, 1864, in the part of *Ninetta* in a drama entitled 'The Woman in Red.' Subsequently, in the same year, Miss Farren joined the company of the Olympic Theatre, under Mr. Horace Wigan's management. Among pieces in which she there appeared during her engagement, 1864–6, the following are entitled to notice, viz. 'The Hidden Hand' (Tom Taylor) ; 'My Wife's Bonnet' (J. M. Morton) ; a burlesque entitled 'Prince Camaralzaman ; or, the Fairies' Revenge'; 'Faust and Marguerite,' also a burlesque ; and Shakespeare's 'Twelfth Night,' in which Miss Farren undertook the part of the *Clown.* On the opening of the Gaiety Theatre, under Mr. John Hollingshead's management, Monday, December 21, 1868, Miss Farren appeared in ' On the Cards.'

During her long connection with this theatre, continuing, it may be mentioned, to the present time (October 1879), Miss Farren has played a principal part in the following, among other plays, viz. 'The Man of Quality' (*Miss Hoyden*) ; 'Dot,' Mr. Boucicault's version of 'The Cricket on the Hearth' (*Tilly Slowboy*) ; 'Love for Love' (*Miss Prue*) ; 'Thespis ; or, the Gods grown Old,' by W. S. Gilbert (*Mercury*) ; 'Shilly-Shally,' by Anthony Trollope and Charles Reade (*Polly Neefit*) ; 'The Battle of Life,' a dramatic version of Charles Dickens's Christmas story of that title, arranged by Charles Dickens, jun. (*Clemency Newcombe*) ; and in the various burlesques :—' Robert the Devil,' ' Princess of Trebizonde,' ' Little Faust,' &c.—produced under Mr. John Hollingshead's supervision within the period 1868–1879.

FARREN, WILLIAM. Son of William Farren, sometimes called the elder Farren, a well-known comedian of the London stage, contemporary with Macready. Previous to his entering the dramatic profession Mr. Farren had appeared in London with some success as a singer at the so-called Ancient Concerts. At the outset of his stage career he performed at the Strand and Olympic Theatres under the name of Forrester, and as William Farren, jun. In January 1851 Mr. William Farren, jun., was a member of the company of the last-named theatre ; and on Monday, 13th of that month, he sustained the part of *Frederick Plum*, first performance of Morton's comedy ' All that Glitters is not Gold.' At the same theatre, in the following year, he was in the original cast of the two following plays, viz. 'The Bag of Gold' (Hillyard), first performed at the Olympic Theatre, June 27, 1852 ; and 'Sarah Blangi' (adapted from the French, ' Sarah la Créole'), first performed there October 27, 1852.

In 1853, on Mr. J. B. Buckstone assuming the management of the Haymarket Theatre, Mr. William Farren became a member of his company. On Easter Monday of that year he made his *début* at the Haymarket as *Captain Absolute*, in ' The Rivals,' and for a great many years took part there in the various revivals of national comedy for which Mr. Buckstone's management was specially distinguished. Mr. Farren was also in the original cast of a number of plays produced at the Haymarket during the period of his engagement. Of these the principal were from the pen of Mr. Stirling Coyne and Mr. Tom Taylor, and included, among others, the following, viz. ' Elopements in High Life' (Stirling Coyne), first performed at the Haymarket Theatre April 7, 1853; ' The Hope of the Family ' (by the same author), first performed December of the same year; ' The Old Château ' (by the same), first performed July 22, 1854 ; ' The Secret Agent' (by the same), first performed March 1855; ' The Man with Many Friends' (by the same), first performed September 3, 1855; ' The Unequal Match ' (Tom Taylor), first performed November 7, 1857 ; ' The Contested Election ' (by the same author), June 29, 1859 ; ' The Overland Route' (by the same), February 23, 1860 ; ' The Family Secret ' (Edmund Falconer), May 9, 1860, &c., &c.

At the Vaudeville Theatre, July 1872, in a revival of ' The School for Scandal,' Mr. Farren sustained the part of *Sir Peter Teazle*, and continued to appear in the character during the very successful run of the comedy. In 1875, on January 16, he played the part of *Sir Geoffrey Champneys*, first performance at the Vaudeville Theatre of H. J. Byron's comedy ' Our Boys,' and continued to play the same character at that theatre nightly without intermission until July 1878. In the autumn of the same year Mr. Farren presented the part of *Grandfather Whitehead*—in later years one of the elder Farren's most successful impersonations—in a revival of the comedy of that name (adapted from the French by Mark Lemon), at the Theatre of the Westminster Aquarium. At the same time and place he acted *Young Wilding* in a revival of ' The Liar ' (altered from Foote). On Saturday, April 19, 1879, first performance at the Vaudeville Theatre of H. J. Byron's comedy ' Our Girls,' Mr. Farren sustained the part of *Josiah Clench*.

FAUCIT, HELEN (Mrs. THEODORE MARTIN), was born in London in 1819, and is the daughter of Mrs. Faucit, and younger sister of Harriet Faucit (Mrs. Bland), both of whom were actresses of considerable repute in London in the third decade of the present century. The first performances which Miss Helen Faucit gave in public were at the Theatre Royal, Richmond (Surrey), in November 1833, in the characters of *Juliet* (' Romeo and Juliet'), *Mariana* (' The Wife'), and *Mrs. Haller* (' The Stranger'). These, however, were mere trial performances, due to the accident of Miss Helen Faucit having been overheard by the manager of the Richmond Theatre (a Mr. Willis Jones) while going through the balcony scene of ' Romeo and Juliet ' with her sister, Harriet, who was at that time an actress in the theatre. The manager was so much struck by what he heard that he urged that Miss Helen Faucit should make the experiment of acting, and she was permitted by her mother to do so. Her success upon the occasions above indicated was so marked that she was allowed to entertain the idea of entering the dramatic profession. In the interval between these performances and her *début* on the stage proper, she received the ordinary instruction in the business of the stage from Mr. Percy Farren, brother of William Farren the elder. Miss Helen Faucit made her first professional appearance on the stage at the Theatre Royal, Covent Garden, Tuesday, January 5, 1836, in the character of *Julia* in 'The Hunchback.' The *Morning Chronicle* (January 6, 1836) noticed the event as follows :—" The only important incident was the appearance of Miss Helen Faucit in the character of the heroine ; and we speak quite within compass when we say that we never witnessed a better first performance, or one in which approbation was more constantly or enthusiastically expressed. . . . What we especially liked in her acting is that she seems to have faith in herself, or, rather, not so much in herself, as in the truth and force of the passion she has to express. She relied upon it in all the principal situations and passages, and found her account in it." A three years' engagement was the outcome of this performance, and the same year she acted at Covent Garden Theatre the character of *Belvidera* in Otway's 'Venice Preserved,' and *Margaret* in an original play by Joanna Baillie, entitled ' The Separation,' a piece which proved unattractive. Mr. Charles Kemble was the leading actor at Covent Garden Theatre during 1836, and Miss Helen Faucit had the advantage of acting with him in the following, in addition to the two parts already noticed : she played *Julia* to his Clifford in ' The Hunchback'; *Mrs. Haller* to his Stranger ; *Mrs. Beverley* to his Beverley in ' The Gamester'; *Lady Constance* to his Falconbridge in ' King John'; *Juliet* to his Mercutio in ' Romeo and Juliet'; *Katherine* to his Petruchio in ' Taming of the Shrew'; *Beatrice* to his Benedick in ' Much Ado About Nothing.' She also performed the counterparts to Mr. C. Kemble in the series of farewell performances at Covent Garden, ending December 3, 1836.

In July 1837 Helen Faucit was engaged by Macready as a member of his company, on his assuming the direction of Covent Garden Theatre. In the various plays performed there for the first time, ' Brian Boroihme ' (Sheridan Knowles) ; ' Walter Tyrrel'; Talfourd's ' Athenian Captive,' &c., and in all of the Shakespearian revivals arranged there under Macready's superintendence, and during his subsequent lesseeship of Drury Lane Theatre, Miss Helen Faucit bore a conspicuous part. These early impersonations included *Constance, Imogen, Cordelia, Desdemona, Rosalind,* and *Hermione.* She was the original representative of the heroines of the most important of the late Lord Lytton's plays. On January 4, 1837, Miss Faucit sustained the part of the *Duchess de Vallière*, in his play of that title, an event which was not left unnoticed by Macready, as appears from the following entry in his diary :—" Acted *Bragelone* (La Vallière) well, with earnestness and freshness; some passages were deficient in polish. Being called for, I did not choose to go on without Miss Faucit, whom I led forward. The applause was fervent."—*Macready's Reminiscences* (New and Revised Edition), p. 406.

On May 1, 1837, Helen Faucit acted the part of the *Countess of Carlisle*, in Robert Browning's play of ' Strafford,' at its first representation at Covent Garden; and on February 15, 1838, the part of *Pauline Deschapelles* at the first performance of 'The Lady of Lyons,' Mr. Macready playing Claude Melnotte. " Macready acted with spirit, and so did Miss Faucit, though she occasionally overdid her part. . . . The piece was eminently successful." (*Times*, February 16, 1838.) On Thursday, March 7, 1839, at the same theatre, she played at the first performance of ' Richelieu' the character of *Julie de Mortemar;* Anderson and Miss Faucit as the *lovers*, Ward as Bouillon, Elton as the King, Phelps as a Capuchin Friar, and Howe as a page, being entitled to especial commendation. The acting throughout was good, records the *Athenæum* (March 9, 1839).

Between the closing of Covent Garden Theatre in 1840, and the opening of Drury Lane by Mr. Macready, Miss Helen Faucit performed with him at the Haymarket. During this engagement, on Tuesday, December 8, 1840, ' Money ' (by Lord Lytton) was first performed there, Miss Helen Faucit playing the character of *Clara Douglas*. Among other plays in which she acted, with Macready, a leading part on the occasion of their first performance, may be mentioned Sheridan Knowles's ' Woman's Wit '; the same author's play of ' The Secretary '; Lord Lytton's ' Sea Captain '; Talfourd's ' Glencoe '; Serle's ' Master Clarke '; Westland Marston's ' Patrician's Daughter '; Byron's ' Marino Faliero '; Zouch Troughton's tragedy ' Nina Sforza.' A prologue by the late Charles Dickens was made a leading feature of the performance of ' The Patrician's Daughter.' It was written with admirable point and feeling, and was spoken by Macready. Miss Helen Faucit performed the part of *Mabel* in the play. In 1842 she accepted an engagement to be a member of Mr. Macready's company on his assuming the lesseeship of Drury Lane Theatre. On the 23rd of February of that year she acted *Sophronia*, first performance of ' Gisippus ' (Gerald Griffin); and in October of the same year *Julia* in ' The Rivals '; and later *Angelica*, in Congreve's ' Love for Love.' On February 11, 1843, she performed the part of *Miss Tresham*, first performance of Browning's ' A Blot on the Scutcheon.' Two years later, viz. in October 1845, Helen Faucit sustained her original character of *Pauline* in a revival of ' The Lady of Lyons ' at the Haymarket Theatre. The progress that she had made in the study and appreciation of the subtilties of the part, in the interval from the date of its first performance, may be estimated from the following criticism : " High as was our previous opinion of her (Miss Helen Faucit), our present estimate of her histrionic talent stands rather in contrast than comparison with the past. . . . She has evidently been taught by self-dependence to think, to feel, to act for herself. The character of *Pauline Deschapelles* is favourable for histrionic development. The heroine's pride is soon forgiven, and, for the rest, she is the sufferer, not the inflictor of wrong, and therefore the natural object of pity. Miss Faucit felt this, and assumed a passive quietness which, in its repose, was charming as well as artistic. In this respect it is altogether different from the *Pauline* to which in former times she accustomed us. That was rage and violence, a fault after all, perhaps, more attributable to the author than the actress. It is not so now. . . . Nor has Miss Faucit only learned to correct the author's mistakes in execution, but to supply his deficiencies of conception. To point out the beauties of her playing were to go through every scene of the drama, and to discriminate between what the author has not done, and what the actress supplies." (*Athenæum*, October 25, 1845.) When Mr. Macready retired from the management of Drury Lane Theatre there was no longer any theatre in London for the representation of the poetical drama. Miss Faucit then sought a field for the exercise of her powers in the provinces. In Dublin, Edinburgh, Glasgow, Manchester, Liverpool, and other important towns her reputation was soon established, and she drew large houses. In 1845 she appeared with Macready in Paris, and at the Salle Ventadour (the theatre at that time usually devoted to Italian Opera) played in a series of English performances, which comprised ' Othello,' ' Hamlet,' ' Virginius,' ' Macbeth,' ' Werner,' ' King Lear,' and ' Romeo and Juliet.'

The effect these performances produced is still vividly remembered by elder students of the dramatic art, and by those who had the privilege of witnessing them in Paris. In a criticism in the *Messager* (January 5, 1845), written by M. Edouard Thierry, brother of the historian, he says :—" Miss Helen Faucit, pour qui la voit en passant, est une jeune femme de formes grêles, mais non pas délicates, grande, et à laquelle manque la fleur de la chair. Cependant, aussitôt qu'elle marche, aussitôt qu'elle fait un geste, qu'elle prend une attitude, une grâce charmante se révèle. Cette jeune femme, qui ne semblait pas avoir la séduction nécessaire de l'actrice, a tout l'attrait, mais l'attrait irrésistible de la femme. Elle est femme, en un mot ; sa grâce particulière ne saurait s'expliquer par aucune autre expression ; et quand elle parle, c'est encore la voix qui convient à cette grâce, c'est la douceur d'organe qui sied bien à cette harmonie de la démarche, et de toute la personne, c'est le son caressant qui accompagne à souhait cette caresse, pour ainsi parler, du regard et des manières décentes. . . . Ajoutez une voix comme celle de Mlle. Mars, et une manière de réciter qui rapproche surtout de notre manière. En général, les artistes anglais ont retenu l'emphase de la tragédie, telle que la jouait Lafont, telle qu'on la déclamait à côté de Talma. Macready lui-même a conservé par moments ce débit pompeux, qu'il accentue d'ailleurs à la façon anglaise, en appuyant sur toutes les syllabes. Miss Helen Faucit parle simplement, naturellement ; la phrase coule limpidement de ses lèvres, et s'échappe d'une seule émission, comme dans notre récitation française.

" Après ' Othello ' sont venus successivement ' Hamlet,' ' Virginius,' ' Macbeth,' ' Romeo et Juliette.' A chacun de ces drames le succès de Miss Faucit s'est accru sans autres artifices. . . . On n'avait imaginé *Ophélia* ni plus touchante, ni plus gracieuse. Notre parterre français est demeuré surpris devant cette pantomime pleine de sens, pleine d'idées, pleine de bonté, pleine de la tendresse, pleine de passion même, mais surtout pleine de mesure et pleine de modestie. Car c'est là une qualité rare ; aussi je reviens sur cet éloge ; il y a dans Miss Faucit, et à un degré éminent, ce que j'appelle la modestie de l'artiste, ce désintéressement précieux par lequel l'artiste préfère l'art à lui-même, et le succès du drame à son propre succès. Quel que soit le rôle, quelle que soit la scène, Miss Faucit prend sa place dans la perspective du tableau, dans l'ensemble de l'œuvre, et cette place elle la garde jusqu'à la fin sans chercher à sortir de la demi-teinte nécessaire ; disparaissant même au besoin, dans l'ombre que le poëte a ménagée."

On January 16, 1845, Miss Faucit acted in 'Hamlet' before King Louis Philippe and the French Court at the Tuileries, and was by the king presented with a costly bracelet. In March 1845, after playing *Antigone* in Dublin, she was presented with the following address by members of the Royal Irish Academy and the Society of Ancient Art :—

"Madam,—We beg to give expression to the unalloyed and sustained satisfaction which we have derived from your late performance at our national theatre.

"We have each and all endeavoured to promote the cultivation of ancient Art in this our city; and we feel that your noble representation of *Antigone* has greatly advanced this important object, by creating a love and admiration of the beauty and grandeur of Ancient Greece.

"With the writings of the Grecian dramatists it is true we have been long familiar, but their power and their beauty have come down to us through books alone. 'Mute and motionless' that Drama has heretofore stood before us. You, Madam, have given it voice, gesture, and life ; you have realized the genius, and embodied the inspiration of the authors and artists of Early Greece, and have thus encouraged and instructed the youth of Ireland in the study of their immortal books.

"We offer the accompanying testimonial to the virtues and talents of one whose tastes, education, and surpassing powers have justly placed her at the summit of her profession.

(Signed) "George Petrie, R.H.A., V.P.R.I.A., Chairman. John Anster, LL.D. } John Francis Waller } Secretaries."

Accompanying this testimonial was a splendid brooch of Irish gold, nearly four inches in diameter, designed by F. W. Burton, R.H.A. In the centre was a medallion exhibiting the figure of Antigone crouching in grief over the funeral urn of Polynices. The success of Miss Faucit's personation of the 'Antigone' led to the production for her in Dublin of the 'Iphigenia in Aulis' of Euripides. In 1845, on the 6th of November, Miss Faucit sustained the part of *Rosalind* in 'As You Like It' at the Haymarket Theatre. The

Athenæum (November 8, 1845) thus commented on the performance :—"On Thursday Miss Faucit performed the part of *Rosalind* in the play of 'As You Like It,' and charmed us by the simplicity, the delicacy, the purity of the delineation. The character, like the play itself, is ideal, and therefore requires a spiritualization in the performance, without which it is apt to become gross and sensual. It is not because she assumes masculine habiliments, and instructs her lover how to woo her, that *Rosalind* is to be taken as a hoyden. In the real world this would undoubtedly be the case, but not in the Forest of Arden, where, as Hazlitt justly says, 'nursed in solitude, under the shade of melancholy boughs, the imagination grows soft and delicate, and the wit runs riot in idleness, like a spoiled child that is never sent to school.' This softness and delicacy we never saw more beautifully represented than in Miss Faucit's performance of *Rosalind*—the caprice of the part never more ethereally embodied."

In 1847 Miss Faucit played a short engagement at the Haymarket, where (October 4) she appeared as *Florence Delmar*, on the occasion of the first performance of Dr. Westland Marston's 'Heart of the World.' The play was saved from immediate condemnation by her acting. Mr. W. J. Fox, then critic of the *Morning Chronicle* (October 5, 1847), thus wrote of it :—"The play last night produced was no doubt so far successful. But will it ever be acted without Miss Helen Faucit to play the heroine? Mr. Westland Marston may have written the drama, but Helen Faucit made it ; Helen Faucit saved it. She was the life and soul of the stage." Three years later (November 5, 1850) Miss Faucit again introduced to public notice a play of Dr. Marston's, 'Philip of France and Marie de Méranie'—a play as thoroughly dramatic as the 'Heart of the World' was the reverse. The piece was produced at the Olympic Theatre and was a complete success. In a notice of the performance in the *Literary Gazette* (November 9, 1850), written by the late G. H. Lewes, he says :—"The engagement of Miss Helen Faucit is a rich boon to the public, for since the days of Siddons and O'Neill she is the most worthy exponent of the lofty poetical drama. She is the Rachel of the English stage. Her fine appreciation of the poetry is equalled by her power of characterization and the exquisite melody of her voice. All the phases of passion find in Helen Faucit a faultless interpretess. She seizes the most delicate *nuances* with a feminine yet firm grasp ; and all the varying emotions of the scene pass before us as truthfully as life, but exalted by the fine intellectuality and exquisite sensibility of the truly inspired artist." The play was taken by Miss Helen Faucit into the provinces and acted with great success. *Marie de Méranie* has not since found any adequate representative, and this fine dramatic work seems to have disappeared for the present from the acted drama. In July 1851 Miss Faucit appeared for twelve nights at the Olympic Theatre, and played *Julia* ('The Hunchback'), *Rosalind*, and *Lady Macbeth*. In 1852 she made her reappearance at Drury Lane Theatre. During the intervening period, on August 25, 1851, she married Mr. Theodore Martin, an author of distinction, whose 'Bon Gaultier Ballads,' and more recent literary labours in connection with 'The Life of the Prince Consort,' are well known to the public. On Wednesday, January 28, 1852, Miss Faucit once more stood on the London boards, in the character of *Juliet.* " Assuredly she acted it with so much care and elaboration," remarked the *Athenæum* (January 31, 1852), "and in a style so superior to all her former efforts in the character, as to challenge on this occasion more than ordinary critical attention. One attribute of her performance it was impossible to overlook—the purpose which pervaded the whole, and which was felt as much in minute points and situations, as in the more prominent incidents and general scope of the action. It was in this particular that Miss Faucit chiefly excelled. She gathered a meaning from every phrase, and sometimes from a word. In the balcony scene she was greatest, both as regards the general impression, and the detail by means of which it was elaborated."

Miss Faucit appeared at the Haymarket Theatre at intervals during the period 1853-5 in several of her more famous characters, *Pauline, Rosalind,* &c. On 25th April, 1853, she performed there the character of *Colombe,* in Browning's 'Colombe's Birthday,' as to which the *Morning Post* (April 26, 1853) wrote:—" Miss Helen Faucit has returned to us in the full possession of those remarkable powers which long ago made her a cherished favourite of the London public. Never did she look or act better than on the present occasion; and the applause that greeted her, though frequent and cordial, was not half so much as she deserved." In June 1855 Miss Faucit again appeared for a short engagement at the Haymarket Theatre, during which (June 12) was produced 'Love's Martyrdom,' from the pen of Mr. John Saunders, a play which had been highly commended by Mr. Landor, Mr. John Forster, and others. It secured, however, only a *succès d'estime,* due in great measure to Miss Faucit's performance of the heroine. "More than to any merits of its own, the success of 'Love's Martyrdom' is due to the admirable acting of Miss H. Faucit in the character of the heroine. Nothing could be more perfect than her delicate delineation, either of her young and hardly conscious love, or of the same love, deeply felt, and impetuously declaring itself; of her wounded pride; of her inflexible devotion to her pledged word; or of the hard struggle between her love and pride. The great 'point' of the performance was a fine scene towards the end of the fourth act, in which, with a wild outbreak of tumultuous emotion, she declares to her cousin with how absorbing a passion she loves the man she believes herself to have lost for ever. It deservedly gained for the artiste the honour of a call at the end of the act." (*Morning Chronicle,* June 12, 1855.) On Friday, July 6, 1855, for the first time in London (having often previously performed the part on the provincial stage), Miss Faucit appeared at the same theatre as *Iolanthe,* in Mr. Theodore Martin's version of 'King René's Daughter.' The *Daily News* (July 9, 1855) noticed the performance as follows:—" Miss Helen Faucit took a benefit at this theatre on Friday night, the result of which must have proved to the lady that the majority of the audience was not at all unwilling to concur in an opinion tolerably well credited, that she stands at the head of living tragic actresses. Her attempt was a bold one, but its success shows that she was right as far as the determination to obtain a recognition of her power was concerned. 'King René's Daughter,' which she chose for the first piece, is, as a dramatic composition, worthless. It is a translation, or rather an adaptation, from the Swedish by Heinrik Herz. The interest depends upon the recovery of sight by a blind princess, under the excitement produced by a tumult of novel sensations. In the year 1849 two translations of this piece were brought forward. Mrs. Stirling and Mrs. C. Kean then undertook to represent the heroine. There is no doubt that the representation by Miss Faucit last night was a far more real thing than that of either of the actresses mentioned. The great defect of the piece is, that it sets the intellect at work to know what would be the nature of the victory achieved over a physical defect. The subject is essentially undramatic. Nevertheless, with a tact which can have its foundation only in genius, Miss Faucit managed to throw ophthalmia into the background, and to bring forward human sensations, which have their source in nature far deeper than those from which physical defects spring. She carried a trumpery piece triumphantly on her shoulders, and flinging it before the audience, dared them to deny its value. The answer was all that she could have desired. Can any actress desire a greater success? She achieved what ought to have been an impossibility."

The record of Miss Helen Faucit's performances, from the year 1855 to the date of her final disappearance from the stage, consists, for the most part, only of repetitions of previous impersonations. These have passed the ordeal of criticism again and again, and are among the familiar facts of the playgoing public.* On Thursday, November 3, 1864, however, during Messrs. Falconer and Chatterton's management of Drury Lane Theatre, she played there the part of *Lady Macbeth*, a character in which she was almost new to London, the direction of her talents having generally led, as we have seen, to the adoption of the gentler heroines created by Shakespeare. In these she had acquired a high reputation; but in severer parts she had yet to justify her pretensions. It is gratifying to be able to record that she was not unsuccessful in the new part. Said the *Athenæum* (November 12, 1864): "Her *Lady Macbeth* is an original conception, elaborately studied and carefully illus-

* Mr. W. Clark Russell, in *Representative Actors* (p. 409), has collected a few criticisms on the acting of Miss Helen Faucit by De Quincey (1843), William Carleton (1846), George Fletcher (*Studies of Shakespeare*), Sir A. Alison, Mr. Arthur Helps (*Realmah*), &c. Mr. George Henry Lewes, in *Actors and the Art of Acting*, incidentally mentions the same lady's name in the article "Macready" (p. 36). The labour and difficulty of searching out the fugitive contributions to journalism of the same writer, on the subject of Miss Faucit's performances, were too great to allow of my attempting the task. I tried, but found it next to impossible to trace them.--ED.

trated with sculpturesque attitudes, which are sometimes too pain-
fully realized. Intent on these expressions of deliberate thought,
the actress is incapable of impulse, which accordingly is throughout
suppressed in favour of an artificial representation. We have
before us a living figure which undergoes a series of modifications
prescribed by the most vigorous art. One of these is the attitude
in which she stands reading the scroll that registers her husband's
meeting with the Weird Sisters on the heath. It is gracefully
marmorean, and gave the preliminary tone to the performance.
The soliloquy was delivered with great energy, and rose to a height
of poetical declamation seldom attained. The interview with Macbeth was rendered impressive by all the aids of style and predetermined emphasis, so that not a single word was bereft of its
due force. . . . All that art could enable her to do Miss Faucit
did; but we have been more strongly impressed with the spiritual
terrors that beset the self-communing sleeper by means more
simple."

During November and December of the same year (1864) she
appeared at the same theatre as *Imogen* ('Cymbeline') and *Rosalind* ('As You Like It'). Touching these later performances of
Miss Faucit, we borrow the following from *Journal of a London
Playgoer*, by Prof. Henry Morley, pp. 346–357 : "November 5,
1864.—At Drury Lane the reappearance of Miss Helen Faucit
brought us 'Cymbeline'; for *Imogen*, the most beautiful of Shakespeare's female characters, is that in which this lady seems most to
delight and to excel, and with this she desired in returning to the
London stage, of which she was some years since a chief ornament,
to make her first impression. . . . In its tenderness and grace of
womanhood; in the simple piety which looks to the Gods when
Imogen commits herself to rest, or is about to read a letter from
her husband; in the wife's absolute love and perfect innocency, void
of false shame, slow to believe ill, strong to resist it, Miss Faucit's
Imogen is eloquent to our eyes, even when she fails now and then
to satisfy our ears. She is an actress trained in the school of the
Kembles, careful to make every gesture an embodiment of thought;
too careful sometimes, as when, after the cry 'What, ho, Pisanio!'
she remains with upraised arm throughout half the speech of
Iachimo that begins 'O happy Leonatus!' There is a graver
fault of excess in the first part of the representation of womanly
fear when, as *Fidele*, she calls at the mouth of the unoccupied
cavern, and runs from the sound herself had made. The warning
of her error might be found in the fact that her pantomime here
excites rather general laughter, where surely Shakespeare never
meant that even the dullest boor should grin. But that short sin
of excess is followed by the entry into the cavern, which is done
most charmingly. Miss Faucit's voice is more often at fault; it
fails her whenever she has a violent emotion to express, and
passion sounds often like petulance. . . . Yet where the mere
emotion to be expressed is more tender than violent she attains
often—though even then, perhaps, with a too visible art—to the
utmost delicacy of expression. . . . On Wednesday Miss Faucit

played *Rosalind* in 'As You Like It.' . . . In all the scenes with Orlando Miss Faucit's acting is delightful. If she has not the art to conceal art, the art she does not conceal is true, is founded on quick and refined perception of the poetry she is interpreting. She can realize line by line, with tone and gesture, more of the spiritual grace and beauty of true poetry than any lady who now acts upon the English stage."

Without attempting categorically to write down every principal incident in Miss Helen Faucit's brilliant career on the English stage, it may be remarked that her greatest impersonations in the Shakespearian drama—in the performance of which she has most excelled as an actress—have been *Juliet, Beatrice, Constance, Desdemona, Hermione, Isabella, Imogen, Portia, Lady Macbeth,* and *Rosalind.* She followed Miss Vandenhoff (the original impersonator of the character in England) as the heroine in 'Antigone,' first produced with Mendelssohn's music at Covent Garden Theatre, January 2, 1845, a part in which Miss Faucit gained, as we have elsewhere remarked, well-merited honour. Her presentation of the character of *Iolanthe* has invariably incited high admiration, however much critics may differ as to the exact value of the play in which that character is cast. The great attractions of Miss Helen Faucit's acting could scarcely, perhaps, be more satisfactorily summed up, than they have been in the following opinion of one of the more famous of her earlier contemporaries. Vandenhoff, in his *Dramatic Reminiscences* (London Edition, p. 40), remarks : " Her expression of love is the most beautifully confiding, trustful, self-abandoning in its tone that I have ever witnessed in any actress. It is intensely fascinating." Miss Helen Faucit's last appearance on the London stage took place June 1876, when she appeared at the Lyceum Theatre in 'King René's Daughter,' Mr. Henry Irving playing the part of *Sir Tristram.* At the Shakespeare Memorial Festival, at Stratford-on-Avon (April 23-30), 1879, she impersonated *Beatrice* in a performance of ' Much Ado About Nothing.'

FERNANDEZ, JAMES, was born at St. Petersburg, Russia, May 28, 1835, and entered the dramatic profession at the Queen's Theatre, Hull, October 1853. Afterwards he played at Stafford, Hanley, Lichfield, Isle of Man, Wolverhampton, Whitehaven, Rochdale, Blackburn, &c. Mr. Fernandez made his first appearance on the London stage at the Queen's Theatre, in 1855. Subsequently he played at the Bower, Queen's, Surrey, and Grecian Theatres ; and returned to the Surrey Theatre and remained there (under the management of Messrs. Shepherd and Creswick) for six consecutive seasons, playing, in conjunction with Charles Calvert, principal "juvenile" parts ; among the number the character of *Walter Hartright*, in the first dramatization of Wilkie Collins's ' Woman in White.' Upon the destruction, by fire, of the Surrey Theatre, in 1864, Mr. Fernandez was engaged by the late E. T. Smith to sustain at Astley's Theatre the part of *Ruby Darrell*, in a new drama entitled 'The Mariner's Compass,' which had a lengthened run. Afterwards he appeared at the Lyceum Theatre

in a drama entitled 'Narcisse.' (*See* BANDMANN, DANIEL E.)
In 1868 Mr. Fernandez was leading actor at the Theatre Royal,
Brighton. The following year he accepted a special engagement
to play the *King o' Scots* at the Alexandra Theatre, Liverpool,
appearing there for the first time Easter Monday, 1869. Shortly
after this Mr. Fernandez became the leading actor at the Amphitheatre, Liverpool, and made his first appearance there as *Shylock*,
to the Portia of Miss Bateman. During this engagement, in a
revival of 'Arrah-na-Pogue,' Mr. Fernandez played the part of
Shaun the Post, of which performance the *Liverpool Daily Post*
(May 1869) remarked as follows :—" None but an actor of sterling
ability could have personated *King James* in 'King o' Scots' as he
did ; and his performance on Saturday was the best confirmation
of the favourable opinion expressed of him when he played in Mr.
Halliday's drama. It is a step indeed from *King Jamie* to *Shaun
the Post-boy*, but the ability to sustain characters so widely different
is a true and severe test. Mr. Fernandez has confidence in himself ;
and his success in *Shaun* is ample justification for it, and another
reason to think that he is one of the best stock actors that have
ever appeared in Liverpool."

Mr. Fernandez reappeared in London, at the Adelphi Theatre,
1871, as *Claude Frollo*, in Halliday's 'Notre Dame,' playing the
character for 270 nights, "with an earnestness and effect which made
his *début* on these boards a triumph of the most unequivocal description." He remained at the Adelphi Theatre for three seasons,
playing principal parts ; among others, *Dagobert*, *Don Salluste*
(to Fechter's Ruy Blas), *Newman Noggs*, *Micawber*, &c. He was
subsequently engaged by F. B. Chatterton for Drury Lane Theatre,
and appeared there as *FitzJames* in the drama of 'The Lady of
the Lake'; and as *Isaac of York* in a revival of 'Rebecca.' He
sustained the part of *Old Tom* in a revival of 'After Dark,' at the
Princess's Theatre in June 1877, and performed the character for
80 nights. Returning to Drury Lane Theatre, September of the
same year, Mr. Fernandez acted the part of *Christian* in W. G.
Wills's drama of 'England'; and afterwards appeared as *Varney*
in a revival of 'Amy Robsart.' Subsequently he was selected by
Mr. Henry Irving to support him, as *Coitier* in the production
of 'Louis XI.' at the Lyceum Theatre, March 12, 1878. Mr.
Fernandez continued a member of the Lyceum company until June
1878 ; he shortly afterwards accepted an engagement at the Globe
Theatre, and thence went into the provinces, where he appeared
with success as *Gaspard* in the English version of 'Les Cloches
de Corneville.'

FISHER, DAVID (the Elder). Born at East Dereham, Norfolk,
one of the towns which formed the circuit of " The Norfolk and
Suffolk Company of Comedians," an association of players established by the grandfather of the present actor, and which continued under the control of Mr. D. Fisher's family (father and
uncle) until about the year 1841. Trained from boyhood to the
stage, but prevented for some years by a severe accident from

following his profession, David Fisher became engaged in various musical pursuits in Norwich at the outset of his career. He appeared at public concerts as a principal violinist, and secured favourable notice for his praiseworthy performances in this direction. In 1849, after his recovery, he joined the company of Mr. Edmund Glover at the Prince's Theatre, Glasgow, meeting, as members of the same, Miss Agnes Robertson (Mrs. Boucicault), Mrs. Ternan, George Everett, &c. Playing a variety of characters during the succeeding four years, receiving during that time offers of engagement from Mr. E. T. Smith of Drury Lane, and Mr. A. Wigan of the Olympic, Mr. Fisher finally arranged with Mr. Charles Kean, and made his first appearance in London at the Princess's Theatre, November 2, 1853, as *Victor* in 'The Lancers.' At the same theatre he played *Windsor Brown* in 'Away with Melancholy'; *De Brissac* in 'Our Wife'; *Faust;* and *Pertinax* in his own production, 'Music hath Charms.' Mr. David Fisher took part in the dramatic performances at Windsor Castle, arranged by the late Charles Kean, playing the *Marquis* in the 'Wonderful Woman,' *Gratiano* in 'The Merchant of Venice,' and *De Brissac* in 'Our Wife.' In 1859 he accepted an engagement at the Adelphi under Mr. Benjamin Webster's management. It was at this theatre that Mr. David Fisher first played many of his most important characters, notably the *Abbé Latour* in Watts Phillips's 'Dead Heart,' *Garroway* in the same author's 'Paper Wings,' *Lanières* in 'Magloire,' *Hulks* in 'The Willow Copse,' and *Kyrle Daly* in 'The Colleen Bawn.'

In 1863 David Fisher produced an entertainment called 'Facts and Fancies' at the Hanover Square Rooms and St. James's Hall, which was noticed in the *Observer* (April 12, 1863) as follows :— "Mr. David Fisher goes through the busy and prolonged programme with amazing spirit and address, and displays a versatile experience which those who knew him on the stage could hardly have expected. His musical attainments are very remarkable. He not only plays on the pianoforte with the skill of a proficient, but is more than respectable as a violinist, while his singing is neat and tasteful." In the autumn of the same year he joined Mr. Vining's company at the Princess's, playing *Mr. Abel Honeydew* in 'Paul's Return'; *Jaques Sabot* in 'Light and Shadow'; and *Mozart Smith* in his own farce of 'Heart Strings and Fiddle Strings,' &c. In 1865 Mr. Fisher was specially engaged for the part of *Orpheus* in Offenbach's opera at the Haymarket. During a part of 1866 and up to July 1868 David Fisher was under the management of Mr. H. J. Byron at Liverpool, and undertook the duties of stage-manager, playing a great variety of characters at the Royal Amphitheatre and Alexandra, including *Sir Peter Teazle, Sir Harcourt Courtly, Autolycus, Stephano,* &c., &c. He engaged for the opening of the Globe Theatre in London, November 28, 1868; and on that occasion undertook the character of *Major Treherne* in H. J. Byron's 'Cyril's Success.' In 1869 he appeared as *Major Jorum* in Boucicault's 'Formosa' at Drury Lane, Henry Irving playing the character of *Compton Kerr.*

"The gem of the evening, so far as acting was concerned, was Mr. David Fisher's admirable impersonation of the *roué* and gamester, *Major Jorum*. Make-up, dress, action, were all perfect. . . . . . Mr. Fisher cannot be complimented higher than he deserves." (*Standard*, August 6, 1869.) In 1870 he accepted an engagement at the Olympic, and played, among other principal characters, *Brigard* in 'Frou-Frou'; *Micawber* in 'Little Em'ly'; and *Lord Claremont* in Tom Taylor's 'Handsome is that Handsome does.' At a performance for his own benefit, August 29, 1870, Mr. Fisher acted the character of *Sir John Falstaff*. Engaged under Mr. H. J. Montague's management, at the Globe Theatre in 1871, he played there *Horace Mervyn* in Byron's 'Partners for Life,' and *Dick Fallow* in Albery's 'Forgiven.' Engagements followed at the Opéra Comique, where in 1872 he acted the *Marquis* in an English version of M. Hervé's 'L'Œil Crevé'; *De Grignon* in Charles Reade's adaptation from the French, 'The Ladies' Battle' ('La Bataille des Dames'); and *Nicholas Flam* in Buckstone's comic drama of that name. At the opening of the Criterion Theatre, March 21, 1874, he played *Ransome Trivass* in 'The American Lady'; at the Mirror Theatre (Holborn), *Jack Paget* in 'The Detective,' May 29, 1875; at Drury Lane, the same year, *Father Dolan* in 'Shaughraun.' Mr. Fisher joined Mr. H. Wigan's company at the Princess's in 1876. Since that year he has been engaged with a company playing 'Dan'l Druce' in the provinces, and as an actor of principal parts in Mr. Gilbert's comedies. In 1879 he was performing in the provinces in the so-called 'Crisis' company.

FISHER, DAVID (the Younger). Professionally known as Walter D. Fisher till 1874, afterwards as David Fisher, jun. Born at Norwich. Was specially educated to the stage by his father, David Fisher the elder, at whose benefit at the Theatre Royal, Glasgow, in 1852, the younger Fisher first appeared on the stage as the boy in 'The Children in the Wood.' His first engagement in the dramatic profession was made at the Theatre Royal, Manchester, September 21, 1862. Afterwards he fulfilled engagements in the provinces, at the Theatres Royal, Brighton, Dublin, Glasgow, Liverpool, Edinburgh, Newcastle, &c. In the summer of 1870 Mr. Fisher became lessee (in conjunction with Miss Marie Rhodes) for a short period of the Theatre Royal, Edinburgh, producing 'Formosa,' 'Lancashire Lass,' 'Prompter's Box,' &c., with considerable success. In 1873 he played at the Athenée Theatre in Paris with an English company of comedians, which included, among others, Messrs. Ryder, Swinbourne, Charles Warner, Miss Viner, Miss Margaret Cooper, &c. In 1874 Mr. Fisher joined Mrs. Herman Vezin's so-called 'Cora' company. He made his first appearance on the London stage July 1875, at the Theatre Royal, Haymarket, as *Moses* in 'The School for Scandal'; and his first important London engagement was at the Globe Theatre, where he acted *Potain* in a play adapted from the French ('L'Article 47') entitled 'Cora,' noticed in the *Times* (March 9,

1877) as "one of the cleverest bits of acting in the piece." On August 12, 1877, Mr. Fisher appeared at the Haymarket Theatre as the *Rev. Horatio Tibbets* in G. F. Rowe's comedy of 'Brass'; subsequently playing at the same theatre in various Shakespearian parts during the engagement (1878) of Miss Adelaide Neilson, and later as *David* ('The Rivals'), *Mr. Taperly* ('Conscience Money'), *Lord William Whitehead* ('The Crisis').

FISHER, WALTER H., is the son of a portrait painter of Bristol, and made his first London appearance on the stage in the play of 'Broken Spells' at the Court Theatre. At the opening of the Olympic Theatre in 1873, under the management of Mr. Henry Neville, he appeared in a piece of H. J. Byron's entitled 'Sour Grapes.' In March 1874 he was the original *Woodstock* in Tom Taylor's play of 'Clancarty,' and in Mortimer's play of 'Figaro' he was *Cherubino* the page. He has appeared as a singing light comedian at the Globe, the Royalty, the Strand, and other London theatres, and has at various times taken the parts of *Marasquin* in 'Giroflé-Girofla,' *Piquillo* in 'La Périchole,' *The Defendant* in 'Trial by Jury,' &c. He played *Frickel* in Lecocq's opera 'La Marjolaine' at the Royalty Theatre, October 1877, and appeared there in the opera bouffe of 'La Belle Hélène' in March 1878. When 'Madame Favart' was first produced at the Strand Theatre, Saturday, April 12, 1879, Mr. Fisher appeared in it as *Hector de Boispreau*.

FITZWILLIAM, KATHLEEN MARY (Mrs. C. WITHALL), was born in November 1826. She studied under the following masters, viz. John Barnett (singing), J. L. Hatton (piano), Balzir Chatterton (harp); and made her first appearance in public in 1845, at the Hanover Square Rooms, as a concert singer, on the occasion of the first performance of an original 'Stabat Mater' composed by her brother, Edward Francis Fitzwilliam. Miss Fitzwilliam made her *début* on the stage the same year at the Theatre Royal, Birmingham, as *Rosina* in the opera of 'The Barber of Seville,' and during the two following and subsequent years fulfilled engagements in Liverpool, Manchester, Edinburgh, Glasgow, Dublin, and other important towns, playing "principal and leading business" with several eminent members of the dramatic profession. With Macready she acted in 'Hamlet,' and sustained the part of *Ophelia*. With Mr. and Mrs. Charles Kean she appeared in 'The Wife's Secret,' as *Maud*, and in 'Strathmore.' With Miss Cushman she played in several important pieces. And on the occasion of the reappearance in Liverpool (1847) of Miss Fanny Kemble (Mrs. Butler), after her long absence in America, Miss Fitzwilliam sustained the part of *Helen* to that lady's Julia in 'The Hunchback.' A contemporary Liverpool journal, alluding to this performance, remarks :—"The lively and volatile *Helen* was personated by Miss Kathleen Fitzwilliam, who, though more than commonly clever, would, we thought, fail in this rather difficult character. What, then, was our delight, our astonishment, to see it played as we never saw it played before.

Amidst all the *Helens* we ever saw, Miss Fitzwilliam ranks first. It was worthy indeed to rank with the Julia she played with. Few who saw Miss Fitzwilliam's perfect acting that night could have credited that she was, in comparison with those by whom she was surrounded, a perfect novice." Among other actors of note with whom Miss Fitzwilliam appeared in the earlier part of her career, Mackay, the celebrated Scotch actor, and Leigh Murray may be mentioned. With the first named she played in 'The Heart of Midlothian' (*Dumbiedikes*, Mackay ; *Madge Wildfire*, Miss Fitzwilliam) ; and, with Mr. Leigh Murray (as *Claude Melnotte*), she personated *Pauline* in 'The Lady of Lyons.'

Miss Fitzwilliam made her first appearance on the London stage, December 1, 1847, at the Lyceum Theatre under Madame Vestris's management, as *Peggy Green* in a comic drama of that title, written expressly for her by Mr. Charles Selby. The original cast included the following well-known names : Charles Mathews (*Mr. Edward Roverly*) ; Harley (*Nicholas*) ; Granby (*Mr. Thomas Tippins*) ; and Mrs. Macnamara (*Mrs. Glover*). "The drama is gay and sprightly throughout," said the *Morning Advertiser* (December 2, 1847), " and it ends with an animated, bustling, good, hearty, homely, honest 'country dance.' The piece is rendered very amusing by the rough, rural acting of Harley ; the juvenile-antique affections and airs of Granby; the dashing, daring doings of the penniless Mr. Edward Roverly, admirably personated by Charles Mathews ; and the holiday adventures of some six fair and frolicsome milliners. Lastly (and yet in importance she should have been first) Miss Kathleen Fitzwilliam was extremely successful throughout this lively little drama. Her acting is *naive*, natural, easy, and unaffected ; and her singing is perfectly charming—from a sweet voice, managed with skill, taste, and feeling. The three elegant songs introduced and executed by her were very effective. The first especially delighted the audience, and was heartily encored. Indeed the *début* was in every respect successful, and the young actress cannot fail, with due attention and care, to secure a very favourable position in public estimation."

Miss Fitzwilliam remained at the Lyceum Theatre for three seasons, playing, among others, the following original parts in the under-mentioned extravaganzas of J. R. Planché, viz. *Prince Humpy* in 'The Golden Branch'; *Prince Florizel* in 'The King of the Peacocks'; *Ariadne* in 'Theseus and Ariadne'; *St. George* in 'The Seven Champions of Christendom.' She appeared also in the following leading parts at the same theatre during this engagement, viz. *Margaret Honeyball* in Shirley Brooks's play 'Anything for a Change'; *Anne Page* in a revival of 'The Merry Wives of Windsor'; and *Polly Peachum* in a revival (June 15, 1848) of 'The Beggar's Opera,' with Madame Vestris as *Lucy Lockit*, W. H. Harrison as *Macheath*, Harley as *Filch*, F. Matthews as *Peachum*, Granby as *Lockit*, and Mrs. C. Jones as *Mrs. Peachum*. The *Literary Gazette* (June 17, 1848) noticed this revival as follows :—" Foreigners beware ! English actors have the remedy in their own hands ; and one of their most effective demonstrations was made at the Lyceum on Thursday evening, when Gay's 'Beggar's Opera,' restored to the pristine shape it bore one hundred and twenty years ago, was reproduced. The characters of the Player and the Beggar in the sort of introduction which prefaces and closes the play were retained, and thus explained away the anomalies of the commencement and conclusion; they could not have been in better hands than those of Messrs. Parselle and Meadows, the latter, as usual, 'made up' to life. The cast was altogether powerfully strong. . . . . The feature of the evening, however, was the *Polly* of Miss Kathleen Fitzwilliam; it was not only graceful and interesting, but occasionally really pathetic ; and her warbling—for her singing of many of the morsels deserves that term—of the beautiful ballads scattered through the part was almost of nightingale sweetness ; she occasionally added some simple ornaments to the vocalization, displaying taste and ability of no ordinary kind, and she was loudly applauded and encored in three or four airs, such as ' Cease your funning,' and ' Oh, ponder well.' She also acted with great judgment and feeling."

Miss Fitzwilliam performed the same part at Drury Lane Theatre in the month of July 1849, with Madame Vestris as Lucy, and Mr. Sims Reeves as Macheath, the occasion being the benefit of Kenney, the dramatist, who unhappily died the same evening. At the Windsor Castle Theatricals, Christmas 1849, Miss Fitzwilliam sustained the part of *Endiga* in the play of ' Charles the Twelfth,' and sang ' Rise, gentle Moon,' on the stage in the Rubens' room, accompanied by an unseen band in another apartment, led by Mr. Anderson, who stood midway, and with his bâton acted as a sort of fugleman between singer and musicians. The Queen, through Mr. Charles Kean, sent a gracious and complimentary message to the actress, saying how pleased Her Majesty had been with the song, and expressing appreciation of " the admirable way in which Miss Fitzwilliam had accomplished, what must have been, a very difficult task." In 1850 (January) Miss Fitzwilliam joined the company of the Haymarket Theatre, under Mr. Benjamin Webster's management; but shortly afterwards transferred her services to the Adelphi Theatre, where she remained for three seasons, playing original parts in ' Mephistopheles,' ' Red Riding Hood,' ' Esmeralda,' ' Jessie Gray,' ' The Tarantula,' ' Sea and Land,' &c., and appearing also in the French operettas of ' Griselda ' and ' Bon Soir, Signor Pantalon,' on their production in England. Miss Fitzwilliam made her last appearance on the stage in August 1852 in the latter operetta, and thenceforward adopted concert singing as a profession. From the last-mentioned date until early in the year 1854 she sang with much success at most of the concerts and musical *réunions* in London and at several in the principal towns of the provinces. In May 1854 she married and left the profession.

FLEET, GEORGE RUTLAND. *See* BARRINGTON, RUTLAND.

* **FLOCKTON, CHARLES P.**, made his first appearance on the London stage as *Holdsworth* in ' Glitter,' at St. James's Theatre

December 26, 1868. In the following year he was engaged at the Charing Cross Theatre, and later at the Royalty and Globe; his performances in W. S. Gilbert's burlesque of ' Norma,' and in the comedies ' Not So Bad After All ' and ' Behind a Mask,' being favourably noticed in contemporary journals. More recently he has fulfilled a lengthened engagement at the Adelphi Theatre.

FOOTE, LYDIA A. (a *nom de théâtre*), niece of the popular actress, Mrs. Keeley, made her first appearance on the London stage at the Lyceum Theatre, April 1, 1852, in a child's part, in a piece entitled ' A Chain of Events.' Twelve years later, viz. on Wednesday, November 2, 1864, at the Olympic Theatre, first performance of Tom Taylor's play ' The Hidden Hand,' Miss Foote successfully sustained the part of *Enid Gryffydd;* and in the following year, Saturday, March 4, at the same theatre, first performance of the same author's play entitled ' The Settling Day,' she acted the character of *Miss Hargrave.* In 1866, Saturday, October 29, Miss Foote sustained the part of *Clara*, in Mr. Wilkie Collins's drama ' The Frozen Deep,' then first performed at the Olympic Theatre. By her graceful and earnest performance of this part she largely enhanced her reputation. Nothing could have been more life-like or interesting than her conception of the character. On Saturday, April 6, 1867, first performance of Mr. T. W. Robertson's comedy entitled ' Caste,' at the Prince of Wales's Theatre, she undertook the part of *Esther Eccles.* " The one ideal personage of the play is *Esther*, who is entirely distinct from her sister Polly, and in whom the boundary marks of ' caste ' vanish, though it is on her account that the battle of ' caste ' is fought. The author has even given her an aristocratic tinge, and when her spirit is roused she does not assert plebeian independence like Polly, but speaks as Mrs. George d'Alroy, mother of a child of ancient lineage. To *Esther* belong the strong situations, and generally what may be called the hard work of the piece. The part is most efficiently filled by Miss Lydia Foote." (*Times*, April 11, 1867.) On Saturday, February 15, 1868, she was in the original cast (as *Amanda*) of ' Play,' first performed on that date at the Prince of Wales's. On Saturday, September 5, 1868, at the Holborn Theatre, first performance of H. J. Byron's drama ' Blow for Blow,' Miss Foote played *Mildred Craddock;* and subsequently the part of *Alice Petherick*, " displaying quiet pathos and real power, together with artistic sense and delicacy not often exhibited " (*Athenæum*, September 12, 1868). In April of the following year, first performance at the Globe Theatre of a play by Mr. H. J. Byron entitled ' Minnie; or, Leonard's Love,' she sustained the part of the heroine, *Minnie Vaughan.* At the same theatre, on Saturday, September 18, 1869, in a new comedy by T. W. Robertson, entitled ' Progress,' adapted from ' Les Ganaches ' of M. Sardou, Miss Foote enacted the part of the heroine. In 1870, Saturday, October 1, at the Holborn Theatre, she played the leading female *rôle* in Sefton Parry's piece entitled ' The Odds.' At the same theatre, in December of the same year, first performance of Dion Boucicault's drama entitled 'Jezebel; or, the Dead Reckoning,' she sustained the part of *Madame D'Artignes.* In 1871, in a revival of 'Caste' at the Prince of Wales's Theatre, Miss Foote played her original character. In 1872 (July), in a revival at the Gaiety Theatre of a version by Boucicault of Colman's comedy of 'John Bull,' she played the part of *Mary Thornberry.* In March 1875, first performance at the Adelphi Theatre of Halliday's dramatized version of Charles Dickens's 'Nicholas Nickleby,' she acted *Smike.* In December 1876 Miss Foote played the part of *Grace Harkaway,* in a revival of 'London Assurance,' at St. James's Theatre; and on Saturday, January 6, 1877, first performance at the same theatre of 'The Danischeffs,' she sustained the part of *Anna.* In 1879 she was engaged at the Adelphi Theatre, appearing in revivals of 'The Hunchback,' 'School for Scandal,' 'Amy Robsart,' and 'Ticket-of-Leave Man.'

FORBES-ROBERTSON, JOHNSTON, eldest son of John Forbes-Robertson, art historian and critic, was born in London in 1853, and educated at Charterhouse, and in France. He was admitted student at the Royal Academy of Arts in 1870. Mr. Forbes-Robertson made his first appearance on the stage at the Princess's Theatre, in March 1874, in the part of *Chastelard* in W. G. Wills's play of 'Marie Stuart.' Subsequently he played *James Annesley* in Charles Reade's 'Wandering Heir,' in London, Manchester, and Birmingham. Respecting this performance of Mr. Forbes-Robertson the following criticism appeared:—"We have rarely heard an actor talk so 'humanly,' with such a refreshing disregard of the arbitrary law of climax which seems to rule the stage. He has great earnestness, and dignified and natural bearing, and the true note of manly emotion." (*Manchester Guardian,* May 19, 1874.) The same year Mr. Forbes-Robertson accepted an engagement at the Prince's Theatre, Manchester, under Mr. Calvert, and played *The Prince of Wales* in the revival of '2nd Part of Henry IV.'; *Lysander* in 'Midsummer Night's Dream,' and *Mercutio,* 'Romeo and Juliet.' Returning to London he played a series of parts at the Gaiety Theatre, supporting Mr. Phelps; afterwards accepting an engagement at the Olympic Theatre. In April 1875, at the Haymarket, he played in Tom Taylor's 'Anne Boleyn.' At the Lyceum, in July 1876, he sustained the part of *The Abbé de Larose,* first performance of Mr. Buchanan's 'Corinne.' "A word of very hearty praise," remarked the *Standard* (July 1, 1876), "must be bestowed upon Mr. Forbes-Robertson, who, throughout the drama, gave a well-considered picture of the *Abbé de Larose,* and displayed real and unexpected power in the last act. His abject terror when brought before Marat's remorseless gang in the prison was most forcibly expressed in his face and trembling limbs. The effort to steady himself and resume his courtly and gracious demeanour is admirably conceived." Mr. Forbes-Robertson returned to the Olympic, Easter 1877, for two seasons, appearing as *Jeremy Diddler, George Talboys, Sir Fred Blake* in 'Money,' &c.; and subsequently at the Haymarket Theatre, in September of the same year, he performed the part of *Geoffrey Wynyard*, in Gilbert's 'Dan'l Druce.' During the autumn season of 1878 he was acting at the Prince of Wales's Theatre in 'Diplomacy.'

FORRESTER, HENRY, was born at Capel, Surrey, and entered the dramatic profession in 1855, at Worthing, in a company under the management of Messrs. Parry and Castle. He made his first appearance on the London stage in 1858 at the Marylebone Theatre under Mr. Cave's management, in the character of *Hassan*, in 'The Castle Spectre.' The same year he accepted an engagement at the Lyceum Theatre under Madame Celeste; Mr. Forrester was the original *Charles Darnay* in the play of 'A Tale of Two Cities,' first performed there. Subsequently he went to Sadler's Wells under Mr. Samuel Phelps, and afterwards joined the Princess's company under George Vining's management, at whose theatre he was the original *Paul Fairweather* in 'The Streets of London.' Mr. Forrester played the part of *Friar Laurence* ('Romeo and Juliet') at Stratford-on-Avon at the celebration of the Shakespeare Tercentenary. Under Mrs. Bateman's management, and during the period of Mr. Irving's engagement, he was a member of the company of the Lyceum Theatre, and on February 14, 1876, appeared there as *Iago* in Shakespeare's tragedy of 'Othello.' The *Times* (February 17, 1876) remarked on this performance as follows:—"The *Iago* of Mr. Forrester is as fine a piece of acting as, perhaps, any actor of to-day could show us in this character. With boldness equalled by his judgment, he discards altogether the conventional idea of fawning craft and servile humility, which has been so often and so erroneously made the prominent feature in this wonderful character, and which could but have disgusted, and never could have imposed on such a man as Othello. He stands up before us fair and square, manly of form, pleasant of voice and face, save when, with no companion but his own thoughts, he lifts for a moment the veil of his villany. 'This fellow's of exceeding honesty' throughout, till his purpose is served, and he has done with honesty for good and all; and it is precisely because he seems of such honesty that we find nothing incongruous in the success of what we know to be so outrageous a piece of treachery. His actions and attitudes, which are most natural and effective, and his voice go hand-in-hand throughout."

Mr. Forrester has played the part of *Dan'l Druce* nearly three hundred times in the provinces with great success. Since 1877 he has appeared in London at the St. James's Theatre in the parts of *Othello, Claude Melnotte, Jaques* ('As You Like It'), &c. When Mr. Irving assumed the management of the Lyceum, on December 30, 1878, Mr. Forrester reappeared there in 'Hamlet' as *Claudius;* and in the following March, during Mr. Irving's temporary indisposition, he played *Hamlet* for three nights, being his first appearance in that character. Subsequently during the season he appeared in the various revivals of Mr. Irving's most successful plays, viz. 'Eugene Aram,' in which Mr. Forrester acted *Housemann;* 'Richelieu,' in which he acted *Barradas,* &c.

FOWLER, EMILY (Mrs. JOHN C. PEMBERTON), was born in Rochdale. At an early age she appeared on the continental stage as a dancer in ballet and spectacle ; but coming to London in 1868, made her *début* on the metropolitan stage at the Royalty Theatre, under Miss Oliver's management, in the burlesque of 'Black-Eyed Susan.' Miss Fowler was afterwards engaged by Mr. John Hollingshead at the Gaiety Theatre, and subsequently by Mr. Wybert Reeve at the Charing Cross Theatre, where she first attracted notice by her painstaking acting in his comedy entitled 'Not So Bad After All.' Miss Fowler then joined the company of the Olympic Theatre, where in March 1874, first performance of Tom Taylor's drama 'Lady Clancarty ; or, Wedded and Wooed,' she acted the part of *Lady Betty Noel.* At the same theatre she appeared in the following plays with considerable success, viz. 'The Ticket-of-Leave Man ' (revival), in which she sustained the character of *May Edwards ;* 'The Two Orphans ' (first perform- ance), in which she played *Louise ;* and 'The Spendthrift ; or, the Scrivener's Daughter,' J. Albery (first performance), in which she acted the leading *rôle.* In September 1876, in a revival of Shake- speare's 'Henry V.' at the Queen's Theatre, Long Acre, Miss Fowler undertook the part of *Katharine of Valois.* In May 1878 she assumed the management of the Royalty Theatre for a brief period, and produced there W. G. Wills's ' Nell Gwynne,' in which she played the heroine with much success. She produced on the same stage 'Scandal,' adapted from ' Les Scandales d'Hier,' by Arthur Matthison, in which she acted the part of *Viscountess Liddesdale.* On Saturday, September 28, 1878, Miss Fowler played *Perdita*, in a revival of ' A Winter's Tale,' at Drury Lane Theatre. Since that time she has been acting in the provinces.

FRANCIS, VIRGINIA (a *nom de théâtre ;* VIRGINIA FRAN- CIS BATEMAN), was born in New York. Fourth daughter of the late H. L. Bateman, formerly of that city, and subsequently lessee of the Lyceum Theatre, London. As a child she appeared, December 22, 1865, at Her Majesty's Theatre, in the character of *Little Daisy*, in the play of that name ; her sister, Miss Isabel Bateman, playing the part of *Diggory Dawdlegrace.* Miss Francis made her first appearance on the stage proper, Monday, October 19, 1868, at the Haymarket Theatre, as *Madelena*, in ' Leah '; her sister, Miss Bateman, playing the title *rôle.* In May 1872, in a revival of that play at the Lyceum Theatre, she played the same character. In June of the same year, at the same theatre, first performance of 'Medea' (W. G. Wills), she sustained the character of *Glaucea.* "As *Glaucea*, Miss Virginia Francis acted with much taste and feeling. Her attitude at the foot of the altar in the second act was singularly graceful and poetical." (*Athenæum*, July 13, 1872.) In April 1876, at the Lyceum Theatre, Miss Francis performed the part of *Princess Elizabeth*, in ' Queen Mary ' (Tennyson) ; and in June of the same year, *Mrs. Racket*, in a revival of ' The Belle's Stratagem.' In April 1878 she sustained the part of *Marie*, revival of Boucicault's version of Casimir Delavigne's play ' Louis XI.'

GAINSBOROUGH, MONTA. Born in the West Riding of Yorkshire. Was educated to the stage from childhood, but severe indisposition prevented her from actively following the duties of her profession until 1869, when she appeared at the Theatre Royal, Leeds. From 1869 to 1872 she fulfilled various provincial engagements, playing during that period all lines of business. Miss Gainsborough's first appearance of importance was at the Queen's Theatre, London, as *Amos*, the boy, in Watts Phillips's drama of 'Amos Clark.' At the Court Theatre, in 1873, she played the original heroine in ' Marriage Lines,' and subsequently, at the Opéra Comique, sustained the characters of the heroines in revivals of H. T. Craven's plays ' Milky White ' and ' Miriam's Crime.' July 1873, at the Haymarket, Miss Gainsborough played *Pauline* (' Lady of Lyons '), Mr. Creswick performing the leading *rôle*. In November 1874, at the Prince's Theatre, Manchester, in a revival of ' Romeo and Juliet,' arranged by Mr. Charles Calvert, she played *Juliet* for twelve nights. Afterwards, in various provincial towns, she performed the part of the heroines in the following plays, viz. ' Lost in London,' ' Notre Dame,' ' Blow for Blow,' ' London Assurance,' ' The Ladies' Battle,' and the leading female *rôle* in several plays of the Shakespearian and poetic drama. In May 1875, at the Standard Theatre, London, she performed *Ophelia* " with much freshness and pathos, and meriting warm praise for the mad scenes, which were acted with remarkable grace and skill " (*Times*, May 17, 1875). The same year, at a morning performance (at the Alexandra Palace) of ' The School for Scandal,' in which Mr. S. Phelps played Sir Peter Teazle, Miss Gainsborough appeared as *Lady Teazle*. June 23, 1877, at the Prince of Wales's Theatre, Birmingham, in a revival by Mr. Charles Calvert of ' Sardanapalus,' she played the character of *Myrrha*, and with so much success that she continued to perform the part during a provincial tour which extended over six months. In November 1877, on the revival of the same play at the Duke's Theatre, Holborn, Miss Gainsborough represented the character in London. Easter, 1878, at the Alexandra Theatre, Liverpool, she played *Hero*, in a revival of ' Much Ado About Nothing,' " with uncommon power and unimpeachable grace " (*Liverpool Daily Post*, April 23, 1878).

GARDEN, EDMUND WILLIAM, was born in London, April 27, 1845, and made his *début* on the stage on the night of the opening of the Theatre Royal, Nottingham, under the management of the late Walter Montgomery. He appeared subsequently for entire seasons at the Amphitheatre, Leeds ; Lyceum Theatre, Sunderland ; Theatre Royal, Croydon (when first opened under George Fawcett Rowe) ; and Theatre Royal, Norwich, playing " light," " eccentric," and " first low comedy," in the entire range of the drama. Mr. Garden made his first appearance on the London stage at the Olympic, under the management of Mr. W. H. Liston, in the character of *Uriah Heep* in the play of 'Little Em'ly,' on the occasion of its revival, October 17, 1870. He remained at that theatre during two seasons, playing, among other characters, *Dicky Duggo* in Craven's 'Milky White,' and the "original" *George Warriner* in Byron's 'Daisy Farm.' He became one of the original members of the Globe company, when that theatre was opened under the late H. J. Montague's management, and played there for nearly three seasons. He was in the original cast of 'Partners for Life,' 'Forgiven,' 'Spur of the Moment,' 'Tourist's Ticket,' 'Arkwright's Wife' (on its first performance in London), and 'Fine Feathers.' In the latter play he was very successful in the part of *Daniel Dole*, a circus clown, known in the programmes as the "celebrated Chaucerian comique." "Skilfully portrayed by the author, this admirable character is wrought by the actor, without the slightest straining after a point, into one of the most impressive pictures the gallery of the stage has exhibited for many years. There is a fine touch of pathos in the last act, where the clown comes to offer the gratuitous services of the company in aid of the broken-down circus-proprietor they have so long faithfully served in better days ; and it may be safely said that, although the marked intelligence of Mr. E. W. Garden has been frequently before noted in other characters, he has here raised himself at once into a high position as a thorough artist." (*Daily Telegraph*, April 28, 1873.) Mr. E. W. Garden was the original representative of *Don Boléro* in Lecocq's 'Giroflé-Girofla,' when that opera was first produced in English at the Philharmonic Theatre. He has visited most of the chief towns in the United Kingdom on several tours, playing original parts and principal characters in such pieces as 'Two Roses,' &c. He was the original representative in the provinces of *Talbot Champneys* in Byron's 'Our Boys,' and *Mr. Gibson Greene* in the same author's 'Married in Haste,' and has played those parts uninterruptedly in nearly every town in the United Kingdom for a period extending over three years.

GARNER, ARTHUR, was born at Bath, February 8, 1851, and entered the dramatic profession in 1870, making his first appearance on any stage October 29th of that year, at the Prince of Wales's Theatre, Liverpool, in a small part in Farnie's burlesque 'The Idle 'Prentice.' On the termination of the season at the Prince of Wales's, in April 1871 he joined a travelling company in Scotland, as "walking gentleman," and afterwards played the same line of "business" under Mr. J. L. Toole during his summer provincial tour in that year. In June 1872 Mr. Garner joined the company of the Amphitheatre, Liverpool, under Mr. Leslie's management, to play the "juvenile leading business." In March 1873 he sailed for Australia, and subsequently appeared at the Theatre Royal, Melbourne, as *Frank Goldsworthy* in Brough's comedy 'Kind to a Fault,' with very considerable success. He remained in Australia about three years, playing for a great part of the time at the Melbourne Theatre all the principal light comedy and juvenile business. May 29, 1875, Mr. Garner sustained the part of *Captain*

Molineux in 'The Shaughraun,' on its first performance in Australia. Having travelled through that country, he returned by way of San Francisco and the United States to England, and appeared November 6, 1876, at the Amphitheatre, Liverpool, as *Tom Spiril* in Paul Meritt's play entitled 'Stolen Kisses,' then performed for the first time. He made his first appearance on the London stage, June 25, 1877, at the Globe Theatre, in the part of *Chandos Bellingham* in 'After Dark.' Subsequently at the same theatre Mr. Garner played his original part of *Tom Spiril* ('Stolen Kisses') for 150 consecutive nights, commencing June 2, 1877. He appeared in the same part on a provincial tour which lasted for forty-five consecutive weeks in 1878, 'Stolen Kisses' being the only piece performed by the company, of which Mr. Garner was a member, during that time. In April 1879 he started for Melbourne to fulfil a lengthened engagement in the Australian colonies.

GARTHORNE, C. W. (CHARLES W. GRIMSTON), is a brother of Mr. W. H. Kendal, and made his first appearance on the stage at the Theatre Royal, Edinburgh, December 1869, in the character of *Adolphus* in 'Bachelor of Arts,' with the late Charles Mathews. He first appeared in London at the Vaudeville Theatre, April 16, 1870, as *Tom Buncombe* in 'For Love or Money.' This play was the first of the Vaudeville successes. On a tour in the provinces with the original Vaudeville company he played *Caleb Deecie* in Albery's 'Two Roses,' having previously played that character in London during Mr. Thorne's absence. After fulfilling an engagement at the Theatre Royal, Brighton, for one season, he played at the Royalty Theatre for six weeks, and was the original *Hudson* in Bertie Vyse's comedy of 'L. S. D.' He also appeared as *Gavis* and *Romeo;* and afterwards at the Olympic Theatre for nine months, under Miss Ada Cavendish's management. For the next six months he was on tour with Mr. Richard Younge, playing *Tom Pogson* in 'Time's Triumph,' *Lord Gadderly* in 'Fine Feathers,' and *Major M'Tavish* in 'Old Soldiers.' From thence he engaged with Mr. Flockton on tour, representing the characters of *Caleb Deecie* in 'Two Roses,' *The Great Baggs* in 'Apple Blossoms,' *Jones* in 'Two Thorns,' *Dick Tallon* in 'Forgiven,' &c., in Mr. Albery's pieces. After playing *Lord Woodstock* on a tour with Mr. Richard Younge's 'Clancarty' company, and a brief engagement at the Opéra Comique Theatre, he rejoined the company at the Vaudeville Theatre in January 1875. In 1876 he played *Charles Middlewick* in Byron's comedy of 'Our Boys' in place of Mr. Charles Warner, the original representative of that part. Mr. Garthorne was the original *Lord Aspland* in the same author's comedy of 'The Girls,' first performed at the Vaudeville Theatre, April 19, 1879.

GEORGE, EDWARD JOHN, was born in London, October 29, 1842, and made his first appearance on any stage, November 1865, at the Theatre Royal, Norwich, as *Winterbottom* (the valet) in

' Arrah-na-Pogue.' He had played in various benefit performances —e. g. at the Royalty Theatre, July 10, 1875, as *Dame Hatley* in ' Black-Eyed Susan ' (F. C. Burnand)—previous to his professional *début* in London, which took place September 22, 1877, at Drury Lane Theatre, in the part of the *Chamberlain* in ' Barbazon,' operetta by Arthur Matthison. In the intervening period Mr. George had undergone " all the drudgery of a provincial actor's life," his first important engagement having been entered into with the late Mdlle. Beatrice, in whose theatrical company he played *Pitou* in the English version of ' Frou-Frou.' At the Hull and Brighton Theatres Royal, Mr. George was for a long time a special favourite in what is known as " character parts." In November 1877 he commenced an engagement in London at the Adelphi Theatre as *Bob Saunders* in ' Formosa '; subsequently succeeding Mr. Emery in the part of *Chamboran*, 'Proof,' and more recently playing at the same theatre *Crabtree* in a revival of ' The School for Scandal.'

GIBSON, JAMES RHIND, was born at Aberdeen, November 28, 1842, and entered the dramatic profession November 18, 1862, appearing first at the Theatre Royal, Sheffield. He afterwards played various parts in the provinces, and for the season 1866–7 was enrolled by Mr. C. Calvert as a member of the company of the Prince's Theatre, Manchester. At that theatre he played *Octavius Cæsar* (' Antony and Cleopatra '), *Edgar* (' King Lear '), *Abbot of St. Maurice* (' Manfred '), *Iago* (' Othello '), &c. In August 1867 Mr. Gibson became stage-manager of the Theatre Royal, Newcastle-on-Tyne, and in April 1868 returned to the Prince's Theatre, Manchester, where he acted various characters of note in the dramas of Boucicault and others. In 1869 he appeared at the same theatre as *Camillo* in a revival of ' A Winter's Tale.' The same year Mr. Gibson became leading actor of the Theatre Royal, Edinburgh, and sustained there, among other characters, the part of *Jaques* to the Rosalind of Miss Helen Faucit at her farewell performance in Edinburgh. In 1870 he went on a six months' tour with Charles Dillon, playing *Iago, Macduff, Petruchio, Gratiano,* and lastly, with great success, at the Theatre Royal, Glasgow, the part of *Bailie Nicol Jarvie* to that actor's Rob Roy. Mr. Gibson was leading actor at the Glasgow Theatre Royal in 1871, and in the following year accepted an engagement in the like capacity at the Opera House, Aberdeen. In 1873 he travelled as a dramatic reader in Scotland. In 1875 (having in the intervening period been incapacitated by severe illness) Mr. Gibson played various " starring " engagements in Scotch *rôles*. In 1876 he sustained the part of *Antigonus* in a revival of 'A Winter's Tale' at the Alexandra Theatre, Liverpool. In 1877 he again performed Scotch *rôles* in leading towns in Scotland. In the year following, on April 6, he made his first appearance in London at the Duke's Theatre, in the character of *Jock Howieson* in the play of ' Cramond Brig,' and was subsequently engaged by Mr. Irving for the Lyceum Theatre, where since December 30, 1878, he has been performing.

GIDDENS, GEORGE, was born at Bedfont, Middlesex, June 17, 1845, and first appeared on the stage at Theatre Royal, Edinburgh, in November 1865, in the part of *Katty* in 'Arrah-na-Pogue.' Afterwards he performed at various theatres in the provinces, and accepted an engagement as "comedian" in the "Swanborough Burlesque" and "United Service Dramatic" companies. In 1871 he went to the United States as a member of "Charles Wyndham's Comedy Company," subsequently fulfilling engagements in "stock companies" at San Francisco, Chicago, and at the Union Square Theatre, New York, where he played *Henry Greenlanes*, first performance in America of 'Pink Dominos.' He has been "on tour" through the Australian colonies. Mr. Giddens made his *début* on the London stage at the Folly Theatre, in August 1878, in the part of *Jenx* in a play entitled 'The Idol.'

GLENNEY, CHARLES HENRY HALL, was born in Glasgow, June 20, 1857, and first appeared on the stage at the Theatre Royal, St. Helen's, in the part of *Montano* ('Othello'). He made his *début* on the London stage at the Duke's Theatre, Holborn, September 7, 1878, in the part of *Theuerdier*, in a piece entitled 'The Barricade,' a dramatic version of 'Les Miserables.' At the same theatre he played with success the character of *Salem Scudder* in a revival of 'The Octoroon,' *Captain Crosstree* ('Black-Eyed Susan'), *Kyrle Daly* ('Colleen Bawn'), and *Mr. Lamb* ("original") in the 'New Babylon,' by P. Meritt.

GLOSSOP, MARIA ELIZABETH. *See* HARRIS, MARIA.

GLOVER, AUGUSTUS (a *nom de théâtre;* SIDNEY DE FIVAS), was born in Edinburgh, May 29, 1846, and is the youngest son of the late Victor de Fivas (formerly of Edinburgh), M.A., LL.D., &c., author of many well-known French educational works. He made his first appearance on the stage, June 1864, at the New Royalty Theatre, as *Bassanio* ('Merchant of Venice'), under the name of 'Gilbert.' Afterwards he became "stock leading-man" for several seasons at various provincial theatres; and was a member of Mr. Walter Montgomery's company when that gentleman opened the New Theatre Royal at Nottingham. On December 26, 1871, at the New Theatre Royal, Bristol, he played the part of *Captain Bill Backashaw* in the pantomime of 'Dick Whittington and His Cat,' with much success. Mr. Glover's first appearance of note in London was made September 21, 1872, at the Adelphi Theatre, as *Wild Murtoch* in a revival of 'The Green Bushes,' Madame Celeste playing Miami, her original part. (*See* CELESTE, MADAME.) At the same theatre he played the following original parts, viz. *Daniel Mandril* in 'Mabel's Life' (H. J. Byron), *Colonel Crafton* in 'Fritz' (Andrew Halliday), *Mr. Pollywiggle* in 'A Yule Log' (Benjamin Webster, jun.), *Captain Cartouche* in 'A Waltz by Arditi' (John Oxenford). Subsequently at the Princess's Theatre he played the part of *Fix*, the detective, during the performance of 'Round the

World in 80 Days,' and at Covent Garden Theatre (1876), *King Hokypokywankyfum*, in the Christmas pantomime.

GLYN, ISABEL (Mrs. E. S. DALLAS), was born in Edinburgh in 1825. She had played in a few rehearsals at Manchester previously to her professional *début*, which took place at the Olympic Theatre, London, Wednesday, January 26, 1848. Miss Glyn made her appearance, specifically, as a pupil of Charles Kemble, in the character of *Lady Macbeth*. The *Athenæum* (January 29, 1848) thus noticed her *début :*—" Miss Glyn is a brunette, rather tall, of a well-proportioned figure and expressive features. Her eyes are large and dark, and she has a prominent intellectual forehead. It was evident from her entrance that she was suffering from excessive nervousness. There was nevertheless in her early scenes a marked intention, not fully brought out. The voice faltered—at times all but failed, and the action was embarrassed. As the play progressed, however, the text was more strongly pronounced, and it was interesting to note the gradual increase of confidence from scene to scene. . . . A course of provincial training would have made Miss Glyn, we doubt not, a great actress ; with proper allowance for the difficulties of her position, and a little generous management, she will, we believe, become so without it. We are content at present to record that her style is eminently natural and unaffected, and free from any tendency to rant or exaggeration."

At the same theatre, on Wednesday, February 16 of the same year, she played *Juliana* in ' The Honeymoon ' ; and on Wednesday, September 27, 1848, at Sadler's Wells Theatre, *Volumnia* to the Coriolanus of Mr. Samuel Phelps. In the following month, at Sadler's Wells, she played *Hermione* (' A Winter's Tale'), and on December 13, *Queen Katherine*. In 1849, on January 29, she appeared as *Constance* (' King John') at Sadler's Wells. " The *Constance* of Miss Glyn is a marked improvement on her early and most crude style. Her grief and her indignation have no lack of intensity, she seems filled with a determination to give all her words and all her by-play their full expression, and some of her points are made with striking effect. Still there is a great deal to learn in the art of concealing art." (*Times*, January 30, 1849.) During the same year, at Sadler's Wells, Miss Glyn appeared (with Mr. Samuel Phelps) in the following characters, viz. *Margaret of Anjou* (' Richard the Third '), *Portia* (' The Merchant of Venice'), *Emilia* (' Othello'), *Isabella* (' Measure for Measure ') ; and, after long preparation of the piece, on October 22, 1849, ' Antony and Cleopatra' was produced for the first time at this theatre, Mr. Phelps acting Antony, and Miss Glyn *Cleopatra*. The following criticism on this performance appeared in the *Athenæum* (October 27, 1849):—" In portraying the enchantress, *Cleopatra*, Miss Glyn had occasion to draw upon the entire resources of her art. The variety and fascination of the character she touched to admiration. The caprice, the grace, the pride of the character were exhibited with a power which exceeded expectation. It was evident that she had made a profound and industrious study of the part. The whole portrait was thrown · out with decision and force, and richly coloured. Those parts in which dignity and anger were expressed —such, as the interview with the messenger after Antony's second marriage—were given with a vehemence and power corresponding to the language she had to deliver. But it was in the fifth act, when preparing for her death, that the better phases of the character and the more refined parts of the action tested the fitness of the actress for this assumption. Indignant majesty, compulsory resignation, heroic resolve, and tender memory, were all adequately pronounced. The death itself was a triumph."

During 1850 Miss Glyn's engagement at Sadler's Wells continued, and she appeared there in the following characters, viz. *Lady Macbeth*, for the second time ; *Isabella*, in Southerne's fine tragedy of that name ; *Bianca*, in Milman's tragedy of ' Fazio ' ; *Juliana* in ' The Honeymoon ' ; and *Beatrice* in ' Much Ado About Nothing.' The production of ' Much Ado About Nothing ' at Sadler's Wells was highly interesting, from the circumstance that it exhibited Miss Glyn in an entirely new light. " Hitherto she had been confined not only to tragedy, but to the sterner section of tragedy, and there was some reason to doubt that a lady who had once adopted the elevated manner of interpretation would be able to realize the vivacious *Beatrice*. The result of her attempt surpassed even the most favourable expectations. *Beatrice*, as represented by Miss Glyn, was full of healthy hilarity, indicated by the play of the countenance and the nimble readiness of the movements ; but she did not overpower her hearers with those incessant bursts of laughter that sometimes become fatiguing. It was the distinctive feature of her interpretation that she thoroughly displayed the mental peculiarities of the character without recourse to violent physical expedients. Her attack on Benedick at the ball, when she rallies him as the ' Prince's jester,' was a remarkable instance of discrimination. She threw out her words with more than ordinary force, making them hit harder and faster, as if aware that she had seized on a happy suggestive notion and was delighted with its capabilities." On Wednesday, November 20, 1850, Miss Glyn played the title *rôle* in R. H. Horne's version of ' The Duchess of Malfi ' with marked success. On the occasion of her first "benefit," at Sadler's Wells Theatre, Tuesday, March 11, 1851, she played *Katharine* (' The Taming of the Shrew ') for the first time. During this year she made her first tour in the provinces and achieved great success ; and in September 1851, for a brief period, entered upon a series of Shakespearian readings. On December 26, 1851, she made her first appearance at Drury Lane Theatre (under Mr. Bunn's management) as *Bianca* (' Fazio ') ; and subsequently, Friday, January 16, 1852, appeared as *Julia* in ' The Hunchback.' The *Times* (January 17, 1852) remarked of this performance :— " Miss Glyn's *Julia* essentially differs from that of any other actress who has sustained the part. As if anxious to avoid the charge of exaggeration, she seems determined to place the character rather within the sphere of genteel comedy than to render it a subject for tragic emotions. She plays with the sentiment of the first act. She does not exhibit a very intense grief when about to accept the Earl of Rochdale, and even the words, 'He never loved me,' often uttered with such deep sorrow, were spoken rather as if they furnished a just pretext for revenge than with any other feeling. It was not till the interview with the humbled Clifford took place that she seemed to trust herself with all the agony of the situation, and the words, 'Clifford, why don't you speak to me?' after the previous quiet, came with terrific effect. In the fifth act, when she resolutely refuses to marry the Earl, and defies Master Walter, the tragic position is beyond a doubt, and Miss Glyn gave herself up entirely to its influence, occasionally at the expense of clearness of articulation. This is a defect she will easily remedy, for distinctness of delivery is one of her great qualifications."

From 1852 to 1854 Miss Glyn rarely appeared on the stage. In the latter year, on Monday, October 2, first performance at St. James's Theatre, of 'The King's Rival' (Messrs. Tom Taylor and Charles Reade) she sustained the part of *Miss Stewart.* In 1855 Miss Glyn accepted an engagement at the New National Standard Theatre, Bishopsgate, and appeared there in a number of her favourite Shakespearian representations, "opening" on March 3 as *Cleopatra* ('Antony and Cleopatra'), and continuing to act at the same theatre from time to time until 1857. In 1859 she had returned to the avocation of a "reader" in public of Shakespeare's plays, her most successful selections being taken from the play last named. She followed this pursuit with unvarying success at intervals during the decade 1859–69. Miss Glyn appeared for a brief season at Sadler's Wells Theatre in 1859 in a "round" of Shakespearian parts, beginning with *Lady Macbeth*, performed there on Saturday, May 28. After some years' absence from the stage, in May 1867, she reappeared at the Princess's Theatre, as *Cleopatra*, and according to the *Athenæum* (May 18, 1867), "the triumph of the evening was the assumption by Miss Glyn of *Cleopatra*. The witchery of the blandishments, the Asiatic undulations of the form, the variety of the enchantments, the changes of mood, the impetuous passion, and in the end the noble resignation—all these points were brought out with an accuracy of elocution and with a force of genius which left no doubt on the mind that Miss Glyn is as great an actress as ever adorned the English stage." The following year (1868), April and May, she accepted a brief engagement at the Standard Theatre, appearing there as *Hermione*, in 'A Winter's Tale,' among other characters. Since the last-mentioned date Miss Glyn has rarely appeared on the boards of a theatre. She has principally devoted herself to the instruction and preparation of pupils for the stage, and to the "readings" already noticed. The first of these given by her in America, were delivered in the autumn of 1870, at Tremont Temple, Boston, and consisted of selections from 'Antony and Cleopatra.' More recently (June 1878), Miss Glyn has been reading from the same play in London; and in March and April 1879 she gave, with much success, "Readings from Shakespeare" at the Steinway Hall, London.

GOODALL, ISABELLA, was born in Liverpool, August 10, 1851, and first appeared on any stage at the Royal Amphitheatre, Liverpool, in 'The Middy Ashore.' She made her *début* on the London stage April 15, 1866, at the Prince of Wales's Theatre as *Coralie* in 'A Winning Hazard.' Miss Goodall has since appeared at the following theatres in London, viz. the Royalty, Alhambra, Strand, Holborn, Opéra Comique, Haymarket, Prince of Wales's, and Gaiety, in most of the popular burlesques produced during the past ten years—'The Black Crook,' 'Field of Cloth of Gold,' 'Idle 'Prentice,' 'Don Giovanni,' &c.

GORDON, GEORGE LASH, was born in London, August 29, 1851, and first appeared on the stage in 1870, at the Theatre Royal, Scarborough; after playing there a season he joined the late Mdlle. Beatrice's Comedy Company. At the termination of that engagement he joined the company of the Theatre Royal, Dublin, remaining there till 1874, "playing a round of light comedy, and devoting spare time to dramatic authorship." In 1874 Mr. Gordon joined the company of the Prince of Wales's Theatre, Liverpool. He made his *début* on the London stage at the Opéra Comique, August 7, 1875, as *Fred Walmsley*, in his own farce, 'Backing the Favourite.' In 1877 he "started a tour," in conjunction with Mr. Joseph Eldred, at the end of which engagement he produced, at the Princess's Theatre, Edinburgh, "a new and original comedy-drama" from his own pen, entitled 'Auld Lang Syne,' which was subsequently (May 26, 1878) placed on the stage of the Park Theatre, London. Mr. Gordon is the author of other dramatic pieces produced at the same theatre in the same year. In 1879 he was engaged at the Duke's Theatre, playing in Mr. Meritt's 'New Babylon.'

GOWARD, MISS. *See* KEELEY, Mrs.

GRAHAME, C., began her professional career at the Hull Theatre, December 26, 1875. Her merits attracted the attention of Mr. and Mrs. Kendal when they were fulfilling an engagement there, and she was engaged by them. On the 4th of January, 1879, she made her first appearance on the London stage at the Court Theatre as *Lucy* in 'A Scrap of Paper.' Subsequently she played the character of *Leonie* in 'The Ladies' Battle,' and *Florence Dalston* in Val Prinsep's sketch entitled 'Cousin Dick.' In each of these parts Miss Grahame showed more than ordinary ability.

GRAHAME, J. G., first appeared at the Holborn (now Duke's) Theatre with Mr. J. S. Clarke in 1874 in 'Red Tape.' He took for a time the character of *Charles Middlewick* in 'Our Boys' at the Vaudeville Theatre, and afterwards appeared at the Strand in Burnand's 'Our Club' and other comedies. Later he appeared at the Folly in 'Retiring,' and in 1879 played at the Globe Theatre with Messrs. Shiel Barry and James Fernandez in 'Bird in Hand.' He has since been playing in the provinces.

GREEN, DOLORES DRUMMOND. *See* DRUMMOND, DOLORES.

GRIMSTON, MRS. W. HUNTER. *See* KENDAL, Mrs. W. H.

GRIMSTON, WILLIAM HUNTER. *See* KENDAL, Mr. W. H.

GRIMSTON, CHARLES W. *See* GARTHORNE, C. W.

GROSSMITH, GEORGE (the Younger), son of George Grossmith, a well-known popular lecturer, was for many years a reporter in the law courts, which he attended with a view of ultimately entering the legal profession. Being, however, possessed of considerable musical ability, Mr. Grossmith, jun., at the suggestion of Professor Pepper, was induced to exchange the toil of the courts for more inviting repose afforded by the Polytechnic Institution. There, in 1869, he made his *début* as a public entertainer in the school of the late John Parry; and in the following year went on tour with Mr. and Mrs. Howard Paul. Subsequently, Mr. Grossmith visited many hundred of Provincial Literary and Mechanics' Institutions, in conjunction with his father, and on his own account, giving recitations, interspersed with songs and character sketches. In 1876-7 he produced an entertainment with Florence Marryatt entitled 'Entre Nous,' for which he wrote and composed the successful musical comedietta entitled 'Cups and Saucers.' During a part of the year it is Mr. Grossmith's custom to give recitals at private houses, and on one of these occasions he attracted the notice of Dr. Arthur Sullivan, who persuaded him to undertake the part of *John Wellington Wells*, in Gilbert and Sullivan's comic opera of 'The Sorcerer,' produced at the Opéra Comique. Mr. Grossmith, jun., first appeared on the stage in that character. In May 1878 he became connected with 'H.M.S. Pinafore' (the very successful opera by the same authors), as *Sir Joseph Porter, K.C.B.*, a character sustained by him in a spirit of the most refined and amusing burlesque. During the "run" of that piece Mr. Grossmith has composed several "drawing-room comic songs" of a popular character, besides his own entertainments and *scenas*, of which the following will suffice as examples, viz. 'The Silver Wedding,' 'Beauties on the Beach,' 'Five Hamlets.'

GROVES, CHARLES, was born in Limerick, December 6, 1843, and first appeared on the stage in the year following (October 1844), at the Theatre Royal, Monmouth, as *Little Peter* in 'Mr. and Mrs. White.'* "My dramatic career," Mr. Groves

---

* Mr. Groves has the advantage of every other player whose name is included in the present edition. He made his first appearance at the age of ten months !—ED.

writes, " commenced at a very early period of my existence, having been born in the profession. My parents were at the time on tour with a company in Ireland, under the management of Mr. Collins. My father (Charles Groves) was a provincial actor of over thirty years' standing ; my mother an actress of even longer experience, she having played children's parts in London theatres in 1830, under the name of Miss Bigg—' Little Bigg,' as she was called. She appeared in ' Peter Bell the Waggoner,' at the old Cobourg, under Mr. Davage's management ; also as *Tom Thumb* at the Haymarket, in Edmund Kean's time, with Mrs. Glover, Mr. Dowton, and the elder Farren in the company." Following his first appearance Mr. Groves does not seem to have been relegated to the nursery ; his services were utilized in "speaking children's parts " until November 1858, when he " first tasted the sweets of salary " as a member of the company of Mr. James Rodgers, manager of the T. R. Worcester, by whom Mr. Groves was engaged, to make himself "generally useful." For several succeeding years he "played all sorts of business, with all sorts of managers, in all sorts of places, experiencing the uphill work and drudgery of a provincial actor's life." In September 1868 Mr. Groves joined the company of the T. R. Bradford under Mr. Charles Rice, as "first low comedian," acting such parts as *Squire Chevy* (' David Garrick '), *Captain Montraffe* (' Home '), *Dr. Botcherby* (' The Unequal Match '), *Michael Feeny* (' Arrah-na-Pogue '), &c. In September 1870 he " opened " at the Theatre Royal, Brighton, as "first low comedian" and stagemanager. During this engagement he played *Mould* (' Not Such a Fool as He Looks '), *Bunter* (' New Men and Old Acres '), *Brown* (burlesque, ' Brown and the Brahmins '), &c., &c. Mr. Groves made his *début* on the London stage, Boxing Night (Christmas), 1871, at Covent Garden Theatre, as *Lebeau* in ' Lost Letter,' and *Sister Anne* in the pantomime of ' Blue Beard.' Subsequently he played a short engagement at the Royalty Theatre ; and in August 1872 " opened " at the Theatre Royal, Plymouth ; following which he joined Mr. C. Bernard's company at the Gaiety Theatre, Glasgow. Here he remained till March 1877, and established himself as a great favourite in burlesque and comedy. He was on tour with Mr. and Mrs. Kendal during the year last stated. October 12, 1878, he joined the company of the Royalty Theatre, London, where he is now (June 1879), acting as *Alderman Jones*, in a comedy entitled ' Crutch and Toothpick,' by G. R. Sims.

HAMILTON, HENRY. Born at Nunhead, Surrey. Youngest son of the late Captain Hamilton, H.E.I.C.S. Educated at Christ's Hospital. Entered the dramatic profession in 1873, appearing first at the Theatre Royal, Edinburgh, under Mr. J. B. Howard's management. Subsequently he joined the following travelling companies of comedians, viz. Mr. Wilson Barrett's in August 1873; Mr. Craven Robertson's so-called 'Caste' company in November 1874; and in April 1876, in conjunction with Mr. H. M. Pitt, he formed the "Pitt and Hamilton Comedy-Drama Company." He made his first appearance in London at the Lyceum Theatre, July 1878, in the character of *Snodgrass* in the revival of 'Jingle' (Albery). During the autumn of the same year Mr. Hamilton was engaged for a brief season at Drury Lane Theatre.

HARCOURT, CHARLES, made his first appearance on the London stage March 30, 1863, at the St. James's Theatre, as *Robert Audley* in George Roberts's dramatic version of Miss Braddon's novel 'Lady Audley's Secret,' first performed at the same theatre Saturday, February 28, 1863. He has since appeared in London with success in the following parts, viz. at Drury Lane Theatre, February 1866, as *Baron Steinfort*, in 'The Stranger'; at the same theatre, January 1867, as *Frank Rochdale*, in a revival of 'John Bull'; at the same theatre, March 1868, as *Count Henri de Villetaneuve*, first performance of Colonel A. B. Richards's drama 'The Prisoner of Toulon'; at the Royalty Theatre, September 1872, as *Young Rapid*, in a revival of Morton's comedy 'A Cure for the Heartache'; at the Charing Cross Theatre, November 1872, as *Captain Absolute*, in 'The Rivals'; at the Globe Theatre, September 1873, as *Lord Zeyland*, first performance of Richard Lee's play entitled 'Chivalry'; at the Haymarket Theatre, May 1876, as *Claude Melnotte;* at the same theatre, in January 1877, as *Pygmalion*, in a revival of Gilbert's 'Pygmalion and Galatea.' On Saturday, April 20, 1878, first performance at the Adelphi Theatre of F. C. Burnand's drama 'Proof; or, a Celebrated Case,' adapted from the French 'Une Cause Célèbre' of MM. Adolphe d'Ennery and Eugène Cormon, Mr. Harcourt played the part of *Count d'Aubeterre.* He has since appeared at the Haymarket Theatre as *Mercutio* in 'Romeo and Juliet,' a part which he acted with infinite spirit and discrimination.

HARE, JOHN (a *nom de théâtre;* JOHN FAIRS), made his first appearance on the London stage at the Prince of Wales's Theatre, September 25, 1865, in the part of *Short* in a play entitled 'Naval Engagements.' At the same theatre, November 11 of the same year, he sustained the part of *Lord Ptarmigant*, first performance in London of T. W. Robertson's comedy entitled 'Society,' originally produced at the Prince of Wales's Theatre, Liverpool. This "bit of character" was made up to the life by

Mr. Hare. The acting throughout was admirable. Mr. Bancroft who performed the hero, Mr. Hare who played the part of a listless middle-aged lord, and Mr. Clarke who represented the vulgar-minded, self-sufficient young man of property, were most artistic. On Saturday, September 15, 1866, first performance at the Prince of Wales's Theatre of T. W. Robertson's comedy entitled ' Ours,' Mr. Hare undertook the part of *Prince Perovsky*. The play was originally performed with great success at Liverpool. Acted with remarkable care by the excellent company of the Prince of Wales's, the comedy produced an effect which was most satisfactorily displayed in warm applause and full and fashionable assemblages. Mr. Hare again distinguished himself as a most skilful delineator of character, and no more complete impersonation had been for some time seen than his embodiment of the Russian *Prince Perovsky*, characterized by the highest polish and the utmost refinement of speech and manner. (*Daily Telegraph*, September 19, 1866.) On Saturday, April 6, 1867, first performance at the same theatre of T. W. Robertson's comedy entitled ' Caste,' Mr. Hare played the part of *Sam Gerridge*. The *Daily News* (April 8, 1867) thus wrote of the performance :—" Mr. T. W. Robertson, whose great dramatic successes have been achieved at this theatre with pieces combining the elements of comedy and domestic drama, produced another play on Saturday night under the title of ' Caste,' which, in our opinion, is the best work he has yet given to the stage. . . . The aristocratic portraits—the mother, the son, and the son's friend, a captain of the 'haw-haw' school—are comparatively weak, more or less wooden, conventional, and stagey, and highly coloured for the sake of contrast. The most natural and powerful character in the play is the drunken father—a selfish sot, partly self-deluded, partly a humbug. Next to him stands the other and the real working man, a mechanic whose flow of speech is not great, but who makes his presence felt by judicious ' business.' . . . Mr. Hare is so refined and perfect an actor, so true an observer of life, that we were not surprised to find him made up a sharp, wiry, veritable working man who might have stepped out of any carpenter's shop in England. His dialogue, however, wants a little more breadth in delivery and less use of the aspirate. The scene in which he reads to his ' intended ' the trade circular he has just composed is the most exquisite and unforced bit of comedy we have seen for years."

In the following year, on Saturday, February 15, first performance at the Prince of Wales's of Mr. Robertson's comedy entitled ' Play,' Mr. Hare sustained the part of *Hon. Bruce Fanquehere*, according to the *Times* (February 17, 1868), another well-drawn part in the piece. " His morals are somewhat lax, but his principles, when a point of honour is concerned, are sound, and when interest does not decidedly pull the wrong way he is an earnest though cool advocate on the side of right. Mr. Hare, always ready to seize on exceptional peculiarities of character, is the very man to perform the character, and the figure he presents, with thin legs, imperturbable demeanour, and a dress which, though plain, borders on the 'slangy,' is entirely new to the stage." On Saturday, January 16, 1869, first performance at the same theatre of Mr. Robertson's comedy entitled 'School,' Mr. Hare played the part of *Beau Farintosh*. Discussing the merits of the players in the "original" cast, the *Daily Telegraph* (January 25, 1869) said :—"Whatever part Mr. Hare undertakes we may be quite assured the utmost amount of pains will be bestowed on every detail ; and this most creditable characteristic of the actor is especially to be noticed in his latest assumption. *Beau Farintosh*, who might have been a young 'buck' in the days of the Regency, but who is now only a padded old man striving to repair the ravages of nature by the appliances of art, must be ranked among the very best of Mr. Hare's impersonations. The carefully made-up face, in which the wrinkles are effaced by the plastering of cosmetics, the affected jaunty air of youth contrasting with the unavoidable feeble gait, and the blundering short-sightedness of which he seems to be so amusingly unconscious, are admirably exhibited. An effective contrast is also produced when he no longer affects to conceal the years he has attained ; and when clasping his long-sought grandchild to his arms with emotions which overpower his utterance, the old beau reappears as a grey-headed old gentleman, inspiring reverence instead of ridicule. The burst of pathos which accompanies this wholesome change favourably displays the power of the actor in a strong situation."

At the same theatre, on Saturday, April 23, 1870, first performance of Mr. Robertson's comedy entitled 'M.P.,' Mr. Hare acted the part of *Dunscombe Dunscombe*, a performance which, in the opinion of the *Times* (April 25, 1870), was the best of its kind then to be seen on the London stage. "Mr. Hare is the most finished actor of old men that our stage has had since the late W. Farren, if we except Mr. A. Wigan, who might, and no doubt will, be pre-eminent in this line of business whenever he takes to it. As it is, Mr. Hare has no rival in our theatres at this moment. . . . The one new incident of the comedy, and the best part intrinsically, of Mr. Robertson's piece, is the scene of the sale by auction in Dunscombe Hall, which may have been suggested by the late R. Martineau's impressive picture of 'The Last Day in the Old House,' but on which as well Mr. Robertson is to be congratulated, both for his choice and his treatment of the incident as his actors —Mr. Hare more particularly—for their perfect realization of the author's intention. We remember no more natural and touching passage of mingled comedy and pathos than the best part of this third act, and it alone would have secured the success of the piece. We have little but praise for all the actors concerned without a single exception. . . . . Mr. Hare's performance in conception and execution was the gem of the piece. Nothing so good is at this moment to be seen in London, unless it be in some of Mr. A. Wigan's admirable impersonations, and *his* material is less artistic than that with which Mr. Robertson has furnished Mr. Hare in this comedy. The scene in which the old squire resents Piers's charge, and that which follows when he listens to the voice of the auctioneer

knocking down his ancestral pictures, rises to the highest rank of
acting in contemporary comedy. Throughout, his performance
illustrated admirably a truth very important to dramatists and
actors, viz. how wide and unoccupied a field there is for effective
impersonation, even in the studiously unmarked and reticent
manners of contemporary life, and among the class most careful to
mask emotion and put the curb on all expression of it." During
the remaining four years of his connection with the Prince of
Wales's Theatre Mr. Hare appeared in the following among other
plays, viz. in May 1872, 'Money,' as *Sir John Vesey;* in February
1873, Wilkie Collins's 'Man and Wife'; and, at Easter, 1874, 'The
School for Scandal,' in which he sustained the part of *Sir Peter
Teazle.* "How loyally and well Mr. Hare would assist such a
performance we all know, and how the performance was in itself
brought into relief by Mr. Hare's good taste we must all be convinced. Without such a *Sir Peter,* who refines everything to a
nicety, who remembers the tone and character of the old English
gentleman and studiously forgets the coarseness, and we may add
the grossness, which has been attached to the character by tradition,
how much less expression would have been obtained in the great
scene with Lady Teazle! Surely a young actor can play *Sir Peter
Teazle* without being obstinately compared with such geniuses as
are identified with the character, and we may well congratulate Mr.
Hare in successfully passing through a most harassing and almost
overwhelming ordeal. It is difficult to shake the conviction of anyone, and with old playgoers old memories are necessarily dear; but
it will be gratefully remembered that in *Sir Peter Teazle* Mr. Hare,
true to his art, discarded those coarse effects which are so telling,
and, remembering his own standard and outlook of the character,
played it with evenness and finish, and like a refined and well-bred
gentleman." (*Daily Telegraph,* April 6, 1874.) At the close of
1874 Mr. Hare retired from the company of the Prince of Wales's
and entered upon the management of the Royal Court Theatre,
which he opened on Saturday, March 13, 1875, with a comedy
by Mr. Charles Coghlan, entitled 'Lady Flora,' in which Mr. Hare
played the part of *Duc de Chavannes.* In addition to the foregoing
he placed on the stage the following "original" plays, namely,
Aïdé's comedy 'A Nine Days' Wonder,' Gilbert's fairy play 'Broken
Hearts,' Mr. Coghlan's 'Brothers,' the late Lord Lytton's play 'The
House of Darnley.' All of these, however, were not equally successful. Among the pieces in which he has performed since he
assumed the management the following are entitled to particular
mention, viz. 'A Quiet Rubber,' adapted from the French 'La
Partie de Piquet,' in which he acted the part of *Lord Kilclare;* 'A
Scrap of Paper,' adapted from the French of M. Sardou, 'Les
Pattes de Mouche,' in which he played *Archie Hamilton;* 'New
Men and Old Acres' (revival), and 'The Ladies' Battle.' One of
the most successful plays produced by Mr. Hare at the Court
Theatre was Mr. W. G. Wills's 'Olivia,' founded on a leading
incident in Oliver Goldsmith's 'Vicar of Wakefield,' first performed
March 30, 1878. In this piece, however, Mr. Hare did not appear.

The character of Dr. Primrose was sustained by Mr. Herman Vezin, and that of Olivia by Miss Ellen Terry. In 1879 Mr. Hare appeared in various revivals of plays already named. On Saturday (afternoon), April 19, he produced at the Court Theatre 'The Queen's Shilling' (G. W. Godfrey), a new version of 'Le Fils de Famille' (Bayard and Bieville), already known on the English stage under the title of 'The Lancers' (1853). In the cast of the new version Mr. Hare appeared as *Colonel Daunt*, generally allowed to be one of the very best of this actor's impersonations. On Saturday, July 19, 1879, Mr. Hare's management of the Court Theatre was brought to a close with a performance for his benefit. In the course of an address spoken on the occasion, Mr. Hare referred to his new venture, as part manager of St. James's Theatre in conjunction with Mr. Kendal, in the following terms :—"Union is strength ; and I feel that in associating myself with an admirable man of business and a most able artist, and at the same time gaining the permanent services of his accomplished wife, there seems a reasonable hope of conducting successfully a theatre which up to the present time has laboured under the stigma of being unfortunate. I assure you we shall work our hardest to reverse its ill-luck, and it will be through no lack or endeavour on our part if we fail. I may tell you that our plan of campaign will be similar to the one adopted by me here. Comedy and comedy-drama will form the staple of our dramatic fare, and we shall endeavour to get the best company together, with a view to giving that which is always, I take it, the most satisfactory thing to an audience—an even all-round performance. Our opening play will be 'The Queen's Shilling,' which has already been received with great favour at matinées ; and in the course of the season we may revive one or more English comedies, and an original play by Mr. Dubourg will also be produced."

HARRIS, AUGUSTUS, eldest son of the late Mr. Augustus Harris, in his day one of the most accomplished and successful stage-managers in Europe. Mr. A. Harris was for a short time in the house of Emile Erlanger and Co. as foreign correspondent. At his father's death he entered the dramatic profession, and accepted an engagement to play *Malcolm* in a revival of 'Macbeth' at the Theatre Royal, Manchester, under the management of Mr. John Knowles (September 1873). From thence he went to the Amphitheatre, Liverpool, and played juvenile and light comedy parts with Mr. Barry Sullivan. During this engagement Mr. Mapleson engaged Mr. Harris as assistant stage-manager to his Italian Opera Company, and after a fortnight appointed him stage-manager, in recognition of the way in which some operas had been by him placed on the stage at the Theatre Royal, Bath, under more than ordinary difficulty.

In 1876 Mr. Harris was sent by Lord Newry as his representative to negotiate with the Odéon Company of Paris to appear in 'The Danischeffs' at the St. James's Theatre, and was complimented by the well-known Parisian stage-manager, M. Boudois, on the effective.

way this play was placed upon the London stage. This engagement was, with the exception of that recently fulfilled by the members of the Comédie Française at the Gaiety Theatre, the most successful ever fulfilled by any French comedy company in London.

Mr. Harris invented, constructed, and produced the pantomime of 'Sindbad the Sailor' at the Crystal Palace in 1876 on behalf of Mr. Charles Wyndham, and introduced some novel effects in the same that were much appreciated. In 1877 he "created" the part of *Henry Greenlanes* in 'Pink Dominos' at the Criterion Theatre, playing the part every night during the long run of the piece.

HARRIS, MARIA (MARIA ELIZABETH GLOSSOP), was born in London, January 13, 1851, and made her first appearance on any stage at the Princess's Theatre, Saturday, October 27, 1860—the date of Mr. Charles Fechter's first appearance in London—in a piece entitled 'The First Night.' Among the various plays in which Miss Harris has subsequently appeared on the London stage the following may be mentioned, viz. 'Don Cæsar de Bazan'; 'Jeannette's Wedding'; 'Silken Fetters'; 'Little Daisy' (T. J. Williams), all produced at the Princess's Theatre within the period 1861–63; and 'The Little Treasure,' in which she acted the part of *Gertrude;* 'The Widow Hunt,' in which she has appeared as *Mrs. Swandown;* 'The Heir-at-Law,' in which she has played the part of *Cicely Homespun;* 'The Rough Diamond,' in which she has acted the character of *Margery;* 'Paul Pry,' in which she has played *Phœbe.* Miss Harris hitherto has only appeared on the London stage.

HARVEY, FRANK, was born in Manchester, April 1842, and made his first appearance on the stage, July 1863, at the T. R. York, under W. S. Thorne's management, where he was for some time the "singing walking gentleman" of the company. Subsequently he went to Plymouth, and was for two seasons a member of Mr. Newcombe's company at the Theatre Royal in that town. At the end of this engagement he joined the circuit of theatres under Mr. Wybert Reeve's management, remaining with him for two years. In August 1866 Mr. Harvey joined the company of the Theatre Royal, Dublin, "opening" there as *Modus* in 'The Hunchback' in the month and year last named, and continuing a member of the company for four successive years. At Dublin he became very popular, and here, during a professional visit, made the acquaintance of the late Mdlle. Beatrice, of whose comedy-company he was the leading member, and the first engaged by that manageress. He made his *début* on the London stage at the Olympic Theatre, in May 1872, in an English version of M. Sardou's 'Nos Intimes,' in the part of *Maurice.* In this character Mr. Harvey showed himself much superior to the average *jeune premier* in an English performance, and his judicious acting of the part won prominent recognition. In conjunction with Mdlle. Beatrice he afterwards appeared in 'The Sphinx' (as *Henri Savigny*), in 'Monsieur

Alphonse' (the title *rôle*), in 'Frou-Frou' (*Valreas*), and in 'The Woman of the People' (*Bertrand*), at the Haymarket, Globe, Standard, and Olympic Theatres.   For some years Mr. Harvey was the manager of Mdlle. Beatrice's company of comedians.   At her death in 1878 he was made, by will, her sole legatee, joined with a request that he would continue the company in her name.   Mr. Frank Harvey has written various plays which have been successfully presented on the stage—'John Jasper's Wife,' 'Jacqueline,' 'Married, not Mated,' &c.   The last was produced at the Olympic Theatre, April 26, 1879, the author in the principal *rôle*.

HAYNES, THOMAS PERCIVAL, has been connected with the stage from boyhood.   In 1871 he was a member of a travelling company on the South Coast, and in that year first appeared at the Theatre Royal, Portsmouth, as first low comedian.   From 1871 to 1876 he was engaged on a tour with various companies.   On September 10, 1877, he made his first appearance at the Princess's Theatre, London, as *Nicholas Dovetail* ('Mischief Making'), and *Tom Sprotter* ('Guinea Gold').   In 1879 at the Princess's he played *Delph* in 'Family Jars' for a "run" of 100 nights.

HAYWELL, F., prior to his entering the dramatic profession, was in practice as a solicitor.   He made his first appearance on the stage at the Marylebone Theatre, 5th March, 1855, with Mr. J. W. Wallack, as *Florizel* in 'A Winter's Tale.'   Shortly afterwards he accompanied Mr. Wallack and his company to the Théâtre Impérial des Italiens in Paris.   For five seasons Mr. Haywell was a member of Mr. Phelps's company at Sadler's Wells, playing various important characters, amongst them *Sebastian* and *Prince Escalus*, in the last of which characters he appeared with Mr. Phelps's company before Her Majesty and the Royal Family at Windsor Castle in November 1859.   He has acted at several of the provincial theatres (the T. R. Dublin, Brighton, the T. R. and Prince's, Manchester, Bristol and Bath, Nottingham, Birmingham, and others), playing the "leading business" at Nottingham, Dublin, and the Manchester theatres.   He was stage-manager at the T. R. Manchester and other theatres, and was the last manager at the T. R. Manchester under Mr. John Knowles.   In London, Mr. Haywell was at the Olympic for a season in 1875-6, and has also appeared at the Princess's as *Lord Dalgarno* in 'The King o' Scots'; as *Master Ford* at the Gaiety; *Iago* at the Opéra Comique; *Mercutio* at the Olympic; and lately as *Asa Trenchard* at the Haymarket.   He is the author of several dramas, which have been played in various provincial towns with some success.

HEATH, CAROLINE (Mrs. WILSON BARRETT), made her professional *début* at the Princess's Theatre, Saturday, September 18, 1852 (having previously appeared as an amateur at the Royalty Theatre), in the character of *Stella*, the heroine of Mr. Dion Boucicault's drama 'The Prima Donna.'   Miss Heath's self-possession on the occasion is noted in contemporary journals as having

been " remarkable." " Although we have not omitted one material
fact in describing the story of ' The Prima Donna,' our description
will give a very faint notion of the impression made by the piece,
so much more does it depend upon character than upon plot. The
personages of *Stella*, Margaret, and Rouble are all elaborately
drawn, and gain additional colour from the very able manner in
which they are acted. *Stella* is the matured woman, proud of her
position, of a sensitive and passionate nature, but constantly regu-
lated by a stern regard for duty. Miss Heath, who represented
her, made her first appearance on any public stage, and she may be
congratulated on the manner in which she accomplished a really
difficult task. The position of *Stella* in the Milan scene is very
delicate, the discovery that she has been ' cut out ' by her little
innocent sister, although affecting, borders on the ludicrous, and
the skill with which Miss Heath went through a variety of *nuances*,
that by turns belong to high comedy and pathetic *drame*, shows
great intelligence in a *débutante*. . . . ' The Prima Donna ' was
received with loud applause, and beyond its intrinsic merits, its
production is highly interesting from the fact that it has shown we
have two young and rising talents, Miss Heath and Miss Agnes
Robertson,* promising to supply the gaps which of late years have
occurred so frequently in histrionic ranks." (*Times*, September 20,
1852.) The piece was produced under the supervision of Mr.
Charles Kean. Miss Heath remained a member of his company
for some years, playing in the various Shakespearian revivals
which brought so much fame to the Keans and to the Princess's
Theatre under their management. On Easter Monday, 1853, Miss
Heath sustained there the part of *Bianca* in ' Marco Spada,'
adapted from Scribe's libretto of Auber's opera of that name.
Monday, June 5, 1854, she played *Rose Walstein*, first performance
of J. M. Morton's piece ' From Village to Court.' The same year,
Monday, October 9, first performance at the same theatre of
Douglas Jerrold's drama ' A Heart of Gold,' she sustained the character of the heroine, *Maude Nutbrown*. Of this play, following his
performance, Douglas Jerrold himself wrote, " With a certain graceful exception (Miss Heath), there never was so much bad acting as
in ' A Heart of Gold.'" He spoke of it despairingly, as his " farewell
to all dramatic doings." The *Athenæum* (October 14, 1854), examining its merits, remarked:—" As a literary production, the play is full
of beauties. . . . we do not hesitate to pronounce it one of the most
intellectual plays—intellectual in conception and in spirit—in the
moral as well as in the literary sense, that the English stage has
added to its repertory for many a season." The *Times* (October
10, 1854) spoke of it as follows :—" Like most of the author's
dramas, this work is placed in an old-fashioned period, the manners
of a century back seeming to give a greater opportunity for quaint
dialogue than those of the present day. . . . . The sole merit of
the piece consists in the eloquence and sparkle of certain portions
of the dialogue. *Maude's* description of London, as seen from the

---

* Now Mrs. Dion Boucicault.

summit of St. Paul's, is a choice bit of fanciful word-painting, in Mr.
Jerrold's best style, and a pretty series of conceits *apropos* of a foam-
ing glass of ale, are put into the mouth of old Yewberry.   For the
rapid exchange of repartee two comic characters are devised,
Michaelmas (Mr. Fisher), a waiter, and Molly Dindle (Miss
Murray), a maidservant, who, though they have little to do with
the plot, being constantly introduced, like the sweethearts of old-
fashioned melodrama, deal out some of those smart 'hits' with
which Mr. Jerrold has often stirred an audience to a roar.   The
acting of the piece was good, but not all on the same level.   Miss
Heath, as *Maude*, a character endowed with varied attributes—
now bounding with joyousness, now strong in indignation, now
oppressed with grief—displayed unwearied energy and abundance of
genuine feeling.   Her unfeigned delight at the recovery of Dym-
mond, when she sprang along the stage to spread the good news
about the neighbourhood, and her eloquent denunciation of Pierce,
were in the best spirit, and appealed irresistibly to the sympathies
of the audience."

In May 1855, in a revival of Shakespeare's 'Henry the Eighth,' at
the Princess's (Mr. and Mrs. Charles Kean in the leading characters), Miss Heath played *Anne Boleyn*.   In January 1858 she
played the part of *Ophelia*.   Said the *Daily News* (January 14,
1858) :—" Miss Heath's *Ophelia* merits a distinct recognition, from
its sweetness and grace.   In characters requiring an elegant and
prepossessing appearance, combined with the power of expressing
the gentler emotions of love and grief in a refined and artistic
manner, this young lady evinces the greatest promise."   On
Monday, April 17, 1858, in a "grand revival" of 'King Lear' at
the Princess's, she sustained the part of *Cordelia*.   During her connection with that theatre she several times played in the series of
dramatic performances arranged by Mr. C. Kean, and given by the
Queen's command at Windsor and Osborne.   Removing to Sadler's
Wells, on Saturday, September 16, 1859, she appeared there for
the first time as *Juliet*.   "The *Juliet* of the evening was Miss
Heath, well known at the Princess's, where she held a respectable
rank, but never had the opportunity of occupying so important a
position.   There, however, she had acquired so much self-con-
fidence that she could go through even so long a part as *Juliet*
without hesitation or fear.   Of course she was unequal; but the
traces of study were evident, especially in the elocution, which is at
present artificial and without enough impulse, and the general outline was commendably accurate.   The chief fault was in the conception, which might more fitly become the Greek Clytemnestra
than the passionate and trusting devotion of the Italian Juliet.
Her action was large and massive, while her speech was wanting in
that full and round tone of delivery which would have better harmonized with the attitudes assumed. . . . She (Miss Heath) is now
in a school the good influence of which has been already shown in
beneficial fruits, and where she will have the utmost opportunities
of completing her histrionic education." (*Athenæum*, September
17, 1859.)   The same month, at the same theatre, Miss Heath

played *Mary Thornberry*, in a revival of 'John Bull'; and in October of the same year, first performance at Sadler's Wells Theatre of Mr. Tom Taylor's play 'The Fool's Revenge,' she sustained the character of *Fiordelisa* "with all maidenly grace and delicacy" (*Daily News*, October 19, 1859). When the late Mr. Augustus Harris entered upon the lesseeship of the Princess's Theatre, he secured Miss Heath's assistance during a portion of Mr. Charles Fechter's engagement. She played there the part of *The Queen of Spain*, first performance of Falconer's version of Victor Hugo's 'Ruy Blas' (Mr. Fechter in the title *rôle*), Saturday, October 27, 1860. "The character of *The Queen* was extremely well delineated by Miss Heath," remarked the *Times* (October 29, 1860). "The rapt delight with which she listened to Ruy's declaration of love was even pictorial in its effect, and the agony and terror with which she watched the fierce struggle of the last scene were marked by the complete abandonment to the situation, which is so necessary when the more overwhelming emotions are to be depicted." Subsequently Miss Heath devoted herself to "star" acting in the provinces, appearing only at intervals on the metropolitan stage. Her most successful impersonations in London, between the last-mentioned date (1860) and the present year (1879), have been *The Witch of the Alps*, in the revival of 'Manfred' at Drury Lane Theatre, in October 1863; *Princess Olimpia*, first performance of Falconer's 'Night and Morn,' at the same theatre, January 1864; *Lady Isabelle*, at the Surrey Theatre, in 'East Lynne,' in June 1867—generally allowed to have been a fine piece of acting ;. *Margaret Ramsay*, first performance of Andrew Halliday's 'King o' Scots,' at Drury Lane, in September 1868; and *Jane Shore* in Mr. Wills's drama of that name, produced at the Princess's Theatre in 1877-8; and subsequently (April–May 1879) at the Surrey Theatre. Miss Heath became identified with the *rôle* when the play was first acted in the provinces. The success of this play, both in London and the provinces, must be mainly ascribed to her admirable impersonation of the heroine. Miss Heath is now the leading actress of the Court Theatre, of which her husband is lessee and manager, in succession to Mr. Hare.

HENDERSON, MRS. ALEXANDER. *See* THOMPSON, LYDIA.

HENRI, BLANCHE MARIAN. Born near Ross, Herefordshire. She made her first appearance on any stage in 1870, at the Charing Cross Theatre, under the management of Miss Fowler. In May 1871 she joined the company of the Theatre Royal, Haymarket, playing, among other characters, *Rachel Grindrod*, in Byron's play 'An English Gentleman,' and *Florence Trenchard* in 'Our American Cousin,' Mr. Sothern sustaining the principal *rôles*. Miss Henri remained a member of the Haymarket company for four years. In 1875 she accepted an engagement with the Vezin-Chippendale Comedy Company, of which Mrs. Vezin, Mr. Compton, and Mr. and Mrs. Chippendale were leading members. During the provincial tour that followed, Miss Henri played many important characters in the old comedies with much success, notably *Lydia Languish, Lydia* ('The Love Chase'), young *Lady Lambert, Miss Neville, Grace Harkaway,* &c., &c. In January 1876 she returned to the Haymarket and played *Lady Rochfort,* first performance of Tom Taylor's historical play of 'Anne Boleyn,' and afterwards proceeded on tour with Mr. J. S. Clarke's company, from that theatre. In March 1877, at the Royal Aquarium Theatre, Miss Henri played *Estella* ('Great Expectations'), and *Mrs. Cuthburt* ('Cyril's Success'). In October of the same year, at the Royal Court Theatre, she appeared in the first performance of Lord Lytton's posthumous drama 'The House of Darnley,' and subsequently sustained the part of *Mrs. Fitzherbert,* first performance of Tom Taylor's comedy entitled 'Victims.' "There is, indeed, not much that is heroic in the story of 'Victims,' unless it be in the case of the generous and devoted wife of *Fitzherbert,* who is represented with such excellent moderation and feeling by Miss Henri that the rather heartless trick to which she is subjected for the mere sake of bringing about the repentance of Mrs. Merryweather, necessarily awakens more sympathy than the author seems to have intended." (*Daily News,* January 28, 1878.) At the same theatre Miss Henri played *Lilian Vavasour,* in a revival of 'New Men and Old Acres.' In April 1878, having accepted an engagement from Mr. and Mrs. Bancroft, Miss Henri became a member of the company of the Prince of Wales's Theatre. Subsequently, for the season 1878–9, she joined the Haymarket company under Mr. John S. Clarke's management, and played there Easter Monday (April 14, 1879) the part of *Lady Breezy,* first performance of 'Ellen; or, Love's Cunning' (W. G. Wills). This part, well performed by Miss Henri, was one of the redeeming features of Mr. Wills's unsuccessful but in some respects clever play. 'Ellen' was reconstructed and produced on the same stage under the title of 'Brag,' but was again unsuccessful.

HERAUD, EDITH, was born in London, and is the daughter of Mr. John A. Heraud, author of two elaborate epics entitled 'The Judgment of the Flood' and 'The Descent into Hell,' as also of the acted dramas 'Videna,' 'Wife or No Wife,' and other pieces. Miss Heraud's genius as an actress was early developed. She was only fourteen years of age when she played the heroine of Hannah More's tragedy of 'Percy,' at a private performance, at which Mr. Charles Kemble was present. In 1851 she accompanied some members of the Sadler's Wells company to Richmond, and acted *Juliet* in the presence of an audience that included Douglas Jerrold, Stirling Coyne, and other celebrated dramatists; this was noticed in the *Era* as an "extraordinary performance." She was now sought for by provincial managers, and appeared at Rochester, Southampton, Woolwich, Winchester, Canterbury, and Cambridge. On the revival of 'Pericles' at Sadler's Wells she was solicited by Mr. Phelps to represent its heroine, *Marina*, in which she was eminently successful. Charles Dickens several times witnessed this performance. The play ran for more than seventy nights, and after an interval was revived. In 1852 she performed *Julia* at the Olympic, then under the direction of Mr. Farren, and afterwards played at the Haymarket in her father's drama 'Wife or No Wife,' and also at the Marylebone Theatre as the heroine of a play by Mrs. Edward Thomas called 'The Merchant's Daughter of Toulon.' Among her important parts was *Ophelia* in 'Hamlet'; her mad songs were peculiarly effective. As a reader of plays Miss Heraud has shown extraordinary capacity. Her 'Antigone' at the Crystal Palace created quite a sensation. The *Daily News* observed that "the effect was immense. Her clear mellow voice reached the ears of the vast audience, as was shown by the bursts of applause that followed her impassioned recitations, and her skill as an actress enabled her to give animation to the scene. In reading the dialogue between the two sisters, the difference in the tones of the voices of Antigone and that of Ismene was clearly defined. The scene where the heroine is dragged away to death, while her cries of grief and despair are echoed by the low wailing sounds of the instruments [Mendelssohn's beautiful accompaniments], was very striking." In 1857 Miss Heraud appeared at Sadler's Wells in 'Medea,' as adapted to the boards by her father, from M. Legouvé's famous tragedy ; in 1859 this piece was revived at the Standard Theatre, and "ran" for three weeks. The *Sunday Times* and the *Morning Advertiser* commended her "truthful and natural manner," and her "full mastery over the passions." "The long conflict that the wronged and unhappy woman suffers was often brought out, and oftener suggested by the actress's powers. She showed the full dignity of suffering and passion ; and whether as the forlorn wife, the outraged woman, or the relenting mother, touched the right key and fully realized the emotion." To which the *Evening Star* adds, "Miss Heraud has evidently a strong poetic sympathy with the part—a vivid conception of what it is she has undertaken to represent ; and speaks far more from impulse than from rule." Other journals mentioned her acting in 'Medea' in high terms. Miss Heraud is also esteemed as an able representative of *Lady Macbeth*, a part in which she has frequently appeared, with Mr. Charles Dillon as the guilty Thane. She also achieved in 1864 a success at the Grecian Theatre in a version of Mosenthal's drama 'Deborah,' which ran for a hundred nights. Previous to this she had appeared at the Polygraphic Hall in a Shakespearian entertainment, in which she enacted twelve of the immortal bard's heroines. These performances continued for nearly forty nights, and were highly commended by the London journals. She has succeeded also in the recitation of Milton's 'Samson Agonistes' at Myddelton Hall and before the Society for the Encouragement of the Fine Arts. As a teacher of elocution, Miss Heraud has, during the past ten years, been singularly successful, the annual reading prizes distributed at the University of Cambridge having been, in divers instances, awarded to her pupils. In 1870 she produced at the Standard a play by Mrs. Edward Thomas, called 'The Wife's Tragedy.' "The piece," said the *Sunday Times*, "is of 'The Duchess of Malfi' school, wherein horror succeeds horror, but it has good scenes and situations, and it has solid merit of dialogue. Miss Edith Heraud showed power as the Duchess." The *Athenæum* states that she "played with tenderness the part of the murdered Duchess, flashing, however, into fire when the motive of her own humiliation became apparent." Miss Heraud for the last few years has been absent from the stage.

HERBERT, LOUISA (Mrs. CRABBE), made her first appearance on the London stage at the Strand Theatre in September 1854, as *Maria Darlington*, in the farce entitled ' A Roland for an Oliver.' In May 1856, at the Olympic, in a new drama called 'Retribution,' in which Mr. A. Wigan acted the part of Count Priuli, "Miss Herbert appeared as a *débutante*, and achieved no small success." (*Journal of a London Playgoer*, H. Morley, p. 134). Miss Herbert's most important performances on the metropolitan boards belong to the period of her connection with the St. James's Theatre. She was a member of Mr. A. Wigan's company when he assumed the management of that theatre in 1860, and afterwards of the company of his successor, Mr. Frank Matthews. Subsequently Miss Herbert herself undertook the management. Among the more noteworthy characters sustained by her during the time she was performing at the St. James's Theatre, 1860–1866, the following are entitled to special mention. On Saturday, January 21, 1863, she played the leading *rôle* in a piece entitled 'The Merry Widow' (Leicester Buckingham), adapted from the French 'Jeanne qui pleure, et Jeanne qui rit,' and "in one situation made the fortune of the little drama." Saturday, February 28, 1863, she sustained the part of *Lady Audley* in George Roberts's dramatic version of Miss Braddon's novel 'Lady Audley's Secret,' then first performed. ". . . . Apart from the interest of the story itself—which, as we have said, proves excellently adapted to the stage—there is this end attained by the production of 'Lady Audley's Secret,' that it provides Miss Herbert with a part worthy of her abilities. Indeed, highly as the merits of this lady are appreciated by all the higher class of playgoers, few, we think, would have given her credit for her finished performance of the bold, bad, fascinating woman whom she personated on Saturday. In most of the dramas that have been chiefly supported by her talent she has been the meek sufferer, with a load of trouble on her mind, to which she does not give verbal expression, and which reveals itself in a thousand mute indications of uneasiness. As *Lady Audley*, on the contrary, she has to do even more than she has to suffer, and terrible are the deeds she does. Her physical force is not always equal to her intentions, but this inequality is overlooked in the amount of intellectual power she bestows upon the impersonation. . . . Miss Herbert's representation of the affectation of indifference is exquisitely true. There is an evident exaggeration of liveliness, an inconsistent attention to the details of her drawing, a hollow flippancy, which no one can take for reality, and the voice is affected by the frightful apprehensions which the accomplished coquette is striving to conceal. By this time the variety of the part is nearly exhausted, and in the last scene, where the guilt of *Lady Audley* is brought home to her, she has only to reassume the air of defiant badness with which she has already met her first husband. Here it is only the power of Miss Herbert that prevents an anti-climax. But there is again a change, when defeated wickedness results in insanity; and the disappearance of all expression whatever from a countenance that a moment before has expressed demoniac rage is remarkably fine." (*Times*, March 2, 1863.)

On Monday, May 29, 1865, in 'Eleanor's Victory,' a dramatization of Miss Braddon's novel of that title, from the pen of Mr. John Oxenford, Miss Herbert played the title *rôle*. "The whole interest is centred in *Eleanor*, who, as embodied by Miss Herbert, retains all the prominence, though losing much of the sympathy, which influenced the reader. The intensity of expression which the actress has at command, and the rare power of delineating the strongest feeling of vindictive hatred with the utmost refinement of manner, communicate a force to her denunciations, and a terrible reality to her emotions, which could not fail to impress the spectator. It may be doubted whether those who had come unprepared by a perusal of the novel clearly understood the pertinacity with which each clue to the offender had been followed up, or could fully appreciate the illustration, even so vividly given, of a stern tenacity of purpose; but there could be no hesitation in recognizing the thorough grasp of the character which Miss Herbert had acquired, nor the artistic completeness of the entire assumption." (*Daily Telegraph*, May 30, 1865.) During the season 1865–6 Miss Herbert played the following characters at St. James's Theatre with great success, viz. *Lady Teazle* in a revival of 'The School for Scandal'; *Miss Hardcastle* in a revival of 'She Stoops to Conquer'; *Beatrice* in 'Much Ado About Nothing'; *Lydia Languish* in 'The Rivals'; *Mrs. Oakley* in 'The Jealous Wife'; and *Letitia Hardy* in 'The Belle's Stratagem.' On Monday, November 9, 1866, first performance in London, at the same theatre, of Dion Boucicault's drama entitled 'Hunted Down,' Miss Herbert sustained the part of *Mary Leigh*. The feeling that is most strongly exhibited in *Mary Leigh* is her affection to her children. That she may not be torn from these she will submit to any sacrifice; and when she is hunted down, and feels that her character is blighted, she will voluntarily leave them, that they may not be affected by her infamy. The expression of this sentiment showed Miss Herbert's talent in a new light, and she was equally successful in its more pathetic and its more violent manifestations. In April 1867, at the St. James's Theatre, Miss Herbert played the heroine in 'Idalia,' then first performed; and in October, at the Adelphi Theatre, the leading *rôle* in Watts Phillips's drama 'Maud's Peril,' then first performed. In 1869 Miss Herbert accepted an engagement at the St. James's Theatre, under Mrs. John Wood's management, and appeared in some of her best-known characters. Since her marriage Miss Herbert has retired from the stage.

HERBERT, WILLIAM (a *nom de théâtre*), son of the late Colonel W. F. Eden, of the Madras Army, was born in India on November 18, 1844. He was for some years in the British Army, and served in H.M. 33rd Foot, both at home and in India. Mr. Herbert entered the dramatic profession in April 1870, and made his first appearance at the Charing Cross Theatre, under the management of Miss Fowler. In August of the same year he was engaged by Mrs. Bancroft for the Prince of Wales's Theatre, and remained with them for four years, playing several important parts. He was the original *Arnold Brinkworth*, in Wilkie Collins's drama 'Man and Wife,' first performed at that theatre in February 1873. At the conclusion of his engagement at the Prince of Wales's he was engaged by Mrs. John Wood to support her on her provincial tour with Mr. Byron's comedy 'The American Lady,' playing *Harold Trivass*, the part created by Mr. Byron in London. Mr. Herbert was afterwards engaged by Mr. Horace Wigan for the reopening of the Holborn Theatre, and later on by Mr. Burnand for the Opéra Comique. At the Court Theatre he played in the successful comedy 'A Quiet Rubber,' and the character of *Hector Placide* in Boucicault's 'Led Astray.' In October 1876 he appeared as a member of the company of the Haymarket Theatre, his most successful impersonations during this engagement being *Prince Philamir* ('Palace of Truth'), and *Tom Dexter* ('Overland Route'), in revivals of those plays. In June 1877 Mr. Herbert went with the Haymarket company on Mr. J. B. Buckstone's farewell tour of the provinces, which lasted six months. During this time he appeared with success at all the principal towns in England, Scotland, and Wales, in the following leading characters, viz. *Charles Surface, Young Marlow, Captain Absolute, Pygmalion* ('Pygmalion and Galatea'), *Prince Philamir, Tom Dexter, Dazzle*, &c. On his return to London, in December, he fulfilled a short special engagement, under Miss Ada Cavendish's management, at the St. James's, playing the character of *Charles Surface*. In January 1878 Mr. Herbert joined Mr. Toole, and acted in Mr. H. J. Byron's comedy 'A Fool and his Money,' having been selected by the author for the *rôle* of *Percival Ransome*.

In August 1878 this actor was selected by Mr. Hare to play "on tour" *Squire Thornhill* in 'Olivia'—an uphill and ungrateful part —in the presentation of which Mr. Herbert evinced much care and judgment. He made his reappearance at the Court Theatre, January 4, 1879, in his "original" character of *Charles Kilclare* in 'A Quiet Rubber,' and on Saturday, February 15 of the same year, at the same theatre, sustained the part of *Henri de Flavigneul* in a revival of 'The Ladies' Battle,' a performance which the *Standard* (February 17, 1879) noticed in the following terms :— "The other hero of the play, *Henri de Flavigneul*, was impersonated by Mr. Herbert, who has we think never before acted with such force and feeling. The animation with which he gave the description of his 'crime'—the fastening upon the breast of his old general a cross in place of that which had been rudely snatched from it—was particularly good. The somewhat constrained action which was once a drawback to Mr. Herbert's performance has disappeared, and the freedom and appropriateness of his gestures are very noticeable improvements."

HERTZ, IDA, was born in London, and made her first appearance on the stage, November 1870, at the Standard Theatre, London, in the part of *Polly Flamborough* in a dramatized version of 'The Vicar of Wakefield.' Subsequently she played at the same theatre various characters in support of Mr. Sothern, Mr. B. Webster, Mr. Creswick, and other leading "stars." Miss Hertz has been a member of two travelling companies of comedians, the 'Two Roses' and the 'Pygmalion and Galatea'; the first under Messrs. Montague, James, and Thorne's management, the second under Mr. J. L. Sefton's. She has fulfilled engagements at the Theatre Royal, Hull, and at the Prince of Wales's Theatre, Birmingham. In July 1876 she became a member of the company of the Prince of Wales's Theatre, London, under Mr. and Mrs. Bancroft's management, and is still (1879) playing there.

HIBBERT, LOUISE, was born May 12, 1855, at Cordova, in Spain. She came to England at an early age, and having a predilection for a dramatic career, studied the rudiments of acting with Mr. Ryder. Having appeared at various theatres in the provinces, on June 20, 1874, she made her *début* on the metropolitan stage at the Queen's Theatre in the character of *Juliet.* The impression she made upon her audience was most favourable, according to the *Times* (June 22, 1874). " Her appearance is very charming. She enters thoroughly into the various emotions of the character, and evidently seizes the meaning of every situation. Most satisfactory were the passages expressive of tenderness or devotion." Afterwards Miss Hibbert accepted an engagement at the Gaiety Theatre, under Mr. John Hollingshead's management, to play *Helena* in 'A Midsummer Night's Dream.' In August 1875 she went to the United States of America with Mr. Barry Sullivan, and with him played in several cities, New York, Boston, Philadelphia, &c., *Ophelia, Lady Macbeth, Pauline* ('Lady of Lyons'), *Mrs. Beverley* ('The Gamester'), &c. She returned to England, and visited the provinces on a "starring" tour, playing *Beatrice, Rosalind, Lady Teazle,* &c. Miss Hibbert sustained the character of *Lady Dedlock* in the drama of 'Jo' (founded on Dickens's 'Bleak House') on the occasion of its first performance at the Globe Theatre in London. (*See* LEE, JENNIE.) She subsequently accompanied Mrs. Stirling on a tour through Liverpool, Edinburgh, Glasgow, Dublin, &c., and acted in those cities the following important parts, viz. *Lydia Languish* ('The Rivals'), *Constance* ('The Love Chase'), and *Mabel Vane* ('Masks and Faces'). In October 1877 she played a special engagement at the Theatre Royal, Bristol, appearing as *Helen* in Charles Reade's drama of 'The Scuttled Ship' with much success. In 1878 she went on tour with George Honey to play the character of *Belinda* in W. S. Gilbert's comedy entitled 'Engaged.'

HILL, CAROLINE L. BROOK, was born at York, and entered the dramatic profession when a child, playing such parts as *Mamilius* in 'A Winter's Tale,' *Arthur* in 'King John,' &c., at Sadler's Wells Theatre, during the last two years of the management of Mr. Samuel Phelps. Afterwards Miss Hill obtained an engagement at the Haymarket Theatre, under Mr. J. B. Buckstone. At this theatre she remained during a long period, playing " original " parts in various comedies placed on its stage, and, it may be added, with uniform success. Among important plays performed in London, in which, on their first presentation, Miss Caroline Hill sustained a leading character, the following are entitled to notice, viz. 'The Favourite of Fortune,' 'Mary Warner,' 'The Palace of Truth,' 'Pygmalion and Galatea,' and 'All for Her.' In the two examples of W. S. Gilbert's " fairy-comedies " mentioned, Miss Hill was especially successful. Her very effective acting in the parts of *Mirza* ('Palace of Truth') and *Cynisca* ('Pygmalion and Galatea') contributed in no slight degree to the popularity which those plays subsequently attained. In 1879 Miss Hill accepted an engagement at the Duke's Theatre, and appeared in a play entitled 'New Babylon' (P. Meritt), a piece described as " a mixture of Moncrieff's 'Tom and Jerry' and Mr. Boucicault's 'Formosa,' " but which was, nevertheless, a considerable success.

*HODSON, HENRIETTA, had earned some repute as an actress in the provinces, chiefly in burlesque, previous to her *début* in London, which took place in the second season of Miss Marie Wilton's (Mrs. Bancroft) management of the Prince of Wales's Theatre, December 26, 1866, in the character of *Prometheus* in H. J. Byron's 'Pandora's Box,' designated by the author " a grand new Christmas comicality." In the following year Miss Henrietta Hodson was engaged at the Queen's Theatre,† Long Acre, and appeared there on the opening night, October 24, 1867, in an unimportant character (*Jacintha*) in Charles Reade's drama 'The Double Marriage,' the late Mr. Alfred Wigan in the leading *rôle*, Captain Raynal. The same season at the same theatre she acted *Arabella Fotheringay* in 'The First Night,' the same actor playing Achille Talma Dufard, one of his most important impersonations. On January 8, 1868, at the same theatre, Miss Hodson was in the " original " cast (the play had been essayed at Liverpool with a view to presenting it on the London stage) of H. J. Byron's 'Dearer than Life' as *Lucy*. Mr. Toole, Mr. Irving, Mr. C. Wyndham, Mr. Clayton, Mr. Lionel Brough, Mrs. E. Dyas, took

† This theatre, after eleven years of variable fortune under a succession of managers, commencing in October 1867, and ending in the Spring of 1878, has now passed into the hands of a Limited Liability Company for commercial purposes.

part in the performance. Miss Hodson appeared in the original cast of the same author's play 'The Lancashire Lass,' first performed at the same theatre July 24, 1868. She also acted, during the term of her engagement here, in various extravaganzas and burlesques, 'La Vivandière' (W. S. Gilbert), 'The Stranger' (Reece), 'The Gnome King' (W. Brough). On May 29, 1869, she took part in the first performance, at the same theatre, of Burnand's play 'The Turn of the Tide,' which had a considerable success. In the following year (January 1870), at the same theatre, she was in the original cast of Tom Taylor's play ''Twixt Axe and Crown,' the late Mrs. Rousby in the leading *rôle*. Completing her engagement at the Queen's Theatre August 10, 1870, on the 3rd of the following month she opened the Royalty Theatre under her management with a comedy by H. T. Craven and a burlesque by F. C. Burnand. During the year following she acted in various pieces, chiefly burlesque, at that theatre, and in 1872 returned to the Queen's, " opening " January 8 as *Nydia* the blind girl in John Oxenford's version of Lord Lytton's 'Last Days of Pompeii.' During the same year at the same theatre Miss Hodson played certain parts in the so-called " legitimate " drama : *Virginia* (' Virginius '), *Imogen* (' Cymbeline '), &c. Of the latter character she gave " a tender and graceful representation, failing only to convey those subtle shades of character, duly to embody which needs an actress of highest intellect and culture. She exhibited much grace and not a little intelligence, but no inspiration." (*Athenæum*, April 6, 1872.) Since this date Miss Hodson has appeared at various theatres in London and the provinces, one of her most successful later impersonations being that of *Dick Wastrell*, in a romantic drama in five acts entitled ' Old London,' adapted from ' Les Chevaliers du Brouillard ' (a French dramatization of Harrison Ainsworth's ' Jack Sheppard '), produced at the Queen's Theatre in February 1873. She was also very successful in a revival of ' Pygmalion and Galatea ' at the Haymarket, in January 1877, in the character of *Cynisca*. Miss Henrietta Hodson is an actress of ability, and has proved herself competent and painstaking in various branches of her art.

HODSON, KATE (Mrs. CHARLES FENTON), is a daughter of the late George Hodson, a favourite Irish comedian. She is a younger sister of Henrietta Hodson, and a niece of Henry Marston. At the Queen's Theatre, Long Acre, when under the management of Mr. Labouchere, she appeared as principal soubrette under the name of Kate Gordon, and has played in other London theatres from time to time.

HOLME, MYRA, made her first appearance on the stage January 10, 1876, at the Olympic Theatre, where she acted minor parts for some months. She was engaged to play *Lady Hamerton* in ' The Great Divorce Case ' at the Criterion Theatre. She was principal " walking lady " in other plays subsequently produced there, and also took part in Mr. Wyndham's revivals of old plays at the Crystal Palace, where she also appeared as *Emily St. Evremond* in 'The Ticket-of-Leave Man' with Mr. Henry Neville. Miss Holme afterwards took the part of *Lady Lennox* in 'Family Ties' at the Strand Theatre. Her next appearance in London was in 'Pink Dominos' at the Criterion. She afterwards accepted an engagement at the Vaudeville, where she has appeared in several light juvenile leading characters. At the reopening of the Lyceum Theatre by Mr. Irving, September 20, 1879, she appeared in 'The Boarding School' and 'The Iron Chest.'

HOLT, CLARANCE, was born in London January 12, 1826, and entered the dramatic profession in 1842, making his first appearance on the stage in that year at the Victoria Theatre as *Timothy* in 'All at Coventry.' After playing in the provinces for some years he went to the Australian colonies and fulfilled several very lucrative engagements. In 1857 he returned to England and assumed the management of the Marylebone Theatre, which he "opened" on October 5 of the same year with John Wilkins's successful five-act drama 'Civilization.' During the season Mr. Holt appeared in 'Hamlet,' 'Othello,' 'Macbeth,' and other characters of the legitimate drama; and on the 15th of February, 1858, produced for the first time in England 'Ruy Blas,' in which he performed the title *rôle*. His lease of the Marylebone having expired in March 1858, he played several starring engagements in the provinces, and in the following June left England to fulfil an engagement at New York. Here he appeared in 'Belphegor' at Burton's New Theatre with great *éclat*. Following this engagement Mr. Holt returned to Australia, once more with very profitable results. In January 1862 he became the pioneer of the English drama in New Zealand. At Dunedin he built a theatre, and opened with a full and efficient company. Here he played for two years and two months with unusual success. Having resolved on again returning to England, on the night of his last appearance a handsome testimonial was publicly presented to Mr. and Mrs. Clarance Holt. "During their stay in Dunedin they had paid away for benefits and charities over 2300*l*. To 'stars' they had paid 6000*l*. during the last fourteen months of the season. Having left Dunedin in August 1864, they appeared, by special desire, for one night only, in a grand performance at the New Haymarket Theatre, Melbourne, given on the 25th of that month, Mr. Holt taking the part of *Rob Roy* and Mrs. Holt that of Helen Macgregor. Lady Don appeared as Francis Osbaldiston—the Philharmonic Chorus, eighty in number, contributing their services. After the performance Lady Don presented Mr. and Mrs. Holt with a handsome silver vase, bearing the names of the company, and wishing them a speedy voyage to Old England." Arriving in London he entered upon an engagement at the Haymarket Theatre, and played with Miss Amy Sedgwick as *Master Walter* to her Julia in 'The Hunchback.' Mr. Holt then appeared in conjunction with Miss Helen Faucit at the Theatre Royal, Manchester; afterwards with Mrs. Scott-Siddons, then with Mdlle.

Beatrice, and other tragediennes of the day, playing the opposite characters to them. He then appeared at the New Adelphi Theatre, London, as *Ruy Gomez* in Planché's favourite comedy ' Faint Heart Never Won Fair Lady,' in which he proved himself a very efficient actor, after which he turned his attention to giving new and popular entertainments from the works of Shakespeare, Scott, and Dickens. In September 1878, in conjunction with Mr. Charles Wilmot (a comedian of standing in the colonies), he entered upon the management of the Duke's Theatre, Holborn, " opening " with an adaptation by Mr. Holt of Victor Hugo's ' Les Miserables ' entitled ' The Barricade.' In February 1879 the management produced " a new and original drama in a prologue and four acts, illustrating scenes and incidents of modern life in London, written by Paul Meritt, entitled ' New Babylon,'" which was very successful.

*HONEY, GEORGE, is generally allowed by dramatic authorities to have made his first appearance on the London stage at the Princess's Theatre in November 1848, as *Pan* in ' Midas.' According to old play-bills, he was engaged at the Adelphi Theatre in the summer season of 1851, acting in a comic opera entitled ' Good Night, Signor Pantalon,' and later in pantomime. At the outset of his professional career he was regarded not only as a comedian of much promise, but was also credited with no ordinary skill as an operatic vocalist. He appeared with considerable success in several of the English operas produced under the joint management of Miss Louisa Pyne and Mr. Harrison at Covent Garden Theatre ; and in Macfarren's ' Robin Hood,' performed at Her Majesty's Theatre under the direction of the late E. T. Smith, Mr. Honey rendered valuable assistance both by his comic acting and excellent singing. Since the decline of English opera, in England, Mr. Honey has devoted himself to performing in comedy and extravaganza, in which he has been very generally popular. Among other pieces that have obtained notice in which he has appeared with more than ordinary success, the following may be enumerated : In ' Miriam's Crime,' first performed at the Strand Theatre, October 9, 1863, " as a discreditable limb of the law Mr. Honey obtained much laughter by an exceedingly grotesque assumption of intoxication " (*Daily Telegraph*, October 10, 1863). In William Brough's burlesque entitled ' Prince Amabel,' performed at the Royalty Theatre in September 1865, Mr. Honey played the part of *Turco the Terrible.* On Monday, July 2, 1866, at the Princess's Theatre, first performance of Watts Phillips's drama ' The Huguenot Captain,' he sustained the part of *Annibal Locust*, " a rather tiresome, Pistol-like part, which is very drunken and very musical, with plenty of work for the lowest notes of the human voice " (*Daily News*, July 3, 1866).

On Saturday, April 6, 1867, at the Prince of Wales's Theatre, first performance in London of Mr. T. W. Robertson's comedy ' Caste,' Mr. Honey played the part of *Eccles.* " Instead of the conventional clowns who are put in by slop-work dramatists to lighten the serious interest of their work, we have real characters who think, speak, and act like human beings, and yet are intensely amusing and interesting. The drunken father, evidently made up from Mr. George Cruikshank's pictures of 'The Bottle,' is admirably played by Mr. George Honey, who made his first appearance at this theatre, and who never acted better. The part wants no such padding as the scraps of song, both comic and serious, given to it in various situations. The make-up, the voice, the manner, the savagery in one part, the hypocritical maudlin grief in another, the toadying to wealth in another, the disgust and abuse when wealth refuses to deposit even a sovereign, the exits and entrances of this character, are things to be gratefully remembered by those whose melancholy duty it is to see all London plays and all London performers." (*Daily News*, April 8, 1867.) On the occasion of the opening of the Vaudeville Theatre under the management of Messrs. Montague, Thorne, and James, Saturday, April 16, 1870, in a comedy entitled 'For Love or Money,' he acted the part of *Major Buncombe*. In May 1875, in a revival at the Prince of Wales's Theatre of ' Money,' he sustained the part of *Graves*. This performance was alluded to in the *Standard* (May 31, 1875) in the following terms :—" A noticeable and welcome feature in the revival is the return of Mr. George Honey, who resumes his part of *Graves*, one of the most genuine and unexaggerated examples of pure humour the modern stage has witnessed. Before Mr. Honey has uttered three sentences the character of *Graves* is distinctly placed before the spectator. The manner in which the sigh of grief for the memory of ' sainted Maria' gives place to the approving criticism on the glass of sherry, and the aspect of bereavement changes to a look of gratification as his eye lights on the pleasant face of Lady Franklin, is irresistibly amusing ; and the subsequent scene between the two is the perfection of comedy acting. Those who have not seen Miss Wilton as Lady Franklin have no idea of the fund of humour which the character contains ; and to see how these two excellent artists play into each other's hands will afford entertainment to the most *blasé* of playgoers. Each look and gesture is replete with significance, and so artfully is Lady Franklin's little plot evolved that the solemn *Mr. Graves* is led into his wild Scotch jig in the most natural manner possible. At the end of the first act those who have refused a few pounds to the poor secretary hasten to offer them to the wealthy heir, and the only fault that can be found with Miss Wilton's Lady Franklin is that she too, like the rest, eagerly puts her hand in her pocket to find the money."

Of Mr. Honey's later impersonations, one of the most popular has been the part of *Cheviot Hill* in W. S. Gilbert's farcical comedy entitled ' Engaged.' Mr. Honey has appeared at various theatres in the United States. In 1879 (January 11) he commenced an engagement at the Prince of Wales's Theatre, appearing in a revival of ' Caste ' as *Eccles*, of which character he was the original representative. The " revival," continuing to May 30 of the year last mentioned, was a complete success.

HORSMAN, CHARLES, was born at Welchpool, Montgomery-shire, October 21, 1825, his first recorded appearance on the stage being at the Theatre Royal, Plymouth, in the year 1835, when he appeared as *Albert* to Mr. Macready's William Tell. He continued from that time, as a boy, to act occasionally such parts as *Young Norval, Selim* in ' Barbarossa,' &c. ; but was principally engaged in studying the rudiments of an artist's profession. In 1839 young Horsman entered the painting-room of William Beverly—the father of the present well-known scenic artist—on the so-called ' Northern Circuit,' and continued to serve under that gentleman for some years. In 1845, on the occasion of the opening of the Theatre Royal, Manchester, an epidemic among some of the members of the company necessitated Mr. Horsman's taking a place on the stage, and, in great measure owing to the genial advice of Mr. Macready, he began to take a serious interest in dramatic work. This was increased by the young actor's subsequent asso-ciation with the late G. V. Brooke ; and in 1847 Mr. Horsman finally adopted a dramatic career, accepting an engagement with Mr. Simpson at the Theatre Royal, Birmingham, as "light come-dian." Remaining at Birmingham and afterwards at Liverpool for a considerable time, he subsequently visited the "York and Worcester Circuits " ; and in 1851 made his first appearance in London at Punch's Playhouse (now the Strand Theatre), as *Henry Thornton* in ' Popping the Question.' After the season there he was mainly engaged as "leading man " and "light comedian " at the Theatre Royal and Queen's Theatre, Manchester. In 1864 Mr. Horsman reappeared on the London stage, at Sadler's Wells, under Miss Marriott's management, as *Sir Rupert* in 'Love.' The following year at the Lyceum Theatre, under Mr. Charles Fechter's management, he was engaged as "light comedian " and stage-manager ; and remained a member of Mr. Fechter's company for two seasons. Afterwards Mr. Horsman joined the "Princess's " company, under Mr. G. Vining, and appeared at the first per-formance of the dramatized version of ' Barnaby Rudge,' in the character of *Black Hugh*—a part which he played with considerable success. Mr. Horsman was manager of the New Theatre Royal, Leeds, for a season. He has played various special engagements with Miss Neilson, Miss Bateman, Miss Kate Rodgers, Mr. Barry Sullivan, and others. In 1875 he joined the Messrs. Gunn as manager of the Gaiety Theatre and Theatre Royal, Dublin, an office which he fulfilled for two seasons, and resigned in May 1877, owing to severe domestic affliction. Mr. Horsman has written various dramatic works and pantomimes, and is the author of a volume of poems descriptive of incidents of Irish life.

HORTON, PRISCILLA. *See* REED, Mrs. GERMAN.

HOWE, HENRY (a *nom de théâtre;* HENRY HOWE HUTCHIN-SON). Born at Norwich, March 31, 1812. He made his pro-fessional *début*, October 1834, at the Victoria Theatre, London, in the part of *Rashleigh Osbaldiston.* Mr. Howe was engaged by Mr. Macready to join his company when he entered upon the management of the Theatre Royal, Covent Garden, in 1837, and played in the numerous pieces, both original and revived, produced there during that eminent tragedian's administration of its affairs. He was in the original cast of 'The Lady of Lyons,' first performed at Covent Garden, February 15, 1838 ; and of 'Richelieu,' played there for the first time March 7, 1839. (*See* FAUCIT, HELEN.) On the occasion of Mr. Macready's farewell performances, Mr. Howe played *Marc Antony* to the tragedian's Julius Cæsar. So success-fully was this part acted that Mr. Macready drew a ring off his finger and presented it to Mr. Howe in token of his appreciation of Mr. Howe's meritorious services. This ring was a valuable one which had been found at Herculaneum.* After concluding his engagement at Covent Garden, Mr. Howe joined the company of the Haymarket Theatre, under Mr. Benjamin Webster's manage-ment, and continued a member of its company for a period of nearly forty years, without a break in the engagement. Such a lengthened term of service to the interests and fortunes of one theatre is unparalleled, we believe, in theatrical annals, and affords very gratifying testimony of Mr. Howe's abilities as a member of the dramatic profession. He was performing nightly at the Hay-market Theatre during the engagement of the late Mr. Charles Mathews and of his wife, Madame Vestris, in 1842–5 ; and he was a leading actor of the same theatre down to the transfer by Mr. J. S. Clarke of the unexpired term of his lease to Mr. Bancroft in the summer of 1879. To mention all the various plays and characters in which Mr. Howe has appeared in the interval would necessitate the preparation of a complete list of all the comedies, tragedies, interludes, and farces produced at the Haymarket during forty years. The following characters, selected from among those in which Mr. Howe first attracted attention as an actor at this theatre, are deserving of being recorded, viz. *Brandon*, in Lovell's comedy 'Look before you Leap,' first performed at the Haymarket, October 29, 1846 ; *Ernest de Fonblanche*, in 'The Roused Lion' ('Le Réveil du Lion'), first performed at the same theatre, November 15, 1847—Mrs. Keeley, Mr. B. Webster, and Mr. A. Wigan were in the cast, and the piece attained an extraordinary success ; *Lord Arden*, in 'The Wife's Secret,' by Lovell, first per-formed at the same theatre January 17, 1848, Mr. and Mrs. Charles Kean acting the principal characters. (*See* KEAN, Mrs. CHARLES.) On Monday, January 23, 1854, Miss Cushman acting the part of Bianca, Mr. Howe sustained the character of *Fazio* in a "revival" of Dean Milman's tragedy of that title. In June 1855 he appeared in a new play entitled 'Love's Martyrdom.' "A few errors of tact in the management of stage effect . . . . caused the success of the play to be somewhat doubtful until after the conclusion of the first three acts. But from that point all was triumph. The conception and management of the fourth act were unexceptionable, the writing was full of force and beauty, opportunity was given for a full display of the powers of Miss Helen Faucit as an actress, and the house was stirred into enthusiasm by her way of using it. In the same act all

---

* Letter from Mr. Howe to the Editor.

the point of the story, until then but dimly shown, was brought out very distinctly, being indebted much for its distinctness, let us say, to the excellent manner in which Mr. Howe delivered speeches that expressed the entire spirit and meaning of the author. The fifth act, although not equal to the fourth, untied the knot of the drama cleverly, and left the audience so thoroughly well pleased, that after the fall of the curtain there was nothing to be heard for some minutes but hearty acclamation." (*Examiner*, June 16, 1855.)

In July 1855 Mr. Howe took part in the revival of Mrs. Centlivre's comedy 'The Busybody,' at the Haymarket, and played the part of *Sir George Airey*. In the following September (3rd) he was the original *Captain Hawkshaw*, first performance of Stirling Coyne's comedy 'The Man with Many Friends'; and in November he played *Lord Townly* in a "revival" of Vanbrugh's comedy 'The Provoked Husband.' "Miss Cushman was carefully supported by Mr. Howe, who, in the part of *Lord Townly*, rose to a degree of excellence that will serve to confirm the steady progress which he has lately been making in the good opinion of the public. In the pathos of the concluding scene he showed a power of producing a state of feeling in the house not always possessed by actors of greater name." (*Athenæum*, November 24, 1855.) The following year (1856), January 5th, Mr. Howe played *Archer* in a "revival" of 'The Beaux' Stratagem'; and in September (4th) *Jaques* in a "revival" of 'As You Like It'—a performance by Mr. Howe so meritorious as to deserve record in a contemporary journal as furnishing "an instance of what long practice and conscientious earnestness in art may ultimately achieve, even with limited means." In 1857 (September 7th) he appeared as *Benedick* in a "revival" of 'Much Ado About Nothing,' "sharing the honour [of an ovation] and deserving it, for his *Benedick* was distinguished by many felicities of expression which commanded the repeated plaudits of the house. Mr. Howe's industry in his professional studies is now bearing its natural fruit, and his assumptions have all the merit of ripened talent." (*Athenæum*, September 12, 1857.) In 1858 (May) he appeared as *Joseph Surface* in a revival of 'The School for Scandal'; and more recently in the characters of *Sir Anthony Absolute*, *Ingot* ('David Garrick'), and *Sir Peter Teazle*. During the succeeding twenty years Mr. Howe's name was seldom absent from the "bills" of the Haymarket Theatre, either in the announcement of new pieces or of revivals of old ones ; and he has performed almost every line of character in comedy and farce included in its dramatic collection.* In August 1879 Mr. Howe,

---

* Mr. Howe writes to me :—" I have been so long at the Haymarket that now I play the 'old men.' I have played *every* part in the male *rôle* in some of the pieces produced on its stage. For instance, in 'The Lady of Lyons' I began with the *First Officer*, then I played *Gaspar*, *Beauseant*, *Claude Melnotte*, and now *Colonel Damas ;* and in many other pieces the same variety, as for instance 'The Stranger,' 'Money,' &c. I am now, and have been for three years, stage-manager. Lately I made a success as *Sir Anthony Absolute* and *Sir Peter Teazle*. I mention these parts, being now *engaged* for the 'first old men,' after playing all the different ranges of character in the one theatre, the Haymarket."—ED.

through changes in the management, ended his long, and in all respects honourable, connection with the Haymarket Theatre. It is gratifying to record that this excellent actor has become associated with a no less popular theatre in London—the Vaudeville. Here he made his first appearance on Saturday, August 16, 1879 in a comedietta by Richard Lee, entitled ' Home for Home,' and as *Josiah Clench* (the part originally played by Mr. W. Farren) in Byron's comedy ' Our Girls.'

HOWSON, EMMA, was born in Hobart Town, Tasmania. She is a daughter of the late Frank Howson,* and niece of Madame Albertazzi (Emma Howson), who some forty years ago was a favourite mezzo-soprano singer at Her Majesty's Theatre; sister also of the under-mentioned John Howson. As a child, Miss Howson was possessed of considerable musical ability, which developed under her father's instruction. At an early age she sang in concerts in Australia in conjunction with him and her brothers. She made her first appearance in English opera, June 1866, at Maguire's Academy of Music, San Francisco, as *Amina* in ' La Sonnambula.' After playing several successful engagements in California and other cities on the Central Pacific Railway route to the Eastern States (*see* HOWSON, JOHN), Miss Howson made her *début* in New York in 1869 in the opera of ' Maritana ' at Fiske's Opera House. A twelve months' season followed with the Riching's " English Opera Combination." Subsequently Miss Howson entered into a contract with Mr. C. D. Hess to play in English opera, and visited all the principal cities of the United States and Canada, playing the *prima donna rôles* in ' Maritana,' ' Fra Diavolo,' ' Bohemian Girl,' ' Martha,' ' Oberon,' ' The Marriage of Figaro,' ' Der Freyschutz,' and ' Trovatore.' At Niblo's Theatre, New York, she acted the character of *Eily O'Connor* in ' The Colleen Bawn.' At the end of 1873 Miss Howson left the United States for Europe, and went to Milan to study the Italian repertory and language under Signor Lamperti. In March 1875 she made her *début* in Italian opera at the Teatro Manoel, Malta, in the part of *Amina* (' La Sonnambula'). Afterwards Miss Howson appeared at the same theatre in ' Martha,' and during the season sang in these two operas. In the autumn of the same year she went to Leghorn, and sang there in Meyerbeer's ' Dinorah ' with considerable success. In the beginning of 1876 she accepted an engagement for a provincial tour in England in Italian opera, during which she performed the *prima donna rôles* in ' Le Nozze di Figaro,' ' Lucia di Lammermoor,' ' Rigoletto,' ' Don Giovanni,' ' Maritana,' ' Der Freyschutz,' ' Les Huguenots.' Her various performances were very favourably noticed in the local

* Mr. Frank Howson was a baritone vocalist of no inconsiderable local reputation, who left England in 1842 for the Australian colonies, where he engaged in theatrical pursuits. He was the first to present complete English and Italian operas to an Australian public. He acted as stage-manager to Madame Anna Bishop and the gifted Catherine Hayes, and other celebrities who visited Australia many years ago. He died at Omaha, Nebraska, U.S.A., September 16, 1869.

press. Miss Howson made her *début* on the London stage at the Opéra Comique, on Saturday, May 25, 1878, as *Josephine*, first performance of 'H.M.S. Pinafore,' comic opera, by MM. W. S. Gilbert and Arthur Sullivan, her "clear and pure soprano voice, and refined and unaffected style, rendering full effect to the music of her part" (*Daily News*, May 27, 1878). In this opera Miss Emma Howson appeared from the date of its first performance down to April 1879. She subsequently went to New York to appear in the same *rôle*.

HOWSON, JOHN, was born in Hobart Town, Tasmania, November 17, 1844, and is second son of the late Frank Howson and brother of the above-named Emma Howson. He first appeared on the stage as a lad at the Royal Victoria Theatre, Sydney, N.S.W., under his father's auspices. During the period of the gold fever in Australia, and the engagement of Catherine Hayes, he sang in the chorus in 'La Sonnambula' at the same theatre. After various fortune incidental to colonial life, "serving for a time in a lawyer's office, then a ship chandler's, afterwards, for two years, as assistant to a fashionable dancing master, devoting spare hours to education, the study of music, and practice of the violin," John Howson formed, in conjunction with other members of his family, a concert company to visit "the Diggings," Ballarat, Victoria, &c. Of this organization he was the principal violinist and "general utility" man. In 1865, at Brisbane, Queensland, "tasting the sweets of applause in a burlesque character, that of *Phineas* in 'Perseus and Andromeda,'" he decided on adopting the stage as a profession. In March 1866 he left Australia with his family for San Francisco. Touching at Tahiti, Society Islands, the Howsons gave two concerts under the patronage of Queen Pomare and other notabilities. Mr. Howson was for three years resident in San Francisco, appearing at the theatre in the "usual round of comedy and character business." In May 1869, *en route* to the Eastern States, he played the part of *General Boom* in 'La Grande Duchesse' at the theatre Great Salt Lake City—"a piece which the Prophet and President, Brigham Young, witnessed on three consecutive nights." Mr. John Howson made his first appearance on the New York stage in November 1869, at Wood's Museum, as *Upton Spout* in the old Adelphi farce 'The Pretty Horsebreaker,' and as the *Widow Twankay* in H. J. Byron's burlesque of 'Aladdin.' He was for a time a member of the company of Booth's Theatre, and in the orchestra of the Grand Opera House as violinist. During the season of 1871–2 he was first comedian of a travelling company (Mr. Mark Smith's) in the United States, playing such parts as *Doctor Ollapod, Bob Acres, Mark Meddle, Zekiel Homespun*, &c. At the Varieties Theatre, New Orleans, he was engaged in the earlier part of 1872 "in the useful capacity of second comedian and character actor," supporting the leading "stars" of the American stage—MM. Joseph Jefferson, John E. Owens, Lawrence Barrett, &c. In the season of 1872–3 he travelled in the United States with a Musical, Drama, and Opera Bouffe Company; Characters:

Sergeant Scalade in Buckstone's version of 'The Child of the Regiment'; *Mons. Choufleuri* in Offenbach's operetta of that name; *Princess Vindicta* in the burlesque of 'Fortunio.' From 1873 to 1877 Mr. Howson was engaged in various theatrical enterprises in the United States which were more or less successful. He first appeared on the English stage at Brighton, September 3, 1877 in 'La Créole,' as *Commodore Patatras*, and made his *début* in London at the Folly Theatre, Saturday, September 15 of the same year, in the same character. "In Mr. John Howson, who made his first appearance in London as the *Commodore Patatras*, a capital comedian has been discovered, and a comedian distinct and apart from the conventional pattern. He does not struggle to be funny— he is funny. He does not struggle to get his effects—they come of themselves. Mr. Howson had clearly sketched out in his own mind the character of the noisy, blustering, determined old gentleman who conceals beneath his autocratic manner a good heart and a kindly disposition, and he produced, without the slightest effort all the fun of which the character was capable, particularly at that notable point where the martinet at the very highest point of his tyranny is continually summoned away to be bullied by somebody else. . . . . [Mr. Howson's] was a comedy success." (*Daily Telegraph*, September 17, 1877.) In February 1878, first performance at the same theatre of Reece and Farnie's version of 'Les Cloches de Corneville,' he acted the *Marquis*. Easter Monday of the same year, at the Prince of Wales's Theatre, Liverpool, he appeared as *Gaspard* in the same piece, playing the *rôle* at several theatres in the provinces. He is now (July 1879) appearing in his "original" (as far as the English version is concerned) part of the *Marquis* at the Globe Theatre, London. "Mr. John Howson is a genuine artist, and one of the best actors that have for some time appeared on our stage. He has a good voice and delivery, sings well and in tune, acts to perfection, and lives in his parts in a way that gives them reality and strength of no common degree." (*Echo*, November 24, 1877.)

*HUDSPETH, HENRIETTA (Mrs. EDMUND PHELPS), is the daughter of John Hudspeth, an actor who was for a long time connected with the old Queen's (now Prince of Wales's) Theatre. Her first London appearance was at the Lyceum Theatre, November 28, 1859, as *Madeline Champi* in 'Paris and Pleasure.' Since then she has played in all the principal theatres in London and in the provinces.

HUTCHINSON, HENRY HOWE. *See* HOWE, HENRY.

* **ILLINGTON, MARIE,** made her *début* at the Haymarket Theatre in the comedy of 'Red Tape' in the autumn of 1875. Subsequently, at the Theatre Royal, Edinburgh, she played many light comedy parts until, attracting the notice of Mr. Walter Gooch, she was engaged to appear at the Princess's Theatre in London. In the play of 'Guinea Gold,' which was produced there September 10, 1877, she sustained an important part. She also appeared in the play of 'Jane Shore' at the same theatre. During the indisposition of Miss Heath she took the place of that lady in the principal character at very short notice. In the summer of 1878 Miss Illington went to the Vaudeville, where she acted the part of *Mary Melrose* in 'Our Boys.' She was in the original cast of Byron's comedy of 'The Girls,' produced April 19, 1879, and has since appeared as *Lottie* in a revival of Albery's 'Two Roses' at the same theatre.

INGRAM, ALICE (Mrs. J. R. CRAUFORD), daughter of Mr. F. Haywell, began her theatrical career at the T. R. Birmingham, and afterwards held engagements at the Tyne Theatre, at Nottingham, and the T. R. Dublin, playing (among numerous other parts) *Mary Wurzel* with Charles Mathews, and the *Duchess Francesca* in 'The Fool's Revenge' with Mr. Phelps. She then joined for a short time Captain Disney Roebuck's company, and afterwards the 'Caste' company with Mr. F. Younge, playing the principal parts in Mr. T. Robertson's pieces—*Esther Eccles, Bella, Amanda* (in 'Play'), *Ruth Daybrooke, Blanche Haye,* &c. Her engagement with the 'Caste' company was continued under Mr. R. Younge, with whom she made a successful appearance at the Charing Cross Theatre as *Milly Petworth* in 'Time's Triumph.' Her subsequent engagements have been at the Prince's, Manchester (*Helen* in 'The Hunchback'); at the Gaiety, Dublin (*Edith* in 'On the Jury' with Mr. Phelps); as *Titania* for a run of five weeks at the T. R. Birmingham; at Plymouth; the Prince of Wales's, Birmingham; the Prince of Wales's, Liverpool; and the T. R. Manchester; on tour with Mr. C. Wyndham (as *Effie Remington* in 'Brighton'); as *Henriette* in 'The Two Orphans' company; as *The Fool* in 'King Lear' with Mr. Creswick at the Standard; at the Corinthian Theatre, Calcutta, for a season of five months; at Bristol as *Eliza* in 'After Dark'; at the opening of the new T. R. Cardiff, as *Cynisca* in 'Pygmalion and Galatea'; and several engagements at the Alexandra, Liverpool, as *Pauline* in 'The Lady of Lyons,' *Olivia* in 'Twelfth Night,' and as *Helen Macgregor.* Miss Ingram has also appeared for short engagements at the Crystal Palace, St. James's, the Court, and Gaiety Theatres in London; and lately with Mr. Sothern on tour, as *Florence* in 'Our American Cousin,' and *Carrie Gresham* in 'A Hornet's Nest.'

IRISH, FRED. WILLIAM, was born in Leicester, 1835, and entered the dramatic profession in 1853, appearing first at the Theatre Royal, Leicester, as *Marcellus* in 'Hamlet.' After a short season there he went to Derby, and from thence to Nottingham, Sheffield, Blackburn, and Belfast, where he secured his first engagement as "principal low comedian." He remained in Liverpool for six years, acting principal low-comedy parts, and then accepted an engagement at Newcastle-upon-Tyne in 1867–8, and acted a leading part on the occasion of the opening night of the new Tyne Theatre. Mr. Irish made his first appearance on the London stage, March 2, 1871, at the Holborn Theatre under Mr. Sefton Parry's management, in the character of *Dan* in 'The Streets of London.' He has since been engaged at the following London theatres: Alhambra, Lyceum, Queen's, Astley's, Charing Cross, Mirror, Princess's, Drury Lane, and Haymarket, and also at the Crystal and Alexandra Palaces. At the Lyceum, under Mr. Bateman's management, April 1872, he played the part of *Sam* in 'Raising the Wind.' In December 1874 he undertook the part of *Widow Mustapha* in 'Aladdin' at the Charing Cross Theatre, and played it with a decided flow of unexaggerated and original humour.

IRVING, JOHN HENRY BRODRIB, was born at Keinton, near Glastonbury, Somersetshire, February 6, 1838, and educated at a private school in London. He was originally intended for mercantile life, and passed some few months in the office of an East India merchant; but having exhibited a strong partiality for a dramatic career, early forsook commerce for the stage, with which he became professionally connected in 1856. He made his first appearance on the stage that year at the Lyceum Theatre, Sunderland, in the part of *Orleans* in 'Richelieu.' Afterwards, at the same theatre, he undertook the part of *Cleomenes* in a revival of 'A Winter's Tale.' Neither of these performances were altogether satisfactory, and subjected Mr. Irving to unfavourable criticism in the local press. Henceforward he earnestly devoted himself to the study of dramatic art. In 1857 he was fortunate enough to secure an engagement at the Theatre Royal, Edinburgh, where he remained for two and a half years; and during their several "starring" tours had the advantage of acting with such admirable artists as Miss Cushman, Miss Helen Faucit, Messrs. Vandenhoff, Robson, Charles Mathews the younger, Benjamin Webster, and Wright. In 1859 Mr. Irving entered upon a brief engagement at the Princess's Theatre, London, then under the management of the late Mr. Augustus Harris; but this engagement being cancelled, he shortly afterwards became attached to the late Mr. Edmund Glover's company at Manchester. In this city, for the first time in his professional career, he essayed the character of *Hamlet*. In 1866, ten years after he had first adopted the stage as a profession, he made his appearance as an actor of recognized merit at the St. James's Theatre in London. On Saturday, October 6 of that year, he played there *Doricourt* in a revival of 'The Belle's Stratagem' (Mrs. Cowley), "his mad scenes being truthfully conceived and most subtilely executed" (*Athenæum*, October 13, 1866). In the following November, at the same theatre, first performance in London of Dion Boucicault's drama ' Hunted Down,' he acted the part of *Rawdon Scudamore* with considerable success. In 1867, on Saturday, February 9, at the same theatre, he undertook the character of *Harry Dornton* in a revival of ' The Road to Ruin '; and, in the succeeding April, the part of *Count Falcon* in a drama entitled ' Idalia.' In January 1868, at the New Queen's Theatre, London, first performance of Mr. H. J. Byron's play ' Dearer than Life,' he sustained the character of *Bob Gassitt*—" a most ungrateful part, acted with scrupulous care and artistic taste " (*Standard*, January 9, 1868). At Drury Lane Theatre, August 5, 1869, Mr. Irving played *Compton Kerr* on the occasion of the first performance of Boucicault's drama ' Formosa '; and in 1870, Saturday, June 4, first performance at the Vaudeville Theatre of Mr. Albery's play ' Two Roses,' he performed the part of *Digby Grant*, the impersonation being so original in conception and so masterly in execution as to entitle the actor to rank among the very best actors on the London stage. " The selfish arrogance, the stuck-up *hauteur*, the transparent hypocrisy, and the utter heartlessness of the character, made all the more odious from the assumption of sanctity, were depicted by Mr. Irving with exquisite truthfulness of detail, and admirable brilliancy and vigour of general effect. His make-up for the part was excellent, and his whole performance spirited, characteristic, and life-like " (*Morning Post*, June 6, 1870).

In 1871 Mr. Irving accepted an engagement at the Lyceum Theatre, under the management of the late H. L. Bateman ; and on Monday, September 11, " opened " there as *Landry*, in a piece entitled ' Fanchette ; or, the Will o' the Wisp.' On Monday, October 23 of the same year, he appeared as *Jingle* in a dramatic version of ' Pickwick,' by Mr. Albery. In the November following, ' The Bells,' a version by Mr. Leopold Lewis of MM. Erckmann-Chatrian's ' Le Juif Polonais,' was first performed at the Lyceum Theatre. In this drama Mr. Irving undertook the character of *Mathias*, as to which the *Times* (November 25, 1871) remarked :— " It will be obvious to every reader that the efficiency of this singular play depends almost wholly upon the actor who represents *Mathias*. . . . Mr. Irving has thrown the whole force of his mind into the character, and works out bit by bit the concluding hours of a life passed in a constant effort to preserve a cheerful exterior, with a conscience tortured till it has become a monomania. It is a marked peculiarity of the moral position of *Mathias* that he has no confidant, that he is not subjected to the extortions of some mercenary wretch who would profit by his knowledge. He is at once in two worlds, between which there is no link—an outer world that is ever smiling, an inner world which is a purgatory. Hence a dreaminess in his manner which Mr. Irving accurately represents in his frequent transitions from a display of the domestic affections to the fearful work of self-communion. In the dream his position is changed. The outer world is gone, and conscience is all triumphant, assisted by an imagination which violently brings together the anticipated terrors of a criminal court and the mesmeric feats he has recently witnessed. The struggles of the miserable culprit, convinced that all is lost, but desperately fighting against hope, rebelling against the judges, protesting against the clairvoyant who wrings his secret from him, are depicted by Mr. Irving with a degree of energy that, fully realizing the horror of the situation, seems to hold the audience in suspense. It was not till the curtain fell, and they summoned the actor before it with a storm of acclamation, that they seemed to recover their self-possession." On Monday, April 1, 1872, in a revival of the farce of 'Raising the Wind,' Mr. Irving played the character of *Jeremy Diddler;* and the same year, Saturday, September 28, 'Charles the First' (W. G. Wills) was first performed at the Lyceum, in which he sustained the leading *rôle.* "Through 'Charles I.' runs a melancholy beauty which finds expression in many musical passages, and which intensifies, as the play proceeds, into absolute pain. During the last act there was scarcely a dry eye in the house. Women sobbed openly, and even men showed an emotion which comported ill with the habitual serenity of the stalls. Much of this uncomfortable gratification was due to the acting of Mr. Irving, the hero of the play, who has once more created a great *rôle.* In intensity of suggestiveness his *Charles I.* will compare with his *Mathias,* while in breadth, dignity, and harmonious colour it surpasses it. . . . Nothing more regal can be desired than his bearing, nothing more harmonious than the effect of every look and gesture, nothing more touching than his delivery of the poetic beauties that abound. From the outward appearance of the king (he might be an incarnate portrait of Vandyke) down to each little detail of posture, everything is elaborated with conscientious care, and the result is a vivid creation of art." (*Daily News,* September 30, 1872.) 'Charles the First' was so great a success that it was performed during nearly seven months.

In April 1873 another of Mr. Wills's plays was undertaken by Mr. Irving, 'The Fate of Eugene Aram.' In this again a remarkable piece of acting was exhibited. Said the *Spectator* (April 19, 1873):—"The acting of Mr. Irving in this character is wonderfully fine, so deeply impressive that once only, by a bit of 'business' with lights and a looking-glass, quite unworthy of the play and of him, does he remind one that he is acting and not living through that mortal struggle; so various that to lose sight of his face for a moment is to lose some expression full of power and of fidelity to the pervading motive of the part. . . . In the second act the anguish of his mind is intensified with every moment, until in the sudden outburst of his fury, his defiance of Houseman, his proud boast of his character in the place and the influence of it, the change, fierce yet subtle, from sad and dreamy quiet to the hard, scoffing, worldly wisdom of the criminal at bay before his accomplice, there is a positive relief for him and for ourselves. Then comes the terror, abject indeed for a while, with desperate, breathless rally, thick incoherent speech, failing limbs, ghastly face, dry

lips and choking throat, as dreadful as only fear can be, and
horribly true. . . . In the concluding scenes, one, in which he
sends Houseman flying from the churchyard, appalled at the sight
of his suffering ; a second, in which, in accents of heartrending
grief and contrition, he implores Heaven for a sign of pardon, and
flings himself down by a cross, with an awful face, the white, mute
impersonation of mental despair and physical exhaustion ; and a
third, in which he makes confession to Ruth and dies—the play of
his features, the variety and intensity of his expression are most
remarkable." On the 27th September, 1873, 'Richelieu' was produced at the Lyceum, Mr. Irving sustaining the part of the
Cardinal. " Those who are familiar with the portrait of the
Cardinal must be at once struck by its presentation in a living
form when Mr. Irving makes his first appearance. . . . His
defence of Julie de Mortemar when the minions of the king would
snatch her from his arms, the weight of sacerdotal authority with .
which he threatens to 'launch the curse of Rome,' his self-trans-
formation into the semblance of a Hebrew prophet of the olden
time, with whom imprecations were deeds, combine together to
produce a most astounding effect. Here is tragic acting in the
grandest style, and it will be borne in mind that although ' Richelieu ' is not a tragedy, it belongs practically to the tragical category,
as none can do justice to it but a tragedian. Before the effect of
the fulmination was subsided came the well-known lines—

> ' Walk blindfold on—behind thee stalks the headsman.
> Ha ! ha ! how pale he is ! Heaven save my country ! '

The scornful laugh by which the flow of indignation is checked,
and which was a great point with Mr. Macready, had told with
surprising force, and when the *Cardinal* had fallen back exhausted
. . . . the old-fashioned excitement which we associate with the
days of Edmund Kean and his ' wolves' was manifested once more
in all its pristine force. Enthusiastic shouts of approbation came
from every part of the house. The pit not only *rose*, but made its
rising conspicuous by the waving of countless hats and handkerchiefs. Not bare approval but hearty sympathy was denoted by
this extraordinary demonstration ; and this sympathy nothing but
genius and thoroughly self-abandonment on the part of the artist
could have produced." (*Times*, September 30, 1873.)

On Saturday, February 7, 1874, Mr. Irving played *Philip* in a
romantic drama of that title from the pen of Mr. Hamilton Aïdé.
In the autumn of the same year 'Hamlet' was placed on the
Lyceum stage, and created a curiosity to witness Mr. Irving's impersonation of the character altogether remarkable. The play had
the unprecedented run of two hundred nights—not only unprecedented, but unapproached in the history of Shakespearian revival. He continued to perform the part from October 30, 1874, to
June 29, 1875. " Mr. Irving's *Hamlet* is original throughout. It
is more than probable that he has never seen any predecessor of
extraordinary eminence enact the part. At all events, it is certain

that the *Hamlet* in the play-book has been realized by Mr. Irving upon the stage without passing through any medium but that of his own thought. . . . The learned will turn over their books to discover what was done by Betterton, what by Kemble, what by Charles Young; but their studies will avail them nothing towards an estimate of Mr. Irving, who stands aloof from the pedigree beginning with Betterton and ending with Charles Kean. . . . Why then is *Hamlet* so irresolute? . . . If we rightly interpret Mr. Irving's performance his reply to the question is to the effect that the nature of *Hamlet* is essentially tender, loving, and merciful. He is not a weak man called upon to do something beyond his powers, but he is a kindly man urged to do a deed which, according to the *lex talionis*, may be righteous, but which is yet cruel. . . . There is a theory to the effect that *Hamlet*, while assuming madness, is really somewhat insane. From this theory we entirely dissent, at the same time admitting that his sensitive nature subjects him to the highest degree of nervous excitement. This could not be more clearly expressed than by Mr. Irving. . . . Most powerfully is the nervous condition exhibited in the scene with Ophelia. The pretended madness, the unquenchable love, and the desire to utter stern truths seemed to hustle against each other. The words seemed to be flung about at random, and the facial movements correspond to the recklessness of the words. The storm of applause which followed this display of genius denoted not only admiration but wonder." (*Times*, November 2, 1874.) Concerning this performance of 'Hamlet,' a writer in the *Dublin University Magazine* of September 1877 thus remarked upon the excitement its announcement produced:—" Mr. Irving's *Hamlet* was not the essay of a tyro, but the culminating point of a career in which genius and arduous study had marked every stride. As early as three o'clock in the afternoon of the 31st of October the crowd began to form at the pit door of the Lyceum, and soon a struggling, seething mass of human beings extended down the covered way right out into the Strand. The pit that night was a memorable spectacle. Never had that tribunal been so highly charged with anxiety, impatience, and enthusiasm. The entire audience was an extraordinary assemblage, for the fact that Mr. Irving had set his reputation on a cast which was also to decide whether the times were indeed too degenerate for Shakespeare to be popular, had brought most of the representatives of art and letters to witness the hazard of the die. The actor's welcome was an outburst of unfeigned admiration of the courage with which he was about to grapple with the most difficult and exacting of Shakespearian creations. But for a time the novelty of the conception and the absolute independence of familiar traditions bewildered the audience. This sad and self-distrustful *Hamlet*, who gave natural and constant expression to his thoughts as they occurred to him, instead of delivering a number of unnatural 'points' like stones from a catapult excited a growing interest; but two acts had almost passed before he began to be understood. It may be remarked here as a striking trait of a conscientious artist, that after

the scene with the Ghost, Mr. Irving came off the stage depressed
not by the silence of the auditory, but by the thought that he had
fallen below his ideal. But when the tender, sympathetic nature of
this *Hamlet* fairly revealed itself, the affections of all were won. It
was the most human *Hamlet* they had ever known. . . . The
performance was now one long success . . . . and when the curtain
fell upon the consummation of the tragedy the immense assembly
clamoured its delight till nearly one o'clock in the morning."

In June 1875 'Hamlet' was erased from the Lyceum play-bills,
and in the following September 'Macbeth' was revived, Mr. Irving
sustaining the principal *rôle*. The *Athenæum* (October 2, 1875),
discussing the merits of the performance, s id:—"In Mr. Irving's
conception there is intention, but it is wrong ; and there are individual
merits which will not compound for systematic error. This objection, might, however, be vanquished in another part—might even
be removed by further study and practice. Mr. Irving must learn,
however, that his mannerisms have developed into evils so formid-
able, they will, if not checked, end by ruining his career. His slow
pronunciation and his indescribable elongation of syllables bring
the whole occasionally near burlesque. In one speech, that in
which *Macbeth* speaks of false Thanes gone to 'mingle with the
English epicures,' absolute laughter was evoked, and a similar
calamity was on another occasion scarcely avoided. Mr. Irving
has youth, intelligence, ambition, zeal, and resolution. These things
are sacrificed to vices of style which have strengthened with the
actor's successes, and like all weeds of ill growth have obtained
excessive development. It is impossible to preserve the music of
Shakespeare if words of one syllable are to be stretched out to the
length of five or six. Mr. Irving's future depends greatly on his
mastery of this defect."

The *Daily News* (September 27, 1875) found more to praise in
the performance, according to the subjoined criticism:—"But the
secret of the spell which this extraordinary actor exercises over the
imaginations of audiences is not difficult to discover. It lies in
the imaginative power with which he is able to depict the most
terrible passions of the human soul in a great crisis of action, and
in the wonderful expressiveness of countenance which on these
occasions never deserts him. To the playgoer whose memory is
haunted with the Macbeths of the past there is a peculiar pleasure
in the total absence in all Mr. Irving's performances of mere conventional details. We believe it has always been customary in the
dagger scene to confront the audience looking upwards, as if the
imaginary weapon were hovering in the air somewhere between the
performer and the audience. Mr. Irving, on the contrary, sees the
dagger at a much lower point as he follows it across the stage,
drawn as it were by its fascination towards the arched entrance to
the chamber of the king—a fine point being his averted hands, as
if the man, 'infirm of purpose,' and conscious of the spell that is
around and about him, could not trust himself to 'clutch' the airy
weapon save in words. . . . The touches of tenderness and of
regretful remorse, which add greatly to the beauty of these latter

scenes, seemed indeed to miss some of their effect; but the final combat and death struggle has probably never been equalled for picturesque force and intensity."

In February 1876 'Othello' was revived at the Lyceum with Mr. Irving as the *Moor*. Probably this has been the least successful of Mr. Irving's impersonations, and was the subject of much unfavourable comment in the public press. It was conceded, however, that there were powerful passages in Mr. Irving's acting, and that he had bestowed his usual careful study upon the representation which he gave. " To ask of one man to represent night after night for many weeks or months such characters as Hamlet, Macbeth, or Othello, is as to require of the English army to fight a battle of Waterloo every day. From Hamlet Mr. Irving proceeded, illadvisedly as, at the time, we thought, to Macbeth, and our anticipations were before long justified by the public verdict. With still greater want of judgment, we fear, has he now attempted *Othello*, for which he either altogether lacks, or at least has failed as yet to exhibit, the qualifications which such a character demands. In his pathos he is monotonous without being tender, in his rage violent without being dignified, while his love for Desdemona has altogether to be taken on trust from the words that are put into his mouth. In many passages, moreover, and especially in the third act, where he demands from her slanderer some tangible proof of his wife's guilt, his violence is such as to render him almost ludicrous, and altogether unintelligible. This latter fault is, indeed, most unhappily prominent throughout the performance. It has been said, and well said, that the great masterpieces of Shakespeare, even when most indifferently acted, cannot altogether fail to please, provided only the actors will suffer the audience to hear the words of the author. But from the mouth of Mr. Irving, unfortunately, we cannot hear them. In repose he is as much too slow of speech as in action he is too tumultuous, while in both he has of late acquired a peculiarity of pronunciation, for which, in all humility, we confess ourselves totally unable to conceive any authority. In his description to the Duke of the only arts he employed to gain Brabantio's daughter, and in that magnificent farewell to content, it is possible indeed to hear what is said ; but throughout the third and fourth acts we are denied even this consolation. Our ears are stunned by an empty noise which only a knowledge of the text can possibly allow us to accept as the passionate outpourings of a noble mind overthrown in the keenest of all mortal anguish. In harmony with so much indeed, but how out of harmony with Shakespeare's *Othello* are the actions and gestures in which Mr. Irving indulges ! The movements of his body are as the movements of his voice ; when slow, so slow as to excite the impatience—when quick, so quick as almost to excite the laughter—of the spectator. Once only did Mr. Irving appear to us to have caught the spirit of *Othello*—and *Othello*, be it remembered, is not, as Hamlet is, a character of many and diverse readings ; there can be but one true *Othello*. As he sits writing at his table at the opening of the third act, and when Iago first begins to pour the 'mixture rank' into his too open ear, both in Mr. Irving's face and in his attitude, and very nearly in his voice, the first faint flushings of the dawn of jealousy are not unskilfully marked. Yet the dawn broadens into no perfect day, but rather into an indescribable chaos of painful and inharmonious elements. In the torrent, tempest, and whirlwind of this passion there is no temperance, and so no smoothness. We can well remember, on the first night this actor played Hamlet, our admiration at the manner in which he delivered the famous counsel to the players ; as we sat the other night through the five acts of ' Othello ' we could not but wonder whether Mr. Irving's memory was as good as ours. It would have been easier, and certainly far pleasanter, to have written in a more complimentary fashion, but we have felt it our duty to speak plainly. We can believe that three years ago Mr. Irving would have pleased us as *Othello*, but for the sake of Hamlet we are sorry he has attempted it now." (*Times*, February 17, 1876.)

In a critical review of Mr. Irving's appearance as *Othello* in the *Standard* (February 11, 1876) the writer found somewhat to praise in it :—"And here Mr. Irving made one of those subtle points which add such remarkable strength to his impersonations. ' If more thou dost perceive, let me know more,' *Othello* says, and then pauses. . . . He turns away that Iago may not see his face, and speaks in a hasty whisper, ' Set on thy wife to observe. Leave me, Iago.' . . . Suddenly Desdemona stands before him. As he looks at her his doubts disperse. . . .

> ' If she be false, oh, then Heaven mocks itself :
> I'll not believe it.'

The utterance of these last words was marvellously fine, and it would be difficult to describe the tremendous effect they had upon the audience. It is impossible to deny the power of an actor who by the delivery of three or four simple words can so deeply move the hearts of a crowded and certainly a critical house. . . . Another special success was made in the speech where, goaded to madness, he seizes Iago by the throat, ' Villain, be sure thou prove.' . . . All that most perilous business of the trance, which must be fatal to any but an actor of very exceptional powers, was most skilfully managed, and the transitions of emotion during the scene with Desdemona, beginning, ' My lord, what is your will ? ' were ingeniously traced in expression of voice and feature. . . . The conclusion of the tragedy may also be warmly commended. . . . The performance will add to the high reputation Mr. Irving has won, but it is gravely affected by the mannerisms of pronunciation, on which comment has been made."

In April of the same year, ' Queen Mary,' an historical play in five acts, by Mr. Tennyson, was performed for the first time, Mr. Irving sustaining the part of *Philip of Spain*. This piece was but a partial success. " To Mr. Irving was assigned the small part of *Philip*, in which there is little to say but much to look. . . . This was indeed the very *Philip*—harsh, cold, satirical, of facile, unrelenting, and exquisite cruelty. His mannerisms apart — those unhappy mannerisms that have been spoken of already—not a touch was wanting to the completeness of the portrait. The play-goer should very specially mark the bitter and dry humour of every taunt and threat, the Spanish and kingly rigidity of *physique* to which the portraits of the time bear witness, the alertness and eager watchfulness of mind, the concentration of purpose, in the scene in which *Philip* broaches the question of the hand of Elizabeth. It is the most complete piece of ' character acting ' now on the stage." (*Academy*, April 22, 1876.)

" Mr. Irving's stately, scornful, and frigid, but yet brutal *Philip*, is as faultless as we could well imagine it. It has been objected that he makes his disgust for the Queen too evident . . . . but that is evidently the self-deception of a mind too haughty and careless of others to be aware of the disgust which his language has really implied. . . . As far as we can judge, it would have been im-possible for Mr. Irving to represent the poet's conception of *Philip* more perfectly than he has done." (*Spectator*, April 22, 1876.) In the autumn of 1876 Mr. Irving played *Hamlet* in the provinces, and his interpretation of the character was everywhere welcomed with acclamation. It was estimated that, during his stay at Manchester, nearly eighteen thousand persons visited the theatre at which he performed. In Scotland and Ireland his reception was no less gratifying. On November 29 an address was presented to him by the graduates and undergraduates of Trinity College, Dublin. "To the most careful students of Shakespeare," they said, "you have, by your scholarly and original interpretation, revealed new depths of meaning in *Hamlet*, and aroused in the minds of all a fresh interest in our highest poetry. . . . Acting such as yours ennobles and elevates the stage, and serves to restore it to its true function as a potent instrument for intellectual and moral culture. Throughout your too-brief engagement our stage has been a school of true art, a purifier of the passions, and a nurse of heroic senti-ments; you have even succeeded in commending it to the favour of a portion of society, large and justly influential, who usually hold aloof from the theatre." The last night of Mr. Irving's engagement in Dublin he played *Hamlet* in compliance- with a "command" from Trinity College.

In 1877, January 29, Shakespeare's ' Richard the Third ' was placed on the Lyceum stage, Mr. Irving as *Richard Duke of Gloucester*. The *Morning Post* (January 30, 1877) thus alluded to the performance :—" There are, of course, blemishes as well as beauties in Mr. Henry Irving's impersonation of *Richard III.*, but viewing it in its entirety—the only fair way of regarding any work of art on which a general opinion is to be pronounced—it is, we think, a fine performance, brilliant, energetic, impassioned, and full of life and character. . . . Mr. Irving would seem to have bestowed minute care upon his personal portrait of *Richard*, in which he reproduces not only the usurper's historic ungainliness of form and feature, but also such smaller singularities as the frequent twitching of the hands—a physical denotement of the restless spirit within. . . . The grim, sardonic humour of the poet, which has always been an element of enjoyment with the populace, is distinctly marked in the present impersonation, though not so distinctly as to become the most salient attribute of the character. Mr. Irving is very judicious in his delivery of the opening speech, ' Now is the winter of our discontent,' &c., which as spoken by him does not sound like a set recital on studied philosophy, but rather resembles what the poet probably intended—the unconscious meditative utterances of a man thinking aloud while wrapt in a fit of profound abstraction. In the courting scene with Lady Anne . . . . Mr. Irving, unlike most of his predecessors in the part, represents *Richard* making love less with the bluntness of a soldier than with the tenderness and impressment of an impassioned suitor. . . . The scornful exultation with which, contemplating his triumph and finding in it a subject for egotistical congratulation, he utters the famous words, ' Was ever woman in this humour wooed ? was ever woman in this humour won?' provokes a shout of derisive applause. . . . The look of concentrated rage and hatred which he cast upon the ' parlous ' young prince, whose doom he foreshadows in the ominous reflection, ' So wise, they say, and so young, ne'er live long,' bespeaks the true character of the usurper more eloquently than could the most poignant words. . . . The apparition scene in the fourth act is exceedingly impressive, and in his representation of the mental anguish which *Richard* endures from the visitation of the shadows Mr. Irving depicts the terrors of a guilty conscience in appalling colours."

In May of the same year Mr. Irving undertook the dual parts of *Joseph Lesurques* and *Dubosc* in the drama of ' The Lyons Mail,' rearranged by Mr. Charles Reade from ' Le Courier de Lyon.' " The difficulties in the way of the adequate representation of two such characters as those of *Lesurques* and *Dubosc* are, as will easily be understood, extremely severe, but they are managed by Mr. Irving with consummate art. . . . Not only in voice, but in expression, in bearing and in gesture, *Dubosc* and *Lesurques* are two people, the latter courteous, suave and gentle in manner, tenderly affectionate to his daughter and pleasantly at ease with his friends ; the former a swaggering ruffian, clumsy and abrupt in action, husky and coarse in voice. The most remarkable feature in the assumption is the final scene in the first floor of a cabaret overlooking the place of execution. *Dubosc* is inflamed by drink, excitement, and the prospect of the sight he is to see, into a state of absolute madness ; his attack on Fouinard is simply an outbreak of the savagery of a wild beast, and after the brutal fury comes despairing terror to find himself tracked, and furious rage against his betrayers. Passion convulses his limbs and distorts his features ; yet scarcely more than ten seconds after *Dubosc* has rushed behind the opening door *Lesurques* enters, calm and collected and utterly free from any trace of excitement. . . . The word marvellous is certainly not too strong to describe the command of feature and demeanour which enables him thus to change his identity, to say nothing of dress, in such a space of time." (*Standard*, May 20, 1877.)

In 1878 (March 9) Mr. Irving appeared for the first time as *Louis XI.*, in a version of M. Casimir Delavigne's play of that title by Boucicault. It was the opinion of the *Saturday Review* (March 16, 1878) that the part might very well have been written for Mr. Irving, who had seldom presented a performance with which there was less opportunity of finding fault. In saying this, the *Saturday Review* did not mean that in *Louis XI.* Mr. Irving had reached a height which he had not attained before. "On the contrary, the character affords no kind of opportunity for the display of that fiery passion and force of inspiration which have asserted themselves sometimes in performances in which on other grounds there has been something to blame. The part of *Louis XI.* never rises to grandeur; it rests on a dead level of hypocrisy, meanness, and craftiness, which the dramatist has been at no pains to diversify, except by touches of grim humour. He has represented only one side of *Louis's* character, and has given no hint of the qualities which enabled him to hold other countries besides his own in his grasp; and it is the actor's merit, not the author's, that the *Louis* whom we see has about him an intangible and mysterious fascination which makes it possible to reconcile the low tone of his speeches and deeds with the gift for government which he must have had. . . . Mr. Irving's appearance was a first sign of the study which he had bestowed on the part. He had managed somehow to disguise his height, and his face indicated the singular mixture of ferocity, cunning, and grotesque sense of the ludicrous which, in the first part of the play, marks *Louis's* character. . . . His worming out of Marie's secret knowledge of the identity of Nemours with Rethel was intensely true to nature, and his delight at finding Nemours within his grasp was most effectively contrasted with his order for the Court to wear mourning for a week for the Duke of Burgundy. Here Mr. Irving brought out with rare skill the characteristic appreciation on the King's part of the grim wit of his own proceedings to which he throughout gives prominence. . . . As a piece of complete mastery of the science of acting in gesture and expression, Mr. Irving's recognition of Nemours' threatening figure, which he sees as he sinks down into his chair, was especially remarkable. The convulsive but restrained grasping of the chair, the look of dumb horror, the low thrilling cry of 'Merciful God!' led finely up to the more noisy and abandoned expressions of terror with which the interview closes, and to the half-insane reaction of violence at the end of the act."

We cannot resist adding here, even at the risk of trying the reader's patience, extracts from an able and thoughtful piece of criticism of Mr. Irving's performance in the same character, published in the *Liverpool Daily Post* (September 17, 1878): "The *Louis XI.* of Mr. Irving will probably be regarded hereafter as his most distinctive masterpiece," remarks the writer. "The play of Casimir Delavigne, as adapted into English blank verse for Mr. Charles Kean by Mr. Dion Boucicault, gives the actor no wings with which to soar. The play is a commonplace and somewhat meagre sketch, crudely outlined, not always with strict conformity to nature, from the traces left by Comines and worked up by Scott and Victor Hugo. But within this bare outline what a marvellous work of creative art has been elaborated by Mr. Irving—bold in conception, strong in light and shade, and filled in with details of infinite nicety and variety! Naturally, the first question that will be asked is how the representation compares with that of Charles Kean, which must be vividly remembered by all who saw it. The answer is, that while as remarkable as Mr. Kean's *Louis* for the vivid strength and truth of its general conception, Mr. Irving's is more delicately and minutely wrought, and the general features of *Louis* have with greater care and closeness of observation been associated with a life-like assumption of increasing senility. But besides this it must be recorded that the last act is vastly superior to anything that it entered into the mind of Charles Kean to effect. If there is any point in which the latest English *Louis XI*. is inferior to the first, it is in the abject pleading to Nemours for life, to which Mr. Kean's peculiar power of rapid and impetuous utterance gave thrilling effect. There is no other point at which Mr. Irving must yield the palm. It was, indeed, suggested by certain of the London critics that the incident of *Louis* suddenly praying to the images of the saints stuck in his hat, when interrupted in his directions for the murder of Nemours by the sound of the Angelus, was spoilt by Mr. Irving's appearance of grimacing insincerity. Remembering well, and with admiration, the intense and superstitious fetishism with which Mr. Kean enacted this episode, we awaited with some curiosity Mr. Irving's treatment of it. The London critics seem to have grossly mistaken him at this juncture. He is just as devout and intense as was Mr. Kean. What these writers took for ironic antics are really earnest movements of the head such as a very superstitious *old* man would make in such a situation. It is only one instance among many in this play in which Mr. Irving uncompromisingly realizes what the *King* must have been in his ill-favoured old age, according to the abundant accounts of him which we possess, and which distinguished novelists have used with great power. Mr. Irving has preferred to follow Victor Hugo rather than Sir Walter Scott. His *Louis* is a shambling, ill-held-together, down-at-heel old man, whose attitudes are never gainly and mostly mean; who slips down miserably with hollowed stomach into the seat of a throne during a critical diplomatic interview, and warms himself squalidly over the fire on a low stool; who, in fact, never thinks of appearances, and never chances to become an agreeable picture. A close skull-cap helps Mr. Irving to assume an aspect of ill-conditioned age, which is supported by a wonderful make-up of the face, while a contemptible and at the same time contemptuous gait and many rude and uncanny gestures and grins complete the study, which, as soon as the actor speaks, is imbued with absolute life and being. This *Louis XI*. is as individual to every spectator who saw him as ever was any human being who was known to his fellow-creatures by his ways and his talk.

"*Louis* does not appear in the first act, which, indeed, is dull and uninteresting. In the second act are illustrated the violence of the old king's rage, tempered by his fear of his doctor; his prompt and ever wily cunning; his readiness to use sentiment, and to throw it cynically aside; his remorseless cruelty and faithlessness, and many other execrable points of his character. Mr. Irving manages all the contrasts and transitions with great art, taking for his guide a clear idea of the character, and developing its many oddly-assorted peculiarities by telling changes of voice and manner. The sudden ' There, that'll do; sit down,' after the Dauphin has just burst forth into patriotic defiance of Burgundy, and the *King* has caressed him as the child of France, must be heard to be appreciated, and it is only one of many illustrations of Mr. Irving's success in realizing the *King's* cynical humour. The third act introduces the episode of the peasants, in which, of course, the actor revels, for *Louis's* varied reception of the supposed sincerities of the rustics affords not a little scope. Equally characteristic is the manner in which the old fox elicits from Marie de Comines the name of her lover, and the fact that the Burgundian envoy is Nemours. Act the fourth is far more onerous. Here the *King* is seen in the solitude of his bed-chamber. Here takes place his extraordinary confession to François de Paule, delivered with great effect in all its blood-chilling frankness and incorrigible impenitence. And here, when the holy father has retired, the monarch is suddenly frozen into abject terror by the appearance of the avenging Nemours. A terrible scene ensues—first of wild pleading for mercy, and then, when Nemours has with contempt and loathing granted the king his life, a fearful paroxysm of rage and hallucination, as the old man, suddenly young again with desperate excitement, rushes up to what he supposes to be the Duc de Nemours, and violently stabs the air until he falls fainting into the arms of those around him—a situation of great power most startlingly enacted. Great as the performance is in every phase, it is grandest in the fifth act, where *King Louis* enters robed and sceptred, with death written in his countenance, and his *physique* reduced to the lowest stage of feebleness. The skull-cap has been abandoned. Long grey locks stream somewhat wildly on the *King's* shoulders. His countenance derives a sort of dignity, not seen before, from these changes—though such a figure can never be truly venerable—and also from the absorbing nature of the conflict which *Louis* wages with visibly declining powers. In this hour of extreme mental exhaustion, deepening momentarily into actual stupefaction and afterwards into coma and then into death, the extraordinary resolution and will of the *King* still display marvellous power. But never was there such a picture of moving prostration and animated decay. The back of a couch lost hold of for a moment, and the tottering form stumbles forward in a manner which sends a painful start through the whole audience. The sceptre drops, after being used head downwards as a staff, and is forgotten. Then the *King* is induced to be seated on a couch, and with extraordinary elaborated graduations of insensibility, violently interrupted occasionally by spasms of vigour, he gradually loses his consciousness. No physical detail is neglected that can help to realize a sinking of mind and body into annihilating death. The voice and articulation have the weird, half-drunken thickness of paralysis. Even the effect observable in age and sickness of drawing the retreating lips in over the sunken teeth is somewhat simulated. The difficulty of carrying out such a conception of dissolution in a scene in the course of which such matters have to be dealt with as the final sentence of Nemours, and an interview with Coitier, the leech, who comes from a dungeon with the rust of fetters on his wrist, at the summons of the *King* who sent him there, must be extreme; but Mr. Irving triumphantly surmounts it, and gives a picture of gradual and placid yet horrible death such as we believe has never been achieved before. Perhaps the greatest success of all is the still and silent impassibility into which the *King* sinks so absolutely that the courtiers and his son suppose it to be death. The actual death is not placid. The *King* struggles on his feet, and falls forward on a cushion, with his head toward the audience, as the low murmur, ' The King is dead, long live the King,' proclaims the close of the long, long struggle of a mind that seemed indomitable with the frailties and tortures of a body racked for years with the worst tortures to which humanity can be a prey, and consoled by none of the assuagements to which the suffering are most indebted. Such, lit up in the earlier passages by infinite comedy and artistically elevated by several tragic episodes of the highest power, is this famous impersonation."

On Saturday, June 8, 1878, a new English version of ' Der Fliegende Holländer,' by Messrs. Wills and Percy Fitzgerald, under the title of ' Vanderdecken,' was produced at the Lyceum Theatre, Mr. Irving sustaining the leading *rôle.* " His appearance was splendidly picturesque and impressive, his aspect in the stronger scenes being absolutely lurid. His performance was, how- ever, wanting in variety, and was marred by the peculiarities which in ' Louis XI.' he appeared to have shaken off. If the play succeeds it must be on the strength of its weirdness and the admirable scenery supplied it. Mr. Irving's performance will certainly not rank with his best efforts." (*Athenæum,* June 15, 1878.) The piece did not prove attractive. In the following month of the year last mentioned the management of the Lyceum Theatre revived Mr. Albery's adaptation of ' Pickwick,' designed to illus- trate the character and career of *Alfred Jingle.* Mr. Irving had appeared in this character before, as has been already noticed, but the setting was a new one. The impersonation, however, was not of a kind to merit critical attention, and was possibly undertaken as a relief to Mr. Irving's more arduous duties.

In the autumn of 1878 Mr. Irving became manager of the Lyceum Theatre, in succession to Mrs. Bateman, and opened Monday, December 30, with a revival of ' Hamlet,' in which Mr. Irving played *Hamlet,* Miss Ellen Terry *Ophelia,* Mr. Chippen- dale *Polonius,* Mr. Mead the *Ghost,* Mr. Forrester *Claudius,* Mr. F. Cooper *Laertes,* Miss Pauncefort *Gertrude.* Mr. Irving's reception was enthusiastic. On Thursday, April 17, 1879, he placed 'The Lady of Lyons' on the stage, himself enacting the part of *Claude Melnotte.* The play was presented with every possible advantage in the way of scenic illustration and appropriate costumes. No applause could have been more vigorous, and no outward marks of appreciation more complimentary than Mr. Irving received on the first night and during the progress of the play. His *Claude* was, in all respects, an interesting performance, and for its own artistic value fully deserved the recognition that it gained; but it can hardly be claimed that it ranks with other characters in which Mr. Irving has appeared, in point either of the general interest it inspired or the permanence of its success.* "Mr. Irving, to tell the truth, is habitually inclined too much to seriously didactic tones and to the use of excited gestures of the sterner kind to attain an ideal standard of excellence in playing the part either of the ecstatic or the penitent lover. That his performance was distinguished by much force of the picturesque sort cannot be denied, and never, perhaps, has the fencing scene been rendered with more graceful dexterity, but *Claude Melnotte* is probably not destined to take high rank among Mr. Irving's impersonations." (*Daily News*, April 18, 1879.)

Another journal, the *Athenæum* (April 26, 1879), remarked of Mr. Irving's performance of *Claude Melnotte* that it "will not add to his reputation. Had his impersonation, indeed, possessed the gifts it lacked, there would have been waste in employing his powers in this supremely artificial work, which has the fatal defect of displeasing more every time it is seen. As it proved, however, the character from the author's standpoint was not realized, the *Claude Melnotte* being a virile and passionate man instead of a dreamy and sentimental boy. . . . In *Claude Melnotte* a triumph, if obtained, would have been uninteresting as regards art, however flattering it might have been to the artist. As it is, the warmest admirers of Mr. Irving speak of it apologetically rather than with open advocacy."

During the continuance of the summer season 1879 Mr. Irving occupied himself with revivals of 'Hamlet,' 'Lady of Lyons,' 'Eugene Aram,' 'Richelieu,' 'Louis XI.,' 'Charles I.,' 'The Bells,' 'The Lyons Mail.' One of these performances, that of 'Richelieu,' attracted the attention of M. Jules Claretie, the eminent French dramatic critic (who was in England during the visit of the Comédie Française in the summer of 1879), in his weekly *feuilleton* to *La Presse* (June 22, 1879). The translated passage of what he wrote is as follows:—"The great Cardinal, lean, eaten up with ambition, less for himself than for France, is admirably rendered by the actor. His gait is jerky, like that of a dying man racked by fever, his eye has the depths of a visionary, a hoarse cough undermines that frail body, which is yet made of steel. When *Richelieu*

---

* Since writing the foregoing I have been informed, on unquestionable authority, that the representations of 'The Lady of Lyons' at the Lyceum Theatre in 1879 have been most successful; and that on every evening during the season when it was played "the theatre was thronged."—ED.

appears in the midst of the courtiers, when he flings scorn in the face of the mediocre man who is to succeed him, when he supplicates and adjures the weak Louis XIII., Irving gives that grand figure a striking majesty. And how profound an artist the tragedian is! I went to see him in his dressing-room after the performance. I found him surrounded by portraits of Richelieu. He had before him the three studies of Philippe de Champaigne, which are preserved in the National Gallery: Richelieu seen full face, right-hand profile and left-hand profile, and also a photograph of the full-length portrait of the Cardinal by the same Philippe de Champaigne. When he plays *Louis XI.* he studies Comines, Victor Hugo, Walter Scott, and all those who have spoken of the bourgeois and avaricious king who wore out the elbows of his ratteen pourpoint on the oak tables of his companions the fell-mongers and shoe-makers. . . .

"Mr. Irving, in spite of his superb, energetic and fine head, has an air rather elegant than robust. He is as charming outside the theatre as he is touching on the stage. His dressing-room, with the pictures that are hung there, and the hospitality that awaits visitors, reminds one of the artistic *loge,* such as it is figured in Madame Sand's novel 'Pierre qui roule,' or in Dumas' famous drama 'Kean.' Only here we must not place as a sub-title 'Désordre et Génie,' for you feel in Irving and in his company the correct rectitude of the gentleman beneath the inspiration of the lettered artiste. We were asking him the other night what historical personage would tempt him, what physiognomy, he who excels in what I call resurrections, he would like to make alive again. 'What personage?' he asked. 'Yes; which is the hero that seduces you?' He reflected a moment, his fine head becoming suddenly pensive. 'French or English?' he asked again. 'French or English, it does not matter.' 'Well,' he replied, after a moment's reflection, I should like to create a Camille Desmoulins.' He has, indeed (adds M. Claretie), the energetic type and also the fineness of the men of the eighteenth century. With his long black hair and his fine, witty smile, he is a very living Camille. Perhaps there is more kindness in his features than there was in those of the malicious author of 'Révolutions de France et de Brabant.' It is the Camille of the 'Vieux Cordelier.' He would gladly incarnate that enthusiastic journalist, and Miss Ellen Terry, who plays Ophelia with him in *Hamlet,* would make a touching Lucile. But the little success obtained by the piece on Camille Desmoulins that was played at Paris deters Henry Irving, who feels himself attracted rather by the physiognomy of André Chénier. He would be, and I hope will be, absolutely admirable if he has confidence in him who writes these lines, and who would regard it as a good fortune to have such an actor for an interpreter." M. Claretie further expressed himself as delighted with Mr. Irving's *Hamlet* and the splendour of the *mise en scène.* He compared the gravedigger's scene to a picture by Jean-Paul Laurens; he had never seen anything so profoundly, so tragically true.

Mr. Irving's first season as manager terminated on July 26.

His annual benefit took place on the 25th and 26th. On the former evening he appeared in the fourth act of ' Richelieu,' and the third act of ' Louis XI.'; also (in association with Miss Ellen Terry) in the first act of ' Richard III.,' the fourth act of 'Charles I.,' and the third act of ' Hamlet,' terminating with the play scene. The entertainments on each evening concluded with the farce of ' Raising the Wind,' in which Mr. Irving represented the leading character. On the last night of the season he and Miss Ellen Terry appeared in Mr. Wills's ' Eugene Aram.' In an address from the stage on the previous evening, Mr. Irving stated that the receipts of the theatre during the seven months it had been opened under his management amounted " to the large sum of 36,000*l.*"

IRWIN, KATHLEEN, was born at Exeter, and was specially educated for the stage. In singing she was a pupil of Mr. Joseph Wood (the husband of Miss Paton) and of Signor Lago, of the Royal Italian Opera. She entered the dramatic profession at Newcastle in 1868, playing there a round of characters with considerable success, and was engaged afterwards for the opening of the Charing Cross Theatre. Miss Irwin made her first appearance in London, June 19, 1869, at that theatre, as *Patty Mayberry* in the operetta ' Coming of Age.' On the same occasion she appeared also as *Ferdinand* in Cheltnam's comedy of ' Edendale,' and as *Adalgisa* in Gilbert's burlesque of ' Norma.' " In each of the three pieces the most unequivocal proof of ability was afforded " (*Daily Telegraph*, June 21, 1869). Since 1869 Miss Irwin has fulfilled important engagements at the Vaudeville, Drury Lane, Globe, Prince of Wales's, and Haymarket Theatres, in London. She has several times accompanied Mr. Toole on his provincial tours, playing leading characters in all his pieces; and was a member of the so-called ' Caste ' company. Among principal parts Miss Irwin has played the following at various theatres in the provinces, viz. : *May Edwards* (' Ticket-of-Leave Man '), *Marguerite* (' Turn of the Tide '), *Little Don Giovanni, Aladdin, Mary Belton* (' Uncle Dick's Darling '), *Maria* (' Twelfth Night '), *Ophelia, Polly* (' Beggar's Opera '), *Phœbe* (' Paul Pry '), and *Little Em'ly* in the play of that name. To these may also be added : *Diana Vernon* (' Rob Roy '), *Clairette* (' Madame Angot '), *Esther* and *Polly Eccles* (' Caste '), *Mary Netley* and *Blanche Haye* (' Ours '), *Bella* and *Naomi Tighe* (' School '), *Black-Eyed Susan, Violet* (' Life of an Actress '), *Lydia Languish*, &c.

During the greater part of 1877 Miss Irwin was a member of the Haymarket company, and accompanied Mr. Buckstone on his farewell tour through the provinces, playing leading parts in ' The Rivals,' ' Pygmalion and Galatea,' &c.

JAMES, DAVID (a *nom de théâtre*), made his first appearance on the London stage at the Princess's Theatre during the management of Mr. Charles Kean in a subordinate part. He was afterwards engaged at the Royalty Theatre, where, in Mr. Burnand's burlesque ' Ixion ; or, the Man at the Wheel,' he played the part of *Mercury*. Mr. James subsequently joined the company of the Strand Theatre, of which he remained a member for nearly six years, and where he attained some distinction as an actor, chiefly in burlesque. Among pieces in which he was more than ordinarily successful during this engagement may be mentioned, ' One Tree Hill ' (H. T. Craven), produced April 1865, in which Mr. James played the part of *Tom Foxer;* an operatic extravaganza by Mr. Burnand entitled ' Windsor Castle,' first performed June 5, 1865, in which he played the part of *Will Somers*, the Court Jester ; the same author's burlesque of ' L'Africaine,' produced November 18, 1865, in which Mr. James was *Neluska;* ' The Heir-at-Law,' revival in February 1870, in which he sustained the part of *Zekiel Homespun* " in a quiet natural manner, which at once brushes from the mind all remembrance of the vigorous dancer of ' breakdowns ' " (*Times*, February 7, 1870). In this part Mr. James achieved a sort of surprise, according to the *Daily News* (February 7, 1870), " by giving to this character, which is merely the conventional and intensely artificial stage-countryman of bygone times, a vitality and interest which few could have expected. The scene in which he rejects with scorn and loathing, mingled with sorrow at the discovery of the baseness of an old friend, the offensive proposal of the Honourable Dick Dowlas for a formal *liaison* with his sister, was really a powerful piece of acting."

In conjunction with Messrs. Montague and Thorne, Mr. James entered upon the management of the Vaudeville Theatre in 1870. On Saturday, April 16 of that year, the management opened the theatre with a farce entitled ' Chiselling '; a new comedy by the late Andrew Halliday entitled ' For Love or Money '; and a burlesque entitled ' Don Carlos ; or, the Infante in Arms.' Since his connection with the Vaudeville Theatre Mr. James has played the following parts with considerable success, viz. *Mr. Jenkins*, in Albery's comedy ' Two Roses,' produced June 4, 1870; *Bob Prout*, in a comedy by the same author entitled ' Apple Blossoms,' first performed September 9, 1871 ; *Sir Benjamin Backbite*, in a very successful revival of ' The School for Scandal,' July 18, 1872 ; *Goldfinch*, in ' The Road to Ruin,' revived in 1873 ; *Sir Ball Brace*, in a comedy by James Albery entitled ' Pride,' first performed April 1874; and *Perkyn Middlewick*, in H. J. Byron's comedy ' Our Boys,' produced at the Vaudeville Theatre Saturday, January 16, 1875, and removed from the playbills Friday, April 18, 1879—the most extraordinary " run " ever attained by a play. " The *Perkyn Middlewick* of Mr. David James and the lodging-house servant of Miss Cicely Richards would be unworthily treated by merely a passing word of conventional praise. The artistic impulse of Mr. David James is so keen that it refuses to be fettered. In spite of the fact that the character of the old butterman is often awkwardly portrayed—though his pathetic utterances are not naturally introduced, springing out of nothing, governed by little motive, and marred by the wilful introduction of some verbal eccentricity—the artist is determined to fix the man vividly on the mind, and to show how thoroughly humour is appreciated. In walk, manner, gesture, intonation, and dress we perceive *Perkyn Middlewick*, the butterman. Clever lines were never more admirably spoken, and caricature seldom conveyed with less exaggeration. Well might the audience appreciate the twinkle of delight with which the old fellow questions his boy on the details of his foreign trip, with an honest sense of pride in the possession of his hard-earned capital; the fussy vulgarity of the ex-tradesman when he finds himself on the same social platform as his friend the baronet; his irritation under correction; his natural and tender love for his boy, which will come welling up, swamping all the obstinacy and determination for which he considers himself famous; his horror to find that the eggs the lad has been taking in his poverty are merely 'shop 'uns,' and that his bread has been buttered with 'Dosset.' These are but few of the points of a thoroughly characteristic and intelligent specimen of acting. One more character has been added to the list of successes achieved by Mr. David James in *Perkyn Middlewick*, the retired butterman." (*Daily Telegraph*, January 18, 1875.)

On Saturday, April 19, 1879, first performance at the Vaudeville Theatre of 'Our Girls,' "a new and original" comedy, by Mr. H. J. Byron, designed to take the place of 'Our Boys,' Mr. James played with great effect the part of *Plantagenet Potter*—a hard and literal representation of an uncultivated, but lucky and powerful, commercial gambler. "In all his actions this individual proves himself a vulgar, illiterate, pretentious hound, without a redeeming feature. Insolent in his prosperity, he is in his defeat cowardly and abject, and he treats with absolute brutality the wife who has sunk herself low enough to share his fate. Inasmuch, however, as this character has to be played by Mr. James, who presents it with artistic truth and sincerity, it is sought to give it some claim on sympathy." (*Athenæum*, April 26, 1879.)

JAMES, MRS. LITHGOW. *See* St. John, Margaret Florence.

JECKS, CLARA, daughter of Mrs. Jecks (Harriet Coveney), commenced her dramatic career in July 1873 at the Opéra Comique in Burnand's 'Kissi-Kissi.' In the same year, during the autumn, she played a round of soubrette parts at Drury Lane Theatre; and at Christmas sustained a leading part there in Blanchard's pantomime of 'Jack-in-the-Box.' She has appeared in other pantomimes at the same theatre. At the Adelphi Theatre in 1877, in the character of *Lord Eden* in 'Formosa,' she "displayed both good taste and spirit in a considerable degree" (*Times*, November 2,

1877) ; and in the two following years acted there in ' Proof,' ' The Crimson Cross' (as *Gontran*), ' The Ticket-of-Leave Man ' (as *Sam*), ' Amy Robsart ' (as *Janet Foster*), &c. Miss Clara Jecks is a promising pianist and vocalist, a pupil of Madame Helene Greiffen-hagen.

JECKS, MRS. *See* COVENEY, HARRIET.

JEFFERSON, JOSEPH, was born in Philadelphia, February 20, 1829. He is descended of an old theatrical family, his grandfather, Joseph Jefferson, comedian, having been a special favourite at the Chestnut Street Theatre in that city in the first years of the present century.* Mr. Jefferson's father was a scenic artist who became, by design, a manager, and subsequently, by accident, a player. It has been remarked of him (' At and After the Play,' L. Clarke Davis, *Lippincott's Magazine,* July 1879), that he began too late and died too early to make a great reputation as an actor, though he was accounted a fair one. The subject of the present record very early entered the dramatic profession in the United States, and earned distinction in a great variety of comic parts, ranging from *Bob Acres,* in the higher range of English comedy, to *Caleb Plummer* in the domestic drama of more recent years. When only three years old he appeared on the stage as *Rolla's* child. Like most English actors, Mr. Joseph Jefferson studied the rudiments of his profession "strolling." In 1849 he entered into partnership with Mr. John Ellsler to take a company over the Southern Circuit, which included all cities south of Richmond between the Atlantic and the Gulf. The writer from whom these facts are quoted (Mr. Clarke Davis) says :—" Now it was that ' hard times ' ceased knock-ing at his door, and for the first time in his life he began to gather in money faster than butcher or baker could take it from him." From 1852 to 1856 Mr. Jefferson was in Baltimore, first at the Holiday Street Theatre, then at the Museum; the next year he was in New York at Laura Keene's Theatre, " opening " the season for her as *Dr. Pangloss.* " But his thorough recognition by the public as a great and original artist of comedy was delayed in that city until the next season, when, on October 18, 1858, was produced for the first time on any stage Tom Taylor's play of ' Our American Cousin.' The cast was a remarkable one, embracing the names of Jefferson, Sothern, Couldock, and Peters ; and Laura Keene and Mary Wells, Effie Germon and Sarah Stevens." Mr. Jefferson

* " Mr. Joseph Jefferson was an actor formed in Nature's merriest mood, a genuine son of Momus. There was a vein of rich humour running through all he did which forced you to laugh despite yourself. . . . His excellent personation of old men acquired for him before he had reached the meridian of life the title of Old Jefferson. . . . His versatility was astonishing—light comedy, old men, pantomime, low comedy, and occa-sionally juvenile tragedy. . . . He was the reigning favourite of the Philadelphia Theatre for a longer period than any other actor ever attached to the city, and left it with a reputation all might envy."—Wemyss's *Theatrical Biography.*

played *Asa Trenchard* on the occasion, and, discarding all the traditions of the theatre, "presented to the audience a Yankee entirely new to them." In 1860 he first began playing his inimitable impersonation of *Rip Van Winkle*, from a play founded on Washington Irving's story by Charles Burke, an American actor of some repute in his day. During the Civil War Mr. Jefferson professionally visited the Australian colonies, and returning home by way of Liverpool, rested for a few days in London, where Mr. Benjamin Webster offered him an engagement at the Adelphi Theatre if he would appear in a new play. Writes Mr. Clarke Davis :—" He had none, but instinctively turned to *Rip*, for he had played the old version of Burke's, as altered by himself, with great success in the British colonies. He asked Boucicault to reconstruct it, and give it the weight of his name. Many of the suggestions of changes came from Jefferson, and one at least from Shakespeare. Boucicault shaped them in a week, and in the end received three thousand pounds for doing it; but he had no faith in the success of his work, and told Jefferson that it could not possibly keep the stage for more than a single month."

It is in the character of *Rip Van Winkle* Mr. Joseph Jefferson is best known to Englishmen, and he made his first appearance in that part before a London audience, at the Adelphi Theatre, on Monday, September 4, 1865. A drama under the same name had been performed at the elder establishment, the old Adelphi, in the month of October 1832. The cast had included the late Mr. Yates —whose representation of *Rip* in old age is mentioned in contemporary journals as having been marvellously fine in its natural and artistic power—and Messrs. John Reeve, J. B. Buckstone, O. Smith, W. Bennett, and Miss Novello. Mr. Bernard was the author of the earlier adaptation. Mr. Jefferson achieved a triumphant success on the first night of his appearance in London. He has now the reputation in this country of being one of the most genuine artists who has at any time appeared on the English stage. "In Mr. Jefferson's hands," remarked the *Times* (September 6, 1865), "the character of *Rip Van Winkle* becomes the vehicle for an extremely refined psychological exhibition. In the first act he appears as a fine hearty man, aged about thirty years, with a frank, open countenance, rendered rather picturesque than otherwise by his dishevelled hair and tattered garments. He is so confirmed a drunkard that he has not so much as a sober interval. He will drink in company or he will drink alone; but under any circumstances, if a cup of schiedam comes within his reach, he will not let it go till it is empty; and yet his vicious inclination can scarcely be called morbid. His potations rather improve than spoil his temper; and, far from seeking to drown care in the bowl, he is such a happy-go-lucky sort of wight that he has no care to drown. He is beaming with a perpetual good nature, to which alcohol seems to be the necessary aliment, and which is rendered additionally unctuous by his dialect—a dialect, we may observe, that seems to be more German than Dutch in its character. Even though he greatly fears his wife, and almost execrates her in the presence of his boon companions, we perceive that there is nothing very harrowing in his terror, and that his dislike cannot approach malignity. The expression of any emotions is accompanied by a chuckle, as if he thought with Rabelais, that life is at best a farce, and was determined to take things easy. It is only when his wife, exasperated by his persistent inebriety, turns him out of doors into a stormy night that he is stricken to the heart, and even then he is only *hurt*—he is neither desperate nor vindictive. This freedom from malice always enlists the sympathies of the audience on the side of disreputable *Rip*, and however the declamations of his wife may delight teetotallers, impartial observers, who see such very good-humoured vice placed in juxtaposition to such very cross virtue, cannot help siding with the former. Let it not be supposed, however, that *Rip* is altogether a fool. A roguish money-lender, who, by making him a shade more drunk than usual, hopes to trap him into an alienation of important rights, is suddenly met by a petrified smile, plainly showing that business is impossible. The man is as void of expression as a toad ; but he is also as immovable. In the short second act, which is occupied by the meeting of *Rip Van Winkle* with the ghostly Hudson and his spectral crew, there is no further development of character ; but when the Dutchman wakes in the third act, after a sleep of twenty years, the portraiture progresses. He is now an aged man, with white flowing hair and beard, who must be seventy or eighty years of age ; and although the change from the *Rip* of the first act is greater than could possibly have been effected by the mere lapse of four lustra, we would rather attribute the completeness of the transformation to the effect of Hudson's infernal beverage than suggest a correction of the seeming exaggeration. . . . The aged *Rip* has not altogether lost the disreputable peculiarities of his younger days. He cannot even now resist the temptation of a cup of schiedam when one is presented to him ; but his former nature is toned down, and his affectionate disposition is more visible on the surface. Thinking that the woman whom he has so often execrated is dead, he honours her with a tear, and his love for the daughter, whom he left a little girl, crying over his expulsion, and whom he finds a full-grown woman, asserts itself with all force."

The Press was unanimous in praise of Mr. Jefferson. The *Saturday Review* (September 23, 1865) thus alluded to the performance :—" If we state that every possible detail of character that could be produced under the circumstances supposed is represented with the most perfect ease—an art that thoroughly conceals art being aided by a happy union of natural qualities—we shall have implied that Mr. Jefferson has already taken a high position among modern theatrical artists. . . . There is no doubt that Mr. Jefferson will for some time to come remain the leading object in the eyes of the playgoing world ; and in the meanwhile we may praise Mr. Boucicault for the clever manner in which he has fitted an old story, twice dramatized already, to the peculiarities of so original an actor." The *Examiner*, September 23, 1865,* considered that the

* Compare *Journal of a London Playgoer*, Professor Henry Morley, p. 380.

drama in the third act was at its poorest, but Mr. Jefferson was at his best. "Retaining his old Dutch English with a somewhat shriller pipe of age in its tone, he quietly makes the most of every opportunity of representing the old man's bewilderment His timid approaches to an understanding of the change he finds ; his faint touch of the sorrow of old love in believing his wife dead, and reaction into humorous sense of relief; his trembling desire and dread of news about his daughter ; and, in a later scene, the pathos of his appeal to her for recognition, are all delicately true. It is doubtful whether, in such a drama, more could be done by the best effort of genius to represent the *Rip Van Winkle* of whom Washington Irving tells. It is certain that in a play more closely in accordance with the spirit of the story, Mr. Jefferson's success, real as it is, would have been yet more conspicuous." Since Mr. Jefferson's first appearance in London as *Rip Van Winkle* he has appeared only in this character during his periodical visits to England, with the following exceptions, namely, at the Prince's Theatre, Manchester, where he appeared, for one night only in May 1866, in a piece by Boucicault called 'The Parish Clerk'; and at Drury Lane Theatre, in March 1877, and at the Haymarket Theatre, in June, when he played *Mr. Golightly* in 'Lend me Five Shillings,' and (at the last-named) *Sir Hugh de Brass* in 'A Regular Fix.'

JOHNSON, SAMUEL, born in Ayrshire; son of a well-known actor and manager of a circuit of theatres in the west of Scotland. He first appeared on the stage at the theatre at Maryport, in Cumberland, at the age of fourteen, in the part of *Bartolo* in 'The Wife.' In 1853 Mr. Johnson became partner with Mr. John Coleman in the management of the Theatre Royal, Sheffield, and produced there a version of 'Uncle Tom's Cabin,' which was played for forty nights, "at that time considered an extraordinary 'run' in the provinces for anything but pantomime." In 1855 he joined Mr. E. D. Davis's company at the Lyceum Theatre, Sunderland, opening as *Touchstone* in 'As You Like It.' After the destruction of that theatre by fire at Christmas in the same year, Mr. Johnson went to Newcastle-on-Tyne under the same management, returning when the "Lyceum," which had been rebuilt in the interval, reopened in September 1856. It was on this occasion that Mr. Henry Irving made his first appearance on the stage. Mr. Johnson made his *début* on the London stage at the Lyceum Theatre in 1859 in the Savage Club burlesque of 'The Forty Thieves,' in which he acted the part of *Cassim Baba*. In 1860 he accepted a three years' engagement at Edinburgh Theatre Royal, where, in addition to the usual round of low comedy, he played an extensive series of Scotch characters, *Nicol Jarvie*, *Dumbiedikes*, *Jock Howieson*, &c. Returning to London, Mr. Johnson was subsequently engaged at St. James's Theatre under the management of Frank Matthews, "opening" in an original farce, 'The Carte-de-Visite,' by Montague Williams, and as *Golden-hair the Good* in a "fairy tale" by H. J. Byron.

In 1864 Mr. Johnson joined the company of the Theatre Royal, Dublin, "opening" there on October 10 as the *First Gravedigger* in 'Hamlet.' He was attached to this theatre for ten years, playing all the legitimate comedy, more particularly *Zekiel Homespun, Dr. Ollapod, Bob Acres, Touchstone, Dogberry,* &c.; and during the summer months visiting the provincial towns in the south of Ireland, adding to his *répertoire* the characters of *Myles-na-Coppa-leen, Shaun the Post, Conn the Shaughraun.* It is worthy of mention that this engagement of Mr. Samuel Johnson is noticed in appreciative terms in an interesting little volume, *History of the Theatre Royal, Dublin,* published in that city in 1870. At the end of his long period of service there, Mr. Johnson went in 1874 to Belfast, opening at the Theatre Royal as *Baillie Nicol Jarvie,* and afterwards, with Mr. Warden's company, visiting Edinburgh and Glasgow and appearing in a series of the old comedies. In July 1878 he was engaged by Miss Bateman for a short season at the Lyceum Theatre, playing *Inspector Follit* in 'Mary Warner'; and on the opening of the same theatre under Mr. Irving's management, December 30, 1878, reappeared there as the *First Gravedigger* ('Hamlet'), a part which he played throughout the summer season 1879 with much success.

JOHNSTONE, JAMES, was born in London, 1817, and made his first appearance on any stage in 1837, at Pym's private theatre, in the character of *Iago.* He made his *début* on the London stage in August 1847, at the Marylebone Theatre, then under the management of Mrs. Warner. as *Polixenes* in 'A Winter's Tale.' He has since appeared "in all the principal theatres of England, Scotland, and Ireland." In the year 1866 he was engaged by Mr. F. B. Chatterton, and was for five years stage-manager under him at Drury Lane Theatre. In 1876 he was stage-manager at the Princess's Theatre during an engagement of Mr. Jefferson (*Rip Van Winkle*). In 1878 Mr. Johnstone was engaged at the Park Theatre (London), playing in Irish drama, 'Peep o' Day,' 'Shaughraun,' &c. At Easter of the same year he accepted an engagement at the Adelphi Theatre, and played in the drama of 'Proof' during the successful run of that piece (241 nights).

JOSEPHS, FANNY (a *nom de théâtre*), entered the dramatic profession at a very early age, under the tutorage of her father, who held a position at the Dublin Theatre. She made her *début* on the London stage Saturday, September 8, 1860, at Sadler's Wells Theatre, in the part of *Celia* in a revival of 'As You Like It.' Afterwards at the same theatre she played *Perdita* in a revival of 'A Winter's Tale.' In 1861 Miss Josephs joined the company of the Strand Theatre, of which she continued a member for some time, attaining considerable popularity, chiefly as an actress in burlesque. In 1866, on the opening night of the Holborn Theatre, under Mr. Sefton Parry's management, Saturday, October 6, she played the part of *Lord Woodbie,* first performance of Boucicault's drama 'Flying Scud.' In 1868 she entered upon the management of the same theatre, and produced on the opening night 'The Post Boy,' by H. T. Craven, and a burlesque by F. C. Burnand entitled 'The White Fawn.' In 1871, October 7, Miss Josephs appeared at the Globe Theatre in H. J. Byron's comedy 'Partners for Life,' then performed for the first time. Two years later she accepted an engagement at the Prince of Wales's Theatre, and in September 1873 appeared there as *Bella* in a revival of 'School'; and at Easter, 1874, as *Lady Sneerwell* in a revival of 'The School for Scandal.' "Special mention should be decidedly reserved for the *Lady Sneerwell* of Miss Fanny Josephs—a small character, it is true, though what character is small in the hands of an artist? Following the example so frequently and unselfishly set by Mrs. Bancroft for so many years, Miss Josephs took the small and, as it is called, ungrateful character, and made her mark. The dancing of Miss Fanny Josephs in the introduced minuet would have astonished the most critical grandmother. One can well believe in the old-fashioned horror of valses and polkas when we see such charming grace and true elegance as this." (*Daily Telegraph,* April 6, 1874.) In 1876 Miss Fanny Josephs appeared at the Olympic Theatre in a play, adapted by Mr. W. Muskerry from the French of M. Barrière, entitled 'The Gascon; or, Love and Loyalty.' On Saturday, March 31, 1877, first performance at the Criterion Theatre of 'The Pink Dominos,' adapted from the French of MM. Hennequin and Delacour ('Les Dominos Roses'), she played the part of *Lady Marie Wagstaff.* Miss Josephs appeared in the same character at the same theatre during the run of the piece. In the summer season of 1879 Miss Josephs became lessee and manager of the Olympic Theatre, "opening" in July with a five-act drama, by Paul Meritt and Henry Pettitt, entitled 'The Worship of Bacchus,' described in a contemporary journal as "a good specimen of a poor class of work, its chief fault being the absence of originality." It proved unattractive. On its withdrawal Mr. Mayo, an American actor of some celebrity, appeared in a piece in which he had been very successful in the United States, entitled 'Davy Crockett,' "an Idyll of the Backwoods." This likewise failed to enlist the support of the public.

KEAN, MRS. CHARLES (*née* TREE, ELLEN), relict of the late Charles Kean ; born in 1806. She first appeared in public at the Theatre Royal, Covent Garden, in the character of *Olivia* in Shakespeare's play of 'Twelfth Night.' Having subsequently fulfilled various engagements at Edinburgh and Bath, in 1826 she was engaged at Drury Lane Theatre, and made her first appearance there as *Violante* in 'The Wonder.' Writing of her in that year, Talfourd remarked of Ellen Tree :—" She has not the vocal power of Miss M. Tree [Maria Tree, afterwards Mrs. Bradshaw], nor that peculiar crispness of tone and delicacy of style which enabled her almost to hint how the women of Shakespeare should be played ; but she is much handsomer, and is better adapted both by figure and manner to represent the heroines of comedy. It has been her misfortune to appear at the commencement of the season when the company was incomplete and when there was occasion for her services in a greater range of parts than she is as yet prepared to fill. She has played successively *Violante, Letitia Hardy, Rosalie Somers, Albina Mandeville, Lady Teazle*, and *Jane Shore*, risking fearful odds in every trial, and, of course, with unequal success, but exhibiting in all good sense, feeling, and taste. Of these we think *Albina Mandeville*—which is an excellent picture of the hoyden softened by the lady—the best, and her *Lady Teazle* considerably the worst. Her *Jane Shore*, graceful, unpresuming, and feeble, gave no reason to believe that tragedy will ever be her *forte*, but afforded assurance that she will beautifully express the milder sorrows of the sentimental drama." In 1829, at Covent Garden Theatre, Miss Ellen Tree sustained the part of *Lady Townley* in 'The Provoked Husband' with much success. She was the " original" *Mariana* in Sheridan Knowles's play of 'The Wife'; the *Countess*, in the same author's play of 'Love'; the heroine of Miss F. Kemble's 'Francis the First,' &c. Between 1836 and 1839 Miss E. Tree visited the United States of America. She was an actress of considerable repute previous to her marriage with the late Charles Kean, which took place on January 29, 1842. In that year she appeared with her husband at the Haymarket Theatre, under Mr. Benjamin Webster's management, in various Shakespearian plays and other examples of the poetic drama— 'Twelfth Night,' 'Hamlet,' 'Macbeth,' 'The Stranger,' 'The Lady of Lyons,' 'The Gamester,' &c. Mrs. Charles Kean was at that time considered, according to the *Athenæum* (April 16, 1842), the most gentle and affecting representative of *Mrs. Beverley* on the stage—" she sets the ladies sobbing for sympathy with her sorrows." On Saturday, June 4, 1842, first performance at the Haymarket of Sheridan Knowles's play 'The Rose of Arragon,' Mrs. Charles Kean sustained the character of the heroine. "The *Olivia* of Mrs. Kean was pervaded by an earnest and thrilling expression of womanly feeling. Her parting with her husband, her terrible scene with Almagro, and that blushing passage in her scene with her brother, where she reveals the outrage that had been committed upon her by Almagro, were alike distinguished by the purity and pathos of their delivery." (*Atlas*, June 11, 1842.)

During the seasons 1842-3, 1843-4 she acted with her husband in the several revivals produced under his superintendence at the Haymarket and Drury Lane Theatres. In 1846, during Mr. and Mrs. Charles Kean's visit to the United States, they produced at the Park Theatre, New York, the play of 'The Wife's Secret,' written specially for them by Mr. Lovell. On Monday, January 17, 1848, this piece was performed for the first time in England at the Haymarket Theatre—*Sir Walter Amyott*, Mr. C. Kean; *Lady Eveline Amyott*, Mrs. C. Kean; *Jabez Sneed*, Mr. Benjamin Webster; *Maud*, Mrs. Keeley; *Lord Arden*, Mr. Howe. The *Times* (January 18, 1848), noticing the performance, said :—"*Lady Eveline*, the wife, is played to perfection by Mrs. Charles Kean. She makes the character exquisitely gentle and feminine, rising on occasion to haughtiness of conscious right, and looking with abhorrent indignation at the imputation of wrong. It was by the admirable preservation of the tenderer side of the character that the sterner traits produced their effect, for in her whole performance there was nothing forced or exaggerated. While conscious that she has a secret which she cannot disclose to her husband, the honest fearlessness with which, in one of the critical situations of the piece, she looks unshrinkingly into her husband's face is beautifully conceived, and when, towards the end, she is plainly accused of infidelity, the change in her countenance, and the deliberate manner in which she says,

> ' I did not think
> I could so nearly hate thee,'

is exceedingly fine. It should be observed that although she is aware she is suspected of harbouring a fugitive, it is not until late that she finds a doubt is entertained as to her virtue, and the disclosure of this doubt comes upon her like a thunderbolt, the shock of which her pure soul is unable to sustain. The intrinsic goodness of the *Lady Eveline* is never lost sight of by Mrs. Kean, who endows virtue with all its cheerfulness and all its indignation." The *Morning Herald* (January 18, 1848) remarked of her acting :— " Mrs. Charles Kean has not lost any of those native traits which were always so becoming and fascinating. . . . Her portraiture of the heroine was a delicate sketch of feminine goodness and purity, winningly gentle in the moments of love and confidence, though weighed down with the burthen of an unwilling 'secret'; but almost sublime in the tearful and impassioned vindication of her truth in the closing scenes of the drama. A more exquisite and touching performance than this is not to be found in the records of the stage."

Commenting upon Mrs. Kean's performance at the Haymarket Theatre, in June 1848, of the part of *Clara Douglas* in ' Money,' a contemporary journal remarks of it that " nothing more perfect was ever witnessed on the stage. It was nature itself, refined and idealized ; but still nature." On November 11 of the same year, at the same theatre, she played *Viola* in a "revival" of Shakespeare's 'Twelfth Night.' "Mrs. Charles Kean was the *Viola*, and her excellent impersonation of the character is now traditional. Of modern actresses Mrs. Kean is the only one who presents it in its sweetness and its depth. The poetry and the melancholy are there, as well as the assumed gaiety. Not a tone of her voice but touches the heart. . . . *Viola* with Mrs. Kean puts not off the woman with her attire, but becomes yet more womanly." (*Athenæum*, November 18, 1848.) On Wednesday, June 20, 1849, she played at the Haymarket the character of *Katharine Lorn*, first performance of Westland Marston's tragedy 'Strathmore.' This piece was a considerable success. The following year, in conjunction with Mr. Keeley, Mr. Charles Kean entered upon the management of the Princess's Theatre, and on the opening night of his first season there produced Shakespeare's 'Twelfth Night,' and a farce entitled 'Platonic Attachment.' In the first-named comedy the cast included the following admirable players :—Mr. Keeley, *Sir Andrew Aguecheek ;* Mr. Harley, the *Clown ;* Mr. Ryder, *Antonio ;* Mr. Addison, *Sir Toby Belch ;* Mr. Meadows, *Malvolio ;* Mr. J. F. Cathcart, *Sebastian ;* Mrs. Charles Kean, *Viola.* The house was crowded to excess. The piece of the evening formed the inaugural performance of a series of Shakespearian representations at the Princess's Theatre produced under Mr. Kean's superintendence, which, in the completeness and magnificence of their display, have never been excelled in the history of the English stage. Mrs. Charles Kean's acting of her favourite character on this occasion was thus spoken of :—" Mrs. Charles Kean's *Viola* is one of those charming impersonations which silence criticism. Skilful distribution of light and shade, mixed gaiety and sadness, naïveté and poetry are the attributes which in this part present her to us as an inimitable actress. These qualities, combined with the touching tones of her voice and the strong passion of her delivery, make her irresistible in characters of the kind. Her power in all these respects was never more perfectly exhibited than on the present occasion." On Monday, September 30, 1850, she played the part of *Ophelia* at the Princess's Theatre ; and on Saturday, November 9 of the same year, the part of *Isoline* in 'The Templar' of A. R. Slous, a play which met with extraordinary success.

During the season Mrs. Kean played *Lady Percy* ('Henry the Fourth') ; *Violante* ('The Wonder') ; *Rosalind* ('As You Like It'), spoken of as being "one of the most original of her performances. In buoyancy, vivacity, and sweetness it can scarcely be surpassed." In 1851, Monday, 17th March, she played the heroine in John Oxenford's drama 'Pauline,' then first performed in London at the Princess's Theatre ; and on Wednesday, June 4, *Mdlle. Lestelle de Belle Isle*, in 'The Duke's Wager' (A. R. Slous), a version of M. Dumas' 'Mdlle. de Belle Isle.' On Monday, February 9, 1852, Mrs. Kean sustained the part of *Constance* in 'King John,' which was produced at the Princess's on a scale of magnificence never before surpassed, either by Macready or Phelps, and with a profusion of accessories that even in those days of special attention to *mise en scène* was pronounced to be unexampled. Said the *Spectator* (February 14, 1852) :—" Altogether, great care and artistic conscientiousness are the leading characteristics of Mr. Charles Kean's present career. They are now even the distinguishing marks in his acting. . . . The same spirit of completeness extends to Mrs. Kean's *Constance.* She has a more complete management of her voice than on many former occasions, and while she gives full play to the rage and pathos of the character, she does not force us to reflect on an inadequacy of physical force to meet the requisition of mental energy." The *Times* (February 10, 1852) wrote of Mrs. Kean's impersonation of *Constance* as follows :—" As for Mrs. Kean, it is long since she had a part displaying her to such advantage as *Constance.* The mother's fondness was constantly kept in view in the earlier scenes, as a preparation for the storms of grief and rage that were to arise when the loved object was snatched away. The tone in which she addressed Austria, after she had vented her first indignation at the French for their desertion of her cause, was finely discriminated. Her wrath had hitherto been vehement, but here it grew calm with intensity and slow of utterance ; it was rage accompanied with contempt. The agonies of grief were commanding in their force, and we seldom see nowadays such a complete abandonment of the actress to the spirit of the scene as in the torrent of woe with which she bewailed the loss of her son. It was a grief exulting in its own abundance, and claiming reverence from all who beheld it."

During the same year two new pieces were produced at the Princess's Theatre, in which Mrs. Kean sustained a principal *rôle,* viz. 'The Trial of Love' (Lovell), on June 7, 1852 ; and 'Anne Blake' (Westland Marston), in October 1852. On Saturday, January 12, 1853, was performed Douglas Jerrold's play 'St. Cupid,' first represented on the stage at Windsor Castle, before the Queen, Prince Consort, and royal household. Mrs. Kean played her original character, *Dorothy Budd.* The *Spectator* (January 29, 1853), examining the merits of this production, said :—" To a man of real literary genius like Mr. Jerrold, the aspect of the drama at the time to which we more especially refer—the time immediately preceding Mr. Macready's management of Covent Garden—must have been particularly revolting. The large theatres were professedly devoted to opera and spectacle. . . . In that evil day Mr. Jerrold stood as one of the very few practical representatives of the literary drama. What wonder, then, that finding 'effects' and the melodramatic aids of the art in the hands of the enemy, he should eschew them and endeavour to make language alone the important affair in a dramatic work ? . . . . Hence originated his good qualities and his defects. The power of repartee has been developed in him to a degree that claims unmixed admiration, the author having so used it as to have formed a distinctive style of his own, almost as peculiar as that of Mr. Thomas Carlyle ; but his story and his characters rarely lay a strong hold on the sympathies. What we have just said generally will apply particularly to Mr. Jerrold's new three-act piece of 'St. Cupid,' played yesterday week before the Queen at Windsor, and on the following night (last Saturday) at the Princess's. It is a sort of pendant to 'The Housekeeper,' having, like that favourite drama, the contest between Hanoverians and Jacobites as an historical background. The heroine of 'The Housekeeper' is a young lady who adopts the position of a superior servant to captivate the heart of a recluse ; the hero of 'St. Cupid' is a young gentleman of fortune and family, who assumes the disguise of an usher to make an impression on the daughter of a suburban schoolmaster. In both the leading female character is one of those combinations of sentiment and repartee which no one can personate better than Mrs. Charles Kean, who so well understands how to convey an emotion by a glance, and a point by an accent. When we look for differences, the advantage is on the side of 'The Housekeeper,' as being the more compact of the two."

On Monday, February 14, 1853, one of the grandest and most original revivals of the Kean *régime* took place at the Princess's Theatre, in the performance of 'Macbeth.' Mrs. Kean played the heroine. According to the *Athenæum* (February 19, 1853), there are two modes of acting *Lady Macbeth*. One is the cool and witheringly sarcastic under which Macbeth writhes and winces, the other the impassioned and determined by which he is attracted and hurried on to the assassination. Mrs. Kean adopted the| latter reading. She employed great action and energy in the temptation scenes, displayed much agitation during the banquet, and in the somnolent soliloquies affected attitudes that were picturesque and imposing. In the embodiment of this impersonation she was remarkably successful ; not at all deficient, as might have been expected, in the requisite physical force.

" The acting of the tragedy," said the *Times* (February 15, 1853), " is perhaps less a subject of curiosity than the decorations, inasmuch as Macbeth and his lady were favourite characters with Mr. and Mrs. Charles Kean shortly before they opened the Princess's Theatre. But unless our memory very greatly deceives us, it seems to us that Mrs. Charles Kean has adopted a version of *Lady Macbeth* which differs essentially from the one which she gave a few years back, as being much more terrible and much more tragic. The countenance which she assumed last night when luring on Macbeth to his course of crime was actually appalling in intensity, as if it denoted a hunger after guilt. When remorse had taken off the first bloom of reckless courage, and she appeared heartsick in the midst of worldly success, her features were less savage, but they were not the less stern ; and her appearance at the banquet, when by a feigned hilarity she strove to divert the attention of the guests from Macbeth's aberrations, was singularly impressive. . . . The sleep-walking scene, calm and dignified, an incarnation of agony, was admirably played, and, what is a great point in this scene, was admirably looked." On Monday, June 13, 1853, Lord Byron's Assyrian tragedy of 'Sardanapalus' was produced at the Princess's. Nothing so gorgeous, striking, and characteristic was ever before put on the boards. It is stated to have

cost the management not less than 3000*l.* in its production
Mrs. C. Kean sustained the part of *Myrrha.* Lord Byron'
'Sardanapalus' had been used by Mr. Charles Kean as a vehicle
for presenting to the public a series of tableaux based on the
researches of Mr. Layard. The scenes were of the most costly and
elaborate kind ; and it was said that the public, who would not
have gone to see the play as a tragic production, were likely to be
tempted to it as a sort of Panorama of Assyria. (*Examiner*
June 18, 1853.) In May 1855, after an absence of many months
from the stage owing to ill-health, Mrs. Charles Kean reappeared
on the stage of the Princess's Theatre as *Queen Katharine,* in a
revival of Shakespeare's 'Henry the Eighth,' produced with a
degree of elaboration in its accessories and illustrations never before
exceeded in the presentation of this play. Said the *Times* (May 17
1855) :—" We will run the risk of being charged with exaggeration by
declaring in most unequivocal terms that the play of 'Henry VIII.
as produced last night at the Princess's Theatre, is the most
wonderful spectacle that has ever been seen on the London stage
Our readers may, if they please, shake their heads and shrug their
shoulders, but when they have become spectators as well as readers
we are perfectly certain of their suffrages. . . . Altogether, it was a
grand occasion at the Princess's. Mrs. Charles Kean, who had
been absent for nearly eighteen months, reappeared as *Queen
Katharine,* and the dignified manner in which she went through
the trial, and the truthful details of the death, rendered this one of
the most striking characters in which she has yet been seen. . .
If we now speak only in these general terms, it is because we
intend, at a future opportunity, to recur to the subject, and to state
in something like detail the merits of this most remarkable production. Such a revival demands a careful study to appreciate its
various excellencies ; we now merely wish to convey the fact of an
extraordinary success." In a second notice of the same performance
—it may be remarked that the revival was eminently successful
and had a " run " of 100 nights—published in the same journal, the
acting of Mrs. Charles Kean is thus reverted to :—" ' Pomp,' says
Dr. Johnson, dribbling out his little meed of praise, 'is not the only
merit of this play ; the meek sorrows and virtuous distress of
Katharine have furnished some scenes which may be justly
numbered among the greatest efforts of tragedy.' The return of
Mrs. Charles Kean to the stage in the part of *Queen Katharine* is
one of the great features of this revival, and her delineation of the
'meek sorrows' and 'virtuous distress' is as refined and touching as
possible. In her first scene (the council chamber), when she tries
to damp the ill-feeling against the Duke of Buckingham, she
conveys by her firmness, and, at the same time, by the mild tone of
her remonstrance, that combination of a strong sense of rectitude
with excessive mildness of disposition which makes the entirety of
her character. The revival of the scene in the third act—omitted
of late years—in which the Queen receives the visit of the two
cardinals, is most judicious, as it gives the part a development
which is generally missed. In the trial scene the wrongs of

Katharine have so completely aroused the dignified element of
her nature, that the gentle constituent is almost forgotten, and she
must be followed to her own apartment in the palace, where she
enjoys a comparative privacy, that the extent of her suffering may
be appreciated. The revelation of sorrow is exquisitely made by
Mrs. Charles Kean. The indignation against her visitors passes
away, and the whole misery of her position rushes upon her at the
words,

> ' I am the most unhappy woman living,'

with an intensity that could not be surpassed. The last scene is, of
course, the most elaborate study of the whole ; she has to indicate,
by visible signs, the gradual but sure approach of death ; and the
feeble movements, the involuntary play of the hands, and the
uncertain gaze, are admirably sustained throughout. The dignity of
character, which has been so prominent at the trial, is now displayed by the offence taken by the *Queen* at the unmannered
entrance of the ' saucy fellow,' as she calls the messenger, and Mrs.
Kean has taken care to show how the high feeling of a lady, who,
though meek, is still an Arragonese, may be tempered down by
physical debility into invalid pettishness ; there is even something
of puerile spite in her request : ' But this fellow let me ne'er see
again ; ' when after being seemingly pacified, she returns to the
subject of offence. This scene is, unquestionably, one of the most
arduous in the whole cycle of the English drama. All the emotions
that have previously influenced the *Queen* are brought together
within its limits, but the expression of these is so much altered by
suffering that each requires a new interpretation. There is, moreover, one failing which is peculiar to the scene, and that is the
sentiment of religious resignation. Mrs. Charles Kean makes this
sentiment especially valuable in completing the effect produced by
the descent of the angels in the vision. The attitude in which,
half rising from her couch, she follows with her eyes the departing
forms, might serve as a study for some picture of a saint's
' ecstasy.' "

On April 28, 1856, ' A Winter's Tale' was represented on the
stage of the Princess's, with such elaboration, completeness, and
skill, as to astonish even those who were familiar with the glories of
' Sardanapalus ' and ' Henry the Eighth.' The fact that the scene of
the play is laid in Sicily had been seized upon with avidity by the
enterprising manager as a pretext for converting the greater portion
of the piece into a most costly exhibition of Grecian antiquities ;
while " Bohemia," changed for stage purposes into Bithynia, was
made to contrast the pastoral life of Asia Minor with the town
existence of Syracuse. In the piece Mrs. Charles Kean sustained
the part of *Hermione*. "The ' Winter's Tale,' produced at the
Princess's Theatre with extraordinary magnificence of decoration,
has revived the question of the artistic legitimateness of those
gorgeous accessories with which Mr. Kean has more than once
decked out the Shakespearian dramas. The point is by no means
settled, as some critics seem to think, by the consideration that

Shakespeare himself could never have, in fact, contemplated such a representation of his play. If any test at all can be applied, it must be furnished by the dramatist's own conception of the scene in which his personages moved—by the manner in which they were ideally presented to his mind; and if we can convince ourselves that Shakespeare—with whatever vagueness—conceived his Leontes, his Hermione, and his Perdita, as surrounded by the very life and scenery of actual Greece, we must be grateful to Mr. Kean for supplying an element which the poet himself was only forced to exclude by the imperfect mechanism of the Elizabethan stage. . . . The first three acts of 'A Winter's Tale' are occupied with the causeless jealousy of Leontes, and the suffering resignation of *Hermione.* This series of scenes could hardly have been written by any dramatist of a period in which the events of Henry the Eighth's reign were not fresh in men's minds, and the modern reader finds them unaccountable and unnatural. The last two acts are, however, among the most charming in Shakespeare; and it is by their performance in this part of the play that the actors will probably be judged. Autolycus—an old part of Mr. Harley's, we imagine—overflows with humour. The beauty and rusticity of Perdita, and the boyish petulance of Florizel, are not unworthy of the exquisite scene in which the dramatist has made them the principal figures. *Hermione*—but it is superfluous to praise Mrs. Kean—is full of womanly gentleness and tenderness." (*Saturday Review*, May 3, 1856.) In 1857, Thursday, March 12, 'Richard the Second' was produced to a crowded audience. This revival was, if possible, more imposing, and even a greater success than its predecessors had been. "Long before the performance had reached its termination the opinion was murmured through the stalls that all past glories were eclipsed by the lustre actually present, and that 'Richard the Second' was, in fact, 'the best thing that Mr. Kean had ever done.'" Mrs. Kean sustained the part of the *Queen*, "a little more than nominal character, but made a vehicle for the finest acting by the mere force of her own genius." "When in front of an admirable picture, representing the 'Traitor's Gate' of the Tower, and coming in mournful contrast with the glittering displays that have preceded it, the *Queen* bids farewell to her deposed husband, we find out at last why Mrs. Charles Kean has undertaken a part so unpromising. The horror which she has evinced in the fourth act, while listening to the gardener's conjectures as to the fate of Richard, is, indeed, finely portrayed ; but one start is, after all, a small object. The character has been left as a mere sketch by the poet, and, far from any historical association being connected with it, an inaccuracy has been committed by making a child of nine years old a full-grown woman. In the parting scene, however, Mrs. Kean shows how a consummate artist can make a great deal out of a scanty material. This shadowy unsubstantial Queen can be supposed a remarkable instance of feminine devotion, and the words she utters, though not many, bear out the supposition. On this hypothesis Mrs. Kean, when Richard is torn from her arms, displays such an agony of tearful grief, is so completely broken up with heartrending sorrow, that, although the pageantry of the play is over, this scene is one of the most effective of the whole performance. When the hapless King has departed she carries out still further her illustration of the feeling by rushing towards the parapet and leaning over it to catch a last glimpse of the beloved object, while the succeeding decoration closes upon her." (*Times*, March 16, 1857.)

Towards the close of Mr. Kean's management of the Princess's Theatre, in March 1859, "naturally desirous of crowning his series of Shakespearian revivals with his greatest effort," he placed upon the stage 'Henry the Fifth.' Mrs. Kean in the play undertook the part of *Chorus*, her acting in which was very highly commended. On Monday, August 29, 1859, the last of the famous Shakespearian revivals of Mr. Charles Kean's administration of the Princess's Theatre took place. His management had continued for nine years, and during that time Mrs. Kean had necessarily shared with her husband all the anxieties inseparable from so great a responsibility. In one season alone fifty thousand pounds were expended in the production of plays. Whilst some of these were being performed the management had given employment, and consequently weekly payment, to nearly five hundred and fifty persons. Each important piece, from the moment it first suggested itself to the mind of Mr. Kean until its first public performance, had occupied not far from a twelvemonth in preparation. Said Mr. Kean, in a farewell address :—"It would have been impossible on my part to gratify my enthusiastic wishes in the illustration of Shakespeare had not my previous career, as an actor, placed me in a position of comparative independence with regard to speculative disappointment. Wonderful as have been the yearly receipts,* yet the sums expended—sums I have every reason to believe not to be paralleled in any theatre of the same capacity throughout the world—make it desirable that I should now retire from the self-imposed responsibility of management, involving such a perilous outlay, and the more especially as a building so restricted in size as the Princess's renders any adequate return utterly hopeless." Mrs. Kean, by her great professional accomplishments, contributed, in no slight degree, to render her husband's period of management eminently prosperous in a monetary sense; and to her a share of the honour also belongs of helping to make it in all respects the most brilliant, and from first to last remarkable, of any in dramatic annals. Mrs. Kean retired from the stage on the death of her husband, which took place January 22, 1868.

KEELEY, MRS. (*née* GOWARD), born at Ipswich, in 1806; relict of the late Robert Keeley, the popular comedian, who died in 1869. She made her professional *début* at the Lyceum Theatre in 1825, as *Rosina* in the operetta of that name. Mr. J. R. Planché, in his *Recollections* (vol. i. p. 81), writing of the production in

---

* 200*l.* was considered a large nightly receipt, and 250*l.* an extraordinary one.

London of Weber's 'Oberon,' remarks :—" A young lady, who subsequently became one of the most popular actresses in my recollection, was certainly included in the cast ; but she had not a line to speak, and was pressed into the service in consequence of the paucity of vocalists, as she had a sweet, though not very powerful voice, and was even then artist enough to be entrusted with anything. That young lady was Miss Goward, now Mrs. Keeley, and to her was assigned the exquisite Mermaid's song in the *finale.*" In 1832 Mrs. Keeley was engaged at the Theatre Royal, Covent Garden, appearing there in such pieces as 'The Tartar Witch and the Pedlar Boy'; 'The Clutterbucks; or, the Railroad of Love,' &c. In March 1833 at that theatre she played a subordinate part in Poole's farce 'A Nabob for an Hour,' with sufficient energy as to merit the following notice from a contemporary journal :—" One joyous, bubbling, triumphant rush of Mrs. Keeley upon the stage to announce *Mr. Frampton* to her mistress is admirable." In 1834 she acted at the old Adelphi Theatre for a season the comic female *rôle* in ' Agnes de Vere ; or, the Broken Heart,' with Mr. Buckstone, the author of the piece, as leading low comedian. At the English Opera House in 1835 she appeared in Serle's drama ' The Shadow on the Wall,' her acting in which was noticed as of a very high order indeed. Said the *Athenæum* (May 2, 1835) :—" If Mrs. Keeley continues to act so admirably in parts like this of domestic pathos there will be a sad struggle for her between the tragic and comic muses of humble life. To those who know how clever she is in low comedy we cannot pay her a greater compliment than we do in saying that as far as the public is concerned it matters little which gets her." The same year at the Adelphi Theatre, the first year of the late Charles Mathews the younger's managerial experiences, Mrs. Keeley appeared on the opening night, September 28, in a new domestic burletta, entitled ' The London Carrier'; Mr. Buckstone, Mr. Keeley, and Mr. O. Smith were in the cast. At the same theatre in the following month she played a part in the late John Oxenford's first melodramatic attempt, ' The Castilian Noble and the Contrabandista.' When Mr. Charles Mathews joined Madame Vestris in the management of the Olympic Theatre, Mrs. Keeley went with them for a brief season, and appeared there in October 1837 in a piece written by Mr. Charles Mathews, entitled ' Truth.' Returning to the Adelphi in November 1838, she played *Smike*, in a dramatic version of Charles Dickens's ' Nicholas Nickleby,' the late Mr. Yates sustaining the part of Mantalini, and O. Smith that of Newman Noggs. The following year (still at the old Adelphi Theatre) she personated with immense success the house-breaking hero in Buckstone's drama of ' Jack Sheppard.' In 1841 Mrs. Keeley was " making merry the visitors at the new Strand Theatre," then recently opened. In January 1842 she took part in the performances inaugurating the Macready management of Drury Lane Theatre, and appeared there as *Nerissa* (' The Merchant of Venice '), and subsequently as *Mrs. Placid* in Mrs. Inchbald's comedy ' Every One has his Fault.' The same year at the same theatre she sustained the part of *Poll Pallmall* in

Douglas Jerrold's comedy ' The Prisoner of War.' Mrs. Keeley's acting of this character confirmed her rising reputation, and stamped her as an artist in critical estimation. In March 1842, at Drury Lane, she played *Thérèse* in ' The Students of Bonn,' with " the ease, volubility, and dryness of Déjazet without Déjazet's effrontery " (*Athenæum*, April 2, 1842).

In the second season of Macready's management of Drury Lane Theatre, Mrs. Keeley appeared as *Audrey* in a " revival" of ' As You Like It.' In 1844 she and her husband entered upon the management of the Lyceum Theatre, which, under their *régime*, became famous for dramatic parodies and burlesques, written, for the most part, by Charles Dance and J. R. Planché. On the opening night, Easter Monday, 1844, ' The Forty Thieves ' was produced; and throughout the season a variety of pieces written especially for Mr. and Mrs. Keeley received well-deserved support. On Saturday, December 20, 1845, Mrs. Keeley played *Mrs. Peerybingle* in ' The Cricket on the Hearth,' dramatized at the request of Charles Dickens, by Albert Smith, with express reference to the Lyceum company. The following year at Christmas a dramatization by Albert Smith of Charles Dickens's story ' The Battle of Life ' was produced, Mrs. Keeley sustaining the part of *Clemency Newcome.* " The acting of Mrs. Keeley is one of those admirable examples of histrionic art which almost reconcile an audience to every fault in the scenes that give occasion to their exhibition. The part of *Clemency Newcome* was the life, the soul, the salvation of the new drama. The actress was unwearied in her exertions. Her costume was picturesque, her action and by-play were everywhere appropriate, her tones were full of feeling, honesty, and earnestness. *There* was the eccentric, hard-working, faithful little body—an unmistakable identity!" (*Athenæum*, December 26, 1846.) In August 1847 Mrs. Keeley retired from the management of the Lyceum Theatre, and accepted an engagement under Mr. Webster at the Haymarket. On Monday, November 15, 1847, she appeared there as *Mdlle. Suzanne Grasset de Villedieu* in ' The Roused Lion,' a comic drama, adapted from the French, ' Le Réveil du Lion.' The extraordinary success of this piece was, in the main, attributable to the acting of Mr. B. Webster and Mrs. Keeley. On January 17, 1848, first performance at that theatre of ' The Wife's Secret ' (Lovell), Mr. and Mrs. Charles Kean in the principal parts, Mrs. Keeley played the waiting-maid *Maud* with great excellence. (*See* KEAN, Mrs. CHARLES.) Said the *Times* (January 18, 1848) :—" That admirable actress, Mrs. Keeley, plays a lady's-maid forced into puritanism by the manners of the time, yet dropping the garb of sanctity at every possible opportunity. The alternation of the nasal twang with her own merry little voice tells with excellent effect, and the piquancy of the actress renders this trifling part one of the most interesting in the piece."

In 1849, during the engagement of the Keans at the Haymarket, Mrs. Keeley played, among other characters, *Nerissa* (' Merchant of Venice '); *Jane* (' Wild Oats '); *Rachel* (' The Rent Day '), &c. On Thursday, May 9, 1850, first performance of Douglas Jerrold's comedy 'The Catspaw,' she sustained the part of *Rosemary*, and the same year, at the Princess's Theatre, *Maria* in 'Twelfth Night.' From 1850 to 1855 Mrs. Keeley was a member of the company of the Adelphi Theatre. On Thursday, March 8, 1855, she appeared there as *Betty Martin*, in a farce of that name, derived from a French vaudeville, 'Le Chapeau de l'Horloger,' from the pen of Madame Girardin, a little piece converted into a great one by the force of Mrs. Keeley's acting. "The little farce of 'Betty Martin,' though its action depends on the smallest possible motive, is remarkable for one of the most perfect histrionic exhibitions that could be found upon the modern stage. *Betty Martin* is a house-maid in the service of Major Miltiades Mohawk, an irascible gentleman who has lately taken unto himself a young and charming wife. *Betty Martin* breaks the family clock, which is a choice work of art, and that it may be mended clandestinely sends for a clockmaker, intending to defray the charges out of her own pocket. Somebody arrives during the interview with the clockmaker, who is accordingly concealed by *Betty Martin* in her mistress's chamber, and leaves his hat behind him. The hat, a very shabby one, is picked up by the peppery major, whose domestic peace is at once annihilated, as from sundry causes he believes that the concealed party is a lover of Mrs. Mohawk's. When he has gone through a due course of jealous anguish he learns the real state of the case, and is so pleased at being relieved from his horrid suspicions, that, far from discharging the destructive *Betty Martin*, he actually doubles her wages. All this drily narrated looks, no doubt, trivial and commonplace; but the filling up of Mrs. Keeley converts the slight sketch into a work replete with life and truthfulness. The agonized terror with which she rushes upon the stage when she has just broken the clock, is all but tragical, and her weeping is such weeping that we feel could not exist in any other situation. The clock has been her fate, and seems to rule all her actions. She steals about like a 'guilty thing'; she is always nervously ready to check any revelation of the dreadful deed; she empties the sugar-basin into the teapot, and commits other discrepancies as if she were possessed by a demon; and when at last the major, believing that she is an accomplice in his wife's infidelity, flings down her wages and bids her quit the house, the reaction is tremendous. She feels that she is no longer a servant, and therefore no longer responsible to the major, a vast load of care has fallen from her heart, and with a haughty, defying look, she bids him take back his money, as it may go towards the damages. The whole character is a complete creation from beginning to end; there is not a weak point about it." (*Times*, March 10, 1855.)

On Monday, February 11, 1856, at the Adelphi, Mrs. Keeley played *Mary Jane*, first performance of Moore's farce 'That Blessed Baby.' In 1857, March, at Drury Lane, revival of Morton's comedy 'A Cure for the Heartache,' she sustained the part of *Frank Oatlands*. As late as 1859 Mrs. Keeley was playing in burlesque at the Lyceum Theatre, as *Hector*, in 'The Siege of Troy,' by Brough. Since that year Mrs. Keeley has rarely appeared on the boards except on benefit occasions, in aid of some deserving player. The late Mr. G. H. Lewes, in his work *On Actors and the Art of Acting* (pp. 80–87), makes mention of Mrs. Keeley as follows :—" Among my very pleasantest recollections of the stage arise the figures of Keeley and his wife, each standing alone as a type of comic acting, and each markedly illustrating the truth so little understood, that acting, because it is a *representative* art, cannot be created by intelligence or sensibility (however necessary these may be for the perfection of the art), but must always depend upon the physical qualifications of the actor, these being the means of representation. It matters little what the actor *feels;* what he can *express* gives him his distinctive value. . . . Mrs. Keeley had little or none of the unctuousness of her husband, but she also was remarkably endowed. She was as intense and pointed as he was easy and fluent. She concentrated into her repartees an amount of intellectual *vie* and ' devil' which gave such a feather to the shaft that authors must often have been surprised at the revelation to themselves of the force of their own wit. Eye, voice, gesture, sparkled and chuckled. You could see that she enjoyed the joke, but enjoyed it rather as an intellectual triumph over others than from an impersonal delight in the joke itself. Keeley was like a fat, happy, self-satisfied puppy, taking life easily, ready to get sniffing and enjoyment out of everything. Mrs. Keeley was like a sprightly kitten, eager to make a mouse of every moving thing. . . . Did the reader happen to see her play the maid-of-all-work in ' Furnished Apartments'? He will not easily forget such a picture of the London ' slavey,' a stupid, wearied, slatternly, good-natured drab, her brain confused by incessant bells, her vitality ebbing under overwork. He will not forget the dazed expression, the limp exhaustion of her limbs, the wonderful assemblage of rags which passed for her costume. There was something at once inexpressibly droll and pathetic in this picture. It was so grotesque, yet so real, that laughter ended in a sigh. . . . It is an inestimable loss our stage has suffered by the departure of two such actors."

Mrs. Keeley's last appearance on the stage was at the " Testimonial Benefit " to Mrs. Alfred Mellon (*née* Woolgar), on May 15, 1878, at Drury Lane Theatre.

KELLY, CHARLES (a *nom de théâtre;* CHARLES WARDELL), the son of a clergyman living in the north of England, was born in 1839. Prior to entering the dramatic profession he held a commission in Her Majesty's Army. He made his first appearance on the stage at the Theatre Royal, Hull, in 1868, in the character of *Montano* (' Othello '). In London he has played at the Surrey, Holborn, Globe, Queen's, Royalty, Court, St. James's, Adelphi, and Haymarket Theatres in many parts, of which the following are deserving of particular mention. In October 1873, at the Globe Theatre, Mr. Kelly sustained his " original " part of *Richard Arkwright* in the drama of ' Arkwright's Wife ' (Tom Taylor), first performed at the Leeds Theatre Royal (*see* BARRY, HELEN).

Mr. Kelly's acting in this part was noticed in the *Globe* (October 7, 1873) as " a genuine surprise. His insight into character and his powers of representation were those of a true artist, who has seen clearly the thought he seeks to realize, and has accurately measured the means at his command. . . . There was room for quiet artistic excellence, and that the actor knew how to supply. His tender, fond enthusiasm for the machine he had invented, and the sudden grief and despair at its destruction, were striking points in a piece of acting which was thoroughly interesting throughout." Having previously appeared in Charles Reade's plays of ' Rachel the Reaper ' and ' Griffith Gaunt ' at the Queen's Theatre in Long Acre, in 1875 Mr. Kelly accepted an engagement at the Court Theatre, under the management of Mr. Hare. On Saturday, March 13 of that year, Mr. Kelly appeared there as *Lord Melton* in an original comedy by Charles F. Coghlan entitled ' Lady Flora,' in which he won the honours of the evening. In January 1876, at the same theatre, first performance of ' A Quiet Rubber ' (C. F. Coghlan), adapted from the French ' La Partie de Piquet,' Mr. Kelly played *Mr. Sullivan.* " In one point at least Mr. Coghlan's version is remarkably happy. By changing the scene to Irish ground he has converted the father of the intended bride into an admirable type of an Irish kind—a good-natured, quick-tempered, retired man of business, with a fund of native wit, and no less abundance of native readiness and warm feeling. These words, it is true, describe nothing new, and yet there is a great freshness in the sketch, thanks partly to the dramatist, but certainly in equal measure to Mr. Kelly, who plays his part with an overflowing, but unforced, vivacity, and with so many modest but effective touches of nature, that it would be difficult to imagine anything more perfect in its way." (*Daily News,* January 10, 1876.) In December of the same year, at the same theatre, in a revival of ' New Men and Old Acres ' (Tom Taylor and A. Dubourg), the part of *Mr. Samuel Brown* was sustained by Mr. Kelly. It may be remarked that the revival of this play was very successful, and that it remained on the " bills " of the Court Theatre for 250 consecutive nights. At the same house Mr. Kelly appeared as *Darnley* in ' The House of Darnley.' At St. James's Theatre, in ' Such is the Law,' he gained further reputation by his careful acting of *Tom Goacher.* At the Adelphi Theatre in 1878 he played for a time the part of *Pierre Lorance* in ' Proof.' The same year, on Monday, December 2, at the Haymarket Theatre, first performance of ' The Crisis ' (James Albery), adapted from M. Emile Augier's ' Les Fourchambault,' Mr. Kelly presented in a remarkably able and finished way the character of *John Goring.* Easter Monday, April 14, 1879, at the same theatre, in an original comedy-drama in five acts, by W. G. Wills, entitled ' Ellen ; or, Love's Cunning,' he played the part of *Thomas Pye* with admirable earnestness. This character and that of Lady Breezy (sustained by Miss Blanche Henri), and the excellent acting which was displayed in their presentation, probably sug-gested to Mr. Wills to reconstruct his play, and reproduce its

" comedy " scenes under the title of ' Brag,' Mr. Kelly playing his
" original " character. ' Brag,' however, like ' Ellen,' failed to
enlist the support of the public, and was immediately withdrawn.

KELLY, MRS. CHARLES. *See* TERRY, ELLEN.

KEMBLE, FRANCES ANN; better known as **FANNY
KEMBLE.** (Mrs. FANNY BUTLER.) Born in London, 1809.
Elder daughter of the late Charles Kemble, and niece of Mrs.
Siddons. She made her first appearance on any stage, Monday,
October 5, 1829, at the Theatre Royal, Covent Garden, then under
the management of her father, in the character of *Juliet* (' Romeo
and Juliet '). Her performance of the part was a great success.
" The house was crowded before the curtain drew up. . . . On
her (Miss Kemble's) first entrance she seemed to feel very sensibly
the embarrassment of the new and overwhelming task she had
undertaken. She ran to her mother's arms* with a sort of in-
stinctive impulse, but almost immediately recovered her composure.
From that time, although there was occasionally something
like timidity in her manner, there was not the slightest portion of awkward-
ness or even want of self-possession which might have been well
pardoned in so young an actress. Her first scene with Romeo was
very delicately and intelligently acted. In the garden scene she gave
the exquisite poetry of the part with a most innocent gracefulness,
and acted quite as well as she spoke. The scene with the Nurse
was full of delightful simplicity. In the scenes which ensue Miss
Kemble rose with the part. . . . Upon the whole we do not
remember to have seen a more triumphant *début*. That Miss
Kemble has been well and carefully instructed, as of course she
would be, is clear ; but it is no less clear that she possesses qualifications which instruction could not create, although it can bring
them to perfection." (*Times*, October 6, 1829.) ' Romeo and Juliet '
was played to crowded houses (with Miss Fanny Kemble in the
leading *rôle*) three times weekly until December 9, when Otway's
' Venice Preserved ' was produced. Miss Kemble played the part
of *Belvidera*. Said the *Morning Chronicle* (December 10, 1829) :—
" *Belvidera*, as our readers are aware, does not enter until near the
close of the third act, and she is first heard speaking without. The
moment the sound of her voice was caught the whole house was
in a tumult, and boxes, pit, and galleries joined in one common
endeavour to grace Miss Kemble's entrance. . . . The conclusion
of the third scene of this act (the fifth) was marked with many
vehement rounds of applause—where *Belvidera* imagines herself
drowning, and the waves ' buzzing and booming round my sinking
head.' We well remember and shall never forget the manner in
which Mrs. Siddons uttered this line, and the fearful action with
which that majestic woman accompanied it. Miss Fanny Kemble
could not venture in her inexperience so near the boundary of the

---

* Mrs. Charles Kemble was acting the character of *Lady Capulet* on this
occasion, after several years' absence from the stage.

sublime; but, nevertheless, her manner was most striking and impressive, and she rushed from the stage with a terrific energy of action that has never been equalled in boldness and picturesqueness from the time of Mrs. Siddons to the present hour."

In January 1830 Miss Kemble appeared as *Euphrasia* in 'The Grecian Daughter.' According to the *Athenæum* (January 23, 1830), her performance of *Euphrasia* confirmed more fully even than her acting in *Belvidera* the opinion formed on her first appearance in *Juliet.* " She has immense power, and cannot fail, if she continue on the stage, to prove an actress of the very first quality. . . . Her own taste will warn her against the effects of public applause when judiciously bestowed. We concur in the opinion which we find general that her *Euphrasia* in ' The Grecian Daughter ' is her *chef-d'œuvre.*" The season closed May 1830, having been a most prosperous one for the management. In the following season Miss Kemble played these among other characters, viz. *Mrs. Haller, Lady Townley, Calista* ('The Fair Penitent '), *Mrs. Beverley, Juliana* (' The Honeymoon '), *Lady Macbeth,* and one or two Shakespearian parts. The year 1832 was a remarkable one in the annals of the Kemble administration of Covent Garden Theatre. On Thursday, March 15, was produced there ' Francis I.,' a tragedy written by Miss Fanny Kemble herself ; and on Thursday, April 5, was performed for the first time Sheridan Knowles's play ' The Hunchback,' in which she was the " original " *Julia.* In the intervening period, Fanny Kemble had played a new part, *The Duchess of Guise,* in Lord Leveson-Gower's adaptation of A. Dumas' (the elder) tragedy, ' Henry III.' This play was unsuccessful. Nor was ' Francis I.,' in which Miss Kemble appeared as *Louise of Savoy,* a satisfactory success. It lacked a general interest, mainly owing to the unalloyed wickedness of nearly all the principal characters. Criticising the work as a literary effort, the *Athenæum* took leave to doubt that it would be permanently successful. It lacked concentration. " There are effective situations and clever scenes, but they have no connecting interest. . . . Much of it is just such dramatic poetry as a girl (a clever girl) of seventeen would write, the language of the poets, not of poetry ; and, as was very natural with a Kemble, the language of Shakespeare, full of ' By my fay,' and ' Sith you say,' and ' Wend your way,' and ' Go to, go to !' and ' Marry, this means,' and all the other outward and visible signs of a school exercise. But of the living, breathing language of passion and nature there is little, and there is less of poetry, hardly the melody of the voice which we had anticipated and believed would have characterized the work, because it is the true mark of poetical *feeling.*" (*Athenæum,* March 17, 1832.) Of Sheridan Knowles's production, the same journal had something of far greater moment to say. ' The Hunchback ' is a most delightful production—" every way a most delightful production ; good in plot, dramatic in composition, elegant, vigorous, and poetical in language, deep in knowledge of human nature, varied in display of the passions and affections which adorn or disfigure it, and admirable in their development."

As to Miss Fanny Kemble's creation of the part of *Julia*, we sub-join the following excerpt :—" Of Miss Fanny Kemble it gives us real gratification to speak in terms of unqualified commendation. She has never appeared to so much advantage. We followed her throughout with constantly increasing satisfaction, and may truly affirm that a more perfect piece of acting has seldom been witnessed than her earnest and impressive appeal to Master Walter in the commencement of the fifth act. Genuine feeling took the place of laboured and measured emphasis—the picture was true to nature—it was difficult to imagine that she uttered any words but those which the emergency of the moment called forth, and at the close of her address, its truth and beauty were acknowledged by shouts of ' Bravo !' from all parts of the house." (*Athenæum*, April 7, 1832.)

During the comparatively short period (three years) that Fanny Kemble was a member of her father's company, she revived the English national attachment to the stage, and achieved for the fallen fortunes of Covent Garden what the genius of the elder Kean enabled him to do for Drury Lane. In the autumn of 1832 with her father she visited America, and made her first appearance on the American stage, September 18 of that year, at the Park Theatre, New York, in the character of *Bianca* in ' Fazio.' Her first appearances at Philadelphia and at Boston were in the same part. From first to last, this joint venture of father and daughter was a triumph. January 7, 1834, Miss Kemble married Mr. Pierce Butler, a Southern planter, who died in Georgia, U.S.A., in 1867. Her married life was not altogether a happy one, and there was a separation, which ended (in 1848) in judicial proceedings for a divorce at Mrs. Butler's instigation. In 1847 she returned to England, and after thirteen years' absence from the stage made her reappearance at the Theatre Royal, Manchester, February 16, 1847, in the character of *Julia* in ' The Hunchback.' She was welcomed with a warmth of applause which must have assured her of the sympathies of her English compatriots in regard to her then recent domestic troubles. " Long before the curtain rose last evening the house was crammed to the ceiling. On Mrs. Butler's entrance the excitement was immense. Round after round of applause, cheer after cheer welcomed her to this her first audience after so long an absence. Her first efforts showed how keenly she felt the warmth of her reception. . . . Her voice has lost none of its exquisite music, her attitudes and action are still as graceful and picturesque. . . . She showed that she had in the retirement of private life lost none of her intelligence, none of that fine poetic spirit with which her remembrance is linked." (*Manchester Courier*, February 17, 1847.)

During the engagement which followed, she appeared in a round of her favourite characters, *Juliana* ('The Honeymoon'), *Lady Macbeth*, *Juliet*, *Queen Katharine*, &c. In May of the same year she reappeared at the Princess's Theatre, in London, and continued to act there during the season. She returned for a brief period to America, and once more came to England. In April 1848 Mrs. Butler commenced a series of Shakespearian readings at Willis's

Rooms, which, although well attended, did not attract the critical attention of the Press. October 1849 she gave her first Shakespearian reading (from ' King John ') in America, at Sansom Street Hall, Philadelphia. After this date she resumed her maiden name, and retired to Lennox, Mass., U.S.A., where she resided for nearly twenty years. In 1868 Miss Fanny Kemble reappeared as a reader at Steinway Hall, New York. In 1873 she went to reside near Philadelphia; and in 1877–8 again returned to England. Miss Kemble is the author of the following works :—' Francis I,' (a tragedy); ' Journal of a Residence in America ' (1835); ' The Star of Seville ' (1837) ; ' A Year of Consolation ' (1847) ; ' Mary Stuart,' translated from the German of Schiller; ' Mademoiselle de Belle Isle,' a paraphrase in prose of Dumas' work; ' Residence on a Georgian Plantation in 1838–9,' published in 1863; ' Records of a Girlhood,' published in 1878. " In the late Justice Halliburton's ' Letter-bag of the Great Western,' giving life-like portraits of individuals, their manners, style, feelings, and expression, will be found ' The Journal of an Actress,' in which the cleverness and audacity, refinement and coarseness, modesty and bounce, pretty humility and prettier arrogance of Miss Fanny Kemble were touched off in a style which all the world could identify, and the lady herself could not turn her lip at except to smile at the skill with which her literary merits and affectations were imitated so as to be like reality." (*Athenæum*, September 22, 1865.)

KEMBLE, HENRY, was born June 1, 1848, and is a son of Captain Henry Kemble (son of Charles Kemble, the eminent tragedian). He was educated at Bury St. Edmunds and King's College, London, and, afterwards, was for a period of two years in the Civil Service of the Crown. He resigned his official appointment, and entered the dramatic profession in 1867, making his first appearance on the stage at the Theatre Royal, Dublin, on the 7th of October of that year. From 1867 to 1869 he was a member of the company of the above-named theatre; from 1869 to 1871 of the company of the Theatre Royal, Edinburgh; and from 1871 to 1873 of the company of the Theatre Royal, Glasgow; the line of " business " ordinarily undertaken by him being " first old men and character parts." During the probationary period of his professional career, Mr. Kemble appeared with success at the Theatres Royal, Newcastle-on-Tyne and Scarborough. He made his *début* in London August 29, 1874, at the Theatre Royal, Drury Lane, in the part of *Tony Foster*, in Andrew Halliday's play ' Amy Robsart.' During the season 1874–5, at the same theatre, he played the following parts, viz. *Cedric the Saxon*, in ' Rebecca '; *Philip of France*, in ' Richard Cœur de Lion '; the *1st Actor*, in ' Hamlet '; *Old Capulet*, in ' Romeo and Juliet '; and *Dr. Caius*, in ' The Merry Wives of Windsor.' This latter impersonation was very successful, and secured for Mr. Kemble favourable notice in various journals. On March 13, 1875, he joined Mr. Hare's company, on that gentleman's entering upon the management of the Royal Court Theatre. Here Mr. Kemble " opened " as *Short*, in a piece entitled 'Short and Sweet,' and as *Binns*, in 'Lady Flora.' This part, although a subordinate one, was performed by Mr. Kemble with excellent judgment, and may be recorded among his legitimate successes on the stage. Another part, also, in which his careful acting received approval, at the same theatre, was that of *Dr. Penguin*, in 'A Scrap of Paper' (A. Wigan), adapted from M. Sardou's play 'Les Pattes de Mouche.' Subsequently Mr. Kemble joined the company of the Prince of Wales's Theatre, of which he still remains a member. He has performed at that theatre the following characters, viz. *Crossby Beck*, in 'Peril'; *Sir Sowerby Honeywood*, in 'An Unequal Match'; *Waddilove*, in 'To Parents and Guardians'; *Sir Oliver Surface*, in 'The School for Scandal'; *John Chodd*, in 'Society'; and *Algie Fairfax*, in 'Diplomacy'—each in a way deserving of recognition.

KENDAL, MRS. W. H. (Mrs. W. HUNTER GRIMSTON, *née* ROBERTSON, MARGARET ['MADGE']), was born at Great Grimsby, March 15, 1848, and was educated to the stage as a profession from early childhood. At the age of four (in 1852) she appeared at the Marylebone Theatre as the *Blind Child*, in 'The Seven Poor Travellers'; and in 1855 at the Bristol Theatre as *Eva*, in a dramatic version of 'Uncle Tom's Cabin.' It may be remarked that Mrs. Kendal's early tuition as an actress was principally received at the Theatres Royal Bristol and Bath, under the management of the late Mr. J. H. Chute. On Saturday, July 29, 1865, she made her professional *début* in London at the Haymarket Theatre as *Ophelia*, in a revival of 'Hamlet' by the late Walter Montgomery, who played the leading *rôle*. Her acting on that occasion created a favourable impression; and on Monday, August 21 of the same year, at the same theatre, she acted the part of *Desdemona*, Mr. Ira Aldridge sustaining the *rôle* of Othello. After fulfilling engagements at Nottingham and Hull, in 1867 Miss Robertson returned to London, and on Easter Monday of that year, at Drury Lane Theatre, played the part of *Edith*, the heroine, on the occasion of the first performance of 'The Great City' (Andrew Halliday). The following year, at the Haymarket Theatre, first performance (Saturday, March 14) of Dr. Westland Marston's play 'A Hero of Romance,' Mr. Sothern in the leading character, she acted the part of *Blanche Dumont*, being "more than equal to the character, and investing it with beauty and pathos" (*Athenæum*, March 21, 1868). At the same theatre, in July, she sustained the part of *Hypolita*, in a revival of Colley Cibber's comedy 'She Would and She Would Not'; and on Monday, December 21, 1868, at the opening of the Gaiety Theatre, appeared in a piece entitled 'On the Cards,' then performed for the first time. In March of the following year (1869), at the same theatre, Miss Robertson sustained the part of *Lady Clara Vere de Vere*, in her brother, the late T. W. Robertson's play entitled 'Dreams.' On Monday, October 25, 1869, at the Haymarket Theatre, first performance of Messrs. Tom Taylor and Dubourg's comedy of 'New Men and Old Acres,' Miss Robertson undertook the character of *Lilian Vavasour*. "The theme of Messrs. Taylor and Dubourg's comedy is the very old one of contrast and conflict between the old class and the new—the aristocratic landed gentry and the wealthy self-made men of our day. . . . The comedy, though wanting anything like that view of serious interest which can alone take hold of the hearts of an audience, is lively and amusing throughout, while the dialogue, which is generally clever and pointed, sometimes attains even higher merits. But the acting of Miss Robertson, who sustained the part of *Lilian*, might alone have sufficed to secure success for a work of far inferior merits. A young lady who talks slang, corrupted by the society of a sporting cousin, would be a dangerous part in ordinary hands; but Miss Robertson's performance in no part degenerated into anything like vulgarity. There was a neatness and a finish not only in her delivery of the words, but in all her movements, including that indefinable filling up of time known to the actors as 'business,' which belong to the very best school of comedy-acting. Nor is she much less at home in the more pathetic portions of her part, particularly in the scene in which, in view of the wealthy *parvenu's* succession to her father's property, she bespeaks his favour and kindness for old objects of her bounty, not forgetting her dog and the peacock with one eye; and, again, in a later portion, in which she freely offers herself, when rich, to the man who loves her, and who had not disdained her when presumptively poor—both of which dramatic situations were greeted by the house with well-merited applause." (*Daily News*, October 26, 1869.)

In 1870, at the same theatre, in a revival of 'The Rivals' (Monday, October 24), Miss Madge Robertson appeared as *Lydia Languish;* and on Saturday, November 19 of the same year, at the same theatre, she sustained the part of *Princess Zeolide*, first performance of Mr. W. S. Gilbert's play 'The Palace of Truth,' which was a complete success. In the same author's play of 'Pygmalion and Galatea,' first performed at the same theatre, Saturday, December 9, 1871, she acted the leading female *rôle*, *Galatea;* and in 'The Wicked World,' by the same author, first performed Saturday, January 4, 1873, Miss Robertson played the part of *Selene.* In each of the three plays Miss Robertson's acting was admirable. On Saturday, January 3, 1874, in a new play by Mr. Gilbert, entitled 'Charity,' she played the principal character, *Mrs. Van Brugh*, and, according to the *Athenæum* (January 10, 1874), obtained at the end of the third act a triumph more spontaneous and overwhelming than has often been accorded an artist. "The audience literally rose to greet her. Delight in finding deeper qualities in an actress known principally for her comic personations must be accepted as the reason for this. In fact, the acting was not equal to the reception. Miss Robertson's pathos was studied. The actions were good but not affecting until the very close of the situation. Momentarily she then reached inspiration, producing upon the audience the marvellous effect described." The *Daily Telegraph* (January 5, 1874), discussing the merits of the same performance, said:—"The *Mrs. Van Brugh* of Miss Robertson was in many respects so admirable, and, from a popular point of view, such a triumph, that we have the less hesitation in asking this most intelligent lady to consider the character as a whole ; to live in it, and breathe in it throughout, and to work up every scene and half-scene to the same pitch of excellence as that great burst of combined power and pathos which took the house by storm at the close of the third act. This great scene was a complete and successful study, and will be still more remarkable a study when the anxious excitement of a first night does not exist. We do so want power ; we do so ask for expression ; we do so demand acting which shall soar above commonplace, that we are grateful for this remarkable outburst. As an example of study of light and shade, it is extremely interesting ; as an instance of change of key and contrast of harmony, it is most creditable. The pleading, agonized despair of the detected woman, the outburst of rage and scorn, the quick hysterical summons to the family, the wealth of love over the innocent child, and the sad, yet solemn confession, are rapid instances of successful art rarely seen nowadays on the stage. The true ring of genius was perhaps wanted, but the acting made a dull English audience leap to its feet, and wave hats and handkerchiefs. The audience was possibly not familiar with inspired genius, and looked for an outburst at the close of the third act. With so much gained, Miss Robertson may surely avoid staginess, *passim*. The perpetual roll of the eyes, the stilted walk, and the seeming neglect of many scenes of high comedy, astonish those who so much admire individual passages. There is acting to be done in moving, in speeches which have no particular weight, and even in listening. The important scene in which Smailey first suggests a fault on the part of *Mrs. Van Brugh* was worth mastering ; and when we remember the true and admirable expression of the actress on hearing of Ted Athelney's love for her daughter, we know well what the actress can do. In these new-fangled days it is not the highest art to rush at the telling speeches, or at the obvious acting positions ; a Desclée has taught us how an actress can live and breathe in a character. Miss Robertson's *Mrs. Van Brugh* is a very remarkable performance, eminently superior to the ordinary run of English art, graceful and highly intelligent. If it were only less stagey in parts, the performance would be more acceptable."

At Christmas 1874 Miss Robertson left the Haymarket Theatre for a short engagement of eight weeks at the Opéra Comique, commencing Monday, January 18, 1875. During this engagement she appeared as *Pauline Deschapelles* in 'The Lady of Lyons'; as *Rosalind* in 'As You Like It'; and as *Miss Hardcastle* in 'She Stoops to Conquer,' considered one of the most successful of her impersonations. In March 1875 she joined the company at the Court Theatre, under the management of Mr. Hare, and played during the season in 'Lady Flora,' 'A Nine Days' Wonder,' 'Broken Hearts,' 'A Scrap of Paper,' 'Uncle's Will,' &c. Subsequently Miss Robertson (now Mrs. Kendal) joined the company of the Prince of Wales's Theatre, and, perhaps, the most noteworthy success she met with there was in the part of *Dora* in the English version of M. Sardou's play of that name, entitled 'Diplomacy,' first performed January 12, 1878. " Of the acting of the play we can speak with more unqualified praise. It does not, it is true, rise to the level of force and pathos demanded by the most passionate and tender of its scenes, but it is always careful and well proportioned, and within the bounds of good taste. It is rather the result of the curtailment of the exposition of the play than the fault of Mrs. Kendal that the exclamation of joyous surprise with which *Dora* receives an offer of marriage fails to produce the simple touching effect of Mdlle. Blanche Pierson's utterance of the same words. The position is an extremely delicate one, for the young lady has really to indicate mingled pleasure and astonishment that at last she has a lover who is an honourable man. For us to feel its spirit it was necessary that the character of *Dora* should be drawn in the first place, not in meagre outline, but in full detail; but this is denied, and hence the exclamation could hardly fail to give a slight shock to the hearer's sense of propriety. Among many excellent details in Mrs. Kendal's impersonation we ought to note the perfectly unsuspecting and unhesitating innocence of her tone and manner when, seated at the table, her husband begins to unfold the suspicions against her." (*Daily News*, January 14, 1878.) On Saturday, January 4, 1879, Mrs. Kendal and her husband "opened" at the Court Theatre in a revival of 'A Scrap of Paper,' Mrs. Kendal resuming her part of *Susan Hartley.* On Saturday, February 15, she appeared as *Countess D'Autreval* in a revival of 'The Ladies' Battle' ('La Bataille des Dames' of MM. Scribe and Legouvé); and on Saturday, April 19 of the same year, at the same theatre, as *Kate Greville* in 'The Queen's Shilling' (G. W. Godfrey), a new version of 'Le Fils de Famille,' first performed in London on the date last mentioned, and afterwards played at the opening of St. James's Theatre.

KENDAL, W. H. (a *nom de théâtre;* WILLIAM HUNTER GRIMSTON), was born in London, December 16, 1843, and entered the dramatic profession in 1861, appearing on the stage for the first time, in London, at the Soho, now the Royalty Theatre. The following year Mr. Kendal joined the company of the Theatre Royal, Glasgow, where he remained until 1866. During this long engagement he had the advantage of acting in association with such well-known "stars" as the late G. V. Brooke, the Keans, the Boucicaults, Mr. Anderson, and Miss Faucit. Mr. Kendal made his professional *début* in London, October 31, 1866, at the Haymarket Theatre, in a piece entitled 'A Dangerous Friend,' and met with gratifying success. On Monday, September 2, 1867, at the same theatre, he appeared as *Orlando* in a revival of 'As You Like It.' "He was well suited to the part, and his style is at once elegant and vigorous, and likely, we think, to become popular." (*Athenæum*, September 7, 1867.) The following year, in July, he played *Don Octavio* in a revival of Cibber's comedy 'She Would and She Would Not'; and on Monday, December 7, 1868, first performance at the Haymarket Theatre of 'Pictra,' adapted from Mosenthal's tragedy of that name—Miss Bateman in the title *rôle* —Mr. Kendal sustained the part of *Manfred.* He was in the original cast of 'Mary Warner' (*see* BATEMAN, KATE), produced at the Haymarket, and of 'Uncle's Will,' a comedietta written expressly for Mr. Kendal and Miss Robertson by Mr. Theyre Smith. Mr. Kendal continued to play at this theatre for some time, taking important parts (*Captain Absolute, Charles Surface*, &c.) in the old comedies, and appearing in Mr. W. S. Gilbert's most successful plays, 'The Palace of Truth' (*Prince Philamine*), 'Pygmalion and Galatea' (*Pygmalion*), 'The Wicked World' (*Ethais*), and 'Charity' (*Frederic Smailey*), on the occasion of their first performance. (*See* KENDAL, Mrs. W. H.)

In January 1875 Mr. Kendal, with his wife, fulfilled a short engagement at the Opéra Comique, under the management of Mr. Hollingshead, the plays in which they appeared together being 'The Lady of Lyons,' 'As You Like It,' and Goldsmith's comedy of 'She Stoops to Conquer.' On March 12 of the same year Mr. and Mrs. Kendal "opened" at the Court Theatre, under the management of Mr. Hare, and appeared in the following pieces, viz. 'Lady Flora,' 'Nine Days' Wonder,' 'Broken Hearts,' and 'A Scrap of Paper.' In 1876 Mr. Kendal went to the Prince of Wales's Theatre, under the management of Mr. and Mrs. Bancroft, and appeared there in 'Peril' and 'London Assurance,' and later in the English version of M. Sardou's play of 'Dora,' entitled 'Diplomacy,' first performed January 12, 1878. In this play Mr. Kendal sustained the part of *Captain Beauclerc*. "The famous 'Scène des trois hommes' could hardly have been received with more enthusiasm when represented by MM. Berton, Train, and Dieudonné to the great delight of a Parisian 'first-night' audience; and though the marvellous dramatic power, variety, and truth of this memorable episode have a necessary tendency to weaken the impression of subsequent scenes, the story was from this point, at least, followed with eager interest until the curtain fell amidst hearty and genuine applause. . . . The performance of the scene [of 'the three men'] by Mr. Kendal, Mr. Clayton, and Mr. Bancroft was exceedingly spirited and nicely marked in all its transitions of passionate feeling. Of the striking effect which it produced we have already spoken." (*Daily News*, January 14, 1878.)

"In the first of the great scenes the acting of Mr. Bancroft, Mr. Kendal, and Mr. Clayton, respectively impersonating the friend, the husband, and the brother, could not well be bettered. The situation is in itself very striking, and presented as it is by these three gentlemen, it brought down, from all quarters of the house, such applause as is seldom heard in this theatre, where satisfaction is wont to be expressed after a somewhat languidly decorous fashion. Mr. Kendal, we confess, fairly surprised us. He has long been credited with the pleasant expression of the easy graces and fancies of the comedian, but for the exhibition of so much feeling and power few were, we suspect, prepared." (*Times*, January 21, 1878.) On Saturday, January 4, 1879, Mr. Kendal and his wife "opened" at the Court Theatre, in a revival of 'A Scrap of Paper,' in which he acted *Colonel White*. Saturday, February 15, in a revival of 'The Ladies' Battle,' he played *Gustave de Grignon;* and on Saturday, April 19 of the same year, at the same theatre, the part of *Frank Maitland* in 'The Queen's Shilling' (G. W. Godfrey), a new version of 'Le Fils de Famille' of MM. Bayard and Bieville. He is now co-manager with Mr. Hare of St. James's Theatre.

KENNEY, ROSA, is the daughter of Mr. Charles Lamb Kenney, a *littérateur* of some distinction, and the grand-daughter of Mr. James Kenney, the dramatist. Miss Kenney made her first appearance on any stage January 23, 1879, in a morning performance at Drury Lane Theatre, in the character of *Juliet* in 'Romeo and Juliet.' Several weeks later she appeared at two matinées at the Princess's Theatre in the same part, and as *Pauline* in 'The Lady of Lyons.' At the reopening of the Royal Court Theatre, September 20, 1879, under the management of Mr. Wilson Barrett, Miss Kenney took the character of *Fernande* in Sutherland Edwards's adaptation of Sardou's 'Fernande'; but subsequently retired from the part.

KING, T. C., was born at Cheltenham in 1825, and entered the dramatic profession at a comparatively early age, making his first appearance on the stage proper at the Theatre Royal, Birmingham, under Mr. Mercer Simpson's management. Afterwards he joined the "York Theatrical Circuit," under Mr. John Langford Pritchard, and played various parts in the Shakespearian and legitimate drama at the Theatres Royal, York, Leeds, and Hull. Subsequently Mr. King fulfilled a lengthened engagement at the Edinburgh Theatre, under Mr. William Murray, appearing principally in Shakespearian characters. He made his *début* on the London stage at the Princess's Theatre, July 22, 1857, when that theatre was under the management of the late Mr. Charles Kean, in the part of *Bassanio* ('Merchant of Venice'), Mr. Kean acting *Shylock*. Remaining a member of the company of the Princess's Theatre for two years, Mr. King, at the end of that period, relinquished his engagement for a "starring" tour in the principal theatres of the provinces, which was attended with gratifying success. At Dublin he became an especial favourite, and his performances at the Theatre Royal in 'Hamlet,' 'Othello,' 'Macbeth,' 'Merchant of Venice,' 'Richelieu,' &c., attracted large and appreciative audiences. In 1868 Mr. King accepted an offer of an engagement from Mr. F. B. Chatterton, and in March of the year following made his reappearance on the metropolitan stage at Drury Lane Theatre in the character of *Richelieu*. "In the later acts, when *Richelieu* sees his fortunes desperate, and places in the hands of the king his resignation, the dignity and pathos of Mr. King's acting were great, and took complete hold upon the audience. Mr. King has a fine presence and commanding look. His voice is musical, his pronunciation is good, and his attitudes are all well chosen and expressive." (*Athenæum*, March 20, 1869.)

On Thursday, March 18 of the same year, he appeared at the same theatre as *Hamlet*, and subsequently as *Othello* and *Iago*, acting those parts alternately with Mr. Charles Dillon. Later, Mr.

King acted the part of *Macbeth*. These performances were favourably noticed in the *Standard*:—" The winter dramatic season was brought to a close on Saturday, the performance during the final week being remarkable for the diversity of the entertainment, and the appearance on the London stage of a tragedian of the first rank in the person of Mr. T. C. King. Of Mr. King's first appearance as *Richelieu* we have already spoken. On the occasion of his second appearance, on Thursday, Mr. King played *Hamlet*, his performance of the Danish prince giving evidence of careful study, together with a thorough comprehension of character. Mr. King possesses many qualifications calculated to make him a good exponent of the part—a tall and commanding figure, graceful and easy movements, an intelligent face, and a full-toned sonorous voice. His impersonation of the mad prince may rank among the highest efforts of the present day; all those touches of tender pathos with which the character abounds were thoroughly, though not obtrusively, brought into prominence, while in all other portions of the play the power of the actor was rendered fully apparent."

During the season 1870, at the same theatre, Mr. King played the following, among other parts, with much success, viz. *William Tell* in Sheridan Knowles's play of that title; *Julian St. Pierre* in the same author's play of 'The Wife'; and *Varney* on the occasion of the first performance, Saturday, September 24, 1870, of 'Amy Robsart.' It has been remarked that, in his portrayal of Shakespearian tragedy, Mr. King is "earnest and impassioned, tender and pathetic, declamatory and conversational, as suits the character he represents, and in all the varying moods and feelings that actuate him he is true to nature." The *Saturday Review*, in a notice of his performance of *Macbeth* at Drury Lane Theatre in 1870, remarked that "Mr. King has all the attributes of a first-class tragedian. No such actor has appeared on the boards of old Drury since Macready bade farewell to the stage in the same character (*Macbeth*)." Since his last appearance in London Mr. T. C. King has fulfilled several successful " starring " engagements in the provinces.

LACY, WALTER, was born in 1809, and made his first appear-ance on any stage at the Theatre Royal, Edinburgh, in 1832 as *Count Montalban* in 'The Honeymoon.' Subsequently he played various engagements in Glasgow, Manchester, and Liverpool; and made his *début* on the London stage in August 1838, at the Hay-market Theatre, as *Charles Surface* ('School for Scandal'), Miss Taylor—an actress who was the "original" Helen in 'The Hunch-back,' and of considerable repute on the London stage in the second quarter of the century—playing Lady Teazle. This lady afterwards married Mr. Walter Lacy, and "for twenty years played leading comedy, tragedy, and Vestris-business at Covent Garden, Drury Lane, or the Haymarket, during the last twelve acting as Mrs. Walter Lacy, and shining especially in Shakespearian women."* Following his first appearance on the London stage Mr. Lacy was engaged for three years at the Haymarket Theatre. After this he accepted a three years' engagement at the Theatre Royal, Covent Garden, "opening" as *Captain Absolute* in 'The Rivals,' Madame Vestris playing Lydia Languish. Among the company of this theatre, during Mr. Lacy's connection with it, were Messrs. George Bartley, Charles Mathews, F. Vining, George Vandenhoff, John Cooper, William Farren, F. Matthews, J. P. Harley, John Brougham, Alfred Wigan, and Mesdames Nesbitt, Vestris, Glover, W. Lacy, Brougham, H. Bland. Later, Mr. Lacy became a member of the company of the T. R. Drury Lane, "opening" there as *Wildrake*, Mrs. Nesbitt acting Con-stance. He was for seven years connected with the Princess's Theatre under Mr. Charles Kean's management, "opening" there Saturday, September 18, 1852, as *Rouble*, first performance of 'The Prima Donna' (Boucicault). During the same evening he played *Chateau Renaud* ('The Corsican Brothers') and *Alfred Highflyer* ('Roland for an Oliver'). "These were brilliantly contrasted characters, affording splendid opportunity for an artist to establish himself. Of such an opportunity the severity of my early training and the varied experience of my career enabled me to take full advantage. . . . After the first act of 'The Prima Donna' Charles Kean came to my dressing-room to congratulate me on my 'make-up' and acting in *Rouble;* and at the conclusion of 'The Corsican Brothers' I was cheered by the whole house. The manager and manageress were delighted, and Mr. Bayle Bernard came on to the stage with the late Douglas Jerrold to compliment me on 'the originality and finish of my acting.' Next morning Charles Mathews and Madame Vestris called me to their carriage in the middle of Regent Street and heartily congratulated me. . . . My 'make-up' hit the house and was the key-note of the new rendering of the

* From a letter addressed by Mr. Walter Lacy to Mr. W. Clark Russell, Editor of 'Representative Actors' (p. 442).

part."* " *Rouble,* the generous, wrong-headed *millionaire,* always fighting for his mistress, and always offending her, was admirably dressed and played by Mr. Walter Lacy, who is a new addition to the company. His ludicrous distress, tempered in the oddest manner by a sort of cold nonchalance, made up one of those characteristic inconsistencies which stand out in the memory from the level of ordinary stage routine. Mr. Lacy is really an artist well known and esteemed by habitués of the theatres, although of late years hidden from the view of the general public. His performance of *Chateau Renaud* in 'The Corsican Brothers,' which followed 'The Prima Donna,' was a great instance of his care and judgment in a part quite out of his usual line, and in which he had all the disadvantage of appearing after an excellent predecessor." (*Times,* September 20, 1852.) Subsequently Mr. Lacy accepted engagements at the Olympic, Lyceum, Strand, St. James's, and Charing Cross Theatres. Of the parts played by him during his long and honourable connection with the London stage the following, in the plays to which each relates, are entitled to special mention, viz. *Benedick, Mercutio, Faulconbridge, Malvolio, Touchstone, Cloten* ('Cymbeline'), *Prospero, Gratiano, Roderigo, Henry the Eighth, Young Marlow, Sir Brilliant Fashion, Goldfinch, Flutter, Tony Lumpkin, Acres, Dazzle, Dudley Smooth, Sparkish, Megrim* ('Blue Devils'), *Ghost* ('Hamlet'), *Lord Trinket, Lord Tinsel, My Lord Duke* ('High Life Below Stairs'), *Jeremy Diddler, Puff* ('The Critic'), *Sir Anthony Absolute.* For a period of sixteen years Mr. Lacy has been Professor of Elocution at the Royal Academy of Music. In April 1879, on the occasion of the revival by Mr. Henry Irving at the Lyceum Theatre of 'The Lady of Lyons,' Mr. Lacy sustained the part of *Colonel Damas.* The *Times* (April 19, 1879) makes mention of his reappearance, after a long period of retirement, as lending an additional feature of interest to the revival. In Mr. Walter Lacy's hands (remarked this journal) "*Colonel Damas* exhibited a nature gentler and more subdued than that with which most actors have been wont to invest that worthy soldier; yet there were still distinctly to be traced those enduring remains of a skilled and careful training which neither time nor long disuse are ever able wholly to efface."

 LARKIN, SOPHIE, made her *début* on the London stage, September 25, 1865, at the Prince of Wales's Theatre as *Mrs. Pontifex* in 'Naval Engagements.' On November 11, 1865, she played, at the same theatre, the part of *Lady Ptarmigant,* first performance of T. W. Robertson's comedy 'Society'; on September 15, 1866, the part of *Lady Shendryn,* first performance at the same theatre of the same author's play of 'Ours'; and on April 6, 1867, the character of *Marquise de Saint-Maur,* first performance at the same theatre of the same author's play of 'Caste.' On January 1 of the following year she "opened" at St. James's Theatre as *Mrs. Erskine Meek* in H. T. Craven's

* 'Representative Actors,' W. Clark Russell, pp. 398-9.

comedy 'The Needful,' then first performed ; and in the following month, at the same theatre, sustained the part of *Patty Probity* in a revival of the same author's play of 'The Chimney Corner.' The same year (1868) Miss Larkin joined the company of Miss Fanny Josephs, who, on April 13, re-opened the Holborn Theatre with Burnand's extravaganza 'The White Fawn,' in which Miss Larkin appeared as *Queen Harmonia*. During 1869 she played *Mrs. Raby* in a revival of H. T. Craven's 'Miriam's Crime' at the same theatre ; and for the benefit of Mr. Lionel Brough (March 15) acted excellently the part of *Mrs. Hardcastle* ('She Stoops to Conquer') at the Queen's Theatre. At St. James's Theatre, in April 1870, Miss Larkin appeared in a version of 'Frou-Frou,' produced by the late Mdlle. Beatrice, as *Baroness de Cambri*. On Saturday, October 7, 1871, first performance at the Globe Theatre of H. J. Byron's comedy 'Partners for Life,' she played the part of *Priscilla Mervyn*. Miss Larkin was also in the original cast of the same author's comedy 'Our Boys,' first performed at the Vaudeville Theatre on January 16, 1875. She sustained the character of *Clarissa Champneys*, and continued to appear in the part during the unprecedented run of the piece. (*See* BYRON, H. J.) On the withdrawal of this play and production at the same theatre of 'The Girls,' a new and original comedy from Mr. Byron's pen, Miss Larkin "created" the part of *Mrs. Clench*.

LA TROBE, MRS. *See* ADDISON, CARLOTTA.

LAVERNE, PATTIE, was born in London, and first appeared in public as a concert-singer, making her *début* at the Hanover Square Rooms, in 1871. Being possessed of a powerful, flexible, and true soprano voice, united with considerable power of expression, she met with some success in oratorio and concert at St. James's Hall, and other places in London, and at the Free Trade Hall, in Manchester. Her first appearance on the stage was made at Preston, in the character of the *Grand Duchess*, in Offenbach's opera of that title, during a tour with Mr. John Russell's company in Lancashire, in 1871. The following year, when Mr. Hingston opened the Opéra Comique in London, for Opera Bouffe, Miss Laverne became a member of his company. In October 1872 at that theatre, she played the part of *Dindorette* in 'L'Œil Crêvé.' "Nothing could have been prettier in its way than the *Dindorette* of Miss Pattie Laverne, a most attractive young lady, with a very decided talent for sprightly acting. Her first song, 'If perchance my lover,' was encored, and fully merited the compliment. The duet at the end of the scene was equally successful, and throughout the opera Miss Laverne was as piquant and sparkling as possible, and added greatly to the success of the piece." (*Era*, October 26, 1872.) At the same theatre, during the season 1872–3, she played the parts of *Little Tom Tug, Guillerette*, in 'The Bohemians,' and *Kissi-Kissi* in the operatic trifle of that title, " deserving all praise for her spirited and piquant impersonation of the boy-girl, *Kissi-Kissi*. Her sprightliness and really admirable singing were of the

most essential service to the success of the little piece; and the
part is one difficult to sustain without offence." (*Standard*, July 14,
1873.)   Upon the production of 'La Fille de Madame Angot,' at
the Opéra Comique, under the joint management of Messrs. John
Hollingshead and Charles Morton, Miss Laverne played the part
of *Clairette*, and during a subsequent provincial tour with Mr.
W. H. Liston sustained the same character with marked success.
She has since represented most of the leading female parts in
Opera Bouffe, including *Giroflé-Girofla*, *Boulotte* in 'Barbe Bleue,'
Trainette in 'Pom,' and the title *rôle* in Cellier's opera, 'Nell
Gwynne,' produced with much success at the Prince's Theatre,
Manchester.   Of the part of *Boulotte*, played by Miss Laverne at
Liverpool, the following criticism was published :—"Miss Pattie
Laverne played, not as is generally done, merely gracefully, but
with great care.   In place of tacitly appealing to the audience,
she set herself to make the most of what is at the best a disagree-
able character.   *Boulotte* being coarsely drawn requires the most
delicate treatment, and there is little doubt that in the hands of
a less skilful player it would have been absolutely disagreeable."
(*Liverpool Daily Post*, August 28, 1877.)

* **LAWLER, KATE,** previous to her *début* on the London stage,
had earned some repute in the provinces as an earnest and painstaking actress; the character of *Smike* in 'Nicholas Nickleby'
being among the parts which she has performed with more than
ordinary success.   Miss Lawler made her first important appearance in London at the Gaiety Theatre, in October 1878, as *Sally
Scraggs* in an amusing trifle entitled 'Stage Struck.'   In this
piece she exhibited humorous talent of a very varied kind.   Miss
Lawler has, during her engagement at the Gaiety, appeared in the
later burlesques placed on its stage.

* **LEATHES, EDMUND,** made his *début* on the London stage
March 1, 1873, at the Princess's Theatre, as *Gratiano* in 'The
Merchant of Venice.'   In November of the same year he played
with considerable success the title *rôle* in Charles Reade's drama
'The Wandering Heir' at the Queen's Theatre, "showing himself a
promising actor, with much grace of presence and purity of style,
and likely to prove a competent representative of the Doricourts
and Wildairs of old comedy, a class of parts lost of late years
to the stage" (*Athenæum*, November 22, 1873.)   In October 1874,
and during the "run" of 'Hamlet' at the Lyceum Theatre, Mr.
Leathes admirably sustained the part of *Laertes*.   Two years later
(September 1876), in a revival at the Court Theatre of Boucicault's
'Led Astray,' he acted *George de Lesparre*.   It is understood that
Mr. Leathes has now retired from the stage.

LECLERCQ, CARLOTTA (Mrs. JOHN NELSON), born in
London; elder daughter of the late Charles Leclercq, for many
years favourably known in dramatic circles in Manchester and
London as a skilful ballet-master, pantomimist, and stage-manager,

and, also, actor in a certain range of parts. Miss Leclercq was educated to the stage from childhood, and, as a child, played in extravaganza at various London theatres. At Christmas, 1850–1–2, she undertook the part of *Columbine* during the "run" of the pantomime at the Princess's Theatre. At Easter, 1853, at the same theatre, first performance of 'Marco Spada,' adapted from Scribe's libretto to Auber's opera of that name, she played the character *Marchesa Maddalena*, "her acting abounding in the spirit in which her fellow-actors were deficient" (*Athenæum*, April 2, 1853). In April 1854 she made her first appearance of any note in the character of *Marguerite* ('Faust and Marguerite') at the Princess's Theatre. This so-called "magical drama" was a close adaptation of a French piece of the same name, written by M. Michel Carré, and brought out at the Gymnase in August 1850. As a spectacle it was one of the most tasteful and elaborate ever seen on the boards of the Princess's Theatre. The *Times* (April 20, 1854), noticing Miss Leclercq's acting in the part, said:—"*Marguerite* served to display to an extraordinary degree the talents of Miss Leclercq. Her appearance, both as the happy innocent girl and as the victim of remorse, was beautifully picturesque, and her pantomime, which was important throughout, was always graceful and expressive. The interior of the cathedral, in which she is disturbed by evil thoughts during her prayer, was exhibited by means of a transparency, and her wild gestures of despair as she knelt conspicuous among the rest of the congregation gave a strik-ing character to the whole tableau."

In March 1855, first performance at the Princess's of 'The Muleteer of Toledo,' adapted from the French of M. Adam's opera of the same title, Miss Leclercq performed the part of *Elvira, Queen of Murcia.* The same year at the same theatre she played the part of *Diana*, first performance of Morton's drama, 'Don't Judge by Appearances' (founded on M. Dutertre's 'Ange et Démon'); and the following year *Beppo* in Morton's play, 'A Prince for an Hour,' and the heroine in the same author's play, 'Our Wife; or, the Rose of Amiens.' On July 1, 1857, she played *Ariel* in a revival of 'The Tempest' at the Princess's; and June 12, 1858, *Nerissa* in a revival of 'The Merchant of Venice.' In June 1860, during a temporary engagement of Mr. Phelps at the Princess's Theatre, Miss Leclercq played *Mrs. Ford* in a revival of 'The Merry Wives of Windsor'; and subsequently (in the follow-ing year) *Mrs. Page*, in the same play. On Saturday, September 28, 1861, first performance in England at the above-named theatre of Brougham's 'Playing with Fire,' she sustained the character of *Mrs. Savage.* Monday, February 10, 1862, at the same theatre, she played *Rosalind* in a revival of 'As You Like It,' as to which the *Athenæum* (February 15, 1862) remarked:—"Miss Carlotta Leclercq is entirely out of place in *Rosalind.* She wants altogether the educational training which such an exquisite creation of poetic fancy requires and implies; nor is her personal appearance suitable to the part. She is too demonstrative, too heavy, too sensuous, where only the ideal, the fantastic, the *spirituel* should prevail." On Saturday, January 10, 1863, first performance of 'The Duke's Motto' at the Lyceum Theatre, under the management of the late Charles Fechter, Miss Leclercq played the part of *Zillah;* and on Saturday, October 22, 1864, first performance at the same theatre of 'The King's Butterfly' (Mr. Fechter in the leading *rôle*), she played *Madame de Pompadour.* December 22, 1865, production at the Lyceum Theatre of Palgrave Simpson's version of 'The Master of Ravenswood,' she personated the part of *Lucy Ashton.* Saturday, April 21, 1866, first appearance at the Lyceum Theatre of Mr. Fechter in the part of *Hamlet*, Miss Carlotta Leclercq performed *Ophelia*, and continued to play that character during the very successful run of the piece. Monday, September 16, 1867, she appeared at the same theatre as *Pauline* in 'The Lady of Lyons,' Mr. Fechter playing Claude Melnotte. On Mr. Fechter's removal to the Adelphi Theatre, and the production there (Saturday, October 17, 1868) of a dramatic version of A. Dumas' novel 'Monte Cristo' (Mr. Fechter as Edmond Dantes), Miss Leclercq played the part of *Mercedes.* In March 1869, first performance at the same theatre of a play entitled 'Black and White,' by Messrs. Wilkie Collins and Charles Fechter, Miss Carlotta Leclercq sustained the part of *Emily Milburn.* During the subsequent seven years, Miss Leclercq acted principally in the United States in the various plays produced there by Mr. Fechter. She returned to England in 1877, and down to the date of her husband's death, in July. 1879, acted with him at the principal theatres in the provinces.

LECLERCQ, ROSE, born in Liverpool ; fourth daughter of the late Charles Leclercq, and sister of Carlotta Leclercq. She made her first appearance of any note Saturday, September 28, 1861, at the Princess's Theatre, London, as *Mrs. Waverly*, first performance in England of 'Playing with Fire' (Brougham). On Monday, September 21, 1863, at Drury Lane, first performance of F. C. Burnand's play, 'The Deal Boatman,' she sustained the part of *Mary Vance* (Mr. Belmore as Jacob Vance). On Saturday, October 10, 1863, on the occasion of the revival at Drury Lane, by Mr. S. Phelps, of 'Manfred' (Byron), she played the part of *The Phantom of Astarté.* "One word uttered by Miss Rose Leclercq—'Manfred !' was the great attraction of that play." (*Athenæum*, April 1, 1871.) On Wednesday, August 12, 1868, she acted the heroine, first performance at Princess's Theatre of 'After Dark' (Boucicault) ; and, in the following year, at the Adelphi, the heroine in the same author's 'Lost at Sea.' Monday, March 7, 1870, at the Princess's Theatre, first performance of Dion Boucicault's play, 'Paul Lafarge,' she sustained the character of the heroine. Saturday, November 26, 1870, revival at the Princess's of 'The Pretty Girls of Stilberg' (Mr. Benjamin Webster in his original character of Napoleon), Miss Rose Leclercq played the part of *Margot.* The following year, at the same theatre, she appeared (February) as *Margaret* in a revival of 'King o' Scots'; (April) as *Marguerite* in a revival of the drama, 'Faust and Marguerite'; (May) as *Mrs. Stirling* in a revival of 'The Clandestine Marriage'; and Tuesday, June 29, 1871, first performance, at the same theatre, of Falconer's drama, 'Eileen Oge; or, Dark's the Hour before Dawn,' she personated the heroine. Saturday, March 2, 1872, revival of 'Ruy Blas' at the Adelphi Theatre, London, with Mr. Fechter in the title *rôle*, Miss Rose Leclercq played the *Queen;* Saturday, September 28, 1872, revival, at the Princess's Theatre, of 'Othello' (Mr. Phelps as the Moor), she performed the part of *Desdemona;* and, in a revival of 'The Merry Wives of Windsor,' at the same theatre, December 19, 1874, she played the part of *Mrs. Ford.* Saturday, September 4, 1875, first performance at Drury Lane of 'The Shaughraun' (Dion Boucicault), Miss Rose Leclercq personated the character of the heroine, *Claire Ffolliott.* "There are at least two characters in this piece which alone would suffice to raise it far above the level of melodrama. The first of these is Conn the Shaughraun, and the other is the heroine, who is not less natural than Conn himself, though in a different way. Her Irish ready wit and sly sense of humour are by a happy exercise of ingenuity not only combined with qualities of a deeper and more earnest kind, but so interwoven with them that they both act and re-act upon each other. The peculiar position of this heroine—admirably performed by Miss Rose Leclercq—is that she is in love with a young gentleman who is not only of the hated Saxon race but a red-coat. What is more, he is actually the officer commanding the detachment who arrest her brother as an escaped rebel. The reluctance with which she perceives the good qualities of this hero and progress of her affection for him, and the hollowness of the coldness with which she receives the young officer's advances, are delightfully portrayed. There is a humorous playfulness even in her sternest moods, and a fertility of resource about her modes of baffling his attempts to look into her secret heart which, together with many other traits of character, are as subtle and refined as they are fresh and pleasing." (*Daily News*, September 6, 1875.)

Since the year 1875 Miss Rose Leclercq has been mostly engaged travelling as "star" in the provinces; appearing in such parts as *Galatea* ('Pygmalion and Galatea'), *Hilda* ('Broken Hearts'), comedies by Mr. W. S. Gilbert; and as *Ruth* in 'Ruth's Romance.' Probably, Miss Rose Leclercq's greatest dramatic triumph has been achieved in the character of *Liz*, 'That Lass o' Lowrie's,' in the drama of that title, a part which she has performed with much success both in London and the provinces. The *Manchester Examiner* noticed this performance as follows :—"Perhaps no other actress could be found on the English stage at the present time so well qualified in every way to assume the difficult part of the title *rôle* as Miss Rose Leclercq. Her commanding presence, her boldness in defying her father, and her courage in rescuing Fergus Derrick from the burning mine, stand out in bold relief against the pathos and tenderness displayed at several stages of the play, and notably in the second act, where her interview with Alice Barholm, the daughter of the mine-owner, is particularly affecting."

LEE, JENNIE (Mrs. J. P. BURNETT), daughter of Edwin George Lee, artist ; born in London. After her father's death she entered the dramatic profession, and first appeared on the stage at the Lyceum Theatre as "a page" in ' Chilperic.' Subsequently, in 1870, at the same theatre, under the Mansell's management, in ' Le Petit Faust ' she played " the crossing-sweeper," and secured favourable notice for her skilful rendering of the part. Miss Lee was afterwards engaged by Mrs. Swanborough, of the Strand Theatre, for " leading burlesque," and appeared there in July 1870 as *Prince Ahmed* in ' The Pilgrim of Love.' She remained at the Strand Theatre for two seasons. Subsequently she accepted an engagement from Mr. Sothern, and accompanied him to the United States, " opening " at Niblo's Theatre, New York, as *Mary Meredith* in ' Our American Cousin.' Miss J. Lee was " leading soubrette " at that theatre until it was destroyed by fire ; and then became a member of the company of the Union Square Theatre, in the same city, playing the same " line of business." She subsequently went to San Francisco, and appeared at the California Theatre, where Miss Lee remained for a period of two years. While at this theatre she appeared for the first time as *Jo* in the play of that title, a version of ' Bleak House,' adapted from Charles Dickens's novel by J. P. Burnett. Miss Lee's impersonation of the part was a remarkable success. In August 1875 she returned to England, and, in London, played at the Surrey Theatre for the Christmas season. Having leased the Globe Theatre for a time, on February 22, 1876, Miss Lee " opened " with *Jo*, playing the part with " a realism and a pathos difficult to surpass. A more striking revelation of talent has seldom been made. In get-up and in acting the character was thoroughly realized ; and the hoarse voice, the slouching, dejected gait, and the movement as of some hunted animal, were admirably exhibited " (*Athenæum*, February 26, 1876). Miss Lee has since acted the same character with unvarying success at all the principal theatres in the provinces.

LEIGHTON, MARGARET, daughter of J. Davies, Esq., J.P. of Brecknockshire ; born in Brecon, South Wales. She made her first appearance on any stage at the Queen's Theatre, London, March 1874, in the character of *Julia*, in ' The Hunchback.' " Miss Leighton has an excellent voice and an expressive cast of countenance ; but what is of greater importance she possesses histrionic power of high order. Her performance was distinguished by tenderness, force, and passion, each point being made the very most of, and securing hearty applause. Miss Leighton was called before the curtain at the conclusion of every act and loudly cheered." (*Daily News*, March 1874.) Subsequently at the same theatre she played various Shakespearian parts. In October 1874 she played *Romeo* at the Prince's Theatre, Manchester, in Mr. Calvert's revival of that play. She next appeared at the Queen's Theatre, London, under Mr. John Hollingshead's management, playing *Evadne* in ' The Bridal ' (Beaumont and Fletcher), and the parts of *Desdemona* (' Othello ') and *Portia* (' Merchant of Venice ').

Shortly afterwards, with her own company, Miss Leighton went on a tour in the provinces, appearing as *Marie Stuart* in the play called 'The Gascon.' She reappeared September 1876 at the Queen's Theatre, London, as *Chorus* in a grand revival there of Shakespeare's 'Henry V.' In a notice of this performance the *Daily Telegraph* (September 1876) said :—" Perhaps the most difficult task was that allotted to Miss Leighton, a young actress of decided and marked ability. To play *Chorus* in this play, and to speak a prologue to the enterprise, means to run the risk of ridicule and to break in more than once upon the patience of the audience. But Miss Leighton held her own bravely. She could not possibly have done so had she been less correct in her elocution or less earnest in her work. The use and meaning of a chorus can only be known to a limited number in a general assembly; but Miss Leighton thoroughly succeeded in banishing laughter and creating attention by the polish of her recitation and the round resonance of her voice."

Miss Leighton played the part of *Haska* on the first performance of Mr. Spicer's play of that name at Drury Lane Theatre ; and, subsequently, the character of the *Countess of Derby* in Mr. W. G. Wills's play ' England,' produced at Drury Lane, September 1877. The following season she sustained the part of *Formosa* in a revival of Boucicault's drama of that name at the Adelphi Theatre, London.

LE THIÈRE, ROMA GUILLON, made her first appearance on the London stage at the New Royalty Theatre, 1865, in the character of *Emilia* (' Othello '). Subsequently she played in ' Hunted Down ' at the St. James's (*see* HERBERT, LOUISA) ; ' Life for Life' at the Lyceum ; ' Ours ' (revival) at the Prince of Wales's Theatre ; the melodrama of ' Rob Roy,' in which she played *Helen Macgregor*, at Drury Lane Theatre ; and after fulfilling an engagement with Mrs. John Wood at the St. James's, on January 12, 1878, sustained the part of the *Marquise de Rio Zares*, first performance of ' Diplomacy ' at the Prince of Wales's Theatre. " Especial attention may be invited to the scene between mother and daughter in the first act, so excellently sustained by Miss Le Thière as the *Marquise de Rio Zares*, and Mrs. Kendal as Dora. We have here a picture of pure and tender affection approached in an earnest spirit and touched by both ladies with graceful skill, a scene instinct with variety, charm, and truth. The dreary doubts of Dora as to the value of such a broken life as her's are with intense expression softened by the abiding presence of her good old mother's love." (*Daily Telegraph*, February 8, 1878.) Miss Le Thière has appeared in revivals of ' Caste ' at the same theatre. In July 1869 she produced at the Haymarket Theatre " a new and original comedy," written by her, entitled ' All for Money,' in which Miss Amy Sedgwick, Mr. Henry Irving, and Mrs. Stephens appeared. The piece was, however, a failure.

LEWIS, MRS. ARTHUR. *See* TERRY, KATE.

*LITTON, MARIE, first obtained notice as an actress by her praiseworthy performance of the part of *Effie Deans*,† in a revival of Boucicault's revised version of the play of 'The Trial of Effie Deans,' presented on the Princess's stage, March 23, 1868, under the title of 'Jeannie Deans.' It may be remarked that the first-mentioned drama was produced at the Theatre Royal, Westminster (Astley's Theatre), January 26, 1863, Mrs. Boucicault in the leading *rôle.* On the occasion of the opening of the Gaiety Theatre, Monday, December 21, 1868, Miss Litton appeared in the English version of MM. d'Ennery and Brevil's 'L'Escamoteur,' entitled 'On the Cards,' the late Mr. Alfred Wigan in the leading *rôle;* and at the same theatre in the following year (December 1869) she appeared in 'Uncle Dick's Darling' (H. J. Byron). Subsequently Miss Litton became connected with the Brighton Theatre for a period. January 25, 1871, she opened the Court Theatre under her management, and produced various plays, among which W. S. Gilbert's 'Randall's Thumb' (first performed on the opening night) ; the same author's 'The Happy Land,' 'Alone,' and 'Wedding March,' and Mr. Bronson Howard's 'Brighton' were conspicuous. In 1873 she was engaged for a time at the Haymarket Theatre, and appeared, Saturday, January 4 of that year, in Mr. Gilbert's play 'The Wicked World' as *Zayda.* In 1875 she was acting at St. James's Theatre, and secured favourable notice for her performance in the comedy of 'Tom Cobb.' At the Prince of Wales's Theatre in 1877 she acted the character of *Mrs. Montressor* in 'The Unequal Match.' In the autumn of 1878 Miss Litton undertook the management of the theatre attached to the Aquarium, Westminster, and appeared during the season in a series of performances of old comedy. This theatre was subsequently (1879), under the same management, opened under the designation of the Imperial Theatre, with an effective company of comedians. Among the revivals of old comedies by Miss Litton in 1878-9, 'The Liar' and 'She Stoops to Conquer' claim notice. Her acting of the part of *Miss Hardcastle* in the first-named play was especially successful.

*LOSEBY, CONSTANCE, had earned some reputation as a public singer previous to her first appearance on the London stage, which took place at the opening of the Gaiety Theatre under Mr. Hollingshead's management, in December 1868, in Mr. Jonas's comic operetta 'The Two Harlequins.' Her *début* was favourably noticed in the *Daily News* (December 23, 1868) as follows :—" Mr. Hollingshead's programme includes several first appearances, one of which at least is the occasion of introducing to the public a valuable acquisition to the stage. We allude to Miss Constance Loseby, a lady whose performances have hitherto, we believe, been confined to the music-halls. As an actress in

† This performance is treated by the *Era* (March 29, 1868) as Miss Litton's first appearance on the stage. In a notice of her acting, published on that date, she is stated to be "not only a stranger to this theatre, but, as we are informed, entirely new to the stage."— ED.

operetta and burlesque Miss Loseby is fully equal to the performance of leading parts, while she possesses a mezzo-soprano
voice of considerable power. This was manifested at once, in
spite of her evident nervousness, by her pleasant rendering of the
song 'When husbands run away.'" She remained at the Gaiety
for six years (1868–74), playing leading *rôles* in various burlesques
placed on its stage : 'Thespis ; or, the Gods Grown Old' (W. S.
Gilbert), 'Aladdin the Second' (Hervé), 'Princess of Trebizonde'
(Offenbach), 'Trombalcazar' (rendered into English by C. H.
Stephenson), &c., &c. Later, Miss Loseby became engaged at
the Alhambra Theatre, where she has since successfully appeared
in several versions of French comic operas.

LYLE, ARTHUR, was born in London, and made his first
appearance on the stage at Brighton in 1863 in one of the minor
parts in 'Society.' Subsequently he performed for some years in
the provinces with more than ordinary success, and made his
début on the London stage at the Standard Theatre in June 1878
in the part of *Phil Lowrie* in the drama of 'Liz' ('That Lass o'
Lowrie's ').

LYONS, EDMUND D., born in Edinburgh, February 29,
1851. He entered the dramatic profession in boyhood under the
auspices of his father, the late Mr. E. D. Lyons, lessee of the
Theatre Royal, Dundee, and of Mr. and Mrs. R. H. Wyndham,
of the Theatre Royal, Edinburgh ; his first appearance in a part
of any importance being at the Dundee Theatre in 1864. He
was a member of the "stock" company of the Theatre Royal,
Edinburgh, in 1870. In 1874 he travelled with J. L. Toole through
the principal provincial towns as *The Judge* in 'Wig and Gown.'
The same year he became a member of the company of the
Alexandra Theatre, Liverpool, under Mr. Saker's management.
On April 15, 1876, he sustained the part of *Captain Manuel* in
Wilkie Collins's 'Miss Gwilt,' on the occasion of the first production of that play at the Globe Theatre in London, and he
was for a short period stage-manager at that theatre. At the
Christmas season 1876 he produced the pantomime at the Theatre
Royal, Bristol, under Mr. James Chute's management ; and afterwards joined the so-called 'Caste' company for a short season
during the summer months of 1877, playing in the provinces the
following characters—*Hon. Bruce Fanquehere, Prince Perovsky*,
and *Beau Farintosh.* On August 29, 1877, he joined the Lyceum
company, under Mrs. Bateman's management, and sustained with
excellent effect the character of *Joseph Buschmann* on the first
production of Wilkie Collins's drama of 'The Dead Secret,' subsequently appearing at the same theatre as *Pierre Choppard*
('Lyons Mail '), and (April 1878) as *Marcel* ('Louis XI.').

LYONS, ROBERT CHARLES, born October 31, 1853 ; son
of the late Mr. E. D. Lyons, of Edinburgh, sometime lessee and
manager of the Theatre Royal, Dundee. He has 'been, more or

less, connected with the dramatic profession from boyhood, and made his professional *début* March 1869, at the Theatre Royal, Edinburgh, under the management of Mr. R. H. Wyndham. He played in the grand revival of 'Rob Roy' at that theatre, August 1, 1871 ("the Scott Centenary Celebration"). Subsequently Mr. Lyons accepted an engagement with Mr. J. L. Toole for a short tour in the provinces in May 1874 ; and afterwards returned to the Theatre Royal, Edinburgh, of the "stock" company of which he remained a member until the theatre was destroyed by fire, February 6, 1875. He opened in Liverpool at the Alexandra Theatre, under the management of Mr. Saker, March 1, 1875, as *Charles Courtly* in 'London Assurance,' subsequently playing during this engagement such parts as *Sir Thomas Clifford, Eugène de L'Orme, Jacques, Mercutio,* &c. During his stay at Liverpool Mr. R. C. Lyons played a special engagement at the Rotunda Theatre in a round of Scotch comedy. On the 9th December, 1875, he played *Allan Armadale,* in Wilkie Collins's drama of ' Miss Gwilt,' first produced at the Alexandra Theatre, Liverpool, prior to its production in London. He made his first appearance on the London stage (in the same character) at the Globe Theatre, April 15, 1876, under the management of Miss Ada Cavendish. He was engaged by Mrs. Bateman for Mr. H. Irving's provincial tour, September 14, 1876; and subsequently joined the company of the Lyceum Theatre in London, and played in the two productions of the seasons immediately following, viz. *Hastings* (' Richard III.'), *Monsieur Couriol* (' Lyons Mail ').

MACKINTOSH, WILLIAM, was born in Melbourne, Australia, July 23, 1855, and first appeared on the stage December 24, 1872, at the Theatre Royal, Elgin, in a subordinate part in a piece entitled ' Christmas Eve.' He entered upon his first important engagement with Mrs. John Wood at the Gaiety Theatre, Dublin, June 21, 1875, appearing as *Crabtree* (' School for Scandal '), *Mark Meddle* (' London Assurance '), &c. In 1876 he played various parts at the Gaiety Theatre, Glasgow, during the engagements of the late Mr. Charles Mathews, Mr. and Mrs. Kendal, &c. In the following year Mr. Mackintosh appeared at the Prince of Wales's Theatre, Liverpool, as *Flop* (' Bounce '), *Jacques Strop* (' Robert Macaire '), *Peckover* (' The Contested Election '), *Whiskerandos* (' The Critic '), *Touchstone* (' As You Like It '), &c., and at other leading theatres in the provinces, for the most part in support of " star " actors. He made his *début* on the London stage at the Royal Court Theatre, January 4, 1879, as *Dr. Penguin* in a revival of ' A Scrap of Paper,' his performance of the part being noticed in the following terms in the *Athenæum* (January 11, 1879) :— " Of the new comers, one, Mr. Mackintosh, seems likely to be of high service to the company at the Court. The get-up of Mr. Mackintosh was admirable, a new and quite recognizable type of comic character being presented. In other respects the performance was excellent, though it was not free from exaggeration in the later scenes." At the same theatre (at a morning performance), Saturday, April 19, 1879, he played the part of *Sam Pilcher* in 'The Queen's Shilling,' a new version, by G. W. Godfrey, of ' Le Fils de Famille.'

MACKLIN, FRANCIS HENRY, was born in London 1848, and entered the dramatic profession under the pseudonym of " F. Manton " in 1873. He made his first appearance on the stage in June of that year, at the Queen's Theatre, Long Acre, under Miss Litton's management, as *Melun* in ' King John.' Afterwards he went on tour with a company of which the same lady was manager ; and in September 1873 joined Mr. Chatterton's Drury Lane and Adelphi companies, playing at the former of these theatres in a revival of ' Antony and Cleopatra,' and at the latter in ' Green Bushes,' with Madame Celeste in the cast. At the Adelphi he played his first original part, *Harry Valentine*, in a play by Paul Meritt, entitled ' Rough and Ready.' Assuming his own name in 1874, Mr. Macklin played several provincial engagements, notably at the Prince's Theatre, Manchester, where, among other parts, he played *Prince John* in a revival of ' Henry the Fourth.' At the Queen's Theatre, in the same city, he played *Romeo* to the Juliet of Miss Ada Cavendish. Afterwards returning to London, in May 1875, at the Mirror Theatre, he played the original *Laurence Lindon* in ' The Detective,' a version of ' Le Parricide,' by Clement Scott. The acting of this character served to bring Mr. Macklin into notice, although the play itself was not a success. Subsequently he fulfilled various provincial engagements. In January 1876, at the Olympic Theatre in London, he performed the leading character of *Tom Mayfield* in J. Hatton's drama entitled ' Clytie '; and in the March following appeared at the Duke's Theatre in Mr. Craven's drama ' Too True.' Mr. Macklin has since undertaken engagements at the Opéra Comique and St. James's Theatre, and at the Globe Theatre, where he appeared in ' Stolen Kisses,' and at various times has played such parts as *Falkland* (' The Rivals '), *Young Marlow* (' She Stoops to Conquer '), *Captain Hawksley* (' Still Waters Run Deep '), *Mr. Chevenix* (' Uncle Dick's Darling '), *Charles Courtly* (' London Assurance '). In April and May 1878 he supported Miss Neilson during her engagement at the Haymarket, playing the following characters : *Mercutio, Angelo,* and *Modus.* In September 1878 Mr. Macklin accepted an engagement at the Olympic Theatre, where he played *Chevalier de Vaudray* in a revival of ' The Two Orphans.' At the same theatre during the same engagement he appeared as *Joseph Goupille* in a new and original comedy-drama by Mrs. Holford, entitled ' A Republican Marriage.' In 1879 he went on tour in the provinces in a company under the management of Miss Helen Barry.

MACLEAN, JOHN, was born in London. He began his professional career on the stage in 1859, at the Theatre Royal, Plymouth. Previous to this he had been engaged in giving dramatic readings in conjunction with Mr. T. J. Searle, one of the literary staff of the *Weekly Dispatch.* During the last provincial tour of Mr. and Mrs. Charles Kean, while they were performing at the Theatre Royal, Plymouth, Mr. Maclean undertook to play the *King* in ' Hamlet ' at very short notice, and was complimented on this occasion by Mr. Kean for the excellent manner in which he had rendered the character. Afterwards Mr. Maclean entered upon engagements at Jersey and Guernsey, and, later, at Birmingham. In 1861 he made his first appearance on the London stage at the Surrey Theatre ; and in 1862 was engaged by the management of the Olympic Theatre to play the part of *Mr. Gibson* in ' The Ticket-of-Leave Man.' Afterwards he became a member of the company of the New Surrey Theatre, under Mr. Shepherd's management. Subsequently Mr. Maclean appeared at the Princess's Theatre in ' The Man o' Airlie.' In 1868 he was enrolled a member of the company of the Gaiety Theatre, under Mr. John Hollingshead's management, and continued to perform there in almost all the various plays produced under Mr. Hollingshead's supervision down to the year 1879 inclusive.

MAISEY, ELISE, commenced her professional career in 1875, when she created a favourable impression by her acting in various *rôles* in the legitimate drama at the Rotunda Theatre, Liverpool. During 1877–8 she was acting with success at Aberdeen and other northern towns, principally in Shakespearian characters, *Juliet,*

Ophelia, Rosalind, &c. She made her *début* on the London stage at the Olympic Theatre, in July 1878, in the part of *Euphrasie Dupont* in 'Vivianne ; or, the Romance of a French Marriage,' adapted, "by the author of 'The Member for Paris' and Mr. George Canninge," from a story published in the 'Cornhill Magazine' entitled " Mdlle. Vivian." Subsequently, in the provinces, Miss Maisey played very effectively the part of *Valentine* in 'Proof; or, a Celebrated Case,' with a company organized under Mr. Wilson Barrett's direction.

MARIUS, CLAUDE (a *nom de théâtre;* CLAUDE MARIUS DUPLANY), born February 18, 1850, at Paris. He entered the dramatic profession in 1865 as an auxiliary at the Folies Dramatiques, playing parts in most of the popular pieces presented there for a brief period. In 1869 he came to London, and appeared at the Lyceum Theatre in the characters of *Landry* in ' Chilperic,' and of *Siebel* in ' Little Faust.' M. Duplany joined the French Army during the Franco-Prussian war; but in 1872 returned to London, and, at the Philharmonic Theatre, appeared as *Charles Martel* and *Drogan* in ' Généviève de Brabant.' Subsequently " M. Marius " joined the company of the Strand Theatre, where he has played and " created " many parts, among them the following : viz. *Major Roland de Roncevaux* in 'Nemesis,' *Rimbombo* in 'Loo,' *Baron Victor de Karadec* in 'Family Ties,' *Orloff* in 'Dora and Diplunacy,' and *Dubuisson* in ' Our Club.' On Saturday, April 12, 1879, first performance at the Strand of an English version of Offenbach's ' Madame Favart,' he sustained the *rôle* of *M. Favart.*

MARKBY, ROBERT BREMNER, youngest son of the late Rev. W. H. Markby, sometime Fellow of Corpus Christi College, and rector of Duxford St. Peter's, Cambridge, received his education at Marlborough College. He had acted on the provincial stage, at Glasgow, Dublin, Liverpool, &c., previous to his first appearance in London, which was made at the Court Theatre, Saturday, October 28, 1871, in the part of *Denis Grant* in W. S. Gilbert's comedy ' On Guard.' In the following year, in May, in a revival of 'Leah' at the Lyceum Theatre, Miss Bateman in the title *rôle,* Mr. Markby acted the character of *Father Hermann* "with great vigour and dramatic force." At the same theatre, Saturday, September 28, 1872, first performance of ' Charles the First ' (W. G. Wills), he sustained the part of *Ireton.* In 1873, in the provinces and in London (at the Charing Cross Theatre), he acted the character of *Rev. Julian Gray* in Mr. Wilkie Collins's drama ' The New Magdalen,' Miss Ada Cavendish in the leading *rôle.* In this part Mr. Markby proved himself a careful and efficient actor, and secured well-merited praise. At the Prince of Wales's Theatre he has appeared in revivals of ' The School for Scandal ' as *Trip,* and of ' Masks and Faces ' as *Snarl,* and at the St. James's Theatre as *Dazzle* in ' London Assurance ' and *Lord Lovell* in ' A New Way to Pay Old Debts.'

MARRIOTT, ALICE (Mrs. R. EDGAR), made her first appearance on the London stage at Drury Lane Theatre in December 1854 as *Bianca* in 'Fazio'; and in the following month, at the same theatre, sustained the title *rôle* in Boucicault's drama 'Eugénie,' then performed for the first time. Miss Marriott remained a member of the company of Drury Lane Theatre for some seasons; but in 1861 entered upon the management of the Standard Theatre for a brief period. Here, on Monday, May 27, 1861, she produced Westland Marston's play 'Anne Blake,' and performed the title *rôle*. In February 1862, at the Princess's Theatre, she undertook the part of *The Angel of Midnight* in Brougham's play of that title, adapted from the French of MM. Barrière and Plouvier. In 1863 Miss Marriott entered upon the management of Sadler's Wells Theatre, and on Saturday, September 5, "opened" with Lovell's play of 'Love's Sacrifice,' herself sustaining the part of *Margaret*. On Monday, November 9 of the same year, she produced, at the same theatre, a play in four acts, by Westland Marston, entitled 'Pure Gold,' in which she acted the part of *Evelyn Rochford*. During 1863-4, at Sadler's Wells, Miss Marriott appeared in the following characters, viz.: November 20, *Virginia*, in the tragedy of 'Virginius'; January 23, 1864, the *Duchess of Malfi*, in Webster's tragedy of that name; February 22, 1864, the character of *Hamlet*, in Shakespeare's tragedy; September 17, 1864, the *Countess*, in Sheridan Knowles's play of 'Love;' and later, *Lady Macbeth* and *Juliet*, "showing the versatility of her talent by sustaining both with such points of discrimination as prove a remarkable power of artistic adaptation. . . . The extent of her range is a qualification which peculiarly fits her for the management of a theatre in which she must herself play the leading Shakespearian characters." (*Athenæum*, October 1, 1864.) Miss Marriott retained the management of Sadler's Wells Theatre for a period of six years. She has appeared with success in the United States in leading *rôles* in the legitimate drama, and is now (1879) travelling in the provinces with a company known as "Miss Marriott's Dramatic Company."

MARSH, HENRY. *See* MARSTON, HENRY.

MARSHALL, FREDERICK, born in Glasgow, November 5, 1848; he was educated to the stage from childhood, appearing as one of "The Marshall Family" in various dramatic pieces written by his father, C. F. Marshall. His first engagement as a member of the dramatic profession proper was at the New Theatre Royal, Bristol. In Easter, 1870, at the Theatre Royal, Bradford, he played the character of *Quilp*, in a version of 'The Old Curiosity Shop,' written by C. Rice. This performance was so far a success that it had a long run on tour in the provinces. Subsequently Mr. Marshall became a member of the company of the New Theatre Royal, Nottingham; and, later on, of the Prince of Wales's, Liverpool. At this theatre he played several important parts in "revivals," notably *Biles* ('Miriam's Crime'), *Peter Probity* ('The Chimney Corner'), *Daniel*

White ('Milky White'), *Sampson Burr* ('Porter's Knot'). March 29, 1875, Mr. Marshall opened at the Philharmonic Theatre, London, in a burlesque entitled 'The Talisman'; and also again enacted the part of *Peter Probity*, in which he was very successful. March 6, 1876, he was engaged by Mr. W. S. Gilbert to play the character of *Mousta* in 'Broken Hearts,' for a lengthened tour through England and Scotland. "The best piece of acting in the performance is undoubtedly that of Mr. F. Marshall as *Mousta*, the dwarf. Highly effective, in a quiet, subdued style, was the expression of feeling in the passages where the deformed creature pleads for the love of the queenly Hilda, and still finer the rendering of utter prostration, physical and mental, as he sinks under her reproaches." (*Scotsman*, July 11, 1876.) In September 1876 Mr. Marshall joined Mr. Duck's so-called 'Our Boys' company of comedians, playing the parts of *Perkyn Middlewick* ('Our Boys') and *Percy Pendragon* ('Married in Haste') with much success. In June 1877 he was engaged as a member of Miss Lydia Thompson's travelling company, and visited the United States, performing at New York, Boston, Philadelphia, Baltimore, &c. Returning to England December 1877, he afterwards fulfilled a two months' engagement (June–July 1878) at the Vaudeville Theatre, London, appearing as *Perkyn Middlewick*. In April 1879 he sailed for a tour in Australia.

MARSTON, HENRY (a *nom de théâtre;* HENRY MARSH), born at Highworth, March 1804; son of Dr. Marsh, a well-known Wiltshire physician. He was educated at Winchester School, and in early life studied law in the chambers of Messrs. Jay and Thomson, of Gray's Inn. Mr. Marston made his first appearance on the stage at Salisbury, in November 1824, as *Florian*, in a play entitled 'The Foundling of the Forest.' For several successive years he played with all the histrionic celebrities of the time, Miss Foote, Miss Smithson, Madame Vestris, Mrs. Glover, the elder Kean, Charles Kemble, Macready, Charles Kean, Dowton, Liston, and John Reeve (*see* CRESWICK), making, in London, eventually a very successful appearance at Drury Lane, October 31, 1839, as *Benedick*, in the comedy of 'Much Ado About Nothing.'* The more prominent part of Mr. Marston's professional career belongs to the period of the late Mr. Samuel Phelps's management of Sadler's Wells Theatre. Of that excellent actor's company Mr. Marston was a conspicuous and popular member, taking a leading part in nearly all the Shakespearian revivals for which (1844–59) the little theatre at Islington became famous. It would be impossible to select for special mention any one *rôle* in the legitimate drama in the presentation of which Mr. Marston excelled over and above another. For fifty-five years he devoted his energies almost solely to the interpretation of that drama (indeed, he might justly be considered the last of the Kemble school), and, during that time, he appeared in more plays of Shakespeare than has fallen to the lot of

* For these particulars I am indebted to the *Era*, April 1879.—ED.

any principal living tragedian.   Of plays, nowadays not so well known to playgoers as when Mr. Phelps "redeemed Sadler's Wells from clowns and waterworks, and made it a not unworthy shrine of Shakespeare," * in which Mr. Marston played a part, 'Timon of Athens,' 'Pericles, Prince of Tyre,' 'The Comedy of Errors,' 'The Taming of the Shrew,' and Beaumont and Fletcher's 'A King and No King,' are entitled to particular notice.   When Mr. Phelps produced the first-named play it had been acted but few times since the days of Shakespeare, and in the revival Mr. Marston acted *Apemantus*, and by his conception of the character "helped much to secure a right understanding of the entire play" (*Journal of a London Playgoer*, Prof. H. Morley, p. 155).   In 'A King and No King,' which attracted the best judges of the drama to Islington, Mr. Marston appeared as *Tigranes.*   The writer just quoted makes mention of the excellent acting of Mr. Marston in Bickerstaff's 'Hypocrite,' at the same theatre, in October 1858, and of his judicious rendering of the part of *Manly* in 'The Provoked Husband,' in the same year.†   He also acted in Shakespearian drama at Drury Lane and Covent Garden, and other theatres in London and the provinces, with success.   On Thursday, May 29, 1879, a special performance of 'Much Ado About Nothing' was given at the Lyceum Theatre for the benefit of Mr. Marston.   It is gratifying to record that many of the best known actors and actresses of the English stage lent their services on this occasion, contributing greatly to its success, and aiding in no small degree, by the pecuniary results of their kindly co-operation, to make smoother the passage of Mr. Marston's declining years, unfortunately somewhat roughly assailed by ill-health.

MARTIN, MRS. THEODORE.   *See* FAUCIT, HELEN.

* **MASSEY, ROSE,** began her professional career at the Haymarket Theatre, July 1, 1867, as *Mary Meredith* in 'Our American Cousin,' but attracted little notice as an actress until her appearance in the pantomime of 'Blue Beard' in 1871 at Covent Garden Theatre, under the management of the late Mr. Augustus Harris, when she played *Fatima*.   Later she appeared as leading lady at the Globe Theatre with the late H. J. Montague, and afterwards

---

* Speech of Mr. W. F. Fox, M.P., at the farewell banquet to Mr. Macready, March 1851.

† A correspondent of the *Daily News*, writing under date April 16, 1879, bears the following testimony to the dramatic ability of Mr. Marston :— "As well as myself, there are, I believe, very many remaining who were habitual frequenters of the performances at Sadler's Wells during the memorable campaign there of Mr. Phelps, and who ever recur to them with a living and grateful memory. . . .   I know it to have been the opinion of the majority (and including the more intelligent and cultured) of the old Wells frequenters, that they were indebted to Mr. Marston's acting, next to that of his chief and manager's, for the excellence of the performances there as a whole, and which, moving and delighting at the time, abide fixed and fresh in the memory."

went to America, where she fulfilled several engagements. She has appeared at all the principal London theatres.

MATHEWS, MRS. CHARLES (formerly Mrs. DAVENPORT), relict of the late Charles Mathews, the younger, was an actress of some note on the American stage previous to her second marriage. She made her first appearance on the London stage Monday, October 11, 1858, at the Haymarket Theatre, as *Lady Gay Spanker* in 'London Assurance,' Mr. Charles Mathews playing *Dazzle*, his original part. Subsequently, at the same theatre, Mrs. Mathews played in various pieces :—*Nannette Didier*, in a play adapted by her husband from a comédie-vaudeville of MM. Bayard and Dumanoir, 'La Vicomtesse Lolotte,' entitled 'The Milliner to the King'; and afterwards in 'Nothing to Wear,' from the French 'En Manches de Chemise.' In March 1859 she played (with Mr. Charles Mathews), at the Haymarket, *Mrs. Featherby* in Stirling Coyne's 'Everybody's Friend.' She was the original *Mrs. Honeybun* of Tom Taylor's 'The Contested Election,' first performed at the same theatre June 29, 1859. September of the same year she played at the Haymarket Theatre *Sophia* in 'The Road to Ruin,' her husband as Goldfinch ; and *Phœbe* in 'Paul Pry,' Mr. Mathews in the title *rôle*. Thursday, February 23, 1860, first performance of Mr. Tom Taylor's comedy 'The Overland Route,' she sustained the character of *Mrs. Sebright*, Mr. Charles Mathews playing Tom Dexter. During 1861 Mrs. Mathews continued to play at the Haymarket Theatre ; and in 1862 for a short season appeared with her husband at the Bijou Theatre then adjoining Her Majesty's Theatre. In 1864 she played at the St. James's Theatre in a burlesque by Burnand entitled 'Faust and Marguerite,' appearing in the latter character. Mrs. Charles Mathews has rarely appeared on the stage since the above date, and finally retired from it some years ago.

MEAD, T., born in Cambridge, August 22, 1819, and entered the dramatic profession in 1841 at the Devonport Theatre, under the management of Mr. James Dawson, making his first appearance as *Orozembo* in 'Pizarro.' Having met with success, he was subsequently engaged by Mr. Roxby, of the Sunderland circuit, in whose company he travelled the provinces for some time, playing any line of business that offered. He made his first appearance on the London stage November 8, 1848, at the Victoria Theatre, in the character of *Sir Giles Overreach*. Afterwards (shortly before Easter, 1849), being engaged by Mr. Shepherd, of the Surrey Theatre, he appeared there during that year as *Othello, Colonna* ('Evadne'), &c., and as *Almagro*, in Sheridan Knowles's 'Rose of Arragon,' being noticed in the *Athenæum* (September 22, 1849) as "an energetic performer of considerable promise." Mr. Mead remained at the Surrey Theatre from 1849 to 1852, and became a great favourite with its habitués. He was shortly afterwards engaged at Drury Lane Theatre, under E. T. Smith's management, and played there, among other parts, *Hamlet, Iago, Macduff,*

Claude Melnotte, Duke Aranza, Wellborn, and *Chateau Renaud.*
Mr. Mead was a member of the company of the St. James's
Theatre (for "leading business and stage-management") under
Mrs. Seymour. In 1858 he was enrolled as leading actor at the
New Grecian Theatre. In subsequent years he fulfilled engage-
ments at Sadler's Wells, playing the leading parts with Miss
Marriott. At the Princess's Theatre he was the "original" *Isaac
Levy* in 'Never Too Late to Mend,' and *Crawly* in 'The Streets
of London.' Afterwards Mr. Mead became lessee and manager
of the Elephant and Castle Theatre for a short period. At the
Queen's Theatre he played the leading part in the first performance
of Charles Reade's drama 'Rachel the Reaper.' He was engaged
at the Lyceum Theatre, under Mrs. Bateman's management, to
perform in the Shakespearian revivals and other plays produced
under the supervision of Mr. Irving. He is still (June 1879) performing there, having appeared during his engagement in the
following parts, viz. *The Ghost* ('Hamlet'), 1st *Witch* ('Macbeth'),
Brabantio ('Othello'), *Lord Howard* ('Queen Mary'), 1st *Murderer* ('Richard III.'), &c., &c. Mr. Mead is the author of a play
produced at the Haymarket, July 8, 1867, under the title of 'The
Coquette,' in which Miss Amy Sedgwick played the leading part.

MELLON, MRS. ALFRED (*née* WOOLGAR, SARAH J.), was born
in 1824, and made her professional *début* in London in September
1843, at the old Adelphi Theatre, in a duologue entitled 'Antony
and Cleopatra.' At the beginning of her career Miss Woolgar's
versatile talents were generally employed in burlesque, in which
she attained great repute. Her name will, however, be more
generally and favourably known in connection with the series of
domestic dramas for which the old Adelphi, under Mr. Benjamin
Webster's management, and during Madame Celeste's popularity,
became famous. Among the more important of those in which
Miss Woolgar played on the occasion of their first performance
may be noted the following :—'The Flowers of the Forest'
(*Lemuel*), 'The Marble Heart' (*Marie*), 'The Willow Copse'
(*Meg*), 'The Dead Heart' (*Catherine Duval*), &c. Besides the
foregoing plays in which Miss Woolgar's acting invariably commanded praise, the following characters and pieces in which she
has also appeared on the London stage are entitled to mention,
viz. on April 9, 1853, at the Adelphi Theatre, the *Widow Somerton*,
in a farce of more than ordinary merit, by Mr. M. Morton, entitled
'A Desperate Game'; on Wednesday, July 20 of the same year,
the leading *rôle* in Mark Lemon's burlesque of 'Sardanapalus';
on Monday, March 30, 1854, *Anne Musgrave*, first performance of
Messrs. Tom Taylor and Charles Reade's drama, 'Two Loves
and a Life,' "a drama built on an interesting story, with many and
various incidents, and with important personages enough to employ
a large number of good actors. In addition to this qualification,
which it has in common with many other effective Adelphi pieces,
it has the strange peculiarity that it is not taken from the French,
but is really spun in the first instance from the brains of Mr. Tom

Taylor and Mr. Charles Reade. It is in four acts. . . . . The assemblage of more incidents than are altogether consistent with the laws of probability, and the nature of the situations themselves, stamp this work with the character of melodrama. But it rises above the ordinary level of that class of entertainment by the carefulness and good taste displayed in the writing. The contrast between the two females, one of more feminine, the other of sterner stuff, is well conceived, as a new element of melodramatic action, while it seems to draw out most advantageously the opposite peculiarities of Miss Woolgar and Madame Celeste." (*Times*, March 21, 1854.) At Easter, 1854, at the Adelphi Theatre, she played *Lord Bateman* in Brough's ' Overland Journey to Constantinople,' &c. " The most marked performance in the piece is that of Miss Woolgar as the famous *Lord Bateman;* particularly in the second part of the drama, where, after an absence from his Sophia for ' seven long years and fourteen days,' his mind reverts to its first love while on the point of contracting a marriage with a new bride, and manifests a state of abstraction and uneasiness peculiarly dramatic. Mr. Brough's burlesques often become serious verities, and for a while sink the fun and bustle in real pathos, with which what is called humour, as distinct from wit, readily coalesces. The scene to which we allude is an instance in point, and was acted by Miss Woolgar with truth and effect. Such painting is like Nature's own, and, we were struck with it in the situation we have described as something worthy of being included with efforts of Art." (*Athenæum*, April 22, 1854.)

In the same year, on Monday, December 11, she played the part of *Marie Blanche* in ' Pierre, the Foundling,' at the Adelphi. Monday, September 15, 1856, the opening night of the Lyceum Theatre, under Mr. Charles Dillon's management, Miss Woolgar played *Florizel* in a burlesque by William Brough, entitled ' Perdita; or, the Royal Milkmaid.' The same year, Tuesday, October 16, first performance at the Lyceum of ' The Three Musketeers,' she sustained the part of *Constance;* and on Saturday, December 6, *Eugénie* (of Beaumanoir), first performance of Ed. Falconer's drama ' The Cagot; or, Heart for Heart.' In March 1857, at the same theatre, she appeared as *Ophelia;* Mr. Charles Dillon performing the part of *Hamlet.* " Miss Woolgar's *Ophelia* was one of the finest performances of the character we have ever seen. It was full of genius, and the pathos of the mad scene was irresistible." (*Daily News*, March 21, 1857.)

On Wednesday, January 20, 1858, at the same theatre, first performance of a play of Leigh Hunt's, entitled ' Love's Amazements,' she played the part of the *Countess de Montelais;* and in the same year (September) succeeded Mrs. Charles Young as *Miss Vavasour* in Falconer's play ' Extremes; or, Men of the Day.' The following year she returned to the Adelphi Theatre, and in January appeared there as *Dorine* in ' Tartuffe.' The following month, in a "revival" of ' Masks and Faces,' she played the character of *Peg Woffington*, noticed in the *Athenæum* (February 19, 1859) as follows: " The performance of *Peg Woffington* for the first time by Miss Woolgar is an event. It was in all respects admirable and thoroughly original. The capricious impulse and natural good-heartedness of the actress, by the manners of the time placed in a false position, oppressed with a sense of degradation, but upheld by a consciousness of superior talent, were distinctly exhibited, not only in the general bearing of the assumption but in the most minute details. Nothing could be more lifelike than the play of light and shadow introduced, and their skilful distribution in the picture. Miss Woolgar has achieved by the performance a triumph, not only with the public but in the estimation of fastidious censors." During the same year, at the Adelphi, she played the following characters, viz. *Don Cleophas Zambullo,* in the burlesque of 'Asmodeus'; *Sir Rowland Macassar,* in a burlesque 'The Babes in the Wood'; and *Catherine Duval* (November), first performance of Mr. Watts Phillips's drama 'The Dead Heart.'

On Monday, September 10, 1860, first performance at the Adelphi of 'The Colleen Bawn' (Mr. and Mrs. Boucicault in the principal parts), Miss Woolgar sustained the character of *Anne Chute.* Monday, April 14, 1862, first performance of Boucicault's dramatized version of 'The Cricket on the Hearth,' entitled 'Dot,' she played the part of *Tilly Slowboy.* " For downright grotesque yet still natural fun, Miss Woolgar's *Tilly Slowboy* could not be surpassed. The drollery of *Tilly's* position is greatly heightened by the perverse pleasure which the now reckless Ned Plummer takes in frightening her out of her wits—an exhibition of comic terror is constantly taking place in the background." (*Times,* April 16, 1862.)

On Monday, August 8, 1864, in a new farce of some interest, by T. J. Williams, entitled 'My Wife's Maid,' Miss Woolgar played the leading character, *Barbara Perkins.* In July 1865, still at the Adelphi, first performance of Mr. Walter Gordon's play 'Through Fire and Water,' she performed the part of *Honnor Bright.* Saturday, May 5, 1866, first performance at the same theatre of Mr. Benjamin Webster junior's version of Victorien Sardou's 'La Famille Benoiton,' entitled 'The Fast Family,' Miss Woolgar sustained the part of *Clotilde.* " Miss Woolgar (Mrs. Alfred Mellon) managed the scene admirably, and to her vigorous performance throughout of this part of *Clotilde,* which is an exceedingly arduous one, the success of the *drame* should in fairness be attributed." (*Athenæum,* May 12, 1866.)

In the following year, Thursday, December 26, first performance at the Adelphi of 'No Thoroughfare' (Messrs. Charles Dickens and Wilkie Collins), Mr. Charles Fechter in the leading *rôle,* Miss Woolgar played *Sally Goldstraw.* From 1867 to 1875 she acted at various theatres in several revivals of plays of more or less interest. In March 1875, first performance at the Adelphi of a dramatic version of 'Nicholas Nickleby,' from the pen of the late Mr. Andrew Halliday, she undertook the part of *Mrs. Squeers.* The same year, in October, reappearance of Mr. Joseph Jefferson at the Princess's Theatre as *Rip Van Winkle,* she played *Gretchen;* and in 1877, at the same theatre, she performed her original character in 'Lost in London,' produced at the Adelphi Theatre in 1867. On Wednesday, May 15, 1878, a performance was given at Drury Lane Theatre in aid of a testimonial benefit to Mrs. Alfred Mellon (Miss Woolgar), in which the principal members of the dramatic profession took part. The result was in every sense most gratifying, and bore ample testimony to her personal worth and considerable merits as an actress. She has recently (June 1879) been acting nightly at her old theatre, the Adelphi, as *Mrs. Candour*, in a revival of 'The School for Scandal.'

Miss Woolgar married the late Alfred Mellon, a gentleman well known in the musical world, and a composer of considerable ability, who inaugurated the series of Promenade Concerts now annually given at the Royal Italian Opera, Covent Garden.

MERVIN, FREDERICK, is the son of a gentleman farmer in Leicestershire. He made his first appearance in London at the St. James's Theatre as *Oscar* in the comedy of 'War,' by Robertson. Afterwards at the Royalty, under Miss Kate Santley's management, Mr. Mervin appeared as *Anibal* in 'La Marjolaine.' He was engaged for a season at the Alhambra Theatre. When 'Les Cloches de Corneville,' in August 1878, was transferred from the Folly Theatre to the Globe, Mr. Mervin performed the character of the *Marquis* for a considerable time. In May 1879 he superseded Mr. Walter Fisher as *Hector* in 'Madame Favart' at the Strand Theatre, and was himself superseded by Mr. H. Bracy about the end of the London season. In September 1879 he was at Edinburgh, performing in the same opera the character of *Charles Favart.*

*MEYRICK, ELLEN, is a niece and pupil of Mr. John Billington. She first appeared in London at the Adelphi Theatre, January 31, 1874, as *Alice May* in 'Rough and Ready.' She has performed in the provinces, and generally in company with Mr. and Mrs. Billington. She took the part of *Miss Neville* in 'She Stoops to Conquer' at the Aquarium (now Imperial) Theatre, February 15, 1879, and during the extended run of the piece. She played *Georgiana Vesey* in 'Money' on the occasion of Mr. E. L. Blanchard's benefit at the Haymarket in 1879, with a very strong cast ; and appeared as *Dorinda* in 'The Beaux' Stratagem,' September 22, 1879, at the Imperial Theatre, at the reopening under Miss Litton's management.

MOODIE, LOUISE M. R., had appeared on the continental stage previous to her *début* in England, which took place Saturday, February 26, 1870, at the Royal Alfred Theatre, London, in the part of *Camille*, in an English version of a drama of the same name by Alexandre Dumas, jun. During the same year she became a member of Sir Charles Young's comedy company, playing, 1870, in the provinces and in London (at the Charing Cross Theatre) the leading *rôle, Beatrice,* in 'Shadows' (Sir C. Young), and, 1871, *Marchesa de Torriano* in ' Charms,' from the pen of the same author. In the first-named character Miss Louise Moodie achieved considerable distinction, and, so to speak, at once earned a reputation for herself on the English stage. It may be remarked that she had undergone no special course of training when she adopted the stage as a profession and first appeared in public as an actress. In October 1871 she joined the company of Sadler's Wells Theatre, under Mr. F. Belton's management, appearing there as *Mdlle. Marco* ('The Marble Heart'), and *Lucrezia Borgia* in a drama of the same title by Mr. F. Belton. At the Alexandra Theatre, Liverpool, Monday, December 4, 1871, she sustained the part of *Esmeralda* in Andrew Halliday's drama 'Notre Dame.' Severe illness having necessitated Miss Louise Moodie's retirement from the stage for a lengthened period, she did not again act in England until June 1873, when she accepted an engagement in the late Mr. Alfred Young's travelling company. During a tour which followed Miss Louise Moodie played *Miss Chester* in the drama of that name by Florence Marryat and Sir Charles Young; *Mrs. Oakley* ('The Jealous Wife'); *Lady Audley* ('Lady Audley's Secret'), &c. She reappeared on the London stage at the Court Theatre under Miss Litton's management, Saturday, February 14, 1874, in "a romantic play" entitled 'The White Pilgrim' (Merivale) as *Thordisa*. This play was unsuccessful on the stage; but the *Times*, in its review of its first representation, remarked that it was "of no uncommon merit, and was possessed of much of the character of antique tragedy." In the same year Miss Moodie joined the late Mdlle. Beatrice's comedy-company, and personated the character of *Berthe de Savigny*, first performance of the English version of M. Octave Feuillet's 'Le Sphinx' ('The Sphinx;' Campbell Clarke), at the Theatre Royal, Edinburgh, August 12, 1874. This piece was subsequently produced at the Theatre Royal, Haymarket, Miss Moodie sustaining her original character. "The palm falls to the share of Miss Louise Moodie, who has a strong character to represent, and succeeds in rendering it forcible by concealing the art which strengthens the illustration of nature. Every phase of the part is artistically represented, and the fine scene in the last act, when *Berthe* threatens to expose Blanche's infamy, is played with remarkable power. . . . Miss Moodie deserves the highest praise for her performance, which we have no hesitation in saying is one of the most forcible the stage has witnessed for a long time past." (*Standard*, August 24, 1874.) She was specially engaged to perform the part of *Aika* in the "spectacular romance" 'The Black Crook,' produced at the Amphitheatre, Liverpool, in May 1875. The same year, in October, she appeared in the characters of *Lady Macbeth*, *Ophelia*, and *Portia*, at the Gaiety Theatre, Glasgow. In 1876 Miss Louise Moodie became connected with the Chippendale Comedy Company, and in the provinces acted such parts as *Lady Teazle*, *Lydia Languish*, *Miss Hardcastle*, &c. Among other characters played by her in the same and following years (1876–8) may be mentioned *Clytie*, in the drama of that name by J. Hatton; *Lady Isabel* and *Madame Vine* ('East Lynne'); *Helen Rolleston* ('The Scuttled Ship'; Charles Reade); *Queen Katherine* ('Henry VIII.'); *Lady Marsden* ('All for Her'); the *Countess Danischeff* ('The Danischeffs'). In April 1878, first performance at the Adelphi Theatre of 'Proof,' a version by Mr. Burnand of MM. D'Ennery and Cormon's 'Une Cause Célèbre,' Miss Moodie personated *Madeleine*, and subsequently, in addition, *Adrienne Lorance*, acting the dual parts with singular care and effectiveness. On Monday, December 2, 1878, first performance at the T. R. Haymarket of 'The Crisis' (J. Albery), founded on ' Les Fourchambault' of M. Augier, she sustained the part of *Mrs. Goring*. In discussing the merits of this performance the *Daily Telegraph* (December 4, 1878) said:—" It will be a pleasure to describe, in some detail, the finished art of Miss Louise Moodie, who emphatically secured the success of the evening by one of those performances so seldom found on the English stage, but when met with so warmly welcomed. A scene so subtle and sympathetic as this must be mastered by art or it becomes ridiculous or commonplace. Suddenly there came out an actress—Miss Louise Moodie—an actress comparatively unknown, save to those who minutely study art, to hold an audience in breathless admiration and sympathy. Unannounced and unexpected, Miss Moodie stood forward to convince the sceptical as to the value of finish, refinement, and grace in high-comedy acting. It was not the words only that *Mrs. Goring* spoke which convinced the listener— it was the pathos of resignation which she displayed. On that weary face were scored the lines of many sorrows. The tired eye contained what Mr. Swinburne has nobly called 'the fire of many tears'; the voice was musical with forgotten memories. The action of the hand, the anxiety of the look, the intonation of the voice, were all in harmony, and the audience seemed hushed to pity as they heard the record of so sad a life. With great grasp and honesty of purpose did Mr. Kelly answer to the call required of him in such a scene. He was as deeply earnest as was Miss Moodie pathetically resigned. He was the type of action; she was the embodiment of regret. The scene from first to last, in short, rivalled the success of the similar situation at the Français, and moved the house to an emotion that can only be accomplished by the most finished art. No one can sit through the scenes in which old *Mrs. Goring* and her son are engaged without being profoundly touched, not by the expression of a careless sentiment, but by the firm, artistic embodiment of a palpable truth. Every word uttered is human, and goes home to the heart, and a far inferior play could be endured for the sake of acting so pathetic, so tender, and so true. Whenever *Mrs. Goring* is on the stage, with her silvered hair and her martyrdom of suppressed sorrow, the audience is moved. The scenes in which Miss Louise Moodie and Mr. Charles Kelly were concerned conspicuously raised the interest of the comedy, and will certainly give it an impetus in public estimation."

MORGAN, WILFORD, occupied the post of second tenor at the Italian Opera, Covent Garden, during the last years of the late Mr. Gye's administration. Mr. Morgan is an educated musician and well-trained tenor. According to the *Athenæum* (September 13, 1879), "He is well versed both in the sacred and secular schools of composition; and his setting of Bunyan's 'Pilgrim's Progress' for solos, chorus, and orchestra, his ballads, &c., have attracted attention in the provinces, if not, as their merits entitled them to do, in the metropolis. For a short period he acted as double for Mr. Sims Reeves at the Alexandra Palace and other places, for he is master of the *répertoire* of our great English tenor. Mr. Wilford Morgan obtained a fair chance at last when he was secured for the Imperial Theatre (Aquarium) for the tenor part in 'H.M.S. Pinafore,' in which he enjoyed great success. His powers were still better displayed at the Globe Theatre, where, on Saturday, September 6, 1879, he appeared at a short notice in 'Les Cloches de Corneville' as the *Marquis.*"

MUNROE, KATE, was born in New York, U.S.A., and entered the dramatic profession in 1870. On October 25 of that year, at Milan, she sang the *rôle* of *Norina* in Donizetti's opera of 'Don Pasquale.' She studied for the operatic stage with some of the best masters in Milan and Naples, and played and sang in Italian opera for three years in various Italian cities. Miss Munroe was engaged for six months at the Théâtre des Italiens in Paris, and came to London in 1874, making her first appearance in London 24th September of the same year at the Gaiety Theatre in opera bouffe. She has played in French opera at the Philharmonic Theatre, Islington, and was engaged for two years and a half at the Alhambra Theatre, sustaining various principal parts, and subsequently at the Folly Theatre, London. Since her *début* in London Miss Munroe has occupied a prominent position in that limited circle of English artistes competent to sing in the more attractive works of the modern French composers. In the autumn of 1878 she went to Paris, where during an engagement of seven months she played with success two different *rôles* in French, in the 'Deux Nababs' at the Théâtre des Nouveautés, and in 'La Marquise des Roues' at the Bouffes-Parisiens.

MURRAY, ALMA, born in London, November 21, 1856, and made her first appearance on any stage in 1869, at the Olympic Theatre, London, as *Saccharissa*, in W. S. Gilbert's 'Princess.' From 1869 to 1875 she played various small parts at London theatres, viz. the Olympic, Royalty, Adelphi, and Drury Lane. From August 1875 to April 1877 she was engaged in the provinces, playing "juvenile lead" characters, such, for example, as *Rose Cudlip* ('Forgiven'), *Lottie* ('Two Roses'), *Kate Garston* ('Lancashire Lass'), *Constance Howard* ('False Shame'), *Clara Douglas* ('Money'), *Gertrude* ('Little Treasure'), &c., &c. In September 1877 Miss Murray reappeared in London at Drury Lane Theatre as *Alice Bridgenorth*, first performance of 'England in the Days of Charles II.,' by W. G. Wills, "rendering the character thoroughly girlish and attractive, and displaying much refinement " (*Sunday Times*, September 30, 1877).

From October 1877 to February 1878 Miss Murray was engaged at the Adelphi, appearing as *Eliza* ('After Dark'), and *Edith Burrowes* ('Formosa'). During a part of 1879 she played in the provinces the part of *Esther Eccles* in ' Caste;' and in June 1879, *Julie de Mortemar* in a revival of ' Richelieu' by Mr. Irving at the Lyceum Theatre, where she is now (October 1879) engaged.

*MURRAY, DOMINICK, made his first appearance on the London stage at Astley's, March 28, 1853. It was not, however, until some ten years later that he attained any considerable success as an actor. His reputation, as far as our own stage is concerned, may be said to date from his connection with the Princess's Theatre, 1864-9, and his appearance in the plays of Boucicault first represented there. He was in the original cast of that author's drama 'The Streets of London,' as *Dan*, first performed at the Princess's Theatre August 5, 1864 ; and of ' Arrah-na-Pogue,' as *Michael Feeny*, first performed at the same theatre March 22, 1865. Mr. Dominick Murray's acting in this latter character is mentioned in contemporary journals as "being excellent, and proving in him the possession of decided tragic powers." During his engagement at the Princess's his name appeared in the original cast of Palgrave Simpson's drama ' Marie Antoinette' (February 15, 1869) as *Turgy*, and he also performed in the following April at the same theatre the character of *Shylock*. In the ensuing August Mr. Dominick Murray went to the United States of America, where he has since remained, and earned for himself the reputation of being an admirable actor.

MURRAY, GASTON, born in London 1826, and first appeared on any stage at the Prince's Theatre, Glasgow, in June 1854, as *Charles* in a piece entitled ' The Happiest Day of My Life.' He made his *début* on the London stage March 2, 1855, at the Lyceum Theatre, as *Tom Saville* in ' Used Up '; the late Charles Mathews acting in his original character, *Sir Charles Coldstream*. During the same year Mr. Gaston Murray proceeded on tour with the Lyceum company, and appeared in the following characters, viz. *Tom Russelton* in ' A Cosy Couple '; *Harry Ringdove* in ' The Ringdoves '; *Faulkland* in ' The Rivals '; *Dick Dowlas* in ' The Heir-at-Law'; *Charles Paragon* in ' Perfection '; *Victor de Mornac* in ' Retribution.' On January 28, 1857, he took part in the Windsor Castle Theatricals, appearing as *Jules de Crussac* in the play entitled ' Secret Service.' During the year 1859 he was engaged at the Manchester Theatre Royal, and played the following characters, viz. *Felix Featherley* in ' Everybody's Friend '; *Faust* in the English version of ' Faust and Marguerite '; *Laertes*, and subsequently the *Ghost* in ' Hamlet '; *George Barnwell* in the drama of that title ; *Orlando* in ' As You Like It '; *Duke Aranza* in ' The Honeymoon '; *Wilford* in ' The Iron Chest.' In 1862

Mr. Gaston Murray was a member of the company of the Olympic Theatre, and appeared with the late Mr. Robson in the following among other plays, viz. ' The Porter's Knot,' as *Stephen Scatter*, and ' Boots at the Swan,' as *Frank Riskly*. In 1863, at St. James's Theatre, he was the " original " *George Talboys* in ' Lady Audley's Secret'; and also played the following characters, viz. *Sir Benjamin Backbite* in ' The School for Scandal '; *Sir George Touchwood* in ' The Belle's Stratagem '; *Silky* in ' The Road to Ruin,' &c. In 1867–8 Mr. Gaston Murray fulfilled engagements at the Strand and Queen's Theatres, and in the year following at the Haymarket, where he played *Edward Ashley* in the original cast of ' All for Money.' In 1871 he was a member of the company of the Lyceum Theatre, appearing there in ' Pickwick ' and ' The Bells.' In 1872 he acted the character of *Pickwick* at the Standard Theatre, and afterwards, in the same year, became treasurer to Lord Londesborough when that nobleman produced ' Babil and Bijou ' at the Theatre Royal, Covent Garden.

MURRAY, MARY FRANCES (Mrs. GASTON MURRAY), daughter of the late Henry Hughes, of the Adelphi and Surrey Theatres, was born near Frankfort, Germany. She first appeared on any stage in 1851, at the Guildford Theatre, as *Sophia* in ' The Rendezvous '; and made her *début* on the London stage in 1853 at the Lyceum Theatre as *Emma Thornton* in 'The Bachelor of Arts.' In 1857 she was engaged at the Olympic Theatre under Mr. Alfred Wigan's management, and afterwards, at the same theatre, for upwards of six years, during the entire management of Messrs. Robson and Emden. During her connection with the Olympic, Mrs. Gaston Murray played the following original parts, viz. : *Esther Hardacre* in ' Daddy Hardacre,' by Palgrave Simpson—she acted this part at Windsor Castle in 1857 with the late Mr. Robson, " and received a special message of approval from Her Majesty; *Alice* in ' The Porter's Knot,' by John Oxenford ; *Emily St. Evremond* in ' The Ticket-of-Leave Man '; *Fair Rosamond* in Burnand's burlesque of that title, and *Galatea* in the same author's ' Acis and Galatea.' Mrs. Gaston Murray has fulfilled various engagements at all the principal theatres in London, and was a member of Mr. Hare's company for the whole period of his management of the Court Theatre, where she personated with much success *Mrs. Primrose* in Wills's play of ' Olivia '; *Miss Tarragon* in Hamilton Aïdé's comedy of ' A Seven Days' Wonder '; *Mrs. Penguin*, also *Susan Hartley* (during the temporary absence of Mrs. Kendal) in ' A Scrap of Paper '; *Lady Matilda Vavasour* in ' New Men and Old Acres,' &c.

* MURRAY, MRS. LEIGH, has been for many years an actress, and has appeared at all the principal London theatres, notably at the Olympic, under the management of Robson ; at the Strand ; and at the Prince of Wales's with Mrs. Bancroft. Her original parts have been various and many. She was acting at the Strand Theatre as early as May 1849 as *Mrs. Bodkin,* a young wife, in Selby's ' Taken In and Done For,' and as *Mrs. Chesterton* in ' John Dobbs,' an amusing farce by Morton. Later, at the Prince of Wales's Theatre (1867), she played the *Marquise de St. Maur* in ' Caste,' and was the original *Mrs. Kinpeck* in ' Play,' February 15, 1868. In August 1879 Mrs. Leigh Murray was engaged by Miss Genevieve Ward to play *Mrs. Foley* in ' Forget-Me-Not ' at the Lyceum, and in September she appeared as *Madame Senechal* at the Court Theatre in a revival of ' Fernande,' under the management of Mr. Wilson Barrett.

NEILSON, LILIAN ADELAIDE, was born in 1850, and made her first appearance on the stage at the Theatre Royal, Margate, at the age of fifteen, in *Julia* ('The Hunchback'). In July 1865 she made her *début* in London at the Royalty Theatre in the character of *Juliet*, but without attracting particular attention. The following year, Monday, July 2, in a drama by Mr. Watts Phillips, entitled 'The Huguenot Captain,' then first performed at the Princess's Theatre, she played the part of *Gabrielle de Savigny*, and was noticed as being "a remarkably pretty and interesting actress, a little stiff and awkward in her movements, but with considerable command of facial expression. Her voice is pleasing, though it appears to have a slight lisp, and with proper tuition and practice she may hope to gain a good position on the London stage." (*Daily News,* July 3, 1866.) The same year, in November, at the Adelphi Theatre, she sustained the part of *Victorine* in the drama of that title, brought out at the old theatre in 1831, when Mr. and Mrs. Yates, Mr. Buckstone, John Reeve, Hemming, and O. Smith played the principal characters. At the same theatre in 1867 (Saturday, March 16), first performance of Mr. Watts Phillips's play 'Lost in London,' she acted the character of *Nelly Armroyd* "with spirit and pathos." On September 25, 1868, at the Theatre Royal, Edinburgh, Miss Neilson appeared for the first time as *Rosalind* in 'As You Like It'; followed, on the succeeding evening by *Pauline* in 'The Lady of Lyons,' and on September 29 by *Julia* in 'The Hunchback.' The *Scotsman* (September 30, 1868) remarked of this performance as follows :—" Miss Neilson as *Julia* opened with little promise of the true heroine she finally developed. There was flatness and insipid commonplace in the early scenes, but with the progress of the piece she fitted herself with artistic aptitude to the highest requirements of the part, and by the time the curtain had risen on the second act she was entirely the personage it was her office to present. The play abounds in opportunities for skilful and effective display, and it is not only in her efficient employment of these, but also in the admirable manner in which she sustains the most incidental links in the plot, that the success of Miss Neilson's ample and accurate delineation of this heroine is to be traced."

On Friday, October 2, 1868, at the same theatre, Miss Neilson acted the heroine's part in a play by Mr. Palgrave Simpson, entitled 'Stage and State,' founded on a French drama, 'Beatrix ; ou la Madone de l'Art' of Legouvé, a play in which Madame Ristori some time before had created a great sensation at the Vaudeville in Paris. The English version was not a success. The following month Miss Neilson appeared at the Theatre Royal, Birmingham, in a play by C. Williams (a Birmingham dramatist), adapted from an early novel of Miss Braddon's, entitled 'The Captain of the Vulture.' In March 1869, at the Lyceum Theatre in London, first performance there of Dr. Westland Marston's play 'Life for Life,' she acted the part of *Lilian.* In this play the *Athenæum* (March 13, 1869) took occasion to speak of Miss Neilson as an actress of great power. " Her method in art is as yet imperfect. The demonstrations of passion are confined to low and emphasized speech, with an accompaniment of appropriate gesture. She has yet to learn that hurried and breathless accents and sharp incisive pronunciation of words are as powerful means of expressing sorrow or fear as those to which she confines herself. Her acting, accordingly, fine as it was, wanted variety. Some movements of her body were over sinuous, a few of her notes were too loud as too sustained, and her transition from tragic grandeur to girlish prettiness of speech and face was too sudden. A tendency to over attitudinizing was also displayed. Here censure ends. In the most important respects the impersonation was finest. It had true tragic fire. Some of the attitudes of Miss Neilson were full of grandeur ; her utterance was musical and impressive, and her face assumed at times a look full of awe and tragic portent. The delivery of some passages had, moreover, very subtle significance. Practice and care are alone required to secure for Miss Neilson a high and enduring reputation." The following October (Monday, the 11th), at the Gaiety Theatre, London, first performance of ' A Life Chase ' (by John Oxenford and Horace Wigan), she played the leading *rôle—Madame Vidal.* In December 1869, at the same theatre, first performance of ' Uncle Dick's Darling,' she sustained the part of *Mary Belton,* and on Monday, April 11, 1870, at the Gaiety Theatre, she appeared as *Julia* in a revival of ' The Hunchback.' During this year—commencing on May 26th—Miss Neilson gave an entertainment, under the title of ' Dramatic Studies,' at St. James's Hall, with great success. " Miss Neilson possesses several very necessary qualifications for a good reader. She has a handsome presence and an expressive face, which are no unworthy adjuncts to the gracious delivery of lofty sentiments. She has a harmonious voice, capable of very great modulation ; and she has a most artistic command of what may be called the *matériel* of elocution—the inflections ; it is not surprising, therefore, that her appearance at St. James's Hall should have proved a decided success, especially as she was aided by a well-selected programme. The readings consisted of scenes from ' The Provoked Husband,' from Schiller's ' Wallenstein,' from ' The Taming of the Shrew,' Racine's ' Phédre,' and Congreve's ' Love for Love.' " (*Examiner,* June 4, 1870.)

In 1870, on Saturday, September 24, first performance at Drury Lane Theatre of the drama of ' Amy Robsart,' she acted the title *rôle.* " For the character of *Amy Robsart* it would certainly have been difficult to find another such a representative as Miss Neilson, who, notwithstanding some faults of nature, is an actress of true dramatic genius. Her passionate appeals to the truth and honour of Leicester were finely contrasted with the tenderness of her love passages. In the great scene with the jealous and suspicious Queen in the garden at Kenilworth, her acting rose to a higher level of pathetic force ; and finally her struggles with Varney, and her womanish terror at the prospect of death, were depicted with an intensity which powerfully excited the feelings of the audience." (*Daily News*, September 26, 1870.) The same year at Drury Lane Theatre, on Monday, December 19, Miss Neilson appeared as *Juliet*, the character in which she had made her earliest appearance on the London stage, and which still remains the impersonation of all others in which she displays her talents to the highest advantage. On this occasion the whole of the tragic scenes were rendered by her with high intelligence, accompanied by a power of interpretation and revelation to which Drury Lane Theatre had long been a stranger. " There is, perhaps, no actress now on the stage who more perfectly understands the routine of the part," remarked the *Times* (December 21, 1870), " and certainly there are none who can give greater force to the scenes in which frequenters of the playhouse look for marked effects. The balcony scene, the ' tiff ' with the nurse, the soliloquy in the chamber, and the death on Romeo's corpse, give evidence of thorough and conscientious study. In an age when tragedy is out of fashion the young and rising actress has determined to make *Juliet* her own, and the applause of a crowded audience bore witness to her success." In March 1871 Miss Neilson entered upon a tour of the United Kingdom, appearing principally in her original part of *Amy Robsart*. On Saturday, September 23 of the same year, she acted the part of *Rebecca* in the drama of that title, founded on Sir Walter Scott's novel of ' Ivanhoe,' then performed for the first time at Drury Lane. On December 18 of the same year she appeared at the same theatre as *Rosalind* in a revival of ' As You Like It.' In the month of September 1872 Miss Neilson gave a series of farewell performances at the Queen's Theatre, Long Acre, prior to her departure for America. In these were included ' Romeo and Juliet,' in which she played *Juliet*, and ' The Lady of Lyons,' in which she acted the part of *Pauline*. Both impersonations were eminently successful. " *Juliet* is Miss Neilson's masterpiece. In this character she made her *début* before a London audience, and upon it she has since bestowed long and conscientious study. . . . Miss Neilson's *Juliet* is now a ripe and sustained performance, ascending in the latter acts of the play to a tragic elevation and fire that seem less art than inspiration. To say that the potion scene has a passionate intensity and a concentrated power such as no modern representation on the English stage has exhibited, is to do it no more than justice. The tenderness and grace of the early scenes are in striking contrast with the gloom and terror of the later. When the last waning faults of self-consciousness are removed, there will be nothing to bring against this fine interpretation. The power of the actress was shown by the manner in which she triumphed over difficulties, and held the audience enthralled in spite of the absurd accessories of the performance." (*Athenæum*, September 21, 1872.)

On November 18, 1872, Miss Neilson " opened " at Booth's Theatre, New York, in her favourite character. Her acting was received with much enthusiasm. During the tour through the

United States and Canada which followed, she appeared in the following characters in addition to *Juliet*, viz. *Beatrice* in ' Much Ado About Nothing '; *Pauline* in ' The Lady of Lyons '; *Lady Teazle* in ' The School for Scandal '; *Julia* in ' The Hunchback '; and *Isabella* in ' Measure for Measure.' Her career in the United States was one of extraordinary success. The *New York Tribune*, in alluding to the last of a series of performances given by Miss Neilson in New York in 1875, remarked that " since the night when Dickens, with slow step and sad face, made his last exit from the stage of Steinway Hall, there had been no theatrical occasion in the American capital at once so animated with chivalry and touching with sense of sorrow and loss as that on which Miss Neilson bade farewell for a time to the good people of New York." In 1876, Monday, January 17, Miss Neilson reappeared on the Haymarket stage, and during the season played *Juliet, Rosalind, Anne Boleyn* (on the occasion of the first performance of Mr. Tom Taylor's play of that title, Saturday, February 5), *Julia* in ' The Hunchback,' and *Isabella* in ' Measure for Measure.' " The announcement that Shakespeare's ' Measure for Measure ' has not been presented in London for ' nearly a quarter of a century ' will make the playgoer rub his eyes and reflect once more upon the swift flight of time. . . . On the first representation of the comedy an enthusiasm was shown which is a direct compliment to the acting of nearly all concerned in it. The *Isabella* of Miss Neilson was particularly admired, and at the conclusion of the prison scene the actress was called before the curtain three times and literally pelted with bouquets. So highly intelligent and carefully studied a performance really deserved some eloquent and marked praise ; and it is certain that our stage is not so rich in actresses capable of attempting *Isabella* that we can afford to dilute the success with many doubts as to the soundness of the verdict. The mere fact that ' Measure for Measure ' has been produced, and has held a critical audience, that a play has been seen that would otherwise have remained in its hiding-place, that *Isabella* has been prettily sketched if not boldly painted, suggested, no doubt, such encouraging and appreciative applause. If at any time it is urged that Miss Neilson's *Isabella* is interesting rather than powerful, graceful rather than intense, unequal in sustained strength, and occasionally, as in the last act, inclined to fade and wane instead of burning brightly with a clear and undimmed light, it must be remembered that the actress still shows traces of exhaustion and prostration from illness, and that the *Isabella* comes after many representations of *Juliet* and *Anne Boleyn*. It is possible that those who cheered so loudly and so generously have not seen *Isabella* at her best; but the experience of many playgoers in the house warranted some cordiality after so unusual and—in these days—so welcome a performance." (*Daily Telegraph*, April 3, 1876.)

In 1877 Miss Neilson again visited the United States. During a season of eight months she appeared there as *Viola*, ' Twelfth Night,' and *Imogene*, ' Cymbeline,' both new characters to her.

She appeared also in the before-mentioned characters, viz. *Juliet, Rosalind, Isabella, Viola,* and *Julia,* during her engagement at the Haymarket Theatre terminating in May 1878. On February 27, 1879, she appeared at the Adelphi Theatre as *Queen Isabella,* first performance of 'The Crimson Cross;' and afterwards, during the summer season at the same theatre, as *Julia* and *Lady Teazle,* and in her "original" part of *Amy Robsart* in Andrew Halliday's well-remembered drama. In October 1879 she again left England for America.

NELSON, MRS. JOHN. *See* LECLERCQ, CARLOTTA.

NEVILLE, HENRY GARSIDE, son of the well-known actor and theatrical manager, the late John Neville, was born in Manchester in 1837. He entered the dramatic profession at an early age under his father's auspices, and made his first appearance on the London stage, October 8, 1860, at the Lyceum Theatre under Madame Celeste's management. On the 12th of the following month he there performed the part of *Victor Savignie* on the production of 'Adrienne; or, The Secret of a Life.' Afterwards he fulfilled a series of engagements at Liverpool, Manchester, Birmingham, and Dublin theatres; and in 1861 was enrolled a member of the company of Messrs. Emden and Robson at the Olympic Theatre in London. At this theatre he remained for four years, playing various leading parts in the plays produced on its stage; and here, in May 1863, made his first important dramatic success as the "original" *Bob Brierly* in Tom Taylor's drama 'The Ticket-of-Leave Man,' adapted from the French 'Léonard,' of MM. Edouard Brisbarre and Eugène Nus. Mr. Neville, who had already won a position in public favour, gained much praise for the earnest, truthful, and natural manner in which he delineated the struggles of a man who, striving to redeem his early folly, and to free himself from the stigma that has been its consequence, finds every avenue to a better life gradually closed against him. The play was eminently successful, and, generally, has proved attractive with a London audience whenever revived in later years. At the Olympic Theatre Mr. Neville has won several other successes, of which the more noteworthy are *Henry Dunbar* in Tom Taylor's version of Miss Braddon's novel of that title, and *Jean Valjean* in the drama of 'The Yellow Passport,' adapted by Mr. Neville himself from M. V. Hugo's 'Les Misérables.'

After a stay of some four years at the Olympic he joined the company of the Adelphi Theatre, and appeared there as *Job Armroyd* in 'Lost in London'; and as *Farmer Allen* in Charles Reade's dramatic version of Tennyson's 'Dora.' The part of *Job Armroyd* was admirably played by Mr. H. Neville, and largely increased his reputation. "*Job Armroyd,* if we do not admire him as an adept in social science, we readily acknowledge as a most effective stage figure; and although Mr. Neville has long distinguished himself as a serviceable actor . . . . he perhaps never played so well as when he represented the elderly miner, uncouth in gait, rough in dialect, but always of a manifestly earnest and affectionate disposition." (*Times*, March 18, 1867.) In the principal *rôle* of 'Put Yourself in His Place,' Charles Reade's adaptation of his own novel of that title, Henry Neville's acting attracted favourable notice. He had evidently studied the intentions of the author very thoroughly, and his impersonation of the hard-working Sheffield mechanic was singularly life-like and truthful in detail. On completing his engagement at the Adelphi Theatre Mr. Neville appeared at various London theatres for short seasons—at the Holborn, the Duke's, and the Globe. In 1873 he returned to the Olympic as lessee, and assumed, in connection with that position, the management of the theatre, which he retained until 1879. The following list of noteworthy plays, produced at the Olympic between the date of Mr. Neville's first entering upon the lesseeship and August 1879, are worthy of being recorded as an indication of his dramatic enterprise : Season 1873-4 —'Sour Grapes' (Byron) ; 'Richelieu Redressed' (Reece) ; 'School for Intrigue' (Mortimer); 'Clancarty' (Tom Taylor). Season 1874-5—'Two Orphans' (Oxenford) ; 'Spendthrift' (Albery)'; 'Ticket-of-Leave Man' (revival). Season 1875-6—'Buckingham' (W. G. Wills) ; 'Clytie' (J. Hatton); 'The Gascon' (Muskerry) ; 'Home, sweet Home' (Farjeon). Season 1876-7—'No Thoroughfare' (Dickens and Collins); 'Si Slocum' (F. Trayne and Tayleur); 'Queen of Connaught' (Buchanan) ; 'Wife's Secret' (revival) ; 'Scuttled Ship' (C. Reade) ; 'Violin Maker of Cremona' (M. François Coppée and Neville) ; 'Lady Audley's Secret' (revival). Season 1877-8—'The Moonstone' (Wilkie Collins); 'Henry Dunbar' (revival); 'Turn of the Tide' (Burnand) ; 'Jealousy' (C. Reade). 1878-9—'The Two Orphans' (revival).

In August 1878 Mr. Neville entered upon an engagement to play *Pierre Lorance* in the drama of 'Proof,' produced at the Adelphi Theatre. In the summer of 1879 he relinquished the management of the Olympic, and appeared nightly at the Adelphi Theatre, playing the parts of *Master Walter* ('The Hunchback') and *Charles Surface* ('The School for Scandal'). During the season he appeared at the same theatre as *Bob Brierly* in a revival of 'The Ticket-of-Leave Man.'

NEWMAN, THOMAS EDMUND. *See* WENMAN, THOMAS EDMUND.

NORTON, FLEMING, appeared at the Olympic Theatre, September 20, 1879, as *Sir Joseph Porter* in 'H.M.S. Pinafore,' in place of Mr. J. G. Taylor.

PATEMAN, ISABELLA, wife of the undermentioned Robert Pateman, made her *début* on the London stage October 28, 1876, as *Lady Clancarty,* in a revival of that play at the Olympic Theatre. She had previously acquired a considerable reputation as an actress in America, and before going to that country had performed in the provinces. The *Times* (November 2, 1876) noticed her *début* in the following terms :—" The present performance possesses, among others, one particular feature of interest in the introduction to the London stage of a new actress. Miss Pateman has hitherto been known only in the theatres of the United States and of our own country towns, and she must be regarded as fortunate in making her first appearance in London in such a character as that of *Lady Clancarty.* For her performance of this character she has been much, and in many respects justly, praised. She has evidently studied with much care, and has made herself a thorough mistress of the mechanical details of her art, the only true means to the attainment of that higher excellence to which we should be sorry to say Miss Pateman may not hope to aspire. At present, however, the results of her study, though perfect in themselves, are a little too apparent. Nor has she as yet mastered the secret of those last delicate touches which make that appear to be nature which we know to be art. Her acting, though artistic, is somewhat formal and cold ; it lacks fire, and at times even grace. We miss the tenderness of *Lady Clancarty,* and though the passion is accurately enough expressed, it scarcely rings true. Nor do we think Miss Pateman has invested the part with quite enough of the 'grand air,' which, by virtue of her birth and courtly training, would belong to the heroine ; this objection, by the way, applies with still greater force to the present representative of Lady Betty Noel, whose archness and piquancy, though not to be denied, belong more to the soubrette than to the lady-in-waiting. We have pointed out the faults which Miss Pateman's acting seems to us at present to show. They are faults, however, from which an actress who has had patience and intelligence enough to thoroughly ground herself in the first principles of her art may be accredited certainly with the desire, and possibly the means, to free herself."

Since her first appearance on the metropolitan boards Miss Pateman has played in various pieces at the Olympic, notably *Lady Eveline* in a revival of ' The Wife's Secret,' and the leading female *rôle* in Charles Reade's drama ' The Scuttled Ship,' first performed there in April 1877. In April 1878 she was in the original cast of ' Proof ; or, a Celebrated Case,' first performed on Saturday, 20th of that month, at the Adelphi Theatre, sustaining the part of *Adrienne.* Later (season 1878–9), Miss Pateman has been playing at the same theatre *Lady Sneerwell* in a revival of ' The School for Scandal' and *Queen Elizabeth* in a revival of ' Amy Robsart.'

*PATEMAN, ROBERT. Made his first appearance on the London stage September 30, 1876, at the Olympic Theatre, as *Carigue* in the play of ' The Duke's Device,' and has for some time been a member of the Adelphi company.

PATTISON, KATE, was born in Chelsea, and made her *début* on the occasion of the late Mr. Compton's benefit at the Theatre Royal, Manchester, March 26, 1877, in the comedietta ' To Oblige Benson.' Miss Pattison had been previously associated with Miss Emily Faithfull in the conduct of the 'Victoria Magazine,' and accompanied that lady during a year's tour in the United States. She made her first appearance in London at the St. James's Theatre in ' A New Way to Pay Old Debts,' Mr. Herman Vezin playing the character of Sir Giles Overreach. Miss Pattison was afterwards engagĕd by Mr. Chatterton and played at the Princess's Theatre, subsequently accepting an engagement at the Lyceum, under the management of Mrs. Bateman. In the autumn of 1878 she accompanied Mr. and Mrs. Kendal on their tour through the provinces, playing the part of *Countess Zicka* in ' Diplomacy ' in a way that obtained very favourable notice :—" Endowed with a fair presence, an expressive face, and a voice of rich tone, she lends valuable natural gifts to a fine histrionic perception in her interpretation of the Hungarian adventuress. In her jealousy, as in her revenge, and again in her remorse, when at the end she makes confession of her deeds, every gesture and every tone had its effect, and were essential elements of the success of her clever and precise impersonation." (*Manchester Examiner.*) In January 1879 she was engaged by Mr. Hare for the Court Theatre, and there played *Lady Ingram* in ' A Scrap of Paper ' and the principal part in Mr. Val Prinsep's comedietta ' Cousin Dick.' More recently (November 1879) she has appeared at St. James's Theatre.

PAULTON, HARRY, was born in Wolverhampton, and first appeared on any stage, in that town, in 1861. Subsequently, for several years he acted there, and at Wakefield, Derby, Northampton, Leeds, York, &c. Having adopted "low comedy" in 1864, Mr. Paulton was in the year following engaged for three seasons at the Theatre Royal, Glasgow, where he became exceedingly popular ; afterwards joining the company of the Theatre Royal, Birmingham ; and, at the termination of that engagement, the company of the Prince of Wales's Theatre, Liverpool. He made his *début* on the London stage June 23, 1867 (appearing for one night only), at the Surrey Theatre, as *Wormwood* in ' The Lottery Ticket,' acquitting himself in a creditable manner. Mr. Paulton's connection with the London stage may be said to have begun in 1870 with his engagement at the Strand Theatre, where he first appeared as *Blueskin* in the burlesque of 'The Idle 'Prentice.' He there became favourably known to the London public as a burlesque actor of considerable quaintness, enlarging his dramatic reputation by an admirable rendering of the part of *Uncle Sedley* in a comedy by Arthur Sketchley entitled ' Up in the World,' first performed at the Strand in February 1871. In April 1872 he joined the company of the Alhambra Theatre, of which he remained a member for five years, appearing during that period for the most part in opera bouffe—'King Carrot,' 'The Black Crook,' 'Don Juan,' 'La Belle Hélène,' &c., &c.

*PAUNCEFORT, GEORGIANA, was a member of the company of the Surrey Theatre under Messrs. Shepherd and Anderson's management in 1862, and was playing there in 'The Medal of Bronze,' 'Effie Deans,' and 'Winter's Tale' in that and the succeeding year. In 1864 she appeared with considerable success at the Surrey as *Jane Grierson* ("an orange girl") in a drama by Henry Leslie and Nicholas Rowe entitled 'The Orange Girl.' She was attached to that theatre for some years as the leading actress, performing in various original dramas placed on its stage and also in revivals of Shakespearian plays. Miss Pauncefort was in the original cast of "'Twixt Axe and Crown,' as *Queen Mary*, when that play was first produced at the Queen's Theatre in January 1870. In the following year she accepted an engagement at the Lyceum Theatre, and "created" the character of *Catherine* in 'The Bells,' first performed in December of that year. At the same theatre in 1872 she was the "original" *Lady Eleanor Davys* in W. G. Wills's play of 'Charles I.,' and later, played there the *Countess de Miraflore* in Aïdé's 'Philip.' In 1874 she sustained at the same theatre the character of *Hecate* in the revival of 'Macbeth.' Miss Pauncefort has also appeared there in other revivals—in 'Hamlet' as *Gertrude*, in 'Richelieu' as *Marion de Lorme*, &c., with success.

PEMBERTON, MRS. JOHN C. *See* FOWLER, EMILY.

*PHILLIPS, KATE (Mrs. H. B. CONWAY [COULSON]), made her first appearance on the London stage at the Haymarket Theatre as *Gabrielle* in a piece with the title of 'Tom Noddy's Secret.' She is a clever and pleasing actress of what are known as "soubrette" parts.

PINERO, ARTHUR WING, born in London 1855; son of a solicitor, and grand-nephew of Captain Thomas Wing, who fought on board the 'Victory' at Trafalgar. Mr. Pinero was educated for the legal profession; but having no particular liking for the law forsook it for the drama. He first appeared on the stage at the Theatre Royal, Edinburgh, on the 22nd June, 1874, and continued at that theatre, under the management of Mr. and Mrs. R. H. Wyndham, until the 6th February, 1875, when it was destroyed by fire. On the 1st March following he joined the company of the Alexandra Theatre, Liverpool, under Mr. Saker. Mr. Pinero made his first appearance in London, April 15, 1876, at the Globe Theatre, in the character of *Mr. Darch* in Wilkie Collins's play of 'Miss Gwilt.' On September 4 of the same year he joined the Lyceum company, and played *Claudius* to Mr. Irving on his first "Hamlet tour," in all the principal theatres in the United Kingdom. Subsequently Mr. Pinero played *Lord Stanley* in the Lyceum

revival of Shakespeare's 'Richard III.'; *Shrowl* in Wilkie Collins's
'Dead Secret,' &c. On December 26, 1877, he played *Marquis of
Huntley* in a revival of 'Charles I.' at the Lyceum Theatre, and as
Montgomery Clutterbuck in his own comedietta 'Two Can Play at
That Game.' June 8, 1878, first performance of W. G. Wills's
'Vanderdecken' at the same theatre, he enacted *Alderman Jorgens.*
During the same year he went on tour with Mr. Irving, and rejoined
his company at the opening of the Lyceum Theatre for the season
1878–9.

Mr. Pinero is author of '£200 a year,' a piece first played at the
Globe Theatre, London, in October 1877 ; of 'La Comète ; or, Two
Hearts,' an original drama in four acts, and of other pieces.

PITT, HENRY MADER, born in Albany, U.S., September
16, 1850 entered the dramatic profession 1865, appearing at the
Theatre Royal, Sheffield, in a comedy entitled 'Under the Rose.'
He was connected with the same theatre, playing various light-
comedy parts, until 1870. In August 1872 he accepted an engagement as stage-manager of the Queen's Theatre, Manchester. In
May 1873 he joined Craven Robertson's 'Caste' company, playing
the following characters, viz. *George D'Alroy* ('Caste'), *Lord
Beaufoy* ('School'), and *Angus McAlister* ('Ours'). Mr. Pitt
made his first appearance on the London stage at the Standard
Theatre, June 1874, as *Lord Beaufoy*, "playing well and carefully,
not the least of his good qualities being his distinct enunciation" (*Standard*, June 1874). In May 1875 Mr. Pitt assumed the
management of 'The Two Roses' company, playing the following
parts : *Jack Wyatt* ('Two Roses'), *Claude Redruth* ('Forgiven'),
Tom Penryn ('Apple Blossoms'), *Jones* ('Two Thorns'). In
April 1876 he appeared at the Theatre Royal, Bristol, as *Lord
Chilton* in Marshall's 'False Shame,' since which time he has
performed this character with much success at nearly every
principal provincial theatre in the United Kingdom. At the Imperial Theatre (attached to the Aquarium), Westminster, in a
revival of 'She Stoops to Conquer' (commencing Easter Monday,
April 14, 1879), he played *Young Marlow.*

PITT, MRS. H. M. *See* ADDISON, FANNY.

POWER, CLAVERING, son of the late Edward Power, Esq.,
of the Middle Temple, barrister-at-law, was born in London 1842,
and educated at King's College, London. He entered the Madras
Army as ensign December 1859, and subsequently joined H. M.
105th Regiment. He served for seven years in India, and retired
from the service as lieutenant in 1870. In that year Mr. Power
entered the dramatic profession, and in October made his *début* on
the London stage at the Victoria Theatre as *Woodcock* in the farce
of 'Woodcock's Little Game.' Afterwards, on tour in the provinces,
he played the part of *Caleb Deecie* in Albery's comedy 'The Two
Roses.' He has been engaged as "leading actor" at several
theatres in the provinces ; and in 1877–8 fulfilled engagements at

the Folly and Alhambra Theatres in London, appearing for the most part in opera bouffe—the 'Grand Duchess,' 'La Fille de Madame Angot,' &c.

POWER, GEORGE, was born in Kilkenny County, Ireland, December 24, 1848, and first appeared on the stage in December 1876, at Teatro Manoel, Malta, in the part of *Almaviva* in 'Barbière di Siviglia.' He made his *début* on the London stage December (Boxing Night) 1877, at Her Majesty's Theatre, in the tenor part in 'Swiss Cottage.' Subsequently he entered upon an engagement at the Opéra Comique, and appeared there, February 1878, in a revival of 'The Sorcerer' (Gilbert and Sullivan), and 'Trial by Jury' (same authors). May 25, 1878, first performance at the same theatre of 'H.M.S. Pinafore' (same authors), Mr. Power "created" the part of *Ralph Rackstraw*, "in concerted pieces displaying a light tenor voice of very agreeable quality, and acting the part of the sentimental lover well" (*Daily News*, May 27, 1878).

RAYNE, LIN, was born in Calcutta. He first appeared on the London stage at the Lyceum Theatre, October 3, 1868, in the part of *Faulkner*, first performance of Lord Lytton's drama 'The Rightful Heir.' After leaving the Lyceum Mr. Lin Rayne joined Mr. Barry Sullivan's company at the Holborn Theatre, where he made his first success in a comedy entitled 'Plain English.' During this engagement he played "leading juvenile and light comedy business." Among "original" parts played by him the following are deserving of mention : *Marquis d'Arcis* in ' Fernande '; *Jones* in 'Two Thorns'; *Tom* in ' Apple Blossoms.' In a revival of ' The School for Scandal ' in April 1874, at the Prince of Wales's Theatre, London, he acted the part of *Sir Benjamin Backbite.*

REDMUND, WILLIAM, was born in London, and first appeared on the stage at the Theatre Royal, Margate, June 1874, in the character of *Brown*, 'New Men and Old Acres.' In the following year, on Easter Monday, he made his *début* on the metropolitan stage at the National Standard Theatre in a drama entitled ' Rank and Fame.' He remained at this theatre for several seasons as "leading man" and stage-manager, meeting with creditable success in such parts as *Nicholas Nickleby*, *Tom Mayfield*, &c., and playing the "juvenile parts" during an engagement of Mr. Creswick. He has also played in the provinces at various leading theatres. In London he has appeared at the Duke's Theatre (as *Landry* in a piece entitled ' Little Cricket '); and at the Haymarket ; at the Court Theatre for a short season as '*jeune premier*'; and at the Princess's, where in a revival of ' Never Too Late to Mend' (1878–9) he appeared as the *Rev. Mr. Eden.* At the same theatre, on Monday, June 3, 1879, first performance of ' Drink' (founded on M. Zola's novel ' L'Assommoir '), an English version of a French play by Charles Reade, he acted the part of *Lantier.*

REED, MRS. GERMAN (*née* HORTON, PRISCILLA), first attracted notice in London as an actress in melodrama at the Victoria Theatre, under the management of Messrs. Abbot and Egerton, and when Mr. Sheridan Knowles and Miss Mitford endeavoured to support its interest by allowing their plays to appear on its boards. She was playing at that theatre in February 1834 as *Kate* in Sheridan Knowles's drama ' The Beggar of Bethnal Green.' In August 1835 she appeared at the English Opera House, in a Scotch ballad opera called ' The Covenanters,' and an agreeable trifle, performed under the title of ' Domestic Arrangements.' In January 1836 Miss Horton zealously contributed to the success of a new burletta first performed in that month at the St. James's Theatre, entitled ' Monsieur Jaques.' In a revival of ' The Tempest,' at the Theatre Royal, Covent Garden, October 1838, she played the part of *Ariel.* At the same theatre, during the following year, Miss

Horton played in English opera. On Tuesday, March 16, 1840, she sustained the part of *Ophelia* at the Haymarket Theatre, under Mr. Benjamin Webster's management, in a "revival" of 'Hamlet,' with Macready and Phelps in the principal parts, "the only striking novelty in the performance being the *Ophelia* of Miss P. Horton, which approached very nearly to the wild pathos of the original in one scene, and was touching and beautiful in all" (*Athenæum*, March 21, 1840). At the same theatre, during the same year (Tuesday, December 8), Miss P. Horton sustained the part of *Georgina Vesey*, first performance of the late Lord Lytton's play of 'Money.' In 1841 she was still a member of the company of the Haymarket Theatre, appearing in various comedies. In 1842 (November 16), at Drury Lane, under Macready's management, she played with some success the part of *Philidel*, in a "revival" of Purcell's 'King Arthur'; and in March of the following year appeared in the title *rôle* of the fairy spectacle 'Fortunio and His Seven Gifted Sisters.' In 1844 (January 1), at the Haymarket, "in one of the neatest and smartest of the elegant series of extravaganza for which the town is indebted to Mr. Planché," Miss P. Horton performed the part of *Graceful*. She continued a member of the Haymarket company until the end of the season 1846. At this period of her career she is mentioned in a contemporary journal as "one who ought to have been by this time the first contralto on our stage, now that Mrs. Shaw has left it." She acted in extravaganza and pantomime, produced annually at Easter and Christmas, and, in fact, was the mainspring of this class of entertainment at the Haymarket under Mr. Benjamin Webster's management. Tuesday, December 7, 1847, Miss P. Horton acted (with the leading players of the day), at Covent Garden Theatre, the part of *Ariel* ('Tempest,' act 1, sc. 2), in aid of the "Fund for the Purchase and Preservation of Shakespeare's House at Stratford-on-Avon." In 1849 she played in the various Shakespearian "revivals" of Mr. and Mrs. Charles Kean at the Haymarket. From 1850 to 1854 Miss P. Horton appeared from time to time at the Haymarket, Drury Lane, and Olympic Theatres, for the most part in extravaganza. The latter year she went on a "starring" tour in the provinces "with a sort of entertainment or medley song, in which the different European styles of singing are represented or parodied," in regard to which the following entry appears in Prof. Morley's *Journal of a London Playgoer*, pp. 113-14:—"March 17, 1855.— An entertainment entitled 'Illustrative Gatherings' was given last Monday at the St. Martin's Hall by Miss P. Horton. The lady who by this name is so widely known as a public favourite is the wife of a skilful musician and composer, Mr. T. German Reed, who assists in the entertainment. Mainly it consists, however, of those characteristic songs and personations by which Miss P. Horton won her reputation on the stage. In one of the latter she admirably represents a dialogue between two old women, being differently dressed on either side so as to put each vividly in turn before her audience. Another of her characters is a singing, laughing dandy in ringlets and moustache, whose *methode* as a dandy singer is hit off with exquisite skill. And throughout it is delightful to hear her fine voice and observe her free, cordial, unaffected manner." This entertainment was the forerunner of the amusing and popular series of drawing-room plays given for so many years by Mr. and Mrs. German- Reed at "The Gallery of Illustration," Regent Street, London, and now (1879) at St. George's Hall, Langham Place. Miss P. Horton's last appearance on the stage proper took place in 1858.

REEVE, WYBERT, was born in London 1831, and entered the dramatic profession at Bradford, Yorkshire, in 1849, playing the part of *Frederick* in ' The Wonder.' Afterwards he joined the York circuit, appearing in various juvenile leading parts, as *Azael, Sir T. Clifford,* &c. In 1852, at Plymouth, he produced his first dramatic piece, a farce, entitled ' An Australian Hoax.' In 1855 he joined the Bath and Bristol company. The same year he wrote and produced a farce entitled ' Supper Gratis,' acted during the summer months in Mr. Roxby's circuit. In 1857 Mr. Reeve became a member of the Theatre Royal, Manchester, company, with whom he acted for four consecutive seasons, as light and eccentric comedian. During this engagement, he produced a comedietta entitled ' A Match for a Mother-in-Law,' and was also part author of the successful pantomime entitled ' Blue Beard.' On leaving Manchester to enter upon the management of the Cardiff, and subsequently of the Swansea and Ryde Theatres, Mr. Reeve was presented with a testimonial by his professional colleagues of the Theatre Royal. In 1862 he managed the Theatre Royal, Sheffield, under the lesseeship of Mr. Charles Pitt, a position which Mr. Reeve resigned in 1865, for the purpose of opening the New South Shields Theatre. In 1867 he became lessee of the Theatre Royal, Scarborough, of which, however, he has now (1879) ceased to be proprietor. At Sheffield he produced ' Pike O'Callaghan,' an Irish two-act piece, which was afterwards played in London at the Surrey Theatre ; a'three-act comedy, ' Not So Bad After All '; and the three successful pantomimes entitled ' The Dragon of Wantley,' ' Robinson Crusoe,' and ' Little Red Riding Hood,' of which pieces he is author. He made his first appearance on the London stage, October 1869, at the Lyceum Theatre, as *John Mildmay* in ' Still Waters Run Deep.' " Mr. Reeve possesses the necessary qualifications to render his assumption of *John Mildmay* essentially popular—a pleasing *physique,* deep sonorous voice, distinct enunciation, gentlemanly self-possession of no common order, and a thorough knowledge of stage business ; all are brought to bear in his representation, the result being a genuine and well-deserved success." (*Standard,* October 1869.) Subsequently Mr. Reeve produced and appeared in his comedies of ' Won at Last,' and ' Not So Bad After All,' at the Charing Cross Theatre, with success. In 1871 (after playing in the provinces) he returned to London and appeared at the Olympic Theatre as *Walter Hartwright,* on the production of Wilkie Collins's play ' The Woman in White.' Shortly afterwards, during Mr. George

Vining's illness, Mr. Reeve sustained the part of *Fosco* in the same play, and so satisfactorily, that he has since performed this character more than fifteen hundred times in various cities of the United Kingdom, Canada, and the United States of America, and more recently (1878-9) in the Australian colonies. His performance of this part in New York was noticed in the following terms in the *New York Tribune :*—" Mr. Reeve's intellect is, manifestly, of an alert order, compact, vital, sympathetic, and fed by a vigorous imagination. His voice is fresh and bright , his individuality is unique and pleasing ; his bearing is notably refined and very agreeable. He used no stage tricks to entrap attention, but, in a mood of quiet power and skilful precision, he embodied the character and lived it out through its experience. He had not been five minutes on the stage before the presence was felt of an original nature, and a dramatic artist of the best school—because the school of simplicity,"

Mr. Wybert Reeve is a member of the Dramatic Authors' Society. He has written, among other pieces, 'Never Reckon Your Chickens, &c.,' a farce performed at the Olympic Theatre, and received with much favour ; ' Parted,' a four-act comedy-drama ; ' The Better Angel,' a four-act play, and a piece entitled ' I Love You '; and he has also produced dramatizations of ' George Geith ' and ' No Name,' the latter made at the request of Mr. Wilkie Collins.

*RICHARDS, CICELY. Since January 1875, when Miss Richards assumed the character of *Belinda* in ' Our Boys,' she has continued a member of the company of the Vaudeville Theatre. She appeared there in a subordinate part in ' The Girls,' April 19, 1879, and through the run of that piece, till the revival in September of ' The Two Roses,' when she essayed the part of *Mrs. Cupps.*

RIGHTON, EDWARD CORRIE, had earned a high reputation in the provinces as an actor previous to his *début* in London, which took place, Wednesday, January 25, 1871, at the Royal Court Theatre. The occasion was the opening of that theatre under Miss Litton's management ; and in the principal piece of the evening, an original comedy by W. S. Gilbert entitled ' Randall's Thumb,' Mr. Righton played *Joe Bangles*, and created a very favourable impression. After a few months he was elected manager of the Court Theatre, a position which he held for two years. During his engagement there he appeared in the following " original " parts, viz. *Joe Gargery* in 'Great Expectations' ; *Boomblehardt* in ' Creatures of Impulse '; *Isaac of York* in a burlesque on Sir W. Scott's novel of ' Ivanhoe ' entitled ' In re-Becca '; *Lutin* in the burlesque of ' The Happy Land '; *Richelieu* in burlesque ' Richelieu Redressed '; *Anthony Tubb,* ' Tale of a Tub ' ; *Weathersby Grandison* in ' Divorce Case '; *Sir Philander Rose,* ' Hot Water '; *Wackford Squeers* in ' Dotheboys Hall '; *Mr. Salmon,* ' About Town ' ; and as ' the bewitched bard *Bracy* ' in the burlesque of ' Christabelle,' in which Mr. Righton very cleverly caricatured a distinguished living tragedian : " The acting all through this scene was passionate and intense, and it was difficult to separate the fun from the real thing. On no former occasion has Mr. Righton so thoroughly proved that any comparison between him and Mr Robson was not a ridiculous compliment. He does not perhaps suggest Mr. Robson in his best days, but it is not an ignoble feather in his cap to suggest Mr. Robson. Another imitation by Mr. Righton of a totally different kind, quite apart from the Mathias travestie, but showing the versatility and humour of the actor, is given in one of the comic dances, in which Mr. Righton suggests, amidst the roars of the audience, the extravagant bound-ings and the irrepressible elasticity of Mdlle. Sara, the Philharmonic dancer. This is really wonderfully clever. Without any petticoat of course, and without any female habiliments whatever, Mr Righton is for the minute the famous Mdlle. Sara. The sudden plunge up of the leg, the strut, the panting desire to be at it again the restlessness, and the little tricks and affectations of this well-known dancer are reproduced with the greatest accuracy. All this we repeat, is burlesque acting. It is worth going to see, and deserves to be talked about. Far indeed is it removed from the tedious insipidity, the everlasting breakdown, the music-hall topical song, and the never-ending sameness of modern burlesque.' (*Observer*, May 19, 1872.)

Among other characters which have been performed by Mr. Righton the following are deserving of notice, viz. *Bob* in 'Old Heads and Young Hearts'; *Major Shoreshot* in a farcical comedy entitled 'Flirtation'; *Dogberry* in 'Much Ado About Nothing, played at the Olympic Theatre, London; *Touchstone* in 'As You Like It,' played at Drury Lane Theatre; *Tony Lumpkin* in 'She Stoops to Conquer,' played at the Globe Theatre; *Bob Acres* in 'The Rivals,' played at the same theatre, of which he was for a time lessee (1877–8). During the period of his management there he produced the two following comedies, which subsequently became very popular—"Stolen Kisses' and 'Dearer than Life.' Since leaving the Globe Theatre, Mr. Righton has appeared with con-siderable success in Manchester, Dublin, and other places.

RIGNOLD, GEORGE, brother of the undermentioned William Rignold, became connected with the stage in boyhood, and was for several years at the Bath and Bristol Theatres. He first attracted notice on the London stage by his praiseworthy performances in 1870 and two following years at the Queen's Theatre, where he first appeared as *Sir John Brydges* in ''Twixt Axe and Crown,' and subsequently as *Father Isambard* in Tom Taylor's drama 'Joan of Arc,' *Wenzel* in W. G. Wills's drama of 'Hinko, &c. During 1872 at that theatre he successively sustained the part of *Posthumus* in a revival of 'Cymbeline,' of *Icilius* in a revival of 'Virginius'; of *M. Théophile Ferron* in Richard Lee's original comedy 'Ordeal by Touch;' of *Romeo* in a revival of 'Romeo and Juliet;' and, lastly, of *Amos Clark* in Watts Phillips's drama of that name. He has twice visited Australia and the United States, in both of which countries he has been very successful, and has largely added to his reputation by his interesting impersonation of the character of 'Henry V.'

*RIGNOLD, SUSAN, sister of the above and under-mentioned George and William Rignold.

RIGNOLD, WILLIAM HENRY RIGNALL, was born in Leicester, December 18, 1836, and first appeared on the stage in his fourth year at the Redditch Theatre in a " Benefit" performance for his mother, who was " starring " there during the vacation at the Theatre Royal, Birmingham. Mr. (then "Master") William Rignold danced a sailor's hornpipe, and Mr. Alfred Mellon was good enough to go over from Birmingham to lead the band on the occasion. Mr. Rignold appeared on the stage as a dancer and in pantomime during his boyhood ; and in 1846, at Newcastle, played the part of *Franco* in ' Guy Mannering,' with Miss Cushman in her great part of Meg Merrilies. Afterwards he studied music, and took his first lessons on the violin from Mr. Coppin, father of the Australian manager. William Rignold entered the orchestra in 1850 at the Queen's Theatre, Hull. In 1855 he was *repetiteur* at New Theatre, Sheffield, under the management of Mr. Charles Dillon. In 1856 Mr. Rignold happened to be " sent to Limerick by Henry Webb to lead the band for ' Rob Roy,' Sir William Don playing the Baillie. The ' heavy gentleman ' lost the train, and I played *Rashleigh* and led the orchestra as well, without being discovered by the crowded audience. This performance made such an impression that all my friends persuaded me to take to the stage ; so I left my much-loved violin, and, in 1857, ' opened ' at the Amphitheatre, Liverpool, under Mr. Copeland, as ' general utility.' At the end of three years I had played the entire round of ' heavy business.' I had the good fortune in many of Mr. Webster's parts to please Celeste, who offered to make me an opening in London. I still practised the violin, hoping the day might come when I should appear as a soloist."* In 1860 Mr. Rignold was acting at the Bath and Bristol Theatres Royal as "high comedian"; second season "juvenile lead"; third and fourth seasons " entire lead." In 1865 he entered into an engagement with the management of the Theatre Royal, Dublin, and played "lead " there for four seasons. In 1869-70 he was playing at the Princess's Theatre, London, where he made his *début* on the metropolitan stage, February 15, 1869, as *Count de Fersen*, in Palgrave Simpson's ' Marie Antoinette.' Since that time he has in the metropolis fulfilled engagements at the Adelphi, Gaiety, and Olympic Theatres, &c. Mr. W. Rignold is at present (November 1879) engaged at the Princess's Theatre, performing in ' Drink,' a version by Charles Reade of a French play founded on M. Zola's ' L'Assommoir.' In the English version Mr. W. Rignold " created " the part of *Goujet*, one of the most successful impersonations in the piece. It is interesting to notice that his acting attracted the attention of M. Francisque Sarcey during that gentleman's visit to London in May 1879. In a letter to the writer of the interesting notes on

* Letter from Mr. W. Rignold to the Editor.

" The Theatres," published weekly in the *Daily News* (July 1, 1879); that admirable dramatic critic writes : " The artist who plays *Gueule d'Or* [a sobriquet of *Goujet*] impressed me by the simple truth of his acting. He has a ' good-bye ' that brings tears into the eyes."

ROBSON, E. M., born in London, January 12, 1855; nephew of the distinguished comedian the late F. Robson. He first discovered a partiality for a dramatic career through being permitted to play one of the children in the burlesque of ' Medea,' with his uncle, during that admirable actor's last " starring " tour in Ireland. His first professional engagement was (1871) at the Elgin Theatre, under Mr. Edward Price's management. He has since played at the leading provincial theatres, notably in Edinburgh, Liverpool, and Birmingham, several of the late Mr. F. Robson's more important conceptions. Mr. E. M. Robson made his first appearance on the London stage at the Aquarium Theatre, August 3, 1878, in the part of *Captain Spooneysoft*, in a piece entitled ' That's Why She Loved Him.'

ROLLS, MRS. ALEXANDER. *See* BARRY, HELEN.

RORKE, MARY, was born in Westminster, and entered the dramatic profession in Mr. Charles Wyndham's company playing at the Crystal Palace, Sydenham, in 1874. She was also temporarily engaged at the Croydon Theatre under Mr. Charles Kelly's management in the same year. Miss Rorke made her *début* on the London stage at the Mirror Theatre, Holborn, under Mr. Horace Wigan's management, in a subordinate part in ' Maids of Honour.' Subsequently she was engaged at the T. R. Haymarket, Prince of Wales's Theatre, Liverpool, Royal Court and Criterion Theatres, London. At the two last named she has appeared in the following characters, viz. *Clara* (' Model of a Wife '); *Fanny Bunter* (' New Men and Old Acres '); *Meg* (' Meg's Diversion '); *Mrs. Dorothy Sterry* (' Truth '). The last-mentioned play, by Mr. Bronson Howard, was produced at the Criterion Theatre January 1879.

ROSELLE, AMY, was born in London in 1854, and first appeared upon the stage in childhood at the Theatre Royal, Exeter, acting with her brother, " Master Percy Roselle." Afterwards she was engaged at the Cardiff, Swansea, and Plymouth Theatres in succession ; and was then engaged by Mr. Sothern to support him in the provinces. In 1871 she made her *début* on the London stage at the Haymarket Theatre as *Lady Teazle ;* and in May of that year appeared with Mr. Sothern at the same theatre in a comedy by H. J. Byron entitled ' An English Gentleman ; or, the Squire's Last Shilling.' Having played at the Haymarket until the end of the season, Miss Roselle accepted an engagement to play with Mr. Sothern in the United States. Returning to London in 1872, in September of that year she was engaged by Mr. Chatterton to support the late Mr. Samuel Phelps and Mr. Creswick in Shakespearian parts at the Princess's Theatre. Among the characters she there undertook were *Portia, Desdemona, Ophelia;* and *Julie de Mortemar* ('Richelieu'). Subsequently she performed at the Haymarket Theatre (January 3, 1874), *Eve Van Brugh* in W. S. Gilbert's 'Charity.' Saturday, January 16, 1875, first performance at the Vaudeville Theatre of H. J. Byron's comedy 'Our Boys,' Miss Roselle sustained the part of *Mary Melrose.* In 1878 she was engaged by Mr. and Mrs. Kendal to support them "on tour" in 'Diplomacy,' playing the part of *Dora.* In 1879 she accepted an engagement at the Prince of Wales's Theatre, and in January appeared there in a revival of 'Caste' as *Esther Eccles,* the part originally played by Miss Lydia Foote, and in which Miss Roselle proved herself a careful and accomplished actress, and increased her professional reputation.

ROSELLE, JULIA, sister of the above-named Amy Roselle, made her first appearance on the stage in the United States in 1871 as *Augusta* ('Our American Cousin'), Mr. Sothern in the leading character. Returning to England in 1873, Miss Julia Roselle played "juvenile leading parts" for three successive seasons at Birmingham, Manchester, and Liverpool; and at Christmas 1876 made her first appearance on the London stage at Covent Garden Theatre. In March 1877 she accepted an engagement at the Royal Aquarium Theatre and played the character of *Biddy* ('Great Expectations') with considerable success. Subsequently (1877-8) Miss Julia Roselle was engaged by the management of the T. R. Haymarket and played *Miss Araminta Brown* in 'David Garrick,' &c.

ROUSBY, WYBERT, was an actor of considerable provincial repute previous to his first appearance on the London stage, which took place at the Queen's Theatre, Long Acre, December 19, 1869, in the part of *Bertuccio* (Triboulet) in Tom Taylor's drama 'The Fool's Revenge.' "Mr. Rousby, who is a gentleman of rather slight figure and proportions, has a face capable of much and varied expression, and is evidently well trained in all the business of the stage. His voice is good, and his delivery clear and resonant. He is a master of the rare art of correct emphasis. He knows how to fill up his time on the stage with the restless activity proper to the character of the jester, with his misanthropic hatred of the frivolous and profligate court of the Duke, his cruel spirit of revenge, and his tenderness for the sole object of his affections— his daughter, whose existence is the secret of his life. Careful elaboration is suggested by every point of Mr. Rousby's acting in this part, from the picturesque Mephistophelean attitudes, of which he has so great a variety, to the manifold wrinkles of his malignant smiles. Indeed the faults of his performance lie on this side, though it was not without some of those bursts which at least appear spontaneous, and which excite the feelings of the audience for that reason. . . . The very completeness of Mr. Rousby's art will, no doubt, detract something from the curiosity with which his future performances will be looked forward to; and many of his points are undoubtedly traceable more to the school to which his style belongs than to the promptings of his own genius." (*Daily News*, December 22, 1869.)

Following the above date Mr. Rousby appeared on the London stage in those plays of importance first produced at the Queen's Theatre in which his wife played the leading *rôle*. In Mr. Tom Taylor's drama ''Twixt Axe and Crown' he was in the original cast as *Courtenay;* in 'Joan of Arc,' by the same author, he played, on the occasion of its first performance, the part of *La Hire;* and (at the Princess's Theatre) in W. G. Wills's drama 'Mary Queen of Scots' the part of *Knox.* In February 1871 Mr. Rousby appeared at the Queen's Theatre as *Orlando* in a revival of 'As You Like It,' Mrs. Rousby playing Rosalind; in April 1873, at Drury Lane Theatre, he sustained the part of *King Lear* in a revival of Shakespeare's tragedy, his wife acting Cordelia. Since 1876 Mr. Rousby has not appeared on the London stage in any part requiring notice.

ROYCE, EDWARD WILLIAM, was born at Eversholt, Beds, August 11, 1841, and entered the dramatic profession in the year 1860, as an auxiliary at Covent Garden Theatre, in the opera of 'Un Ballo in Maschera,' having specially studied operatic and character dancing. In 1861 he was engaged at the Lyceum Theatre, and danced in the "Fair Scene" of Edmund Falconer's drama 'Peep o' Day.' Christmas, 1863, at the old Theatre Royal, Leeds, he first sustained the part of *Harlequin* in the pantomime of 'The Yellow Dwarf.' Mr. Royce has since played *Harlequin* with great success at theatres at the following principal towns, viz. Leeds, York, Sheffield, Hull, Lincoln, Nottingham, Manchester, Glasgow, Edinburgh. While playing the character at the York Theatre in 1868 he was happily able to save the life of a little girl of the ballet whose skirts had unfortunately become ignited. For this act of bravery he received a testimonial from the Royal Society for the Protection of Life from Fire.

At Leeds Mr. Royce performed the "original" *Welch* in Charles Reade's drama of 'Foul Play,' concerning which the author, in a letter to the editor of the *Manchester Examiner* (June 26, 1868), said that "it owed a large share of its success to the talent and zeal of the performers, and especially of those who played the minor characters." Mr. Royce has been a member of the travelling companies of Mr. John Coleman and Captain Disney Roebuck. In 1872, at the Prince of Wales's Theatre, Liverpool, he played the part of *Varney* in Halliday's revived burlesque of 'Kenilworth,' entitled 'Little Amy Robsart.' The same year, having accepted an engagement from the management of the Gaiety Theatre, in London, he first appeared at that theatre in September, in the part of *Whiskerandos* in 'The Critic.' At the St. James's Theatre, during the management of Miss Litton, he played *Tom Cobb*, first performance of W. S. Gilbert's farcical comedy of that title. At the Gaiety Theatre he has since played the following original parts, viz. *Dick Evergreen* ('My Awful Dad'), *Derrick* ('Young Rip

Van Winkle'), *José* (' Little Don Cæsar de Bazan'), *Count Smiff* (' The Bohemian Gyurl'), *Valentine* (' Little Doctor Faust'), *Elvino* (' Il Sonnambulo'), and *Radapolam* (' Rajah of Mysore'), &c., &c. In 1873 and 1874 Mr. Royce produced the Christmas pantomime for the Messrs. Gunn, of the New Gaiety Theatre and Theatre Royal, Dublin, and on various occasions he has undertaken the responsible duties of stage-manager and master of the ballet. He is still (1879) a member of the Gaiety company.

RUSSELL, HOWARD, was born in London, January 6, 1835, and entered the dramatic profession in 1858, making his first appearance in London, September 28, 1867 (having previously studied the rudiments of acting in the provinces), at the Victoria Theatre, in a drama entitled ' The Sin of a Life.' Subsequently he became engaged by Mr. F. B. Chatterton for his theatres, and played various characters in the late Andrew Halliday's plays represented at Drury Lane, the Princess's, and Adelphi Theatres. He has had the advantage of supporting at those theatres some of the leading players of the day, including Messrs. Phelps, Fechter, Creswick, Anderson, King, Barry Sullivan, Mesdames Helen Faucit, Neilson, Herman Vezin, Wallis, Genevieve Ward. Mr. Russell played the character of *Derrick* with efficiency, to the Rip van Winkle of Mr. Jefferson, during his last engagement at the Princess's Theatre. He has taken leading parts in some of the plays produced at the Crystal Palace, notably, *Polonius* (' Hamlet'), and *Phocian* (' Antigone'), the first produced by Mr. Tom Taylor, the second under Mr. Wyndham's superintendence ; and has also played the character of *Claudius*, with Mr. Fechter in the title *rôle* (' Hamlet'), at the Princess's Theatre in June 1872. The production of ' The Wandering Jew' at the Adelphi, and revival of the play of ' Uncle Tom's Cabin' at the same theatre, brought Mr. Russell under notice of the public as a painstaking and efficient actor. He sustained the part of *Eros* on the occasion of the revival of ' Antony and Cleopatra' at Drury Lane Theatre, in 1876 ; and later (1878) has enacted the part of *Richard, Duke of Gloucester*, with considerable success, in a revival of ' Jane Shore' at the Princess's Theatre.

*RYDER, JOHN, was born in 1814. He had attracted notice as an actor of much promise in the line of legitimate drama previous to his being enrolled in Mr. Macready's company, during that eminent tragedian's management of Drury Lane Theatre. This engagement was the first step in Mr. Ryder's advancement. In October 1842, in a revival at that theatre of ' As You Like It,' with Messrs. Macready, Anderson, Keeley, Phelps, and Mesdames Nisbett, Stirling, and Keeley in the caste, Mr. Ryder played the *Duke.* He appeared in most of the plays, original and revivals, produced under Mr. Macready's superintendence during his period of management. At the Princess's Theatre, October 13, 1845, Mr. Macready playing Hamlet, Mr. Ryder sustained the part of *Claudius.* At the same theatre, in the year following, first performance, 20th March, of ' The King of the Commons' (White),

Mr. Macready as James V. of Scotland, Mr. Ryder acted the character of *Sir Adam Weir of Lachemont.* In 1847, on Monday, November 22, at the same theatre, in a play by Taylor (abridged by Macready), entitled ' Philip Van Artevelde,' Mr. Ryder played *Van den Bosch ;* Mr. Macready and Miss Susan Cushman were in the cast. In 1850, Monday, January 28, he played *Œnarus*, first performance of John Oxenford's version of Corneille's ' Ariadne.' When Messrs. Charles Kean and Keeley entered upon the management of the Princess's Theatre, in 1850, Mr. Ryder became a member of their company, and on the opening night of their first season, Saturday, September 28, appeared as *Antonio*, in a revival of ' Twelfth Night.' He subsequently took part in many of the performances for which Mr. Charles Kean's administration became famous. On Saturday, November 9, 1850, first performance at the Princess's of ' The Templar' (A. R. Slous), he sustained the part of *Aymer de la Roche, Grand Master*, with much success.

During 1851 Mr. Ryder appeared in various Shakespearian plays at the Princess's Theatre, and in February of that year acted the part of *Captain Channel*, in a revival of Douglas Jerrold's ' Prisoner of War.' On February 9, 1852, in a revival of ' King John,' he sustained the character of *Hubert*, a part which he played subsequently at the same theatre in October 1858. The same year, Monday, June 7, first performance of Lovell's play, ' The Trial of Love,' at the Princess's, he played *Colonel Boswell.* In 1853, on Monday, February 14, in a revival of ' Macbeth,' Mr. Ryder acted the part of *Macduff.* On Monday, June 13, 1853, Mr. Ryder sustained the part of *Salamenes*, in the grand performance of Byron's tragedy, ' Sardanapalus,' commented upon, at the time, as " the one piece of acting in that play on which there could not be two opinions in regard to its excellence." In the autumn of 1854 Mr. Ryder left the Princess's Theatre for a brief period and accepted an engagement to lead the " heavy business," supported by an efficient company, selected from other metropolitan theatres, at the Bower Saloon, Lambeth, under Miss Lydia Pearce's management. As to which engagement it was remarked in a contemporary journal that " he and his companions on this despised stage may easily find more laudable business to perform than that to which he, and others of respectable name, have lately been condemned at other establishments. In all probability at the popular saloon the higher drama will be preferred." The first week of his engagement, commencing Monday, August 21, 1854, Mr. Ryder appeared in three different characters :—*Macbeth, Othello*, and the *Stranger.* The first-mentioned part he had once before performed at the Princess's during the temporary indisposition of Mr. Charles Kean, and had earned great applause. In October 1854, Mr. Ryder rejoined the company of the Princess's Theatre, and reappeared on its stage the 9th of that month, as *Dymond*, first performance of Douglas Jerrold's play, ' Heart of Gold.' In January 1855, ' Louis the Eleventh,' translated by Dion Boucicault from Casimir Delavigne's historical play of that name, was performed at the same theatre, Charles Kean as Louis ; Mr. Ryder, *Coitier.*

In May of the same year, in a revival at the Princess's Theatre of 'Henry the Eighth,' on an unexampled scale of grandeur, Mr. Ryder sustained the part of *Buckingham*, and was grand and imposing. "His first scene was marked with laudable care, and his final address to the spectators of his execution was a fine example of oratorical speaking, and might be consulted as a lesson by those to whom eloquence is a mission." (*Athenæum*, May 19, 1855.) On April 28, 1856, still at the Princess's Theatre, he appeared as *Polixenes*, in a sumptuous revival of 'A Winter's Tale'; and the following year, May 12, as *Bolingbroke*, in 'Richard the Second,' and July 1, as *Caliban*, in 'The Tempest.' On April 17, 1858, he acted the character of *Edgar* in a revival of 'King Lear'; and in 1859, *Williams*, on the production of 'Henry the Fifth.' When Mr. Kean retired from the management of the Princess's Theatre in August 1859, Mr. Ryder remained a member of its company with Mr. Kean's successor, Mr. Augustus Harris.

On Wednesday, November 2, 1859, Mr. Ryder played at the Princess's the part of *Giovanni Orseolo*, first performance of Edmund Falconer's drama 'The Outlaws of the Adriatic.' On Saturday, September 28, 1861, first performance in England of Brougham's 'Playing with Fire,' he acted the character of *Timothy Crabstick*. The same year, during the first engagement at the Princess's Theatre of Mr. Fechter, Mr. Ryder played *Iago* to that gentleman's Othello. The *Times* (October 24, 1861) noticed this performance as follows :—" Mr. Ryder's *Iago*, Mephistophelean in appearance, quick in thought, picturesque in gesticulation, is probably a creation of Mr. Fechter's, inasmuch as it could scarcely have emanated from a veteran of the London stage. It was admirably fresh and finished, and the disciple, for such we presume he is, has this advantage over the preceptor, that he is able to give the old-fashioned English weight to his language. He is placed in a new position by the peculiar interpretation given by Mr. Fechter to the concluding speech of the play. Othello, instead of allowing Iago to retire, drags him towards the bed, and compels him to kneel before the murdered Desdemona. When he draws his dagger, all suppose that the author of mischief will be the victim, and the suicide therefore occasions more than usual surprise."

In the following year, March 3, Mr. Ryder played *Othello* and Mr. Fechter Iago. In November 1861, at the Princess's, Mr. Ryder acted the part of *Falstaff* in a revival of 'The Merry Wives of Windsor." Said the *Athenæum* (November 30, 1861): "Mr. Ryder has certain advantages of figure for the assumption, and though he lacks the unction which would be shown by a humorous actor, presents an outline that is at once intelligent and effective. He makes the most of the text, and throws the entire force of his conception into the character. The whole is evidently the effect of much study on the part of the actor, and is therefore the more deserving of special notice. What he has thoroughly thought out in the closet, he carefully depicts on the stage. The knightly qualifications of the jovial wassailer he marks with capital discrimination, while he solicitously softens the grosser features."

In 1862, February 10, at the same theatre, Mr. Ryder played *Jaques*, in a revival of ' As You Like It.' The same year, at Drury Lane Theatre, first performance of Boucicault's play, ' The Relief of Lucknow,' he sustained the part of the *Rajah Gholam Bahadoor.* The following year, Monday, January 26, at the Theatre Royal, Westminster (Astley's), under Mr. Boucicault's management, first performance of that author's version of ' The Heart of Midlothian,' Mr. Ryder sustained the character of *David Deans.* At Drury Lane, Saturday, October 10, 1863, revival of ' Manfred' by Mr. Samuel Phelps, Mr. Ryder acted the part of the *Abbot of St. Maurice.* He played in various parts at the Lyceum during Mr. Fechter's management of that theatre, 1863-7, and has since appeared as a " star" actor in London and the provinces. His latest (October 1878) appearances of importance on the metropolitan stage have been at Drury Lane Theatre in ' A Winter's Tale' and ' Macbeth.'

SANGER, RACHEL MARY, was born in London. As a child she appeared on the stage (the Olympic) in 1851 in a dramatic version of ' Uncle Tom's Cabin.' After a considerable period of study and practice in the provinces she made her professional *début* in London at the opening of the Bijou Theatre (Highbury) in the part of *Ernani* in the late W. Brough's burlesque of that title. She was engaged for the two succeeding annual pantomimes at Covent Garden—' Aladdin,' and ' The Forty Thieves,' and afterwards became a member of Miss Herbert's company when that lady was lessee of St. James's Theatre. (*See* HERBERT.) At the Princess's Theatre Miss Sanger played *Lucy Fairweather* in a revival of ' The Streets of London '; and, during the temporary indisposition of Mrs. Boucicault, the part of *Arrah* in ' Arrah-na-Pogue.' (*See* BOUCICAULT.) Having at Liverpool originally acted the part of *Lina* in Mr. T. W. Robertson's ' Dreams,' she was chosen by the author to play the same part on the production of this piece at the Gaiety Theatre in London. In July 1870, in a revival at the Olympic Theatre of ' Little Em'ly,' Miss Sanger played the heroine. Subsequently she accepted a position as "leading" lady at the Amphitheatre, Liverpool, and there played the opposite parts to Mr. Barry Sullivan, in this respect developing unexpected dramatic resources. Under Mr. Alexander Henderson's management, at the Globe Theatre, London, she was the original *Fatima* in ' Blue Beard ' (Farnie) produced there at Christmas 1874. At the same theatre she played *Lady Isabel* in a revival of ' East Lynne '; and at the Adelphi Theatre, *Mabel Truegold* in a revival of ' True to the Core.' At the Strand in 1878 Miss Sanger played the leading *rôle* in the burlesque ' Diplunacy.' More recently (1879) she has been engaged at the Gaiety Theatre, Dublin, where she created the part of *Annie* in a play entitled ' Pair o' Wings ' (Paul Meritt and E. Righton).

SANTLEY, KATE, had earned some success in London as a public singer previous to her adopting the stage as a profession. She made her *début* as an actress at Edinburgh, and there, on the occasion of a "starring" visit of the late Charles Kean, played *Jessica* to his Shylock. She made her first appearance on the London stage at the Queen's Theatre in a burlesque on the well-known drama of ' The Stranger.' Afterwards Miss Santley accepted engagements at the Drury Lane and Strand Theatres, and then made a professional tour through the chief cities of the United States. Miss Santley's *rentrée* on the metropolitan boards at the Alhambra Theatre in 1872, when she assumed the character of *Cunégonde* in ' Le Roi Carotte,' was very successful. Since that time she has enacted principal parts in many of the opera-bouffes produced in London which have attained popularity, notably in ' La Belle Hélène,' ' Don Juan,' ' La Jolie Parfumeuse,' and ' La Marjolaine.' In 1877-8 Miss Kate Santley undertook the management of the

New Royalty Theatre for a season, but relinquished it to fulfil various engagements at the principal theatres in the provinces. In April 1879, she commenced an engagement at the Globe Theatre, London, and played the leading female *rôle* in 'Les Cloches de Corneville.'

SAUNDERS, CHARLOTTE, was born in London. She began her professional career in childhood, and first appeared on the stage in May 1833 at Wakefield (Yorkshire), in the part of *Duke of York* in Shakespeare's 'Richard III.' Afterwards she acted many children's parts—*The Spoiled Child, The Climbing Boy, Oliver Twist,* &c., and first attracted notice in the profession by her admirable rendering of the part of *Tilly Slowboy,* on the occasion of the opening of the Theatre Royal, Manchester, in January 1846. Noticing this performance the *Manchester Guardian* (January 4, 1846) said :—" How shall we limit our eulogistic and side-aching admiration of the extraordinary performance of *Tilly Slowboy* by Miss Charlotte Saunders who has most certainly made the part her own ? Miss Turner is stated to have realized the part to perfection in London, but some persons who have seen both award the palm to Miss Saunders. Certainly it is difficult to conceive anything more exquisitely in the spirit of the original than the acting of Miss Saunders throughout. Her fondling of the baby, her slovenly dress and awkward motions, her begrimed face and vacant, open-mouthed stare, are altogether in the richest resemblance to the *Tilly* of Mr. Charles Dickens. Her by-play is really admirable; she is never perfectly quiet ; always doing something perfectly in character, and thus keeping up the true action of the piece. Her scalding her mouth with hot potato while rocking the cradle with her foot; her exclamations at not being able to make the guest hear; her delight at the wedding-cake ; her joy at receiving from Gruff and Jackleton his wedding-ring to put in the fire, but resolving to keep it till she wants it herself; and lastly, her unique dancing in the finale, formed a succession of tableaux, inimitable in their exquisitely grotesque and truly laughable breadth of humour." After some years' practice in Liverpool, Manchester, Birmingham (where she played *Albert* to Mr. Macready's William Tell in a way which secured high commendation from that distinguished tragedian), Glasgow, and Edinburgh, Miss Saunders made her first appearance on the London stage at the Marylebone Theatre under Mrs. Warner's management in August 1847 as *Mopsa* in 'A Winter's Tale.' Miss Saunders also performed here the well-known *rôle* of *Guy Fawkes* in Albert Smith's most amusing burlesque of that title. Afterwards, at the Princess's Theatre, in October 1849, she appeared in the original performance of 'The First Night' (adapted from the French 'Le Père de la Débutante '), in which Mr. Alfred Wigan made such a success as *Dufard.* Criticizing her acting of a part in a farce at the early period of her career, the *Morning Post* (January 30, 1849) speaks of her as " a rapidly rising actress who will take the lead in the *soubrettes.*" In December 1851, Miss Saunders reappeared in London at the Strand

Theatre (then Punch's Playhouse), under Mr. Copeland's management, as the "original" *Chang* in Francis Talfourd's burlesque of
'The Willow-pattern Plate.' Having completed her engagement
here in 1852 she returned to the provinces, and, in conjunction with
that inimitable actor the late F. Robson, became a great favourite
at the Theatre Royal, Dublin. At this time Miss Saunders was
acting what were then known as 'the Vestris parts' in Planché's
burlesque extravaganzas, and in which she gained considerable
reputation. In December 1858 she was once again engaged at the
Strand Theatre, and appeared there in the following among other
pieces, viz. in Halliday and Lawrence's burlesque of 'Kenilworth'
(as *Tresilian*), H. J. Byron's burlesques of 'The Lady of Lyons'
(as *Claude Melnotte*), 'Miller and his Men,' 'Aladdin,' &c., &c.
In September 1863, at Drury Lane Theatre, Miss Saunders was in
the "original" cast of Falconer's play, 'Nature above Art.' In the
following year in December she appeared at St. James's Theatre as
Hercules in W. Brough's burlesque of 'Hercules and Omphale.'
Saturday, October 6, 1866, at the Holborn Theatre (the opening
night), first performance of Boucicault's drama, 'Flying Scud,' Miss
Saunders played the character of *Bob Buckskin* the jockey. This
piece had a long run, and was revived at the same theatre in 1868,
Miss Saunders in her "original" character. In 1868 she joined
Miss Oliver's company at the Royalty Theatre, and appeared
during the following seasons in many original parts in burlesque
—*Billy Taylor* in Burnand's burlesque of that name; *Lord Ronald*
in the same author's burlesque 'Claude du Val,' &c., &c. Among
Miss Saunders' more recent successes her impersonation of *Madame
Guichard* in the three-act comedy, 'Love and Honour,' founded on
Dumas the younger's 'Monsieur Alphonse,' is entitled to high
praise. The English version by Mr. Campbell Clarke was first
produced by the late Mdlle. Beatrice and her comedy-drama company in the provinces, and in August 1875 was placed on the stage
of the Globe Theatre in London. With respect to Miss Saunders'
acting of the part of *Madame Guichard*, the *Times* (August 20,
1875) remarked as follows :—"Miss Charlotte Saunders, as *Madame
de Guichard*, abandons herself to every side of the character with
surprising facility, and nothing can be better in its way than her
simulation of the contending feelings with which the innkeeper's
widow dismisses the adventurer. Altogether, her *Madame Guichard*
is one of those portraitures of character which if once seen is not
to be forgotten."

SAVILLE, ELIZA HELENA, youngest daughter of the late
John Faucit Saville, formerly of the Haymarket and Adelphi, and
afterwards manager of the Nottingham, Sheffield, and other theatres
in the midland counties, and sister of Miss Kate Saville who was
an actress of considerable repute on the London stage prior to her
marriage in 1872. Miss Eliza Saville made her first appearance
on the stage at a very early age, playing children's parts at
the Theatre Royal, Nottingham, under her mother's management.
Having studied and practised at that theatre she was afterwards

engaged as "leading lady" in Manchester, Sheffield, and Dublin (1870–72). In 1873, on tour with Mr. Wybert Reeve's company, she acted "with power and ability" the part of *Marian Halcombe* in 'The Woman in White,' adapted by Mr. Reeve from Mr. Wilkie Collins's novel of that name. During 1874–5 she fulfilled several short special engagements in the provinces. In May 1878, at the request of the late Mdlle. Beatrice, she undertook the title *rôle* in 'The Woman of the People,' and sustained that and other leading parts of the *répertoire* of the Beatrice company up to the close of the year. In the spring of 1879 she rejoined that company under Mr. Frank Harvey's management; and, on Easter Monday (April 14) of the same year, made a very successful *début* in London at the Olympic Theatre in the *rôle* and play last mentioned ('Woman of the People').

SAVILLE, KATE, sister of the above-mentioned Eliza Helena Saville, made her first appearance on the London stage September 24, 1859, at the Princess's Theatre, as *Camilla Wiley* in 'Ivy Hall,' adapted by John Oxenford from the French 'Le Roman d'un Jeune Homme Pauvre' of Octave Feuillet. On Monday, January 30, of the following year she acted the part of *Lucie Manette*, first performance at the Lyceum of 'The Tale of Two Cities,' one of the most important of Madame Celeste's productions when she had the management of that theatre. Miss Kate Saville was likewise in the original cast of another of the plays produced there by the same lady, namely, 'The House on the Bridge of Notre Dame,' in which Miss Saville sustained the part of *Mélaine de St. Ange*. In the two following years she was engaged at the Olympic Theatre, where she "created" the part of *Martha Gibbs* in Tom Taylor's 'All that Glitters is not Gold'; of *Lady Camilla Hailstone* in Watts Phillips's play, 'Camilla's Husband'; and *May Edwards* in Tom Taylor's 'Ticket of Leave Man.' At the Strand Theatre, in October 1863, Miss Saville played the leading *rôle*, first performance of H. T. Craven's 'Miriam's Crime.' In the following year, on February 15, at the Princess's Theatre, she acted the character of *Beatrice*, first performance of Watts Phillips's comedy, 'Paul's Return.' On Monday, April 2, 1866, at the Haymarket Theatre, she played, at the first performance in London of Westland Marston's comedy entitled 'The Favourite of Fortune,' the part of *Hester Lorrington*. In the same year, September 8, first performance at the Surrey Theatre of "the T. P. Cooke prize drama," by A. R. Slous, entitled 'True to the Core,' she acted the leading female *rôle, Mrs. Truegold*. Miss Kate Saville has also acted with great success in the provinces. She retired from the stage on her marriage in 1872.

SCOTT-SIDDONS, MARY FRANCES, great-grand-daughter of the famous actress Sarah Siddons, one of whose three sons, George, held a high civil appointment in India. A son of George Siddons, Captain William Siddons, 35th Bengal Native Infantry, married the daughter of Lieut.-Colonel Earle; and of this marriage came Mary Frances Scott-Siddons, the subject of this record. She first appeared on the stage at Edinburgh as *Juliet* in the early part of 1866. In the year following, in London, she gave public readings at the Hanover Square Rooms from Shakespeare's plays. She made her *début* on the metropolitan stage, Monday, April 8, of the same year, at the Haymarket Theatre, in the character of *Rosalind* ('As You Like It'). This performance was thus noticed in the *Daily Telegraph* (April 10, 1867):—"The favourable opinion of the histrionic qualifications of Mrs. Scott-Siddons formed by the distinguished auditory who listened last week with so much satisfaction to that lady's Shakespearian readings at the Hanover Square Rooms, was on Monday evening fully confirmed by a fashionable and crowded audience, assembled to witness her *début* on the metropolitan stage as *Rosalind*. A lady who can boast of a direct descent from the most illustrious of our actresses, comes accredited with the strongest recommendation to all who hold in reverence the names which adorn our Thespian annals; but Mrs. Scott-Siddons has a fair claim to theatrical distinction apart from hereditary honours. Well-trained in the business of the stage through a course of provincial practice, there is nothing in the *débutante* which betrays the inexperience of the novice. Possessed of a fine expressive face, which may be called classical in its profile, and endowed with the advantages of a neat symmetrical figure, Mrs. Scott-Siddons effectively supplies the external requisites for this most fascinating of Shakespeare's heroines. Her delivery of the text, on which she has manifestly bestowed much thoughtful study, is characterized by earnestness and intelligence, and her action is appropriate and unrestrained. Judging by the enthusiastic plaudits so frequently bestowed through the evening, her performance would seem to have exceeded the most sanguine expectations her friends had entertained; but the good sense of the actress may be safely trusted to discriminate between the liberal applause which is intended to encourage a young aspirant, and a fervent spontaneous acknowledgment of a great triumph fairly won in the world of art. It is when *Rosalind* dons the doublet and hose that Mrs. Scott-Siddons gives her impulses full play; and the bantering of Orlando in the forest and the vivacious raillery of the imitative wooing were as effective as could be desired. That the young actress who has been received with so warm a welcome is deservedly entitled to the highest position on the metropolitan boards, it would be too much to affirm; but Mrs. Scott-Siddons is unquestionably a valuable acquisition to any theatre in which comedy is performed, and there may be latent powers which only need time and opportunity to favourably develop."

The *Daily News* (April 9, 1867) expressed the opinion that "Mrs. Scott-Siddons's neat figure, pretty face, and pleasing arch delivery, qualified her for light comedy, and her ease, confidence, and freedom of gesture showed that she had an aptitude for acting. Her reading of *Rosalind* was saucy and attractive. She lacked the grand air of the *tragédienne*, which is not always an agreeable air, and many persons, missing this, will vote her unequal to the embodiment of Shakespeare's lighter heroines. Her reception last night by a friendly audience will doubtless encourage her to adopt the stage as a profession, and her sprightliness and evident intelligence will make her path easy. Her future will depend upon herself, her capacity for instruction, and the discretion of her advisers. If she is not exactly the shining star we were led to expect, she is a very lively and promising actress, who may be as easily spoilt as improved." On Monday, September 2 of the same year, Mrs. Scott-Siddons reappeared at the Haymarket in the same character. In the autumn of 1868 she made her first professional appearance in America, giving readings at Steinway Hall, New York, from 'Macbeth' and 'As You Like It.' Subsequently, Mrs. Scott-Siddons entered upon an engagement at the Fifth Avenue Theatre in the same city. After a long absence from London she entered upon a brief engagement at the Haymarket Theatre in 1870, reappearing there on Monday, July 11 of that year, as *Pauline* in 'The Lady of Lyons,' and, during the same month, acting the part of the heroine in Dance's comedietta 'Delicate Ground.' Mrs. Scott-Siddons's next appearance of importance in London took place on Saturday, May 4, 1872, at the Queen's Theatre, on which occasion, "in the first original piece in which she had ever acted," viz. 'Ordeal by Touch' (Richard Lee), she played the part of *Coralie.* The piece was not a satisfactory success. Following the last-mentioned date Mrs. Scott-Siddons was engaged on a "starring" tour in the United States and Australia. In 1879, on Saturday, June 21, she reappeared on the London stage at the Olympic Theatre for the benefit of George Coleman, and recited two lyrical pieces.

SEDGWICK, AMY (Mrs. GOOSTRY), was born in 1835. She had acquired reputation as an actress and much stage experience in the provinces previous to her first appearance on the London stage, which took place Monday, October 5, 1857, at the Haymarket Theatre. The character chosen by Miss Sedgwick for her *début,* which was most successful, was *Pauline* in 'The Lady of Lyon's.' The *Spectator* (October 10, 1857) noticing the performance said : " This week we have had a *début* of more than ordinary promise. Miss Sedgwick, an actress well-known in the northern counties, has made her appearance as *Pauline* in 'The Lady of Lyons.' The intelligence that she displays is no rare qualification, for most of the new candidates for public favour who have lately solicited applause, have shown that they tolerably well understand the meaning of the part undertaken. It is in passing from the conception to the execution that a difficulty has been found, and as our recent *débutantes* have not been of the audacious kind, the difficulty has been revealed, not by desperate leaps over the limits prescribed by Nature, but by a timid unwillingness to use the length of tether which Nature liberally accords. Now Miss Sedgwick acts not only with propriety, but with force; she makes her words and gestures tell, and, though in a quiet manner, marks out her character thoroughly. We suspect she is an actress whose progress will be worth watching."

The week following, on Tuesday, October 13, she acted the character of *Constance* in 'The Love Chase,' as to which the *Athenæum* (October 17, 1857) remarked, " Miss Sedgwick is not without qualifications for the part, and her assumption of it has proved that her natural attributes belong to the comic rather than the tragic art, and that in the former she can display vigour and feeling, as well as the possession of stage artifices. It was needful to show this. . . . With a full intelligence of the character and its conditions, Miss Sedgwick trusted to her native vigour for filling up the usual theatrical outline, and impressed the audience with the opinion that she *acted* well. She must get beyond this point and render them unconscious that she is acting at all, while realizing all the points of character with the utmost elaboration."

On Saturday, November 7, 1857, first performance at the Haymarket of Mr. Tom Taylor's comedy, 'The Unequal Match,' Miss Sedgwick sustained the part of *Hester Grazebrook*, afterwards, in the play, *Lady Arncliff*. This according to Prof. Morley (*Diary of a London Playgoer*, p. 198), was Miss Sedgwick's first appearance here in a part for the acting of which she was without help from traditions of the stage. " Her success was great and it was fairly earned." The play met with a most unequivocal success. " Although flat in some of its earlier parts, and weighted with two or three very uninteresting minor characters, it is, on the whole, spirited and entertaining, and the last of the three acts is new, amusing, and lively. The plot turns on the history of a blacksmith's daughter, who marries a baronet and disgusts her husband by her inaptitude for fine society, and finally, learning the lesson he wishes her to acquire, disgusts him still more by the change in her manners, her principles, and her feelings. At the end she throws off the mask of affectation, and having convinced her husband that simplicity is best, shows that she is simple still. This is the moral of the ' Unequal Match.' But another sense is also given to the words. There is a hollow-hearted coquette, who has once rejected the baronet before he came to his honours and his wealth, who sneers at his humble choice, and determines to win back the heart she has once had offered her. She succeeds so far as to entangle her old lover in a desperate flirtation, but in the end the wife makes her husband feel the superiority of honest affection and genuine worth, and the coquette is discovered to have entered on an ' Unequal Match.' . . . Miss Amy Sedgwick played *Lady Arncliff*. It is a difficult part to play, as she had to sustain three characters so different as those of a village maiden, a bride frightened by her guests, and a fine lady triumphing over a rival. She shows herself quite equal to the task she has undertaken, and acts throughout with an evenness of success which proves that her merits are many and high. There is not, we think, any very great promise in her performance ; she will not console veteran playgoers for the loss of their old favourites, but she is a very useful accession to the strength of the London stage." (*Saturday Review*, November 14,

1857.) Another contemporary (the *Times*, November 9, 1857), discussing the merits of the performance remarks, "The character of *Hester* requires no small ability on the part of the actress who sustains it. In the first act she is the pretty rustic, placed amid a scene that brings additional lustre to her charms—a village beauty, marred by no humiliating contrast. In the second, she is the pretty rustic out of place, and not a little petted, but still fond and affectionate as ever, until jealousy of Mrs. Montresor converts her into an indignant wife. In the third act the rustic is lost altogether and we have the woman of fashion, with whom manner is everything. Now, when we say that Miss Amy Sedgwick went through all these phases in a most satisfactory manner, as if perfectly at home in each of them, and marking out each of them as distinctly as possible, we give this young and rising actress 'the highest commendation.'"

In February 1858, Miss Sedgwick, after some two months' absence, appeared as *Beatrice* in a revival of ' Much Ado About Nothing' at the Haymarket Theatre. The performance was a very satisfactory one, but, said the *Daily News* (February 23, 1858), "the *ars celare artem* is still the one thing requisite; a little less artificial, a little less stagey in look, voice, and feature, and Miss Sedgwick would be the best high-class comedy actress on the boards." The author of *The Diary of a London Playgoer* records the following opinion under date February 27, 1858, Haymarket :—"*Beatrice*, in ' Much Ado About Nothing,' is not one of Miss Amy Sedgwick's best characters. In the earlier scenes the stage laugh is too forced and too frequent, but in the latter scenes she succeeds better. . . . Miss Sedgwick shows in *Beatrice* behind the mask of a gay mockery the gentle spirit of a woman. In the garden scene, after listening to *Hero* and *Ursula*, she shows that her heart had not been filled with a new thought, but only opened,—

> ' For others say thou dost deserve ; and I
> Believe it *better* than reportingly.'

Miss Sedgwick's *Beatrice* is in fact hearty in her love as in her mirth, and that is right. The distinct representing of this is the best feature in her performance."

At the same theatre, in the following month, she sustained the part of *Julia*, in ' The Hunchback,' and " still further strengthened her position with the theatrical public. When so many ephemeral successes take place, when an apparent triumph in one character is commonly followed by mere toleration in another, it is a great distinction on the part of Miss Sedgwick that she never loses ground. Her *Constance* and her *Julia* have more than confirmed the favourable impression made by her *Pauline*, to say nothing of the efficient support she gave to Mr. Tom Taylor's last new work, ' The Unequal Match.' After a close observation of her *Julia* we should say that the more tender side of this varied character is the most completely depicted. Of the indignation with which she listens to Helen's sneers at the fallen Sir Thomas, of the many passionate passages at the commencement of the third act, and even during the interview with Clifford, more might be made. There is an absence of that thorough abandonment to the feeling of the moment that can render *Julia* one of the most powerful characters of the modern drama. On the other hand, the softer emotions are adequately expressed. The lingering look at the shreds of the torn letter, the gentle appeals to Clifford's memory of a past affection, are exceedingly pretty and natural. During the interview with Master Walter in the fifth act she moreover attains a degree of power that could scarcely be anticipated in the acts preceding ; and the commanding position which she assumes in respect to her guardian as she warns him against the sacrifice of her happiness, is extremely well sustained. The whole character is, indeed, most creditably represented, and the impression it makes upon the public is, to all appearance, genuine." (*Times,* March 8, 1858.)

On June 30 and July 7, 1858, Miss Sedgwick performed the part of *Lady Teazle,* in a revival of ' The School for Scandal,' at the same theatre, in the presence of a crowded audience, "who listened with the most profound attention to the masterpiece of Sheridan, and applauded its many admirable points with genuine enthusiasm. The excellent qualities which have distinguished Miss Sedgwick's recent dramatic experiences in the metropolis—the vivacity and intelligence which have marked all her exertions, and the fascinating and artistic expression which she has at all times so largely at command—were plentifully exhibited in her embodiment of *Lady Teazle.* Stately and emphatic in her delivery of the serious passages of the text—light, graceful, and dexterous in the humorous sallies in which her ladyship indulges—ever equal to the situation, and fully adequate to a proper appreciation of the author—it may be justly acknowledged that Miss Sedgwick's performance of the part will rank with the best successes which she has hitherto achieved. Her interview with Sir Peter in the third act, in which she wins him over to the fulfilment of her pecuniary desires, and her dignified explanation of the mystery of the screen, were highly effective, and conceived and executed with abundant thought and care, and were warmly and deservedly applauded. Miss Sedgwick was several times recalled before the curtain, and was greeted with enthusiasm and loaded with floral offerings." (*Daily Telegraph,* July 8, 1858.)

On Saturday, March 12, 1859, still acting at the Haymarket, Miss Sedgwick supported the characters of *Juliana,* in ' The Honeymoon,' and *Kate Robertson,* in a new comedy written expressly for her by Mr. Palgrave Simpson, entitled ' The World and the Stage.' " The house was crowded in every part, and the tone of the audience was as enthusiastic as if a popular favourite of many years' standing had claimed the annual tribute to her exertions for the recreation of the public. Yet about a year and a half ago the very name of Amy Sedgwick was unknown to the great body of London playgoers. So striking an instance of rapidly-acquired popularity in a department of histrionic art that may fairly be called ' legitimate ' has not been known for a very long time. Not content with impersonating *Juliana* in 'The Honeymoon,' one of the leading characters in her repertory, Miss Sedgwick produced a new comedy, entitled 'The World and the Stage,' in which she played a part so prominent that she made herself thoroughly responsible for the success of the piece. As might be inferred from the title, the object of this work is to vindicate the heroines of the stage from the aspersions frequently cast upon them by the 'world.' With similar purpose Mr. Tom Taylor composed his 'Masks and Faces,' but *Kate Robertson*, the imaginary actress, represented by Miss Sedgwick, is a far more solemn personage than the historical Peg Woffington, and the new drama is throughout more serious in tone than its predecessor. . . . As far as the acting is concerned, the serious part of the piece rests entirely with Miss Amy Sedgwick." (*Times*, March 14, 1859.) In 1859, in September, she appeared as *Rosalind* in 'As You Like It,' and the same month as *Miss Dorillon* in Mrs. Inchbald's comedy, 'Wives as they Were and Maids as they Are.' In a notice of her acting in the first-named character the *Standard* (September 20, 1859) said that throughout it was greeted with considerable applause, and at the termination of the comedy she was called before the curtain. " Notwithstanding this, it must be fairly owned that the applause was due rather to Miss Sedgwick's past success than to her impersonation of *Rosalind*, which, in many respects, was far from an effective performance. It needed life and flippancy ; there was little or no archness or vivacity ; indeed, the key-note struck was of a lugubrious nature. Fancy and by-play were utterly wanting, and the sprightly *Rosalind* was divested of most of those charming characteristics with which Shakespeare has invested her. It must be admitted that Miss Sedgwick has achieved legitimate successes, but *Rosalind* cannot be added to their number."

During 1860 (February) Miss Sedgwick appeared at the Haymarket as *Mrs. Haller* in 'The Stranger' with some success. On Wednesday, May 9 of that year, she acted the part of *Una*, first performance of Edmund Falconer's play, 'The Family Secret'; and on Saturday, June 23, *Miss Vandeleur* in the same author's drama, 'Does He Love Me?' In 1861 she accepted an engagement at the Olympic Theatre, " opening " on Monday, May 20, as *Lady Teazle*, and subsequently playing there in various original pieces and revivals until 1862. In that year she appeared at the Princess's in two of her well-known impersonations, *Julia* ('The Hunchback') and *Constance* ('The Love Chase'). In 1863 Miss Sedgwick renewed her engagement at the same theatre. In February she appeared there in the following plays, viz. 'One Good Turn Deserves Another (*Phœbe Topper*) ; 'The Winning Suit' (*Princess Orelia*) ; and Mr. Cheltnam's dramatized version of 'Aurora Floyd' (the title *rôle*). In October 1866 she acted the character of *Lady Macbeth* at Drury Lane during the engagement there of Mr. S. Phelps and Mr. Barry Sullivan. Her performance of this part showed cleverness and merit, but was not equal to the ability she displayed in comedy.

The following year, in a new piece entitled 'The Coquette' (Mead), first performed at the Haymarket, July 8, she sustained the part of the *Countess Blanche de Raincourt*. In May 1877 Miss Sedgwick reappeared on the Haymarket stage as *Constance* in 'The Love Chase.' Since that date she has not played in London. It may be remarked that Miss Amy Sedgwick has given "dramatic recitals" in London and the provinces with much success.

SHORE, J. G., first attracted notice on the London stage as a member of the company of the Adelphi Theatre in 1856. On Monday, February 11 of that year, he appeared there with the Keeleys in a farce entitled 'That Blessed Baby' (Moore), in which he played the part of *Mr. Finicle.* The year following he joined the company of the Lyceum Theatre, and among other pieces first produced there, acted in a pleasant little play by Leigh Hunt entitled 'Love's Amazements; or, How will it end?' the part of *Chevalier de Torsey.* This play was first performed on Wednesday, January 20, 1858. The *Daily News* (January 22, 1858) considered the dialogue throughout to be admirably written, rising occasionally to the very highest flight, and being filled with many quaint conceits and pretty tropes and metaphors. "The acting was excellent. Mr. Dillon is never so well suited as in the character of absorbing mystery with a handsome person, a good heart, and very little brains. He played with great spirit and *verve*, and some of his bits of by-play were specially good. Mr. J. G. Shore, who is undoubtedly the most promising actor in that most difficult and most ungrateful line, the *jeune premier*, deserves special commendations for his gentlemanly bearing, careful reading, and clear utterance." In 1859 Mr. Shore became a member of the company of the Princess's Theatre, under the late Mr. Augustus Harris's management, and continued to act at that theatre for some years. In November 1861, in a revival there of 'The Merry Wives of Windsor,' Mr. Shore sustained the part of *Master Slender.* In 1864, at the Lyceum Theatre, in the revival by Mr. Charles Fechter of 'Hamlet,' he played *Horatio.* Afterwards he joined the company of the Royalty Theatre, under the management of the Misses Pelham. At that theatre, on Monday, January 16, 1865, in a little comedy of more than usual brilliancy, from the pen of Mr. John Oxenford, entitled 'Billing and Cooing,' Mr. Shore played the part of *Sir Thomas Turtle.* When Miss Marie Wilton, in conjunction with Mr. H. J. Byron, entered upon the management of the Prince of Wales's Theatre, Mr. Shore became a member of their company. On Monday, May 1, 1865, in a comedietta by Mr. J. P. Wooler, entitled 'The Squire of Ringwood Chase,' then performed there for the first time, he sustained the title *rôle.* The following year (1866), at the Princess's Theatre, in a dramatic version of Mr. Charles Dickens's 'Barnaby Rudge,' performed there for the first time on Monday, November 12, he sustained the part of *Sir John Chester.* At the same theatre, on Wednesday, February 6, 1867, first performance of an original drama by Mr. T. Robertson, entitled 'Shadow Tree Shaft,' he played the part of *Captain Mildmay*. Since that time Mr. Shore has appeared at several theatres in the provinces, and, at intervals, on the stage of almost every theatre in London in a number of original plays, and revivals of plays, always exhibiting that same degree of care in his acting for which he was distinguished in the early part of his career.

SINCLAIR, HENRY, was born in 1834, and entered the dramatic profession in 1853 at Ipswich Theatre, under the management of Mr. Hooper. He played at various provincial theatres, Bristol, Plymouth, Birmingham, Sheffield, and Liverpool, during that and the succeeding year, and first appeared in London at Drury Lane Theatre in the character of *Cassio* in Shakespeare's tragedy of 'Othello.' At the same theatre he has played various Shakespearian leading and second parts, creating a very favourable impression in the character of *Macduff*. Mr. Sinclair has rendered good service to the histrionic art in such characters as *Richmond, The Ghost* (in 'Hamlet'), *Prince Hal* (to Mr. Phelps's Falstaff), *Henry VIII., Romeo, Roderick Dhu, Fabian dei Franchi* ('Corsican Brothers'), and *Bassanio* ('Merchant of Venice'). He was the "original" *Henri de Sartorys* in Benjamin Webster junior's adaptation from the French of 'Frou-Frou,' a part which he acted with much success. In George March's adaptation of Victorien Sardou's comedy-drama 'Nos Intimes' ('Our Friends'), Mr. Sinclair was a very able representative of *Dr. Tholosan*, a part which he has played with much ability at the Olympic Theatre in London. As a light comedian and character actor Mr. Sinclair is possessed of considerable merit. He has taken the "leading business" at several leading provincial theatres: Birmingham, Plymouth, Sheffield, and Liverpool Theatres Royal; and was for three years a member of the travelling company of the late Mdlle. Beatrice.

SOTHERN, EDWARD ASKEW, was born in Liverpool April 1, 1830, and made his first appearance on the stage at the Jersey Theatre. In 1851 Mr. Sothern went to the United States and made his *début* on the American stage (with which he has been so long and profitably connected) at the National Theatre Boston, in September 1852, in the part of *Dr. Pangloss* in a version of the younger Colman's comedy 'The Heir-at-Law.' Subsequently Mr. Sothern went to New York, which may be regarded as his dramatic birthplace, since it was here he first began in earnest to study the histrionic profession. He became a member of the company of Wallack's, and afterwards of Laura Keene's Theatre. At this latter establishment, on May 12, 1858, he made his great hit in the character of *Lord Dundreary*, in a piece by Tom Taylor, entitled 'Our American Cousin.' So great was its success, that previous to the production of the play in London Mr. Sothern had acted *Lord Dundreary*, the character in which the sole interest of 'Our American Cousin' centres, not less than a thousand times. On Monday, November 11, 1861, he played the part at the Haymarket Theatre for the first time. Said the *Athenæum* (November 16, 1861), in a notice of the performance :— "Whether the character [*Lord Dundreary*] by itself would sustain any degree of interest we much doubt; but in the hands of Mr. Sothern, the gentleman who has been acting in it for so many hundred nights over the water, it is certainly the *funniest* thing in the world. The part is abstractedly a vile caricature of an inane nobleman, intensely ignorant, and extremely indolent. The notion once accepted by the audience that such an absurd animal could be the type of any class whatever, the actor was free to exaggerate to any extent the representation of the ridiculous. Mr. Sothern, in the quietest way, takes full advantage of his position, and effectually subdues the audience to his mood. Laughter, at all times irrepressible, finally culminates in a general convulsion, which to our ears seemed quite a peculiarity—it was so strange, and yet so natural. The occasion was simply the reading of a letter from a brother in America, containing literally nothing more than that he feared a former letter had miscarried from his having forgotten to direct it. This, with certain inane comments on its contents, sufficed to enable Mr. Sothern to produce the prodigious effect we have indicated. We are therefore disposed to believe that Mr. Sothern, as an eccentric actor, is a man of no ordinary genius, and reasonably desire his further acquaintance. The public, we have no doubt, will be of the same opinion."

In December of the same year Mr. Sothern appeared at the Haymarket in a comedietta adapted from the French by himself, entitled 'Aunt's Advice.' In March 1863, in a piece called 'The Little Treasure,' selected for the *début* of Miss Ellen Terry, he played the part of *Captain Walter Maydenblush.* In February 1864 he appeared as *Bunkum Muller* in "a piece of extravagance" of the same title. On Saturday, April 30 of the same year, at the same theatre, in 'David Garrick,' a play of some pathos, for which the stage is indebted to the ingenuity of the late T. W. Robertson (who in his turn was indebted to the French drama 'Sullivan' for the main points of his play), Mr. Sothern acted the title *rôle.*

The character of *David Garrick* was the first that had really tested Mr. Sothern's powers beyond the Dundreary sphere. Its peculiarity lies in the second act, where an assumption of the most extravagant form of drunkenness is perpetually brought into contact with the real agony of mind which is now on the point of casting aside the mask of debauchery. The acting of Mr. Sothern in this difficult situation was very fine. The inebriety was furious; the manifested repugnance equally intense. On Monday, June 13 of the same year, 'Lord Dundreary Married and Done For' (H. J. Byron) was produced at the Haymarket—Mr. Sothern as *Dundreary.* During his accustomed autumn tour in the provinces in 1864, Mr. Sothern acted in 'Used Up'; and later in the year, at the Prince of Wales's Theatre, Liverpool (Monday, December 19), played the leading part, *Frank Jocelyn,* in a new play by Watts Phillips, entitled 'The Woman in Mauve.' It was a decided and brilliant success in the provinces, and was performed in London at the Haymarket Theatre for the first time, Saturday, March 18, 1865, Mr. Sothern appearing in his original character. In May of the same year he played the part of the *Honourable Sam Slingsby*, in a piece composed for him by Mr. John Oxenford, entitled ' Brother Sam.' In March 1866, in Glasgow, Mr. Sothern played for the first time *Frank Annerly*, in a new comedy by Mr. Westland Marston, entitled ' The Favourite of Fortune.' This piece was afterwards produced in London (April 2, 1866) at the Haymarket Theatre. Discussing the merits of the performance, the *Daily News* (April 3, 1866) said :—" Mr. Marston is one of the very few living playwrights who trust to their own invention for plots and characters, and who has made a reputation second only to that of Sheridan Knowles as a writer of the poetical drama. His laurels have been chiefly won in the latter capacity ; and much as the modern stage is indebted to him for works which are a credit to our dramatic literature, the present production is, we believe, the first regular comedy, properly so called, which he has given to the boards. . . . Mr. Marston may be congratulated upon the ingenious construction of his comedy, the boldness with which he terminates his first three acts without having recourse to conventional ' situations,' the purity and beauty of his dialogue, and the addition which he has made to our stock of stage-characters in the person of a wealthy widow whom he calls ' Mrs. Lorrington.' With singular good taste and judgment he has drawn a woman who is vulgar, and shows her vulgarity, not by Malapropisms and a liberally false use of the aspirate, but by the natural working of the story. If not intended to be the ' head centre ' of the comedy, she becomes that centre, in our opinion, by the skill with which she is drawn ; though those who surround her, with very few exceptions, are sketched with almost equal felicity. . . . The chief characters were thus distributed : *Frank Annerly*, Mr. Sothern ; *Tom Sutherland*, Mr. Buckstone ; *Mr. Bromley*, Mr. Chippendale ; *Hester Lorrington*, Miss Kate Saville ; *Lucy Lorrington*, Miss Nelly Moore ; *Mrs. Witherby*, Mrs. E. Fitzwilliam ; and *Mrs. Lorrington*, Mrs. Chippendale, late Miss Snowdon. *Frank Annerly*, if it had not been admirably acted by Mr. Sothern, and Mr. Sothern had not given it all the advantage of his well-deserved popularity, would scarcely have struck the critical portion of the audience as what is called a strong part. Mr. Sothern's great merit consisted in his perfect naturalness. Tom Sutherland, though represented by Mr. Buckstone, is no more of a low comedy character than Captain Maydenblush in ' The Little Treasure,' but it plays such an agreeable and important part in the comedy that it stands upon an equality with *Frank Annerly*. . . . Mr. Sothern has shown equal taste in selecting and appearing in an intellectual comedy in which the characters are well balanced. The piece was deservedly successful."

In November of this year, at Edinburgh and Glasgow, Mr. Sothern appeared as *Claude Melnotte ;* his acting of the part is described in a contemporary local journal as having been "thoroughly successful, and impressed with a humour of its own." The *Glasgow Herald* (November 23, 1866) said that it had " all the quietness and grace, the naturalness and the power that the most fastidious critic could desire." In December 1866 at the Haymarket Theatre, he sustained the part of *Harry Vivian* in a three-act comedy of Mr. Tom Taylor's, then first performed, entitled ' A Lesson for Life,' in noticing which the *Daily Telegraph* (December 29, 1876) said :—" As an earnest student in his profession Mr. Sothern has worked with a zeal which has rarely been excelled. The prominent characteristic of his style is the air of modern refinement with which he surrounds the personage represented. There is nothing conventional about his movements, nothing which belongs to the stilted mannerism of the past school of histrionic art. We have the polished ease of good society faithfully illustrated, the reality of nature in place of the artificiality of the stage, and a life-like portrait painted in vivid colours as an acceptable substitute for the faded caricature which has too often passed current with hasty observers for the semblance of a gentleman." On Monday, April 29, 1867, he acted the character of *Robert Devlin*, in a piece produced under the title of ' A Wild Goose.' In July (" opening " the 8th) 1867 Mr. Sothern appeared on the Paris stage as *Lord Dundreary*, but met with scanty encouragement. On Saturday, March 14, 1868, at the Haymarket Theatre, first performance of ' A Hero of Romance ' (Westland Marston), an adaptation of M. Octave Feuillet's ' Roman d'un Jeune Homme Pauvre,' he sustained the part of *Marquis Victor de Tourville.* " The story has not much originality or robust strength, but it is interesting, though much of the interest is forced out of the petty details of servitude and the etiquette of the servants' hall. The *Marquis de Tourville*, a ruined gentleman, accepts the advice of a friend, and consents to become a steward in a rich family named Dumont. He falls in love with Mdlle. Dumont, a young lady of the class known on the stage as haughty beauties. She treats him sometimes as a footman —sometimes as a friend ; and the audience are shocked when they hear her order him in a pet to call her carriage, and delighted when he silently reproves her by ringing in a servant in livery. The disguised marquis is known to a plotting governess in the family, who is anxious to share his title, and, by a variety of arts which need not be related, she does all she can to show him in the light of a fortune-hunter and adventurer. By an accident the marquis-stewart and the haughty beauty are locked up in a ruined tower by moonlight, and the young lady, somewhat hastily, but naturally, accuses him of having plotted to get her in that awkward and compromising position. To show his good faith, with equal hasti-ness he leaps off the top of the tower into an unknown abyss below, dressed in strapped riding trousers. The reception of this scene, at the close of the fourth act, shows that theatrical audiences have not yet lost their appetite for ' sensational headers,' and the per-formance of it by Mr. Sothern, dressed as we have indicated, was both creditable to the actor and his tailor. This gymnastic proof of good faith is not, however, sufficient for the young lady, and it is not until the hero has done several other noble things, including the burning of a document which proves him to be the rightful owner of the Dumont estates, and a tottering old grandfather, Dumont, to be a villain, that he is allowed to marry the haughty beauty. . . . The comedy of the play has been well developed, and the character of a soft-headed, thick-speaking 'man of the world,' admirably played by Mr. Compton, is one of the few things to look back to with satisfaction. Mr. Sothern has one great qualification for the character he has chosen—that of the *Marquis*—he always acts like a thorough gentleman. In all the scenes requiring earnestness and dignity, he was good ; in the few scenes requiring pathos, he was bad." (*Daily News*, March 16, 1868.)

On Thursday, January 14, 1869, he played at the Haymarket the part of *Colonel John White*, on the occasion of the first performance of Mr. T. W. Robertson's comedy entitled 'Home,' founded on a French piece, 'L'Aventurière.' In May of the same year Mr. Sothern acted the part of *Hugh de Brass* in Morton's farce 'A Regular Fix.' In May 1871, first performance in London of Mr. H. J. Byron's play 'An English Gentleman,' he performed the part of *Charles Chuckles*. Mr. Sothern's most important impersonations are, undoubtedly, *Lord Dundreary* and *David Garrick*, and these he has presented on the American and English stage over and over again during the past fifteen years, and, it may be added, with invariable success.

In 1878 (Saturday, May 11) he reappeared at the Haymarket, after a long absence in the United States, in a piece called 'The Crushed Tragedian,' by H. J. Byron, converted from the same author's play of 'The Prompter's Box,' originally produced at the Adelphi Theatre in 1870. Mr. Sothern assumed the leading *rôle*, *Fitzaltamont*. "Mr. Sothern's appearance was the signal for a storm of applause, and for a long-continued roar of laughter. His *Fitzaltamont*, we may say at once, is, like his Dundreary, neither more nor less than an extravagant caricature. He has broadened the lines laid down by Mr. Byron, who himself originally played the part, and the character is now taken into the regions of uproarious farce. From the crown of his head to the sole of his foot there stood the very ideal of what a crushed tragedian should be. He was husky of voice, as became an actor who in one night was wont to play Richard III., and the Stranger, and William in 'Black-Eyed Susan,' to wind up with ; he was melancholy of countenance, as became the poor devil, condemned to study nineteen parts a week ; the sepulchral tones, the glaring eyeballs, the long hair, the wonderful 'stage walk,' and the melodramatic attitudes—all made this character stand prominently forward, to tickle the fancy of the audience, and to elicit repeated shouts of laughter. The part now is unmistakably broad farce, and there may be some to object that broad farce, carried through five acts, is just a little too much. *Fitzaltamont's* tragical declaration of love in the first act, and the sudden Richelieu-like inspiration upon which the 'drop' came down; his expressed scorn of a critical ruffian's rude remarks; his chagrin as he hears a London manager describe how heartily he laughed over his attempts at pathetic acting ; and his reply to the remark of the banker who has not been in a theatre for twenty years, ' It is about the same time since I was in a bank,' in the second act ; his determined efforts in the third to arouse the drunken actor who is to support the daughter of his old friend ; his appearance after a histrionic triumph in the fourth ; and his determination to marry Miss Mountcashel in the fifth, all caused great hilarity ; and, although everybody had to admit that the ' business ' was extravagant, there seemed to be no doubt existing as to its comicality." (*Era*, May 19, 1878.) The following month Mr. Sothern played the part of *Sidney Spoonbill*, in a new comedy by Mr. H. J. Byron entitled ' The Hornet's Nest.' This impersonation, however, cannot be said to have brought any additional lustre to Mr. Sothern's fame as an actor. His present popularity in England rests almost wholly upon his admirable rendering of the two characters already specially indicated, viz. *Dundreary* and *David Garrick*. In May 1879, after a few farewell performances of characters already discussed, Mr. Sothern returned to the United States. He has himself stated that it is to the Americans he is indebted for whatever position he has attained in his profession, since without their encouragement he would long ago have abandoned the stage. His dramatic life, he has remarked, has not been altogether so cloudless as many perhaps have imagined. "The early part of it was chiefly occupied in getting dismissed for incapacity." It was his nature, however, to fight against obstacles. His present high position in the dramatic profession offers assurance that he has not worked and studied in vain.

SOTHERN, LYTTON EDWARD, born June 27, 1856, is son of the above-named Edward Askew Sothern. He first appeared on the stage Wednesday, July 24, 1872, at Drury Lane Theatre, for the benefit of the Royal General Theatrical Fund, as *Captain Vernon* in ' Our American Cousin,' and made his first professional appearance at the Walnut Street Theatre, Philadelphia, in 1873, as *Viscount Veandore* in ' The Marble Heart.' He subsequently played the "light comedy" and "juvenile" business at that theatre for one season. The following year Mr. Lytton Sothern organized a company for, and went on tour with, his father in the United States. Having returned to England in the autumn of 1874, he played for one season, at the Theatre Royal, Birmingham, all the so-called "juvenile" business. In February 1875, at the Haymarket Theatre, in a revival of Robertson's comedy ' Home,' he appeared as *Bertie Thompson*. Subsequently he was engaged at the Olympic Theatre. Following this Mr. L. Sothern went to the Australian colonies, and presented certain of the characters " created " by his father : *Lord Dundreary*, *David Garrick*, &c. April 14, 1879, he " opened " at the Royalty Theatre, London, in a comedy by Mr. G. R. Sims entitled ' Crutch and Toothpick ' (designed to satirize some of the fashionable foibles of the day) as *Cecil Leighton*. Mr. Sothern afterwards appeared at the Criterion Theatre in ' Betsy,' sustaining the part of Mr. Adolphus Birkett.

SOUTAR, MRS. R. *See* FARREN, ELLEN.

SOUTAR, ROBERT, eldest son of the late Robert Soutar, journalist, is a comedian of established position ; has written several farces, and is the author of various pantomimes which have been produced with success at the Brighton, Marylebone, and Victoria Theatres. Mr. Soutar has for some time held the position of stage-manager at the Gaiety Theatre, under the lesseeship of Mr. John Hollingshead.

STANDING, HERBERT, was born in Peckham, Surrey, November 13, 1846, and first appeared on the stage in 1858, at the Queen's Theatre, under the late Mr. Alfred Wigan's management, as *Langford* in ' Still Waters Run Deep.' At the conclusion of this engagement he played *Prince Hal* in selections from ' Henry IV.' to the Falstaff of the late Mark Lemon on a tour through the United Kingdom. After spending considerable time in provincial towns, Mr. Standing was engaged by Mr. Dion Boucicault for the part of *Don Manuel* in ' A Dark Night's Work ' at the Princess's Theatre. Mr. Boucicault relinquishing the management, Mr. Chatterton engaged Mr. Standing to support the late Mr. Phelps ; and he appeared as *Cassio* in ' Othello,' *Lovewell* in ' The Clandestine Marriage,' *Valentine* in ' Faust and Marguerite, and other characters, with success. Subsequently he became a member of the company of the Lyceum Theatre, under Mr. Bateman's management, acting *Christian* in ' The Bells ' (Mr. Irving as Mathias) ; and afterwards appeared at the Prince of Wales's Theatre in a revival of ' The Merchant of Venice.' Following this engagement, Mr. Standing appeared for a brief season at the Mirror Theatre, Holborn, under Mr. Horace Wigan's management ; and then joined the company of the Criterion Theatre, where, Saturday, March 31, 1877, first performance of ' The Pink Dominos ' (adapted by Mr. Albery from MM. Hennequin and Delacour's ' Les Dominos Roses '), he played *Sir Percy Wagstaff.* The piece had a considerable " run." At the same theatre Mr. Standing acted a leading *rôle* in ' Truth ' (Bronson Howard), produced there January 1879.

STANHOPE, ADELINE (Mrs. AMORY SULLIVAN), daughter-in-law of Barry Sullivan, was a pupil of Mr. John Ryder, and first appeared in small parts at the Haymarket Theatre about 1872. She afterwards went to America, playing in ' The Woman in White ' with Mr. Wybert Reeve. After two seasons in Edinburgh, during which time she played the entire round of "leading business," she joined Mr. Barry Sullivan as leading lady, and went with him on two tours through the provinces. In September 1879 she was playing leading parts in San Francisco, California.

STANLEY, LEONORA ALMA, daughter of Stuart Stanley, captain in the body-guard of the late Emperor Maximilian of Mexico, was born at St. Helier's, Jersey, October 26, 1860. She made her first appearance on the stage in December 1873 in the pantomime of 'Cinderella,' at the Theatre Royal, Hull, in the following year playing in 'Black-Eyed Susan' and 'The Rose of Auvergne' at Cremorne Gardens. Afterwards she joined Mr. Hollingshead's "Gaiety" company, of which she remained a member till March 1875, performing such parts as *Amaranthe* in 'Madame Angot,' *Regina* in 'Princess of Trebizonde,' &c. With a short interval of engagement at the Philharmonic Theatre, she rejoined the Gaiety company, and appeared in the burlesque 'Little Don Cæsar de Bazan.' In 1876 she appeared in the pantomime arranged by the Messrs. Sanger; and subsequently played at various theatres with the late Mr. S. Phelps such characters as *Julie de Mortemar*, in 'Richelieu'; *Anne Boleyn*, in 'Henry VIII.'; *Lady Sneerwell*, in 'School for Scandal.' Miss Alma Stanley has successfully fulfilled engagements at the Olympic, Royalty, Folly, and Crystal Palace Theatres in addition to the Gaiety. She has performed the following parts with success, namely, *Zephyrina*, in 'Belphegor'; *Lady Betty Noel*, 'Clancarty'; *Georgy de Burgh*, 'Turn of the Tide'; *Julia*, 'Life of an Actress'; ·*Lady Valeria*, 'All that Glitters is not Gold,' &c., &c.

STEPHENS, MRS. JANE, made her first appearance on the stage at the Olympic Theatre, under Samuel Buller's management, in a small soubrette part. Afterwards she went into the provinces, and "worked hard, playing everything and anything for nearly three years." Returning to London, she was engaged by Mr. Samuel Phelps "for boys and walking ladies" at Sadler's Wells Theatre, and remained a member of the company (with an interval of a season under Mrs. Warner at the Marylebone Theatre) for four seasons, namely, from 1847 to 1852. Afterwards Mrs. Stephens (who, it may be remarked, has always played in her own name, although she was married previous to her adopting the stage as a profession) joined the company of the Lyceum Theatre, under Mr. Charles Mathews's management. When Mr. Alfred Wigan assumed control of the affairs of the Olympic Theatre (1858), Mrs. Stephens was engaged by him, and she remained connected with that theatre for fourteen consecutive seasons, the management changing four times during this period. Of the more successful impersonations of Mrs. Stephens at the Olympic Theatre, we may select the following as being worthy of special recognition. In June 1854 (the second season of Mr. A. Wigan's management), in a revival of 'Hush Money' (George Dance), the part of Jasper Touchwood being performed by the elder Robson, Mrs. Stephens * acted the character of *Mrs. Crab*. In March 1857 she "embodied the part of an old country servant with great unction and marked expression" in the original performance of 'Daddy Hardacre' (probably Robson's greatest impersonation), an adaptation by Mr. Palgrave Simpson of MM. Bayard and Duport's 'La Fille de l'Avare.' In May 1863, first performance at the Olympic

* In the play-bills 'Miss Stephens.'

Theatre of 'The Ticket-of-Leave Man' (Tom Taylor), Mrs. Stephens played the part of *Mrs. Willoughby*, "an amusingly prominent personage . . . . whose flow of anecdote is unceasing, and whose conversational powers resemble those of the memorable Sairey Gamp. Her life is embittered by her boy Sam, to whose enormities the vagaries of the incorrigible 'Bailey' are venial eccentricities ; but under the influence of Robert Brierly's teaching he ultimately reforms, and thus gives additional point to the moral. Mrs. Stephens made a clever bit of character out of the first, which the house enjoyed amazingly." (*Daily Telegraph*, May 29, 1863.) Another contemporary journal alludes to *Mrs. Willoughby* as being *the* character of the play, an old woman "whose inveteracy and 'everlasting rotation of tongue,' interlarded with multitudinous 'which's,' kept the audience in roars of laughter every time she opened her mouth in speech. Mr. Tom Taylor has apprehended the style and manner of the renowned 'monthly,' Mrs. Gamp, with extraordinary fidelity. Nor could the part by any possibility have been entrusted to better hands than those of Mrs. Stephens, who, in her new performance, if nothing else, has proved herself one of the very best 'character' actresses of the day." (*Morning Herald*, June 1, 1863.) In August 1867, on the occasion of Miss Kate Terry's farewell performances at the Adelphi Theatre, Mrs. Stephens acted the *Nurse* in a revival of 'Romeo and Juliet' with much excellence.

During the same year Mrs. Stephens accepted an engagement at the Holborn Theatre, under Mr. Sefton Parry's management, "opening" there in October, in an unsuccessful drama by the late T. W. Robertson, entitled 'For Love.' In this piece Mrs. Stephens played *Mrs. Mountflathwoult*, "a master sketch of one of the most amusing creations of modern comedy." (*Standard*, October 7, 1867.) She was a member of the same "actor-manager's" company during his connection with the Globe Theatre, where, on November 28, 1868, first performance of a new and original five-act comedy, by H. J. Byron, entitled 'Cyril's Success ; an Everyday Story,' Mrs. Stephens acted *Miss Pamela Grannet* (*Mrs. Pincher*), "an old schoolmistress, whose mission in this life is the hatred of all men, and the inoculation of that hate amongst all the womankind of her acquaintance. . . . *Miss Grannet's* description of the separation from her husband is delicious. The culminating point will become a proverb : 'But, my dear, when it comes to the question of the man wanting more than his fair share of the thin part of the salmon, it is time to part. Share and share alike—thick and thin— say I—and I said it—and we parted upon a question of incompatibility.'" (*Glowworm*, November 30, 1868.) In November 1869, first performance at the same theatre of Mr. T. W. Robertson's comedy 'Progress,' Mrs. Stephens sustained the part of *Miss Myrnie*. At the same theatre, in October of the same year, in 'Not Such a Fool as He Looks' (H. J. Byron), the author himself acting the principal part (*see* BYRON, H. J.), Mrs. Stephens played *Mrs. Mould*, presenting the public "with another of her admirable portraits of old women." On Mr. S. Parry's returning to the Holborn Theatre in 1870, Mrs. Stephens reappeared there in her "original" part of *Mrs. Willoughby*. In January 1871 she accepted an engagement from Miss Litton, and on the occasion of the opening of the Royal Court Theatre, Wednesday, January 25, 1871, first performance of 'Randall's Thumb' (W. S. Gilbert), Mrs. Stephens sustained the character of *Mrs. Scantlebury*, Mr. Frank Matthews playing Mr. Scantlebury. At the same theatre she appeared in 'Broken Spells' (Dr. Westland Marston and W. G. Wills); 'Dotheboys Hall' (Mr. Daly Besemere), as *Mrs. Squeers*; 'Playing with Fire,' as the widow *Crabstick*, &c. In October 1873 she "opened" at the Olympic Theatre, under Mr. H. Neville's management, and continued to play there for three consecutive seasons. In Mr. H. J. Byron's comedy of 'Sour Grapes,' first performed there in October 1873, she sustained the part of *Mrs. Gunn*, and she also appeared, with her usual success, at the same theatre in the original casts of 'Lady Clancarty' and 'The Spendthrift.' Later Mrs. Stephens appeared in the very successful revival of 'New Men and Old Acres' at the Court Theatre, and has been recently (1879) acting at the Adelphi and Criterion Theatres. Mrs. Stephens is generally allowed to be the best actress of what are technically known as "old women's parts" at present on the English stage.

STEPHENS, WILLIAM HENRY, was born in London, and made his first appearance on the stage at the Theatre Royal, Derby, April 11, 1839. After playing for some considerable period in the provinces, he was engaged at the Theatre Royal, Glasgow, under J. H. Alexander's management, and at the Queen's Theatre, Manchester, under the management of John Knowles, appearing for the most part as "leading old man" and "eccentric comedian." In 1854 Mr. Stephens left England for Australia; at Sydney, he built the present Queen's Theatre. In 1858 he played in San Francisco, New York, &c., returning to Sydney in 1860. Finally leaving the colonies in that year, and making his *début* in London, January 1861, at St. James's Theatre, under J. Vining's management as the *Marquis* in 'Self-made.' Mr. Stephens has appeared, with more or less success, at the following metropolitan theatres, viz. Sadler's Wells, Princess's, Royalty, Olympic, Astley's, Lyceum, Vaudeville. In August 1875 he went as stage-manager of a dramatic company to Calcutta, and returned to England in 1876. Since that date he has appeared on the London stage at various theatres.

STEWART, JULIA, daughter of a well-known Scotch comedian resident in Edinburgh, David ('auld Davie') Stewart, was born in London, June 1862. She was educated to the stage from childhood, having made her first appearance at the Glasgow Theatre in 1868, in the child's part of *Sybil* in 'A Wolf in Sheep's Clothing.' Thereupon she was engaged by the managers, Messrs. Glover and Francis, for a term of years, and under their auspices played at the Theatre Royal, Glasgow, and in Newcastle-on-Tyne, children and boys' parts. In 1876 this engagement was concluded, and, in the year following, being then a member of Miss Sarah Thorne's dramatic company, Miss Stewart played her " first grown-up part," that of *Emma Marigold* in ' My Awful Dad,' the late Mr. Charles Mathews in the leading *rôle*. Wednesday, October 3, 1877, being specially selected for the part, she played *Maggie Macfarlane*, first performance of Mr. W. S. Gilbert's comedy ' Engaged,' at the Haymarket Theatre. This was Miss Stewart's London *début*, and it was in every way successful. She played the same part during the "run" of the piece in London, afterwards in the provinces, and again in its revival at the Strand Theatre in the summer season 1878. At the end of her " Strand " engagement she "opened" at the Haymarket as *Mary Meredith*, in a revival by Mr. Sothern of ' Our American Cousin.' Afterwards, on tour 1878–9, with the same comedian, she played the like character, and that of *Ada Ingot* in ' David Garrick.' In both of these parts she appeared to advantage, and secured the good report of local journals.

*STIRLING, ARTHUR, was for many years a leading actor in legitimate drama at the Bristol and Bath theatres, where he was a great favourite. His first appearance on the London stage took place at the St. James's Theatre, January 3, 1863, when he played *Philip Austin* in ' Dark Cloud.' Since then he has appeared in many London and provincial theatres with distinguished success. Among his more recent impersonations in London may be mentioned *Patrick Carroll* in ' The Omadhaun' (a version of ' Idiot of the Mountain') November 1877, and *Antonio* in a burlesque of ' The Merchant of Venice,' March 1878, at the Queen's Theatre ; and the villain *Lazare* in ' Proof,' April 1878, at the Adelphi Theatre.

*STIRLING, MRS. ARTHUR (*née* CLEVELAND), first attracted notice as an actress at the Marylebone Theatre, then under Mr. J. W. Wallack's management, as *Juliet*, Mrs. Wallack playing *Romeo*. After her marriage to Mr. Charles Vyner (an actor who was held in much esteem) she went with her husband to Australia, and appeared for a long time in many other characters of the legitimate drama in Australia and New Zealand. After the sudden death of Mr. Vyner, who was killed by a fall from his horse in Australia, Mrs. Vyner returned to England. She subsequently married Mr. Arthur Stirling, and has appeared with that actor in various theatres in London and the provinces, especially at Bath and Bristol under the management of the late Mr. J. H. Chute. Mrs. Arthur Stirling has been for many years an actress of considerable reputation in legitimate drama, and is favourably known for her impersonations of *Lady Macbeth, Hermione, Portia,* and other Shakespearian heroines, and also for her considerable power as an elocutionist. Concerning her late appearances, it may be mentioned that she was the original *Countess de Linière* in ' The Two Orphans' in 1874 at the Olympic Theatre, and that she took the character of *Madame Deprets* in ' Proof' at the Adelphi Theatre in April 1878.

STIRLING, MRS. (*née* CLIFTON, FANNY), was born in London, July 1816, and made her first histrionic essay at the Coburg Theatre. Afterwards she appeared at the Pavilion, playing a variety of parts in tragedy, comedy, and melodrama. On January 1, 1836, Mrs. Stirling first appeared at the Adelphi Theatre, then under the management of Mr. and Mrs. Yates, as *Biddy Nutts*, in 'The Dream at Sea.' The same month she played in a drama by Mr. Serle entitled 'The Ghost Story.' Mrs. Stirling acted at the Adelphi the succeeding season in various pieces produced there, melodramatic and farcical : 'Luke Somerton,' 'The Doom of Marana,' 'Catching an Heiress,' &c. Her qualifications as an actress were thus referred to in a contemporary journal :—"Without becoming too prolix by going into particulars, we may safely assert that she (Mrs. Stirling) possesses in an eminent degree every requisite for a low-comedy performer ; that she uses all with admirable tact and discretion, and that she is withal a very pretty woman." In 1836 she accepted an engagement at the St. James's Theatre, playing there, in May, the leading character in " a very pleasing and neatly-written burletta, entitled ' Love and Charity.' " In 1839 (November), at Drury Lane Theatre, she sustained, "with limited success," the part of *Beatrice* in a revival of 'Much Ado About Nothing ' ; and the same year, at the same theatre, the leading female *rôle* in a piece entitled ' A Night in the Bastile.' The year following Mrs. Stirling took the place of Miss Helen Faucit at the Haymarket Theatre as *Clara Douglas* in ' Money,' and in 1841, at the same theatre, sustained Mrs. Glover's character of *Mrs. Franklin* in the same play. During Mr. Macready's second season at Drury Lane, October 1842, Mrs. Stirling appeared there as *Celia* in ' As You Like It,' as *Sophia* in Holcroft's ' Road to Ruin,' and as *Mrs. Foresight* in Congreve's ' Love for Love.' She also acted with great spirit with the late Charles Mathews the younger in a farce written by him under the title of ' The Eton Boy.' In 1845 she joined the company of the Princess's Theatre, and appeared there with Mr. Macready, Mr. Wallack, Mr. and Mrs. Charles Mathews, Mr. Compton, Mrs. Ternan, in several plays produced under Mr. Macready's superintendence. She acted at the same theatre with Miss Cushman during the first visit of that accomplished actress to England, on April 19, 1845, appearing as *Helen* (to Miss Cushman's Julia) in ' The Hunchback.' Wednesday, October 15, 1845, at the same theatre, she sustained the part of *Cordelia* (' King Lear '), Mr. Macready in the leading *rôle*. The following year, Wednesday, May 20, she acted the character of *Madeline Weir*, first performance of ' The King of the Commons ' (White), the part of James V. of Scotland being undertaken by Macready. In 1847, Tuesday, December 7, Mrs. Stirling took part in the special Shakespearian performances at the Theatre Royal, Covent Garden, arranged in behalf of the fund for the purchase of Shakespeare's house at Stratford-on-Avon. She played on this occasion *Mrs. Ford* in a selection from ' The Merry Wives of Windsor ' (Act 3, Scs. 3 and 4 ; Act 4, Sc. 2). In 1848 Mrs. Stirling joined the company of the Olympic Theatre, and appeared there, September 4, as *Laura Leeson* in ' Time Tries All,' then performed for the first time. This, according to a contemporary journal, was Mrs. Stirling's first appearance on these boards, and she was received with high welcome, which she merited by her able tracings of the finer shades of the part. " No character could well be better suited to Mrs. Stirling's style than that of a fantastic maiden, who, mistaking the bias of her own feelings, banishes from her presence and his country the man whom she really loves. The drama is one in which the interest is mental and sustained by the heroine." The same year (1848), at the Olympic, she appeared as *Juliana* in ' The Honeymoon,' *Kate* in ' The Taming of the Shrew,' and, with distinguished success, as *Cousin Cherry* in the farce of that title. After the destruction by fire of the Olympic (March 29, 1849), Mrs. Stirling accepted an engagement at the New Strand Theatre, under Mr. Henry Farren's management. On October 10 she played there the leading *rôle* in ' The Reigning Favourite,' a piece translated by Mr. John Oxenford from Scribe's tragedy of ' Adrienne Lecouvreur.' " Probably Mrs. Stirling never acted so finely as in the character of *Adrienne*, originally played by Mademoiselle Rachel. It is a very difficult part, since, although a number of passions are to be displayed with great intensity, they must at the same time be expressed with quietness. Excepting in the death scene at the last, when she is alone with Maurice and Michonnet, her emotions are in a state of constant suppression. The intelligence with which Mrs. Stirling seized on points not of themselves salient, and the great, though quiet, force with which she gave them, were admirable. There was a whole history of internal emotion, without anything like violent ebullition. In the cited speeches which she had to deliver in the course of the piece she laboured under a difficulty which did not exist on the Parisian stage. To the French public these speeches are all familiar, but to the English they were only rendered significant by Mrs. Stirling's excellent delivery." (*Times*, October 10, 1849.)

The same year Mrs. Stirling appeared as the heroine in Mr. Theodore Martin's version of ' King René's Daughter,' and as *Olivia* in a version by Tom Taylor of ' The Vicar of Wakefield.' In 1850, October 14, at the Olympic, she sustained the principal *rôle* in Stirling Coyne's ' My Wife's Daughter,' a version of ' La Femme de Quarante Ans.' Monday, January 13, 1851, at the same theatre, she played the part of *Martha Gibbs* in ' All that Glitters is not Gold ' (Morton). The following April, in a dramatic version of Addison's ' Sir Roger de Coverley,' produced at the Olympic, Mrs. Stirling undertook the part of the *Widow*. The piece, though interesting, was not successful. After fulfilling a short engagement at the Olympic Theatre, she returned to the Haymarket, and reappeared there, April 21, 1852, as *Fanny Morrison*, first performance of Mark Lemon's play ' Mind Your Own Business.' On Saturday, November 20, 1852, first perform-ance at the Haymarket Theatre of ' Masks and Faces,' Mrs. Stirling played the part of *Peg Woffington*. " The plot of this piece is its weakest point. The nominal hero, Vane, is a poor creature, weak as well as wicked, who excites no interest whatever, and does not deserve an amiable and loving wife. The principal figure is *Mrs. Woffington*, who is admirably drawn, and charmingly represented by Mrs. Stirling. The character is a delightful combination of grace, wit, spirit, nobleness of nature, and generosity. But this ideal *Woffington* is just such a creature as the still more celebrated Mrs. Clive was in reality; while Kitty Clive (who is also one of the *dramatis personæ*) plays an insignificant part. Triplet, the poor denizen of Grub Street, is an excellent sketch, embodied by Mr. Webster in that artistic and masterly manner for which he is distinguished, with fine touches of homely pathos." (*Daily News*, November 22, 1852.)

Mrs. Stirling, it may be noted, was the original *Mrs. Trotter Southdown* in Taylor's comedy 'To Oblige Benson,' first performed at the Olympic, Monday, March 6, 1854. This successful piece was an adaptation of 'Un Service à Blanchard,' by MM. Moreau and Delacour. Among other characters assumed by Mrs. Stirling during her long connection with the Olympic the following are deserving of being specially mentioned, viz. *Lady Teazle* (June 22, 1855); *Mrs. Bracegirdle*, in the comedietta of 'The Tragedy Queen' (May 1856); *Miss Dorrillon*, in Mrs. Inchbald's comedy 'Wives as they Were and Maids as they Are' (the same month); *Mrs. Levenson*, in Mr. A. C. Troughton's 'Leading Strings' (first performed October 19, 1857). In a notice of this play in the *Saturday Review* (October 31, 1857) it is stated that Mrs. Stirling, as the mother (*Mrs. Levenson*), exhibited one of the most finished and sustained pieces of drawing-room acting that had been seen in London for some years, and, from one end to the other, her part was excellent.

In February 1857, at the Lyceum, Mrs. Stirling played the leading female *rôle*, first performance of Mr. Tom Taylor's play 'A Wolf in Sheep's Clothing,' an adaptation of Madame Girardin's 'Une Femme qui déteste son Mari.' At the Olympic, in October 1858, in a melodrama by Mr. Wilkie Collins, entitled 'The Red Vial,' Mrs. Stirling sustained the part of *Madame Bergmann.* This play was of the most repulsive kind, and is alluded to in contemporary criticism as "the most brilliant failure of the day." Mrs. Stirling's acting was its one redeeming feature. Since 1858 Mrs. Stirling has appeared mostly in the position of a "star" actress in characters in which she had already secured fame. In the spring of 1869 she gave her first dramatic reading in London, consisting of selections from the 'Midsummer Night's Dream.' She has since occupied herself principally with this work, and with her duties as Professor of Elocution at the London Academy of Music, but later (1879) returned to the stage, and has been acting in 'She Stoops to Conquer,' 'The Beaux' Stratagem,' &c., &c., at the Imperial Theatre.

STIRLING, FANNY, daughter of Mrs. Stirling (Fanny Clifton), made her *début* on the London stage July 25, 1860, as *Miranda*, in 'The Enchanted Isle.' On Monday, January 7, 1861, she appeared at the same theatre in her first important part, viz. *Miss Vandeleur*, in Falconer's comedy 'Does He Love Me?' Noticing this performance the *Athenæum* (January 12, 1861) remarked as follows :—" Miss Stirling has great natural powers, and merely requires cultivation in the art which she has chosen to realize a decided success. Her portraiture of the heroine was exceedingly natural, full of girlish impulse, and occasionally revealing extraordinary powers of fascination. In person and style she much resembles her mother, and in time will probably become as attractive an actress." In March of the same year, at the Haymarket, she played in a new piece, 'A Duke in Difficulties,' written by Mr. Tom Taylor expressly for Mrs. and Miss Stirling, both of whom appeared in it—the former as La Jocunde, the latter as *Colombe*. Miss Stirling has appeared on the boards of all the principal theatres in London.

ST. JOHN, MARGARET FLORENCE (Mrs. LITHGOW JAMES), was born in Plymouth. At quite an early age she sang in public at St. James's Hall in that town, and attracted much attention by her unusual accomplishments as a singer and pianiste. For her early training she was indebted to her father, himself a musician of no mean ability; afterwards she completed her studies in London. Miss St. John made her first appearance on the stage in English opera at Preston, as one of the sisters in Rossini's comic opera 'Cinderella,' and secured her first public success in that department of dramatic art at Norwich, on Easter Monday of the same year as *Arline* in Balfe's 'Bohemian Girl.' She subsequently for a season played contralto parts in English opera under Mr. Duraud, and afterwards joining Blanche Cole's company sustained, in the provinces, the mezzo-soprano and contralto parts in the various operas which formed that lady's stage *répertoire*. At the end of this engagement Miss St. John joined the Rose Hersee Opera Company, and performed with much success in a series of operas at the Crystal Palace in August and September 1877. Among the *rôles* which she acted there, the following may be mentioned, viz. *Cherubino* ('Figaro'); *Urbano* ('Les Huguenots'); *Azucena* ('Trovatore'); *Maritana* (in the opera of that name); *Lelia* ('Satanella'); *Cinderella* (in Rossini's opera of that name); the *2nd Goatherd* ('Dinorah'); *Adelgisa* ('Norma'); *Donna Carmen* ('Rose of Castile'); *Lady Allcash* ('Fra Diavolo'), &c. At Easter 1878, Miss St. John made her *début* in London at the Folly Theatre as *Germaine* in 'Les Cloches de Corneville,' a *rôle* which she had previously performed very successfully in the provinces. Her first " original" part was that of *Madame Favart* in the English version of Offenbach's comic opera of that title, produced at the Strand Theatre, Saturday, April 12, 1879. Referring to this performance, the *Daily News* (April 14, 1879) remarked as follows :—" The caste includes at least one lady who, though hitherto practically unknown, may be expected to take a leading position in the interpretation of operatic works of a light kind. We refer to Miss

Florence St. John—a young actress of very pleasing appearance, who acts with remarkable vivacity and grace, possesses a mezzo-soprano voice of really fine quality, and sings in a style that indicates a thoroughly sound training. Miss St. John has, we believe, been recently a member of one of those peripatetic opera companies which are better known to playgoers in provincial towns and cities than they are to frequenters of the London theatres; if we mistake not, she was not very long since even put to such ' base uses ' as the enactment of a part in a pantomime at Brighton. If so, however, the greater is the credit due to those who, discerning her rare and pleasing talents, have boldly introduced her to a London audience in the leading part in this latest work of a popular composer." The same journal adds : " Among the most successful of the songs is the soprano solo, ' Hearts clad in white,' in which the salutation of the novice and the response of the Abbess are contrasted with dramatic effect; ' The Artless Thing,' a solo in G and B flat, also sung by Miss St. John with very pleasant humour ; and, above all, the vocal minuet, ' To age's dull December,' sung by the same lady—a very pretty and harmonious effect being here produced by the simultaneous dance of the minuet by the company." Miss St. John's voice partakes of three qualities, contralto, mezzo-soprano, and soprano. She sings with comparative ease from G below the stave to high C above it, clear and sympathetic throughout, and is, besides, an excellent musician.

SUGDEN, CHARLES, was born at Cambridge in 1850, and entered the dramatic profession in 1869 under the pseudonym of " Charles Neville," first appearing at the Theatre Royal, Brighton, in ' Nobody's Child,' and subsequently at the same theatre in other small parts. During one week at that theatre he acted clown in the pantomime. From Brighton Mr. Sugden proceeded to Dublin and Edinburgh, enacting *Laertes* and other young men's parts in Shakespearian plays, comedy, &c. He next appeared at the Prince of Wales's Theatre, Liverpool, as *Bertie* in ' New Men and Old Acres.' Mr. Sugden made his first appearance on the London stage Saturday, October 7, 1871, as *Ernest* in H. J. Byron's comedy ' Partners for Life,' at the Globe Theatre, then under Montague's management. In 1873 he appeared at the Gaiety as *Frank Rochdale* in the revival of Colman's ' John Bull,' in which Phelps, Charles Mathews, Toole, Vezin, Lionel Brough, &c., took part. In 1874 he accepted an engagement at the Olympic, and played *William III.* in Tom Taylor's ' Clancarty ' (for the first time appearing under his real name, Charles Sugden), and *Chevalier* in 'The Two Orphans.'

On January 16, 1876, Mr. Sugden appeared as *Charles Middlewick* in ' Our Boys '—first performed at the Vaudeville Theatre— a character which he sustained during three hundred nights. At the Prince of Wales's Theatre he has played *Captain Bradford* in 'Peril,' *Algie Fairfax* in ' Diplomacy,' and *Sir Harry Arncliff* in ' The Unequal Match,' " a part thoroughly well suited to a style which errs occasionally on the side of over-repression. The studiously subdued tones of Mr. Sugden's acting was in place here, and its admirable ease and simplicity are well known." (*Pall Mall Gazette.*)

* SULLIVAN, BARRY, was born at Birmingham in 1824, and made his first appearance on the stage at Cork in 1840. After studying for some time he joined the company of the Theatre Royal, Edinburgh. Previous to his appearance on the metropolitan stage he had earned distinction in the provinces—notably at Manchester and Liverpool—as an actor of the poetic drama. Mr. Sullivan made his *début* in London, at the Haymarket Theatre, in the part of *Hamlet*, Saturday, February 7, 1852. The *Athenæum* (February 14, 1852) thus notices this performance :—" Mr. Sullivan is slender of figure and graceful in his attitudes, but his vocal organ is very limited. His evident good taste prevented him from any attempt to strain it ; but however well harmonized were the tones, the effects produced could of course be proportioned only to the capacity of the organ, and the result was a series of minute points and crotchety new readings as substitutes for physical powers. That Mr. Sullivan has mind, and can act well—that he possesses originality of conception and beauty of movement—that he has studied hard and practised long—all this is evident. . . . His interview with the Ghost was, in its expression of reverence, grace, and significance, very fine ; and than his 'closet scene,' we never remember anything more pathetic as well as picturesque. In a word, Mr. Sullivan acts with great care and pains." In a lengthy criticism of Mr. Fechter's performance of the character of Hamlet the *Saturday Review* of April 6, 1861, dwelling upon the novelties introduced by that actor into the generally received reading of Shakespeare's play, remarked : " When Mr. Barry Sullivan came out as *Hamlet* a few years ago, many persons attended the Haymarket for the mere purpose of hearing him say, ' I know a hawk from a herne—Pshaw ! ' instead of the ordinary reading ; and there is no doubt that the novelties of Mr. Fechter are far more important and interesting. But young critics may be usefully warned that the conventional is not necessarily wrong, and that a great artist is not bound, as a matter of duty, to scorn the teachings of his predecessors. A schoolboy who commenced reciting the first book of ' Æneid ' with the words 'Armorum virique cano,' would be the most unconventional Latinist in his class ; but his originality would hardly exempt him from the penalties prescribed by the ancient code of birch."

At the Haymarket, February 14, 1852, Mr. Barry Sullivan acted the character of *Angiolo*, in a five-act drama by Miss Vandenhoff, entitled ' Woman's Heart.' On the 19th of April of the same year, at the same theatre, he played the part of *Evelyn* in a revival of 'Money.' On Saturday, February 12, 1853, first performance, at the Haymarket Theatre, of Lord Lytton's play ' Not so Bad as we Seem ' (written for, and originally played by, members of the Guild of Literature), Mr. Sullivan sustained the part of *Hardman*. " Mr. Stuart played the Duke of Middlesex with volcanic energy and oppressive sense of ducal dignity, and Mr. Barry Sullivan that of *Hardman* in a manner which will not allow him to be dismissed at the tail of a sentence. The impression left by this gentleman's acting is, that he possesses a strong and clear dramatic intellect, but lacks somewhat of the flexibility required by the characters of comedy. Hence his playing in the earlier and more level scenes was somewhat stiff and cumbrous, though always judicious ; but in the last act, the burthen of which rested mainly upon him, he came out with energy and fire, excited and sustained the interest of the audience all through, and obtained a succession of well-merited plaudits." (*Daily News*, February 14, 1853.)

In April of the same year, first performance, at the same theatre, of Mr. Browning's play of ' Colombe's Birthday,' Mr. Sullivan acted the character of *Valence.* The same year he accepted an engagement at the Standard Theatre, and played a leading *rôle* in Bennett's drama ' Retribution ' (revived). In 1855 he returned to the Haymarket Theatre, and in May appeared as *Claude Melnotte*, to Miss Helen Faucit's Pauline (' Lady of Lyons '); in June as *Franklyn* in ' Love's Martyrdom ' ; and subsequently, in the same month, as *Jaques* in ' As You Like It,' Miss Faucit playing Rosalind. On Monday, October 8, 1855, at Drury Lane Theatre, Mr. Barry Sullivan appeared as *Tihrak*, in " a grand Egyptian drama" by Mr. J. Fitzball, then performed for the first time. He continued to play at the same theatre during the year following, and in 1857 accepted an engagement at Sadler's Wells, where he sustained several important parts in the line of the legitimate drama. Subsequently he fulfilled various engagements in the United States. On Monday, August 20, 1860, he reappeared on the London boards, at the St. James's Theatre, acting the character of *Hamlet*, in which, eight years before, he had made his first appearance on the metropolitan stage. In the interval Mr. Sullivan had devoted himself with assiduity to the active duties of his calling, and had reaped all the advantages that inevitably accrue from painstaking labour in any profession. The *Times* (August 22, 1860), noticing his reappearance on the London stage, said :—" The summer performances at the most western of the theatres (the St. James's) take this week a tragic direction, in consequence of the engagement of Mr. Barry Sullivan, who has just returned from America. As on the occasion when some years ago he made his first appearance before the London public, he has chosen *Hamlet* for the inauguration of his career. All the qualities that have rendered his memory estimable in the minds of playgoers he retains to their full extent. He is a careful, correct, and perspicuous declaimer, turning to good account his natural advantages of voice and figure, and he is, moreover, thoroughly versed in the routine of the part, which he has evidently studied with laudable assiduity. Though he makes no particular attempt to startle his audience, he is neither tame nor listless, and all that he does is well considered and quite to the purpose. A numerous audience witnessed his performance of *Hamlet*, and greeted him with a hearty welcome."

From 1860 to 1866 Mr. Sullivan devoted himself to dramatic affairs in Australia, where for some time he was the chief actor and manager of one of the principal theatres. In the latter year he once more returned to the London stage, and reappeared, on September 22, at Drury Lane Theatre, as *Faulconbridge*, in a revival, by Messrs. Falconer and Chatterton, of ' King John,' and in the month following as *Macbeth*. Mr. Sullivan also played other characters in the drama of Shakespeare during the same engagement. " The new *Faulconbridge* was safe with his audience from his very first utterances," remarked the *Athenæum* (September 29, 1866). " Mr. Sullivan's conception of the character is nearer to that of Charles Kemble than of any other actor within the memory of contemporaries. There is an abundance, but not a superabundance of spirit in it ; the utmost freedom, without vulgarity ; a graceful ease, and not a braggart swagger. . . . Mr. Sullivan's success was not confined to the comedy or melodramatic element of the character. There were other portions, in which his display of feeling was given with a quiet but telling effect, no jot of which was lost with the critical part of his audience, who were closely scanning his speech, action, bearing, and expression. His by-play was equally good ; that is, his part in the drama was never forgotten. His very bow to King John was of a real Sir Richard to a substantial King ; and when he bent over the body of the dying monarch there was earnestness of significance in the action, as if the gallant knight felt a respectful sorrow for the condition of his uncle. ' Old Drury,' in short, may be congratulated on its acquisition of Mr. Barry Sullivan. Some time has passed since he won golden opinions by his impersonation of Hamlet ; but a certain lack of strength and want of practice were observable. Since then, however, his experience in the colonies has made a considerable difference in this respect. As manager and chief actor of an Australian theatre he was compelled to venture what in England he might have avoided ; and having, by his excellent conduct of his establishment, secured an extensive patronage, was enabled to make essay of his powers in the most trying parts. He succeeded, and now has so manifestly improved in health and physique, that he supported the part of *Faulconbridge* with the utmost ability and success."

Another contemporary journal, the *Daily Telegraph* (October 3, 1866), thus discusses the merits of his acting in ' Macbeth ':—" Mr. Barry Sullivan's rendering of *Macbeth* is much less familiar to the playgoing public of this country ; but if the sustained applause of such a strong gathering as that of last evening be any criterion, the admiration of the earnest lovers of Shakespeare, who are nightly making ' Old Drury' their trysting-place, will be found pretty equally divided. Without attempting an elaborate analysis of the character as presented by Mr. Sullivan, it would be difficult to indicate the numerous points of departure from those readings with which the town is familiar. It may be briefly stated, however, that Mr. Barry Sullivan strongly impresses his auditory with the conviction that, from the first supernatural soliciting of the witches, *Macbeth* is fully resolved to remove all obstacles in the way of his ambition, and that the letter to his wife conveys that intention. Lady Macbeth readily becomes the partner of his crime, but is thus hardly to be accused of being its instigator, and on those passages in the text which tend to support this view the tragedian places very forcible emphasis. There are some notable variations also from the usual mode of delivering the most familiar lines which will interest if they do not convince the hearer ; and of these, ' *Tide* and the hour run through the roughest day,' may be quoted as a fair specimen. The performance throughout exhibits the characteristics of an actor who has at least had the courage to venture on novel ground, and who possesses the power to render justice to his own conception. It may be fairly objected to Mr. Barry Sullivan's notion of the rapidity with which the thought of the murder entered the mind of *Macbeth*, that his wife, who considers him ' too full o' the milk of human kindness,' could have had but little knowledge of the darker moods of his disposition, or else we must be enforced to believe that his nature entirely changed on being accosted by the witches. Whatever opinion may be entertained it is in favour of the *Macbeth* of Tuesday night that he was unconsciously assisted by Miss Amy Sedgwick, who, venturing for the first time in London on the personation of Lady Macbeth, gave a suggestive rather than a powerful rendering of the character. Her performance is not lacking in intelligence, but it is deficient in force, and much less decided in form and colour than could be desired."

In 1868 Mr. Barry Sullivan entered, for a brief period, upon the management of the Holborn Theatre, "opening" there, Saturday, May 1, as *Evelyn* in ' Money.' Since that date he has principally occupied himself with "starring" in the United States, Canada, Australia, and in England. In 1875, after various farewell dinners given in his honour at the Alexandra Palace and elsewhere, Mr. Barry Sullivan again sailed for the United States and made his first appearance at Booth's Theatre, on August 30 of that year, in *Hamlet.* *Appleton's Journal* (No. 338, vol. xiv., pp. 345-6) published the following criticism on his acting of the part :—" Mr. Sullivan is a long way from being a great actor. He has a very pleasing face and presence, a fine, mellow voice, and he knows how to pose in very picturesque attitudes, and to fill the eye with a succession of well-studied stage-pictures. He unites in these particulars the instincts of the sculptor and the painter ; his eminently picturesque make-ups show a fine taste for colour, and his attitudes evince a plastic grace that would make him always an attractive actor in purely picturesque parts. Nor is he without a calm, balanced intelligence. But there is absolutely no fire and no imagination. His cool judgment keeps him always from rant or turbulence ; he never ' oversteps the modesty of Nature'; in truth, Nature with him is rather closely veiled, and one can get no more than faint glimpses of her true form and being. He errs altogether on the side of tameness. His grasp of *Hamlet* is of the stage, stagey— that is, it is just that perception of the part that a thoroughly trained actor would have who has limited his study to all the external arts—of how he shall walk, how he shall stand, how he shall sit, how he shall do this and that piece of ' business,' how

and where he shall deliver this and that line—but there is no sub-
jective insight, no heed of the fires that burn within, no psychological study, no imaginative grasp for the character of the melancholy and philosophic prince. His conception is that *Hamlet* is
wholly sane, but he never succeeds in catching even the spirit of
the assumed madness ; no 'antic disposition' confounds the court;
he never 'unpacks his heart with words,' for his heart carries no
burden. So sedate, so calm, so sane, so balanced, so fine and
courtly a *Hamlet* would never have given king, queen, or courtiers
a moment's uneasiness. He listens to the players in their trial-
speeches coolly, and when he finds himself alone gives no hint, in
the most impulsive and passionate speech in the play, either in
manner or expression, of the tumult of feeling which the words
describe. In the play-scene he makes a telling picture by graceful
posing on the floor ; and in fact throughout this actor is always
good in a stage-sense, but never really any thing more. He is not
vigorous enough to please the untutored, nor introspective enough
to charm the lovers of Shakespeare's great creation." He has
accepted brief engagements in London in the intervening period,
1875–79; his last performances of importance in the metropolis
having been at Drury Lane Theatre, in 1876, as *Richard III.*, in
Cibber's version of Shakespeare's play, and in the character of
Macbeth, and (August 1879) as *Benedick* at the Haymarket Theatre,
when he appeared for the benefit of Mr. Buckstone.

SWANBOROUGH, ADA, was born in London, and made her
début in November 1861, at the Strand Theatre, as *King Christian*,
in a comedietta adapted from the French by Mr. T. L. Greenwood,
entitled 'Is it the King?' Miss Ada Swanborough has played
many parts and "created" not a few at this theatre, long established
as the home of English burlesque and the domestic drama. Of
leading characters which she has from time to time undertaken the
following may be mentioned among the more important :—*Cicely
Homespun* in 'The Heir-at-Law'; *Estelle Fitzwalter* in 'My
Preserver'; *Matilda Gushington* in 'Marriage at Any Price';
Blanche in the burlesque of 'The Duke's Motto'; *The Caliph*
in Mr. W. Brough's 'Caliph of Bagdad'; *Lady Constance de Grey*
in 'The Field of the Cloth of Gold'; *Countess d'Estrella* in J. P.
Wooler's 'Maid of Honour'; *Mabel Lyndwood* in Burnand's burlesque 'Windsor Castle.' In Burnand's extravaganza 'Der Freischutz' Miss Ada Swanborough played the part of *Agnes*, and in
Brough's 'Pygmalion ; or, The Statue Fair,' the part of *Venus*.
At the Strand Theatre she sustained the part of *Alexina* in a two-
act drama by Sheridan Knowles entitled 'Alexina ; or, True unto
Death,' respecting which the *Athenæum* wrote : "The weight of the
acting fell on Miss Ada Swanborough, who sustained the part of
the heroine with so much feeling and judgment, that, familiar as
we are with the general character of the persons and incidents,
she created quite an interest in her fortunes and destiny." Other
principal characters played by Miss Ada Swanborough at various
periods of her career have been—*Pauline* in 'The Very Latest
Edition of the Lady of Lyons'; *Leonie* in 'The Ladies' Battle';

Hardress Cregan in the burlesque 'Eily O'Connor'; *Inez* in Burnand's burlesque of 'L'Africaine'; *Kate McTavish* in 'Old Soldiers,' &c. On May 6, 1875, Byron's three-act comedy 'Weak Woman' was produced at the Strand, Miss Ada Swanborough undertaking the part of *Helen Gaythorne.* December 5 of the same year she appeared as *Mrs. Sutherland* in C. T. Cheltnam's comedy 'A Lesson in Love.' In all the more successful comedies, comediettas, burlesques, and extravaganzas produced at the Strand Theatre under the present and past managements (1861–1878) Miss Ada Swanborough has borne a principal *rôle.* In the spring of 1879 she went on tour in the provinces.

SWINBOURNE, THOMAS, was born in Birmingham, and entered the theatrical profession at the age of eighteen. Four years later he was playing the "leading business" on Mr. Jackman's circuit of theatres, comprising Northampton, Gloucester, Stratford-on-Avon, and Newcastle in Staffordshire, the last of the old theatrical "circuits." In 1850 he was leading actor at Newcastle-on-Tyne. During his connection with the theatre in that town he played *Othello* to the Iago of Macready. Afterwards Mr. Swinbourne joined Mr. Alexander's company at the T. R. Glasgow, acting in all the leading Shakespearian and other legitimate dramas, and was next engaged at the T. R. Manchester, where he remained four years. He made his first appearance on the London stage, Monday, September 15, 1862, as *Captain Randal Macgregor,* in Boucicault's spectacular drama 'The Relief of Lucknow,' then first performed. Previous to his *début* in London, Mr. Swinbourne had "starred" in the provinces and in the United States with the late Miss Vandenhoff, and obtained the good report of local journals. The following, among other characters from time to time played by Mr. Swinbourne in London, will serve to illustrate the position held by him in the dramatic profession. He became a member of Mr. Boucicault's company when that gentleman opened Astley's Amphitheatre as the 'Theatre Royal, Westminster.' On Monday, January 26, 1863, he appeared there as *Geordie Robertson* in Boucicault's dramatic version of 'The Heart of Midlothian,' then performed for the first time. In the following year, Monday, January 30, at the Adelphi Theatre, he sustained the character of *Master Walter* in a revival of 'The Hunchback,' Miss Bateman playing Julia. He appeared at Drury Lane, September 23, 1865, as *Macduff,* to the Macbeth of Mr. Phelps and of Mr. Anderson, alternately. The "revival" continued for six weeks. October 28 of the same year, at the same theatre, he acted *Caius Cassius* ('Julius Cæsar') for six nights; Mr. Phelps, Brutus; Mr. Anderson, Marc Antony. November 4 of the same year, at the same theatre, he played *Hubert* in a revival of 'King John'; Phelps, King John; Anderson, Faulconbridge; Percy Roselle, Arthur; Miss Atkinson, Constance. At Easter 1866 he "opened" at Sadler's Wells as *Belphegor,* and played during the season *William* ('Black-Eyed Susan'), *John Peerybingle* ('Dot'), *Pierre Leroux* ('The Poor Strollers'). At the same theatre, June 16, 1866, first performance of Mr. Farnie's version of Mr. Charles

Dickens's ' Our Mutual Friend,' entitled ' The Golden Dustman,' Mr. Swinbourne acted the part of *John Harmon.* In 1867, Monday, January 21, at Drury Lane, in a revival of ' John Bull,' he played *Peregrine.* He reappeared at Drury Lane Theatre September 22 of the same year, and played, among other parts during the season, *Petruchio* (' Katherine and Petruchio '), *Jaques* (' As You Like It '), *Walter* in ' The Hunchback '; Miss Faucit as Julia, and the late Walter Montgomery as Sir Thomas Clifford. September 25, 1870, Mr. Swinbourne appeared at the Royal Holborn Theatre, as *Edmund Kean* in the play of that name. October 31, 1874, he appeared at the Lyceum Theatre as *Claudius* in ' Hamlet,' which ran for 200 consecutive nights. At the same theatre (September 25, 1875) he acted *Macduff.* In 1876 he went on tour with Mr. Irving, and appeared as the *Ghost* in ' Hamlet,' *Cromwell* in ' Charles I.,' &c. September 17, 1877, appeared at the Olympic Theatre as *Sergeant Cuff* (' The Moonstone '). December 30, 1878, commenced an engagement at the Lyceum Theatre under Mr. Irving's management, appearing as *Horatio* in a revival of ' Hamlet,' previously to which he had appeared as *Othello* at the Park Theatre :—" Mr. Swinbourne is, as all play-goers are aware, one of the soundest and most legitimate actors of the day. His style, based upon the best traditions of the past, is not so absolutely wedded to tradition as to become rigid or mechanical. In choosing such a character as *Othello* he was certainly well-advised. Quiet, easy, and natural in the opening scenes, he was not wanting in force when occasion required, but he did not make a hurricane of passion the principal feature of the delineation. Passion, wisely and temperately employed, was present, and in ample degree, but the vehemence of *Othello's* jealousy was always tempered by tenderness. If he doubts, he also doats—if he suspects, he also fondly loves ; and never in the very tempest and whirlwind of the Moor's fiery rage do we forget his former tenderness, his ever lingering devotion to the ideal in which he had so devoutly believed, until the base tongue of the ' honest Iago ' had done its terrible work but too surely, aided as it was by circumstances favouring the designs of a villain. To enumerate the chief points of Mr. Swinbourne's impersonation, we may mention the clear and admirable manner in which the speech to the Senate was delivered. This was given with excellent emphasis and feeling, and evoked hearty applause. The pathos of the effective speech ending with ' *Othello's* occupation's gone ' also gained due recognition, and the scenes between *Othello* and Iago proved in the strongest possible manner Mr. Swinbourne's claim to be regarded as a legitimate actor of a high class. The tenderness and gentleness of the interviews with Desdemona, and the dignity displayed in the scenes with Cassio, were further examples of artistic and thoughtful work, deserving the warmest commendation. We have only to add that the audience throughout fully endorsed our own opinion respecting the ability Mr. Swinbourne displayed by applauding repeatedly, and by calling him before the curtain many times during the evening." (*Era*, October 6, 1878.)

TAYLOR, FREDERICA, was born in Philadelphia, U.S.A., of English parents, and brought to England in early childhood, where she was educated for the stage, and entered the dramatic profession in 1869 at the Oxford Theatre. Miss Taylor was subsequently engaged by Mr. Sefton Parry for a short season. In 1872–3 she fulfilled various engagements in the provinces, and afterwards at the Brighton Theatre, under the management of the late Mr. H. Nye Chart, where she appeared as *Ophelia, Helen* ('The Hunchback'), *Lydia* ('Love Chase'). At the end of 1873 she was specially engaged by the management of the Theatre Royal, Birmingham, to personate *Oberon* in a revival of 'The Midsummer Night's Dream.' "As *Oberon,* Miss Taylor had the advantage of a clear and natural expression, even in singing, so that nearly every word and syllable were heard distinctly ; and her vocal illustrations were greatly effective. She evidently took more trouble than singers usually do to act as well as sing, and hence every scene in which she appeared was an excellent success." (*Birmingham Daily News.*) From 1873 to 1875 Miss Taylor was on tour in the provinces, playing various important parts, notably *Amy Robsart* in Andrew Halliday's drama of 'Kenilworth.' In 1876 she was specially engaged to play *Paulina* in Shakespeare's 'Winter's Tale,' revived at the Royal Alexandra Theatre, Liverpool. At the Theatre Royal, Birmingham, the same season, she played *Hermione* ('Winter's Tale'). Among other important parts played from time to time by Miss Taylor, the following may be noticed, viz. *Miss Hardcastle* ('She Stoops to Conquer'), *Lady Isabel* ('East Lynne'), *Margaret Wentworth* ('Henry Dunbar'), *Esmeralda* ('Notre Dame').

TAYLOR, JAMES GOULDE, was born in Manchester, and first became connected with the stage as "walking gentleman" at Aberdeen Theatre in 1858. The following year, at the same theatre, he entered upon the *rôle* of "low comedy," a department of stage work which he has followed with gratifying success ever since. He made his first appearance on the London stage November 2, 1864, at the Olympic Theatre, as *Timothy Topknot* in a new farce entitled 'My Wife's Bonnet.' During his engagement there, continuing till 1869, he played *Gillenormand* in 'The Yellow Passport,' and *Pedrigo Potts* in an English adaptation of Boildieu's comic opera 'John of Paris' in a way that obtained for him warm commendation. In a notice of the latter play the *Examiner* (August 7, 1869) remarked of Mr. Taylor's acting in it that it "might challenge comparison with Liston's—his [Mr. Taylor's] *Pedrigo Potts* was a bit of true comedy, thoroughly humorous and enjoyable from first to last, and yet never dashed with those 'gags' of coarse farce upon which too many comedians rely." At the termination of his engagement at the Olympic he went to the Adelphi, and afterwards to the Strand, Covent Garden, and Gaiety Theatres. At the latter he "opened" in March 1871 as *Christopher Pym* in Byron's domestic drama 'Wait and Hope.' He brought himself prominently into notice by his admirable acting at this theatre in various parts, of which the following may be selected as examples, namely, *Verges* in 'Much Ado About Nothing'; *Isaac of York* in Byron's burlesque of 'Ivanhoe'; *Jim Brass* in 'Off the Line'; *Cabriolo* in 'The Princess of Trebizonde'; *Bertram* in W. S. Gilbert's burlesque 'Robert the Devil'; *Sergeant Bouncer* in Arthur Sullivan's operetta of 'Cox and Box,' &c. It has been remarked of Mr. Taylor that he is an actor who plays equally well in drama, farce, burlesque, opera, and opera-bouffe. He has successfully appeared in the United States and Canada, and largely increased his reputation by his performance there in the part of *Sir Joseph Porter, K.C.B.*, in Gilbert and Sullivan's comic opera 'H.M.S. Pinafore.'

TEARLE, GEORGE OSMOND, was born at Plymouth, March 8, 1852, and entered the dramatic profession March 26, 1869, at the Adelphi Theatre, Liverpool, appearing as *Guildenstern* in 'Hamlet.' He afterwards travelled through the provinces and Scotland, accepting engagements at various theatres. In 1871 he acted the part of *Hamlet* at Warrington. Mr. Tearle made his first appearance on the London stage at the Gaiety Theatre, March 26, 1875, in the play entitled 'Rose Michel.' Returning to Liverpool, he again acted the part of *Hamlet* with some success. Subsequently he played in 'Rip Van Winkle' at the Princess's Theatre, London, during the last engagement of Mr. Jefferson. Since 1877 he has been fulfilling various engagements in the provinces.

TEESDALE, HENRY ROBERT, was born in London, January 28, 1841, and made his first appearance on the stage at the Margate Theatre in the autumn of 1867 for the benefit of Miss Amy Sedgwick. On that occasion he played the part of *Sir Harry Arncliff* in 'The Unequal Match.' Mr. Teesdale entered the dramatic profession January 1868, at Liverpool, under the management of Mr. H. J. Byron, and played a variety of characters at the Amphitheatre and Alexandra Theatre, including *Polixenes* in a revival of 'The Winter's Tale,' and *Antonio* in 'The Merchant of Venice.' Afterwards he joined the comedy company of Miss Marie Wilton in the provinces, and sustained the parts of the *Graf von Staufenberg* and *The Croupier* in Robertson's comedy of 'Play,' and *Captain Hawtree* in the same author's comedy 'Caste.' He made his first appearance in London at the Gaiety Theatre, December 21, 1868, on the occasion of its opening under Mr. John Hollingshead's management, in the character of *Guy Chilstone* in 'On the Cards.' Mr. Teesdale remained at this theatre during a year and eight months, and in 1870 went to the United States of America, and entered upon an engagement at the Varieties Theatre, New Orleans. He played there *Digby Grant* in Albery's 'Two Roses.' Afterwards he went to New York, and appeared at the

Olympic, Niblo's, and Wallack's theatres; at the latter theatre sustaining the part of *Bob Evans* in Boucicault's play of ' Elfie.' Returning to England in June 1872, he played a short engagement at the New Royalty Theatre under Miss Bertram's management, and afterwards rejoined Mr. Hollingshead's company at the Gaiety for a season. Subsequently, he accepted an engagement at the Haymarket Theatre to play the part of *Ted Thelney* in Gilbert's play entitled ' Charity,' and, following this, appeared at the Vaude-ville Theatre as *Dazzle* in the second revival of ' London Assur-ance.' In the spring of 1875 Mr. Teesdale entered into an engage-ment with Mr. and Mrs. Bancroft to join the company of the Prince of Wales's Theatre, an engagement which continued to the close of the summer season 1878. He played *Henry Beauclerc*, ' Diplo-macy,' on tour with Mr. and Mrs. Kendal in the autumn of 1878. In December 1878 he joined the company of the Lyceum Theatre, and has been playing there *Howard Leslie* in the comedietta ' Book the Third, Chapter the First,' &c.

TEMPLE, RICHARD (a *nom de théâtre;* RICHARD COBB), was born in London, March 2, 1847. At the outset of his career he was in the office of his father, a stockbroker in the city of London ; but, having a great partiality for the art, subsequently studied music with a view of practising it as a profession. In 1868 he sang in public at several concerts, and for a short time studied Italian opera on the Continent, the death of his father precluding the necessary arrangements for a lengthened stay in Italy. He played as an amateur at a benefit performance at the Theatre Royal, Haymarket, in April 1868 ; and made his pro-fessional *début*, May 31, 1869, at the Crystal Palace Theatre, as *Count Rodolpho* in ' La Sonnambula.' Afterwards he went on tour in the provinces to study parts, appearing as first baritone in several English opera and opera-bouffe companies. November 17, 1877, Mr. Temple appeared at the Opéra Comique, London, as *Sir Marmaduke Pointdextre* in ' The Sorcerer ' (Gilbert and Sullivan), and was the "original" *Dick Deadeye* in the same authors' popular comic opera ' H.M.S. Pinafore,' first performed at the same theatre Saturday, May 25, 1878, which character he continued to represent for a lengthened period with very great success.

Mr. Temple "is a competent vocalist, always efficient, and fre-quently very effective ; but he owes his position and popularity in a great measure to his facility in stage business, and to his readi-ness in seizing the humorous features of a new character" (*Era,* December 9, 1877).

TERRISS, WILLIAM (a *nom de théâtre*), son of the late George Lewin, Esq., barrister-at-law, and nephew of the eminent historian the late George Grote, was born in London 1849, and educated at Windermere College and Jesus College, Oxford. He was for a short time in the Royal Navy ; but subsequently entered the dramatic profession, October 1869, at the Prince of Wales's Theatre, Birmingham. After playing various minor parts there for some months, he became a member of the company of the Prince of Wales's Theatre, London, under Mr. and Mrs. Bancroft's management. Subsequently (1871) he removed to Drury Lane Theatre, playing in the late Andrew Halliday's drama of 'Rebecca,' and later on as *Malcolm Græme* in 'The Lady of the Lake.' Afterwards he joined the Strand company, enacting *Doricourt* in 'The Belle's Stratagem' during the 250 consecutive representations of the play at that theatre. Having returned to Drury Lane Theatre on the production there of 'Richard Cœur de Lion,' he sustained the part of *Sir Kenneth*. Following the withdrawal of this play, Mr. Terriss essayed *Romeo* to the Juliet of Miss Wallis, and subsequently played *Captain Molyneux* in Boucicault's 'Shaughraun.' The drama last named had an extended run, and, after the Drury Lane season, was removed to the Adelphi stage. Mr. Terriss has played in various revivals at the Adelphi and Princess's Theatres, and was selected by Mr. W. G. Wills to sustain the part of *Julian Peveril* in his drama 'England,' first performed at Drury Lane. On March 30, 1878, at the Royal Court Theatre, he played *Squire Thornhill* in the same author's play of 'Olivia,' then first performed. On Monday, September 16, 1878, first performance at the Haymarket Theatre of H. J. Byron's "comedy-drama" entitled 'Conscience Money,' Mr. Terriss acted the part of *Sydney Sefton*, and was excellent in it, "giving an altogether new presentation of villany. It is difficult to imagine an improvement more rapid or more distinct than that this young actor has made since he quitted melodrama for comedy." (*Globe*, September 17, 1878.) On Thursday, October 3, 1878, in a revival at the same theatre of 'The Rivals,' Mr. Terriss sustained the part of *Captain Absolute ;* and on Monday, December 2, in the first performance at the same theatre of 'The Crisis,' by Mr. Albery, he acted *Fawley Denham*. On April 14, 1879, he appeared as *Walter North* in W. G. Wills's play 'Ellen,' then first performed, and on Thursday, June 12, 1879, in 'Brag,' by the same author, he took the part of *Hugh Merryman*. Mr. Terriss is now (November 1879) engaged at the St. James's Theatre, playing *Comte de la Roque* in 'Monsieur le Duc,' and *Jack Gambier* in 'The Queen's Shilling.'

TERRY, EDWARD O'CONNOR, was born in London, March 10, 1844, and made his first appearance on any stage, August 15, 1863, at the Mechanics' Institute, Christchurch, Hants, as *Wormwood* in 'The Lottery Ticket.' Afterwards (1864) he appeared at the following places, viz. Rochester, Guernsey, Sheffield, Newcastle, and the Isle of Man. At the Theatre Royal, Belfast, in the following years (1865-6), he played, among other parts, *Tom Twig* in 'Catching an Heiress,' *Touchstone*, *Asa Trenchard* ('Our American Cousin'), *Squire Chivey* ('David Garrick'), *Tony Lumpkin*, &c. Mr. Terry made his first appearance on the London stage, at the Surrey Theatre, September 1867, as *Finnikin Fussleton* in 'A Cure for the Fidgets.' Afterwards, the same year, he appeared at the Lyceum Theatre, under Mr. E.

T. Smith's management, as the *First Gravedigger* in a revival of
' Hamlet.' In 1869 (August) Mr. Terry joined the company of the
Strand Theatre, and, in a revival of Mr. Byron's burlesque ' The
Pilgrim of Love,' played the part of the *King of Toledo*. " But
the great man of the performance," remarked the *Times* (August
1869), " is Mr. Edward Terry, who has at once made his mark as a
grotesque actor of most singular qualifications. His slim figure
recalls to mind the four French dancers who appeared at the
Princess's some two years ago. His habitual melancholy, which
is itself expressed by the oddest postures, is relieved by frantic
Terpsichorean explosions, varying the routine of the ordinary
' breakdown' with eccentricities after the manner of Callot. As a
comic singer he is also a proficient ; and a dismal ditty, in which
the unhappy monarch recounts the maladies he has suffered with
very sorrowful mirth, is encored no less than three times amid roars
of laughter. Mr. Terry has fashioned for himself a character out
of the *King of Toledo*, and about the impression made by this
there can be no mistake." At the Strand Theatre, during the time
he was a member of its company, Mr. Terry played the following
original parts, viz. *Kalyba* in Burnand's burlesque of ' Sir George
and A Dragon '; *Polyphloisboio* in the same author's burlesque of
' Orion '; *Cassidy* in Byron's comedy of ' Old Soldiers '; *Lieutenant
Lamb* in the same author's comedy of ' Old Sailors '; *Calino* in a
burlesque under the title of ' Nemesis,' written by Mr. Farnie ; the
Widow Sheppard in ' Little Jack Sheppard ' (burlesque), also by
Mr. Farnie ; *Joe Sally* in ' Dolly's Delusion ' (R. Reece) ; and
Captain Ginger in Byron's comedy ' Weak Woman.' After fulfilling his long engagement at the Strand, Mr. Terry became a
member of the company of the Gaiety Theatre, under Mr. John
Hollingshead's management. In 1877–8 he played there the
following original parts, viz. *King of Spain* in ' Little Don Cæsar
de Bazan ' (Byron) ; *Devilshoof* in ' The Bohemian Gyurl ' (Byron);
and *Mephistopheles* in ' Little Doctor Faust' (Byron). On Monday,
September 2, 1878, at the Gaiety Theatre, Mr. Terry played the
leading *rôle* in Burnand's comedy entitled ' Jeames,' founded on
' Jeames's Diary ' of W. M. Thackeray. He is still a member of
Mr. Hollingshead's company.

TERRY, ELLEN (Mrs. CHARLES KELLY, *a nom de théâtre*
[WARDELL]), was born in 1848. Towards the termination of Mr.
Kean's memorable period of management of the Princess's Theatre
she made her first appearance on the stage in a child's part, that
of *Mamilius* in ' The Winter's Tale,' April 28, 1856. The *Times*
(May 1, 1856), making note of the fact, remarks : " Miss Ellen
Terry plays the boy *Mamilius* with a vivacious precocity that
proves her a worthy relative of her sister, Miss Kate." On Monday,
October 18, 1858, she acted the part of *Arthur* in the second revival of ' King John,' under Mr. Kean's superintendence, at the
Princess's, " with great sweetness, clearness of enunciation, and
delicate light and shade." In March 1863 Miss Ellen Terry made
what may be termed her professional *début* at the Haymarket

Theatre, in the part of *Gertrude* in 'The Little Treasure'—Mr. Sothern as Captain Maydenblush. "The version of that charming little piece 'La Joie de la Maison,' which is well known in London as 'The Little Treasure,' has within the last few weeks been found pre-eminently useful. Revived at the Adelphi, it enabled Miss Marie Wilton to display talent for a wider range of impersonation than had been usually associated with her name. Performed now at the Haymarket, where it was originally produced, it presents Miss Ellen Terry in an entirely new light. But a short time since this young lady was known as the successor of her sister, Miss Kate Terry, in the representation of the most juvenile characters ; and now she is matured into one of the happiest specimens of what the French call the *ingénue* that have been seen on any stage. There is nothing conventional or affected in her performance of the *Little Treasure*, but the young girl of buoyant spirits, kindly heart, impulsive emotions, and somewhat remiss education is presented in her natural shape, free and uncontrolled as her long back-hair. Particularly excellent is her assumption of that perfect confidence which arises from complete innocence of evil. Well may poor Captain Maydenblush be stricken with terror when she makes him an offer of her hand, with an audacity that the most impudent citizen of the *demi-monde* might strive in vain to acquire." (*Times*, March 25, 1863.) Her next appearance on the London boards requiring notice took place October 24, 1867, on the occasion of the opening of the new Queen's Theatre, Long Acre. The piece of the evening, by Charles Reade, was entitled 'The Double Marriage,' in which Miss Ellen Terry sustained the part of *Rose de Beaurepaire*. From the last mentioned date down to 1874 Miss Ellen Terry seems to have accepted no professional engagements in the metropolis. In the last mentioned year, on February 28, she made her reappearance on the stage, at the Queen's Theatre, as *Philippa Chester* in a revival of Charles Reade's drama 'The Wandering Heir.' Discussing the merits of this performance the *Daily Telegraph* (March 2, 1874) said : "Miss Ellen Terry possesses exactly the qualifications demanded by such a character as *Philippa*, and the undiminished brightness and buoyancy of her style became at once apparent in the scene when the hoyden dwells with such delight on her love of boyish pastimes, yet shows how much she retains of girlish modesty and simplicity. Hardly less effective when the action is transferred to America, and *Philippa* appears in male attire, was her generous devotion to the interests of James Annesley ; . . . . while the struggle under masculine garb to veil repeated signs of strong womanly affection was most artistically indicated. Mr. Charles Reade's drama of 'The Wandering Heir,' which possesses a highly interesting story wrought out with remarkable ingenuity, has thus become endowed with an additional element of attraction, and the prosperous career of a piece having a peculiar significance at the present time promises to be prolonged far beyond the hundred nights it has already nearly attained."

In the last mentioned year, on Saturday, April 18, at Astley's Theatre, she played a leading *rôle* (*Susan Merton*) in Mr. Charles

Reade's drama ' It is Never Too Late to Mend.' In 1875 (April), in a revival, at the Prince of Wales's Theatre, of ' The Merchant of Venice,' she acted the character of *Portia*. Respecting this revival the *Daily News* (April 19, 1875) was of opinion that there was not much to be said of any individual performer in it with the single exception of Miss Ellen Terry. " But that is a large exception. This is indeed the *Portia* that Shakespeare drew. The bold innocence, the lively wit and quick intelligence, the grace and elegance of manner, and all the youth and freshness of this exquisite creation, can rarely have been depicted in such harmonious combination. Nor is this delightful actress less successful in indicating the tenderness and depth of passion which lie under that frolicsome exterior. Miss Terry's figure, at once graceful and commanding, and her singularly sweet and expressive countenance, doubtless aid her much ; but this performance is essentially artistic. Nor is there to be found in it a trace of the ' pedantry and affectation' which distinguished critics have erroneously imagined to be essential features of the character. The lady clearly does not belong to the school who imagine that the whole art of acting consists in not acting at all. She is, on the contrary, very inventive in what the players call 'business'—her emphasis is carefully studied, and her action and movements all receive that subtle infusion of colour which raise them into the region of art, and always prevent them from becoming commonplace. But, instead of being less natural on this account, sincerity and truth are stamped upon her entire performance."

In May of the same year, at the same theatre, Miss Ellen Terry sustained the part of *Clara Douglas* in a revival of ' Money,' acting with " an emotional power in which she is now unequalled " (the *Athenæum*, June 5, 1875). " Nothing, however, will distinguish this revival so favourably as the exquisitely graceful, tender, and charming performance of *Clara Douglas* by Miss Ellen Terry. Not only are voice and gesture alike winning and sympathetic, but in a hundred little details which would escape the notice of any but an actress of the very highest capacity does Miss Terry prove her power. The expression of her face during the reading of the will which gives fortune to Evelyn is supremely beautiful, her moan of anguish as she hears the proposal to Georgina irresistibly touching, and the final reconciliation intense in its blissful serenity. Miss Terry has the rare gift of identifying herself with the personage she presents, and neither on our own stage nor on the French do we remember any exemplifications of womanly self-sacrifice and tenderness which surpasses the *Clara Douglas* at the Prince of Wales's." (*Standard*, May 31, 1875.)

On Saturday, August 7, 1875, acting for one night only at the Princess's Theatre, she played *Pauline* in ' The Lady of Lyons.' The effect of this performance, according to the *Athenæum* (August 14, 1875), was to set the seal upon a growing reputation, and to make evident the fact that an actress of a high, if not the highest, order had arisen in our midst. Said that journal : " One of the pleasantest, inasmuch as it is one of the rarest, tasks the critic is called upon to fulfil is that of heralding to the world the advent of genius. So vast a space separates, ordinarily, aspiration from accomplishment, the critic's duty becomes merged in that of the censor, and the public comes to regard him as one whose sole function is to point out inequalities of workmanship and failure of effort. In the case of things dramatic and histrionic, it is rarely indeed the critic can do more than suggest some promise of talent behind crude performance —some glimpse of meaning or intention in a commonplace rendering. There is, accordingly, a pleasure of no ordinary kind in announcing a fact Miss Terry's recent performances have fully established, viz. that an actress has developed in whom there is that perception of analogies, that insight into mysteries, and that power of interpretation, on which the world has bestowed the name of genius. Circumstances took Miss Terry from the stage at a time when men dimly perceived in her the promise which has since been realized. It is probable that some delay in that maturity of style indispensable to perfection in histrionic art has resulted from this break in her career. The interval can scarcely have been misspent, however, since Miss Terry reappeared on the stage with ripened powers and with improved method. After one or two attractive performances in parts which showed one side only of her talent, Miss Terry went to the Prince of Wales's Theatre and played *Portia* in ' The Merchant of Venice,' and *Clara Douglas* in ' Money.' To these *rôles* is now added a third, the result of the three being to prove Miss Terry a subtle interpreter of poetic character, and an admirable exponent of various phases of passion. Physical advantages are, of course, an all-important portion of the stock-in-trade of an actress. The long, tender lines of a singularly graceful figure add wonderful picturesqueness to the illustrations Miss Terry affords.

" Her presentation of *Pauline* comprised a series of pictures each more graceful than the preceding, and all too good for the lackadaisical play in which she appeared. They would have been perfectly in place as illustrations to some border ballad or legend of ' The Round Table.' More important, however, than this gift of picturesqueness, magical as is its effect in illustrating art, is the power of getting inside a character and revealing it to the public. This, in the case of *Portia*, Miss Terry did, showing one of the loveliest of Shakespearian creations in colours in which few, among students even, had dressed it, flooding it, so to speak, with a light of illumination. As interpretation, her *Pauline* was less successful. Pride, which in the character of *Pauline* divides the empire with Love, in the interpretation makes scarcely a fight. Conceding, however, that the conception is wrong to this extent, the impersonation is singularly fine. A score of natural and artistic touches reveal the tenderness and longing of the woman's heart ; while the rendering of the fourth act, in which *Pauline* seeks to force herself from the environing arms of her parents and join her lover, whose words of farewell sting her to madness, is one of those pieces of electrical acting that produce upon the mind an effect of which art in other developments seems scarcely capable. It is too early yet to gauge fully the talent which has revealed itself. It seems probable that Miss Terry's powers will be restrained to depicting the grace, tenderness, and passion of love. In the short scene in the third act, in which *Pauline* chides her lover for treachery, the actress scarcely rose to the requisite indignation. Limiting, however, what is to be hoped from her within the bounds indicated, what chance is there not afforded? Juliet in the stronger scenes would be, we should fancy, outside the physical resources of the artist. Beatrice, Rosalind, Viola, Imogen, Miranda, and a score of other characters of the most delicate and fragrant beauty, are, however, all within what appears to be her range. In the present state of public feeling respecting the Shakespearian drama, it will be strange indeed if some manager does not take the opportunity of mounting some of those plays for which her talent is so eminently adapted. The period during which an actress can play such parts with effect is brief; and a portion of Miss Terry's career has already been lost so far as the stage is concerned. There will be regretable waste if talent so specially suited to the Shakespearian drama is confined to Lord Lytton's facile sentiment and sparkling rhetoric."

In November 1875, in a revival at the Prince of Wales's Theatre of 'Masks and Faces,' she supported the character of *Mabel Vane;* and in the following year (May), at the same theatre, *Blanche* in a revival of T. W. Robertson's comedy ' Ours.' In 1876 she joined the company of the Royal Court Theatre, and appeared there, in November, in a revival of ' New Men and Old Acres.' At the same theatre, March 30, 1878, first performance of W. G. Wills's play of ' Olivia,' founded on 'The Vicar of Wakefield,' Miss Ellen Terry played the title *rôle.* Said the *Daily News* (April 1, 1878) : " To do justice to the tact of the author, to his thoroughly skilful handling of his materials, and to the poetical taste and feeling, and the dramatic energy of the dialogues which he has written, would require far more space than can here be given. A similar remark may with equal justice be applied to the acting of the play. Miss Ellen Terry suppresses something of the pertness and vanity of *Olivia's* character while giving prominence to her confiding innocence. Her temporary hesitation and distrust of her lover's rakish language are nevertheless distinctly and finely marked. Mr. Wills has introduced a pretty and touching scene, in which she takes leave of her family one by one, bestowing small presents and many kisses for the little ones ; and herein the simple feeling of the actress was touching in a high degree. The crowning scene, however, is that in the inn, where by an irresistible impulse *Olivia* is seen to thrust from her violently, with both hands, the man who has outraged, betrayed, and insulted her. This outburst produced upon the audience a powerful effect." Miss Ellen Terry continued to play the part during the very successful " run " of the piece.

On Monday, December 30, 1878, the " opening " night of Mr. Henry Irving's management of the Lyceum Theatre, she appeared as *Ophelia* in the revival of ' Hamlet,' the play chosen for the occasion. The cast included, besides the manager himself (in the title *rôle*), Mr. Forrester, as Claudius ; Mr. Chippendale, Polonius ;

Mr. Mead, the Ghost; Mr. Swinbourne, Horatio; Miss Pauncefort, The Queen. The *Saturday Review* (May 24, 1879) considers
that it is as *Ophelia* that Miss Terry has won for herself a place in
the first rank of actresses. In this performance is found the same
" power of conception of a tragic part, and of execution so perfect
that every word seems to be spoken, every gesture to be made,
from the emotion of the moment, on the importance of which we
have already insisted. The pathos of the mad scene is not more
thought out or more natural than the emotion shown in the scene
where Polonius dismisses Laertes to his ship, a scene of which
Miss Terry relieves the possible tedium by exhibiting, during
Polonius's speech, the interest which a sister would naturally feel
in her brother's prospects. Miss Terry's performance begins by
striking a note of nature, and is natural and complete throughout,
with one exception. Throughout one is impressed by the consistency of the actress's conception, and by the perfect expression
given to her idea. These qualities are especially remarkable in the
mad scene. Here, instead of the incoherent outpouring of imbecile
unconnected phrases which has too often passed for Shakespeare's
representation of *Ophelia's* madness, Miss Terry shows us an intelligible and (if one may use a seemingly paradoxical term) consistent state of dementia. That is, her power of facial expression,
her action, and her intonation, combine to show us the origin in
her disordered state of mind of each wild and whirling word that
she utters. Every broken phrase and strange image is suggested
by some recollection of the time before she was distraught. The
intense pathos with which this catching up of interrupted threads of
thought is presented it is impossible to describe, except in the
words of Laertes :—

> ' Thought and affliction, passion, hell itself,
> She turns to favour and to prettiness.'

The exception referred to above occurs in the scene where *Ophelia*
returns Hamlet's presents. Here Miss Terry is too much given to
tears, too little to amazement. But this is a very small blemish, if
it is a blemish, in a performance full of beauty."

Apropos of this performance *Punch* (January 11, 1879, p. 10)
published the following :—" *Punch* lately read the very sapient
criticism that ' *Ophelia* is a part into which it is impossible to put
much fresh significance.' He especially admires this wise saw, when
he thinks of the entirely fresh significance put by Ellen Terry into
the great scene of the third act in which Hamlet does his best to
wrench the love of her out of his heart and breaks hers in the
effort ; when he retraces the delicate shades by which this admirable
actress distinguished the pangs of despised love from the worse
pangs which follow the discovery that the noble mind she has so
worshipped is overthrown—a misery summed up in the exquisite
closing lines of the scene, which are the epitaph, not of her lost
love, but of Hamlet's shattered reason.
" If anything more intellectually conceived or more exquisitely

wrought out has been seen on the English stage in this generation, it has not been within *Punch's* memory."

On Thursday, April 17 of the same year, Mr. Irving revived 'The Lady of Lyons,' in which Miss Terry acted *Pauline.* "Certainly a more truthful or touching, a more refined or more exquisitely womanly performance of the character has not been witnessed. It differs from that of most preceding representatives of the part chiefly in the predominance of the quality of tenderness. Those who are fortunate enough to have seen this actress's performance in Mr. Wills's play of 'Olivia' cannot have forgotten the terrific power of her expression of hatred and aversion for the man who had so basely betrayed a trusting nature. If, therefore, Miss Terry chooses to moderate those fierce denunciatory tones, to soften down those bitter sarcasms and angry taunts which it has been customary rather to colour highly than to subdue, she will not be suspected of falling short of the occasion from any lack of means. She chooses, apparently, rather to exhibit the love of the woman still struggling to show itself in spite of the cruel fraud of which she is the victim, and to appear as crushed for awhile by a sensitive woman's dread of the mockery of idle tongues, rather than moved by fierce resentment towards her betrayer. All this is very beautiful, and the inexpressible grace of all her movements and attitudes, the perfect simplicity, truth, and directness of all her utterances, add to the performance a singular charm. · Yet it must be confessed that nature portrayed so moderately and with so much sweetness and truth is a little out of keeping with the somewhat artificial character of the play. The old and more emphasized style was unquestionably that which was in the mind of the author when he wrote the speeches that are assigned to the proud lady in the hour of her humiliation." (*Daily News*, April 18, 1879.) In the revival of 'Eugene Aram' during June of the same year Miss Terry acted the part of *Ruth Meadows* with considerable tenderness and grace.

TERRY, KATE (Mrs. ARTHUR LEWIS), was born in 1844, and made her first appearance on the stage at the Princess's Theatre, during the management of Mr. Charles Kean. On Monday, February 9, 1852, she acted there the part of *Arthur* in a revival of 'King John.' According to the *Times* (February 10, 1852), "Hubert, one of the most interesting characters in the piece, was played by Mr. Ryder with a great deal of manly pathos, to the effect of which the clever acting of Miss Terry as *Arthur* greatly contributed. Here and there marks of training might be traced in this little girl; but she was much more easy and natural than is usually the case with juvenile performers." In Lord Macaulay's diary of February 6, 1852 (see Trevelyan's *Life of Lord Macaulay*, vol ii. page 301), he alludes to Miss Kate Terry's performance of *Prince Arthur* at Windsor Castle in these terms: "The scene between King John and Hubert, and that between Hubert and *Arthur*, were very telling. . . . The little girl who acted *Arthur* did wonders." In a footnote to this passage the author says: "It is almost worth while to be past middle life in order to have seen

Miss Kate Terry in *Arthur.*" Miss Kate Terry's first public performance of importance took place at the same theatre, April 17, 1858, in the character of *Cordelia* (' King Lear '); Mr. Charles Kean played the King—one of his most marvellous impersonations —on the occasion. Miss Kate Terry gained praise for the "simple, beautiful style in which she expressed the natural feelings proper to the situations assigned to her in this wonderful drama " (*Athenæum,* April 24, 1858). In the previous year she had played the part of *Ariel* in a revival of ' The Tempest,' at the same theatre. With an enterprise and liberality rare in theatrical annals, Mr. Kean had produced three of his Shakespearian revivals within nine months. ' The Tempest ' was even more remarkable as an effort of labour and invention than its predecessors. " In this revival of ' The Tempest ' the whole interest of the play is concentrated and the whole burden thrown on *Ariel.* The task which Mr. Kean appears to have set himself is to show *Ariel* in the greatest possible variety of situations, keeping up the notion of a spiritual being by the dazzling light with which he is surrounded, the suddenness of his appearance, and the swiftness with which he passes from spot to spot. . . . The part was taken by Miss Kate Terry, who brought to it youth, grace, and intelligence. In one point alone was there a departure from the conception of Shakespeare—*Ariel* did not sing." (*Saturday Review,* July 4, 1857.)

In March 1859, towards the close of Mr. Charles Kean's long term of management, he produced Shakespeare's tragedy of ' King Henry the Fifth,' in which Miss Terry appeared. " The union of England and France in one kingdom is the ambitious sentiment of the play, and the heroism of the English character the spirit that pervades the scenes. This is exemplified in the small as well as the great incidents ; and in none, in acting, did it come out more significantly than in the little part of the boy belonging to the Pistol group of characters at the end of the first act. Miss Kate Terry, as the impersonator of the brave youth, in the heroic and pleasing attitude with which he listened to the sound of the drum, and the measured march with which he followed delightedly the spirit-stirring music, showed us at once the sympathetic gallantry of the English lad going to the wars. There was in it an intelligible indication of the wonderful daring by which the battle of Agincourt was won. To men who were once such lads as he nothing was impossible. The trait was well brought out ; and that little bit of acting, in regard to its completeness. was the gem of the performance." (*Athenæum,* April 2, 1859.) In the year 1862 Miss Terry joined the company under Mr. Alfred Wigan's management at the St. James's Theatre, and subsequently under that of Miss Herbert when the theatre passed into her hands. It was during this engagement that Miss Terry, then only eighteen years old, had her first chance of playing a leading part before a London audience, and at once made her mark as an actress of exceptional gifts, when, owing to the sudden indisposition of Miss Herbert, she was called upon at a few minutes' notice (being then actually dressing for the stage to play a new part in ' Under the Rose ') to take the part of *Mrs. Union* in 'Friends or Foes.' This performance was so excellent, and especially so considering the peculiarly trying circumstances in which it was presented, as to advance Miss Terry at once to the front rank of her profession. The *Daily News* (March 29, 1862), discussing the merits of the play, thus wrote of Miss Terry's part in it : "Mr. Horace Wigan's extremely clever adaptation of 'Nos Intimes' to the English stage continues to attract large audiences to this pretty little theatre (St. James's). . . . Our present intention is not, however, to repeat a favourable notice of a comedy which has drawn all Paris to the 'Vaudeville' for the last few months, and is scarcely less enjoyed in its new dress at the St. James's ; but to record with all the praises it so well deserves the performance of the young and rising actress who has undertaken the part of *Mrs. Union.* Since Monday last, in consequence of the regretted sudden illness of Miss Herbert, Miss Kate Terry has risen at a bound to the highest rank in her profession by her performance of *Mrs. Union.* We confess it fairly surprised us, and no doubt has equally surprised the few among the audience who were not misled by the name of Miss Herbert in the playbill. Miss Kate Terry was, if we mistake not, the *Ariel* of 'The Tempest,' at the Princess's Theatre, under Mr. C. Kean's management, and many of our readers will remember the tender grace of her impersonation of that 'blithe spirit.' She is now in all respects an accomplished dramatic artist ; and there is no actress on the English, or even on the French, stage who could have surpassed her in the part of *Mrs. Union* in 'Friends or Foes.' It is a part that demands exceptional qualifications in an actress— charm of looks, mobility of expression, grace and dignity of manner, and that nameless ease and self-possession which is usually described as 'high-bred.' But the part requires much more than all this. Once and again, *Mrs. Union,* virtuous and honest, but attractive and fond of admiration, hovers on the brink of that precipice over which innocent flirtations are so apt to slide ; and to preserve her character with the audience that too facile and indulgent sympathy which is her besetting danger must never appear self-conscious or in the slightest degree meretricious. Miss Kate Terry manages these inflections of character with so happy an instinct that the audience never for a moment loses confidence in the wife whose gravest error is a momentary imprudence. It is altogether a most charming delineation, and we believe could not be surpassed on any stage. The English theatre is not so rich in promising actresses that we can afford to withhold a word of hearty and sincere encouragement when it is so justly due as in the present instance. Miss Kate Terry in this performance has displayed qualities as an actress in sentimental comedy which have vanished from the English stage since the retirement of Miss Fortescue."

Having fulfilled various engagements in the provinces, Miss Kate Terry joined, in 1863, the company of the Lyceum Theatre, under Mr. Charles Fechter's management, and, on January 15, appeared there as *Blanche de Nevers,* first performance of 'The Duke's

Motto' (John Brougham). On October 31 of the same year, first performance of ' Bel Demonio ' at the same theatre, she sustained the part of *Lena*, " not only like one who has received instruction, but who has impulses of her own, or which, at all events, seem spontaneous." Saturday, May 21, 1864, at the Lyceum, in a revival by Mr. Charles Fechter of ' Hamlet,' in which he played the title *rôle*, Miss Terry supported the part of *Ophelia*. The same year she joined the company of the Olympic Theatre, and at the first performance there, Wednesday, November 2, of 'The Hidden Hand' (Tom Taylor), played the part of *Lady Penarvon*, "in which character she proved that she is already a good actress, and contains the promise of being a better." The following year (1865), Saturday, March 4, first performance of a play entitled ' The Settling Day ' (Tom Taylor), at the same theatre, Miss Terry undertook the character of *Mrs. Markland*. The same year (1865), in June, at the same theatre, in a revival of Shakespeare's ' Twelfth Night,' she acted the dual parts of *Viola* and *Sebastian;* and in July the character of the *Countess de Mauléon* in Tom Taylor's drama ' The Serf; or, Love Levels All.' " Miss Kate Terry, with that bright intelligence which illumines every character she undertakes, played the proud but devotedly-loving countess, and exhibited a grace of expression and an intensity of feeling which deservedly elicited the warmest recognitions of a thoroughly sympathetic audience." (*Daily Telegraph*, July 3, 1865.)

In December 1865 Miss Terry sustained the part of *Margaret Wentworth*, first performance of Tom Taylor's dramatic version of Miss Braddon's novel ' Henry Dunbar.' In May 1866, still at the Olympic Theatre, she performed the part of *Edith Trevelyan*, the heroine, in a play by Leicester Buckingham entitled ' Love's Martyrdom'; and on Monday, October 1, the leading female *rôle* in 'A Wolf in Sheep's Clothing,' then first performed at the Adelphi Theatre. The same year, in a play by Dion Boucicault entitled 'Hunted Down,' first performed at Manchester, Miss Terry undertook the part of *Mary Leigh;* and in November of the same year, at the Adelphi Theatre, London, she appeared as the heroine, in a piece called ' A Sister's Penance,' by Messrs. Tom Taylor and A. W. Dubourg. " Of Miss Kate Terry's acting in this interesting drama it is impossible to speak too highly, and the situation in the third act is especially interpreted by her with a force and tenderness of expression which it is not too much to say no other actress on the stage could equal. Heartily welcomed on her recovery from her late severe indisposition, her performance was throughout greeted with the warmest plaudits and the most unequivocal signs of admiration ; and for real pathos, deep sensibility, and true feeling her achievement has never been surpassed." (*Daily Telegraph*, November 27, 1866.) In 1867, on Saturday, June 1, first performance at the same theatre of Charles Reade's adaptation of Mr. Tennyson's ' Dora,' she sustained the title *rôle*. " The second act . . . is remarkable chiefly for the variety and ingenuity of the touches of true life with which Miss Terry proceeds in her embodiment of *Dora*. Still thoroughly a country girl, simple, yet shrewd, with depths of womanly feeling and little feminine piquancies ; meek as a mouse, but with something in her of the power of angels, she trips on her way of quiet loving kindness in a shabby hat and cotton gloves, and morsel of silk cape over a dress with narrow skirt. Her uncle gives her money for fine dress ; but of that, and of all that she can call hers to give, the utmost toll is taken for the sustenance of the unhappy outcasts. How touching it all is, and true with the real poetry of life, we feel throughout ; the interest in the character rises steadily as the play goes on, and culminates as it should in the last scene." (*Examiner,* June 18, 1867.)

On August 31 of the same year, at the Adelphi Theatre, Miss Kate Terry made her farewell of the stage in the character of *Juliet,* and received an extraordinary ovation. The *Athenæum* (September 7, 1867) thus summed up Miss Terry's professional merits :—" She is certainly a charming actress. Without much physical power, she could nevertheless give, without ostensible effort, great force by an apparently involuntary gesture or motion to the expression of feeling or sentiment. As an artist she gained her ends by an economy of means, and never wasted her powers by overstepping the modesty of nature. Her strength, however, was tried in original parts, which she invested with grace and tenderness. Accordingly our popular dramatists were ambitious to write characters for her. The last of such in which she appeared was Mr. Charles Reade's *Dora,* which, though not exactly the same as Mr. Tennyson's, was still a stage portrait of distinctive elegance. These parts, however, did not give Miss Kate Terry that standing with the public which she deserved, and she was justly desirous of showing her skill in more severe art before finally leaving the stage. She therefore commenced a series of parts from Shakespeare, Bulwer Lytton, and Sheridan Knowles. The public at once responded to the appeal, and were charmed with the delicate interpretation which she gave to *Beatrice, Pauline, Julia,* and *Juliet.* In all these parts Miss Terry was remarkable for the independence of her conceptions, as well as for her spirit or her pathos. They had not in some instances, perhaps, the energy of which actresses of more robust *physique* are capable ; but there was in all a fine poetic appreciation and a subtle judgment which satisfied the taste of the more refined among the audiences which she was now capable of commanding. These were both numerous and fashionable." To the *Daily News* (August 28, 1867), Miss Terry's acting had always seemed to be more intellectual than emotional—to have had more head than heart in its composition. " There has been a want of blood, of vitality, in many of her clever and highly-elaborated impersonations. Her voice and face have to a certain extent been against her ; the former is thin and slightly heady ; the latter wants openness and breadth of effect about the eyes. She is seen to most advantage in parts requiring repose of manner ; but stage repose is, after all, a mere second-rate artificial trick that has no claim to stand by the side of force and passion. . . . Miss Terry's *Juliet* is one of her best impersonations. Nearly everything she does in it is done with apparent effort; but the intention is excellent, and the execution only fails in parts from pure physical weakness. The potion scene in the chamber, for example, requires more bodily force than she is able to throw into it. The point in the scene with the Nurse at the close of the third act, where *Juliet* ceases to be a weak, loving girl, and becomes suddenly a strong, self-reliant woman, was admirably marked. The balcony scene was a little artificial, but very charming; not perhaps girlish enough, and not so demonstrative as Mdlle. Stella Colas made it. In elocutionary grace and power it was equal to Miss Helen Faucit's recent performance of the same character."

According to the *Examiner* (September 7, 1867): "In 'The Hunchback' the acting of Miss Kate Terry was, in the country-bred phase of the part of *Julia*, full of charming touches, and without straining for points, but rather an avoidance of strain, had a true pathos in the close of the third act which drew many tears. The failure in the scene in the fourth act, with Clifford as a secretary, was no failure of conception, but a want of strength to cover with the actor's art the tediousness of the writing by which an attempt was made to pile up the agonies of the situation. The long argument with herself of *Julia*, before she will look at the secretary who has Clifford's voice, remained with her as dull on the stage as in the book."

The following interesting account of Miss Terry's farewell performance appeared in the *Times* (September 2, 1867):—"It is seldom that the theatrical chronicler has to describe a scene like that at the New Adelphi on Saturday, when Miss Kate Terry took her farewell of the stage as *Juliet*. Successes, demonstrations, and ovations of a kind, may be made to order; but the scene of Saturday was one of those genuine, spontaneous, and irrepressible outbursts of public recognition which carry their credentials of sincerity along with them. The widespread feeling that the stage is losing one of its chosen ornaments had been manifested by the full houses, more and more crowded on each successive night, which, even at this deadest of the dead season, have been attracted to the New Adelphi by Miss Terry's farewell performances. Their attraction came to its climax and its close on Saturday, when the theatre was crammed, from the orchestra to the remotest nook in the gallery where a spectator could press or perch, with such an audience as we have never before seen gathered within its walls. At the conclusion of the tragedy, in the course of which Miss Terry was called for at the end of each act except the fourth, when the good taste of the more intelligent part of the audience suppressed the demand, Miss Terry came on before the curtain in obedience to a thundering summons from every part of the house, and, almost overcome with the combined excitement of the part and the occasion, stood for some moments curtseying and smiling under the shower of bouquets and the storm of kindly greeting. Nor when she had retired with her armful of flowers—looking, in the white robe and dishevelled hair of *Juliet's* death-scene, as she used to look in Ophelia—was the audience satisfied. Again Miss Terry was recalled, and again she appeared to receive the loud and long-continued plaudits of the crowd. Then the stalls began to clear. But the storm of voices and clapping of hands continued from pit, boxes, and gallery, through the overture of the farce, swelling till it threatened to grow into a tempest. The curtain rose for the farce; still the thunder roared. One of the actors, quite inaudible in the clamour, began the performance, but the roar grew louder and louder, till at last Mr. Phillips came on in the dress of Friar Lawrence, and, with a stolidity so well assumed that it seemed perfectly natural, asked, in the stereotyped phrase of the theatre, the pleasure of the audience : 'Kate Terry !' was the reply from a chorus of a thousand stentorian voices ; and then the fair favourite of the night appeared once more, pale, and dressed to leave the theatre, and, when the renewed roar of recognition had subsided, in answer to her appealing dumb-show, spoke, with pathetic effect, a few hesitating words, evidently the inspiration of the moment, but more telling than any set speech, to this effect :—' How I wish from my heart I could tell you how I feel your kindness, not to-night only, but through the many years of my professional life. What can I say to you but thanks, thanks, and good-bye !' After this short and simple farewell, under a still louder salvo of acclamation, unmistakably proving itself popular by its hearty uproariousness, the young actress, almost overpowered by the feelings of the moment, retired with faltering steps, and the crowded audience poured out of the house, their sudden exit *en masse* being in itself one of the most flattering tributes to the actress whose last appearance had drawn them together.

" This remarkable manifestation of popular favour and regard is worth recording, not only as a striking theatrical incident, which those who were present can never forget, but because it proves that the frequenters of even the pit and gallery of a theatre where, till Miss Terry came, the finer springs of dramatic effect have very rarely been drawn on, can rapidly be brought to recognise and value acting of a singularly refined and delicate kind—so refined and delicate indeed, that some of those who profess to guide the public taste have been apt to insist on its wanting physical power. On Saturday night it was made evident to demonstration, if other evidence had been wanting, that Miss Terry had wrought her spells over the frequenters of pit and gallery, as well as of boxes and stalls. In the interests of refined dramatic art this is a cheering set-off to many indications that seem to make the other way. It shows that if the theatrical ' masses '—those who are roughly lumped as the ' British Public '—are unable to discriminate nicely between diamonds and paste, and so take a good deal of coarse glassware for real stones, they are, nevertheless, susceptible to the influence of refined, earnest, intelligent and conscientious acting when they have the rare opportunity of seeing it.

" How well Miss Terry's acting merits all these epithets has been abundantly proved, not only through her recent course of farewell performances, in which she has filled a range of parts so widely different as to show a variety of power in itself as rare as the grace, refinement, intelligence, and feeling she has put into her acting, but through the whole of a career extending from four years old to four-and-twenty. If it is worth saying anything precise of her performances now, we may note here that she never gave a more triumphant answer to the critics who have charged her with want of power than in her acting of *Juliet* on Saturday. It was striking to observe the marked improvement on her first performance of the part last Tuesday. On Saturday her finest scenes were, unquestionably, those of fiercest (not of tenderest) passion, beautiful as were the latter in themselves. Perhaps the excitement of the occasion wrought most in unison with the feeling of *Juliet's* more violent passages of emotion. Perhaps the actress wished in this closing performance to assert her power in the point in which alone it had been questioned by fair and competent critics. But whatever the cause, in the scene where *Juliet* learns Romeo's banishment, in her agonised pleading with her parents, in her subsequent interview with Friar Lawrence, and—crown of the series—in the scene where she drinks the sleeping-draught, Miss Terry rose on Saturday to a height she never touched before, and left us more than ever under the impression that the stage is losing in her more than even her warmest admirers have hitherto been content to believe."

Following her retirement from the stage, Miss Kate Terry married Mr. Arthur Lewis.

TERRY, MARION, made her professional *début* at Manchester, in July 1873, as *Ophelia* in ' Hamlet,' arranged by Mr. Tom Taylor. The same year, October 4, she appeared for the first time on the London boards, at the Olympic Theatre, in a revival of a piece entitled ' A Game of Romps '; and the following year, at the same theatre, played *Hero*, in a revival of Shakespeare's ' Much Ado About Nothing.' Subsequently she joined the company of the Strand Theatre, and performed there in various plays of H. J. Byron—as *Clara Mayfield* in ' Old Sailors '; *Lilian Gathorne* in ' Weak Woman,' &c. At the Haymarket, in September 1876, first performance of W. S. Gilbert's drama ' Dan'l Druce, Blacksmith,' Miss Marion Terry played the part of *Dorothy*. At the same theatre, on January 20, 1877, in a revival of the same author's play ' Pygmalion and Galatea,' she sustained the latter character, *apropos* of which performance the *Athenæum*, January 27, 1877, published the following :—" Miss Terry possesses what Mr. Ruskin calls ' a serenity of effortless grace.' Her expression has purity and earnestness in combination. The original charm which is her distinguishing attribute is no mere mask for incapacity. Depth and tenderness of feeling are discovered behind it, and the manner in which power is expressed is surprising in one so young. These are the principal attributes of *Galatea*. . . . . Miss Terry's performance displays at points a little crudeness. It is none the less, as a whole, an admirably suggestive representation." During the same engagement she appeared as *Zeolide* (the part originally played by Mrs. Kendal) in ' The Palace of Truth '; *Lydia* in Sheridan Knowles's ' Love Chase '; in the original part of *Belinda* in W. S.

Gilbert's comedy ' Engaged '; and as *Florence Bristow* in ' The Crushed Tragedian' (Byron). In the Spring of 1878, at the Olympic Theatre, she enacted the heroine in W. S. Gilbert's 'Vagabond.' In August 1878, at the Court Theatre, she took the place of her sister, Miss Ellen Terry, as *Olivia* in the play of that name ; and in October of the same year, at the Olympic, played *Louise* in a revival of ' The Two Orphans.' Miss Terry was the " original" *Marie de Courcelles* in a new play in five acts, entitled ' A Republican Marriage ' (Mrs. Holford), first performed at the Olympic, Saturday (afternoon), November 8, 1878.

TERRY, FLORENCE, made her *début* on the London stage Wednesday, June 15, 1870, at the Adelphi Theatre, as *Louison* in an English version of Molière's ' Le Malade Imaginaire,' entitled ' The Robust Invalid.' She has fulfilled various engagements at London theatres since that time. Florence Terry was the "original" *Little Nell* of Halliday's play of that title, first performed at the Olympic, Saturday, November 19, 1870. " Much interest was manifested in the appearance of Miss Florence Terry as *Nell.* She has evidently been subjected to a severe training, and with an intelligent face and manner, has all the business at her fingers' ends. A slight staginess and artificialness will probably disappear as the young lady grows older." (*Daily News,* November 21, 1870.) In 1876–7, in the provinces, she played *Lady Betty Noel* in Tom Taylor's play 'Clancarty'; and *Cynisca* (' Pygmalion and Galatea'); *Myrza* (' Palace of Truth'); *Dorothy* (' Dan'l Druce'); *Jenny Northcote* (' Sweethearts'), during the same year at various theatres in the provinces. At Christmas 1877 she played the heroine in a revival of ' The Turn of the Tide ' at the Olympic ; and in the spring of 1878 *Olivia* in the play of that name in the provinces. She was the " original" *Ellen* in Mr. Wills's unsuccessful play of that name produced at the Haymarket, April 14, 1879.

THOMPSON, LYDIA (Mrs. ALEXANDER HENDERSON), was born in London. At the outset of her stage career she earned a considerable reputation as a skilful and accomplished dancer. in fairy spectacle and burlesque. She made her professional *début* as a principal dancer in the ballet at Her Majesty's Theatre in 1852. The following year (December 26) Miss Thompson began her career in that line of dramatic " business" in which, afterwards, she took the lead in London, in acting *Little Silverhair,* in the Christmas piece produced at the Haymarket Theatre, entitled ' Little Silverhair ; or, Harlequin and the Three Bears.' In 1854 she played *Little Bo-Peep,* in the Christmas piece of that title produced at the same theatre. In December 1856, a contemporary journal, noticing the absence of Miss Lydia Thompson's name from the theatrical playbills of the Christmas season, remarked : " Persons who miss from the pantomime ballets that popular and promising artist [Miss Lydia Thompson], may be appeased by hearing that she is dancing her way through the theatres of Germany with pleasant success." In 1859 (November 16) Miss Thompson appeared at the St James's Theatre in a fairy spectacle, which was received with much favour by the playgoing public, entitled 'The Swan and Edgar'—*Cygnetta*, Miss Lydia Thompson, "by whom the dancing, of course, was exquisitely executed." At the same theatre, the following year, in a "ballet-*cum*-burlesque," entitled 'My Name is Norval,' she played the part of *Young Norval.* Monday, April 9, 1860, Miss Thompson appeared at the Lyceum Theatre in a burlesque, originally played by members of the Savage Club for a charitable purpose, entitled 'The Forty Thieves'; and subsequently, November 5, 1860, as *Fanchette* in 'The Pets of the Parterre,' written by Stirling Coyne. In 1861, August 19, first performance at the same theatre of Falconer's play 'Woman ; or, Love against the World,' she acted the character of *Norah ;* and in an after-piece by the same author, entitled 'The Fetches,' the part of *Mary Brady.* But Miss Lydia Thompson will be best remembered as a sparkling and extremely clever actress in burlesque, in which, for many years, few excelled her on the London stage. Perhaps the best examples of her excellence in this department of the histrionic art have been witnessed in such pieces as 'Der Freischutz' (H. J. Byron) ; 'The Field of the Cloth of Gold' (W. Brough) ; and 'Blue Beard.' Miss Lydia Thompson, it may be added, has met with well-deserved success on the American stage. She has several times visited the United States with her so-called "burlesque troupe." In October 1878 she appeared at the Folly Theatre, London, of which her husband was proprietor and manager ; and in the spring of 1879 accepted an engagement at the Imperial Theatre, and played during the season *Pauline* in a burlesque of 'The Lady of Lyons' (W. Younge).

THORNE, EMILY, sister of the under-mentioned Sarah and Thomas Thorne, made her first appearance on the English stage at the Strand Theatre (then Punch's Playhouse), in a benefit performance, in the part of *Sally Scraggs* in 'Stage Struck,' and with such success that she was induced to enter the dramatic profession. Her first engagements were at the Theatres Royal, Manchester and Bristol. Miss Emily Thorne made her *début* in London, Easter Monday 1859, at the Adelphi Theatre, in the title *rôle* of 'The Fair One with the Golden Locks.' She was engaged at the Adelphi for three years. In 1862 she went to the United States, opening at the Winter Garden, New York, in an impersonation of *The Goddess of Liberty.* She remained in America for seven years, and travelled there extensively as an English ballad singer. After her return to London she fulfilled engagements at St. James's, Opéra Comique, Criterion, and, later, the Haymarket Theatres, where she appeared in May 1879 as *Mrs. Malaprop* in 'The Rivals.'

THORNE, SARAH, was born in London, and entered the dramatic profession when a child, playing in pantomime, and various children's parts, at the Pavilion Theatre, London, during the time it was under the management of her father. She made her professional *début* in London at the Surrey Theatre under the management of Messrs. Shepherd and Creswick, and afterwards accepted an engagement as "leading lady" at the Theatre Royal, Dublin, where she had the advantage of being associated in the representation of principal Shakespearian characters with the late G. V. Brooke and Charles Kean. Among important characters assumed by Miss Thorne during this engagement, and the "starring" tours in Ireland and Scotland immediately succeeding it, may be mentioned the following :—*Desdemona* in 'Othello,' *Pauline* in 'The Lady of Lyons,' *Portia* in 'The Merchant of Venice,' *Mrs. Haller* in 'The Stranger,' the *Duchess de Torre-nueva* in 'Faint Heart Never Won Fair Lady,' *Helen Macgregor* to Lady Don's *Diana Vernon* in the operatic play of 'Rob Roy'; *Margaret Aylmer* in 'Love's Sacrifice,' and *Juliet* in 'Romeo and Juliet.' At the Brighton Theatre, August 1863, Miss Thorne played *Lady Audley* in the dramatic version of 'Lady Audley's Secret,' and *Zoe, the Octoroon,* in the melodrama of that name. April 1865 she appeared as *Leah* and *Juliet* at the Paisley Theatre Royal, subsequently enacting the same characters at the Prince of Wales's Opera House, Edinburgh. In the summer of 1865 Miss Thorne accepted an engagement at the Jersey New Theatre Royal. From October 1865 to March 1866 she was engaged at the Royal Standard Theatre, London, performing the more popular of Shakespeare's plays with Messrs. Creswick and Ryder. After the retirement of Mr. Thorne from the management of the Margate Theatre Miss Sarah Thorne became the lessee, conducting its affairs with more or less prosperity for a period of seven years. Retiring from the lesseeship she undertook the management of the Worcester theatre until it was destroyed by fire in November 1877. More recently she formed a company for the purpose of supporting the late Mr. Charles Mathews on his provincial tours, afterwards renewing her management of Margate Theatre. Miss Thorne is now (November 1879) lessee of Astley's Amphitheatre.

THORNE, THOMAS, brother of the above named Sarah Thorne, first attracted notice on the London stage in 1862 as an actor at the Surrey Theatre. On Saturday, October 4 of that year, he appeared there in a comic drama entitled 'Tom's Life,' in "which he played a number of characters suited to show the comprehensiveness of his capacity as a comic actor." Two years later, 1864, he joined the company of the Strand Theatre, with which he was connected until 1870, playing leading parts in many of the various farces, burlesques, and dramas produced there during the protracted term of his engagement. In 1870, in conjunction with Messrs. Montague and James, he entered upon the management of the Vaudeville Theatre, and produced there on the opening night 'For Love or Money' (Andrew Halliday), and a burlesque entitled 'Don Carlos ; or, the Infante in Arms.' Saturday, June 4, 1870, first performance at the Vaudeville Theatre of Albery's play 'Two Roses,' he acted the part of *Caleb Deecie.* On Saturday, September 9, 1871, first performance at the same theatre of Albery's play 'Apple Blossoms,' he sustained the part of the *Great Baggs.*

Mr. Thorne took part in the successful revivals of 'The School for Scandal' and 'Road to Ruin' at his theatre during the years 1872-3. The first-named comedy had the unprecedented "run" of 412 nights, and he acted in it the part of *Crabtree.* On April 1, 1874, first performance at the Vaudeville of Albery's comedy entitled 'Pride,' Mr. Thorne played the part of *Barnabas Smith.* On Saturday, January 16, 1875, first performance at the same theatre of H. J. Byron's comedy 'Our Boys,' Mr. Thorne sustained the part of *Talbot Champneys.* This piece was performed nightly at the Vaudeville Theatre from Saturday, January 16, 1875, to Friday, April 18, 1879. Saturday, April 19, 1879, first performance at the Vaudeville Theatre of a new and original comedy by Mr. Byron entitled 'Our Girls,' Mr. Thorne sustained the part of *Tony Judson.* In the revival of 'Two Roses' (September 24, 1879) he reappeared as *Caleb Deecie,* and was the only representative of the original cast of the piece.

TITHERADGE, GEORGE SUTTON, was born at Portsmouth, December 9, 1848, and entered the dramatic profession in October 1866, at the Theatre Royal, Portsmouth. From 1867 to 1872 he was engaged at various theatres in the provinces, viz. at the Theatres Royal, Stockton-on Tees, Bath, Croydon, Glasgow, Southampton, and at the Lyceum Theatre, Sunderland. During a part of this time he travelled with Charles Dillon, personating juvenile parts in Shakespeare's plays, and subsequently became engaged as "leading actor" at the Theatres Royal, Bradford and Newcastle-on-Tyne. In 1874 Mr. Titheradge played in the provinces the heroes in Albery's comedies, under the direction of Mr. Flockton. In 1874-5 he was "leading actor" at the Theatre Royal, Bristol, and afterwards, the same year, joined Miss Marriott on a provincial tour, playing such parts as *Matthew Elmore, Master Walter, Rob Roy,* &c. Mr. Titheradge was "leading actor" at the Theatre Royal, Birmingham, 1875-6; and subsequently, in the latter year, became stage-manager and "leading actor" of the Chippendale Comedy Company, acting the parts of *Dr. Cantwell, Dr. Pangloss, Joseph Surface,* &c. In 1876-7 he was "leading actor" of Mr. G. Anderson's company at the Corinthian Theatre, Calcutta. During this engagement he was selected by the authorities to proclaim Her Majesty the Queen "Empress of India" at the Calcutta Durbar, January 1, 1877. He first performed on the London stage, October 6, 1877, at the Royal Court Theatre, as *Sir Francis Marsden* in 'The House of Darnley.' In 1878 Mr. Titheradge appeared at the St. James's Theatre, playing the parts of *Clancarty, Iago,* &c., and "creating" the part of *Captain Saxby* in Taylor and Meritt's play 'Such is the Law.'

TOOLE, JOHN LAWRENCE, was born in London in 1832. He first attracted notice as an actor during his connection with an amateur dramatic club which gave periodical entertainments at the Walworth Institution. Mr. Toole made his first appearance on the stage proper at the Ipswich Theatre Royal; and in 1852 adopted the stage as a profession, accepting during that year an engagement at the Queen's Theatre, Dublin. Subsequently he acted in the provinces for some eighteen months, principally in the Irish and Scotch cities. He made his *début* on the London stage July 22, 1852, at the Haymarket Theatre, as *Simmons* in 'The Spitalfields Weaver.' On Monday, October 2, 1854, at the St. James's Theatre, under Mrs. Seymour's management, he played *Sam Pepys* in 'The King's Rival' (T. Taylor and C. Reade), acting the same evening in a farce by Charles Selby, entitled 'My Friend the Major,' the part of the hero—"a sheriff's officer disguised as a friend, showing an amount of humour in his odd ball-room adventures which was well appreciated by the house." At the same theatre, the same year, Mr. Toole played *Pierre*, in a piece entitled 'Honour before Titles.'

From the St. James's Theatre Mr. Toole went to the Lyceum, and in September 1856 played there, with considerable success, the parts of *Fanfarronade* in 'Belphegor' (Mr. Charles Dillon acting the title *rôle*), and *Autolycus* in a burlesque by William Brough entitled 'Perdita ; or, the Royal Milkmaid.' Subsequently, at the same theatre, he appeared in a farce entitled 'Doing the Hansom,' in which he increased his reputation by his spirited eccentricities. Mr. Toole remained a member of the company of the Lyceum Theatre until 1859, when he accepted an engagement under Mr. Benjamin Webster at the New Adelphi Theatre. There, in January of that year, he acted in the burlesque of 'Asmodeus' the title *rôle*. On May 9, 1859, at the same theatre, he "created" the part of *Mr. Spriggins*, in the amusing farce of 'Ici on parle Français,' a part which became subsequently, when acted by Mr. Toole, an especial favourite with the public. In August of the same year he performed with great success at the same theatre *Augustus de Rosherville*, in a revival of 'The Willow Copse' (of this eccentric character Wright was the original personator). In January 1860, at the Adelphi, Mr. Dickens's 'Christmas Carol' introduced Mr. Toole for the first time as an actor capable of more than amusing extravagance. "His *Bob Cratchit* contains homely, natural touches that enable it to stand its ground beside the Mrs. Cratchit of Miss Woolgar (Mrs. Mellon), one of the neatest possible stage pictures of a bustling, bothered, scolding, and kind-hearted mother of a poor man's family, at home with many cares." (*Journal of a London Playgoer*, Prof. Henry Morley, p. 243.) During the same year, in the first performance at the same theatre of Watts Phillips's drama 'Paper Wings,' Mr. Toole sustained the part of *William Kite;* at Drury Lane Theatre, in a drama by the same author entitled 'A Story of '45,' he acted the character of *Enoch Flicker*, "a character that stands out from the rest, and is so well performed by the excellent comedian to whom it is confided, that it is likely to be the main attraction of the drama" (*Athenæum*, November 17, 1860). March 1, 1862, first performance at the Adelphi of 'The Life of an Actress,' he played *Wapshot;* and in the same year, Monday, April 14, at the same theatre, *Caleb Plummer*, in Dion Boucicault's dramatic version of 'The Cricket on the Hearth,' entitled 'Dot.' His performance of this part was noticed in contemporary journals as being of the highest merit.

In 1864 Mr. Toole played the leading character in a farce by Brough and Halliday entitled 'The Area Belle,' first performed at the Adelphi Theatre, Monday, March 7 of that year. The point of this piece was the singing by Mr. Toole of an amusing ditty, ' The Horrible Tale,' which attained considerable popularity. In August (Monday, 8th) of the same year he played *Mr. Lysimachus Tootles*, in a farcical piece entitled 'My Wife's Maid.' The following month, at the same theatre, in a piece written specially for him by Mr. John Oxenford, entitled ' Stephen Digges' (adapted from Balzac's novel ' Le Père Goriot'), Mr. Toole acted the title *rôle*. *Stephen Digges* is a serio-comic character, whose peculiarities at first excite laughter, then beget esteem, and at last the warmest sympathy. "Mr. Toole had a character to sustain which made the utmost demand on his powers, and the masterly manner in which he accomplished a very arduous task will be accepted as a convincing proof that the range of his talents has not even yet been properly estimated. Thoroughly true to nature, the performance was replete with evidence of the highest kind of art. . . . The drama was a complete success." (*Daily Telegraph*, September 16, 1864.)

In 1865, January 30, in a revival of 'The Hunchback,' at the Adelphi (Miss Bateman as *Julia*), he acted the part of *Fathom*. At the same theatre, July 1865, first performance of ' Through Fire and Water' (Walter Gordon), he sustained the character of *Joe Bright*. "Although the majority of characters to which Mr. J. L. Toole devotes his talents belong to the region of broad farce, and for the most part only derive their reality from the special ability of the actor to delineate individual peculiarity, he generally strikes into another line whenever he would make an impression of more than ordinary strength, as if convinced that his proper vocation was to follow the late Mr. F. Robson in semi-pathetic illustrations of plebeian life. . . . The action takes place in a stratum of society which is respectable, though humble, the groupings are simple, and the personages have all more or less of marked character, and are all more or less important, the principal figure in whom the interest of the piece culminates being more strongly marked than the rest, and so conceived as to command by turns the laughter and compassion of the audience, and to exhibit the most violently contrasted emotions. This figure is *Joe Bright*, a fireman, who is of course represented by Mr. J. L. Toole. He is a thoroughly honest fellow, who achieves infinite honour and wins innumerable medals by a gallant discharge of his perilous duties, and is, withal, so modest, that he cannot bear to hear himself even slightly praised. . . . All the parts are good and all are well acted. That Mr. J. L. Toole, as *Joe Bright*, would represent to perfection the honest plebeian, good at heart, and thick of head, might easily be foreseen ; but there is novelty in the drunken outburst that brings the first act to its close. Droll inebriety is common enough upon the stage, and Mr. B. Webster in 'Janet Pride' gives an admirable picture of the habitual drunkenness by which a man endeavours to silence the voice of an evil conscience. But the effect of ardent spirits rapidly imbibed by a man who is already distressed in mind, and who is suddenly converted from a comparatively rational being into an ungovernable savage, ready to commit any deed of violence, has been seldom, if ever, represented, and Mr. Toole has never more forcibly displayed his faculty for profitable observation than in his terrific exhibition of this peculiar phase of human frailty." (*Times*, July 3, 1868.)

In May 1866, first performance of 'The Fast Family' (B. Webster, jun.), adapted from M. Victorien Sardou's comedy 'La Famille Benoiton,' Mr. Toole acted the part of *Prudent.* In January 1868 he joined the company of the new Queen's Theatre, Long Acre, and in a comedy by H. J. Byron, entitled 'Dearer than Life,' "created" the part of *Michael Garner.* "The plot of 'Dearer than Life' is comparatively simple. Its hero, *Michael Garner*, is an industrious tradesman who has acquired a comfortable subsistence by long years of honest labour. A strange compound of shrewdness and good-nature, a man whose natural quickness of perception is a little clouded by an unusually affectionate and trusting disposition, it is his lot to be married to a woman whose whole hopes are bound up in an only son. This son, at the commencement of the story, is about twenty-five years of age, employed in a merchant's office in the city. It is the old tale of temptation and weakness. By the influence of a wily and unscrupulous associate Charles Garner is led into betting and silly speculation. He is not deficient in good feeling, but he has ideas above his station. The story commences on the twenty-seventh anniversary of old *Garner's* wedding. By the 'scratching' of a favourite, Charles has been irretrievably ruined. He is engaged to a pretty cousin, and this young lady, Lucy Garner, is loved with a strange earnestness by his worthless and perfidious friend, Bob Gassit. A curious old uncle appears in the form of Mr. Ben Garner, who is chronically under the influence of gin. Lucy is one of those true and constant lovers of whose existence plays and romances inform us. She knows her Charley is wild, but she is bent on redeeming and reforming him. She is quite proof against the insidious advances of Mr. Bob Gassit, and though she does not share Mrs. Garner's blind confidence on her side, she contrives to minister to the old lady's weakness. Old *Garner* has a shrewd suspicion that his son has not been doing right, but he never imagines that he has committed a crime. After a while it appears from Charlie's embarrassed manner that he is in trouble. Lucy finds this out, and taxes him with being in difficulties, and promises to relieve him by obtaining a sum of money which has been carefully hoarded up by his mother.

"In the meantime, the company invited to assist in celebrating the anniversary of the marriage arrives. Chief amongst these is Mr. Bolter, an old friend of *Michael's*, who has gained some small reputation for convivial talents. Young Garner, rather refined by intercourse with sharpers, sneers at Bolter, but *Michael* fraternizes with him, talks of old times, and sings a song about the grip of an honest man. The party adjourn to dinner, but while they are enjoying themselves, Mr. Kedgeley, the employer of Charles, appears, demands an interview with *Michael Garner*, and informs him that his son has forged and embezzled. The heart-broken father calls for the reprobate, urges him to fly from justice, and accuses himself of the crime. The last act is in a garret in Lambeth. The whole family have been reduced from comparative comfort to starvation. Old *Garner* is a messenger earning a few shillings per week. Lucy is a seamstress ; Mrs. Garner is bedridden, and Gassit is still persecuting Lucy with his suit. True to her old love, the heroine resists all the devices of Gassit, and though her landlady is fighting for rent, bears out patiently to the last. Ben Garner, in a fit of maudlin repentance, comes up to the garret, begs his brother to forgive him, and leaves a bottle of gin, which the despairing messenger swallows. In the intoxication which follows *Michael* loses all control of himself, and indulges in a bitter invective against his worthless son. This is overheard by Mrs. Garner, who shrieks out and falls as if dead. This misfortune sobers *Garner ;* but at an opportune moment the long-lost son turns up, with abundance of money, to save his starving relatives. The piece ends with the defeat of the schemer, Gassit, and the reward of virtue in the persons of old *Garner*, his wife, and Lucy.

"Of course, the burden of the drama rests upon the shoulders of Mr. J. L. Toole, for whom it was written. Long ago, in Caleb Plummer, Mr. Toole proved that he not only possessed the quaintest and most genial humour, but that, like most genuine humorists, he had a large fund of pathos. Nothing could have been more natural, more touching, more effective than his representation of *Michael Garner*, the honest tradesman, the loving husband, the courageous and self-sacrificing toiler. The character may be rare, but that it is real was proved by the actor. Every situation in the piece was made striking and successful by Mr. Toole's thorough earnestness and his artistic attention to detail. The second act bears a dangerous resemblance to the second act of 'The Porter's Knot,' and with any other actor it might have been a failure. But Mr. Toole is thoroughly original, and the resemblance of the piece to that in which the late Mr. Robson achieved his greatest success only serves to show the contrast between the styles of the two actors. In some of the scenes he far excelled his impersonation of the old toy-maker, great as that was. The finest points were in the close of the second and the beginning of the third acts. The intense grief of the father when his son's guilt is revealed, the outburst of passionate affection when he implores him to fly from justice, and the utter despair which follows, were wonderfully realized. In the garret scene Mr. Toole improved upon himself. His delineation of the brave old man who could endure starvation with a pleasant face, and could be cheerful under the heaviest burden of misery, was only surpassed by the sudden exhibition of passion when, excited by the drink which his worthless brother has brought him, *Michael* flamed out into a denunciation of his son's guilt. Again, on the conclusion of the drama, when the old man's ready wit, inspired by an unexpected good fortune, obtained a fair opportunity, Mr. Toole contrived to mingle, with consummate skill, the humour and the pathos of the situation." (*Standard*, June 9, 1868.)

The following year, at the same theatre, he played *Jack Snipe*, in a drama by Watts Phillips entitled 'Not Guilty'; and later (December 13, 1869), at the Gaiety Theatre, in a play expressly written for him by Mr. H. J. Byron, under the title of 'Uncle Dick's Darling,' the part of *Dick Dolland.*

After a long and very successful tour in the provinces, Mr. Toole reappeared on the London stage at the Gaiety Theatre, in November 1871, and played in 'Paul Pry' (the title *rôle*), 'The Spitalfields Weaver,' &c. Tuesday, December 26 of the same year, at the same theatre, he played *Thespis*, in a Christmas piece by W. S. Gilbert, entitled 'Thespis; or, the Gods Grown Old.' In April 1872, still at the Gaiety, he performed the part of *Neefit*, first performance of 'Shilly-Shally' (A. Trollope and C. Reade); and in December 1873, *Mawworm*, in a revival of Bickerstaffe's comedy 'The Hypocrite.' In 1874 (April), at the Globe Theatre, first performance of Mr. Albery's comedy 'Wig and Gown,' he acted the character of *Hammond Coote.* In 1875 Mr. Toole went to the United States, and represented his best known impersonations in the principal American cities. His latest, and perhaps one of his most complete successes for some years past, has been in the part of *Chawles,* in Mr. Byron's comic drama 'A Fool and his Money.' It was in this character that Mr. Toole reappeared before a London audience on November 17, 1879, on the opening of the Folly Theatre under his management.

TYARS, FRANK, was born in Kent, 1848, and entered the dramatic profession in 1870, first appearing on any stage at the Standard Theatre, Bishopsgate. Subsequently he joined the companies of the Pavilion and Portsmouth Theatres, and remained with them for some months. In 1876 he was again connected with the "stock" company of the Portsmouth Theatre as "leading man." Mr. Tyars appeared at the Theatre Royal, Drury Lane, September 23, 1876, as *Norfolk* in 'Richard III.,' and afterwards as *Rosse* in 'Macbeth.' In January 1877 he played the character of *Kinchela* in 'The Shaughraun,' at the Adelphi Theatre; and in May was engaged to perform at the Lyceum Theatre, under Mrs. Bateman's management, *Dorval* in 'The Lyons Mail.' Subsequently Mr. Tyars accompanied Mr. Henry Irving on tour through the provinces, playing *Claudius* ('Hamlet'), *Cromwell* ('Charles I.'), *Richmond* ('Richard III.'), &c. He reappeared at the Lyceum in December 1877 as *Dorval* ('The Lyons Mail'), followed by *Cromwell* in 'Charles I.,' and later (April 1878) as *Nemours* in the revival of 'Louis XI.' More recently (1878–9) he has been acting at the same theatre as *Claudius* in a revival of 'Hamlet,' *Armstrong* in 'The Iron Chest,' and the *Prince of Morocco* in 'The Merchant of Venice.'

VANDENHOFF, CHARLES, was born at Hammersmith, Middlesex, and made his *début* at Drury Lane Theatre, September 15, 1862, under the direction of Mr. Dion Boucicault, as *Geordie Macgregor* in 'The Relief of Lucknow.' At the termination of the Drury Lane season he accompanied Mr. Boucicault to the Theatre Royal, Westminster (formerly Astley's, and now Sanger's Amphitheatre), where he continued till June 1863. Still associated with Mr. and Mrs. Boucicault, on Easter Monday 1864 he appeared with them at the Theatre Royal, Dublin, as *Hardress Cregan,* during an engagement of four weeks. On the 3rd of May in the same year he represented the character of *Cassio* at the Shakespeare Tercentenary Festival. The two succeeding years were passed in active provincial practice in Liverpool, Sheffield, &c. In 1866 Mr. H. L. Bateman, chancing to visit Oxford, where Mr. Vandenhoff was acting, engaged him to support Miss Kate Bateman (Mrs. Crowe) in a starring tour through the United States. The severe illness of the latter prevented the contract being carried into effect, and Mr. Vandenhoff's services were transferred to the Olympic Theatre, New York, where in October 1866 he played *Lord Dundreary* to the Asa Trenchard of Mr. Joseph Jefferson. Subsequently he became "leading man" at Baltimore, Washington, and Richmond Theatres; and after accepting an engagement at Philadelphia to appear with Mr. Jefferson as *Lord Dundreary* and *Dick Dowlas,* he commenced a summer season at Montreal on the 4th of June, 1868. After three months of hard work and close study in Canada, Mr. Vandenhoff was selected to fill the position of leading juvenile and light comedian at Selwyn's Theatre, Boston, a house famous for its representations of old and modern comedy. After a series of comedy representations at the Fifth Avenue Theatre and Wallack's, New York, where Mr. Vandenhoff sustained the part of *Luke Blomfield* in Charles Reade's charming drama of 'Dora,' he returned, in September 1869, for a second season to Boston, and renewed his successes in the old comedies which still formed the chief attraction. He next accompanied Miss Maggie Mitchell, an accomplished American actress, on a tour through the States, and in September 1870 commenced, at an increased salary, his third engagement at Selwyn's Theatre, which had been rechristened "The Globe" and committed to the management of the late Charles Fechter. The new departure was not prosperous. 'Monte Christo,' though retained in the bills for many nights, had a depressing effect on the treasury, and after five months' reign of the new dictator he was displaced. A more active director ruled in his stead, and the Globe returned to its first love, the old comedies at once restoring the prosperity of the theatre. In May 1871 Mr. Vandenhoff sailed for England, and in August of the same year appeared at the Theatre Royal, Dublin, as leading support to Mr. J. L. Toole. In September he travelled with the popular comedian to Cork and Limerick, and in October returned to Dublin to act with Miss

Bateman. The production of Halliday's 'Great City' followed Miss Bateman's representations of 'Leah,' and Mr. Vandenhoff was successful in his assumption of *Jacob Blount*. Mr. Vandenhoff continued in the provinces till December 1874, when he returned to America, and where he remained for two years. On May 17, 1876, he returned to London, and was selected by Mr. F. B. Chatterton to enact the *Duke of Buckingham* in the revival of 'Richard III.' at Drury Lane. At the end of his London engagement Mr. Vandenhoff accepted the leading position in a company organized for the presentation of Mr. W. S. Gilbert's comedies. In 'Sweethearts,' 'Tom Cobb,' 'The Wedding March,' and 'The Vagabond,' Mr. Vandenhoff interpreted the chief characters. Mr. Vandenhoff remained with this organization till December 7, 1878, and after a rest resumed his professional labours at the Theatre Royal, Brighton, early in February 1879, appearing there as *Tom Robinson* in Mr. Reade's drama of 'Never Too Late to Mend.'

*VAUGHAN, KATE, an actress who has earned some distinction in burlesque, was a member of Miss Litton's company at the Court Theatre in 1872, and appeared there in a subordinate part in the burlesque extravaganza '*In re*' Becca.' She afterwards appeared in pantomime at Drury Lane Theatre, and is at present a member of the company of the Gaiety Theatre, where her graceful dancing forms, generally, one of the leading attractions in the burlesques placed on its stage.

*VENNE, LOTTIE, was a member of the company of the Nottingham Theatre in 1869, and in the year following of the Brighton Theatre, where she attracted notice by her acting in the part of *Robin Hood* in the pantomime of 'The Babes in the Wood,' Christmas 1870. In 1873 she was a member of Miss Litton's company at the Court Theatre, and appeared there as *Zayda* in the burlesque 'The Happy Land.' She afterwards joined the company of the Holborn, Strand, and later (1879) of the Criterion Theatres, where on August 6 she appeared as 'Betsy' at the first performance of Mr. Burnand's comedy of that name.

VEZIN, HERMAN, was born in Philadelphia, March 2, 1829, and graduated at the University of Pennsylvania in 1847 ; being admitted to the degree of M.A. three years later. In 1850, partly through the influence of the late Charles Kean, Mr. Vezin entered the dramatic profession in England by accepting an engagement at the Theatre Royal, York, under the management of John Langford Pritchard. He played there various subordinate parts, including the character of *Balthasar* in 'Much Ado About Nothing,' during Mr. and Mrs. Charles Kean's representation of that play at the York Theatre. Afterwards he accepted an engagement at Southampton, during which he had the opportunity of acting with the celebrated Mrs. Nesbitt ; and subsequently at the Theatre Royal, Edinburgh. In 1851 Mr. Vezin joined Mrs. Barnett's company on the "Ryde, Guildford, and Reading circuit," playing leading characters,—*Richelieu, Claude Melnotte, Young Norval,* &c. He made his first appearance in London on Easter Monday, 1852, at the Princess's Theatre, in the part of *Pembroke* in 'King John,' when Mr. Charles Kean had the management of that establishment. During the season 1852–3 Mr. Vezin played *Chatillon* in 'King John,' *Rosse* in 'Macbeth,' and *Montgiron* in 'The Corsican Brothers.' In 1857 he visited America. On his return to England in 1859 he took the Surrey Theatre, playing *Hamlet, Othello, Shylock, King John, Louis XI.,* &c. The first most important engagement undertaken by Mr. Vezin was in 1860, at Sadler's Wells, then under Mr. Phelps's management. He played afterwards, with marked success, the character of *Laertes,* to Mr. Fechter's Hamlet, for seventy-three nights at the Princess's Theatre, in 1861. Subsequently he "opened" at the Lyceum with Mr. Falconer as *Mr. Arden* in his comedy of 'Woman; or, Love against the World,' and afterwards acted the part of *Harry Kavanagh* in the same author's drama 'Peep o' Day.' In 1863 Mr. Herman Vezin married Mrs. Charles Young, an actress of considerable reputation. After playing various important engagements at metropolitan and other theatres, in 1867 he produced 'The Man o' Airlie' (W. G. Wills) at the Princess's, playing *James Harebell,* a character with which Mr. Vezin's name will always be associated in dramatic annals. In a notice of this play appearing in the *Spectator* (July 27, 1867) great praise is awarded him for having ventured, "in an era of burlesque, melodramas, and great triumphs of carpentering, to bring out on the stage a genuine and modern English tragedy, in which the main interest is of a kind the mass of playgoers necessarily cannot appreciate, yet which produces on the majority of them the most overpowering effect.

"The writer," continues the article, "had strolled, on the second night of the performance, into the pit, knowing nothing of the piece or its author, rather expecting, in fact, a Highland melodrama, and he can bear unbiassed testimony to the depth of feeling several times displayed. Women, evidently of the lower middle class, who scarcely understood the bad Scotch in which the dialogue is carried on, were sobbing unrestrainedly; and if the stout Scotch tradesman who stood next him was not crying, why he ought to consult an oculist about the state of his eyes. The value of this emotion, as a test of the value of the piece, is increased by the fact that it was due exclusively to sympathy with mental pain of a rare and spiritual kind—the agony of a ruined and maddened poet; agony, no doubt, in part that of a bereaved husband, and therefore common to mankind, but in part also that of a blasted literary and poetic ambition, which might, under other treatment, have seemed ridiculous. To make shop-girls care—care to pain—because an ignorant simpleton in a plaid cannot get his 'sangs' published, seems to us a triumph of art.

"Mr. Herman Vezin has taken Burns for his model—as, perhaps, the only model obtainable—and acts the character well. He looks the simple, not ungainly Scotchman, with a genuine independence and a slight trace of vanity, and creates a sympathy for him in the audience which in the pit showed itself in the oddest forms. 'Oh! hang it!' said a man near us, 'that's a fine beggar!—what is he saying?' and then, and all through the piece, extempore translations were offered in audible tones in four or five parts of the pit. His anxiety about his book; his fear for his wife, who cannot live in towns; his dread of dependence; his credulous simplicity—simplicity pierced by a vein of Scotch canniness as silk by a coloured thread—are all admirably brought out; and so is the nervous, impressionable nature of the man—the sensitiveness which may endanger his reason. In the third act the action quickens. *Harebell* has accepted a situation as private secretary; his wife has died of the close city air, and the poet, frenzied by her loss, saddened and bewildered by the prostration of his hope of literary fame, wearied with the incessant copying of letters and memoranda, gradually loses his reason; wakes for a moment to refuse to betray the man who has plundered him, and finally fancies he sees his dead wife, and walks over the stage with his arm in that of her invisible spirit, his face expressing a bewildered fondness, his left hand patting the air where her hand should have been, in the strained affection of insanity.

"Mr. Vezin did the scene well. There was no applause except from one fool of a claqueur, who, we hope, will read this opinion of his judgment; but over the house, dropping as it were from gallery to pit, descended a dead, strained silence—a silence such as we never but once remember in a theatre—succeeded, as *Harebell* vanished, by a roar of recall. Every side of an emotion of extraordinary complexity—insanity produced by grief, but shot as it were with literary vanity and regret, and tempered by natural sweetness, courtesy, and simplicity of nature—had, we are satisfied, been caught by the least trained portion of the audience.

"The exit is supposed to be followed by a suicide; an interval occurs of twenty years, during which the 'sangs' have become the delight of the people, and the curtain draws up on the preparations for inaugurating, by the side of the loch he loved, a statue to the poet of the poor. Under the stone representative of himself—the light gleaming on the graven young face and the living aged one, gibbering and mourning, amid starts of half recollection—sits the supposed suicide, a lunatic beggar, till the ceremonial includes one of his own ballads. The well-known sounds clear the clouded memory; he adds the last verse; is recognized, and dies a beggar at the foot of the statue raised to celebrate his glory as a poet. No words can fairly express the dramatic power of the scene to any cultivated mind. The blasted life of a poet culminates in a situation which makes his failure and his grand success, the fulfilment and futility of his hopes, his misery and his pride, his triumph and his utter fall, patent to men who, in all probability, never read a line of poetry in their lives. To make such a destiny so manifest—to show an artist utterly beaten down by a fate as remorseless as ever Æschylus imagined, yet in the moment of utter prostration, by the innate power of his art, beating that fate down, rioting in the rapture of a victory which leaves him an idiot beggar—is an effort for which, in an English playwright, we were not prepared; as little prepared as we were for its success. There is nothing whatever to break the unity of the work. The hope, and the failure, and the triumph of a poet, furnish the beginning and the end of a tragedy of which a great poet might be proud."

Another character which greatly increased the reputation of Mr. Herman Vezin as a painstaking and judicious artist was that of *Doctor Davey*, in a comedy of that name, adapted from the French ' Le Docteur Robin ' :—" The points in the performance are three : one where he (*Doctor Davey*) tells a tale of a child on the roof of a house in pursuit of a flower, to the terror of her mother and the crowd in the street, in order to show that acting may exist without reference to the adjuncts of the stage ; another where he assumes the garb of a physician, and counsels the young lady on the state of her affections ; and the third, where he feigns inebriety in order to disgust her with himself and induce her to accept the lover selected for her by her father." The delineation was admirable in each of its phases. On October 3, 1868, Mr. Vezin sustained the part of *Sir Grey de Malpas*, first performance of Lord Lytton's drama ' The Rightful Heir ' ; and subsequently the character of *Philip Earnscliffe* in Burnand's play ' The Turn of the Tide '—a piece which had a considerable " run."

In 1869 Westland Marston's ' Life for Life ' was produced at the Lyceum Theatre, in which Mr. Herman Vezin played *Murdock Mackane*. His representation of the part was admirable in all respects. " It has those qualities in which our tragic acting is most deficient." (*Athenæum*, March 1869.) On July 4, 1870, at the Gaiety, he played *Dubosc* and *Lesurques* in ' The Courier of Lyons.' " The double impersonation of Mr. Herman Vezin is marked by much more refinement than is ordinarily imparted to either character. His *Dubosc* is a thoroughly cold-blooded villain, but not of the low and repulsive type generally shown, while his *Joseph Lesurques* is a high-minded, honest gentleman in every speech and action. Both these characters have been the medium for a good deal of ranting and extravagant declamation. It is, perhaps, needless to say that Mr. Herman Vezin indulges in no such propensity. Even in those passages where the flood of feeling is most let loose, as in the second act, when the evidences of condemnation gather thick around him, and every clue to his innocence seems lost, his energy and action are consistently those of an innocent man wrongly accused and in despair of succour. His repeated calls before the curtain the first night testified the appreciation of the audience to a performance equally powerful, pathetic, and pleasing." (*Examiner*, July 9, 1870.)

On September 9, 1871, Wills's ' Hinko ' was performed for the first time at the Queen's Theatre, Mr. Vezin undertaking the principal character. In 1872 he played the part of *Martel* in ' The Son of the Soil ' at the Court Theatre ; during 1873 *Robert Audley* in ' Lady Audley's Secret,' and *Peregrine* in ' John Bull ' ; and in 1874 *Sigurd* in ' The White Pilgrim,' and *Ford* in ' The Merry Wives of Windsor.' In 1875, at the Opéra Comique, he played

Jaques in 'As You Like It.' "The *Jaques* of Mr. Vezin almost merits to be termed a creation. Even the elderly 'make-up' is new, and every line uttered gives evidence of thought." (*Times*, February 27, 1875.) At the Haymarket Theatre, October 2, 1875, he "created" the part of *Percy Pendragon* in Byron's 'Married in Haste.' The piece ran for a considerable time. By far the most noteworthy performance in the comedy, according to the *Daily News* (October 4, 1875), was that of Mr. Herman Vezin in the part of an eccentric uncle. "Choleric uncles, who disown their nephews on slight provocation, and take them to their arms again on equally slender grounds, cannot be classed among dramatic novelties, nor does the addition in this case of a passion for *bric-à-brac* hunting, which often borders on the ludicrous, add any valuable touch of art to a long familiar creation. The effect which was produced by Mr. Vezin's acting was indeed almost entirely due to the earnestness of his manner, to the just emphasis of his delivery, and to the sincerity which was suggested by numberless details of action and expression, almost too subtle to be noted separately, yet in their entirety impressive in a high degree. His face and figure had been admirably 'made up' to represent age without exaggeration or caricature. This is a kind of impersonation in which Mr. Vezin has not often been seen ; but it is in every respect a piece of acting of a very remarkable kind."

During the year 1876 he acted *Macbeth*, at Drury Lane ; *Othello*, at the Alexandra Palace ; the *Man o' Airlie*, at the Haymarket ; and *Dan'l Druce* (the first performance of that play, September 11, 1876), at the same theatre, with very great success. On the production at the Crystal Palace, June 13, 1876, of Sophocles' 'Œdipus Colonos,' the title *rôle* was assigned to Mr. Vezin, who won distinction by the performance. "As a declaimer of English Mr. Vezin has no equal on our stage," remarked the *Times*. "If he could only have been permitted to speak the language which Sophocles has put into the mouth of *Œdipus* we can imagine few performances of the sort to which we should listen with greater pleasure. . . . We have used the word declaimer in this place advisedly, for of acting in its modern sense there is in the Greek drama no need, nor is there room for it. It is with his voice only that Mr. Vezin has here scope to show his powers as an actor, and he shows them to very excellent advantage." In 1877 he played *De Taldé* in 'The Danischeffs' at the St. James's Theatre, followed by the character of *Sir Giles Overreach*. Both were important successes. On March 30, 1878, Mr. Vezin sustained, at the Royal Court Theatre, the character of *Dr. Primrose* in Wills's 'Olivia,' a play which met with remarkable favour. "Mr. Herman Vezin's vicar has, by the very nature of the play, become a somewhat sententious and didactic person. Necessarily he loses in great measure that tempering power of humorously half-conscious revelation of his own weaknesses which is afforded him in the story as the supposed writer of the narrative ; and, as we have said, he exists in the play chiefly as the father of the injured Olivia. But the figure of the vicar is always impressive, and no more pathetic performance could well be imagined than that of Mr. Vezin during and after the finding of his daughter ; and again when he sinks to rest in the old simple but refined home, from which Mr. Wills's story does not permit the family to be removed." (*Daily News*, April 1, 1878.) It may be added that 'Olivia' "ran" for 136 nights, finishing September 6, 1878. September 23 Mr. Vezin "opened" at the Adelphi Theatre as *Pierre Lorance* in 'Proof,' a version of 'Une Cause Célèbre,' and continued to play the part till February 1, 1879. At the same theatre, during the season, he appeared as *Master Walter*, alternating with *Sir Thomas Clifford*, in 'The Hunchback,' and as *Joseph Surface* in 'The School for Scandal'; and at morning performances as *Richelieu*.

Mr. Herman Vezin is entitled to be ranked among the few refined and accomplished actors of the poetic drama now on the English stage. He has from the beginning of his career conscientiously studied acting as an art, and has devoted his talents, as far as the opportunity has been afforded him, to the thoughtful impersonation of Shakespearian character, and of such parts as belong to the higher range of our dramatic literature. In the representation of these he has been in the main successful, and has succeeded in enlisting the attention of the critical, and the sympathy and appreciation of the thoughtful portion of the audience in whatever theatre he has appeared.

VEZIN, JANE ELIZABETH (formerly Mrs. **CHARLES YOUNG**), previous to her appearance on the English stage, had gained a reputation as an actress in the "legitimate" drama in Australia. She made her *début* in London at Sadler's Wells Theatre, on September 15, 1857, in the part of *Julia* in 'The Hunchback.' The *Times* (September 16, 1857), noticing her first appearance, said :—" Of all the female characters in the ordinary English repertory there is none that affords greater room for display than this favourite creation of Mr. Sheridan Knowles ; but on that very account it is one that renders prognostication respecting the future career of an artist peculiarly difficult. Several actresses have made it their especial aim to 'get up' *Julia* for a first part, and after producing a great effect in it have disappointed the public in their subsequent impersonations. With respect to Mrs. Charles Young, her performance was so promising that, were it not for the prudential considerations just named, she might be safely declared a decided acquisition to our histrionic force. From stage-trick she is thoroughly free ; her expression, even of the most intense emotions, is easy and unexaggerated ; and her delivery throughout is unaffected and natural. The overwhelming grief of *Julia* in the latter half of the play is most touchingly and truthfully delineated ; but in the force that is required to give some of the great 'points' of the character the young lady is deficient. The deficiency, we should say, is purely physical, for a more thorough apprehension of the meaning of the part, in all the situations belonging to it, could scarcely be desired." The same month she appeared at Sadler's Wells in the characters of *Imogen* in ' Cymbeline,' and the *Princess of France* in ' Love's Labour Lost '; and in the following month as *Rosalind* in ' As You Like It,' performing the latter part " not without some sweetness and considerable impulse, pleasant enough in its way, but without that art which is necessary to give variety to the perpetual wit which it is her province to utter. It is not by always speaking in a high key that the sayings of *Rosalind* can be made emphatic ; there is in such a style of elocution the danger of monotony to be avoided." (*Athenæum*, October 31, 1857.) During the same year Mrs. Charles Young appeared at the same theatre in the following characters : *Clara Douglas* (' Money '); *Desdemona* (' Othello '); *Portia* (' Merchant of Venice '); *Cordelia* (' King Lear '); *Mrs. Haller* (' The Stranger '); *Juliana* (' The Honeymoon '); *Mrs. Ford* (' Merry Wives of Windsor '); *Lady Mabel* (' Patrician's Daughter '); *Mrs. Oakley* (' Jealous Wife '); *Pauline* (' Lady of Lyons '); *Virginia* (' Virginius ').

In 1858 Mrs. Charles Young accepted a brief engagement at the Haymarket, returning to Sadler's Wells for the following season. In September of that year she appeared at the latter theatre as *Lady Townley* in ' The Provoked Husband,' respecting which performance the following entry appears in Prof. Morley's *Diary of a London Playgoer*, p. 222 :—" If the play has been produced for the special increase of any one artist's reputation, it has been produced for the credit of Mrs. Charles Young. This lady won her first laurels at Sadler's Wells, and is provided there with the best opportunities of triumph. In ' The Provoked Husband ' she is as truly the high-bred lady as her husband is the high-bred lord. . . . She is fascinating in her folly, innocent even in the seeming heartlessness of her frivolity, so light that none can hope to fix her attention long enough to find a passage through it to her heart ; and when her attention is at last riveted by the strong measure that her husband is compelled to take, she is a woman with a woman's nature, beautiful, after all, in its distress. *Lady Townley* is perhaps the part in which Mrs. Charles Young has found herself most free to exercise her skill." In 1859 (February 24) she appeared at the same theatre as *Juliet;* and on March 21 at the Lyceum, as *Pauline* in ' The Lady of Lyons.' In September of the same year, on the occasion of the opening of the Princess's Theatre, under Mr. Augustus Harris's management, she sustained the character of *Amoret*, in a play adapted from the French of Octave Feuillet (' Le Roman d'un Jeune Homme Pauvre '), by John Oxenford, entitled ' Ivy Hall.' She repeated her impersonation of *Rosalind* (' As You Like It ') on the occasion of the opening of Sadler's Wells Theatre under Mr. Phelps's sole management, September 8, 1860. April 22, 1861, first performance at the Haymarket Theatre of Mr. Stirling Coyne's play of ' Black Sheep,' Mrs. Charles Young supported the part of *Ethel Maynard*, and on August 19, at the Lyceum, first performance of Edmund Falconer's drama ' Woman ; or, Love against the World,' she acted the part of *Geraldine D'Arcy*. The same year, Monday, September 30, on the occasion of Edwin Booth's *début* at the Haymarket Theatre in the character of *Shylock*,

Mrs. Charles Young played *Portia* ('Merchant of Venice'). At the same theatre in 1862 (Monday, March 10), first performance of Westland Marston's drama 'The Wife's Portrait,' she sustained the character of *Clara Lindsay*. In 1863 Mrs. Charles Young was married to Herman Vezin, and thenceforward appeared on the stage under that name. In January 1864, at the Princess's Theatre, in Westland Marston's 'Donna Diana,' a poetical English version of Joseph Schreyvogel's 'Donna Diana' (a version of 'El Desden con el Desden' of Moreto), Mrs. Herman Vezin played the leading *rôle*, *Diana*, in a way "which assured the success of this play on the London boards" (*Journal of a London Playgoer*, Henry Morley, p. 326). Saturday, October 8, 1864, at Drury Lane, under Mr. Phelps's management, 'Othello' was produced with the strongest cast that the profession then afforded. Mr. Phelps played *Othello;* Mr. Creswick, *Iago;* Mr. Walter Lacy, *Roderigo;* Mrs. Herman Vezin, *Desdemona;* Miss Atkinson, *Emilia.* In 1866 Mrs. Herman Vezin appeared at Drury Lane Theatre, in January, as *Mrs. Oakley* ('The Jealous Wife'); and in February as *Mrs. Haller* ('The Stranger'). Both impersonations were remarkably successful. The same year she sustained the part of *Cordelia* in a "revival" of 'King Lear' at the same theatre, and of *Lady Constance* in a revival of 'King John.' Saturday, October 20, 1866, first performance at the same theatre of Bayle Bernard's English version of 'Faust,' Mrs. Vezin sustained the part of *Margaret*. The following year (1867), at Drury Lane Theatre, on Monday, January 21, she acted the part of *Mary Thornbury* in a revival of George Colman's comedy of 'John Bull'; and on August 22, at the Princess's Theatre, for the first time in London, *Peg Woffington* in a revival of 'Masks and Faces.' According to the *Athenæum* (August 31, 1867), Mrs. Vezin had now attained such a position on the boards that her assumption of a new part was a matter of importance, and the merit shown by her in the versatile character referred to (*Peg Woffington*) demanded notice. "Mrs. Vezin is rather an actress of serious and poetic heroines, yet not of so stern a cast as to make it incongruous in her to attempt the lighter creations of the minor drama. In fact, *Peg Woffington* in her hands lost none of her vivacity, but revelled in her sportive humours and benevolent impulses to the delight of a sympathizing audience. Every scene, indeed, was marked by some special beauty; but in that with Triplet's children and guests in his garret, she was remarkably impressive. In all she was careful to preserve the moral as well as the comic element, and thus secured the respect of her admirers for the inner goodness of her heart as well as the outward gaiety of her conduct. The personal and professional were judiciously blended and distinguished, showing 'both in their union and partition' that as an artist Mrs. Herman Vezin has claims on critical estimation."

On Saturday, October 3, 1868, at the Lyceum Theatre, Mrs. Vezin sustained the part of *Lady Montreville*, first performance of Lord Lytton's drama 'The Rightful Heir,' an amended version of the author's play 'The Sea Captain,' in which Miss Helen Faucit originally sustained the leading female *rôle* at its first production by Macready at Covent Garden Theatre. In 1871, March 4, first performance of Albery's play of ' Two Thorns ' at St. James's Theatre, Mrs. Herman Vezin sustained the part of *Mrs. Minton ;* and the same year, September 9, at the Queen's Theatre in ' Hinko,' by W. G. Wills, the character of *Markitta.* Since 1871 Mrs. Vezin has appeared in various Shakespearian revivals at Drury Lane (September 1876 as *Queen Elizabeth* in Cibber's version of Shakespeare's ' Richard III.'), and at other theatres, with her usual success. On Saturday, September 28, 1878, at Drury Lane, she acted *Paulina* in a revival of the ' Winter's Tale,' in which she " stood out among the rest by her perfect elocution and good acting" (*Times,* September 30, 1878.) Discussing the merits of this revival the *Standard* (September 30, 1878) said :—" But if it cannot be denied that some of the parts were badly filled, it must be cordially admitted that one in particular was wholly admirable. To say that any important Shakespearian character could not possibly have been better acted must seem an extremely bold assertion ; but it is more than difficult to see wherein an improvement could have been made in the *Paulina* of Mrs. Herman Vezin. In broad conception and in detail her performance was alike of the highest excellence. Every line is made to convey its fullest meaning, and her beautifully distinct enunciation renders it unmistakable. In the midst of her violent tirade against the King, and even in her threat to the Lords,

> ' Let him that makes but trifles of his eyes
> First hand me : '

this *Paulina* never loses her dignity ; and the womanly tenderness with which she strives to soften her words when an anguish of remorse has overwhelmed Leontes is most true and touching. No warmer praise could be given than to say, as may justly be said, that perfect justice was done to the noble speech which Shakespeare puts here into *Paulina's* mouth :—

> ' I am sorry for 't ;
> All faults I make when I shall come to know them
> I do repent. Alas ! I have show'd too much
> The rashness of a woman,' &c.

In the grand scene which ends the play, the exhibition of Hermione's statue to the Court, and its descent from the pedestal into the arms of the repentant husband, Mrs. Vezin's tenderness, and subtle exhibition of repressed joy, excitement, and triumph, aided greatly to produce the due effect."

Among other parts in which Mrs. Herman Vezin has from time to time appeared on the London stage, the following are entitled to mention, viz. *Constance* (' Love Chase ') ; *Viola* (' Twelfth Night ') ; *Lady Vavasour* (' Extremes ') ; *Charlotte* (' The Hypocrite ') ; *Marianna* (' The Wife ') ; *Hypolita* (' She Would and She Would Not ') ; *Juliet* (' Romeo and Juliet ') ; *Lydia Languish* (' Rivals ') ; *Miss Hardcastle* (' She Stoops to Conquer ') ; *Miranda* (' The

Tempest') ; *Donna Violante* ('The Wonder') ; the *Lady* in 'Comus'; *Constance* ('King John') ; *Lady Macbeth* ('Macbeth').

VOKES, FAWDON, made his professional *début* in London as one of "The Vokes Family," December 26, 1868, at the Lyceum Theatre, in the pantomime of 'Humpty Dumpty.' (*See also,* FREDERICK, JESSIE, and VICTORIA VOKES.)

VOKES, FREDERICK MORTIMER, was born in London, January 22, 1846, and made his first appearance on any stage at the Surrey Theatre, in 1854, as the *Boy* in a farce entitled 'Seeing Wright.' In 1868, December 26, he made his professional *début* in London, at the Lyceum Theatre, as one of "The Vokes Family," in the pantomime of 'Humpty Dumpty.' The most successful pieces presented on the stage by "The Vokes Family" have been the following, viz. 'The Belles of the Kitchen,' 'Phœbus's Fix,' 'The Wrong Man in the Right Place,' 'Fun in a Fog,' 'Bunch of Berries.' It is worthy of note that the pieces in which "The Vokes Family" appear are for the most part invented and written by themselves, and many of the incidents presented are simply illustrations of droll events and adventures that have been met with during their travels. (*See also,* JESSIE and VICTORIA VOKES.)

VOKES, JESSIE, born in London, was educated to the stage from childhood. At the age of four she first appeared at the Surrey Theatre, and subsequently played there a round of juvenile characters. From time to time during the first period of her professional career she performed the following parts, viz. *Teddy* in 'Dred,' with Mr. Creswick in the leading *rôle; Florence* in 'The Dumb Savoyard,' with Mr. Flexmore ; *Mamillius* in 'A Winter's Tale' (at Sadler's Wells), with Mr. S. Phelps ; *Tyoe* in 'The Pirates of Savannah,' with Mr. Charles Mathews ; *Prince Arthur* in 'King John,' with Messrs. Phelps and Creswick ; *Prince of Wales* in 'Richard III.,' with Mr. Barry Sullivan. Her first laurels were won as one of the children in 'Masks and Faces,' in which character she and her sister danced a jig with Mr. Benjamin Webster and the late Mrs. R. Honner, during a performance of that play at the Standard Theatre. In 1861 she started her career with her brothers and sisters as "The Vokes Children" (subsequently changed to "The Vokes Family") at the Operetta House in Edinburgh. The success of that combination is now so well known, and has been so widely circulated, that it is unnecessary to enumerate in detail its history during a period now extending over ten years. "The Vokes Family" made their *début* in London at the Lyceum Theatre, December 26, 1868, in the pantomime of 'Humpty Dumpty.' The travels of the "family" have taken them over half the world. The Vokes's have crossed the Atlantic ten times, and the Rocky Mountains twice, have sojourned among the Mormons in Salt Lake City for a month, have passed through the great Yosemite Valley, and have viewed the Pacific Ocean from the bold headlands sheltering the Bay of San Francisco. They have played in every city of importance in Great Britain, Ireland, the United States, and Canada. Miss Jessie Vokes had the advantage of Mr. Creswick's instruction and friendship in educating her in the business of the stage, and of the late Mr. Flexmore's teaching in the art of dancing. The most successful on the whole of the pieces in which the Vokes Family have appeared has been 'The Belles of the Kitchen.' (*See also*, FREDERICK and VICTORIA VOKES.)

VOKES, ROSINA (Mrs. CECIL CLAY), appeared on the stage as one of the "Vokes Family"; but retired from it on her marriage. (*See* FREDERICK, JESSIE, and VICTORIA VOKES.)

VOKES, VICTORIA, was born in London, and began her professional career at the Royal Surrey Theatre, London, when scarcely two years old, in a drama entitled 'The Avalanche.' She subsequently there shared with her sisters all the children's characters, making her first decided "hit" as the *Duke of York* in 'Richard III.' She afterwards played the same character with Mr. Barry Sullivan at the St. James's Theatre, and became popular in such characters as *Albert* in 'William Tell'; *Henri* in 'Belphegor'; and in such pieces as 'The Four Mowbrays,' 'Little Pickle,' &c. In 1861, with her brothers and sisters, she first appeared at the Operetta House, Edinburgh, as one of "The Vokes Children," afterwards changed to "Vokes Family." Victoria Vokes won her earliest laurels as a vocalist ; but she has also displayed some proficiency as a dramatic artiste, as exhibited by her excellent performance of *Amy Robsart* at Drury Lane, on Monday, February 27, 1871, and her later assumption of *Margery* in 'The Rough Diamond.' During eight years she has been a special attraction in the Christmas pantomimes at Drury Lane. (*See also* FREDERICK and JESSIE VOKES.)

VOLLAIRE, JOHN, was born in Marylebone, December 4, 1820, and made his first appearance on the stage in 1832, his *début* in London taking place at the old Surrey Theatre, October 3, 1854, in a drama entitled 'The Avalanche.' At the outset of his professional career he was well known as a careful and conscientious actor at the Bristol, Bath, and Nottingham Theatres. At Birmingham in 1850, on the occasion of Macready's farewell performance at the Theatre Royal in that town, Mr. Vollaire acted the part of *Sextus Dentatus* to the distinguished tragedian's Virginius. Among the more important characters essayed by Mr. Vollaire during his long connection with the London and provincial stage, the following may be selected for notice, namely, *Sir John Falstaff* in the 'Merry Wives of Windsor' and 'First Part of Henry IV.,' *Old Crumbs* in 'The Rent Day,' *Squire Broadlands* in 'The Country Squire,' *Polonius* in 'Hamlet,' *Adam Greenleaf* in Brougham's comedy 'While there's Life there's Hope,' *Stephano* in 'The Tempest,' *Van Gratz* in 'The Workmen of Paris,' *Mo Davis* in Dion Boucicault's drama 'Flying Scud,' *Dr. Botcherby* in 'The Unequal Match,' *Peter Grice* in Watts Phillips's drama 'Nobody's Child,' *Old Wilding* in Foote's comedy of 'The Liar,' &c.

WADMAN, MISS. A member of Mr. Hollingshead's Gaiety company, where for some time she has successfully taken parts in light comedy and burlesque.

WALLIS, ELLEN (Mrs. LANCASTER), made her first appearance on the London stage at the Queen's Theatre, Long Acre, September 28, 1872, as *Marguerite de Montcalm* in Sir Charles Young's drama entitled 'Montcalm.' At the same theatre, on October 19 of the same year, she played the part of *Mildred Vaughan*, first performance of Watts Phillips's drama 'Amos Clark.' In September 1873, at Drury Lane Theatre, in Shakespeare's 'Antony and Cleopatra,' arranged by Andrew Halliday, she sustained the part of *Cleopatra;* and on January 31 of the year following, in a revival at the same theatre of Halliday's romantic drama of 'Amy Robsart,' Miss Wallis represented the heroine with "a power and pathos which completely controlled the sympathies of the spectators." In September 1874, at Drury Lane Theatre, she enacted the character of *Edith Plantagenet*, first performance of Andrew Halliday's drama 'Richard Cœur de Lion.' "The dramatic interest of the piece is very properly centred in *Edith Plantagenet*, who is personated by Miss Wallis in a highly effective manner. With a command of expression in tone and feature, giving the fullest meaning to every line, the actress unites a gracefulness of demeanour, which becomes especially prominent in this character. The statuesque attitude at the altar, where her lover overhears her vow never to accept the hand of Saladin; the presentation of the standard of her own embroidery with the impassioned ejaculation, 'Oh! that I were a man to wear a sword'; and her interview with Sir Kenneth when he appears as the mute Nubian slave, furnished available opportunities to Miss Wallis of confirming the audience in a high opinion of her ability." (*Daily Telegraph*, September 28, 1874.) In February 1875, in a version by Colonel Richards of the drama of 'Norma,' produced in Edinburgh, Miss Wallis played the heroine. On Saturday, September 28, 1878, in a revival at Drury Lane Theatre of Shakespeare's 'Winter's Tale,' she sustained the part of *Hermione*, the statue scene being specially well played.

WARD, GENEVIÈVE, born in New York; grand-daughter of Gideon Lee, one of the so-called "Fathers of the City." In the early part of her career, under the name of Madame Guerrabella, she sang successfully in Italian opera at Havanna. Miss Ward made her first appearance in England as a tragic actress at the Theatre Royal, Manchester, October 1, 1873, in the character of *Lady Macbeth.* "Perfect ease and a most scrupulously exact knowledge of her part must be conceded to the *débutante.* Miss Ward has a voice of great power; she has besides a good accent and a fluent utterance; her features are expressive, and she gesticulates with ease and grace." (*Manchester Guardian*, October 3,

1873.) The character of *Constance* in ' King John ' was played by Miss Ward at the same theatre during her first engagement. She went to Dublin the same year as a " star," appearing at the Theatre Royal in the principal parts of *Medea, Lucrezia Borgia, Adrienne Lecouvreur, Actress of Padua, Juliana* in ' The Honeymoon,' &c. Miss Ward made her first appearance on the London stage at the Adelphi Theatre in ' The Prayer in the Storm,' March 28, 1874. Miss Ward undertook the double parts of *Blanche de Valois* and *Unarita* in this drama, which ran for 162 nights, " displaying an amount of power, a command over attitude, and a mastery of elocution which warrant the belief that our stage has received a valuable addition " (*Times*, March 30, 1874). In October of the same year she commenced a series of performances at the Crystal Palace as *Julia* in ' The Hunchback,' and in the year following played *Rebecca* at Drury Lane. Afterwards Miss Ward entered upon a provincial tour, beginning April 1875, producing in Dundee, Lewis Wingfield's play ' Despite the World,' and in Dublin, June 7, W. G. Wills's ' Sappho,' both written for her. On September 20, 1875, she commenced another tour through Scotland. In December 1875, Miss Ward played *Antigone* at the Crystal Palace ; and on February 4, 1876, *Lady Macbeth* at Drury Lane, for the benefit of the Philadelphia Centennial Fund. In the same year she appeared in a series of *matinées* at the Gaiety Theatre. She went to Paris in 1877, and studied with Regnier, of the Comédie Française, all the French classical *répertoire* and much of the modern, appearing at the Porte-Saint-Martin, February 11, 1877, as *Lady Macbeth* in Paul Lacroix's French translation of the tragedy. " Dans la scène du somnambulisme du quatrième acte, elle a été positivement admirable, jamais le remord, ni les terreurs de l'hallucination n'ont été interprétés d'une façon aussi poignante ; la salle toute entière était suspendue à ses lèvres et frissonnait avec elle." (*Revue Britannique*, March 1877.)

On August 29, 1877, Miss Ward appeared as *Queen Katharine* in Charles Calvert's revival of ' Henry VIII.' at the Theatre Royal, Manchester. There, and in Liverpool, she played this character for fifteen weeks, appearing also at the same places in the characters of *Lady Macbeth* and *Beatrice* in ' Much Ado About Nothing.' At the Queen's Theatre, London, March 2, 1878, Miss Ward sustained the part of *Emilia* (' Othello '). Subsequently she fulfilled a farewell engagement, previous to her departure for America (in August 1878), in Dublin and in Manchester, enacting the character of *Meg Merrilies* to Sims Reeves's *Henry Bertram* at the Theatre Royal of the latter city. Alluding to this performance the *Liverpool Daily Post* remarked as follows :—" Miss Ward, by a marvellously weird make-up, magnificent declamation, and a death scene of rare and ghastly power, placed her *Meg Merrilies* in the highest category of dramatic performances." In April 1879 Miss Ward returned from the United States, and in August of the same year " opened " the Lyceum Theatre for a brief season with ' Zillah,' a romantic drama in three acts by J. Palgrave Simpson and Claude Templar, in which she acted the heroine. The play proved unattractive, and was removed from the play-bills after a few nights' performance. 'Lucrezia Borgia,' a four-act drama by William Young, replaced it, Miss Ward acting the title *rôle* with considerable power. Afterwards, in the same month, Miss Ward produced another new drama, 'Forget-Me-Not,' by Messrs. Herman Merivale and F. C. Grove, in which she acted the part of *Marquise de Mohrivart.*

WARDELL, CHARLES. *See* KELLY, CHARLES.

WARDELL, MRS. CHARLES. *See* TERRY, ELLEN.

WARDEN, J. F., was born in Hull, December 12, 1836, and entered the dramatic profession in August 1854, at the Theatre Royal, Scarborough, then under the management of Mr. Samuel Roxby, his first appearance being in the part of *Lemuel* in 'The Flowers of the Forest.' After remaining in Roxby's company for about eighteen months, Mr. Warden joined Charles Gill's circuit, playing during the season all the principal juvenile and light comedy characters. He was next engaged for the York circuit, under the management of the late Mr. Addison, playing *Evelyn* in 'Money,' and other important leading characters. Afterwards at Edinburgh, at the Queen's Theatre and Opera House, during a season of ten months, he played *Romeo, Claude Melnotte,* &c., with the several lady "stars" who visited the city. In August 1858 he joined the Theatre Royal, Plymouth, and afterwards accepted an engagement at the Exeter Theatre, undertaking important parts, such as *Hamlet, Othello, Romeo, Richard III., Macbeth.* Mr. Warden entered upon management at Torquay, Easter 1860, and joined the Jersey and Guernsey company in the May following. In September 1860 he made his first appearance in London at the Surrey Theatre, under the management of Messrs. Shepherd and Creswick ; and in May 1861 accepted an engagement at the Queen's Theatre, Dublin, playing there for over two years the entire range of the leading business, legitimate and melodramatic. He entered as lessee and manager of the old Theatre Royal, Belfast, in September 1864, and built a new theatre on the same site, which was opened in September 1871. He also built the Londonderry Theatre, which was opened in August 1877. During Mr. Warden's lengthened management in Belfast he has played several "starring" engagements at Dublin, Cork, Londonderry, Sunderland, Liverpool, Halifax (Yorkshire), Bolton, Glasgow, Edinburgh, &c.

WARDEN, MRS. J. F. (*née* BELLAIR, JENNY), wife of the above-named, was born in Norwich, May 15, 1837, and entered the dramatic profession at an early age at the Theatre Royal, Dublin, under the management of John Harris. Afterwards she joined the company of her father, John Bellair, who, in 1857, was the lessee of the York theatrical circuit, and played "principal comedy and singing chambermaids." She first appeared on the London stage at the Surrey Theatre in 1860 as *Cinderella* in the Christmas pantomime of that year. In 1861, having returned to

Dublin, she played "principal comedy and burlesque" at the Theatre Royal for three years. Mrs. Warden has been associated with her husband in the management of the Belfast and Londonderry Theatres, and is a great favourite with the playgoers of those towns.

WARNER, CHARLES, was born in Kensington, Middlesex, 1846. He was for a short period in the office of an architect, whose profession it was intended he should follow, but having no special inclination towards this end, and " supposing that the pursuit of a theatrical career would not be sanctioned at headquarters, he ran away, and took an engagement in a small provincial town as ' utilitarian.' " After remaining in the provinces for some time studying the rudiments of the dramatic art, he came to London in 1864, and made his *début* on the metropolitan stage at the Princess's Theatre as *Romeo* (' Romeo and Juliet'). Thence he went to Drury Lane, where he was engaged for three years, under Mr. Chatterton's management, and played in various Shakespearian revivals. Subsequently Mr. Warner became a member of Mr. Liston's company at the Olympic Theatre, and there, in the part of *Charley Burridge* in a comedy by H. J. Byron entitled ' Daisy Farm,' won his first success on the London stage. In 1872 he was a member of the late Mr. Bateman's company at the Lyceum Theatre. In July of that year, in an adaptation of ' Medea in Corinth,' by Mr. W. G. Wills, Mr. Warner enacted *Orpheus*. He remained with the Lyceum company for two years, and afterwards joined the company of the Vaudeville Theatre, under Messrs. James and Thorne's management, and attracted favourable notice there by his painstaking acting in various parts. Of these the following, in the revivals to which each relates, are deserving of mention, viz. *Puff* (' The Critic') ; *Charles Surface* (' School for Scandal') ; *Harry Dornton* (' The Road to Ruin '). Mr. Warner was the " original " *Charles Middlewick* in ' Our Boys,' first performed at the same theatre Saturday, January 16, 1875. A character in the presentation of which Mr. Warner secured well-merited praise was that of *Vladimir* in ' The Danischeffs.' (*See* WOOD, Mrs. JOHN.) In 1878 he was engaged at the Princess's Theatre, appearing as *Henry Shore* in Mr. Wills's drama of ' Jane Shore.' In a revival (1879) at the same theatre of Charles Reade's drama ' Never Too Late to Mend ' he performed the part of *Tom Robinson*. On Monday, June 2, 1879, first performance at the Princess's Theatre of Mr. Charles Reade's version of the French play constructed out of M. Zola's novel ' L'Assommoir,'* and entitled ' Drink,' Mr. Warner

---

* ' L'Assommoir,' it may be interesting to remark, was a great success on the Parisian stage ; and M. Zola's novel was, if possible, a greater. The production of this English version of the French play, originally performed at the Ambigu, was looked forward to with immense curiosity by London playgoers. Possibly this desire to note the success or failure of a play whose merits are purely, or perhaps it would be more correct to say impurely, "sensational" from beginning to end, was heightened by the repeated advertised warnings of the management of the Princess's Theatre

acted the part of *Coupeau*. According to the *Daily News* (June 3, 1879), the powerful part which had been assigned to Mr. Charles Warner overshadowed all else in the drama. "In this piece Mr. Warner rises to heights of dramatic power which far exceed expectation based upon any other of the characters in which he is familiar to a London audience. It is doubtless true that he follows with unvarying fidelity the conception of the character created on the stage of the Ambigu. But the impersonation is none the less a striking and overmastering effort of mimetic genius. The entry of *Coupeau* in the sixth act, when he returns to his beggared home, sent a sensible thrill of horror through the crowded and excited audience. His make-up is wonderful, and his voice, looks, and gestures are even horribly realistic. The unsteady walk, the thin yet bloated face, the wandering eyes, the lean, live fingers that clutch at nothingness and are never quiet, tell without need of spoken words the story of his fall. The scene grows in intensity as it progresses. When the eager and tremulously joyous wife goes out to find work for him, and hopes to get a small advance of money to buy bread, *Coupeau* is left alone with the supposed bottle of claret which the treacherous Virginie has sent in. Shall he have half a glass just to warm him? The thought of the generous liquor infuses animation into his miserable body, and with trembling hands he unwraps the bottle and takes out the cork. 'What a body it has got for claret,' he says, as he sniffs at it. Then a spasm of horrible delight thrills him as he makes the discovery that it is brandy. He recoils from it and crouches at the other end of the room, putting all the space possible between table and wall between him and the tempter. The doctors say it will kill him, 'but, then, doctors tell such lies.' He will just taste it. With

that the right to adapt 'L'Assommoir' had been purchased "for a large sum of money," and that any attempt to pirate this subject would be "severely resisted." The *Times* (June 4, 1879) thus commented on its value as an addition to the English melodramatic *répertoire* :—" Most of our readers, as we have already said, have, it may safely be presumed, a more or less distinct idea of the nature of M. Zola's tale, of which the play is a sufficiently faithful transcript. We may, therefore, spare ourselves the disagreeable task of entering into details which it may interest some people to read, but can surely give pleasure to no one to discuss. What moral end is to be gained by the spectacle of two passionate women drenching each other with buckets of water, or of a man dying of *delirium tremens*, when these spectacles are merely the illusions of the stage, we confess ourselves unable to comprehend ; but from the advertisements that have heralded the piece it is only reasonable to suppose that some such end is contemplated by the gentlemen interested in its production. It has been long the fashion in some quarters to assume that it is an open question how far true art is concerned with that which is directly and physically brutal and degrading— hard words, indeed, but not unduly hard, as all who have read M. Zola's novel will allow. But, as a matter of fact, the question is no more an open one than is the question of the authenticity of the Epistles of Phalaris, or of the Rowley Poems. Exact and competent judges have long ago pronounced this verdict, that such subjects have no place in the legitimate province of art."

horrible gleaming eyes and convulsive fingers he approaches the table, seizes the bottle, and drinks. At first the spirit revives and strengthens him, and with new vigour he rushes out of the room, carrying the bottle with him. When he comes back his wife has returned, and finds him a raving maniac with the empty bottle. So he dies on the stage, the audience being spared no detail of *delirium tremens.* Whether this is legitimate art or desirable effect is a matter for individual opinion. But there can be no question of the power and intensity with which Mr. Warner re-presents the most terrible scene ever presented on the English stage."

M. Francisque Sarcey, in a private letter to the writer of the interesting notes on " The Theatres " published weekly in the *Daily News*, remarked that he had seen ' Drink ' at the Princess's Theatre. " The actor who represents *Coupeau* (Mr. Charles Warner) struck me as having a great command of natural ex-pression in the scenes of domestic life. His performance is, in my opinion, superior, indeed altogether superior, to that of our Gill-Naza, the original representative of this character on our stage. I have but little to say about the famous *delirium tremens* scene. It disgusted me in Paris ; in London it inspired me with a sense of horror. I hear that at the great Flemish theatre in Antwerp this scene has obtained as striking a success as in Paris and in London. It would probably have excited in me there only the same feeling of repulsion. Those furious outbursts, those rollings of haggard eyes, that contorted mouth, those lips wet with un-wholesome saliva, may belong to nature, but they have no affinity with art." (*Daily News*, July 1, 1879.)

WARREN, A. H., prior to September 16, 1876, had fulfilled various engagements at provincial theatres in studying the rudi-ments of his profession. On that date he first appeared in London, at the Queen's Theatre, in the character of the *Duke of Exeter* in Shakespeare's ' Henry V.' Having remained at that theatre for six weeks, he afterwards went to the Amphitheatre, Liverpool, to " create" the part of *Walter Temple* in Paul Meritt's drama ' Stolen Kisses.' Returning to London, for a brief season he played the characters of *Sir Leicester Dedlock* and *Lambkin* (' The Tailor Makes the Man ') with Miss Jennie Lee and the Globe company, at the Standard Theatre. On Easter Monday, 1877, he appeared as the Spanish admiral *Don Diego de Valdez* in ' True to the Core' (revival), at the Adelphi Theatre. Subsequently Mr. Warren entered upon an engagement at the Aquarium Theatre to play in ' In-constant'; and on September 22 of the same year commenced a three months' engagement at the Globe Theatre to play *Viscount Trangmar* in ' Stolen Kisses.' On January 3, 1878, he personated the part of the *Prince of Orange* in ' Fatherland,' at the Queen's Theatre ; and on the withdrawal of that play, and the revival of ' 'Twixt Axe and Crown,' acted the character of *Sir John Brydges*. On March 11, 1878, he started on tour through the provinces to play with the ' Stolen Kisses' company.

WEBSTER, BENJAMIN, was born at Bath, September 3, 1798. As early as the year 1818 he was acting in London, at the Regency Theatre, with Gough and Santer, and Strickland, Osborn, Lewis, Mortimer, and the Beverleys. He made his first London success in 'Measure for Measure.' He was one of the leading actors of the Olympic Theatre during its management by Madame Vestris. In 1832 he was acting there in a highly successful farce, entitled 'Kill or Cure' (Charles Dance), with Liston and Mrs. Orger; and, at the same theatre, in November of that year, in a farce adapted from the French ('L'Homme de Soixante Ans') by himself, "took the part created by the inimitable Potier." The following year Mr. Webster became a member of the company of the Haymarket Theatre, and was in the original cast of Douglas Jerrold's play of 'The Housekeeper; or, the White Rose,' first performed there Wednesday, July 17, 1833. In October of the same year, at the same theatre, he acted with the elder Farren and Mrs. Glover in Buckstone's farce 'Uncle John,' then first produced. In December 1833 he was in the original cast of Douglas Jerrold's comedy 'The Wedding Gown,' then performed for the first time at Drury Lane Theatre. In May 1834, at the same theatre, in a revival of the 'Second Part of King Henry IV.'—Macready as the *King*, Blanchard as *Justice Silence*, Farren as *Justice Shallow*—Mr. Webster acted the character of *Bardolph*. In July of the same year, at the Haymarket Theatre, he played with Mr. Buckstone in Douglas Jerrold's three-act comedy 'Beau Nash.' In 1835 (June), at the same theatre, he appeared with Charles Kemble in a revival of 'Much Ado About Nothing'—*Dogberry*, Mr. Benjamin Webster; *Verges*, Mr. Buckstone. In October 1835 Mr. Webster made his first appearance at the old Adelphi Theatre in a piece entitled 'The Yellow Kids,' and "displayed so much original humour as," in the opinion of the *Athenæum* (October 31, 1835), "clearly to entitle him to be taken by the Press out of the class of 'useful actors,' and to be placed among the attractives." On Wednesday, January 4, 1837, he sustained the part of the *Marquis de Montespan*, first performance of the late Lord Lytton's drama the 'Duchess de la Vallière,' at the Theatre Royal, Covent Garden; Messrs. Macready and Vandenhoff and Miss Helen Faucit were of the original cast.

In June 1837 Mr. Webster entered upon the management of the Haymarket Theatre, and produced, on the opening night of the season, a tragedy entitled 'The Bridal' (adapted from 'The Maid's Tragedy' of Beaumont and Fletcher), with Mr. Macready and Miss Huddard in the principal parts. In October 1837 Sheridan Knowles's play 'The Love Chase' was first performed at the Haymarket Theatre; Mrs. Nesbitt supported the character of *Constance;* Mr. B. Webster undertook that of *Wildrake*. This play was one of the most successful of Mr. Sheridan Knowles's works, and soon became a permanent favourite at the theatre. Noticing its first performance, the *Athenæum* (October 14, 1837) said:—"We must inquire of Mr. Webster what on earth could have induced him to cast himself into *Mr. Wildrake?* It is as great a piece of insanity as if he had cast himself into the Thames. We should as soon have thought of his playing Lady Macbeth. It is a part which, to be properly filled, requires such an actor as Mr. Charles Kemble was in his youngest and best day. . . . Mr. Webster is a clever man in his way, but he should not do such out-of-the-way things as this." In October 1838, on the anniversary of the first performance of 'The Love Chase,' another of Mr. Sheridan Knowles's plays was produced at the Haymarket Theatre, namely, 'The Maid of Mariendorpt.' The season 1839-40 was a very successful one for Mr. Webster's management. He had the good fortune to have a most brilliant company of players at his theatre, who succeeded in attracting to it large audiences. Among the company were Messrs. Macready, Warde, and S. Phelps, Mesdames Glover, Warner, Miss Helen Faucit, and Miss P. Horton. During the season Talfourd's play 'Glencoe ; or, the Fate of the Macdonalds,' was produced ; and on Tuesday, December 8, 1840, the late Lord Lytton's play of 'Money.' Mr. Webster sustained the part of *Graves* in the original cast. In 1841-2 Shakespearian and other revivals of the poetic drama were produced at the Haymarket Theatre ; and it was remarked in a contemporary journal (May 1842), that it remained the only place in London where the banners of the national drama still waved— Covent Garden had ended disastrously for Charles Mathews and his wife, Drury Lane for Macready—"the minor rallying points for the scattered troops being merely outposts for the skirmishers."

On Saturday, June 4, 1842, S. Knowles's play 'The Rose of Arragon' was produced by Mr. Webster ; Mr. and Mrs. Charles Kean playing the leading parts. It had not the seeds of stage existence, and was a failure. The following season Mr. Webster opened his theatre with Mr. and Mrs. Charles Mathews (Madame Vestris), Mr. Farren, Mrs. Glover, Madame Celeste, and Mr. Buckstone, of his company. In June 1843 he performed for the first time, with Madame Celeste, in a piece called 'Louison,' an adaptation from the French ; and subsequently (November 1843), with the same actress, as *Victor* in 'Victor and Hortense,' a French vaudeville. The same year Mr. Webster offered, for the encouragement of dramatic literature, the sum of 500*l.* for the best modern comedy, illustrative in plot and character of British manners and customs. A committee of dramatic authors (not competitors), dramatic critics, and actors (male and female), awarded the prize on Saturday, May 18, 1844. Among the judges were the veteran actors Charles Young and Charles Kemble, and Messrs. G. P. R. James, P. R. Moran, H. Ottley, J. Clarke Searle, and the Rev. Alexander Dyce. Ninety-eight comedies had been sent in and examined, and the judges were unanimously in favour of a piece entitled 'Quid pro Quo ; or, the Day of Dupes.' The author was Mrs. Gore. The play was produced, with a strong cast, on Tuesday, June 18, 1844, and was received with uproar and ridicule. In his farewell address of the season 1843-4, Mr. Webster stated, that "for three years no comedy was to be got for love or money"; and that Mrs. Gore's was the best out of a hundred. None of the judges had ever supposed it could have been so egregious a failure. In August of this year Mr. Webster was presented with a costly *épergne* by the actors and actresses engaged at the Haymarket Theatre, "as a mark of their esteem for his private and professional worth." In September 1844 he became proprietor of the old Adelphi Theatre, at the same time continuing his lesseeship of the Haymarket. At the latter theatre, Monday, November 18, 1844, ' Old Heads and Young Hearts' (D. Boucicault) was produced—*Littleton Coke*, Mr. Charles Mathews ; *Bob*, his clerk, Mr. Buckstone ; *Tom Coke*, Mr. B. Webster ; *Jesse Rural*, Mr. Farren ; *Lady Alice Hawthorn*, Madame Vestris. In the following year (1845), April 26, at the same theatre, Douglas Jerrold's comedy ' Time Works Wonders' —" a genuine and legitimate piece of dramatic writing, thoroughly up to the mark, rich in wit, and overflowing with talent "—was performed for the first time. The play was a great success. The following were in the original cast : *Bessy Tulip*, Madame Vestris ; *Florentine*, Miss Fortescue ; *Miss Tucker*, Mrs. Glover ; *Clarence Norman*, Mr. H. Holl ; *Olive*, Mr. Tilbury ; *Goldthumb*, Mr. Farren ; *Felix Goldthumb*, Mr. Charles Mathews ; *Professor Truffles*, Mr. Strickland. On January 6, 1846, Mr. Webster produced a dramatic version, by himself, of ' The Cricket on the Hearth,' and played in it the part of *John Peerybingle*, " precisely the kind of part for which the manager is most qualified by his talents as an actor. It was genial and touching ; vigorous and true ; highly finished in its details, yet natural in its general impression. The performer was at home in it ; and, in its way, nothing could have been better."

The same year, at the Haymarket, Mr. Webster played *Cymon Foxall*, first performance of Sullivan's comedy ' The Beggar on Horseback '—a play which proved a satisfactory success ; and the *Clown* in ' Twelfth Night,' the Misses Cushman (Charlotte and her sister) sustaining in the play the parts of Viola and Olivia. On Saturday, October 17, 1846, ' Queen Mary's Bower' (J. R. Planché), an adaptation of the libretto of M. Halévy's opera ' Les Mousquetaires de la Reine,' was produced, and owed much of its success to the excellent acting of Mr. Webster as the *Laird of Killiecrankie*. The same year, in a revival at the Haymarket Theatre of Lovell's play ' Look before you Leap,' he performed the part of *Jack Spriggs*. The following year (1847) Mr. Boucicault's comedy ' A School for Scheming,' and Robert Bell's comedy ' Temper,' were produced. In the first-mentioned Mr. Webster played *Job Sykes, M.P.* ; in the second the part of *Mr. Hope Emerson*. This same year (1847) ' The School for Scandal ' was revived, with Mr. Farren, Mr. H. Farren, Mr. A. Wigan, Mrs. Glover, Mrs. Nesbitt, and Miss Helen Faucit in the cast ; Mr. Webster himself playing *Moses*. On Wednesday, October 20, 1847, Westland Marston's play ' The Heart and the World ' was first performed at the Haymarket Theatre. Of this play a contemporary journal remarks :—" The prominent faults of the play are a too great subjectivity in the motives, dialogue, and characters, and an occasional defect of continuity in construction. The action is of so subtle a kind that it demands performers of nice perception and polished manners adequately to carry out the dramatic idea. The French stage might supply an appropriate *troupe;* but the English is so deficient of real artists that we know of no existing company capable of enacting such a drama with the requisite grace." On November 15, 1847, Mr. Webster produced, at the Haymarket Theatre, 'The Roused Lion' (from the French 'Le Réveil du Lion'), and played in it the part of *Stanislas de Fonblanche.* This piece attained an extraordinary success.

On Tuesday, December 7, 1847, Mr. Webster took part in the performances at the Theatre Royal, Covent Garden, arranged in behalf of the fund for the purchase of Shakespeare's house at Stratford-on-Avon, and acted the character of *Petruchio* in a selection from 'The Taming of the Shrew' (parts of Acts i. and iv.). In 'The Wife's Secret,' performed at the Haymarket Theatre for the first time, Monday, January 17, 1848 (with Mr. and Mrs. Charles Kean in their original characters), Mr. B. Webster performed the part of *Jabez Sneed.* In April of the same year he sustained the character of *Michael Bradshaw* in Morton's play of ' Old Honesty,' first performed at the Haymarket on Thursday, the 6th of that month. In his customary annual address, delivered on the 10th of July, 1848, at the close of the summer season, Mr. Webster stated, that since January 1847 he had incurred a deficiency of 8000*l.* in his annual receipts, which he attributed to the encouragement of a second Italian Opera House. In 1848–9 Mr. Webster took part in the plays produced under the superintendence of Mr. Charles Kean at Windsor Castle, before H.M. the Queen and the late Prince Consort. On Wednesday, June 20, 1849, Marston's tragedy of ' Strathmore ' was produced at the Haymarket, with Mr. and Mrs. Charles Kean in the principal parts.

The Haymarket Theatre season 1849–50 opened on October 1, with the following among its higher artists, viz. Mr. Macready, Mr. and Mrs. Charles Kean, Mr. Wallack, Mrs. Warner, and Mrs. Nesbitt. On the opening night 'The Love Chase' (S. Knowles) was performed. On the 30th of the same month 'The Serious Family' (M. Barnett), adapted from the French 'Le Mari à la Campagne,' was produced, and was a triumphant success. Mr. Webster played *Mr. Charles Torrens* in the original cast. Thursday, May 9, 1850, Douglas Jerrold's comedy 'The Catspaw' was first performed, Mr. Webster as *Coolcard.* During the next season (Monday, February 3, 1851), Macready made his last appearance at the Haymarket in the part of King Lear, the Queen and Prince Albert being present. In March of the same year Mr. B. Webster played *Tartuffe,* in a literal version of Molière's comedy by Mr. John Oxenford. " The power and finish of this performance were excellent." The same month (March 3, 1851) an original piece by Douglas Jerrold, entitled 'Retired from Business,' was performed, Mr. Benjamin Webster acting the part of *Captain Gunn.* This play was a great success. In 1852 a season of English opera was inaugurated at the Haymarket Theatre. The same year, April 24, Mark Lemon's play 'Mind your own Business' was first performed, Mr. Webster playing in it the part of *Verdon.*

On Saturday, November 20, 1852, first performance at the Haymarket of ' Masks and Faces,' he sustained the part of *Triplet*. (*See* STIRLING, Mrs.) " That is a charming scene," writes Prof. Morley (*Journal of a London Playgoer*, p. 58), " where Peg visits the poor poet in his garret, while his ailing wife and starving children are sadly interrupting the flow of its comic muse. Nothing here was lost in Mr. Webster's hands—the angry fretfulness followed by instant remorse, the efforts of self-restraint which are but efforts in vain, the energy that fitfully breaks out and then pitifully breaks down, and the final loss of hope, even of faith in a better providence which is to set right all that misery and wrong—the picture was complete, and set forth with its immemorial Grub Street appendages of no shirt and ragged but ample ruffles." Saturday, February 12, 1853, the late Lord Lytton's comedy ' Not so Bad as we Seem ' (originally written for and played by members of the Guild of Literature) was produced ; *Sir Geoffrey Thornside*, Mr. B. Webster. The production of ' Not so Bad as we Seem ' was eminently successful, which was attributable 'to the merits and exertions of his company. " Mr. Webster threw a great deal of intensity into the character of *Thornside*, but it is a character that defies all attempts to raise it into significance. . . . The scenery and dresses are exceedingly beautiful ; and certainly everything that could be done for a comedy has been done in this case by Mr. Webster." (*Times*, February 14, 1853.)

On Monday, March 14, 1853, Mr. Benjamin Webster's management of the Haymarket Theatre was brought to a close with the performance of ' The Roused Lion,' ' A Novel Expedient,' and ' The Pretty Girls of Stilberg.' In a review of the period of his management, delivered from the stage on the closing night of the season, Mr. Webster told his audience that without the assistance of a single farthing beyond what he had saved by rigid economy out of a very small income, he had maintained the longest lesseeship on record—one of sixteen years. During that period he had secured theatrical seasons varying from ten to twelve months. He had paid 30,000*l*., if not more, to authors ; expended at least 12,000*l*. in improving the theatre, and disbursed more than 60,000*l*. for rent. His most successful ventures had been ' The Bridal ' and ' Love Chase ' of Sheridan Knowles, ' Money ' of Lord Lytton, ' Used Up,' illustrated by the vivacity of Mr. Charles Mathews as *Sir Charles Coldstream ;* a revival of ' The Taming of the Shrew,' with the simple appointments of the ancient stage ; and ' The Wife's Secret,' with the Keans. He had relied almost wholly on a succession of " star " actors for attracting the public to his theatre—Mr. Macready, Mr. Charles Kean, Miss Ellen Tree, Mrs. Warner, Mrs. Nesbitt, Mrs. Glover, Miss Helen Faucit, Miss Charlotte Cushman, Mr. and Mrs. Keeley.

On Easter Monday, 1853, Mr. Benjamin Webster inaugurated his new management of the Adelphi Theatre with ' A Novel Expedient,' ' To Parents and Guardians,' ' The Pretty Girls of Stilberg,' and ' Pepine, the Dumb Boy.' On June 8 the same year he produced at the Adelphi Mr. Boucicault's drama ' Généviève ; or,

the Reign of Terror,' playing in it the part of *Lorin.* On Monday,
March 20, 1854, was performed for the first time Tom Taylor and
Charles Reade's play 'Two Loves and a Life,' in which Mr.
Webster acted the part of *Father Radcliffe,* a Jesuit, who, having
been disappointed in a love affair in early youth, is now wholly
devoted to the interests of the Church and his order. "The
sacrifice of an individuality to an idea, which is implied in a
thorough devotion to a large principle, was most eloquently illus-
trated in the more solemn passages uttered by *Father Radcliffe,*
who was most carefully and impressively personated by Mr.
Webster." (*Spectator,* March 25, 1854.) The same year, on
Monday, May 22, he produced 'The Marble Heart,' adapted by
Mr. C. Selby from MM. Barrière and Theboust's drama 'Les
Filles de Marbre,' Mr. Webster performing the dual parts of
Diogenes and *Ferdinand Volage.* In 1855, Monday, February 5,
'Janet Pride' (D. Boucicault) was first performed at the Adelphi
Theatre, Mr. Webster sustaining the part of *Richard Pride;* and
on Wednesday, June 20, 1855, 'Helping Hands,' by Tom Taylor,
Mr. Webster acting the part of *Lorentz Hartmann.* In 1858,
Monday, January 18, first performance of Mr. Watts Phillips's
drama 'The Poor Strollers,' Mr. Webster played the part of *Pierre
Leroux.* On Wednesday, June 2, 1858, the last performance took
place at the old Adelphi Theatre, which was pulled down in the
same year, and the present edifice erected in its place. The new
Adelphi Theatre was opened at the Christmas season of 1858, for
the performance of that class of drama for which the older house
had been so long famous. In 1859, Saturday, August 6, Mr.
Benjamin Webster played the part of *Penn Holder,* first performance of a piece adapted from the French by himself, entitled 'One
Touch of Nature.' *Penn Holder* was one of Mr. Webster's best
assumptions, and showed more favourably than any other character,
except Triplet and Luke Fielding, the eminently artistic gifts he
possessed. No living English actor could elicit more completely
the pathos of such scenes as those in the play between the daughter,
who is counterfeiting love for a father she does not know, and the
father who, while speaking, apparently, the words of a written part,
is, in reality, claiming his child in anxious and sorrowful earnest.
Nor did any actor of his day attain his ends by means more simple,
direct, and free from exaggeration. "The scene of the play is laid
in the chambers of Mr. Beaumont Fletcher, a dramatic author, the
elegance of whose furniture, and whose command over an exceedingly smart footman, must have excited the surprise, not to say the
envy, of any member of the London Dramatic Authors' Society who
happened to be present. This fortunate Mr. Fletcher is so much
dissatisfied with the manner in which Miss Constance Belmour, an
actress, has represented the principal French character in a new
drama during rehearsal, that he is resolved to give the part to some
other artist. However, his copyist, *Mr. Holder* (Mr. B. Webster),
a poverty-stricken creature of the 'Triplet' aspect, who has flattered
his vanity by praising his work, pleads so strongly in Miss Belmour's favour, that he abandons his intention, and resolves to give

her a rehearsal in his own room. In the meanwhile the excessive interest with which the young artist inspires the old copyist becomes more and more apparent. He has laid out his scanty earnings in the purchase of bouquets, and he is detected by Fletcher in the act of kissing her shawl. At last he confesses that Constance, though herself unacquainted with the fact, is his own daughter. The mother abandoned him, with a paramour, after a short term of domestic happiness, and took with her the child, who was but three years old ; but he has since been able to identify his offspring with the rising actress, and has watched over her, unseen, with the tenderest anxiety.

" Now the scene which is to be rehearsed in Mr. Fletcher's room embodies the recognition of a father by a daughter who has not seen him since childhood, and Miss Belmour's chief fault is the coldness which she displays on this important occasion. Mr. Fletcher, who has heard *Holder's* story, gladly avails himself of the offer of the copyist to take part in the critical scene, and the rehearsal commences in due form. The father is impassioned in his fondness, and though he cannot follow the words set down by the author, he substitutes others so much more natural that he causes an emendation of the text. Miss Belmour, on the other hand, listens with her wonted coldness to the attempts of the father to raise before her images of a rustic childhood, and Fletcher is almost in despair at the want of animation, when *Holder* suggests a temporary alteration in the words. He was a working tailor when his wife deserted him, and therefore, in repeating the situation, he abandons the description of the rural scene, and depicts instead the interior of a poor work-room in Long Acre. The attention of Constance is fixed ; her awakening memory bears witness to the fidelity of *Holder's* descriptions, and the real and feigned recognition takes place at the same instant, with wonderful effect. There is this fault about the piece, that in transferring the scene of action from Paris to London, Mr. Webster, who has avowedly adapted it from the French, has not sufficiently removed the tones of its native soil. Mr. Fletcher is manifestly a Parisian despot of the stage, exercising a power far beyond that of the English dramatist ; and the position of Mr. Belgrave, a ridiculous fop and a jealous admirer of Constance, belongs rather to Gallic than to British life. But these defects, conspicuous in the early part of the piece, are forgotten when the grand situation towards which the whole action is directed, occupies the attention of the audience. Never did Mr. Webster play more finely than in this difficult position. While hurried along by a storm of passionate affection, *Holder* is constantly forced to think of his merely artificial character, and his most violent outbreaks are checked by a prosaic attention to business. This complexity is represented with marvellous truth and power by Mr. Webster, who works at the character as if he liked it, and who, by the great applause he received, will doubtless abandon his intention of performing the piece for 'one night only.' " (*Times*, August 8, 1859.)

In November 1859 Mr. Watts Phillips's drama ' The Dead Heart ' was performed for the first time at the Adelphi, Mr. Webster acting the part of *Robert Landry.* Said the *Athenæum* (November 19, 1859) :—" Such a part as this, embracing many phases, and presenting the memorabilia of a life, gives to Mr. Webster that variety of expression of which he ever takes such advantage. As an artistic delineation his *Robert Landry* stands in the present day alone. There is no London actor who can compete with it in its rough strength and its intense feeling." In 1867, on Thursday, December 26, first performance of Messrs. Charles Dickens and Wilkie Collins's drama of ' No Thoroughfare,' Mr. Webster played the part of *Joey Ladle.* Subsequent to this date he seldom appeared on the London boards in any but revivals of those plays in which he had already secured reputation. In February 1874 Mr. Benjamin Webster finally retired from the stage ; and in the following month a farewell benefit performance—in which all the principal living actors took part—was given to him at Drury Lane Theatre. The amount said to have been realized was 2000 guineas.

WENMAN, THOMAS EDMUND (a *nom de théâtre;* THOMAS EDMUND NEWMAN), was born at Manchester, March 21, 1844, and first appeared on the stage at the Theatre Royal, Burnley, 1862, as *Captain Blenheim* in the ' Rough Diamond.' He was afterwards engaged (1863-9) at the Theatre Royal, Manchester, on the North Shields " circuit," and at the Theatres Royal, Nottingham and Glasgow, and had the advantage of playing with several " star " actors, the late Walter Montgomery, Miss Madge Robertson (Mrs. Kendal), Miss M. Reinhardt, Miss H. Faucit, &c. In June 1870 he joined the late Mdlle. Beatrice's comedy company, and during his engagement, extending to June 1878, appeared in all the principal towns in the United Kingdom, and at the Haymarket, Olympic, and Globe Theatres in London. Among the more noticeable characters played by Mr. Wenman during his long connection with Mdlle. Beatrice's company, the following are deserving of mention, viz. *M. Brigard* (' Frou-Frou '), *M. Marecal* (' Our Friends '), *Joseph Ironsides* (' Nine Points of the Law '), *Matthew Lambert* (' Married, not Mated '), *Adam Jasper* (' John Jasper's Wife '), *Duke of Alva* (' Patrie '), *John Prescott* (' Glitter '), *Remy* (' The Woman of the People '). In 1878 he joined Mr. Hare's company on tour in the provinces to play *Burchell* in ' Olivia,' and subsequently, on January 4, 1879, " opened " at the Court Theatre, London, as *Sir John Ingram* (' A Scrap of Paper '), and *Mr. Sullivan* (' A Quiet Rubber '), and subsequently *Sergeant Sabretache* (' The Queen's Shilling '), which part he is now (November 1879) playing at the St. James's Theatre.

WESTLAND, HENRY, was born in London, September 14, 1838, and entered the dramatic profession at the Theatre Royal, Leamington, Easter Monday, 1861. In the winter of the same year he joined the company of the Theatre Royal, Dublin, and played there during the " starring" engagements of the late Mr. Charles Mathews, Mr. G. V. Brooke, Mr. Charles Kean, and Mr. John Drew, in the various plays in which those actors played the leading *rôle.* For the season 1862-3 Mr. Westland was re-engaged for the same theatre; but afterwards joined the Theatre Royal, Brighton, under the late H. Nye Chart's management, for the seasons 1863-4-5. In the autumn of 1865 he played at the Lyceum Theatre, under Mr. Fechter's management; and in August and September 1866, at the Haymarket, during an engagement of Miss Amy Sedgwick, the following parts, viz. *The Baron* ('The Stranger'), *Glavis* ('The Lady of Lyons'), *Trueworth* ('The Love Chase'). For the winter season 1866-7 he was engaged by Mr. Sefton Parry for the New Holborn Theatre, and at the same theatre, in the following season, played *Captain Grindly Goodge* in 'Flying Scud.' Mr. Westland remained at the Holborn Theatre during part of Miss Fanny Josephs' management; and in 1869-70 fulfilled an engagement at the Globe Theatre, under Mr. Sefton Parry. Subsequently he was engaged on various tours, viz., in 1870, with Mr. Boucicault; in 1871, with Mr. Arthur Garner's so-called "Royalty Company"; and during the winter season 1872-3, for "leading business" at the Amphitheatre, Liverpool. In 1874 he was engaged by Mr. John Hollingshead for tour with Mr. Lionel Brough and Miss E. Farren; and in 1875 went to the United States with Mr. J. L. Toole, to play with him during his American engagement. He has been on tour with several other well-known players, and is at present acting with Mr. J. L. Toole at the Folly Theatre.

* **WIGAN, HORACE**, made his first appearance on the London stage at the Olympic Theatre, May 1, 1854, in the character of *Paddy Murphy*, in a piece entitled 'The Happy Man,' and first attracted notice as an actor there in 1858. He was the original *Mr. Smoothly Smirk* of John Oxenford's play 'The Porter's Knot,' first performed at that theatre Saturday, December 4, 1858. On April 11, 1859, at the same theatre, in Tom Taylor's drama 'Nine Points of the Law,' then first performed, he acted the character of *Mr. Cunninghame;* and in Madison Morton's play 'A Husband to Order,' first performed at the Olympic, Monday, October 17 of the same year, he played the *Baron de Beaupré*. Monday, April 23, 1860, at the same theatre, Mr. H. Wigan sustained the part of *William Hogarth*, in a piece of pathos entitled 'The Christmas Dinner,' from the pen of Mr. Tom Taylor. In February 1861 he acted the part of the elder *Probity*, first performance of H. T. Craven's play 'Peter Probity,' and subsequently, during the serious illness of Mr. Robson, sustained the leading *rôle* in the piece. In June 1863, first performance of Mr. Tom Taylor's drama 'The Ticket-of-Leave Man,' Mr. H. Wigan acted the part of *Hawkshaw*. In September 1864 he became sole lessee and manager of the Olympic Theatre, "opening" on November 2 with three new pieces, viz. 'The Girl I Left Behind Me' (John Oxenford); 'The Hidden Hand' (Tom Taylor); and 'My Wife's Bonnet' (J. M. Morton), all adapted from the French. After the drama ('The Hidden Hand,' adapted from a French melodrama called 'L'Aïeule'), Mr. Wigan expressed his managerial intentions in an address, wherein he said:—" As for the style of entertainment in store for you, I think that the word 'mixed' will be the best general description. I shall not exclude any dish from our Olympic 'spread,' provided it be wholesome, pleasant, and well-dressed ; from the whipped cream of burlesque, very good in its proper time and place, to the *pièce de résistance* in the shape of drama, with removes of comedy, vaudeville, farce, and comedietta. I shall not even be frightened by the name of sensation, so long as it mean strong interest, exciting incident, and powerfully conceived situation. But I never mean to put the cart of Thespis before the horse, or, in other words, to consider the scenery, dresses, and decorations of more importance than the actors and the piece. In short, if an English manager may be allowed to adopt a maxim from the Roman dramatist, I would say, 'Manager sum, et boni nil a me alienum puto,' or, translating for the benefit of the ladies, I am a manager, and whatever brings me a bonus I shall make a point of producing." (*Journal of a London Playgoer*, Prof. Henry Morley, p. 348.) Saturday, March 4, 1865, 'The Settling Day,' by Tom Taylor, was produced, Mr. H. Wigan sustaining the part of *Meiklam*. The same year, in a revival at the Olympic Theatre of Shakespeare's 'Twelfth Night,' he acted the character of *Sir Andrew Aguecheek*. In July of the same year Mr. Wigan produced Tom Taylor's drama of 'The Serf; or, Love Levels All.' In May 1866 he produced a play by Leicester Buckingham, entitled 'Love's Martyrdom,' and acted in it the part of *Trevelyan*. In 1868, November 7, first performance of Mr. Henry Neville's drama 'The Yellow Passport,' Mr. H. Wigan played the character of *Jouvert*. In 1869 he joined the company of the Gaiety Theatre, and enacted the leading *rôle* in a play written by himself in collaboration with Mr. John Oxenford, entitled 'A Life Chase.' Since 1870 Mr. Horace Wigan has appeared at various London Theatres—the Olympic, Vaudeville, and Strand—in parts of more or less importance in the line of comedy. In the early part of 1875 Mr. Wigan entered upon the management of the Holborn Theatre (re-naming it the 'Mirror'), and produced on the first night an original comedietta 'Maids of Honour' (C. L. Kenney), 'The Hidden Hand,' and a farcical trifle entitled 'Make Yourself at Home' (A. Maltby). He is the author of several farces, some of which have attained fair success on the stage. A piece of his, adapted from the French of M. Sardou ('Nos Intimes'), entitled 'Friends or Foes,' produced at the Olympic Theatre, March 8, 1862, was of more than usual merit, very cleverly constructed, and completely successful.

WIGAN, LEONORA, wife of the late Alfred Sidney Wigan, is descended of an old theatrical family—the Wallacks. She was educated to the stage from early childhood, and was a popular and clever member of the company of the Keeleys when they had the management of the Lyceum Theatre, 1844-7 ; and, with her husband, performed with more than ordinary success at other London theatres previous to his entering upon the management of the Olympic Theatre in 1853. Here Mrs. Wigan actively interested herself in the various and important duties of stage-management; and it would be no injustice to her husband's memory to say that the success which attended his lesseeship of the Olympic Theatre was largely due to the care, energy, and taste with which she performed those duties. Mrs. Wigan may be said to have inaugurated, under Mr. Alfred Wigan's auspices, that more finished style of acting which of recent years has happily become the guiding principle of the London theatres.

WILLES, LOUISE, was born in Cleveland, Ohio, U.S. She left America when quite a child, and was educated in England for the musical profession ; but forsook it for the stage, and made her *début* at the Prince of Wales's Theatre, Liverpool, February 10, 1868. Having studied the various grades of theatrical work until September 1870, Miss Willes then accepted an engagement at the New Theatre Royal, Bristol, as "leading lady." Since that time she has played that business in all the principal towns of the United Kingdom. Her greatest provincial successes have been in the parts of *Edith Dombey, Rosalind,* and *Lady Clancarty.* Miss Willes made her first appearance in London at the Olympic Theatre, July 13, 1875, in the part of *Camille,* in a play entitled ' One Hundred Years Ago.' Subsequently she fulfilled engagements at the Criterion, Globe, Adelphi, and Drury Lane Theatres, in the following principal parts : *Lady Dedlock, Mary Leigh* (' Hunted Down '), *Mrs. Royal* in ' The Golden Plough,' *Fenella* in ' England,' *Amy Robsart,* and *Lady Clancarty.* During the latter part of 1878 and earlier months of the following year she acted with considerable success in Calcutta.

WILTON, MARIE. *See* Bancroft, Marie Effie.

WOOD, MRS. JOHN, daughter of Mrs. Henry Vining, for some years a well-known actress in domestic drama at the Surrey Theatre. She made her first appearance on any stage at the Southampton Theatre, and was an actress of considerable repute in the United States (whither she had gone after a slight experience in the English provinces), prior to her *début* in London, which took place at the Princess's Theatre, Monday, November 12, 1866. The character in which Mrs. John Wood appeared on the occasion was that of *Miss Miggs* in a dramatic version by Watts Phillips of ' Barnaby Rudge.' In 1869, in October, Mrs. John Wood entered upon the management of the St. James's Theatre, and "opened" with ' She Stoops to Conquer,' and an operetta entitled ' Treasure Trove.' Subsequently she appeared at the St. James's Theatre with great success as *Pocahontas* in a burlesque entitled ' La Belle Sauvage.' On Monday, June 20, 1870, at the St. James's Theatre, she played *Phœbe* in a revival of ' Paul Pry,' and in the following month of the same year fulfilled an engagement at the Standard Theatre, appearing in her original character in the burlesque before mentioned. On Saturday, October 15, 1870, at the St. James's Theatre, she played the part of *Georgette* in ' Fernande,' an adaptation by Mr. Sutherland Edwards of M. Sardou's play of that title. Criticising this performance, the *Daily News* (October 17, 1870) said :—" Few actresses have risen as rapidly in the public favour as Mrs. John Wood ; only twelve months since, when this theatre was first opened under her management, her name was practically unknown to English audiences. In the United States she had long enjoyed a high reputation in the field of burlesque ; but her appear-ances here had been confined to the performances of a character in an adaptation to the stage of Mr. Dickens's 'Barnaby Rudge,' produced a few years ago at the Princess's Theatre, and in this she could hardly be said to have been successful. Discouraged appa-rently by her reception, Mrs. Wood shortly afterwards returned to America. Even favourites of the public are quickly forgotten ; but an actress who had made so little impression could hardly be remembered by any but those whose duty it is to chronicle dramatic events. It cannot, therefore, be said that she came among us last year under any very favourable circumstances. Yet a very few weeks sufficed to show that the London theatre had gained the services of a lady of decidedly original powers. People of delicate constitution whispered that her style was 'coarse'; aristocratic loungers in the stalls fancied that they detected an objectionable flavour of Republican freedom in her tone and manner ; but the indisputable cleverness of the lady, her strong sense of humour, her versatility, quaint drollery, and, above all, her never-flagging vivacity, soon reduced her objectors to an unpopular minority. Added to this, Mrs. Wood has exhibited a talent scarcely less rare as a theatrical manager. She has not only amused the public, but has studied the comfort and conveniences of her visitors, until the St. James's, so long regarded as hopelessly out of favour with play-goers, has become one of the most successful of London houses. . . .

"The theme of ' Fernande' is the old one of a woman raised from a position of shame, who finds the secret of her past career still haunting her, and marring her enjoyment of a purer life. In the original, Fernande is the young mistress of a low gambling-house keeper, who, after an attempt to commit suicide in disgust at the degraded condition to which early neglect has reduced her, is rescued by Clotilde, a wealthy lady of generous sentiments. Clotilde herself, however, is not a person of immaculate propriety. She is, in fact, the mistress of a young marquis, who, by an unfortunate coincidence, has seen and fallen in love with her *protégée*, in igno-rance of her antecedents. Having reason to suspect her lover's infidelity, Clotilde feigns to have lost her affection for him, by which he is induced to confess to her the facts with heartless cool-ness. Thenceforth, Clotilde's feeling toward Fernande is changed ; and she resolves on a revenge which bears some resemblance to that of the rejected suitors of the Lady of Lyons. She encourages the match with Fernande ; waylays a letter in which the latter had made full disclosures of her past life to her lover ; and when the union is complete and the honeymoon over, appears on the scene with the astounding proofs that the Marquis has married a woman of antecedents of the vilest kind. Both in the English version and in the original the Marquis finally takes the penitent wife to his arms, on the discovery that she had not after all attempted to deceive him; but it will be easily conceived that the plot we have sketched has undergone, in preparation for our stage, considerable changes. It is, in fact, the old story of taking away an objectionable foundation, while the edifice it supported is expected to stand. In brief, not only is Clotilde at the St. James's a respectable lady to whom the fickle Marquis has been paying his addresses, but Fernande is, from the first, a model of purity; her only association with the low gaming-house being the fact that her mother's second husband is its proprietor. Decency is thus strictly observed, but the point of the plot is obviously gone; the only fault of poor Fernande having been that she had happened to have a very cruel and wicked stepfather. . . .

"The success of the play was in no small degree due to the acting. Mrs. John Wood's part, though merely incidental, is amusing. Her suspicion of her husband, and habit of discovering love letters deposited in his hands as the legal adviser of a lady suing for a divorce, and of regarding them as damnatory proofs of marital infidelity, were depicted with a sprightliness which gave a decidedly new touch to the typical jealous wife of the stage."

In January 1871, at the same theatre, in a revival of 'Jenny Lind at Last,' Mrs. John Wood played *Jenny Leatherlungs;* and, in April following, *Anne Bracegirdle*, in an English version of M. Fournier's play 'Tiridate; ou Comédie et Tragédie,' entitled 'An Actress by Daylight.' After a visit to the United States, Mrs. John Wood reappeared on the London stage in November 1873, at the Queen's Theatre, as *Philippa Chester* in Charles Reade's drama 'The Wandering Heir.' On Saturday, March 21, 1874, on the occasion of the opening of the Criterion Theatre, she played the leading *rôle* in Byron's comedy 'An American Lady'; and on December 19 of the same year, at the Gaiety Theatre, *Mrs. Page* in a revival of 'The Merry Wives of Windsor.' Mrs. John Wood was for a period of eight years manageress of St. James's Theatre. Among pieces produced there during the latter part of her management, 'The Danischeffs,' first performed on Saturday, January 6, 1877, and in which she played *Princess Lydia*, is entitled to special mention. In 1878, on Monday, December 2, at the Haymarket Theatre, first performance of Mr. James Albery's version of 'Les Fourchambault' of M. Augier, entitled 'The Crisis,' Mrs. John Wood sustained the part of *Mrs. Denham*, "a character well and humorously conceived, and expressed with great vivacity and truth by the actress" (*Times*, December 4, 1878).

WOOLGAR, SARAH JANE. *See* MELLON, MRS. ALFRED.

*****WYNDHAM, CHARLES** (a *nom de théâtre*), first appeared on the stage, in New York, at Mrs. John Wood's Olympic Theatre, in 1861, as "walking gentleman." Afterwards he did duty in the Southern States as a surgeon during the Civil War. On May 21, 1866, he made his *début* on the London stage at the Royalty

Theatre as *Sir Arthur Lascelles* in 'All that Glitters is not Gold.' Subsequently (April 1867) he appeared at the St. James's Theatre, during Miss Herbert's management, as *Hugh Stoneleigh* in a play entitled 'Idalia.' Returning to New York in 1869, on September 15 of that year he made his *début* at Wallack's Theatre as *Charles Surface* in 'The School for Scandal.' Mr. Wyndham has appeared at various theatres in London since that date in pieces which have attained more or less success. During his management of the Criterion Theatre he produced, on Saturday, March 31, 1877, 'The Pink Dominos' (adapted by J. Albery from 'Les Dominos Roses' of MM. Hennequin and Delacour), in which he played the part of *Charles Greythorne.* The English version attained much popularity. In January 1879, at the same theatre, Mr. Wyndham produced 'Truth' (Bronson Howard), in which he played the leading *rôle*, and on August 9, 'Betsy,' a comedy adapted from the French by F. C. Burnand.

YOUNG, MRS. CHARLES. *See* VEZIN, JANE ELIZABETH.

YOUNG, SOPHIE, made her first appearance as a child at the Haymarket Theatre in the character of *Prince Edward* in 'Richard III.,' Edwin Booth, the American tragedian, and Mrs. Herman Vezin sustaining the principal parts. She afterwards was a pupil of Mr. John Ryder, and about twelve years ago had control of Astley's Theatre for a season. Miss Young appeared at the Queen's Theatre in the first performance of Burnand's 'Turn of the Tide,' May 29, 1869, in the character of *Lady Clara*, and afterwards joined Mdlle. Beatrice's company, playing leading business in the provinces for about two years. In August 1873 Miss Young produced at the Theatre Royal, Edinburgh, an English version by Mr. Wills of 'Patrie,' by Sardou, under the title of 'Betrayed,' in which she appeared as *Dolores.* Owing to severe illness, however, Miss Young was obliged to retire for a time, and did not reappear on the stage until December 1877, when in the revival of 'The Turn of Tide' at the Olympic Theatre she sustained her original part of *Lady Clara.* She afterwards (1878) appeared in the leading part in Charles Reade's 'Jealousy,' produced at the Olympic. In June 1878 she replaced Mrs. Bancroft in the *rôle* of *Countess Zicka* in 'Diplomacy,' at the Prince of Wales's Theatre, returning again in May 1879 to the Olympic to play *Maud Penreath* in Mr. Frank Harvey's comedy 'Married, not Mated.'

APPENDIX,

BIOGRAPHICAL NOTICES OF THE PRINCIPAL ACTORS AND ACTRESSES

WHO HAVE DIED SINCE THE ISSUE OF THE FIRST EDITION

OF

' THE DRAMATIC LIST.'

———◆———

BEATRICE, MDLLE. (a *nom de théâtre;* MARIE BEATRICE BINDA), born at Lucca, in Italy, August 5, 1839; died in London December 22, 1878. Her father, Chevalier Binda, was for many years the British Consul at Florence and Leghorn, and afterwards in the service of the Imperial Court of Napoleon III. Political offences at an early period of his life caused him to visit England, where he remained for seventeen years, passing much of his time between Chatsworth, the seat of the Duke of Devonshire, and Holland House. Here he made the acquaintance and formed a friendship with most of the political, literary, and aristocratic celebrities of the day. He was a man of polished wit and great literary attainments (the Binda library being famous both in France and Italy), and could claim a personal friendship with Lord Byron and Madame Guiccioli. The family on Mdlle. Beatrice's mother's side was even of higher distinction, Madame Binda being the grand-daughter of the famous Marquise de Lage de Volude, the sincere friend of the Princess de Lamballe, and the principal maid of honour to Marie Antoinette. Her party figured notably in the Revolution of '93. While attached to the Imperial Court of France Chevalier Binda was seized with paralysis. His income being considerably reduced, Mdlle. Beatrice determined to adopt the stage as a profession for the purpose of assisting her family. She entered herself as a scholar of the Conservatoire, obtained a first prize within the year, and made her first appearance at the Théâtre de l'Odéon as the heroine in the French version of Kotzebue's 'Stranger.' From the Odéon she passed on to the Vaudeville, where she became the second and under-study of Mdlle. Fargeuil. She appeared, by special command of the Empress, at Versailles as *The Countess* in 'The Marriage of Figaro'; and was selected by Alexandre Dumas *fils* for the heroine in his play 'L'Ami des Femmes,' but was prevented from accepting it by the death of her father. Four years were thus passed in study, rehearsals, acting, and sharing alternate nights of watching with her sister at her father's bedside. Many of her father's old friends now came to her assistance, and amongst them none were kinder than the present Empress of the French. Mdlle. Beatrice was induced to try her fortunes on the English stage. She was brought to this country under the escort of Lady Holland and the late Mr. Henry Greville, and was for some time a guest at Holland House.* Mdlle. Binda made her *début* on the London stage in the name of Lucchesini at the Haymarket Theatre on Monday, October 3, 1864, in the principal *rôle* in Mrs. F. A. Kemble's (Mrs. F. Butler) stage adaptation of 'Mademoiselle de Belle Isle.' In November 1864 she appeared at the same theatre in 'The Stranger.' Noticing this performance, the *Athenæum* (November 5, 1864) said :—" The new actress at this theatre has put her claims to the test of a second character, and has better satisfied the public than in the first. Mdlle. Beatrice as *Mrs. Haller* is fitted with a part that might have been invented for such an actress. Beautiful, elegant, and Italian, highly polished in her style of art, with manners extremely refined, we have almost the ideal of Kotzebue's heroine. Her last act has never been surpassed ; it is wrought to a climax in an apparently natural manner which conceals the skill by which the effect is secured. Mdlle. Beatrice prefers a happy catastrophe, and throws herself into the arms of 'The Stranger,' who is thus compelled to pardon the erring wife. It is not always that the prejudices of an English audience permit such a consummation of the action ; on this occasion, however, they did, and Mdlle. Beatrice's triumph was not questioned."

In the same month and year Mdlle. Beatrice appeared at the same theatre as *Hilda* in a play called 'Sunny Vale Farm,' adapted by Mr. J. V. Bridgman from the German of Dr. Mosenthal ('Der Sonnenwendhof'). In 1865, Monday, April 17, in a revival of 'Belphegor' at the Lyceum Theatre (Mr. Fechter in the title *rôle*), she sustained the character of *Madeleine.*

After that year Mdlle. Beatrice appeared oftener at provincial theatres than on the London stage. In 1867 she played with very great success in the provinces in Mrs. Fanny Kemble's (Mrs. F. Butler) English version of Schiller's 'Mary Stuart.' Two years later, in February 1869, she reappeared on the London boards for a brief season as *Marie Antoinette* in the drama of that title by Mr. Palgrave Simpson ; but Mdlle. Beatrice entered into no permanent engagements in the metropolis following the five years of her first connection with its stage. She occupied herself principally in travelling in the provinces with a company of her own, which she had organized in the year 1870, appearing from time to time in London with that company in the summer season. The plays which she produced consisted chiefly of translations from the French. " She invested the characters she portrayed with a grace, a refinement, and a charm peculiarly her own, and in her own particular line she had no rival. Her company, too, was always

---

* For the foregoing facts I am indebted to the *Era*, December 29, 1878, p. 13.—Ed.

noted for its excellence, many of its present members being in it from its organization." (The *Era*, December 29, 1878, p. 13.) Among her later appearances on the metropolitan stage the following are to be noted : In May 1872 she presented at the Olympic Theatre 'Our Friends,' a version of M. Sardou's 'Nos Intimes,' and acted in it the part of *Madame Caussade*. On Saturday, August 22, 1874, she opened the Haymarket Theatre for a brief period with her " Comedy-Drama Company," and produced ' The Sphinx,' from ' Le Sphinx' of M. Octave Feuillet ; ' Frou-Frou' ; and 'Our Friends.' In August 1875, at the Globe Theatre with her company, she presented an adaptation of M. Dumas *fils*' 'Monsieur Alphonse,' under the title of 'Love and Honour ; or, Monsieur Alphonse,' by Mr. Campbell Clarke, in which she sustained the part of *Madame Guichard*. In July 1876, at the Haymarket Theatre, she produced a revival of some of the plays above mentioned ; and in August 1878 appeared at the Olympic Theatre for four weeks in the leading *rôle* in a melodrama entitled ' The Woman of the People,' which had been performed by her company with great success in the provinces. The *Era* of the date already quoted, in an obituary notice of Mdlle. Beatrice, remarked of her as follows :—" Mdlle. Beatrice did not count her admirers amongst her audience alone. Her great kindness of heart, her high sense of justice, her charm of manner, made her a special favourite with everyone with whom she came in contact. And her loss will be deeply felt by many. Italian on the father's side, and French on the mother's, she inherited the qualities of both countries—though her sympathies lay all with France. She was highly educated, a first-rate linguist, a true politician, and could converse freely on almost any subject, whilst her wonderful business capacity surprised all those with whom she had dealings." A solemn requiem mass for the repose of the soul of the deceased actress was celebrated at the Pro-Cathedral, Kensington, on Tuesday, January 31, 1879. The remains were afterwards conveyed to Paris for interment in the family vault at Père Lachaise.

CLARKE, JOHN, born *cir.* 1830 ; died 20th of February, 1879. In early life Mr. John Clarke showed a strong predilection for the stage, and eventually he gave up a photographic establishment in Farringdon Street, which he had opened with some prospect of success, and went as " general utility " to several country theatres in succession. He made his first appearance on the London stage at the Strand Theatre, January 1852, as *Master Toby* in Wilkins's play 'Civilization.' At Drury Lane Theatre, October 7, 1852, he played the part of *Fathom* in 'The Hunchback' ; and the same year accepted an engagement at the Strand Theatre (then known as " Punch's Playhouse"), with which he subsequently became connected as a leading actor in burlesque and the domestic drama, its leading specialities. Among the more successful pieces in which Mr. Clarke sustained a leading *rôle* during the first period of his long connection with the London stage the following may be mentioned, viz. 'Electra' (*Lycus*), a burlesque by Francis Talfourd, first performed at the Haymarket Theatre in April 1859; 'The Very Latest Edition of the Lady of Lyons' (*Beauseant*), first performed at the Strand Theatre in 1859; a burlesque entitled 'The Maid and the Magpie,' first performed at the same theatre; a play entitled 'Appearances,' from the pen of Mr. Palgrave Simpson, produced at the same theatre in May 1860; 'The Old Story' (*Mr. Waverly Brown*), by Mr. H. J. Byron, performed at the same theatre in April 1861; 'Aladdin; or, the Wonderful Scamp,' produced the same month; 'Orange Blossoms' (*Septimus Symmetry*), by Mr. J. P. Wooler, performed at the same theatre in February 1862. To mention in detail the numerous characters in which Mr. Clarke appeared during his engagement at the Strand Theatre would necessitate the compilation of a list of the various stage pieces produced there from 1858 to 1862. It may be sufficient to remark that in the most successful of these Mr. Clarke's acting was a principal attraction, conducing largely to their popularity and success. During an engagement at the St. James's Theatre in 1864, on Wednesday, May 11, first performance of Mr. Boucicault's play entitled 'The Fox Chase,' Mr. Clarke played the part of *Twining, alias the Fox.* On Saturday, April 15, 1865, on the occasion of the opening of the Prince of Wales's Theatre under the management of Mr. H. J. Byron and Miss Marie Wilton, in an extravaganza by the former entitled 'La! Sonnambula! or the Supper, the Sleeper, and the Merry Swiss Boy,' Mr. Clarke played the part of *Amina.* On September 25 of the same year (1865) he played *Lucia de Lammermoor* in Mr. H. J. Byron's burlesque of that title, then first performed at the same theatre. On Saturday, November 11, 1865, Mr. Clarke sustained the part of *John Chodd,* first performance of T. W. Robertson's comedy 'Society.' On Saturday, September 15, 1866, at the Prince of Wales's Theatre, he undertook the character of *Hugh Chalcot,* first performance of T. W. Robertson's comedy entitled 'Ours,' "a character affording no scope for the exuberant humour which is usually expected from this clever comedian, but sustained by him with an amount of artistic skill which is thoroughly appreciated by his audience" (*Daily Telegraph,* September 19, 1866).

On Monday, March 2, 1868, at the Olympic Theatre, he sustained the part of *Sarah Gamp* in a dramatic version of 'Martin Chuzzlewit'; and on Saturday, November 28 of the same year, on the occasion of the opening of the Globe Theatre, he played the part of *Matthew Pincher,* first performance of Byron's comedy 'Cyril's Success.' "The chief humour of the play," said the *Daily News* (November 30, 1868), "is sustained by Mr. John Clarke, whom it is a pleasure to meet for once out of that region of oily hypocrisy and smirking roguery in which he at one time threatened to degenerate into a mere mannerist. His hard but distinct voice, and slow manner, told well in the part of *Matthew Pincher,* the cynical critic. The scene in the last act, in which he is reconciled with his wife, coming together after twenty-three years' separation, just as they had parted on a question of 'incompatibility of ideas on the subject of cookery,' was one of the drollest in the play—the humour being heightened by the incomparable acting of Mrs. Stephens." On Saturday, October 23, 1869, first performance at the Globe Theatre of Byron's comedy 'Not Such a Fool as He Looks,' Mr. Clarke played the part of *Mould.* On Monday, June 10, 1872, at the Princess's Theatre, in a revival by Mr. Charles Fechter of 'Hamlet,' Mr. Clarke personated the *First Gravedigger.* On Saturday, March 21, 1874, on the occasion of the first opening of the Criterion Theatre, he played *Shrew*, first performance of Byron's comedy 'An American Lady.' In 1875, first performance at the Adelphi Theatre of Andrew Halliday's dramatic version of 'Nicholas Nickleby,' he played the part of the schoolmaster, *Squeers.* Mr. John Clarke during his career appeared at all the principal theatres in London, and was very successful in the provinces.

Mr. Clarke's last regular engagement in London was at the Court Theatre, under Mr. Hare's management, in the early part of 1878. He there played *John Butterby* in Tom Taylor's comedy 'Victims,' and *Bunter* in a revival of 'New Men and Old Acres.' His last appearances on the London stage were as follows :—On May 8, 1878, at the Gaiety, as *John Chodd, Jun.*, in 'Society,' for his own benefit; on May 18, 1878, at the St. James's, as *Solomon Isaacs* in 'London Assurance,' for Mr. S. Hayes's benefit; on May 25, 1878, at the Globe, in the same character, for Mr. E. Righton's benefit ; and at the Globe, on Saturday morning, June 8, 1878, when he played *Smiler* in 'A Regular Fix,' for Mr. J. L. Toole's benefit. Mr. Clarke was married to Teresa Furtado, a graceful and talented actress, whose death preceded her husband's some two years.* John Clarke lies buried at Highgate Cemetery, in the grave which enclosed the remains of his wife. His memory will be long preserved by all who were frequenters of the Strand Theatre during the brightest period of its prosperity. As a grotesque singer and dancer he had rare advantages (says the *Era*, February 23, 1879), and his embodiments were always characterized by singular care bestowed on what is technically termed "the making-up." Mr. Clarke suffered from a lameness which somewhat interfered with his professional work, added to which he was possessed of a singularly harsh and unpleasing voice. But he was a clever actor, and a man of a singularly kind and generous disposition.

FALCONER, EDMUND, born in Dublin about the year 1813, and died in London in 1879. Before appearing on the London stage he was known as a provincial author of repute, and as the author of a volume of poems which at the time of their publication attracted some attention. On Saturday, December 6, 1856, he produced at the Lyceum Theatre his first play of importance, entitled 'The Cagot; or, Heart for Heart,' in which Mr. Charles Dillon enacted the principal character, Raoul. The *Athenæum*

* Teresa Furtado died August 9, 1877, aged 32.

(December 13, 1856) reported that the play was enthusiastically received. "The dialogue is remarkable for noble sentiments; a religious vein is also observable; and the style is frequently poetic, though the verse is not always correct." On Monday, May 4, 1857, Mr. Falconer appeared at Sadler's Wells Theatre, in a piece written by himself, entitled 'The Lady of St. Tropez.' Both play and player were successful. The same year, in the following month (Monday, June 1), he produced a piece entitled 'A Husband for an Hour,' at the Haymarket Theatre. In 1858 he undertook the management of the Lyceum Theatre for a brief period; and on Thursday, August 26, produced there his play of 'Extremes; or, Men of the Day.' It had an extraordinary success. This was owing in great measure to the earnest endeavour of the author to portray the manners of the time, and his constant introduction of topics currently discussed in society, though not commonly on the stage. "A numerous audience attended on the occasion, and, though the comedy lasted nearly four hours, it seemed

'As if increase of appetite had grown by what it fed on,'

for gratification at the first act increased to delight at the second, and had mounted up to positive rapture by the conclusion of the third. The title of his (Mr. Falconer's) fortunate work is 'Extremes; or, Men of the Day,' and we rejoice to say that it is inaccurate as far as the second part is concerned. If 'men of the day' behaved to each other in the manner exhibited by this portrait of modern life, a dinner party would become an absolute impossibility, for the half-hour preceding the announcement of the meal would be so filled up with bluff repartees and insulting rejoinders, that the master of the house would feel it his bounden duty to ring the bell and order the carriages of all his guests, long before the soup-tureen was placed on the table. It really did one's heart good to hear the wicked gentlemen of fashion insult the man of unpretending virtue, and then to hear the man of unpretending virtue pay back the wicked gentlemen of fashion in their own coin. Refreshing, too, was it to learn that the practice of duelling had become obsolete, for if the ancient code of honour had been in force the whole of the male *dramatis personæ* would have undergone the fate of the renowned Kilkenny cats long before the fall of the curtain. The motive of the plot is furnished by the will of an eccentric old gentleman, who, having risen from the lowest position in society to a condition of affluence, has left the bulk of his fortune to his nephew, *Frank Hawthorne* (Mr. Falconer), and his wife's niece, Lucy Vavasour (Mrs. Charles Young), on condition that they shall marry each other. Six months are allowed for them to make up their minds. If the lady refuses, the gentleman is to have the whole of the money, and *vice versâ*. By this arrangement a mutual suspicion is engendered between the legatees. The gentleman, whose parents were of lowly condition, is regarded by the lady's friends as a mere clodhopper, who may be maltreated as pleasure or profit may dictate; while he, on the other hand, is dreadfully afraid that love may be feigned to prevent the loss of a handsome fortune. Both are the noblest creatures in the world, but neither understands the other. Hence, when the six months have expired, and Miss Vavasour has signified her assent to the proposed marriage, Mr. Hawthorne formally declares his refusal. At last, however, the disinterestedness of the lady is clearly demonstrated by her own offer to marry Hawthorne, when the fortune is clearly in her own hands. . . . . We should not be at all astonished if this piece, with all its crudities and improbabilities, had a long 'run,' and if so, the success will be almost entirely due to the writing. The dialogue is far too abundant, but the repartees are fresh and vigorous, and even the sermonizing Mr. Hawthorne, amid much twaddle, makes several remarks that evince reflection on some of the social questions of the day. The characters, too, though drawn from stage tradition, are sharply defined, and are exactly of a kind to be perfectly intelligible to a large audience." (*Times*, August 27, 1858.) In 1859, on Monday, January 3, at the Lyceum, in 'Marion de L'Orme,' translated from the French by Mr. Falconer, he played the part of *Cardinal Richelieu;* and the same year, on Thursday, March 31, he produced at the Lyceum his play of 'Francesca,' in which he played the part of *Gradinigo;* and on Wednesday, November 2, at the Princess's Theatre, 'The Master ; or, the Outlaws of the Adriatic,' of which he was likewise the author. In 1860 he produced two plays : Wednesday, May 9, at the Haymarket, a drama in three acts, entitled 'The Family Secret'; and on Saturday, June 23, at the same theatre, a play in three acts, entitled 'Does He Love Me ?'

On Monday, September 10, 1860, on the occasion of the first performance at the Adelphi Theatre of Dion Boucicault's 'Colleen Bawn,' Mr. Falconer played the part of *Danny Man* with marvellous truth and accuracy. The same year Mr. Falconer produced a translation of Victor Hugo's effective play 'Ruy Blas,' which was first performed at the Princess's Theatre on Saturday, October 27, with much success, Mr. Charles Fechter sustaining the principal character. In 1861 Mr. Falconer once more entered upon the management of the Lyceum Theatre, and produced there on the opening night (Monday, August 19) a play written by himself, entitled 'Woman ; or, Love against the World.' On Saturday, November 9 of the same year, at the same theatre, he produced 'Peep o' Day ; or, Savourneen Deelish,' founded upon one of the 'Tales of the O'Hara Family.' Of this play Mr. Falconer was the author, and he performed in it the part of *Barney O'Toole.* The success of the new piece, which was very great, depended far more upon two or three grand effects than on the general interest. "The dialogue, though written with more than average care, is often ponderous, and of a kind which even experienced actors can with difficulty render effective. Indeed, though the cast is decidedly strong, only two characters really become conspicuous, namely, the peasant *Barney,* capitally played by Mr. Falconer himself, and the unfortunate Kathleen, sustained by Mrs. Bowers, the American lady, who, starting well in 'legitimate' plays, now distinguishes herself as an excellent melodramatic actress. The great 'sensation scene,' representing the 'Old Quarry in the Foil Dhuiv, or Dark Valley,' together with the business done therein, more than answered expectation, and is likely to attract all London. . . . The customary forms of applause were gone through with far more than wonted enthusiasm, and a 'long run' may be predicted for 'Peep o' Day,' if the paternal sentiments of Mr. Falconer do not prevent him from shortening his own dialogue." (*Times*, November 11, 1861.) In 1864 Mr. Falconer entered upon the management of Drury Lane Theatre, conjointly with Mr. F. B. Chatterton, and in January produced there a drama of which he was author entitled 'Night and Morn,' as to which Mr. Morley enters the following note in his *Journal of a London Playgoer*, pp. 328-30 :—" Here I stop for to-day, but to spare three lines and a half to say that Mr. Falconer's new play 'Night and Morn,' at Drury Lane, is certainly the best he has yet written. . . . . Mr. Falconer I never liked so well as in his 'Night and Morn,' which has had a good run at Drury Lane."

The same year, at the same theatre, he produced 'The O'Flahertys,' a farce, in which he acted the principal character. The following year (1865), Wednesday, May 3, at Drury Lane, was performed for the first time his drama of 'Love's Ordeal,' in which he played the part of *Maximilian Robespierre*. On Saturday, November 25 of the same year, he produced at Drury Lane an adaptation of Mr. Lever's 'Charles O'Malley,' under the title 'Galway Go Bragh ; or, Love, Fun, and Fighting,' and acted in the play the part of *Mickey Free*. In 1866 Mr. Falconer opened Her Majesty's Theatre for a brief dramatic season, and on Saturday, November 19, produced there a new drama written by himself, entitled 'Oonagh ; or, the Lovers of Lisnamona,' in which he played *Fardorougha O'Donovan*. The play was a failure, and the theatre was closed on December 1 following. Mr. Falconer afterwards went to New York, where he produced the same play, with others of his authorship. In 1868 he had returned to England, and in December, at the Haymarket, produced a new comedy, entitled 'A Wife Well Won,' in which Mr. Sothern played the leading *rôle*. After that date Mr. Falconer only produced two plays of importance, viz. 'Innisfallen ; or, the Men in the Gap,' first performed at the Lyceum Theatre, Saturday, July 17, 1870 ; and 'Eileen Oge ; or, Dark's the Hour Before Dawn,' performed for the first time at the Princess's Theatre, June 29, 1871. Mr. Falconer's later career was not altogether so successful as his earlier. He, however, appeared at intervals on the London stage after the withdrawal of the last-mentioned drama, but not in any original part of importance.

FECHTER, CHARLES ALBERT, born in London in 1822 ; died at Richland Centre, near Quakertown, Pa., in the United States of America, August 5, 1879. Mr. Fechter was of mixed parentage —his father being a German, and his mother an Englishwoman. At a very early age his parents removed to France, and there he was brought up and educated. He made his *début* on the stage at the Salle Molière in Paris in 'Le Mari de la Veuve,' and afterwards joined a travelling company on a tour through Italy. Previously to his appearing on the English stage he had been for some time the leading actor of the Porte St. Martin Theatre, Paris. He made his professional *début* as an English actor in London—having already appeared some years before in French Plays at the St. James's Theatre—on Saturday, October 27, 1860, at the Princess's Theatre, in the principal *rôle* in Falconer's version of Victor Hugo's drama 'Ruy Blas.' "As to the manner in which Mr. Fechter would speak English, the mind of the audience was soon at ease," wrote the *Times* (October 29, 1860). "His accent and his gesticulations are entirely of France, but his articulation is perfectly clear, and there is that music in his voice which would sound equally well through the medium of any language. *Ruy's* narrative of his sufferings and his love, and the small delicate touches by which he indicated his uneasiness under a master's control, carried him well through the first act, and though the great scenes of the piece were yet to come, it was easy to foresee that the manner of their execution would be in every way satisfactory. The second act (comprising two acts of the French piece) was an immense advance on the first. Nothing could be finer of its kind than *Ruy's* declaration of love to the Queen, so exquisitely was the fire of passion tempered by the feeling of respectful devotion, and with such eloquence of words and actions were the words poured forth. There are not many actors who succeed even in ordinary love scenes, and few indeed could effect an exhibition of the idolatrous form of passion which inspired so many poets of the chivalric ages, and which is typified in *Ruy Blas*, though he nominally belongs to an unromantic period. But it was in the last act that the triumph of the actor reached its culminating point—the act in which the valet appears as the defender of the Queen against the machinations of his villainous master. The concentration of passionate rage with which he accosted his oppressor, the obvious feeling that he was throwing from his soul a burden that had long crushed it to the dust, elicited that continued succession of plaudits which is only heard when an audience is excited in the highest degree. From the moment when *Ruy* snatches the sword from his master's side (an action which of itself produced an electrical effect) to the fall of the curtain, when the valet dies happy in the conviction that he is loved not under false colours, but with the livery actually present to the mind of his royal mistress, Mr. Fechter had the audience completely in his grasp, and could do with them as he pleased. The shouts which invited him to the front of the curtain were the certain indications of an unequivocal and brilliant success."

The following year (1861), in January, at the Princess's Theatre, he appeared as the twin brothers *Louis* and *Fabian dei Franchi* in 'The Corsican Brothers,' of which (at the Théâtre Historique in Paris) he was the original representative; and on Monday, February 11, Mr. Fechter played the character of *Don Cæsar de Bazan* at the same theatre in the drama of the same name. "When this piece, adapted from the French, was first brought out in 1844 at the Haymarket, under the title of 'A Match for a King,' with Mr. Charles Mathews as the hero, it at once achieved great popularity, and versions were forthwith produced at nearly all the London theatres. Every actor of importance within whose range of parts such a character was comprised seemed to consider it a duty to himself and his admirers to add Don Cæsar to his *réper-toire;* and moreover everyone was successful in it, because, although requiring very great talent to embody it to perfection, a moderate amount of stage knowledge and practice was enough to secure an effective, if not a satisfactory personation. Next to M. Frédéric Lemaître himself, the creator of the part, who frequently played it in London, at the St. James's, the most effective representation was that of Mr. Wallack, at the Princess's Theatre. Mr. Fechter's reading differs greatly from both those of Mr. Wallack and M. Lemaître. To characterize the three briefly, M. Lemaître's may be called the humorous, Mr. Wallack's the melodramatic, and Mr. Fechter's the chivalric version. The situation in which Don Cæsar encounters the King was treated by Mr. Fechter in a manner quite different to that of either of his predecessors above-named. When the King has announced himself to be Don Cæsar de Bazan, and the latter in reply declares himself to be 'Philip, King of Spain,' M. Lemaître did so in a careless tone, as if not deeply impressed with the humour of the situation, and Mr. Wallack threw himself into a chair, and assuming a regal attitude and tone, declared himself to be the King; but Mr. Fechter seems to view his assumption of the King's name as almost a logical result from the King's assumption of his, and subsequently, with mock gravity, puts on a regal deportment for a short time only. This was, perhaps, the most natural of the three modes of treatment, if less effective than Mr. Wallack's, and less consistent with the ruined Don Cæsar of M. Lemaître. In the concluding scene Mr. Fechter rose to the highest point of stage demeanour and of theatrical expression. His earnestness, his manly and graceful deportment, the spirit with which he reproved the King without abating the respect due to the monarch, bringing him down to his own level without detracting from his dignity, could scarcely be surpassed. Not a point throughout the character was missed, yet no effect was unduly thrust forward into notice ; every gesture and look and tone was allowed to bear its own force with the audience, and its significance was left to their appreciation, the whole evidently the result of great artistic perception, and of powers completely under control, the great art, after all, of concealing art predominating." (*Standard,* February 18, 1861.)

In March 1861 Mr. Fechter appeared for the first time in England as *Hamlet.* His interpretation of the character excited great attention, and the performance was in every sense a remarkable success. " Mr. Fechter does not act ; he is *Hamlet,*" wrote the *Athenæum* (March 23, 1861). " The soliloquy was finely delivered without declamation, but with the most passionate feeling. In the scene with the Ghost there was none of the conventional routine. . . . What we principally remarked in the first act was the intense and unmistakable sorrow that is displayed, which exceeded every demonstration of the kind that we had ever witnessed in the character. It showed itself in every tone of the voice as well as in the general gesture, and created a deep sympathy in the audience. . . . We never heard the soliloquy on death better spoken—and of the soliloquies in general we may remark that they were in the finest taste, and extorted the admiration of the most judicious. The plaudits were frequent and prolonged."

The *Times* (March 22, 1861) was no less laudatory in its remarks :—" Mr. Fechter's performance of *Hamlet* should unquestionably be seen by everyone who takes an interest in the higher departments of histrionic art. At all events it is a theatrical curiosity. A Parisian artist, unrivalled in his own line, which is not that of French classical tragedy, essays the most arduous of Shakespearian characters. With the conventions of our stage, with the 'points' which, to us, seem almost as needful to the play as the words of the text, he has had nothing to do. He goes straight from the book to the boards, and, though possibly he has received a few hints as to the general conduct of the business, there is every reason to believe that all his details are entirely the result of his own thought. His very entrance makes a completely novel impression. After the fashion of the German stage, he indicates *Hamlet's* Scandinavian nationality by a profusion of flaxen hair, and carries to perfection an assumption of that dreamy, unpractical look which is scarcely to be associated with a dark complexion. There is no doubt that to him the meditative element in *Hamlet's* nature has seemed most essential. The manner in which he throws out his answers, like one unwillingly awakened from a continued abstraction, into which he presently relapses, is admirably truthful, and the pretence of madness little changes this manner, beyond the addition of a light tone of irony. Through the predominance given to the meditative element the soliloquies acquire a very remarkable character. He has elaborated these at a vast expense of thought, and his delivery is marked by the subtlest variations. But the novelty of his rendering consists in the peculiarity that the stronger passions intrench as little as possible upon his solitude, and that he is chiefly occupied with a play of the intellect. The birth of his thoughts is more visible than the influence of his emotions. The gentleman-like side of *Hamlet* stands also high in the considerations of Mr. Fechter. Throughout the whole tragedy he is the very perfection of courtesy, and this quality is especially shown in his scenes with the players. . . . Indeed, all the 'genteel comedy' which belongs to *Hamlet* is admirably sustained ; and though we can never forget that the part is played by a Frenchman, the Frenchman seems perfectly at home in his new atmosphere, and, indeed, has been qualified for it by the polished comedy of his own stage. In those scenes, on the other hand, in which passion cannot be resolved into meditation, but must speak out loud and strong, the fact that *Hamlet* is played by a foreigner is less advantageously apparent. It is not that he lacks passion, or is deficient in purpose, but that physical force, which we find in the words of Shakespeare, when wielded by a native seems to be beyond the reach of an alien ; and while we admire his general conception it is impossible not to feel that passages to which we have been habituated to attach great importance slip away comparatively unobserved. The merits and deficiencies of Mr. Fechter cannot be better illustrated than by the fact that the 'play scene' and the 'closet scene' are those with which he produces the least effect, whereas in the second act he makes a most powerful impression. We have already said that such a performance is worth seeing as a curiosity. It is also estimable from a higher point of view. The pains which Mr. Fechter has taken to master the diction of Shakespeare and fully to understand every line set down for him are laudable in the highest degree, and the slips which he makes are so rare that they may simply be regarded as monuments of creditable toil. The finish of his performance is not the less real because it has the nature of French polish, and because many of his gestures are unlike those to which we have been accustomed on our own stage. Probably 'Shakespeare' never had been, or will be, played so well by a foreign artist as Mr. Fechter has played 'Hamlet,' and it would be wholly incorrect to measure him by an English standard."

On Wednesday, October 23, 1861, at the same theatre, he appeared in the character of *Othello*, for the first time in England. Mr. Fechter's conception of *Othello* is severely criticised by Mr. G. H. Lewes in 'Actors and the Art of Acting' (a collection of magazine articles), and also by Prof. Henry Morley in his *Journal of a London Playgoer*.

The *Saturday Review* (November 2, 1861) thus discussed the performance :—" M. Fechter is a most logical actor. With all his determination to be original and unfettered, he does not deviate from the prescribed path without warrant from the text, or, at any rate, without full conviction that there is nothing in the text that can be opposed to his innovations. But is not his logic a little at fault in his broad theory respecting tradition? While he denies the authority of every actor of Othello down to this year of grace, 1861, he lays down a rule for the future Othellos far more stringent than any which is based upon ancient precedent. The old path was, at all events, but vaguely defined, whereas we have now a routine from which it is impossible to stray one inch without violating a pointed law. . . . Perhaps we should say that something like an application of imperial logic is to be found in this seeming inconsistency. The Frenchman has overthrown all the traditions of the Bourbons—*ergo* he is free. The artist who ignores the pre-cedent of Kembles and Keans is free likewise. As for the Napoleons and Fechters, they are, of course, symbols of perfect liberty. . . . That M. Fechter's *Othello* will prove more attractive to public curiosity than his *Hamlet* is likely enough. The bait offered is much more tempting on the present than on the former occasion, the whole business of the play being completely remodelled, and the novelty of some of the readings being striking enough to pro-voke general discussion. . . . With regard to his own personation, we should say that, in M. Fechter's view, *Othello* is more affec-tionate than impassioned, and more logical than either. Far from being naturally suspicious, he does not grow uneasy till he has ample ground for annoyance, and, consistently with this belief, that he would not turn mad-jealous for a trifle, the character of the courtesan Bianca, commonly omitted, is restored. Such an *Othello* as M. Fechter conceives would require the evidence of Desdemona's guilt, conveyed by the overheard words of Bianca, before he could be nerved to crime. . . . The growth of distress is portrayed with all the minuteness of which M. Fechter is so great a master ; though we think he is most to be admired in his passages of tenderness, which are charmingly rendered, and not without a tinge of old French gallantry. In some of his innovations, we should say M. Fechter is impelled less by the force of conviction than by the love of novelty for its own sake. . . . As for the alteration of the catastrophe, which consists in making *Othello* drag Iago to the bedside of Desdemona, that he may do homage to her corpse, and leads the ignorant to suspect that the villain, not the Moor, will die like the turbaned Turk at Aleppo, it cannot in any way be justified. There is not one word in the text to indicate that *Othello*, in his last despair, was actuated by the strange wish of making the virtual murderer kneel before the victim, and surely if the poet had conceived such a wish he would have allowed it to have some influence on the dialogue. . . . However, apart from all questions of detail, this much is certain, that a performance like that of *Othello* at the Princess's is of infinite use to theatrical art. An intelligent innovator like M. Fechter gives people something to talk about. The volume of Shakespeare is taken down from the library shelf, and whenever the majority agree or disagree with the new interpreter, the work of the great poet becomes a subject of serious consideration."

In 1863 Mr. Fechter entered upon the management of the Lyceum Theatre, and on Saturday, January 10, "opened" with 'The Duke's Motto' (altered from 'Le Bossu' of Paul Féval, by John Brougham), and played the part of *Henri de Lagardère*. The piece was eminently successful. Said the *Daily Telegraph* (January 12, 1863): "The acting of this drama is very forcible throughout. Mr. Fechter finds in its hero a character that not merely brings out all his known ability, but which has the advantage of placing him also in a new and striking light. For the gay and graceful bearing of the young captain of cavalry, who so well reflects the adventurous and daring spirit of his time, of course we were prepared; but his assumption of the *Hunchback*, with his bent shape, his crippled gait, and his furtive and sardonic glances, was a contrast that came upon us with as much enjoyment as surprise. Still more striking was the dash of humour that he threw into the impersonation of the deformed, and which gave him at times a grotesque jollity that was almost diabolical. That character will be numbered among Mr. Fechter's best successes. We need not dwell on his acting of the *Captain*, whose leading features so well contrasts, in the buoyant spirit displayed throughout his adventures, and the generous ardour with which he responds to the love confession of Blanche. Mr. Fechter was received with great enthusiasm on his first entrance, and was loudly called for at the close of every act as well as at the termination of the drama."

On Saturday, October 31, 1863, at the same theatre, he performed the character of *Angelo,* first performance of ' Bel Demonio ' (John Brougham). In 1864, on Saturday, May 21, he " revived " ' Hamlet ' at the Lyceum with great success ; and the same year, on Saturday, October 22, first performance of ' The King's Butterfly,' he played *Fanfan.* On January 21, 1865, still at the Lyceum, Mr. Fechter produced a version of M. Frédéric Lemaître's ' L'Auberge des Adrets,' under the title of ' The Roadside Inn,' and acted in it the part of *Robert Macaire.* The same year, Monday, April 17, he played *Belphegor,* in Mr. Charles Webb's translation of the French drama originally adopted by Mr. Charles Dillon. (*See* DILLON, CHARLES.) Mr. Fechter's son acted with him in the play. Mr. Fechter's representation of the character was pronounced to be " a masterly piece of acting, replete with a variety of phases, and manifesting much profound feeling."

During 1865 Mr. Fechter produced two plays by Mr. Palgrave Simpson, viz. on Monday, November 6, ' The Watch Cry,' adapted from the French drama ' Lazare le Pâtre ' ; and on December 22 a new version of an old subject, under the title of ' The Master of Ravenswood.' In both Mr. Fechter sustained the leading *rôle :* in the first the part of *Leone Salviati;* in the second that of *Edgar of Ravenswood.* During 1866 Mr. Fechter again " revived " ' Hamlet ' at the Lyceum with success ; and in May of the same year he " revived " ' The Corsican Brothers.' His impersonation was marked by superior refinement and the direct action of an intelligence that had conceived for itself the characters that it supported, independent of imitation ; an affirmation not to be made of any other representative of the parts. The *Daily News* (May 22, 1866), discussing the merits of Mr. Fechter's acting as the twin brothers, said : " One of the greatest ' sensations ' of 1851, a year fruitful in novelties and excitement, was the production of a romantic drama at the Princess's Theatre, entitled ' The Corsican Brothers.' This drama, adapted from the French of Alexandre Dumas by Mr. Boucicault, was most effectively put upon the stage, and Mr. Charles Kean's double assumption of Louis and Fabian dei Franchi, and Mr. Alfred Wigan's Chateau Renaud, were, unquestionably, the great theatrical successes of that season. The drama was often performed at the same theatre during Mr. Kean's long lesseeship, and when Mr. Fechter was engaged by Mr. Harris at the same house in 1862 it formed one of the few French melodramas that relieved his Shakespearian impersonations. Mr. Fechter was naturally anxious to appear before an English audience in the two characters—Fabian and Louis—which he had originally represented at the Théâtre Historique in Paris, when the drama was first produced about 1846, and he had a pardonable preference for an English version which followed the original more closely than Mr. Boucicault's. When Mr. Vining took the Princess's he revived ' The Corsican Brothers ' in 1864, and played the two brothers himself in the old Princess's version, his Chateau Renaud being Mr. Walter Lacy. Last night Mr. Fechter revived the play at the Lyceum, still keeping to the French version, excluding the famous sliding-trap, and making very little use of that popular ghost melody which we believe was composed for the drama by Mr. Stoepel. . . . The strength of Mr. Fechter's performance of the two Corsicans is shown most in the third and fourth acts; the third act in which he is the gay and superstitious young hunter, and the fourth act in which he seeks revenge for his brother's death with concentrated earnestness."

In January 1867 'Rouge et Noir,' by Henry Leslie, was performed for the first time at the Lyceum, Mr. Fechter sustaining in the play the character of *Maurice D'Arbel*. In the following September, on Monday the 16th, he performed *Claude Melnotte* in 'The Lady of Lyons,' at the same theatre. In November he withdrew from the management of the Lyceum Theatre; and the next month (Thursday, December 26, 1867) appeared at the Adelphi, first performance of Messrs. Charles Dickens and Wilkie Collins's play No Thoroughfare,' in the part of *Obenreizer*. "In the fourth act the excitement of the play culminates. The first scene is laid in the room in the Swiss inn, where *Obenreizer* tries to drug his victim and secure his papers; the second, perhaps the finest bit of realistic scenery which the skilled hand of Mr. Grieve has ever placed upon the stage, is the mountain pass where *Obenreizer* taunts Vendale with his approaching doom, until the latter, to foil his would-be robber, springs over the precipice. This scene was acted with the greatest spirit by Mr. Fechter and Mr. Neville; and the manner in which the leap was taken by the last-named gentleman was highly artistic and effective. . . . The weight of the piece lies mainly on the shoulders of Mr. Fechter, who, for the first time since his sojourn in England, has been fitted with a part in which his foreign accent is in his favour. He played throughout with the greatest earnestness and skill, and while the softer passages of his love-making were as graceful and tender as ever, he gave due emphasis to the darker side of the character." (*Daily Telegraph*, December 27, 1867.) It may be mentioned that a French version of this play, entitled 'L'Abîme,' was produced in 1868 in Paris; in this Mr. Fechter sustained the same character. Saturday, October 17, 1868, at the Adelphi, he played *Edmond Dantes*, in a dramatic version of 'Monte Christo,' then first performed. In 1869 (March), at the Adelphi, he appeared as the *Count de Layrac*, in a piece written by himself in collaboration with Mr. Wilkie Collins, entitled 'Black and White.' On Monday, November 29 of the same year, he commenced a series of twelve farewell performances at the Princess's Theatre, previous to his departure for the United States, which took place shortly afterwards. He remained in America until 1872, in which year, on Saturday, March 2, he reappeared on the London stage at the Adelphi, in 'Ruy Blas'; and subsequently, Monday, June 2, at the Princess's, as *Hamlet*. From 1872 until his death in August 1879 Mr. Fechter resided in America.

KEMBLE, ADELAIDE (Mrs. SARTORIS), born *cir.* 1816–17; died August 4, 1879. Daughter of the late Mr. Charles Kemble, and niece of Mrs. Siddons. She was educated principally with a view of entering the musical profession as a public singer, and without any preconceived intention of appearing on the stage. She sang at the York Musical Festival in 1834, having previously made a *début* at a concert in London. Neither of these earliest public appearances seem to have been altogether successful. Subsequently Miss Adelaide Kemble went to the Continent to pursue her education under competent instructors in France, Germany, and Italy, and first appeared on the operatic stage at the Fenice, Venice, with satisfactory success. She also sang in opera at various Italian cities, notably Trieste, Padua, and Milan (at La Scala), and in 1841 returned to London with a considerable reputation. The *Athenæum* (July 3, 1841) thus wrote of her prospects at this period of her career :—" If we mistake not she (Miss Kemble) will one day occupy a place never before occupied by English *cantatrice*. Her voice is a soprano of sufficient extent, reaching to, and resting upon, the C sharp above the line with the firmness and certainty of Grisi in her best days. Neither power nor flexibility are wanting, and the capacity of passionate expression which we found in it three years ago has since then been thoroughly developed. In short, it is a voice for a large stage, and the highest order of parts."

Miss Kemble made her first appearance on the English stage November 2, 1841, at the Theatre Royal, Covent Garden, under the management of Madame Vestris and Mr. Charles Mathews, in the title *rôle* in Planché's revised English version of Bellini's opera 'Norma.' " The audience that was collected last night to witness the *début* of Miss Adelaide Kemble was one of those crowded assemblages that are seldom collected but on the most special occasions. . . . Her reception was magnificent ; the inert black mass in the pit burst into a waving sea of hands and handkerchiefs, one welcoming sound was uttered by hundreds of voices, and her entrance was rather that of the chief person in a triumph than of a yet untried vocalist about to undergo the ordeal of public opinion. . . . Miss Kemble seemed for a moment overcome by the excess of applause, and rested on the altar before the sacred oak. . . . In ' Casta Diva ' she at once took her position as a *prima donna*, which she sustained all the evening, and which places her beyond comparison with any singers on the English stage that have been heard for many years. The cultivation of her voice, the command she has acquired over it, the power of subduing it, are Italian ; in her very tones there is a sound of Italy. . . . There are times when her high notes are of the most exquisite quality. . . . She takes her position as an artiste trained in the highest school, and in that school she stands alone. Her acting is to be praised with far more qualification than her singing. It is in fact little more than a clever imitation of Grisi." (*Times*, November 3, 1841.) A contemporary journal, the *Morning Chronicle* (November 3, 1841), wrote of her as follows :—" Highly as we estimate Miss Kemble's qualities as a singer, we estimate her powers as an actress still higher. She is a Kemble worthy of the name. . . . Miss Kemble's impersonation of *Norma* is the finest we have ever seen. With the force and grandeur of Grisi it combines a delicacy and tenderness which Grisi cannot reach. In depicting 'the fury of a woman scorned' Grisi cannot be surpassed ; but in the scene where the wretched *Norma* hangs over the bed of her sleeping infants, Miss Kemble's tenderness was something of which Grisi did not even give an idea."

So great, indeed, was the triumph of Adelaide Kemble that the opera of 'Norma' had the unprecedented run of nearly forty nights.* It was repeated three times a week from the first week of November 1841 to the second week of February 1842. On January 15, 1842 ('Norma' being still retained on the bills of Covent Garden Theatre), Adelaide Kemble appeared in a tragic opera of Mercadante, entitled 'Elena Uberti.' The work itself was unsuccessful. At the same theatre, on March 15, 1842, she sustained the part of *Susanna* in 'The Marriage of Figaro,' then for the first time completely rendered in English, in a manner that set at rest all cavil as to the soundness of her musical attainments. The performance from first to last was a great success. April 2, 1842, she appeared, also at the same theatre, as *Amina* in ' La Sonnambula.' During the same season (1842) Adelaide Kemble appeared in two other operas, viz. 'Semiramide' and ' Il Matrimonio Segreto,' and finally retired from the stage December 1842. The season had not been a financial success ; but Miss Adelaide Kemble lent her aid towards making it so by offering to be " the last paid, or to play for nothing," rather than deprive the company of the only chance of keeping together till Christmas. The burst of feeling with which, it is said, the green-room resounded when this generous action was communicated to the performers, must have been worth all the plaudits that greeted Miss Kemble before the curtain—intensely gratifying and emphatic as these had invariably been. She married, early in 1843, Mr. Edward John Sartoris, some time M.P. for Caermarthenshire. Within the limited period during which Miss Adelaide Kemble appeared at the Theatre Royal, Covent Garden (latterly under her father, Charles Kemble's management), she successfully performed the characters of *Norma, Elena Uberti, Susanna, Amina, Semiramide,* and *Carolina,* in the operas already mentioned. Before her appearance, with the one exception of 'Artaxerxes,' no recitative opera had ever succeeded

---

* " Miss Kemble's performance of the heroine was admitted on all hands to be worthy of ranking with the greatest of the many triumphs achieved by her gifted family in other branches of the dramatic profession."— *Recollections, &c.,* of J. R. Planché, vol. ii., p. 53.

" In the theatre which had been the scene of the Kemble-and-Siddons triumphs the *furore* she created was unbounded. The aristocracy and fashion of the metropolis filled the private boxes nightly, and the public vied with each other for seats in the general boxes and body of the house. It is a pleasure to say she fully merited the enthusiasm she excited. . . . She was a thorough artist, with a fine voice under admirable control, and with perfect purity of intonation. Add to this, that she possessed considerable dramatic power as well as sang with great *abandon* and natural passion."—*Dramatic Reminiscences* of G. Vandenhoff (London Ed.), p. 51.

on the English stage. Adelaide Kemble was the first to accustom English playgoers, not merely to admit and enjoy the expression of passion in music, but to require of the artist impassioned acting as well as musical feeling. Judged even by the exceptional standard of Pasta, Malibran, Schrœder, and Grisi, Adelaide Kemble was able to maintain her own high place on the operatic stage, whether as a singer or an actress ; but measured against her English predecessors she stood alone and supreme, as the one union of high dramatic and musical power that the annals of the English stage of her day can record. Mrs. Sartoris, who had continued the practice of her marvellous gift in private until the time of her death, achieved a very decided success in literature by her story of " A Week in a French Country House," which appeared anonymously in the ' Cornhill Magazine,' and was published separately in 1867. The style of this little novel was singularly bright and accomplished, the humour original, and the characters sharply drawn. The fact that certain persons very well known in the world of art were understood to have sat unconsciously to Mrs. Sartoris for their portraits gave a further popularity to an exceedingly clever and genial book. She published ' Medusa and other Tales ' in 1868.

MATHEWS, CHARLES JAMES, born at Liverpool, December 26, 1803 ; died in Manchester, June 24, 1878. Only son of the well-known comedian, Charles Mathews. He was for a short period of his boyhood on the foundation of Merchant Taylors' School, but subsequently became a pupil of Dr. Richardson, of Clapham Road, who seems to have enjoyed somewhat of a specialty in educating the sons of distinguished actors. On quitting school in 1819 he entered the office of Mr. Pugin, the eminent architectural draughtsman, to whom Charles James Mathews was articled for four years. He pursued his professional studies for a short time with considerable perseverance in England and Italy, and in 1832 was elected to the office of District Surveyor of Bow and Bethnal Green (London). Charles Mathews had from time to time performed with success as an amateur at fashionable assemblies, and had written various dramatic pieces previous to his adopting the stage as a profession. In May 1832 he produced ' The Wolf and the Lamb,' a farce ; in July of the same year ' The Court Jester,' a clever trifle adapted from the French ; in the following year, July 1833, ' My Wife's Mother,' and shortly afterwards ' Pyramus and Thisbe,' described in a contemporary journal as " a light and slight, but bright and tight little trifle—good for a thirty minutes' laugh to as many as may choose to draw upon it to that amount." Each of the foregoing pieces was first performed at the Haymarket Theatre. In 1834-5 Mr. Mathews turned his attention to painting for a while, and was successful in procuring admission for an example of his skill in this direction at the annual exhibition at Somerset House. In September 1835 he entered for a brief period upon the joint management with Mr. Yates of the Adelphi Theatre, which was opened on the 28th of that month, with the following bill :—"' Mandrin,' a grand Romantic, Melodramatic,

Burletta Spectacle ; ' The Christening,' a favourite one-act farce ; and a domestic burletta, 'The London Carrier.'" The first and third were novelties, with Buckstone, Mr. and Mrs. Keeley, and Mr. O. Smith in the cast. This theatrical venture was unsuccessful, and Mr. Mathews retired for a time from managerial responsibility. On the 7th December, 1835, he made his *début* on the stage proper at the Olympic Theatre, London. " The principal theatrical feature of the week has been the first appearance of Mr. Charles Mathews on the stage. To say that he is the son of the late excellent comedian, and inimitable imitator of man and manners, is merely to say what everybody knows ; but it is necessary that we should allude to the circumstance in order that we may express the pleasure it gave us to witness the cordiality with which he was cheered on. His first essay was most appropriately preceded by an introductory address by Mr. Liston, the friend and fellow-labourer of his father. Mr. Charles Mathews acted in two pieces, one written by himself, and called ' The Humpbacked Lover,' the other by Mr. Leman Rede, called 'The Old and New Stager.' . . . This theatre may be proud of having introduced to the stage one who brings the education and manners and habits of a gentleman to back an evident fondness for his profession." (*Athenæum*, December 12, 1835.)

In 1836 Charles Mathews had joined Madame Vestris in the management of the Olympic, and the two were playing nightly to crowded houses. We find the former giving a Neapolitan Reminiscence by dancing the *Tarantella*, "with an elegance, a force and correctness sufficient to bring the ballet company from the Académie Royale over in a body to see and to envy him." In October 1836 Charles Mathews produced ' He would be an Actor,' a piece which he had adapted from the French. In 1837 the earliest of the late John Oxenford's dramatic successes, 'The Rape of the Lock,' was first performed at the Olympic, with Charles Mathews in a leading part. The same year, ' The Truth,' written by himself, was performed ; and in the following January (1838), 'The Black Domino,' of which he was also author (very successful). In July 1838 Charles Mathews married Madame Vestris, and shortly afterwards sailed for the United States. In May 1839 the Vestris-Mathews management of the Olympic terminated. In September 1839 the two, conjointly, entered upon the lesseeship and management of the Theatre Royal, Covent Garden, and on Monday, September 30, produced for the opening, ' Love's Labour Lost.' Madame Vestris played *Rosalind;* Mr. Keeley, *Custard;* Mrs. Nesbitt, *The Princess of France*, &c. The same week Charles Mathews played the part of *Charles Surface* in ' The School for Scandal.' In November 1839 the first performance of Sheridan Knowles's play of ' Love ' took place, respecting which the author wrote, " Mr. and Mrs. Charles Mathews have granted me the highest terms I ever yet received for a play." In February 1840 the management produced Leigh Hunt's first dramatic venture, under the title of ' A Legend of Florence,' the success of which was unequivocal. April and May 1840 Charles Mathews took a personal part in the various Shakespearian revivals at Covent Garden Theatre, playing *Master Slender*, &c. In September 1840 the management produced there another of Sheridan Knowles's plays, entitled 'John of Procida ; or, the Bridals of Messina,' and the following season (Tuesday, February 9, 1841), Douglas Jerrold's 'White Milliner,' in which Charles Mathews was the original *Lord Ortolan*. Thursday, March 4, 1841, 'London Assurance' (*see* BOUCICAULT, DION) was played for the first time—Charles Mathews as *Dazzle*, the elder Farren as *Sir Harcourt Courtly*, Mrs. Nesbitt as *Lady Gay Spanker*, Madame Vestris as *Grace Harkaway*. Notwithstanding the adverse criticisms of the Press, the piece was a great success, being kept on the bills till May 1841. On September 28, 1841, Mark Lemon's 'What Will the World Say?' was first performed, and early in the following month Sheridan Knowles's comedy 'Old Maids,' but neither was successful. In February 1842 Boucicault's comedy 'The Irish Heiress' was first performed, and on the 25th of that month Douglas Jerrold's comedy 'Bubbles of the Day' was produced, but in the following April the Vestris and Mathews management of the Covent Garden Theatre terminated, having proved a financial failure. The new dramas placed on the stage had been few, and with the exception of 'London Assurance,' not particularly striking. They, however, had been represented with a degree of taste, splendour, and finish in the *mise en scène* that gave to the Vestris-Mathews management of old Covent Garden Theatre an importance second to none in the annals of the British stage.

As an illustration of the strength which was deemed necessary at a leading London theatre thirty-seven years ago, the following list of the company of the Theatre Royal, Covent Garden under the above management (1841–2) may be found of interest:—

Acting and Stage Manager.
GEORGE BARTLEY.

Light Comedy and Eccentrics.
CHARLES MATHEWS. F. VINING.
WALTER LACY.

Leading Business.
GEO. VANDENHOFF.
JOHN COOPER.

Old Men.
WM. FARREN. F. MATTHEWS.
C. W. GRANBY.

Low Comedy.
J. P. HARLEY. D. MEADOWS.

Irish Characters.
JOHN BROUGHAM.

Heavy Business.
C. DIDDEAR. J. BLAND.

Walking Gentlemen.
C. SELBY. A. WIGAN. H. BLAND.

Pantomime and General Business.
PAYNE. HONNER. T. RIDGWAY.
MORELLI. J. RIDGWAY.

Ladies.
Mrs. NESBITT. Mrs. SELBY.
Madame VESTRIS. Mrs. H. BLAND.
Mrs. GLOVER. Miss LEA.
Mrs. W. LACY. Mrs. W. WEST.
Mrs. BROUGHAM. Mrs. J. C. JONES.
Miss COOPER.

Columbines.
Miss FAIRBROTHER.
The Misses KENDAL.

In addition to the foregoing, there was a company, which included Miss Adelaide Kemble, engaged for English Opera.

In October 1842 Charles Mathews joined Mr. Macready's company at Drury Lane Theatre, and first appeared on the boards there October 7 of that year, in a lively, bustling piece, ' The Follies of a Night' (Planché), and as *Fag* in ' The Rivals.' Afterwards, at the same theatre, he played *Goldfinch* in Holcroft's ' Road to Ruin,' and *Roderigo* in Shakespeare's ' Othello.' Monday, November 14, 1842, he made his first appearance at the Haymarket Theatre as *Charles Surface* in ' The School for Scandal.' The same year Mr. Mathews played *Witwould* in Congreve's ' Way of the World,' and at Christmas appeared in a fairy extravaganza called ' Riquet with the Tuft.' The season 1843-4 he performed *Puff* (' The Critic '), concerning which the *Athenæum*, April 1843, made note that " ' The Critic ' promises to be a standing dish at the Haymarket feast of fun, the condiments with which *Mr. Puff* seasons, *à discrétion*, the *sauce piquante* of Sheridan's wit being very much to the taste of the audience." In February 1844 ' Used Up ' was first performed at the Haymarket—*Sir Charles Coldstream*, Mr. Charles Mathews. November 18, 1844, he was the original *Littleton Coke*, first performance at the same theatre of Boucicault's comedy ' Old Heads and Young Hearts.' March 1845, at the Haymarket, he enacted the part of *Chorus* in a burlesque, suggested by the then revival of ' Antigone,' called ' The Golden Fleece,' a parody of the ' Medea of Euripides.' Saturday, April 26, 1845, he was the original *Felix Goldthumb*, first performance of Douglas Jerrold's comedy ' Time Works Wonders,' at the Haymarket.

Monday, October 18, 1847, Charles Mathews entered upon the lesseeship and management of the Lyceum Theatre in conjunction with Madame Vestris ; Messrs. Buckstone, Leigh Murray, and Roxby being of the company. The season commenced with two translated pieces, ' The Pride of the Market' (' Le Bouquetière ') and ' Light Dragoons' (' Les Mousquetaires '). Tuesday, December 7, 1847, Charles Mathews took part in the Shakespearian performances at Covent Garden Theatre arranged for providing funds for the purchase of Shakespeare's house at Stratford-on-Avon. He played *Slender* (' Merry Wives of Windsor,' act iii, sc. 3 and 4; and act iv., sc. 2). The Vestris-Mathews management of the Lyceum Theatre continued until 1855, a period of nearly eight years. It may be affirmed that Madame Vestris was the first in England to pay due attention to the *mise en scène* and other accessories of a play. Mr. Charles Mathews fully acted up to the wisdom of his wife in this respect. So successful did the Mathews' management of the Lyceum Theatre proceed on this plan, that it was seldom found necessary there to change the programme for weeks together, and sometimes not for the entire season. The pieces selected for representation were generally of the drawing-room kind, and interspersed with the vaudeville productions of the French stage. However slight in texture or in subject were the examples of the former, they were always remarkable for a careful and pointed literary manipulation. The acting was, of its kind, always first-rate ; the performers being selected with the utmost judgment, and attached to the theatre from year to year. Mr. Mathews's tenure of the joint management of the Lyceum was, however, not without its difficulties and financial troubles (1853 and 1854); and in March 1855 he announced his secession from the theatre, and "from all management at once and for ever." As a pecuniary speculation it had not been profitable. Almost immediately following his retirement from the Lyceum he entered upon the more successful and profitable career of a theatrical "star" in the line of light comedy, a career which he pursued with indomitable energy till within a few days of his death. That career began with his appearance, in the spring of 1855, at the City of London Theatre. Wednesday, October 10, 1855, he appeared at Drury Lane as *Mopus*, in a three-act play 'Married for Money,' a modification of Poole's comedy 'The Wealthy Widow.' In the following month, at the same theatre, he sustained two parts, which have since been closely identified with his name—*Puff* and *Sir Fretful Plagiary* in 'The Critic,' "distinguishing each with such peculiar characteristics, that the identity of the performer is traced with difficulty" (*Athenæum*, November 10, 1855).

At the close of the week ending August 9, 1856, Madame Vestris (Mrs. Charles Mathews) died, aged 59. In 1857 Charles Mathews once more left England for America, where he married his second wife, Mrs. Davenport, a lady of considerable ability and experience as an actress. Monday, October 11, 1858, Mr. and Mrs. Charles Mathews made their first appearance after their marriage at the Haymarket, in a revival of 'London Assurance'—Charles Mathews as *Dazzle;* Mrs. Charles Mathews as *Lady Gay Spanker.* For the three following seasons they remained attached to the Haymarket company, playing in the various comedies and stage revivals produced under the direction of Mr. J. B. Buckstone. In 1862 Charles Mathews quitted the stage for a time, and commenced a series of 'At Home' entertainments at the Bijou Theatre (Her Majesty's) in the Haymarket. In October of that year these terminated, and he afterwards transferred them to the provinces. In 1863 Charles Mathews appeared at the Théâtre des Variétés, Paris, in the principal characters of a French version, executed by himself, of 'Cool as a Cucumber,' entitled 'L'Anglais Timide.' This was so far a success that he was induced to repeat his visit two years later, when a French version of 'Used Up,' under the title of 'L'Homme Blasé,' was played by him for fifty nights at the Vaudeville. In the interval between 1865 and 1870 he fulfilled various "starring" engagements; and in the latter year started on a tour round the world with Mrs. Mathews, which was completed in 1872. From 1872 to 1875 he remained in England, performing at intervals in London and the provinces. In September 1875 he produced a new two-act comedy at the Gaiety Theatre, London, entitled 'My Awful Dad,' in which, as *Adonis Evergreen*, he secured his usual success. In November 1875 Charles Mathews again set forth on a foreign tour, this time for India. He appeared with great *éclat* at Calcutta, during the visit of the Prince of Wales to that city, it being reported that on the occasion of a "special performance" by Charles Mathews ("by desire of His Royal Highness"), the house realized the unprecedented sum of 2000*l.*

A list, furnished by himself, shows that Mr. Charles Mathews wrote, or adapted from the French for the stage, forty-three pieces—one piece in eight acts, one in five acts, six in three acts, thirteen in two acts, and twenty-two in one act. He, besides, "created" the chief parts in one play of nine acts, one of eight acts, in ten of five acts, twenty-six of three acts, in forty-five of two acts, and in seventy-eight of one act; in all, one hundred and sixty-one parts. His most successful dramatic productions were 'Black Domino,' 'The Milliner to the King,' 'Bachelor of Arts,' 'Court Jester,' 'My Wife's Mother,' 'Serve Him Right,' 'Little Toddlekins,' 'Patter *versus* Clatter,' and 'My Awful Dad.' His most successful impersonations were *Puff* and *Sir Fretful Plagiary, Charles Surface, Mr. Affable Hawk, Sir Charles Coldstream, Dazzle, Twiggleton, Adonis Evergreen,* and his parts in 'Cool as a Cucumber,' 'Woodcock's Little Game,' 'Patter *versus* Clatter,' and 'If I'd a Thousand a Year.' His clever version of Foote's comedy 'The Liar' (produced at the Olympic in 1867) had a very successful run, and furnished proof of his practical skill as a dramatist. In polite comedy Mr. Charles Mathews was one of the most popular and successful actors of the century.

PARRY, JOHN, born in London, 1810; died at East Moulsey, Surrey, February 20, 1879. Only son of John Parry, for many years honorary treasurer of the Royal Society of Musicians, editor of the "Welsh Melodies," and composer of numerous songs, ballads, and dramatic pieces. The *Era* (February 23, 1879) gives the following particulars of his early career :—"As a vocalist he made his *début* May 7, 1830, at the Hanover Square Rooms, on the occasion of Mr. F. Cramer's concert, when he sang Handel's 'Arm, arm, ye brave,' with great success. His voice was then a baritone of fine and rich, though not powerful, quality. Having received lessons from Sir George Smart in sacred and classical music, Mr. John Parry was in great request at the Ancient and Philharmonic Concerts, and also at musical festivals in town and country. For him the Chevalier Neukomm composed 'Napoleon's Midnight Review,' and several other songs, but his forte was simple ballads. In 1833 Mr. John Parry visited Italy, and received instructions from the great Lablache at Naples, where he resided some time. Here he became a great favourite with De Beriot, Madame Malibran, and a number of distinguished personages, who attended a special concert which he gave at Posilippo, in a beautiful theatre belonging to the celebrated Barbaja, who granted him the use of it. The first part of the concert consisted of vocal *morceaux,* sung by Lablache and most of the principal singers belonging to the San Carlos ; and the second part comprised a burlesque on 'Othello,' Lablache sustaining the part of Brabantio, Calvarola—the Liston of Naples—the Moor, and John Parry, Desdemona, dressed *à la* Madame Vestris, and introducing in one of the most pathetic scenes

the then popular song of 'Cherry Ripe,' an effect which gave rise
to uproarious merriment. This burlesque burletta was repeated at
the San Carlos for the benefit of Sanvarola, and went off with
renewed success. At this time, to comply with Malibran's frolicsome request, John Parry gave at an evening party an imitation of
Lablache, Rubino, and lastly, of Malibran herself, in a mock Italian
trio, and this created such an excitement that he was asked to
repeat it in the presence of the King and Queen, who were, like the
rest, immensely delighted by this notable display of musical mimicry.
One evening, when a large party had assembled at a nobleman's
mansion, where a concert was to take place, a fellow stood in front
of the house grinding away at a hurdy-gurdy. This annoyed the
company very much, and Malibran said, 'We'll have a hurdy-gurdy
of our own.' Accordingly, she requested John Parry, Lablache,
and others to sustain notes forming a kind of drone on the common
chord, at the same time to pinch their noses, while she herself gave
a capital imitation of the sonorous tones of that mellifluous instrument. The itinerant outside, believing that he had no chance of
competing with his more powerful rival within the mansion, shifted
his position, and the more harmonious portion of the concert was
resumed. In July 1836 Mr. John Parry gave his first benefit
concert at the Hanover Square Rooms, when he engaged Malibran,
whose terms were twenty guineas, to sing for him. This she did,
and at her own request gave in addition Mazzinghi's lively duet,
'When a little farm we keep,' which had been often sung by her
and John Parry at Naples. The two sang it on this occasion, and
it was, of course, repeatedly encored. When John Parry called
upon her next morning with the twenty-pound note in payment for
her services, Malibran took it, and then seizing him by the hand
and returning it, exclaimed in her own energetic way, 'Take that
as my mite for you to commence life with. I have passed many
happy hours and merry moments with you in Naples. Prosperity
attend you. God bless you, John Parry.' After visiting Rome,
Florence, Milan, and Paris, John Parry returned to England in
1834, after an absence of fourteen months, during which time he
had made himself a perfect master of the Italian language. In
1835 his marriage took place with an accomplished lady, the
daughter of an eminent physician. Persuaded to try the stage, he
offered his services to his father's old friend, John Braham, who
had then just built and opened the St. James's Theatre." He made
his *début* on the London stage September 29, 1836, at that theatre.
In December of the same year he appeared there in a piece by
Poole, entitled 'Delicate Attentions,' and in an operatic burletta,
'The Village Coquettes,' announced in a contemporary journal as
"the second production of the gentleman who writes under the
name of 'Boz.'" The music of the piece was by John Hullah, and
the parts in it were sustained by Messrs. Harley (as *Martin Stokes*),
Braham (as *Squire Norton*), Bennett (as *George Edmunds*), and
Mr. John Parry ; Mesdames Smith, Rainsforth (as *Lucy Benson*),
and others. Four songs in 'The Village Coquettes' subsequently
became popular :—'The child and the old man sat alone'; 'Love

is not a feeling to pass away'; 'Autumn Leaves'; and 'There's a charm in Spring.' The book of the words was published by Mr. Bentley, and dedicated to J. Pritt Harley in the following terms :— " My dramatic bantlings are no sooner born than you father them. You have made my 'Strange Gentleman'* exclusively your own ; you have adopted Martin Stokes with equal readiness." " Boz " proceeds to excuse himself for appearing before the public as the composer of an operatic burletta, in the following words:—" ' Either the Honourable Gentleman is in the right or he is not' is a phrase in very common use within the walls of Parliament. This drama may have a plot or it may not ; and the songs may be poetry or they may not ; and the whole affair from beginning to end may be great nonsense or it may not ; just as the honourable gentleman or lady who reads it may happen to think. So, retaining his own private and particular opinion upon the subject (an opinion which he formed upwards of a year ago, when he wrote the piece), the author leaves every gentleman or lady to form his or hers, as he or she may think proper, without saying one word to influence or conciliate them. All he wishes to say is this—that he hopes Mr. Braham, and all the performers who assisted in the representa- tion of this opera, will accept his warmest thanks for the interest they evinced in it from its very first rehearsal, and for their zealous efforts in his behalf—efforts which have crowned it with a degree of success far exceeding his most sanguine anticipations, and of which no form of words could speak his acknowledgment. It is needless to add that the *libretto* of an opera must be to a certain extent a mere vehicle for the music ; and that it is scarcely fair or reasonable to judge it by those strict rules of criticism which would be justly applicable to a five-act tragedy or a finished comedy."

Subsequent to his engagement at St. James's Theatre, Mr. John Parry was for a brief season at the Olympic. In 1842 he had for- saken the stage for the concert-room, and was singing in pieces written expressly for him by the late Albert Smith, having as supporters Madame Anna Thillon and Herr Staudigl, well-known artists of their day. In 1850 Mr. Parry originated an entertain- ment in London under the designation, " Mr. John Parry's Notes," thus spoken of in a contemporary journal :—" There is mirth in the words, wit in the music, and a versatility of power and accomplish- ment put forth in the execution of both, which will raise Mr. Parry's reputation even with those with whom it has already stood the highest. He talks, he sings in half-a-score of different voices and styles ; he plays the pianoforte more boldly and brilliantly than ever. . . . . He changes his dress with the rapidity of sorcery ; and, we repeat, entertains his company better than anyone single-handed since Mathews." Mr. Parry continued his entertainment in London with very great success until 1853, when he advertised his intention of bidding farewell to public exhibition, being compelled to retire

---

* The first dramatic production of the late Mr. Charles Dickens, per- formed at St. James's Theatre, September 29, 1836, Mr. Pritt Harley in the title *rôle*. John Parry and Madame Sala (the distinguished vocalist, and mother of Mr. George Augustus Sala) appeared in the pieces.

owing to ill-health. Following upon this announcement these comments appeared in the *Athenæum* of August 13, 1853 :—" By his departure music and merriment sustain no ordinary loss ; since (as the *Athenæum* has again and again pointed out) there was something besides, and far beyond the ordinary buffoon, in Mr. John Parry's performances—a spirit of quaint humour told in, and aided by, music, nothing short of artistic, the like of which we have never met save perhaps in the comicalities of that eccentric genius, M. Vevier. It should be recorded that John Parry's drolleries have been as delightful to the most scientific and most fastidious of musicians as to the general audiences that flocked to listen to the 'Accomplished Young Lady' and Fair Rosamond, or to assist at the wondrous amateur singing and pianoforte playing so shrewdly and mirthfully reproduced in his later entertainments. Mr. John Parry's whimsies were started, if we mistake not, under the aid and by the abetting of Madame Malibran at Naples ; but we have seen Mendelssohn sit to listen by the hour with the eager face of an enjoying child, and we have heard Chopin laugh till he was almost 'ready to die' (so frail in his case was the machine) at the travesties, parodies, imitations, and *amphigouris** of the racy humorist. If, indeed, Mr. John Parry must cease his performances, we trust that, in some form or other, we may still profit by a genius which is as delicate as it is genial." Mr. Parry's retirement was only temporary. He returned to London after a period of rest, and in conjunction with Mr. and Mrs. German Reed gave his admirable performances for many years at the Gallery of Illustration, Regent Street. In a leading article published in the *Daily News*, July 20, 1878, Mr. John Parry's power of entertaining is thus alluded to : " The comic singer of our modern music halls is at his best lamentably and offensively bad. The talent, however, of Mr. John Parry was of a different order to that which belongs to the so-called ' Comics,' distinguished in their advertisements by such epithets as ' Great' and ' Jolly.' Nor had Mr. John Parry anything of the ' Lion comic' about him. His humour was of the quiet, suggestive, subtle kind. He could invent, and himself impersonate, characters which became accepted as types. ' Impersonate' is, perhaps, not the word ; for Mr. Parry contented himself with indicating peculiarities, and never for any length of time sustained a part. Those who have not had the advantage or disadvantage of seeing him (for he was in his prime many years ago) will get a better notion of his genius by remembering that he was the originator of the style which has found able followers in Mr. Corney Grain, Mr. Arthur Cecil, and Mr. George Grossmith. The comic song, as treated by Mr. John Parry, ceased to be musical buffoonery, and became a comedy scene with musical illustrations. It seems, moreover, to be an understood thing that the ' entertainer' of the school founded by

---

* " A term popular in Paris at the beginning of the century. An *amphigouri* is not a ' medley,' as we understand the term, so much as a macaronic compound of music and words—of the sublime and the ridiculous—of the antique classical modes and the nonsense of the minute." —*Athenæum*, August 13, 1853, p. 971.

John Parry shall invent his own entertainment, which is usually a mixture of prose and verse; that he shall compose his own music, play his own accompaniments, and, as a matter of course, sing his own songs, Now that Mr. Arthur Cecil has abandoned the entertainment, specially so called, for the drama, and that Mr. George Grossmith has, in some measure, followed his example, the only artist who can be looked upon as a worthy continuer of the John Parry tradition is Mr. Corney Grain. Excellent as this gentleman's performances are, those of Mr. John Parry were still more admirable, if only from the fact that Mr. John Parry invented, not merely his own entertainments, but the whole style of which each of these entertainments was an example."

PAUL, MRS. HOWARD (*née* ISABELLA FEATHERSTONE), born at Dartford, Kent, 1833; died in London, June 6, 1879. She was well known in London as an actress and singer of great promise five-and-twenty years ago. It was remarked of her (*Athenæum*, April 25, 1868) that she sacrificed for second-rate objects an amount of natural vocal endowment rarely combined (at least in this country) with such genius for the stage as she possessed, which might have made her the Malibran of England, and as such an artist of European renown. One of Miss Featherstone's most important parts was *Captain Macheath* in 'The Beggar's Opera,' which she played at the Strand Theatre in 1853. She also appeared at the Haymarket Theatre in this character with great success, Monday, October 24, 1854. The same year Mr. and Mrs. Howard Paul first appeared together in a dialogue play which attained a considerable degree of success in the provinces. It was entitled 'Locked Out,' and was from the pen of Mr. Howard Paul. Later, in 1858, husband and wife appeared in an "entertainment" entitled 'Patchwork,' described in a contemporary journal as "a clatter of fun, frolic, song, and impersonation carried on by performers of unfailing dash." For some years Mr. and Mrs. Howard Paul conducted this entertainment in London and elsewhere with well-merited support from the public. Mrs. Howard Paul returned to the stage in 1869, and in February of that year appeared at Drury Lane, doubling the parts of *Lady Macbeth* and *Hecate*, with Mr. Phelps and Mr. Charles Dillon acting on alternate nights the leading *rôle*. She afterwards performed in other plays on the London and provincial stage, her last appearance being at the Opéra Comique as *Lady Sangazure* in 'The Sorcerer,' comic opera by Arthur Sullivan, produced November 17, 1877.

PHELPS, SAMUEL, born at Devonport, in 1804; died in London, November 6, 1878. He was apprenticed to a printer in early life; but relinquished the printing trade for the dramatic profession, which he entered in 1828, making his first appearance at York. Mr. Phelps made his professional *début* on the London stage at the Haymarket Theatre, under Mr. Benjamin Webster's management, August 28, 1837, as *Shylock* in 'The Merchant of Venice.' "His representation of the character was correct and judicious, but

not remarkable or striking. . . . Kean threw something of sub-
limity into the character of Shylock ; we felt as if an incarnate fiend
stood before us. Such an effect as this Mr. Phelps had no power
to produce. . . . He performed the trial scene very ably and gave
great effect to several passages. . . . Upon the whole, Mr. Phelps'
performance of this part is entitled to considerable praise, and
shows him to be a valuable acquisition to the London stage. He
was extremely well received." (*Morning Chronicle,* August 29,
1837.) From 1837 to 1839 Mr. Samuel Phelps was one of the
leading actors at Covent Garden Theatre, under Mr. Macready's
management, appearing in most of the original pieces first produced there under that distinguished tragedian's auspices. (*See*
FAUCIT, HELEN.) In August 1839, at the Haymarket, Mr. Phelps
played *Iago* ('Othello'), with Mr. Macready, Mr. Power, Mr.
Benjamin Webster, Mrs. Warner, and Miss Helen Faucit in the
cast. During 1840 and 1841 Mr. Phelps was engaged at the Haymarket, and occasionally at Drury Lane Theatre (sometimes with
Mr. Charles Kean), playing in the poetic drama such parts as
Darnley in ' Mary Stuart' (January 1840) ; *Gabor* in 'Werner'
(October 1840); *Macduff,* &c. In January 1842 he took part in
the performances inaugurating Mr. Macready's management of
Drury Lane, playing *Antonio* (' Merchant of Venice ') ; *Lord Nor-
land* in Mrs. Inchbald's comedy ' Every One Has His Faults'; and,
subsequently, the same month, *Stukeley* in ' The Gamester.' Later
in the year (July), he appeared at the Haymarket Theatre in the
character of *Sir Giles Overreach,* the elder Farren playing *Marall;*
and at Drury Lane as *Faulkland* ('The Rivals') ; *Old Dornton*
(' The Road to Ruin ') ; and *Iago,*—" the best we have seen since Mr.
Young," remarked the *Athenæum* (October 22, 1842) ; " his rugged
looks and plainness of speech became the assumed blunt honesty of
the knave extremely well, and his chuckling levity, though at times too
obvious, was in keeping with the character ; still it was not perfectly
satisfactory, wanting the higher attributes of the ideal character."

The same year (December 10), at the same theatre, he sustained
the part of the *Earl of Lynterne,* first performance of Westland
Marston's ' Patrician's Daughter.' This was one of the most careful
impersonations in that unsuccessful but clever play. During 1843
Mr. Phelps played the following original parts, viz. *Lord Tresham*
in Browning's poetic melodrama ' A Blot on the Scutcheon '; *Lord
Byerdale* in Sheridan Knowles's play ' The Secretary '; *Dunstan*
in Smith's tragedy of ' Athelwold '; and (at Covent Garden Theatre)
Gaston de Foix, in Boucicault's drama ' Woman.'

In 1844, the " New Theatres Regulation Act " * having come into
operation, placing all theatres upon an equal footing of security and
respectability, leaving no difference, except in the object and conduct
of the managements, Mr. Samuel Phelps, in conjunction with Mrs.
Warner, entered upon the lesseeship of Sadler's Wells Theatre,

* Mr. Phelps was the first London manager to take advantage of this
Act, by which all theatres were enabled to do what the so-called patent
theatres had been privileged to attempt, namely, the performance of the
five-act poetic drama.

then dilapidated and almost forgotten. He re-established the house, and, in time, promoted it to a position second to no other theatre in London. It became the home of the Shakespearian drama. It was opened under its new *régime*, Monday, May 27, 1844, with the representation of ' Macbeth.' " Mr. Phelps we have never before seen in *Macbeth*, and it was certainly the ablest performance in which he has yet exhibited. Since Edmund Kean's we have seen nothing better for vigour and vivid effect. It is essentially distinct from, and stands in contrast with Mr. Macready's, which, however fine and classical in its conception, is but too obviously open to the Scotch sneer of presenting ' a very respectable gentleman in considerable difficulties,' so studied is it in all its parts and subdued into commonplace by too much artifice. . . . The straightforward and right earnest energy of Mr. Phelps' acting, on the contrary, made all present contemplate the business as one of seriousness and reality, while the occasional pathos of his declamation thrilled the heart within many a rude bosom with delight. The spectators were visibly agitated and incapable of resisting the impulse." (*Athenæum*, June 1, 1844.) The experiment was a success. Sadler's Wells Theatre was now crowded night after night, not merely by the denizens of suburban Clerkenwell and of the neighbouring Islington, but by visitors from the remote and more aristocratic quarters of western London. Mr. Phelps's principal characters, before he entered upon theatrical management, had been *Macbeth, Shylock, Othello, The Stranger, Mr. Oakley, Werner, Sir Peter Teazle*, and last, not least, *Virginius.* The Werner and Virginius Macready had hitherto completely appropriated to himself; but Mr. Phelps showed that these characters had now found a second competent representative, albeit not attached to the theatres royal. The foregoing characters, and many more to be enumerated, Mr. Phelps introduced for the first time to an audience at Sadler's Wells Theatre. On Monday, July 29, 1844, he appeared there, for the first time, as *Hamlet;* and in the following October he produced ' King John,' with a degree of spectacular effect not exceeded by Mr. Macready's doings at Drury Lane.

Mr. Phelps soon established a reputation which placed him in the front rank of his profession. " He is not only a modest and intelligent man," remarked a contemporary journal, " but a skilful and able performer—an actor of intense passion. In the more pathetic passages of a part, comic as well as tragic, he gives a tone of reality to the action that commonly transports the audience into the precise spirit of the scene." In 1845 (March) he performed *Richard III.* for the first time ; and, on the 16th of June of the same year, *Richelieu* (of this play Mr. Phelps was the original *Joseph : see* FAUCIT, HELEN). In regard to the way in which it was put on the stage, the whole of the costumes, scenery, and accessories were appropriate, and the performers carefully studied and well-drilled throughout. On the 27th August, 1845, he produced ' The Fatal Dowry ' of Massinger ; and, in November, ' King Lear.' It was said of Mr. Phelps's performance of *Lear* that it might be easily excelled in royal dignity and in physical vigour ; but as a pathetic piece of acting it was unrivalled. " Mr. Phelps never forgets the father—never seeks to surprise, but contents himself with exciting pity for the wrongs that the outraged parent suffers, and the natural relations that are insulted in his person. It is much to the actor's credit that he sacrificed his professional ambition to the proprieties of the scene. Having restored the curse to its original place in the drama, Mr. Phelps was judiciously careful not to give it undue effect by being too vehement. He chastened and toned it down to the proper emphasis required by its rightful position. Was it on that account less effective with the audience? Not a whit." (*Athenæum*, November 8, 1845.) The same year he placed ' The Winter's Tale' on the stage at Sadler's Wells. Saturday, July 25, 1846, having vastly improved the theatre in the recess externally and internally, he opened the season with ' Henry IV.,' himself playing the part of *Falstaff*. " Mr. Phelps, whose particular *forte* is the pathetic, and who can represent some man of solid worth stricken down by adverse circumstances, as well as anyone on the stage, selects the character of *Sir John Falstaff*. Seek not for an unctuous reading of the part in Mr. Phelps, for his very *physique* denies it ; but do not fail to recognize the hearty enjoyment of the humour in the manager's delineation. He does not look very fat or talk very fatly, but there is much fun of a peculiar order about, and as he is usually alive to the pathetic natural, so does he enter into the fun natural likewise. His lecture to the prince, in the character of the king (is not this lecture often omitted in the acting version?), was amusingly pompous, and his soliloquy on honour, with the modulations of the word ' No,' capitally delivered. It was not the least entertaining part of the exhibition to watch how the audience took the part of *Falstaff*. They welcomed him not with the frigid acknowledgment of those who are merely curious to see how a new actor interprets a character, but they hailed the character itself. It was the comic part of the evening, and the pleasantries, the rhodomontades and dilemmas of ' plump Jack' created the sort of laughter which, in Westminster, pertains to a new broad farce." (*Times*, July 29, 1846.)

In the following year (1847), Wednesday, January 13, Mr. Phelps produced, at Sadler's Wells, Beaumont and Fletcher's play of ' A King and No King,' with that diligent care and those appropriate appointments of scene and costume which made famous the little theatre under his management. The interest excited by the announcement of the play was immense. The house was crowded. The best judges of the drama were present. The performance was a complete success. The "revival" was heralded as the most important step which had yet been taken in the serious task of restoring the poetic drama to the English stage. Mr. Phelps acted the character of *Arbaces*, Mr. Marston that of Tigranes, Mr. Bennet Bessus, Miss Laura Addison Panthea, and Miss Cooper Spaconia. On Wednesday, June 2, 1847, Mr. Phelps closed the season with Lovell's ' Provost of Bruges.' The following, his fourth season, he " opened " with ' Cymbeline,' playing *Posthumus*. Tuesday, December 7, 1847, Mr. Phelps took part in the performances at Covent Garden Theatre in behalf of a fund for the purchase of Shakespeare's house at Stratford-on-Avon. He played *Prospero,* in a selection from 'The Tempest' (act 1, sc. 2). January 1848, at Sadler's Wells, he "revived" 'Twelfth Night,' sustaining the character of *Malvolio,* which the *Athenæum* (January 29, 1848) mentioned as a part by which Mr. Phelps will be remembered. "The making-up is so complete that the actor's person cannot be identified until he speaks. The execution of the part is equally complete; elaborately finished—thoroughly carried out to the minutest particular." During the season 1849-50 he placed on the stage 'The Honest Man's Fortune,' remodelled from Beaumont and Fletcher by Mr. Horne (author of 'Gregory VII.'), Mr. Phelps playing *Lord Montague,* 'the honest man'; and, on Monday, October 22, 1849, 'Antony and Cleopatra,' on a scale of expense and effect exceeding all the former efforts of the management. Mr. Phelps acted *Marc Antony,* Miss Glyn *Cleopatra.* (*See* GLYN, ISABEL.) In 1851, on the occasion of Mr. Macready's farewell of the stage at Drury Lane Theatre, Mr. Phelps played *Macduff* to the great actor's *Macbeth.* Saturday, December 6, 1851, at Sadler's Wells, Mr. Phelps played, with remarkable success, the part of *Sir Pertinax Macsycophant* in 'The Man of the World.' In 1852 he revived 'All's Well That Ends Well,' and gave the character of *Parolles,* one of his most important and interesting impersonations. In 1853, Saturday, October 8, he produced the 'Midsummer Night's Dream,' and played *Bottom.* "Every reader of Shakespeare is disposed to regard the 'Midsummer Night's Dream' as the most essentially unactable of all his plays. It is a dramatic poem of the utmost grace and delicacy; its characters are creatures of the poet's fancy, that no flesh and blood can properly present—fairies that 'creep into acorn cups,' or mortals that are but dim abstractions, persons of a dream. . . . In some measure we have found reason to modify our opinion on these matters since we have seen the 'Midsummer Night's Dream' as produced by Mr. Phelps. . . . Mr. Phelps has never for a minute lost sight of the main idea which governs the whole play, and this is the great secret of his success in the presentation of it. He knew that he was to present merely shadows; that spectators, as Puck reminds them in the epilogue, are to think they have slumbered on their seats, and that what appeared before them have been visions. Everything has been subdued as far as possible at Sadler's Wells to this ruling idea. The scenery is very beautiful, but wholly free from the meretricious glitter now in favour. . . . Nor should we fail to remark upon the very perfect taste shown in the establishment of a harmony between the scenery and the poem. . . .

"It remains for us only to speak of the success of Mr. Phelps as *Bottom,* which he presented from the first with remarkable subtlety and spirit, as a man seen in a dream. In his first scene, before we know what his conception is, or in what spirit he means the whole play to be received, we are puzzled by it. We miss the humour, and we get a strange, elaborate, and uncouth dream-figure, a clown restless with vanity, marked by a score of little movements, and speaking ponderously with the uncouth gesticulation of an unreal thing, a grotesque nightmare character. But that, we find, is precisely what the actor had intended to present, and we soon perceive that he was right. Throughout the fairy scenes there is a mist thrown over *Bottom* by the actor's art. The violent gesticulations become stillness, and the hands are fixed on the breast. They are busy with the unperceived business of managing the movements of the ass's head, but it is not for that reason they are so perfectly still. The change of manner is a part of the conception. The dream-figure is dreaming, there is dream within dream; *Bottom* is quiet, his humour becomes more unctuous, but *Bottom* is translated. He accepts all that happens quietly as dreamers do; and the ass's head we also accept quietly, for we too are in the middle of our dream, and it does not create surprise. Not a touch of comedy was missed in this capital piece of acting, yet *Bottom* was completely incorporated with the 'Midsummer Night's Dream,' made an essential part of it, as unsubstantial, as airy and refined, as all the rest. Quite masterly was the delivery by Mr. Phelps of the speech of *Bottom* on awakening. He was still a man subdued, but subdued by the sudden plunge into a state of unfathomable wonder. His dream clings about him, he cannot sever the real from the unreal, and still we are made to feel that his reality itself is but a fiction. The pre-occupation continues to be manifest during his next scene with the players, and his parting, ' No more words ; away ; go away,' was in the tone of a man who had lived with spirits and was not yet perfectly returned into the flesh. Nor did the refinement of this conception, if we except the first scene, abate a jot of the laughter that the character of *Bottom* was intended to excite. The mock play at the end was intensely ludicrous in the presentment, yet nowhere farcical. It was the dream. *Bottom* as *Pyramus* was more perfectly a dream-figure than ever. The contrast between the shadowy actor and his part, between *Bottom* and *Pyramus*, was marked intensely ; and the result was as quaint a phantom as could easily be figured by real flesh. We have said a good deal of this revival, for it is very doubtful whether the 'Midsummer Night's Dream' has ever yet, since it was first written, been put upon the stage with so nice an interpretation of its meaning. It has pleased us beyond measure to think that an entertainment so refined can draw such a throng of playgoers as we saw last Saturday sitting before it, silent and reverent, at Sadler's Wells." (*Examiner*, October 15, 1853.) *

In 1854, Saturday, October 14, Mr. Phelps produced ' Pericles, Prince of Tyre,' the most laborious and the most ambitious of the " revivals " for which his management had now become famous. The following year he dealt with ' The Comedy of Errors,' which was received with remarkable favour ; and, in 1856, ' The Merry Wives of Windsor ' was performed, concerning which, and his representation of *Sir John Falstaff*, the following criticism

---

* Compare *Journal of a London Playgoer*, pp. 69-72, Professor Henry Morley.

appeared :—"We have been sometimes tempted to think that if Mr. Phelps had early taken to comedy, and particularly to what are technically termed character-parts, he would have accomplished a more profitable reputation than that he now enjoys as a tragedian. Mr. Phelps's successes in such characters as *Mr. Justice Shallow*, *Bottom*, the weaver, *Sir John Falstaff*, and *Sir Pertinax Mac-sycophant*, are all manifestly the result of consummate art, bearing the marks of elaborate study as they do. They may be thought deficient in the points of spontaneity and mellowness, and are subject to the green-room charge of 'hardness'; but the thorough-going earnestness with which the delineation is made complete, even to the minutest details, must be accepted as a compensation." (*Athenæum*, October 11, 1856.) The same year, on Saturday, November 15, he placed 'The Taming of the Shrew,' with the Induction, upon the stage, and acted in it the part of *Christopher Sly*. This play numbered the twenty-ninth of the Shakespearian dramas introduced by Mr. Phelps to the audiences of Sadler's Wells during the twelve years he had now held the theatre. "An excellent type of low, dogged, habitual inebriety is presented by Mr. Phelps in his impersonation of *Christopher Sly*, the comic hero of the 'Induction' to 'The Taming of the Shrew.' The play, revived at Sadler's Wells on Saturday, has not been acted in its entirety, save at the Haymarket in 1844, within the memory of many generations—although 'Katherine and Petruchio,' as Garrick's abridgment is called, has always been a favourite after-piece. From the effect of the representation at Sadler's Wells we may gather the inference that our immediate ancestors were not such mere blockheads in theatrical affairs as rigid Elizabethans would have us suppose. The story in which Katherine and Pe-truchio are the principal figures shakes the audience with laughter; and the 'Induction,' with the tinker of Mr. Phelps, is a choice little bit of low comedy; but the dull tangled tale of Bianca and her sisters is scarcely worth the trouble of reviving, lacking as it does all the practical fun and ingenuity which belong to 'The Comedy of Errors,' while it is marked by the same puppet-like treatment of the personages that belong to that primitive work." (*Spectator*, November 22, 1856.)

In October 1859 Mr. Tom Taylor's play 'The Fool's Revenge' was brought out by Mr. Phelps, who sustained the part of *Bertuccio the Jester*, which became afterwards one of his favourite and most popular impersonations. Saturday, September 8, 1860, he com-menced his first season of sole management of the theatre with the performance of 'As You Like It,' himself playing *Jaques*. In 1861 he appeared for a brief season at the Princess's in *King Lear*, *Hamlet*, and other parts; and, on Saturday, September 21, at his own theatre, performed, for the first time, *Louis XI*. in a version of Casimir Delavigne's play of that name. "From the first entrance to the fall of the curtain the assumption of character was complete; perhaps at times a little too much care was apparent; such a determination to give full force to certain passages resulted in a weakening of the general effect, in a want of concentration, and, if the word may be here used, of lubricity—faults which, as they are the very opposite of slovenliness, a few evenings' practice will no doubt remove. The dying scene, so horrible in its exhibition of physical suffering in conjunction with the highest degree of moral depravity, was most truthfully portrayed, not only in feebleness of manner, but in an expression of face that was almost terrible in its weakness and suffering, and in that unmistakable look of exhaustion which it would seem next to impossible to counterfeit. Mr. Phelps's performance of *Louis XI.* cannot fail to be looked upon as one of the most remarkable of his numerous successful personations; and as another proof of his conscientious devotion to his art, at a time when finished acting is certainly not the rule upon the stage." (*Standard*, September 23, 1861.)

In 1862 (October) Mr. Phelps commenced a series of farewell performances at Sadler's Wells, by way of taking a formal leave of his Islington patrons. He appeared in the first of the series as the *Cardinal* in 'Richelieu.' Thursday, November 6, 1862, his farewell benefit took place. The play was 'Julius Cæsar'; Mr. Phelps acting *Brutus*, Mr. Creswick Cassius, Mr. Edmund Phelps Marc Antony. Mr. Samuel Phelps had conducted Sadler's Wells Theatre for a period of eighteen years, during which time he had placed no less than thirty-four of Shakespeare's plays before the public. For some years Sadler's Wells maintained itself exclusively by the performances of the Shakespearian drama, and it would have been in vain to have gone elsewhere for such plays as 'Antony and Cleopatra,' 'Timon of Athens,' 'Pericles,' and 'Love's Labour Lost.' On its humble stage these, with many other of the poet's plays, were conscientiously enacted, and among them all those which were afterwards produced as spectacles by Mr. Charles Kean at the Princess's. Subsequent to the year of his retiring from the management of Sadler's Wells Theatre Mr. Phelps appeared in a few new characters of importance. Saturday, October 10, 1863, 'Manfred' was revived at Drury Lane, after a slumber of thirty years, and he played in it the title *rôle*. "His performance of the character was chiefly remarkable for his careful enunciation of the text; the harmony of the numbers and the distribution of the emphasis evidently claiming the first place in his attention. To variety of action and the transitions from thought to passion and from passion to description with which the dialogue abounds he was less attentive; indeed nearly ignoring their necessity. The best acting scenes were the second in the first act and the fourth of the second." (*Athenæum*, October 17, 1863.) Mr. Phelps's last original part of any note was that of *Trapbois* in 'King o' Scots,' performed at Drury Lane in October 1868. He appeared at London theatres at intervals after that date in some of his favourite and best known characters.

ROUSBY, CLARA MARION JESSIE, born at Parkhurst, Isle of Wight, 1852; died at Wiesbaden, April 19, 1879. Fourth daughter of the late Dr. Dowse, D.I.G.H. Army Medical Department. Married to Mr. Wybert Rousby, at the Catholic Church, Plymouth, in 1868. She made her first appearance on the London stage at the Queen's Theatre, Long Acre, December 20, 1869, as

Fiordelisa in Tom Taylor's drama 'The Fool's Revenge,' founded upon Victor Hugo's 'Le Roi s'Amuse.' Her *début* was noticed in the *Daily News* (December 22, 1869) as follows :—" Persons who take interest in theatrical events have for some time past looked forward with curiosity to the appearance in London of Mr. and Mrs. Rousby, two performers hitherto of provincial reputation, whose merits, discovered by a sort of accident in an obscure corner of the kingdom by a distinguished dramatist and man of letters, were by him generously proclaimed to the world a few months ago. The play chosen for the occasion of what is, we believe, virtually their first metropolitan appearance, was Mr. Tom Taylor's 'Fool's Revenge.' . . . A fresher and more genuine interest was awakened by Mrs. Rousby's performance of the part of *Fiordelisa*. A fine countenance, a lithe and graceful figure, and a voice capable both of soft utterances and of passionate declamation, are not the only, nor even the chief stage qualifications possessed by this lady, who, judging from her appearance on Monday, can hardly be said to have emerged from girlhood. Her style of acting is essentially refined. In proof of this let anyone note carefully her artless confession of interest in the young cavalier who plays at night under her balcony ; or her simple appeal to the old duenna to permit her to finger her lute with just ' one touch, to show him I am listening'; and let him compare this, in his memory, with the detestably artificial utterances, the offensive self-consciousness and transparent coquetry of the powdered and rouged young *ingénue* of the French stage. And yet that the gamut of this young actress's powers has a wider range than all this indicates must have been evident to anyone who heard her cry of terror at the approach of the libertine Duke, or witnessed her flushed and startled look as he came nearer to lay his hand upon her, or the shrinking and repugnance, mingled with something of the fascination with which the mind contemplates inevitable danger, manifest in her attitudes and gestures throughout this powerful scene."

In January 1870 Mrs. Rousby sustained the part of the *Princess Elizabeth* in a five-act historical play, in blank verse, by Mr. Tom Taylor, entitled ''Twixt Axe and Crown,' first performed at the Queen's Theatre, London. "The chief figure is the *Princess Elizabeth*, who through the entire course of the action is floating ''twixt axe and crown,' her enemies constantly seeking to crush her with a charge of high treason. The foibles proper to 'Queen Bess' in her later days are as yet undeveloped, and the Princess is shown as a being scarcely short of absolute perfection, who, far from encouraging the conspiracies formed for her sake, remains unshaken in loyalty to her sister. By the introduction of Courtenay, Earl of Devonshire, a romantic tinge is given to her character. The 'White Rose,' as he is called, is the type of the *preux chevalier*. On him the Princess bestows her heart without reserve, and when the death of her sister has raised her to the throne, the first intelligence she receives is that of his death in a foreign land. But the feelings of the woman are not allowed to predominate over the dignity of the Queen, and when shouts have announced the accession of *Elizabeth*, she is aroused from her grief, and determines that henceforth her country shall be her only love. This extremely ideal view of the Princess's character is, of course, open to all sorts of objections, but the consistency with which it is carried out cannot be too highly appreciated. Not only indeed is the author consistent with himself, but he has found an actress who completely realizes his lofty conception. This is Mrs. Rousby, who, not long ago, made her *début* in 'The Fool's Revenge,' and who now, as the *Princess Elizabeth*, gives a delineation of character in which the natural and the ideal are combined with a harmony to which it would be hard to find a parallel. That the features are those which might be supposed to belong to *Elizabeth* in her early days is a mere accident, but it is an accident that adds to the truthfulness of the performance. Mrs. Rousby, however, is an artist who has no need to rely on fortuities. Without rant or exaggeration she closely portrays all the varied emotions to which the royal maiden is subjected; and while by her melodious delivery she gives full value to the verse, she speaks in that thoroughly natural manner which, under like circumstances, is rarely to be found beyond the precincts of the Théâtre Français." (*Times*, January 27, 1870.)

Among other noteworthy plays in which Mrs. Rousby appeared on the London stage the following are entitled to special mention, viz. 'Joan of Arc' (Tom Taylor), first performed at the Queen's Theatre in April 1871, Mrs. Rousby sustaining the leading *rôle;* 'Griselda' (Miss Braddon), produced at the Princess's Theatre in November 1873, Mrs. Rousby in the title *rôle;* 'Mary Queen o' Scots' (W. G. Wills), first performed at the same theatre in February 1874, Mrs. Rousby in the title *rôle;* 'The Gascon; or, Love and Loyalty' (adapted by W. Muskerry from the French of M. Barrière), produced at the Olympic Theatre in February 1876, Mrs. Rousby playing the part of *Mary Stuart*. Mrs. Rousby also performed leading parts (of which the following will suffice as examples) in various revivals of the legitimate drama in London. In February 1871, at the Queen's Theatre, she acted *Rosalind* ('As You Like It'); in April 1873, at Drury Lane Theatre, she sustained the part of *Cordelia* ('King Lear'); in May 1876, in a revival of 'The Wife' (Sheridan Knowles) at the Olympic Theatre, she played *Mariana*. Mrs. Rousby appeared with much success at the principal theatres in the provinces in the various plays already enumerated. The *Daily News* (April 28, 1879) remarked of her that she was probably the most beautiful woman upon the stage in her time; and, perhaps, this should be accounted a misfortune, for her triumphs came by degrees to be dependent less on her art, and more and more upon her picturesque presence and fine expressive features. Her last appearances on the stage were associated with her brief and unfortunate management of the Queen's Theatre, Long Acre, in the summer of 1878.

WIGAN, ALFRED SIDNEY, born at Blackheath, Kent, March 24, 1818; died November 29, 1878. His education was classical, and his early training scholastic. For a time he was a tutor in a public school. He began his dramatic career as assistant-secretary to the Dramatic Authors' Society in 1834, and in the year following appeared on the stage at the Lyceum Theatre. It was not, however, till the year 1842 that Mr. A. Wigan excited special notice by his acting. On February 12 of that year, in the first performance of Dion Boucicault's play of ' The Irish Heiress,' at the Theatre Royal, Covent Garden, he sustained the part of the French valet in the piece, with much taste, and corresponding success. On September 10 of the same year, at the same theatre, he played the character of *Alcibiades Blague*—" captain of the ragged regiment of guides and relic vendors on the field "—on the occasion of the first performance of an after-piece of Douglas Jerrold's, entitled ' Gertrude's Cherries ; or, Waterloo in 1835.' " This character (*Alcibiades Blague*) was personated by Mr. A. Wigan with a closeness to the original, both in appearance and manner, evidently the result of observation and study ; the mixture of politesse and effrontery, of sentiment and scoundrelism, and the fine French accent of broken English, are traits that mark the race of *chevaliers d'industrie*. Frenchmen have been so grossly cari-catured on the English stage, that a true and finished portrait embodied from life, even to the bronze of the cheek, and the cut of the hair, is the more to be appreciated." (*Athenæum*, September 17, 1842.)

Mr. Wigan remained a member of the company of Covent Garden Theatre from 1842 to 1844, mostly engaged in playing English-French characters ; in the season 1843–4 he acted the part of *Lawyer Meddle* in a revival of ' London Assurance.' In the latter year he joined Mr. and Mrs. Keeley's company at the Lyceum Theatre, where he attracted attention by his peculiar aptitude for the delineation of foreign manners in such parts as *Pygmalion Bonnefoi* in ' A Model of a Wife ' ; *Chevalier du Guet* in ' Watch and Ward ' ; *Balthazar* in ' Taking Possession,' &c. On May 12, 1845, at the same theatre, in a burlesque piece by Messrs. Albert Smith and Tom Taylor, entitled ' Cinderella,' Mr. A. Wigan sus-tained the part of the *Prince*, as to which a contemporary journal remarked that the intellectual attraction of the performance rested with Mr. Wigan, who in the course of it indicated " some powers as an actor of which he is, perhaps, not generally suspected." At the same theatre, during 1845–6–7, Mr. Wigan produced various farces from his own pen—' Luck's All,' ' A Model of a Wife,' '£500 Reward,' &c., in which he also acted. In the latter year he accepted an engagement at the Haymarket Theatre, under Mr. Benjamin Webster's management, " opening" there Saturday, October 4, as *Sir Benjamin Backbite* in a revival of ' The School for Scandal.' During the time he was at the Haymarket he played the following among other important characters, viz. *Osborne*, first performance of Westland Marston's drama ' The Heart and the World ' (October 20, 1847), *Hector Mauléon*, first performance of ' The Roused Lion ' (November 15, 1847), *Dudley Smooth* in ' Money ' (revival), *Goldfinch* in ' The Road to Ruin ' (revival), and *Tattle* in

'Love for Love' (revival). On Wednesday, July 12, 1848, at the Olympic Theatre, in a musical drama entitled 'Monsieur Jacques,' he played the hero. His presentment of the character "was touching, true, characteristic, minutely finished in its specialities, and in its more general qualities appealing to those sources of sympathy which make the whole world kin." The same month he produced one of his own farces, 'Law for Ladies,' at the same theatre. The same and following year (1848-9) he acted with Mr. and Mrs. Charles Kean in Shakespearian and other revivals at the Haymarket Theatre, viz. *The Clown* in 'Twelfth Night,' *Bassanio* in 'The Merchant of Venice,' *Tom Purple* in Douglas Jerrold's play of 'The Housekeeper,' one of the *Witches* (in conjunction with Mr. Buckstone and Mr. Tilbury) in 'Macbeth.' In October 1849, at the Princess's Theatre, he acted *Dufard* in 'The First Night,' adapted from the French piece 'Le Père de la Débutante.' In a criticism of this performance the *Athenæum* (November 3, 1849) said :—" Mr. Wigan's personation has sufficient originality, refinement, and heartiness to challenge any version of this character, past, present, or to come. It is highly finished without finicality, instinct with feeling (as every humorous personation should be) without sickliness, conversational without meagreness or frivolity, and excellently droll without grimace. He gives us, in short, a character, not an actor ; and this performance, with all who think as we do of stage personation, will establish the claim of the artist who presents it to a place in the foremost rank of comedians."

In 1850 Mr. A. Wigan produced at the Olympic Theatre a farce from his pen, entitled 'A Dead Take-in.' The same year he became a member of the Princess's Theatre company, under the Kean-Keeley management, and "opened" there on Saturday, September 28, as *Tom Rawlings* in 'Platonic Attachments,' with Mr. and Mrs. Keeley in the cast. On the following Monday he appeared as *Osric* in 'Hamlet,' with Mr. Charles Kean as the Prince of Denmark. In February 1851 he acted the part of *Orlando* in 'As You Like It,' with remarkable success ; and on June 4 of the same year the *Duc de Richelieu*, first performance of Mr. Slous's drama 'The Duke's Wager,' founded on M. Dumas' piece 'Mdlle. De Belle Isle.' On Monday, February 9, 1852, Mr. Wigan sustained the character of *Faulconbridge* in Mr. Charles Kean's grand revival of Shakespeare's 'King John.' "*Faulconbridge*, the bluff, straightforward, 'physical-force' man, not over scrupulous as to peccadilloes, but endowed with a native horror of crime, and faithful to the death when he has once given his allegiance, was played in the best spirit by Mr. Alfred Wigan, who readily entered into the humour of the part, and most aptly caught up that tone of sudden defiance which bespeaks the readiness to follow up a word with a blow." (*Times*, February 10, 1852.) On Tuesday, February 24, 1852, 'The Corsican Brothers' (adapted from the French 'Les Frères Corses') was performed at the Princess's Theatre—Mr. Charles Kean was *Louis dei Franchi*, and Mr. A. Wigan sustained the part of *De Chateau Renaud*. On Saturday, March 6 of the same year, he played *Richard Hazard*, first performance of Tom

Taylor's comedy 'Our Clerks'; and in May, *Paul Raimbaut,* on the occasion of the first performance of 'A Lucky Friday.' This last-named character was afterwards performed "by command," at Windsor Castle, and was considered one of the most perfect of Mr. A. Wigan's earlier assumptions. In a revival of 'The Merry Wives of Windsor,' at the Adelphi Theatre, on Wednesday, May 18, 1853, Mr. Wigan undertook the part of *Dr. Caius;* and in June of the same year, at the same theatre, he acted the character of *M. Dixiner,* first performance of Mr. Boucicault's play 'Généviève; or, the Reign of Terror.'

In the autumn of 1853, Mr. Wigan, who for many years previously had been quietly and steadily advancing in the public esteem, as a careful and conscientious actor, entered upon the management of the Olympic Theatre. On Monday, October 17, 1853, he "opened" there with an extravaganza by Mr. J. R. Planché, entitled 'The Camp,' and a play written by Mr. Tom Taylor, in conjunction with Mr. John Lang, entitled 'Plot and Passion,' in which Mr. Wigan acted the leading *rôle.* On Monday, May 14, 1855, 'Still Waters Run Deep' was first performed at the same theatre, Mr. Wigan taking the part of *John Mildmay,* afterwards one of his most excellent impersonations. Said the *Times* (May 16, 1855): "The acting of Mr. Wigan as *John Mildmay* exactly corresponds with Mr. Tom Taylor's dialogue, in which everything like common-place exaggeration is shunned, and the language is made to approximate as much as possible to that of real life. He does not aim at a violent contrast between the supposed dolt and the man of proved intellect, but he allows the impression of superiority to be gradually conveyed, and make his audience feel that he has a right to the position he acquires at the end. Seldom do we see acting so rigidly truthful."

In 1857, in the very midst of popularity and prosperity, Mr. A. Wigan announced his intention of taking leave of the public on account of the delicate state of his health. It was stated in the journals of the day that he had realized a fortune of 10,000*l.* by his management of the Olympic; but this is an error. His share of the profits was large, but did not amount to this sum.

Mr. Wigan retired for some time from any active part in theatrical matters; but on Monday, February 23, 1859, reappeared on the London boards at the New Adelphi Theatre. Professor Morley (*Journal of a Playgoer*) notices the event as follows:—"March 5, 1859.—The theatrical event of the past week has been the return to the London stage of Mr. Alfred Wigan, who appeared with Mrs. Wigan for the first time on Monday evening at this theatre [the Adelphi] in one of his best characters, that of *John Mildmay* in 'Still Waters Run Deep.' Mrs. Wigan, who supported him most admirably in the part of Mrs. Hector Sternhold, was visibly affected by the cordiality of the welcome showered down upon her husband when the curtain rose. There was more in the plaudits of the public than expression of a selfish pleasure at the recovery of one of its best entertainers. It meant a true sympathy well founded upon personal respect and genuine congratulation." He continued to appear at the Adelphi in various pieces—'Paper Wings,' 'It's an

Ill Wind that Blows Nobody Good,' &c., until the latter part of the
same year, when he undertook the management of the St. James's
Theatre for a brief season, producing there, in April, ' A Scrap of
Paper,' adapted from the French ' Les Pattes de Mouche.' In 1863
(May 16), at the Haymarket Theatre, he sustained the part of *Dr.
Bertrand,* in a play by Lady Dufferin, entitled ' Finesse ; or, Spy
and Counterspy.' In 1864, in conjunction with his wife, Mr. A.
Wigan gave a series of dramatic readings in London. In 1867, at
the opening of the new Queen's Theatre, Long Acre, on Thursday,
October 24, he acted the part of *Captain Raynal* in Charles Reade's
drama entitled ' The Double Marriage.' The following year
(1868), on the occasion of the opening of the Gaiety Theatre,
Monday, December 21, he played *Adolphe Chavillard* in a piece
entitled ' On the Cards,' an adaptation of MM. D'Ennery and Bresil's
five-act *drame* entitled ' L'Escamoteur,' brought out in 1860, and
of which a version was presented at the Adelphi soon afterwards,
bearing the appellation of ' Magloire, the Prestidigitator.' The
prominent merit of the piece, according to the *Daily Telegraph*
(December 24, 1868), was to be found in the opportunity it afforded
Mr. Alfred Wigan of delineating one of those delightful old Frenchmen who stir the sympathies sometimes by the depth of their
emotion, and sometimes by the grotesque form of its expression.
" Those who have cherished pleasant memories of *Achille Talma
Dufard,* the fond father who forces his daughter on to the stage in
spite of obstacles that seemed insurmountable, will give a cordial
welcome to *Adolphe Chavillard,* professor of legerdemain, who, at
first simulating parental affection, afterwards feels it as a reality.
The foundation of this drama, as of so many others, is the circumstance of a wealthy baronet having brought up as his own child the
offspring of a poor woman who died soon after giving birth to a
girl. The particulars of the story, related on the stage with sufficient minuteness of detail, we need here only refer to as being
associated with the most kindly motives on the part of the baronet.
An unscrupulous cousin, who seeks to repair his damaged fortune
by a marriage with the supposed wealthy heiress, possesses himself
of the secret by the somewhat clumsy mode of overhearing the
baronet reveal this mysterious passage of the family history. The
young lady, who for the last eighteen years has passed as Florence
Ethelward, Sir Gilbert's daughter, is thus known to have a father
named Sir Charles Marjolaine ; and the crafty Guy Chilstone,
whose attentions are far from being favourably received, takes
advantage of the pecuniary needs of a conjurer, who is engaged at
the baronet's mansion for an hour's entertainment, to bribe him to
personate the long-lost parent.

" The temptation of the money is too strong to be resisted ; and
Adolphe Chavillard consents, receiving for his assistance a cheque
for 50*l.,* altered by Guy Chilstone so as to represent 150*l.,* and
hurriedly endorsed by the conjurer with a signature which makes
him amenable to a charge of forgery. The sinister cousin thus
believes he has the conjurer in his power, and with this advantage
proceeds to renew his persecution of Florence, when she has been

taken to a new home; but in a box, conveyed to her from Sir Gilbert's apartment, she finds a letter from her mother which explains her assumed name, and reveals the identity of *Adolphe* with her real father. In the last act the cunning Mr. Chilstone discovers that he has overreached himself; Sir Gilbert, by a private mark upon the cheque, is enabled to trace the falsification of the amount to the baffled rogue; *Adolphe* is cleared of all suspicion; and Florence, now made happy with a lover worthy of her, is left to retain the affection of the old Frenchman, her father, with the addition, as we are left to suppose, of the large fortune she would have inherited as the supposed daughter of the baronet. The strength of the drama lies in the second act, where a powerful situation occurs. The old conjurer has been proprietor of a travelling circus in his better days, and has only turned to leger-demain as a means of livelihood when no longer able to pursue his profession as an equestrian. When he finds the intentions of Chilstone are dishonourable, and that he has unconsciously been called upon to aid in the abduction of his own daughter, he contrives to foil the scheme of the villain by bringing into re-quisition some of his early experiences. A dexterous twist of the arm prevents Chilstone from moving, whilst Florence makes her escape at the door, which is then locked on the outside; and *Adolphe*, darting through the open window on to a scaffold, in the fashion of a trapezist, drops safely to the ground, whilst the baffled scoundrel is left in the conjurer's lodgings to liberate him-self as he best may.

" Throughout the drama Mr. Wigan displayed that perfect mastery of his art which always renders his acting so wonder-fully real and so thoroughly enjoyable. The most powerful effects are produced without any visible effort, and whether the tribute to his talent be a laugh or a tear, it is always yielded as spontaneously as it seems to be exacted unconsciously. To see Mr. Wigan in an impersonation of this kind is to be made aware of the resources at the command of a performer who has taken nature for his model, and acquired the skill of faithfully reproducing every shade of expression."

In October 1869, at the same theatre, Mr. Wigan sustained the part of *Bertrand Alvimar*, first performance of ' A Life Chase,' an adaptation from the French play by M. Belot entitled ' Le Drame de la Rue de la Paix,' which was produced at the Odéon Theatre, Paris, in November 1868. Mr. Alfred Wigan played the part of *Bertrand* with powerful effect. In 1872 Mr. Alfred Wigan finally retired from the stage. A farewell performance for the benefit of himself and his wife, in which both took part, was given at Drury Lane Theatre on July 6 of that year.

INDEX.